*Rethinking Risk Measurement
and Reporting: Volume II*

Rethinking Risk Measurement and Reporting: Volume II
Examples and Applications from Finance

Edited by Klaus Böcker

Published by Risk Books, a Division of Incisive Financial Publishing Ltd

Haymarket House
28–29 Haymarket
London SW1Y 4RX
Tel: + 44 (0)20 7484 9700
Fax: + 44 (0)20 7484 9797
E-mail: books@incisivemedia.com
Sites: www.riskbooks.com
         www.incisivemedia.com

© 2010 Incisive Media

ISBN 978-1-906348-50-2

British Library Cataloguing in Publication Data
A catalogue record for this book is available from the British Library

Publisher: Nick Carver
Commissioning Editor: Lucie Carter
Managing Editor: Jennifer Gibb
Designer: Lisa Ling

Copy-edited and typeset by T&T Productions Ltd, London

Printed and bound in the UK by PrintonDemand-Worldwide

Conditions of sale

All rights reserved. No part of this publication may be reproduced in any material form whether by photocopying or storing in any medium by electronic means whether or not transiently or incidentally to some other use for this publication without the prior written consent of the copyright owner except in accordance with the provisions of the Copyright, Designs and Patents Act 1988 or under the terms of a licence issued by the Copyright Licensing Agency Limited of 90, Tottenham Court Road, London W1P 0LP.

Warning: the doing of any unauthorised act in relation to this work may result in both civil and criminal liability.

Every effort has been made to ensure the accuracy of the text at the time of publication, this includes efforts to contact each author to ensure the accuracy of their details at publication is correct. However, no responsibility for loss occasioned to any person acting or refraining from acting as a result of the material contained in this publication will be accepted by the copyright owner, the editor, the authors or Incisive Media.

Many of the product names contained in this publication are registered trade marks, and Risk Books has made every effort to print them with the capitalisation and punctuation used by the trademark owner. For reasons of textual clarity, it is not our house style to use symbols such as TM, ®, etc. However, the absence of such symbols should not be taken to indicate absence of trademark protection; anyone wishing to use product names in the public domain should first clear such use with the product owner.

While best efforts have been intended for the preparation of this book, neither the publisher, the editor nor any of the potentially implicitly affiliated organisations accept responsibility for any errors, mistakes and or omissions it may provide or for any losses howsoever arising from or in reliance upon its information, meanings and interpretations by any parties.

Contents

About the Editor	vii
About the Authors	ix
Introduction	xix

PART I   MARKET RISK AND FINANCIAL TIME SERIES — 1

1   Efficient Bayesian Estimation and Combination of Garch-Type Models   3
David Ardia; Lennart F. Hoogerheide
aeris CAPITAL AG Switzerland; Erasmus University Rotterdam

2   Bayesian Inference for Stochastic Volatility Modelling   31
Hedibert F. Lopes, Nicholas G. Polson
The University of Chicago Booth School of Business

3   Bayesian Prediction of Risk Measurements Using Copulas   69
Maria Concepcion Ausin; Hedibert Freitas Lopes
Universidad Carlos III de Madrid;
University of Chicago Booth School of Business

4   Bayesian Inference for Hedge Funds with Stable Distribution of Returns   95
Biliana Güner; Svetlozar T. Rachev; Daniel Edelman; Frank J. Fabozzi
Yeditepe University; FinAnalytica; UBS Alternative and Quantitative Investments LLC; Yale School of Management

5   Model Uncertainty and Its Impact on Derivative Pricing   137
Alok Gupta, Christoph Reisinger, Alan Whitley
University of Oxford

PART II   CREDIT RISK — 177

6   Predictions Based on Certain Uncertainties: A Bayesian Credit Portfolio Approach   179
Christoff Gössl
UniCredit

7   Uncertainty in Credit Risk Parameters and Its Implication on Risk Figures   199
Christina R. Bender; Ludger Overbeck
d-fine GmbH; University of Giessen

8 Lessons from the Crisis in Mortgage-Backed Structured
   Securities: Where Did Credit Ratings Go Wrong?   241
   Erik Heitfield
   Federal Reserve Board

9 Rethinking Credit Risk Modelling   269
   Christian Bluhm; Christoph Wagner
   Technische Universität München; Allianz Risk Transfer

10 The Bayesian Approach to Default Risk: A Guide   319
   Michael Jacobs Jr; Nicholas M. Kiefer
   US Department of the Treasury, Office of the Comptroller of the
   Currency; Cornell University

11 Bayesian Modelling of Small and Medium-Sized
   Companies' Defaults   345
   *Mathilde Wilhelmsen, Xeni K. Dimakos; Tore Anders Husebø,
   Marit Fiskaaen*
   Norwegian Computing Center; Centre of Excellence Credit Risk
   Modelling, Sparebank 1

PART III OPERATIONAL RISK   **369**

12 Measuring Operational Risk in a Bayesian Framework   371
   Luciana Dalla Valle
   University of Milan

13 Operational Risk: Combining Internal Data, External Data and
   Expert Opinions   401
   Pavel V. Shevchenko; Mario V. Wüthrich
   CSIRO Mathematics, Informatics and Statistics;
   RiskLab ETH Zurich

14 Bayesian Estimation of Lévy Copulas for Multivariate
   Operational Risks   439
   Philipp Gebhard, Gernot Müller; Klaus Böcker
   Technische Universität München; UniCredit Group

   Index   465

About the Editor

Klaus Böcker works as a senior risk controller in UniCredit Group and is the team head of Risk Analytics and Methods. In this capacity, one of his primary responsibilities is overseeing the quantitative aspects of UniCredit Group's economic capital model, in particular business risk, real-estate risk, financial investment risk and risk aggregation as well as stress testing encompassing different risk types.

Klaus is also a research fellow at the Center for Mathematical Sciences at the Technische Universität München. He is conducting research in various fields of finance where he has authored and co-authored several articles that have been published in various recognised finance and mathematical journals.

Klaus is also a frequent speaker at international risk conferences and at seminars about risk management and quantitative finance. In 2007, 2008 and 2010, he won the PRMIA Institute's Award for New Frontiers in Risk Management related to his research activities. In August 2007, Klaus was inducted by his peers as a charter member of the international Risk Who's Who honour society. He holds a degree in Theoretical Physics and a PhD in Mathematics from the Technische Universität München.

About the Authors

David Ardia works as a quantitative analyst and conducts research on financial econometrics. Previously, he was a postdoctoral researcher at the Econometric Institute, Erasmus University Rotterdam, and at CORE, Louvain-la-Neuve. In 2008, he received the Chorafas prize for his book *Financial Risk Management with Bayesian Estimation of Garch Models*. He is the author of several statistical packages for R. David holds an MSc in applied mathematics, an MAS in finance and a PhD in Bayesian econometrics.

Maria Concepcion Ausin is assistant professor of statistics at Universidad Carlos III de Madrid. Her research interests are mainly related to the applications of computational Bayesian methods in insurance and financial problems. She has published in international journals like *Journal of Business and Economic Statistics*, *Mathematical Finance* and *Computational Statistics and Data Analysis*. Maria holds a mathematics degree from Universidad Complutense de Madrid and a PhD in statistics from Universidad Carlos III de Madrid.

Christina Bender works as a senior consultant for d-fine GmbH, Frankfurt, Germany. She consults banks and other financial institutions in quantitative and technical implementation of mathematical models in risk management. In particular, she is interested in managing projects in market risk management, credit portfolio modelling and option pricing. Until June 2008 Christina worked for the active credit portfolio management department at UniCredit's Markets & Investment Banking. Christina is also a visiting lecturer for mathematical methods in risk management at the stochastics group at Saarland University. She is conducting research in various fields of finance where she has authored and co-authored several articles that have been published in recognised finance and mathematical journals. Christina holds a Master's degree in mathematical finance and a PhD in mathematics from the University of Konstanz. For both theses she received several awards from academia and industry.

Christian Bluhm has worked in credit risk and portfolio management for more than 10 years. He has worked for Deutsche Bank in Frankfurt and McKinsey & Company and HypoVereinsbank in

Munich. From 2004–9 he worked for Credit Suisse in Zurich, where he was a managing director and head of credit portfolio management. Together with his business partners he has since founded a consulting company specialising in financial services. Christian studied mathematics at the University of Marburg and the University of Erlangen, where he received his Master's and Doctoral degrees in mathematics. He spent his postdoctoral time at the mathematics department of Cornell University. He regularly publishes in the field of mathematical finance and gives lectures on probability and finance at the University of Technology, Munich.

Luciana Dalla Valle earned a PhD in statistics from the University of Milano-Bicocca in 2007. She holds a post-doctoral position at the department of economics, business and statistics at the University of Milan, where she teaches statistics and data analysis. Luciana is interested in Bayesian statistics, Markov chain Monte Carlo methods, statistical models for financial risks, copula modelling for financial applications, statistical models for internationalisation and sampling techniques.

Xeni K. Dimakos is assistant director of the department of research at Vox, the Norwegian agency for lifelong learning. Previously she was chief research scientist at the Norwegian Computing Center, working mainly with statistical modelling in finance and insurance. Xeni has a broad experience as a project manager and has lead major research projects financed by the Norwegian Research Council. She holds a PhD in statistics from the University of Oslo.

Daniel Edelman is executive director and head of research at Alternative Investment Solutions (AIS), the US-based hedge fund-of-funds that is part of UBS's Alternative and Quantitative Investments platform. His responsibilities include risk management, asset allocation and quantitative research. In 1995, Daniel joined Swiss Bank Corporation as a project manager in the foreign exchange. In 1997, he joined UBS Investment Bank's Alternative Asset Management Group, the predecessor of AIS. Daniel has over 15 years of investment industry experience and holds a BA (Hons) from Harvard University and an MBA from Columbia University. He is a Chartered Financial Analyst.

ABOUT THE AUTHORS

Frank J. Fabozzi is professor in the practice of finance in the Yale School of Management and an affiliated professor at the University of Karlsruhe's Institute of Statistics, Econometrics and Mathematical Finance. Frank serves on Princeton's Advisory Council for the department of operations research and financial engineering. Books he has coauthored include *Quantitative Equity Investing* (2009), *Institutional Investment Management* (2009), *Finance: Capital Markets, Financial Management and Investment Management* (2009), *Bayesian Methods in Finance* (2008), *Advanced Stochastic Models, Risk Assessment, and Portfolio Optimization* (2008), *Robust Portfolio Optimization and Management* (2007) and *Financial Econometrics: From Basics to Advanced Modeling Techniques* (2007).

Marit Fiskaaen works as senior analyst in Centre of Credit Risk Modelling in Sparebank 1 since joining in 2005. Previously, she worked as an actuary in Nordea Liv and NOR Forsikring. Marit holds a CandScient degree in Statistics from the University of Bergen and actuary certification from the University of Oslo.

Philipp Gebhard studied mathematical finance and economics at Technische Universität München and Concordia University, Montreal, with focus on statistics for multivariate time series. He finished his diploma thesis during the time of writing of his chapter. He gained practical experience at Dresdner Bank, in the Group Risk Architecture division.

Christoff Gössl studied Statistics at the Ludwig Maximilians University in Munich and wrote his diploma thesis about Bayesian approaches to measurement error problems in logistic regression models. The subject of his PhD thesis at the Max Planck Institute for Psychiatry in Munich was the application of spatio-temporal Bayesian models in the analysis of functional magnetic resonance imaging data. He started working for HypoVereinsbank AG in 2001 in the Group Credit Portfolio Management department. In 2004 he went on to join the Fixed Income Portfolios Group in London as Senior Quantitative Analyst and worked from 2008 in the Credit Financial Engineering Group at the credit derivatives trading desk. In his career he has worked on many credit portfolio related questions, including general credit portfolio risk management and risk assessment for structured credit products, as well as contributing to a bank-wide structured credit derivatives pricing library.

Biliana Güner obtained her PhD in statistics with emphasis on empirical finance from the University of California, Santa Barbara, in 2007. Her research interests are in the areas of risk and portfolio management and financial econometrics. She co-authored the book *Bayesian Methods in Finance* (Wiley 2008). Biliana is currently an assistant professor in finance at Yeditepe University, Turkey.

Alok Gupta holds degrees from the University of Cambridge, Imperial College London and the University of Oxford. He has worked at HSBC, Deloitte, BNP Paribas, Nomura and FTSE. A Post-Doctorate at Oxford, Alok is investigating applications of Bayesian approaches to problems in mathematical finance. Specifically, he calibrates high-dimensional non-parametric financial models, extracting a distribution of prices and hence some measure of the uncertainty in the prices. Alok further constructs optimal Bayesian hedging strategies and is working on applying his techniques to the problem of optimal portfolio selection for a variety of return-risk objectives.

Erik Heitfield is a senior economist in the Federal Reserve Board of Governors' Risk Analysis Section, where he conducts research on the measurement and management of credit risk in complex financial institutions. He has worked on a broad range of issues relating to financial services regulation, including antitrust policy, risk-based regulatory capital standards and, most recently, clearing and margin requirements for over-the-counter derivatives. In 2006 and 2007 Erik served as a senior staff economist for the President's Council of Economic Advisors. Erik received his PhD in economics from the University of California, Berkeley, in 1998.

Lennart F. Hoogerheide is assistant professor of econometrics at the Econometric Institute of Erasmus University Rotterdam. His research is mainly focused on flexible models and computational methods for analysis of risk and treatment effects in finance, micro- and macroeconomics. His publications have appeared in international journals such as *Journal of Econometrics*, *International Journal of Forecasting*, *Journal of Forecasting* and *Journal of Statistical Software*. In 2006, he received the *Journal of Applied Econometrics* scholarship for his dissertation chapter on the effect of education on income. Lennart holds an MSc (cum laude) in econometrics and a PhD in Bayesian econometrics.

Tore Anders Husebø is head of credit risk modelling at SpareBank 1, Norway. His work focuses on analysis and management of credit risk, including Bayesian econometrics of credit risk on retail and small loans. Tore previously worked at the Norges Bank (Central bank of Norway) on monetary policy and financial stability issues for several years. He holds a MSc in economics.

Michael Jacobs is a senior financial economist. He has worked in the credit risk analysis division/department of economics and international affairs at the Office of the Comptroller of the Currency (OCC) since June 2005. He is a researcher in financial economics, specialising in empirical studies of wholesale credit risk (loss given default, exposure at default, ratings migrations and PD modelling for large corporate loans and bonds; also performance of distressed debt, credit derivatives and correlation forecasting). He has participated in examinations as an advisor in quantitative modelling issues for credit risk rating processes, allowance and economic capital modelling at several large and mid-sized banks. He has also been involved in projects related to the development of policy and guidance for the Basel II capital framework, including the AIGV Research Task Force on vendor models. Prior to joining the OCC, Michael was a vice-president at JPMorgan Chase Risk Methodology for five years, leading the empirical research programme in credit risk for the wholesale bank, publishing several articles in the *RMA Journal*; he spent three years as a quantitative analyst at the Sumitomo-Mitsui Banking Corporation, implementing economic capital and RAROC models, and five years as an instructor and assistant professor at Baruch College, lecturing and performing research in financial economics, having several publications in the *Journal of Futures Markets*. Michael holds a BS in engineering science, an MA and ABD in mathematical economics, both from SUNY Center at Stony Brook; and a PhD in finance from the City University of New York; he is also a Chartered Financial Analyst.

Nicholas M. Kiefer is the Ta-Chung Liu Professor at Cornell University, where he is a member of the departments of economics and statistical science. He is also a senior financial advisor to the Office of the Comptroller of the Currency. He is widely known for his theoretical and applied contributions in the econometric modelling of duration data and financial market microstructure and the specification, identification and estimation of dynamic programming models. His research includes applications in financial economics, credit scoring and risk management. Nicholas advocates the Bayesian approach to modelling and incorporating expert information in risk management applications in banks and related financial institutions. He is an internationally recognised expert, having published in excess of 100 journal articles, books and reviews. His most recent book, co-authored with Bent Jesper Christensen, is *Economic Modeling and Inference* (Princeton University Press 2009). He is a fellow of the Econometric Society and a past recipient of the Guggenheim Memorial Foundation Fellowship.

Hedibert Freitas Lopes conducts research in Markov chain Monte Carlo techniques and sequential Monte Carlo methods applied to multivariate econometrics and time-series models, modelling time-varying covariance of multivariate time series through latent factor analysis, Choleski decomposition and other factorisations, dynamic models and Bayesian inference and computation. He is mainly interested in the implementation of the Bayesian paradigm to solve real large-scale problems in econometrics and other fields of economics. Hedibert serves on several Master's and PhD committees and referees for the majority of leading statistics and econometrics journals. Hedibert earned his Bachelor's degree in statistics in 1991 and Master's degree in statistics in 1994 from the Federal University of Rio de Janeiro. He also earned a Master's degree in statistics and decision sciences in 1998 and a PhD in 2000 from Duke University.

Gernot Müller is a research assistant at the Chair of Mathematical Statistics at the Center for Mathematical Sciences of the Technische Universität München. His research covers various topics, in particular statistical methods for discrete-time and continuous-time models, Bayes inference and computational statistics. Gernot is interested in applications in economics, finance, and insurance.

Ludger Overbeck holds a professorship of mathematics at the University of Giessen in Germany. His main interests are quantitative finance, risk management and stochastic analysis. Until June 2003 he was head of risk research and development in Deutsche Bank's Credit Risk function. Ludger's main responsibilities included development and implementation of the internal group-wide Credit Portfolio model, the EC/RAROC-methodology for all risk types except market risk, and risk assessment of credit derivatives and portfolio transactions like CDO and ABS. Before that he was with the banking supervision department of the Deutsche Bundesbank. Ludger was consultant for Unicredit (HVB) as head of portfolio analytics and pricing of the Active Credit Portfolio Management Division and is currently consultant for Commerzbank as head of quantitative credit portfolio management. He publishes in many academic and applied journals and magazines, including *Risk Magazine*. He has co-authored two books on credit risk modelling.

Nicholas G. Polson is professor of econometrics and statistics at the Chicago Booth School of Business. He obtained his undergraduate degree from Worcester College, Oxford and his PhD from the University of Nottingham. Nick's research interests are Financial econometrics, stochastic volatility, Bayesian methods, MCMC and particle learning.

Svetlozar (Zari) Rachev is a co-founder and president of BRAVO Risk Management Group, the originator of the Cognity methodology, which was acquired by FinAnalytica, where he serves as chief scientist. Zari holds chair-professorship in statistics, econometrics and mathematical finance at University of Karlsruhe, and is the author of 14 books and over 300 published articles on finance, econometrics, probability, statistics and actuarial science.

Christoph Reisinger is a university lecturer in Mathematical and Computational Finance at the University of Oxford, and is director of the MSc programme in Mathematical Finance. He holds a doctorate in Mathematics from the Interdisciplinary Center for Scientific Computing at the University of Heidelberg. His current research includes the development and analysis of numerical methods for the pricing and hedging of financial derivatives, as well as parameter and model identification problems in finance together with their implications on risk management.

Pavel V. Shevchenko is a principal research scientist in the Division of Mathematics, Informatics and Statistics of the Commonwealth Scientific and Industrial Research Organisation (CSIRO) of Australia, based in Sydney. Pavel joined CSIRO in 1999 to work in the area of financial risk modelling. He leads research and commercial projects in the area of financial risk, particularly modelling market, credit and operational risks; option pricing; insurance; modelling commodities and foreign exchange; and the development of relevant numerical methods and software. He received an MSc from the Moscow Institute of Physics and Technology and Kapitza Institute for Physical Problems in 1994 and a PhD in theoretical physics from The University of New South Wales, Sydney in 1999.

Christoph Wagner is global portfolio manager for structured finance at Allianz Risk Transfer, Zürich. His main responsibilities there are structured credit products, insurance-linked securities, securitisations and alternative assets. He has been active in the fields of risk and portfolio management for more than 10 years, and prior positions were with Deutsche Bank, Allianz and Unicredit. Christoph holds a PhD in theoretical physics from the Technical University of Munich, and he is a certified actuary and financial risk manager (GARP). Before entering the financial industry, he spent several years in postdoctoral positions, both at the Center of Nonlinear Dynamics and Complex Systems, Brussels, and at the Siemens Research Department in Munich. He regularly speaks at conferences and he is a lecturer at the Ludwig-Maximilians-University in Munich.

Mathilde Wilhelmsen works as a research scientist at the Norwegian Computing Center, in the field of applied statistical modelling, especially within finance, insurance and commodity markets. She has a masters' degree in statistics.

Alan Whitley is a DPhil student at the University of Oxford, having completed an MSc in Mathematical and Computational Finance at the same institution in 2009. His first degree was a BA in Mathematics from the University of Cambridge and he also holds an MSc in Petroleum Engineering from the University of Strathclyde. Prior to returning to academic studies in 2008, Alan pursued an extensive and varied career in the oil and gas industry, where he worked in Research and Development, Petroleum Engineering, Financial and Strategic Planning, Economics and Corporate Governance roles. His research interests lie in the area of model risk.

Mario Wüthrich holds a PhD in mathematics from ETH Zurich (The Swiss Federal Institute of Technology Zurich) and completed postdoctoral work in 2000 at the University of Nijmegen in The Netherlands. From 2000 to 2005, he held an actuarial position at Winterthur

Insurance and was responsible for claims reserving in non-life insurance, as well as developing and implementing the Swiss Solvency Test. Since 2005, Mario has served as senior scientist at RiskLab in the Department of Mathematics at ETH Zurich, with teaching duties in actuarial mathematics. He serves on the board of the Swiss Association of Actuaries (SAA) and is editor of *Bulletin SAA, Blaetter DGFVM* and has just joined the editorial boards of *ASTIN Bulletin* and *European Actuarial Journal*.

Introduction

Welcome to the second volume of *Rethinking Risk Management and Reporting*. The first volume introduces Bayesian analysis and expert elicitation as excellent tools to assess measurement uncertainty and also presents some finance applications, including, among others, stress testing and risk aggregation. Moreover, it discusses important non-technical aspects such as the nature of risk or cognitive psychological fundamentals of uncertainty, and gives valuable practical insights provided by leading figures of risk management. Therefore, Volume I arms the reader with the necessary technical skills to perform measurement uncertainty analysis successfully on its own, while at the same time it raises the awareness of why model uncertainty is an issue and so helps to develop a culture of managerial accountability and responsibility when using and disclosing financial numbers.

STRUCTURE OF VOLUME II

This second volume consists of three parts and discusses a broad spectrum of financial applications including market risk, credit risk and operational risk. Compared with the chapters of the first volume, the chapters of Volume II are on average at a more technical level, providing a complete set of cutting-edge tools and techniques for the reader as follows.

Part I focuses on issues related to market risk, the estimation of time-series and derivative pricing. Usually, in market risk, there is an abundance of empirical data available, which can be used to parameterise the often quite involved and complex models for pricing stocks, commodities and market indexes. The chapters in this part of the book show that in this field Bayesian analysis provides valuable benefits when modelling, parameterising, analysing and predicting financial market data. For this reason Chapter 1, by David Ardia and Lennart Hoogerheide, gives an up-to-date review of estimation strategies available for the Bayesian inference of Garch-type models; one of the most important model classes used for fitting financial time-series. In Chapter 2 Hedibert Lopes and Nicholas Polson move on to the other famous type of modelling approaches that have been introduced to reflect the significant variability and uncertainty in the instantaneous volatility of traded assets: stochastic volatility models. This chapter is an exhaustive review of Bayesian analysis for stochastic volatility models and also provides a detailed explanation of efficient Markov chain Monte Carlo and sequential Monte Carlo algorithms in this context. Maria Concepcion Ausin and Hedibert Lopes present in Chapter 3 an interesting framework on the Bayesian estimation of a Garch–copula model that enables capture of temporal dependency in multivariate time-series. Using a portfolio of DAX and DJ indexes, they also examine how Bayesian analysis allows the impact of parameter uncertainty on the variance, the VaR and the expected shortfall to be estimated in a quite straightforward fashion. In Chapter 4, Biliana Güner *et al* provide one of the rare examinations that exist, where Bayesian analysis is used to improve our understanding of the risk of hedge funds. By employing an Arma–Garch model with alpha-stable disturbances, they conclude that Bayesian estimation outperforms other techniques in terms of predicting large hedge fund losses, such as the ones seen in September and October 2008. Finally, Chapter 5 by Alok Gupta *et al* examines model uncertainty in the context of derivative pricing, an area that is not typically yet considered adequately enough in banks' trading rooms but, on the other hand, has merited increasing attention by researchers during the last few years. Including a variety of examples via the famous Black–Scholes model, this chapter is included to make this subject accessible to a wider audience.

In Part II we move on to dealing with one of the most important risk types within financial risk management, namely credit risk. There is a vast amount of literature available on general credit risk modelling. However, only a few authors have commented on model and parameter uncertainty for credit risk applications. This part of the book aims to fill this gap by presenting such analyses for single name and portfolio credit risk, certainly with an emphasis on Bayesian methods and expert judgement but also providing a couple of chapters that critically review existing credit models with a focus on uncertainty and model flaws. In Chapter 6, Christoff Gössl investigates the impact of parameter uncertainty by using a Bayesian credit one-factor model. Gössl, who is one of the early supporters of model uncertainty in risk management, wrote the first version of the paper on which this chapter is based in 2005. Even though the ideas in this paper were not largely accepted by the industry at that time, the idea of parameter uncertainty is now much better received and, furthermore, is even sought out as a likely solution. A related analysis about credit portfolio risk is given in Chapter 7, by Christina Bender and Ludger Overbeck, which contains an empirical study based on loss data from Standard & Poor's (1981–2008), where the measurement uncertainty of typical risk figures such as expected loss, VaR and expected shortfall for a large homogeneous credit portfolio is analysed. Chapter 8, by Erik Heitfield, throws light on the role of credit structured products (and mortgage-backed structured securities in particular) in the 2007–9 subprime crisis. Chapter 9, by Christian Bluhm and Christoph Wagner, is the last chapter in Part II that is concerned with credit portfolio risk. This chapter reconsiders credit risk modelling approaches from a quite general perspective, focusing on how default dependence between different obligors is constructed. They pay particular attention to the potential problems and pitfalls, which may easily lead to false risk figures and, thus, to bad decision making. The last two chapters in Part II are devoted to the estimation of default probabilities. Michael Jacobs and Nicholas M. Kiefer present in Chapter 10 a Bayesian approach for default-rate estimation illustrated using annual default rate data from Moody's (1999–2009) and a prior distribution elicited from an industry expert. Finally, Chapter 11 by Mathilde Wilhelmsen *et al* investigates accounting-based bankruptcy prediction using a Bayesian logistic regression model to estimate the default probability of small and medium-sized companies. They also show how the uncertainty in the regression estimation translates into uncertainty for the predicted default probabilities, something which is too often neglected in current practice.

Part III is devoted to operational risk. This risk type is particularly suited to Bayesian methods because a bank usually only has scarce internal information about its own severe loss events, so external data and expert judgement have to be used in addition. Therefore, this part of the book presents effective and reliable techniques to combine the different data sources as well as to analyse the model uncertainty in the final risk figures. Chapter 12, by Luciana Dalla Valle, presents a complete framework for how to calculate operational risk by adopting a Bayesian version of the popular loss distribution approach. Using a real bank's empirical data, this chapter illustrates the huge impact that model assumptions and parameter uncertainties may have on the final operational VaR. In Chapter 13 Pavel Shevchenko and Mario Wüthrich demonstrate the usefulness of the Bayesian approach to combine internal loss data, external data from other banks and expert opinions to determine the parameters of a loss distribution approach model. Finally, Chapter 14 by Klaus Böcker, Philipp Gebhard and Gernot Müller investigates a multivariate operational risk model based on the modern concept of Lévy copulas. Besides assessing measurement uncertainty of risk figures, this chapter provides an illuminating example of Bayesian model selection: one of the key advantages of Bayesian statistics.

To summarise, this volume tackles a wide range of topics relating to market risk, credit risk, operational risk and asset management, which are necessary for developing a theoretically sound, practicably feasible and trustworthy framework of risk measurement and management. Essentially, this volume provides the reader with the tools and techniques to incorporate an understanding of uncertainty in risk measurement and modelling.

ACKNOWLEDGEMENTS

Producing a book requires the effort of many individuals, and I am extremely thankful to the following people for their help and support with this book: Nick Carver, Jennifer Gibb, Sarah Hastings and, in particular, Lucie Carter at RiskBooks for their continuing support and guidance throughout this project (Lucie, without your initiative and your call on March 31, 2009, this book would not have been realised); Emma Dain at T&T Productions Ltd, London, for being so thorough in editing, typesetting and producing the chapters in this book.

I am especially grateful to all the authors for their professional and fruitful collaboration and the fact that they actively supported the idea motivating this book. Finally, I would like to thank Katharina, David, Simon and Antonia for giving me the time to work on this book – chained to my desk in the deepest, darkest corner of my cellar – and, thus, I look forward to reacquainting myself with my family and daylight following the much anticipated publication of this book.

Klaus Böcker
Munich, August 2010

Part I

Market Risk and Financial Time Series

1

Efficient Bayesian Estimation and Combination of Garch-Type Models

David Ardia; Lennart F. Hoogerheide

aeris CAPITAL AG Switzerland; Erasmus University Rotterdam

Volatility forecasting plays an essential role in empirical finance, financial risk management and derivative pricing. Research on modelling volatility dynamics using time-series models has been active since the creation of the original Arch model by Engle (1982). Since then, multiple extensions of the standard Arch scedastic function have been proposed in order to reproduce additional stylised facts observed in financial markets. These so-called Garch-type models recognise that there may be important non-linearities, asymmetries, and long memory properties in the volatility process.[1] Well-known extensions are the exponential Garch model by Nelson (1991), the GJR model by Glosten *et al* (1993) and the TGarch model of Zakoian (1994), which account for the asymmetric relation between stock returns and changes in variance (Black 1976). In parallel to the development of alternative scedastic functions, numerous types of disturbances have been used. The Gaussian distribution and Student-*t* distribution are common choices, while more sophisticated parameterisations such as the skewed Student *t* or the mixture of Gaussian distributions allow us to model skewness and fat tails in the conditional distribution of returns (Ausin and Galeano 2007). Recent interest has focused on regime-switching Garch models. In this framework, the Garch parameters are functions of an unobservable state variable and can change over time. These processes provide an explanation of the high persistence in volatility observed with single-regime Garch models.[2] Furthermore, as shown by Dueker (1997), Klaassen (2002)

This chapter is dedicated to Johannes Frans Kaashoek (1943–2010), whose friendly and wise advice contributed crucially to the development of our methods.

and Marcucci (2005), for instance, the regime-switching Garch models allow for a quick change in the volatility level, which can lead to significant improvements in risk forecasts.

Until recently, Garch-type models have mainly been estimated using the classical maximum likelihood technique. However, the Bayesian approach offers an attractive alternative. It enables small sample results, probabilistic statements on non-linear functions of the model parameters, selection and combination of non-nested models. Due to these numerous advantages, the study of Garch-type models from a Bayesian viewpoint can be considered to be very promising.

This chapter proposes a review of simulation techniques used in the literature to perform the Bayesian estimation of Garch-type models. The emphasis is put on a novel approach referred to as AdMitIS. The algorithm constructs a mixture of Student-t distributions to perform an efficient estimation of models via importance sampling. The methodology is fully automatic and has proved to require less computing time for precise estimation results than several well-known alternatives. We describe in some detail the steps of the algorithm. In an empirical application to S&P 500 Index log returns, we show how it can be used to estimate and combine distribution forecasts of non-nested Garch-type models.

The chapter proceeds as follows. In the following section we survey the existing simulation techniques available for Bayesian Garch-type models. We then present the AdMitIS algorithm in the next section and provide an empirical illustration in the penultimate section, before presenting our conclusions.

BAYESIAN ESTIMATION OF GARCH-TYPE MODELS

The maximum likelihood (ML) estimation technique is the most commonly used scheme of inference for Garch-type models. ML is easy to understand and to implement. Much econometric software contains a Garch toolbox and ML estimation of standard Garch models takes less than one second on a modern computer. This is highly desirable for automated trading strategies, for instance, where several models are fitted on thousands of data many times per day. From a theoretical viewpoint, ML estimators benefit from being asymptotically optimal under certain conditions (Bollerslev *et al* 1994; Lee and Hansen 1994).

Despite these appealing features, we face practical difficulties when dealing with the ML estimation of Garch-type models. First, the maximisation of the likelihood function must be achieved via a constrained optimisation technique since some (or all) model parameters must be positive to ensure a positive conditional variance. It is also common to require that the covariance stationarity condition holds. This leads to complicated non-linear inequality constraints which render the optimisation procedure cumbersome. Moreover, the convergence of the optimisation is hard to achieve if the true parameter values are close to the boundary of the parameter space and if the Garch process is nearly non-stationary. Optimisation results are often sensitive to the choice of starting values.

Second, in standard applications of Garch models, professional interest usually centres not directly on the model parameters but rather on possibly complicated non-linear functions of the parameters. For instance, a trader might be interested in the unconditional variance implied by a Garch model, which is a (highly) non-linear function of the model parameters. In order to assess the uncertainty of such a quantity, classical inference involves tedious delta methods, simulation from the asymptotic Gaussian approximation of the parameter estimates or the time-consuming bootstrap methodology.

Third, the conditions for the optimal asymptotic properties of ML estimators to hold are fairly difficult to satisfy, while often being assumed to hold in practice. Moreover, since Garch-type models are highly non-linear, the asymptotic argument would require a very large number of data in order to hold. This is obviously not always the case in practice.

Finally, in the case of Garch with mixture disturbances or regime-switching Garch models, testing for the number of mixture components or the number of regimes is not possible within the classical framework due to the violation of regularity conditions (Frühwirth-Schnatter 2006, Section 4.4).

Fortunately, those difficulties disappear when Bayesian methods are used. First, any constraints on the model parameters can be incorporated in the modelling through appropriate prior specifications. Second, appropriate Markov chain Monte Carlo (MCMC) procedures can explore the joint posterior distribution of the model parameters. These techniques avoid local maxima (ie, non-convergence or convergence to the wrong values) encountered via ML estimation of sophisticated Garch-type models. Third, exact distributions of non-linear functions of the model parameters can be obtained at low cost by simulating from the joint posterior distribution. Fourth, the issue of determining the number of mixture components in mixtures disturbances or the number of regimes in regime-switching Garch model can be addressed by means of marginal likelihoods and Bayes factors. Marginal likelihoods can also be used for model selection and model combination of non-nested Garch-type models. The latter case is especially interesting in the context of financial risk management, since it allows us to integrate out model uncertainty, thus accounting for model risk in the forecasts.

The choice of the sampling algorithm is the first issue when dealing with MCMC methods and it depends on the nature of the problem under study.[3] In the case of Garch-type models, due to the recursive nature of the conditional variance, the joint posterior and the full conditional densities are of unknown forms, whatever assumptions are made on the scedastic function or the model disturbances. That is, there exists no conjugate prior under which the parameters' (conditional) posterior distributions fall within a known class. Therefore, we cannot use the simple Gibbs sampler and need more elaborated procedures. Hereafter, we review the different techniques currently available to perform the Bayesian estimation of Garch-type models and discuss their advantages and drawbacks. For a numerical comparison of some of these approaches in the context of Garch-type models, we refer the reader to Asai (2006) and Ardia et al (2009a).

Griddy–Gibbs

The Griddy–Gibbs sampler of Ritter and Tanner (1992) is a variant of the Gibbs sampler where each parameter is updated by inversion from the full conditional distribution computed by a deterministic integration rule. The algorithm is intuitive and very simple to implement. However, the procedure is extremely time-consuming due to the numerical integration steps required at each sweep of the sampler. While this can still be acceptable for simple Garch specifications, this becomes a real burden for sophisticated and highly parameterised Garch-type models. Moreover, for computational efficiency, we must limit the range where the probability mass is computed so that the prior density has to be somewhat informative. In our viewpoint, the Griddy–Gibbs sampler is attractive for its simplicity and remains a useful tool for "one-shot" studies. It is, however, not relevant in real-world applications, where the models need to be estimated many times on a large number of times series. The Griddy–Gibbs approach is used in the context of Garch-type models by Bauwens and Lubrano (1998, 2002), Bauwens *et al* (2000, 2010), Wago (2004), Tsay (2005, Chapter 10), Ausin and Galeano (2007) and Bauwens and Rombouts (2007).

Importance sampling

Importance sampling (IS), due to Hammersley and Handscomb (1965), was introduced in econometrics and statistics by Kloek and van Dijk (1978). The IS approach relies on an importance density which approximates the posterior density of the model parameters. Draws are generated from this importance density and weighted, with higher weights given to draws for which the importance density is relatively small compared with the posterior. Then, quantities of interest of the posterior distribution (or predictive distribution) are estimated by weighted averages of (functions of) draws. This methodology leads to a fast estimation since it only requires generating and weighting draws. Moreover, it generates uncorrelated draws, so that the whole posterior sample can be used for Bayesian inference (ie, no burn-in or "thinning" is necessary), and so that the precision of the estimators is easily assessed. However, the key issue for applicability and efficiency is the choice of the importance density. Finding this can be a bit of an art, especially if the posterior density is asymmetric or multi-modal. For instance, in the case of a Garch model with mixture disturbances, the posterior distribution is multimodal. In this case, a (standard) unimodal importance density may imply that some draws have huge weights, leading to large inefficiencies in the estimation or, worse, that relevant parts of the parameters space are completely "missed". The importance distribution should be close to the posterior distribution and it is especially important that the tails of the importance density should not be thinner than those of the posterior. Bayesian estimation of Garch-type models using importance sampling is proposed by Geweke (1988, 1989b) and Kleibergen and van Dijk (1993).

Metropolis–Hastings

The Metropolis–Hastings (MH) algorithm was introduced by Metropolis *et al* (1953) and generalised by Hastings (1970). The approach constructs a Markov chain by generating draws from a candidate density; the candidate draw is then accepted (or rejected) based on an acceptance probability. If the candidate is accepted, the chain moves to the new value; otherwise the chain stays in the current state. After a burn-in period, which is required to make the influence of initial values negligible, draws from the Markov chain are considered as (correlated) draws from the joint posterior distribution of interest. Two variants of the MH approach are most common:

- the independence chain MH and

- the random-walk MH.

In the former case, candidate draws are generated from an unconditional candidate distribution, whereas in the latter draws are generated from a distribution conditional on (and around) the current value of the chain. In both variants the candidate distribution must be tuned to achieve a reasonable acceptance rate and to explore sufficiently the domain of the posterior distribution. This tuning process requires preliminary runs and some knowledge of MCMC techniques from the user. Hence, the method is not automatic, which is not a desirable property. In addition, for interpreted languages such as R, MATLAB or MATHEMATICA,[4] the MH algorithm can be significantly slower than the importance sampling strategy. This is because the probability of acceptance of the new draw depends on the current state of the Markov chain; hence, the algorithm cannot be vectorised. Finally, the MH algorithm creates a sequence of correlated draws from the posterior distribution. Therefore, robust techniques must be used to assess the precision of the estimators and more draws are required to achieve the same degree of (numerical) precision as the importance sampling approach. The MH algorithm is used in the context of Garch-type models by Müller and Pole (1998), Vrontos *et al* (2000), Tsay (2005, Chapter 10), Gerlach and Chen (2006), Miazhynskaia and Dorffner (2006), Aussenegg and Miazhynskaia (2006), Miazhynskaia *et al* (2006), Chen *et al* (2008, 2009) and Chen and Gerlach (2008).[5]

An interesting strategy has been proposed to automate the MH algorithm and improve its efficiency in the case of Garch-type models. This approach was proposed by Nakatsuma (1998, 2000) and consists of an MH algorithm where the proposal distributions are constructed from auxiliary autoregressive moving average (Arma) processes on the squared observations. In addition, to be fully automatic and more efficient than naive MH approaches, the methodology can be extended to regime-switching Garch models.[6] Note, however, that the construction of the proposal distributions strongly depends on the form of the scedastic function and is not applicable to all Garch-type models. Moreover, the algorithm requires filtering steps which significantly increase the computational burden for highly parameterised models. The approach of Nakatsuma (1998, 2000) is used in Nakatsuma and Tsurumi (1999), Kaufmann and Frühwirth-Schnatter (2002), Kaufmann and Scheicher (2006), Rachev *et al* (2008, Chapter 11), Henneke *et al* (2009), Ardia (2008b) and Ardia (2009). The algorithm is implemented in the "R" package BAYESGARCH (Ardia 2008a; Ardia and Hoogerheide 2009) for the Garch(1,1) model with Student-t disturbances.

AdMitIS

Ardia *et al* (2009a,c) rely on a special case of the adaptive approach proposed by Hoogerheide (2006) and Hoogerheide *et al* (2007) for performing the Bayesian estimation of Garch-type models. The methodology, named ADMITIS for "importance sampling with adaptive mixture of Student-t distributions", consists of two steps. First, the algorithm fits adaptively a mixture of Student-t distributions to the kernel of the posterior density. Then, importance sampling is used to obtain quantities of interest for the target posterior distribution, using the fitted mixture as the importance density. The estimation procedure is fully automatic. Moreover, Ardia *et al* (2009a) compared the methodology with standard cases of importance sampling and MH algorithm using a naive candidate, and with the Griddy–Gibbs approach. Overall, they demonstrate the superiority of the ADMITIS approach in terms of both efficiency and reliability.

Due to its flexibility, the adaptive algorithm is able to provide a suitable importance distribution for non-elliptical, possibly multi-modal, posterior distributions. But it is not only useful for sophisticated Garch-type models. For large samples and/or simple scedastic specifications, the posterior distribution of the model parameters is likely to be roughly elliptical. In these cases, the adaptive approach will stop with one or two mixture components, leading to a simple unimodal symmetric importance density. The adaptive fitting together with the importance sampling estimation is achieved fairly quickly. Therefore, models can be re-estimated many times on many data sets without practical issues. This is clearly an appealing aspect for practitioners. Moreover, Ardia *et al* (2009c) show that the approach allows an efficient and reliable estimation of marginal likelihood, which lies at the heart of model selection and model combination. The approach can therefore be used to estimate, select and combine Garch-type models in a simple, quick and efficient fashion.

THE ADAPTIVE MIXTURE OF STUDENT t METHOD

The adaptive mixture of Student-t distributions (ADMIT) procedure has been developed by Hoogerheide and co-workers.[7] The ADMIT methodology consists of the construction of a mixture of Student-t distributions which approximates a target distribution of interest. The fitting procedure relies only on a kernel of the target density, so that the normalising constant is not required. In a second step, this approximation is used as an importance function in importance sampling (ADMITIS) or as a candidate density in the independence chain MH algorithm (ADMITMH). Both ADMITIS and ADMITMH strategies have been implemented in the "R" package ADMIT (Ardia *et al* 2008), which is freely available from the Comprehensive R Archive Network (CRAN).[8] The use of the package with empirical examples is discussed in Ardia *et al* (2009a,b).

Hoogerheide *et al* (2007) mention several reasons why mixtures of Student-t distributions are natural importance or candidate distributions. Indeed, a Student-t mixture

- provides an accurate approximation of a wide variety of target distributions, with substantial skewness and high kurtosis (it can deal with multi-modality and with non-elliptical shapes),
- can be constructed in a quick, iterative procedure and is easy to sample from,
- has fatter tails than the Gaussian distribution (especially if we specify Student-t components with few degrees of freedom) and therefore the risk that the tails of the importance or

candidate are thinner than those of the target distribution is small.

Moreover, from a purely theoretical framework, the mixture of Student-t densities can approximate any density function to arbitrary accuracy under certain conditions (Zeevi and Meir 1997).

Because of its superiority over several alternative methods, in terms of both efficiency and reliability of posterior estimation (Ardia *et al* 2009a; Hoogerheide 2006; Hoogerheide *et al* 2007) and of marginal likelihood estimation (Ardia *et al* 2009c), we will make use of the ADMITIS approach in the following.

For a given Garch-type model, we denote by $\boldsymbol{\theta} \in \Theta \subseteq \mathbb{R}^d$ the vector of parameters, $p(\boldsymbol{\theta} \mid y)$ the posterior density of $\boldsymbol{\theta}$ and $y \doteq (y_1, \ldots, y_T)'$ the vector of log returns. The joint posterior density of $\boldsymbol{\theta}$ is then obtained by Bayes's Theorem as

$$p(\boldsymbol{\theta} \mid y) = \frac{p(y \mid \boldsymbol{\theta})p(\boldsymbol{\theta})}{\int_\Theta p(y \mid \boldsymbol{\theta})p(\boldsymbol{\theta})\,d\boldsymbol{\theta}} \qquad (1.1)$$

where $p(y \mid \boldsymbol{\theta})$ is the joint density of y given $\boldsymbol{\theta}$, ie, the likelihood, and $p(\boldsymbol{\theta})$ is the exact prior density of $\boldsymbol{\theta}$, ie, not merely a prior kernel. In Expression 1.1, we define $k(\boldsymbol{\theta}) \doteq p(y \mid \boldsymbol{\theta})p(\boldsymbol{\theta})$ as the kernel function of the joint posterior and

$$p(y) \doteq \int_\Theta k(\boldsymbol{\theta})\,d\boldsymbol{\theta} \qquad (1.2)$$

as the marginal likelihood. It is clear that the marginal likelihood is equal to the normalising constant of the joint posterior density (Equation 1.1). As the key ingredient in Bayes factors, the marginal likelihood lies at the heart of model selection and model combination in Bayesian statistics.[9]

The ADMIT methodology constructs a mixture of Student-t distributions in order to approximate the posterior density $p(\boldsymbol{\theta} \mid y)$. The density of a mixture of Student-t distributions can be written as

$$q(\boldsymbol{\theta}) = \sum_{h=1}^{H} \eta_h\, t_d(\boldsymbol{\theta} \mid \boldsymbol{\mu}_h, \Sigma_h, \nu)$$

where $\{\eta_h\}$ are the mixing weights of the Student-t components ($0 \leqslant \eta_h \leqslant 1$ and $\sum_{h=1}^{H} \eta_h = 1$) and $t_d(\boldsymbol{\theta} \mid \boldsymbol{\mu}_h, \Sigma_h, \nu)$ is a d-dimensional Student-t density with mode vector $\boldsymbol{\mu}_h$, scale matrix Σ_h, and ν degrees of freedom. The adaptive mixture approach determines H,

$\{\eta_h\}$, $\{\boldsymbol{\mu}_h\}$ and $\{\boldsymbol{\Sigma}_h\}$ based on the kernel $k(\boldsymbol{\theta})$. It consists of the following steps.

Step 0. Compute the mode $\boldsymbol{\mu}_1$ and scale $\boldsymbol{\Sigma}_1$ of the first Student-t distribution in the mixture as $\boldsymbol{\mu}_1 = \arg\max_{\boldsymbol{\theta}\in\Theta} \log k(\boldsymbol{\theta})$, the mode of the log kernel function, and $\boldsymbol{\Sigma}_1$ as minus the Hessian of $\log k(\boldsymbol{\theta})$ evaluated at its mode $\boldsymbol{\mu}_1$. Then draw a set of N points $\{\boldsymbol{\theta}^{[i]}\}$ from this first stage candidate density $q(\boldsymbol{\theta}) = t_d(\boldsymbol{\theta} \mid \boldsymbol{\mu}_1, \boldsymbol{\Sigma}_1, \nu)$, with small ν to allow for fat tails. N is typically a very large number, eg, $N = 100{,}000$.

Then add components to the mixture iteratively by performing the following steps.

Step 1. Compute the importance sampling weights

$$w(\boldsymbol{\theta}^{[i]}) \doteq \frac{k(\boldsymbol{\theta}^{[i]})}{q(\boldsymbol{\theta}^{[i]})} \qquad (1.3)$$

for $i = 1, \ldots, N$. In order to determine the number of components H of the mixture, we make use of a simple diagnostic criterion: the coefficient of variation, ie, the standard deviation divided by the mean, of the importance sampling weights $\{w(\boldsymbol{\theta}^{[i]})\}$. If the relative change in the coefficient of variation of the importance sampling weights caused by adding one new Student-t component to the candidate mixture is small, eg, less than 10%, then the algorithm stops and the current mixture $q(\boldsymbol{\theta})$ is the approximation. Otherwise, the algorithm goes to step 2.

Step 2. Add another Student-t distribution with density $t_d(\boldsymbol{\theta} \mid \boldsymbol{\mu}_h, \boldsymbol{\Sigma}_h, \nu)$ to the current mixture. The new component is based on the ratio of the previous mixture of Student-t densities and the target density kernel $k(\boldsymbol{\theta})$. It is located where this ratio is relatively high, which does not depend on the normalising constant of the target density. Since for most Garch-type specifications the region of integration Θ is bounded, it may occur that $w(\boldsymbol{\theta})$ attains its maximum at a boundary of Θ. In this case, minus the inverse Hessian of $\log w(\boldsymbol{\theta})$ evaluated at its mode (which would otherwise provide $\boldsymbol{\mu}_h$ and $\boldsymbol{\Sigma}_h$) may be a very poor choice; in fact this Hessian may not even be positive definite. Therefore, in order to avoid any numerical problem, $\boldsymbol{\mu}_h$ and $\boldsymbol{\Sigma}_h$ are obtained as the estimated mean and covariance based on a subset of draws corresponding to a certain percentage of largest weights. More precisely, μ_h and Σ_h are obtained as

$$\mu_h = \sum_{j \in J_c} \frac{w(\theta^{[j]})}{\sum_{j \in J_c} w(\theta^{[j]})} \theta^{[j]}$$

$$\Sigma_h = \sum_{j \in J_c} \frac{w(\theta^{[j]})}{\sum_{j \in J_c} w(\theta^{[j]})} (\theta^{[j]} - \mu_h)(\theta^{[j]} - \mu_h)'$$

where J_c denotes the set of indices corresponding to the c percentage points of the largest weights using the sample $\{w(\theta^{[j]})\}$ from $q(\theta)$ we already have. Since our aim is to detect regions with relatively too little candidate probability mass compared with the target distribution (eg, a distant mode), the percentage c is typically a low value, eg, 5%.

Step 3. Choose the probabilities $\{\eta_h\}$ in the mixture

$$q(\theta) = \sum_{h=1}^{H} \eta_h \, t_d(\theta \mid \mu_h, \Sigma_h, \nu)$$

by minimising the coefficient of variation of the importance sampling weights.

Step 4. Draw a sample of N points $\{\theta^{[i]}\}$ from the new mixture of Student-t distributions

$$q(\theta) = \sum_{h=1}^{H} \eta_h \, t_d(\theta \mid \mu_h, \Sigma_h, \nu)$$

and go to step 1.

The coefficient of variation of the importance sampling weights is a natural and intuitive measure of quality of the candidate as an approximation to the target. If the candidate and the target distributions coincide, all importance sampling weights are equal, so that the coefficient of variation is zero. For a poor candidate that does not even roughly approximate the target, some importance sampling weights are huge while most are (almost) zero, so that the coefficient of variation is high. The better the candidate approximates the target, the more evenly the weight is divided among the candidate draws and the smaller the coefficient of variation of the importance sampling weights.[10]

The mode and Hessian of the log kernel function (step 0), the coefficient of variation of the importance sampling weights (steps 1 and 3) and the scaled weights $w(\boldsymbol{\theta}^{[j]})/\sum_{j\in J_c} w(\boldsymbol{\theta}^{[j]})$ (step 2) do not depend on the normalising constant of the target density, which explains why the whole ADMIT procedure only requires a target density kernel (which is also a property of the MH algorithm).

Once the adaptive mixture of Student-t distributions has been fitted to the target density $p(\boldsymbol{\theta} \mid y)$ through the kernel function $k(\boldsymbol{\theta})$, the approximation $q(\boldsymbol{\theta})$ is used in importance sampling to obtain quantities of interest for the posterior $p(\boldsymbol{\theta} \mid y)$ or to perform model selection and model combination. The importance sampling technique is based on the relationship

$$\mathbb{E}_p[g(\boldsymbol{\theta})] = \frac{\int_\Theta g(\boldsymbol{\theta}) p(\boldsymbol{\theta} \mid y) \, d\boldsymbol{\theta}}{\int_\Theta p(\boldsymbol{\theta} \mid y) \, d\boldsymbol{\theta}}$$

$$= \frac{\int_\Theta g(\boldsymbol{\theta}) w(\boldsymbol{\theta}) q(\boldsymbol{\theta}) \, d\boldsymbol{\theta}}{\int_\Theta w(\boldsymbol{\theta}) q(\boldsymbol{\theta}) \, d\boldsymbol{\theta}}$$

$$= \frac{\mathbb{E}_q[g(\boldsymbol{\theta}) w(\boldsymbol{\theta})]}{\mathbb{E}_q[w(\boldsymbol{\theta})]} \qquad (1.4)$$

where $g(\boldsymbol{\theta})$ is a given function (integrable with respect to $p(\boldsymbol{\theta} \mid y)$), $\mathbb{E}_p$ denotes the expectation with respect to the posterior density $p(\boldsymbol{\theta} \mid y)$ and $\mathbb{E}_q$ denotes the expectation with respect to the Student-t mixture $q(\boldsymbol{\theta})$. The importance sampling estimator of $\mathbb{E}_p[g(\boldsymbol{\theta})]$ is given by

$$\hat{\mathbb{E}}_p[g(\boldsymbol{\theta})] = \frac{\sum_{l=1}^L g(\boldsymbol{\theta}^{[l]}) w(\boldsymbol{\theta}^{[l]})}{\sum_{l=1}^L w(\boldsymbol{\theta}^{[l]})} \qquad (1.5)$$

where $\{\boldsymbol{\theta}^{[l]}\}$ is a sample of L independent and identically distributed (iid) draws from the importance density $q(\boldsymbol{\theta})$. Under certain conditions, $\hat{\mathbb{E}}_p$ is a consistent estimator of $\mathbb{E}_p$ (Geweke 1989a). The choice of the function $g(\boldsymbol{\theta})$ allows us to obtain different quantities of interest; for instance, the posterior mean is obtained with $g(\boldsymbol{\theta}) \doteq \boldsymbol{\theta}$ and the posterior probability of a set $S \subseteq \mathbb{R}^d$ is obtained with $g(\boldsymbol{\theta}) \doteq \mathbf{1}_{\{\boldsymbol{\theta} \in S\}}$, where $\mathbf{1}_{\{\cdot\}}$ denotes the indicator function.

As for any time-series model, prediction is essential. The Bayesian framework allows us to obtain predictive densities that by construction incorporate parameter uncertainty when forecasting future observations. For instance, the one-step-ahead predictive density is obtained by setting $g(\boldsymbol{\theta})$ to the density of the one-step-ahead observation y_{T+1} in Expression 1.4. Formally

$$p(y_{T+1} \mid y) = \int_\Theta p(y_{T+1} \mid \boldsymbol{\theta}, y) p(\boldsymbol{\theta} \mid y) \, d\boldsymbol{\theta} \qquad (1.6)$$

This quantity is easily estimated using Equation 1.5 since $p(y_{T+1} \mid \boldsymbol{\theta}, y)$ is known in closed form for any Garch-type model. For multi-step-ahead forecasts, the predictive density is of unknown form and we must rely on simulation in conjunction with the method of composition. We refer the reader to Ardia (2008b, Chapter 6) for an illustration.

The Bayesian framework is also appealing for selecting and combining models, which is achieved through the computation of the posterior model probability. Assume that we have M (possibly non-nested) Garch-type models $\mathcal{M}_i$ with marginal likelihood $p_i(y)$ and prior model probability $p(\mathcal{M}_i)$. Usually, the prior model probability is equal for all models or favours parsimonious specifications. The posterior model probability of model $\mathcal{M}_i$ is then given by

$$p(\mathcal{M}_i \mid y) = \frac{p_i(y)p(\mathcal{M}_i)}{\sum_{i=1}^{M} p_i(y)p(\mathcal{M}_i)}$$

where the importance sampling approach immediately provides the estimator for the marginal likelihood $p_i(y)$

$$\hat{p}_i(y) = \frac{1}{L} \sum_{l=1}^{L} w_i(\boldsymbol{\theta}_i^{[l]}) \qquad (1.7)$$

as shown by Kloek and van Dijk (1978), for instance. In Expression 1.7, $w_i(\boldsymbol{\theta}_i)$ denotes the weight function (Equation 1.3) based on the kernel $k_i(\boldsymbol{\theta}_i)$ and the Student-t mixture density $q_i(\boldsymbol{\theta}_i)$ corresponding to model $\mathcal{M}_i$, and $\{\boldsymbol{\theta}_i^{[l]}\}$ are L iid draws generated from $q_i(\boldsymbol{\theta}_i)$, where $\boldsymbol{\theta}_i \in \Theta_i \subseteq \mathbb{R}^{d_i}$. Therefore, the estimator of Equation 1.7 is simply obtained as the sample counterpart of Equation 1.2 for $\mathcal{M}_i$, which can be expressed as

$$\begin{aligned} p_i(y) &= \int_{\Theta_i} k_i(\boldsymbol{\theta}_i) \, \mathrm{d}\boldsymbol{\theta}_i \\ &= \int_{\Theta_i} \frac{k_i(\boldsymbol{\theta}_i)}{q_i(\boldsymbol{\theta}_i)} q_i(\boldsymbol{\theta}_i) \, \mathrm{d}\boldsymbol{\theta}_i \\ &= \int_{\Theta_i} w_i(\boldsymbol{\theta}_i) q_i(\boldsymbol{\theta}_i) \, \mathrm{d}\boldsymbol{\theta}_i \end{aligned}$$

For model discrimination, the model with the largest posterior probability will then be selected. The posterior probability can also be used to produce a combination of the predictive distributions, an approach referred to as Bayesian model averaging (BMA) in the literature (Kass and Raftery 1995). For instance, the one-step-ahead

BMA predictive density is given by

$$p_{BMA}(y_{T+1} \mid y) = \sum_{i=1}^{M} p_i(y_{T+1} \mid y) p(\mathcal{M}_i \mid y) \quad (1.8)$$

where $p_i(y_{T+1} \mid y)$ denotes the predictive density of model $\mathcal{M}_i$, which is easily obtained using Equation 1.6 with the density $p_i(y_{T+1} \mid \theta_i, y)$ and the posterior $p_i(\theta_i \mid y)$ corresponding to $\mathcal{M}_i$. Expression 1.8 is merely the weighted average of the M single-model one-step-ahead predictive densities, where the weights are the posterior model probabilities. This distribution of the one-step-ahead observation accounts for uncertainty in both parameter values and model choice.

EMPIRICAL ILLUSTRATION

This section proposes an illustration of the AdMitIS strategy with the Bayesian estimation of two non-nested Garch-type models. The posterior model probabilities are estimated and used to combine the predictive densities of the one-day-ahead log returns. This case study aims at describing in a real-life example the mechanics of the AdMitIS strategy and demonstrating its effectiveness.

We apply our Bayesian estimation methods to daily observations of the S&P 500 Index log returns. The sample period is from April 28, 1995, to October 27, 1997, for a total of 633 observations. The reason for this particular data window of two and a half years, which is long enough to estimate Garch-type models, is that it ends with an extremely negative return, which makes the differences between forecasts from the two models more clearly visible. Further, for this data set the typically imposed restrictions on the models (for ensuring stationarity and positivity of the volatility process) seem to be supported by the data. The analysis of the correctness of the model restrictions falls outside the scope of this chapter. The time series has been de-meaned and the nominal returns are expressed in percent. Robust autocorrelation tests do not exhibit any autocorrelation in the returns, whereas significant autocorrelation is detected for the squared log returns, thus suggesting Garch effects in the data.

The two models are based on two non-nested scedastic functions. For the variance dynamics, we use the parsimonious but effective

GJR(1,1) (Glosten et al 1993) and EGarch(1,1) (Nelson 1991) specifications. These models are well known in univariate Garch modelling for their ability to reproduce the asymmetric behaviour of the conditional variance observed in equity markets. For the model disturbances, we consider Student-t innovations, which allow us to reproduce fat tails in the conditional distribution.

Formally, the log returns $\{y_t\}$ can be expressed as

$$y_t = \sigma_t \varrho \varepsilon_t, \quad t = 1, \ldots, T$$

where the scedastic function σ_t^2 can be of either GJR type

$$\sigma_t^2 \doteq \omega + \alpha y_{t-1}^2 + \gamma y_{t-1}^2 \mathbf{1}_{\{y_{t-1}<0\}} + \beta \sigma_{t-1}^2, \quad \omega > 0, \ \alpha, \gamma, \beta \geqslant 0$$

or EGarch type

$$\log(\sigma_t^2) \doteq \omega + \alpha \left[\left| \frac{y_{t-1}}{\sigma_{t-1}} \right| - \mathbb{E}\left(\left| \frac{y_{t-1}}{\sigma_{t-1}} \right| \right) \right] + \gamma \frac{y_{t-1}}{\sigma_{t-1}} + \beta \log(\sigma_{t-1}^2)$$

and where the disturbances ε_t are iid Student-t variates

$$p(\varepsilon_t) \doteq \frac{\Gamma(\frac{1}{2}(\nu + 1))}{\Gamma(\frac{1}{2}\nu)(\pi\nu)^{1/2}} \left(1 + \frac{\varepsilon_t^2}{\nu}\right)^{-(\nu+1)/2}, \quad \nu > 2$$

The scalar ϱ is the normalising factor $\sqrt{(\nu-2)/\nu}$ to ensure that the conditional variance is σ_t^2. For the Student-t variates y_{t-1}/σ_{t-1} that are normalised to have variance 1, we have

$$\mathbb{E}\left(\left| \frac{y_{t-1}}{\sigma_{t-1}} \right| \right) = \frac{\sqrt{\nu-2}\,\Gamma(\frac{1}{2}(\nu-1))}{\sqrt{\pi}\,\Gamma(\frac{1}{2}\nu)}$$

Note the positivity constraints on the model parameters in order to ensure a positive conditional variance, and the constraint on the degrees of freedom parameter to ensure the existence of a finite conditional variance. Moreover, we require the process to be covariance stationary, ie, $\alpha + \frac{1}{2}\gamma + \beta < 1$ for the GJR(1,1) model and $|\beta| < 1$ for the EGarch(1,1) model. Note that the model specifications are used for illustrative purposes only; checking for possible model misspecification is beyond the scope of this chapter.

For both models we specify weakly informative, proper prior distributions on the parameters that can roughly be interpreted as the proper versions of the improper priors used by Vrontos et al (2000). We use proper priors for computing posterior model probabilities and performing Bayesian model averaging. For the GJR(1,1) model, we specify a Gaussian distribution for $\log(\omega)$ with mean $\log(0.01)$

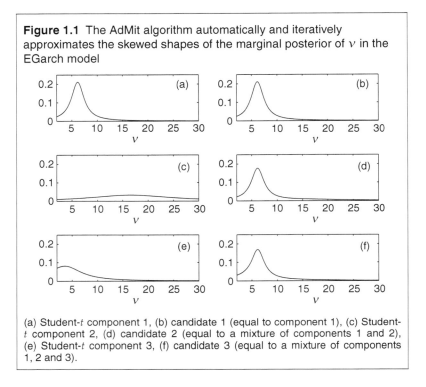

Figure 1.1 The AdMit algorithm automatically and iteratively approximates the skewed shapes of the marginal posterior of v in the EGarch model

(a) Student-t component 1, (b) candidate 1 (equal to component 1), (c) Student-t component 2, (d) candidate 2 (equal to a mixture of components 1 and 2), (e) Student-t component 3, (f) candidate 3 (equal to a mixture of components 1, 2 and 3).

and standard deviation $\log(10)$, which amounts to a 95% prior interval for ω between 0.0001 and 1. For α, γ and β we use a uniform prior on the subspace with $\alpha > 0$, $\gamma > 0$, $\beta > 0$, $\alpha + \frac{1}{2}\gamma + \beta < 1$. We specify an exponential prior distribution with mean 20 for $(v - 2)$. For the EGarch$(1,1)$ model we choose a uniform prior on $[-1, 1]$ for β. For ω, α and γ we use Gaussian priors with zero mean and standard deviation 0.1. Again we specify an exponential prior distribution with mean 20 for $(v - 2)$.

The priors are combined with the likelihood function, leading to the posterior kernel functions. These kernels are used in the ADMIT algorithm. For each model, ADMIT was applied with $N = 100,000$ draws. For both models, the algorithm led to a mixture of three Student-t distributions as the importance sampling distribution. Figure 1.1 illustrates the steps of the ADMIT algorithm for the marginal posterior of v in the EGarch model. The first candidate is a Student-t distribution around the posterior mode. Second, a Student-t component is added that is located in the right tail, yielding a right-skewed

Table 1.1 Posterior results for the two non-nested models using AdMitIS

θ	$\hat{\mathbb{E}}_p(\theta)$	NSE	RNE	$\hat{\mathbb{V}}_p^{1/2}(\theta)$
\multicolumn{5}{c}{$\mathcal{M}_1$: GJR Student-t}
ω	0.0205	0.0002	0.0927	0.0147
α	0.0349	0.0002	0.1232	0.0240
γ	0.1124	0.0005	0.1404	0.0566
β	0.8898	0.0004	0.1207	0.0424
ν	6.4843	0.0201	0.0693	1.6745
\multicolumn{5}{c}{$\mathcal{M}_2$: EGarch Student-t}
ω	−0.0105	0.0001	0.1198	0.0117
α	0.1384	0.0002	0.2525	0.0367
γ	−0.0737	0.0002	0.2230	0.0318
β	0.9733	0.0002	0.1201	0.0201
ν	6.6905	0.0140	0.1844	1.9667

$\hat{\mathbb{E}}_p(\theta)$, posterior mean estimate; NSE, numerical standard error of the posterior mean estimate; RNE, relative numerical efficiency of the posterior mean estimate; $\hat{\mathbb{V}}_p^{1/2}(\theta)$, posterior standard deviation estimate. The number of importance sampling draws is $L = 100{,}000$.

candidate. This consists of a substantial improvement of the approximation to the posterior, shown in Figure 1.3, so that the ADMIT algorithm continues. Third, a Student-t component is added that is placed in the short left tail. This is only a minor improvement of the candidate, so that the ADMIT algorithm stops at three components. Notice that the ADMIT algorithm provides an approximation of the joint posterior in the five-dimensional parameter space; Figure 1.1 displays the one-dimensional marginal candidate distribution of ν only for illustration.

The densities constructed by ADMIT for each models are used to perform the Bayesian estimation of the model parameters via importance sampling (ADMITIS) using $L = 100{,}000$ draws. Results are reported in Table 1.1 and marginal posterior densities are shown in Figures 1.2 and 1.3. We notice the strong evidence for the leverage effect in the time series ($\gamma > 0$ in GJR, $\gamma < 0$ in EGarch), as well as conditional leptokurticity in the data with a rather small ν. The standard deviations of the parameters are quite large. We also report the numerical standard errors (NSEs), ie, the square root of

Table 1.2 Posterior results for the two non-nested models using naive importance sampling

θ	$\hat{\mathbb{E}}_p(\theta)$	NSE	RNE	$\hat{\mathbb{V}}_p^{1/2}(\theta)$
\multicolumn{5}{c}{$\mathcal{M}_1$: **GJR Student-t**}
ω	0.0202	0.0003	0.0271	0.0148
α	0.0350	0.0003	0.0890	0.0241
γ	0.1112	0.0008	0.0516	0.0565
β	0.8903	0.0006	0.0427	0.0424
ν	6.5077	0.0291	0.0337	1.6884
\multicolumn{5}{c}{$\mathcal{M}_2$: **EGarch Student-t**}
ω	−0.0106	0.0001	0.0608	0.0117
α	0.1389	0.0003	0.1722	0.0372
γ	−0.0734	0.0002	0.1710	0.0318
β	0.9732	0.0003	0.0467	0.0202
ν	6.6508	0.0180	0.1028	1.8265

Models use naive importance sampling (ie, a Student-t distribution around the posterior mode). See Table 1.1 for explanations.

Figure 1.2 Marginal posterior densities for parameters in the GJR model

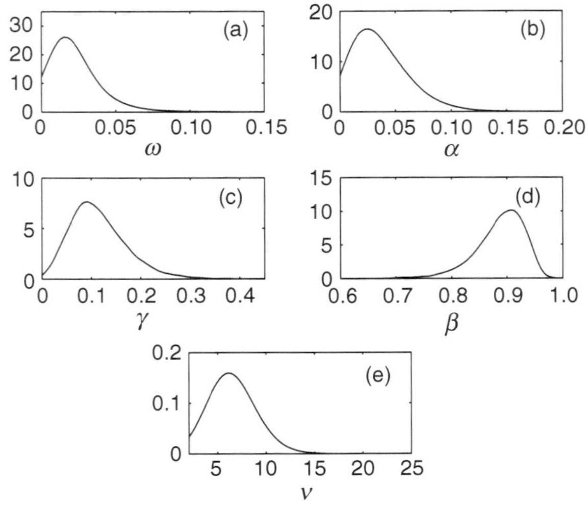

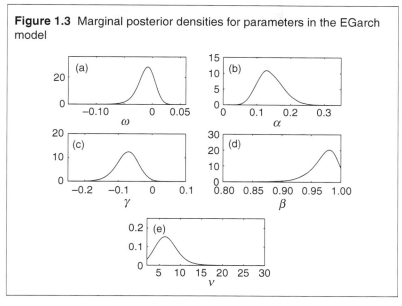

Figure 1.3 Marginal posterior densities for parameters in the EGarch model

the variance of the estimates that can be expected if the simulations were to be repeated with different random numbers. The relative numerical efficiency (RNE) of the estimate is the ratio between an estimate of the variance of a hypothetical estimator based on direct sampling and the importance sampling estimator's estimated variance with the same number of draws. It is an indicator of the efficiency of the chosen importance function; if the target and importance densities coincide, RNE equals 1, whereas a very poor importance density will have a RNE close to zero. Both NSE and RNE are estimated by the method given in Geweke (1989a). The numerical standard error and relative numerical efficiency indicate a reasonable degree of efficiency for the methods, which may be difficult to achieve for non-elliptical, skewed, multidimensional posterior distributions. Table 1.2 reports estimation results for importance sampling using a naive importance density, ie, a Student-t distribution around the posterior mode. Note the lower RNE for all coefficients in both models, as compared with ADMITIS. For the GJR parameter ω and EGarch parameter v, for which the marginal posteriors are substantially skewed, the RNEs are 3.4 and 2.6 times higher in the ADMITIS approach. Further, note the lower estimate of the posterior standard deviation of the EGarch parameter v. Even for $L = 100{,}000$ draws, the naive approach may hardly cover some relevant regions

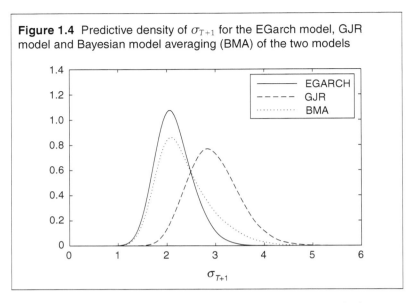

Figure 1.4 Predictive density of σ_{T+1} for the EGarch model, GJR model and Bayesian model averaging (BMA) of the two models

of the parameter space. This failure of the naive approach does not show up in the NSE and RNE, as these only concern the parameter subspace that is visited by the draws. It should be mentioned here that the models that are used in practice often have more than five parameters, and that posterior shapes can be much further from normality than those in our application (eg, we have not only skewness but also curved ridges or even multimodality). In such cases, the naive simulation method's problem of neglecting relevant parts of the parameter space can be even worse. Then estimation, prediction and risk measurement can suffer from substantial biases.

As explained in the previous section, the ADMIT algorithm also delivers a suitable importance density for marginal likelihood estimation. The natural logarithm of the ADMITIS estimate of the marginal likelihood is given by -725.6930 and -724.5382 for the GJR and EGarch model, respectively. This implies a Bayes factor of 3.1734 in favour of the EGarch model, given the observed data. Under equal prior model probabilities, ie, a prior odds ratio of 1, the posterior probabilities for the GJR and EGarch models are estimated as 0.2396 and 0.7604, respectively.

In Figures 1.4 and 1.5, we display the predictive densities for the volatility σ_{T+1} and log return y_{T+1} for October 28, 1997, for the GJR and EGarch models as well as for Bayesian model averaging (BMA), which combines the predictive densities from the models via the

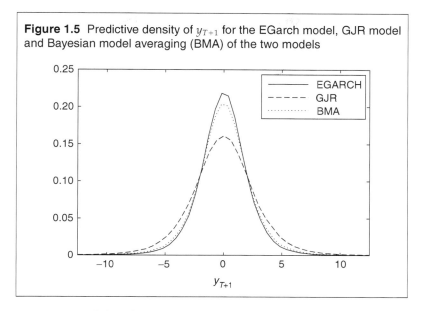

Figure 1.5 Predictive density of y_{T+1} for the EGarch model, GJR model and Bayesian model averaging (BMA) of the two models

posterior model probabilities. Approximate values of risk measures such as the value-at-risk (VaR) can be read from the figure.

Precise estimation of the VaR at the $100\alpha\%$ risk level can be obtained via importance sampling as follows. First, L draws $\{\boldsymbol{\theta}^{[l]}\}$ are simulated from the importance density, and the corresponding importance weights $\{w(\boldsymbol{\theta}^{[l]})\}$ are computed. Second, for the $\tilde{L}$ ($\tilde{L} \leqslant L$) draws with non-zero weights, a log return $y_{T+1}^{[l]}$ is simulated from its distribution given the model and parameter values. Third, the simulated log returns $y_{T+1}^{[l]}$ are sorted ascending as $y_{T+1}^{(i)}$ ($i = 1, \ldots, \tilde{L}$) and the VaR is estimated as $y_{T+1}^{(k)}$ with $S_k = (1 - \alpha)$, where

$$S_k \doteq \sum_{j=1}^{k} \tilde{w}(\boldsymbol{\theta}^{(j)})$$

is the cumulative sum of scaled weights

$$\tilde{w}(\boldsymbol{\theta}^{(j)}) \doteq \frac{w(\boldsymbol{\theta}^{(j)})}{\sum_{i=1}^{\tilde{L}} w(\boldsymbol{\theta}^{(i)})}$$

(ie, scaled to add to 1) corresponding to the ascending log returns. In general there will be no k such that $S_k = (1 - \alpha)$, so that we interpolate between the values of $y_{T+1}^{(k)}$ and $y_{T+1}^{(k+1)}$ where S_{k+1} is the smallest value with $S_{k+1} > (1 - \alpha)$. For importance sampling estimation of VaR in the case of more general profit and loss functions,

Table 1.3 Estimates of the $100\alpha\%$ one-day-ahead value-at-risk for the GJR model, EGarch model and Bayesian model averaging of the two models

α	$\mathcal{M}_1$	$\mathcal{M}_2$	BMA
0.95	−4.7124	−3.4304	−3.7524
0.99	−7.6982	−5.6465	−6.3128

$\mathcal{M}_1$, GJR Student's t; $\mathcal{M}_2$, EGarch Student's t; BMA, Bayesian model averaging.

see Hoogerheide and van Dijk (2010). Hoogerheide and van Dijk (2010) also introduce an additional approximation step, targeted particularly on generating high loss scenarios, that can make the simulation-based estimation of VaR even more efficient.

Table 1.3 reports the values for the one-day-ahead VaR for October 28, 1997, for both models and BMA. Figures 1.4 and 1.5 and Table 1.3 show that the GJR model predicts higher risk than EGarch, with BMA results naturally taking a position in between. Accounting for both the uncertainty on estimated parameters and the uncertainty on model choice, we obtain BMA estimates of VaR (at the 95% risk level) at −3.7524%.

Finally, note that instead of integrating out the parameter (and model) uncertainty in the VaR forecast, we could also determine the impact of the parameter (and model) uncertainty on the VaR estimate. We do not investigate this point here but refer the reader to Chapter 2. See also Ardia (2008b, Chapter 6) for an illustration of the impact of the parameter uncertainty to the VaR and expected shortfall term structures.

CONCLUSION

The study of Garch-type models from a Bayesian viewpoint is relatively recent and can be considered very promising due to the advantages of the Bayesian approach over classical techniques. In particular, the Bayesian framework enables small sample results, robust estimation and probabilistic statements on non-linear functions of the model parameters and model discrimination. Moreover, the Bayesian paradigm allows a combination of model forecasts, thus accounting for model risk in the predictions, which is crucial from a risk management perspective.

This chapter reviewed existing methods for the Bayesian estimation of Garch-type models. We focused our presentation on a novel approach, named ADMITIS, which performs importance sampling with an adaptive mixture of Student-t distributions as the importance distribution. The methodology allows a quick and efficient estimation of any kind of Garch-type models. Moreover, with this approach, it is easy to combine forecasts of non-nested models. The estimation procedure is fully automatic and is achieved within a reasonable computational time compared with alternative MCMC techniques. This is of primary importance for automated trading systems, for instance, where models are estimated frequently and for numerous data sets.

The ADMITIS algorithm was described in detail and we provided an application to S&P 500 Index log returns. We illustrated how two non-nested Garch-type models can be estimated and combined in order to forecast the next-day-ahead log returns distribution.

> The views expressed in this chapter are the sole responsibility of the authors and do not necessarily reflect those of aeris CAPITAL AG or any of its affiliates.

---

1 See Bollerslev *et al* (1992), Bollerslev *et al* (1994) and Engle (2004) for a review.

2 See, for example, Lamoureux and Lastrapes (1990).

3 For a general introduction to MCMC methods, see Chapter 2 of Volume I.

4 See R Development Core Team (2009), http://www.mathworks.com and http://www.wolfram.com/, respectively.

5 See also Chapter 3.

6 See Ardia (2008b, Chapter 7) and Ardia (2009).

7 See Hoogerheide (2006), Hoogerheide *et al* (2007) and Hoogerheide and van Dijk (2008).

8 See http://cran.r-project.org/package=AdMit.

9 See, for example, Kass and Raftery (1995) and Chapter 1, Volume I, page 18.

10 We refer the reader to Ardia *et al* (2009a) for theoretical reasons justifying the coefficient of variation.

REFERENCES

Ardia, D., 2008a, "'BAYESGARCH': Bayesian Estimation of the Garch(1,1) Model with Student-t Innovations in R", URL: http://CRAN.R-project.org/package=bayesGarch.

Ardia, D., 2008b, *Financial Risk Management with Bayesian Estimation of Garch Models: Theory and Applications*, Lecture Notes in Economics and Mathematical Systems, Volume 612 (Springer).

Ardia, D., 2009, "Bayesian Estimation of a Markov-Switching Threshold Asymmetric Garch Model with Student-*t* Innovations", *Econometrics Journal* 12, pp. 105–26.

Ardia, D., and L. F. Hoogerheide, 2009, "Bayesian Estimation of the Garch(1,1) Model with Student-*t* Innovations in R", MPRA Working Paper, URL: http://mpra.ub.uni-muenchen.de/17414/.

Ardia, D., L. F. Hoogerheide and H. K. van Dijk, 2008, " 'AdMit': Adaptive Mixture of Student-*t* Distributions for Efficient Simulation in R", URL: http://CRAN.R-project.org/package=AdMit.

Ardia, D., L. F. Hoogerheide and H. K. van Dijk, 2009a, "Adaptive Mixture of Student-*t* Distributions as a Flexible Candidate Distribution for Efficient Simulation: The R Package AdMit", *Journal of Statistical Software* 29(3), pp. 1–32.

Ardia, D., L. F. Hoogerheide and H. K. van Dijk, 2009b, "AdMit: Adaptive Mixtures of Student-*t* Distributions", *The R Journal* 1(1), pp. 25–30.

Ardia, D., L. F. Hoogerheide and H. K. van Dijk, 2009c, "To Bridge, to Warp or to Wrap? A Comparative Study of Monte Carlo Methods for Efficient Evaluation of Marginal Likelihoods", Report 09-017/4, Tinbergen Institute.

Asai, M., 2006, "Comparison of MCMC Methods for Estimating Garch Models", *Journal of the Japan Statistical Society* 36(2), pp. 199–212.

Ausin, M. C., and P. Galeano, 2007, "Bayesian Estimation of the Gaussian Mixture Garch Model", *Computational Statistics and Data Analysis* 51(5), pp. 2636–52.

Aussenegg, W., and T. Miazhynskaia, 2006, "Uncertainty in Value-at-Risk Estimates under Parametric and Non-Parametric Modeling", *Financial Markets and Portfolio Management* 20(3), pp. 243–64.

Bauwens, L., and M. Lubrano, 1998, "Bayesian Inference on Garch Models Using the Gibbs Sampler, *Econometrics Journal* 1(1), pp. C23–46.

Bauwens, L., and M. Lubrano, 2002, "Bayesian Option Pricing Using Asymmetric Garch Models", *Journal of Empirical Finance* 9(3), pp. 321–42.

Bauwens, L., M. Lubrano and J. F. Richard, 2000, *Bayesian Inference in Dynamic Econometric Models*, Advanced Texts in Econometrics, First Edition (Oxford University Press).

Bauwens. L., A. Preminger and J. V. K. Rombouts, 2010, "Theory and Inference for a Markov Switching Garch Model", *The Econometrics Journal* 13(2), pp. 218–44.

Bauwens. L. and J. V. K. Rombouts, 2007, "Bayesian Inference for the Mixed Conditional Heteroskedasticity Model", *Econometrics Journal* 10(2), pp. 408–25.

Black. F., 1976, "The Pricing of Commodity Contracts", *Journal of Financial Economics* 3, pp. 167–79.

Bollerslev, T., R. Y. Chou and K. Kroner, 1992, "Arch Modeling in Finance: A Review of the Theory and Empirical Evidence", *Journal of Econometrics* 52, pp. 5–59.

Bollerslev, T., R. F. Engle and D. B. Nelson, 1994, "Arch Models", in *Handbook of Econometrics*, Chapter 49, pp. 2959–3038 (Amsterdam: North Holland).

Chen, C. W., and R. Gerlach, 2008, "Bayesian Inference and Model Comparison for Asymmetric Smooth Transition Heteroscedastic Models", *Statistics and Computing* 18(4), pp. 391–408.

Chen, C. W., R. Gerlach and M. K. P. So, 2008, "Bayesian Model Selection for Heteroscedastic Models", in S. Chib, G. Koop, B. Griffiths and D. Terrell (eds), *Bayesian Econometrics*, Advances in Econometrics, pp. 567–94 (Bingley, UK: Emerald Group).

Chen, C. W., M. K. P. So and E. M. H Lin, 2009, "Volatility Forecasting with Double Markov Switching Garch Models", *Journal of Forecasting* 28(8), pp. 681–97.

Dueker, M. J., 1997, "Markov Switching in Garch Processes and Mean-Reverting Stock-Market Volatility", *Journal of Business and Economic Statistics* 15(1), pp. 26–34.

Engle, R. F., 1982, "Autoregressive Conditional Heteroscedasticity with Estimates of the Variance of United Kingdom Inflation", *Econometrica* 50(4), pp. 987–1008.

Engle, R. F., 2004, "Risk and Volatility: Econometric Models and Financial Practice", *The American Economic Review* 94(3), pp. 405–20.

Frühwirth-Schnatter, S. 2006, *Finite Mixture and Markov Switching Models*, First Edition, Springer Series in Statistics (Springer).

Gerlach, R., and C. W. S. Chen, 2006, "Comparison of Nonnested Asymmetric Heteroscedastic Models", *Computational Statistics and Data Analysis* 51(15), pp. 2164–178.

Geweke, J. F., 1988, "Exact Inference in Models with Autoregressive Conditional Heteroscedasticity", in E. R. Berndt, H. L. White and W. A. Barnett (eds), *Dynamic Econometric Modeling*, International Symposium in Economic Theory and Econometrics, Volume 3, pp. 73–103 (Cambridge University Press).

Geweke, J. F., 1989a, "Bayesian Inference in Econometric Models Using Monte Carlo Integration", *Econometrica* 57(6), pp. 1317–39. (Reprinted in *Bayesian Inference* (1994), G. C. Box and N. Polson (eds), Edward Elgar Publishing.)

Geweke, J. F., 1989b, "Exact Predictive Densities in Linear Models with Arch Disturbances", *Journal of Econometrics* 40(1), pp. 63–86.

Glosten, L. R., R. Jaganathan and D. E. Runkle, 1993, "On the Relation Between the Expected Value and the Volatility of the Nominal Excess Return on Stocks", *Journal of Finance* 48(5), pp. 1779–801.

Hammersley, J. M., and D. C. Handscomb, 1965, *Monte Carlo Methods* (London: Chapman & Hall).

Hastings, W. K., 1970, "Monte Carlo Sampling Methods Using Markov Chains and Their Applications", *Biometrika* 57(1), pp. 97–109.

Henneke, J. S., T. Rachev Svetlozar, F. J. Fabozzi and M. Nikolov, 2009, "MCMC-Based Estimation of Markov Switching Arma–Garch Models", *Applied Economics* DOI:10.1080/00036840802552379.

Hoogerheide, L. F., 2006, "Essays on Neural Network Sampling Methods and Instrumental Variables", PhD Thesis, Tinbergen Institute, Erasmus University Rotterdam (Tinbergen Institute Research Series, Volume 379).

Hoogerheide, L. F., J. F. Kaashoek and H. K. van Dijk, 2007, "On the Shape of Posterior Densities and Credible Sets in Instrumental Variable Regression Models with Reduced Rank: An Application of Flexible Sampling Methods using Neural Networks", *Journal of Econometrics* 139(1), pp. 154–80.

Hoogerheide, L. F., and H. K. van Dijk, 2008, "Possibly Ill-Behaved Posteriors in Econometric Models: On the Connection between Model Structures, Non-elliptical Credible Sets and Neural Network Simulation Techniques", Discussion Paper 2008-036/4, Tinbergen Institute, URL: http://www.tinbergen.nl/discussionpapers/08036.pdf.

Hoogerheide, L. F., and H. K. van Dijk, 2020, "Bayesian Forecasting of Value at Risk and Expected Shortfall using Adaptive Importance Sampling", *International Journal of Forecasting* 26(2), pp. 231–47.

Kass, R. E., and A. E. Raftery, 1995, "Bayes Factors", *Journal of the American Statistical Association* 90(430), pp. 773–95.

Kaufmann, S., and S. Frühwirth-Schnatter, 2002, "Bayesian Analysis of Switching Arch Models", *Journal of Time Series Analysis* 23(4), pp. 425–58.

Kaufmann, S., and M. Scheicher, 2006, "A Switching Arch Model for the German DAX Index", *Studies in Nonlinear Dynamics and Econometrics* 10(4), no. 3, pp. 1–35, URL: http://www.bepress.com/snde/vol10/iss4/art3/.

Klaassen, F., 2002, "Improving Garch Volatility Forecasts with Regime-Switching Garch", *Empirical Economics* 27(2), pp. 363–94.

Kleibergen, F., and H. K. van Dijk, 1993, "Non-Stationarity in Garch Models: A Bayesian Analysis", *Journal of Applied Econometrics* 8(S1), pp. S41–61.

Kloek, T., and H. K. van Dijk, 1978, "Bayesian Estimates of Equation System Parameters: An Application of Integration by Monte Carlo", *Econometrica* 46(1), pp. 1–19.

Lamoureux, C. G., and W. D. Lastrapes, 1990, "Persistence in Variance, Structural Change, and the Garch Model", *Journal of Business and Economic Statistics* 8(2), pp. 225–43.

Lee, S. W., and B. E. Hansen, 1994, "Asymptotic Theory for the Garch(1,1) Quasi-Maximum Likelihood Estimator", *Econometric Theory* 10(1), pp. 29–52.

Marcucci, J., 2005, "Forecasting Stock Market Volatility with Regime-Switching Garch Models", *Studies in Nonlinear Dynamics and Econometrics* 9(4), no. 6, pp. 1–53, URL: http://www.bepress.com/snde/vol9/iss4/art6/.

Metropolis, N., A. W. Rosenbluth, M. N. Rosenbluth, A. H. Teller and E. Teller, 1953, "Equations of State Calculations by Fast Computing Machines", *Journal of Chemical Physics* 21(6), pp. 1087–92.

Miazhynskaia, T., and G. Dorffner, 2006, "A Comparison of Bayesian Model Selection Based on MCMC with Application to Garch-type Models", *Statistical Papers* 47(4), pp. 525–49.

Miazhynskaia, T., S. Frühwirth-Schnatter and G. Dorffner, 2006, "Bayesian Testing for Non-Linearity in Volatility Modeling", *Computational Statistics and Data Analysis* 51(3), pp. 2029–42.

Müller, P., and A. Pole, 1998, "Monte Carlo Posterior Integration in Garch Models", *Sankhya: The Indian Journal of Statistics* 60, pp. 127–44.

Nakatsuma, T., 1998, "A Markov-Chain Sampling Algorithm for Garch Models", *Studies in Nonlinear Dynamics and Econometrics* 3(2), pp. 107–117, URL: http://www.bepress.com/snde/vol3/iss2/algorithm1/.

Nakatsuma, T., 2000, "Bayesian Analysis of Arma–Garch Models: A Markov Chain Sampling Approach", *Journal of Econometrics* 95(1), pp. 57–69.

Nakatsuma, T., and H. Tsurumi, 1999, "Bayesian Estimation of Arma–Garch Model of Weekly Foreign Exchange Rates", *Asia-Pacific Financial Markets* 6, pp. 71–84.

Nelson, D. B., 1991, "Conditional Heteroskedasticity in Asset Returns: A New Approach", *Econometrica* 59(2), pp. 347–70.

R Development Core Team, 2008, *R: A Language and Environment for Statistical Computing* (Vienna, Austria: R Foundation for Statistical Computing).

Rachev, S. T., J. S. J. Hsu, S. Bagasheva Biliana, and F. J. Fabozzi, 2008, *Bayesian Methods in Finance* (Chichester: John Wiley and Sons).

Ritter, C., and M. A. Tanner, 1992, "Facilitating the Gibbs Sampler: The Gibbs Stopper and the Griddy–Gibbs Sampler", *Journal of the American Statistical Association* 87(419), pp. 861–8.

Tsay, R. S., 2005, *Analysis of Financial Time Series*, Wiley Series in Probability and Statistics, Second Edition (Hoboken, NJ: John Wiley and Sons).

Vrontos, I. D., P. Dellaportas and D. N. Politis, 2000, "Full Bayesian Inference for Garch and EGarch Models", *Journal of Business and Economic Statistics* 18(2), pp. 187–98.

Wago, H., 2004, "Bayesian Estimation of Smooth Transition Garch Model Using Gibbs Sampling", *Mathematics and Computer in Simulation* 64(1), pp. 63–78.

Zakoian, J. M., 1994, "Threshold Heteroskedastic Models", *Journal of Economic Dynamic and Control* 18(5), pp. 931–55.

Zeevi, A. J., and R. Meir, 1997, "Density Estimation Through Convex Combinations of Densities: Approximation and Estimation Bounds", *Neural Networks* 10(1), pp. 99–109.

2

Bayesian Inference for Stochastic Volatility Modelling

Hedibert F. Lopes, Nicholas G. Polson
The University of Chicago Booth School of Business

This chapter reviews the major contributions to the literature on the Bayesian analysis of stochastic volatility (SV) models (univariate and multivariate) since 1990. Bayesian inference is performed by tailoring Markov chain Monte Carlo (MCMC) or sequential Monte Carlo (SMC) schemes that take into account the specific modelling characteristics.

The popular univariate stochastic volatility model with first-order autoregressive dynamics is introduced in the next section, which provides a detailed explanation of efficient MCMC and SMC algorithms. We briefly describe several extensions to the basic SV model that allow for fat-tailed, skewed, correlated errors as well as jumps (Markovian or not, smooth or not) in both observation and volatility equations and the leverage effect via correlated errors.

Multivariate SV models are then discussed (see page 46), with particular emphasis on Wishart random processes, Cholesky stochastic volatility models and factor stochastic volatility models. The next section (see page 51) contains several illustrations of both univariate and multivariate SV models based on both MCMC and SMC algorithms. In the last section we give our conclusions.

UNIVARIATE STOCHASTIC VOLATILITY MODELS

Univariate SV asset price dynamics results in the movements of an equity index S_t and its stochastic volatility v_t via a continuous-time diffusion by a Brownian motion (Rosenberg 1972; Taylor 1986; Hull and White 1987; Ghysels $et\ al$ 1996; Johannes and Polson 2010):

$$d \log S_t = \mu\, dt + \sqrt{v_t}\, dB_t^P \qquad (2.1)$$

$$d \log v_t = \kappa(\gamma - \log v_t)\, dt + \tau\, dB_t^V \qquad (2.2)$$

where the parameters that govern the volatility evolution are $(\mu, \kappa, \gamma, \tau)$ and the (possibly correlated) Brownian motions (B_t^P, B_t^V). One extension of the above model is the stochastic volatility jump (SVJ) model, which includes the possibility of jumps to asset prices. Here the equity index S_t and its stochastic variance v_t replaces Equation 2.1 by

$$d \log S_t = \mu \, dt + \sqrt{v_t} \, dB_t^P + d\left(\sum_{j=n_{t-1}}^{n_t} Z_j \right) \quad (2.3)$$

where the additional term in the above equity price evolution describes the jump process with jump sizes Z_j (Eraker et al 2003; Johannes and Polson 2010). We now show how to perform Bayesian inference for a wide class of models.

The SV model

Data arises in discrete time, so it is natural to take an Euler discretisation of Equations 2.1 and 2.2. This is then commonly referred to as the SV autoregressive model and is described by the following non-linear dynamic model (West and Harrison 1997)

$$y_t = e^{x_t/2} \varepsilon_t \quad (2.4)$$
$$x_t = \beta_0 + \beta_1 x_{t-1} + \tau \eta_t \quad (2.5)$$

where y_t are log returns, and log variances $x_t = \log v_t$, ε_t and η_t are independent and identically distributed (iid) standard normal errors. We take $\mu = 0$ for simplicity, and $\beta_0 = \kappa \gamma$, $\beta_1 = 1 - \kappa$. The initial log-volatility state $x_0 \sim N(m_0, C_0)$, for known prior moments m_0 and C_0. An alternative specification assumes that

$$(x_0 \mid \beta_0, \beta_1, \tau^2) \sim N\left(\frac{\beta_0}{1 - \beta_1}, \frac{\tau^2}{1 - \beta_1^2} \right)$$

with $|\beta_1| < 1$.[1] The centring parameterisation moves β_0 to the observation equation and centres log variances. This parameterisation only marginally affects posterior inference in most cases, while creating an unnecessary computational burden. We will thus keep the simpler, less restrictive, more general specification with m_0 and C_0.

The SV model is completed with a conjugate prior distribution for $\theta = (\beta, \tau^2)$, ie, $p(\theta) = p(\beta \mid \tau^2) p(\tau^2)$, where $(\beta \mid \tau^2) \sim N(b_0, \tau^2 B_0)$ and $\tau^2 \sim IG(c_0, d_0)$, for known hyperparameters b_0, B_0, c_0 and d_0. An alternative specification where β and τ^2 are independent *a priori* can easily be implemented with negligible additional computational cost.

Given a set of observed asset returns $y^n = (y_1, \ldots, y_n)$ and Equations 2.4 and 2.5, the posterior distribution of the hidden volatility states and parameters (x^n, θ) is given by Bayes's Rule

$$p(x^n, \theta \mid y^n) \propto p(\theta) \prod_{t=1}^{n} p(y_t \mid x_t, \theta) p(x_t \mid x_{t-1}, \theta) \quad (2.6)$$

which is analytically intractable because of the nonlinearity of Equation 2.4. Approximate posterior inference for the SV model based on an MCMC algorithm and an SMC algorithm are discussed in the next two sections. We also provide several references on MCMC and SMC methods.

Posterior inference via Markov chain Monte Carlo

Following the seminal paper of Jacquier et al (1994), an abundance of MCMC algorithms have been proposed for the SV model as well as several of its univariate and multivariate extensions. In this section we present one of these algorithms and argue that the derivations of majority of the existing alternatives/extensions follow roughly the same route.[2] The MCMC algorithm cycles through the main two full conditional distributions, $p(\theta \mid y^n, x^n)$ and $p(x^n \mid y^n, \theta)$, in order to produce draws from $p(x^n, \theta \mid y^n)$ (Gamerman and Lopes 2006; Migon et al 2005).

Sampling parameters

Sampling θ from its full conditional distribution is rather standard since it is based on the Bayesian analysis of the normal linear regression (Gamerman and Lopes 2006, Chapter 2). Given $y^t = (y_1, \ldots, y_t)$ and $x^t = (x_1, \ldots, x_t)$, for $t = 1, \ldots, n$, it is straightforward to show that the full conditional distribution of θ is given by

$$p(\theta \mid y^t, x^t) = p(\theta \mid s_t) = f_N(\beta; b_t, \tau^2 B_t) f_{IG}(\tau^2, c_t, d_t) \quad (2.7)$$

where $f_N(x; \mu, \sigma^2)$ is the density function of a normal distribution with mean μ and variance σ^2 evaluated at point x. The sufficient statistics $s_t = (b_t, B_t, c_t, d_t)$ can be determined recursively as

$$b_t = B_t^{-1}(B_{t-1}^{-1} b_{t-1} + x_t z_t), \qquad B_t^{-1} = B_{t-1}^{-1} + z_t z_t' \quad (2.8)$$

$$c_t = c_{t-1} + \tfrac{1}{2}, \qquad d_t = d_{t-1} + \tfrac{1}{2}(x_t - b_t' z_t) x_t + \tfrac{1}{2}(b_{t-1} - b_t)' B_{t-1}^{-1} b_{t-1} \quad (2.9)$$

for $z'_t = (1, x_{t-1})$. It is worth mentioning that we keep the recursive nature of these moments, since it will be useful when deriving an SMC, or "particle filter", in the next section.

Sampling states one at a time

Sampling x^n from its full conditional distribution is a bit more complicated because of the nonlinearity in the observation in Equation 2.4. Jacquier et al (1994) introduced the general MCMC algorithm to SV models that sample x_t one at a time, and conditional on $x_{-t} = (x_1, \ldots, x_{t-1}, x_{t+1}, \ldots, x_n)$, from

$$p(x_t \mid x_{-t}, \theta, y^n) \propto p_N(y_t; 0, e^{x_t}) p_N(x_t; \beta_0 + \beta_1 x_{t-1}, \tau^2)$$
$$\times p_N(x_{t+1}; \beta_0 + \beta_1 x_t, \tau^2)$$
$$\propto p_N(y_t; 0, e^{x_t}) f_N(x_t; \mu_t, \omega^2)$$

as the conditional only depends on x_{t-1} and x_{t+1} and we can combine the state evolution densities. Here

$$\mu_t = \frac{\beta_0(1 - \beta_1) + \beta_1(x_{t+1} + x_{t-1})}{1 + \beta_1^2}$$

for $t = 1, \ldots, n-1$ $\mu_n = \beta_0 + \beta_1 x_{n-1}$ and $\omega^2 = \tau^2/(1 + \beta_1^2)$. A simple random-walk Metropolis algorithm with tuning variance v_x^2 and current state $x_t^{(j)}$ would work as follows. For $t = 1, \ldots, n$, sample x_t^* from $N(x_t^{(j)}, v_x^2)$ and accept the draw with probability

$$\alpha = \min\left\{1, \frac{f_N(x_t^*; \mu_t, v_t^2) f_N(y_t; 0, e^{x_t^*})}{f_N(x_t^{(j)}; \mu_t, v_t^2) f_N(y_t; 0, e^{x_t^{(j)}})}\right\}$$

Alternatively, x_t could be sampled via an independent Metropolis–Hastings (MH) algorithm with a normal proposal density

$$q(x_t \mid x_{-t}, \theta, y^n) = f_N(x_t; \tilde{\mu}_t, v_t^2)$$

where $\tilde{\mu}_t = \mu_t + 0.5 v_t^2 (y_t^2 e^{-\mu_t} - 1)$ and $v_t^2 = v^2$ for $t = 1, \ldots, n-1$ and $v_n^2 = \tau^2$. The independent MH algorithm would work as follows. For $t = 1, \ldots, n$ and current state $x_t^{(j)}$, sample x_t^* from $N(\tilde{\mu}_t, v_t^2)$ and accept the draw with probability

$$\alpha = \min\left\{1, \frac{f_N(x_t^*; \mu_t, v_t^2) f_N(y_t; 0, e^{x_t^*})}{f_N(x_t^{(j)}; \mu_t, v_t^2) f_N(y_t; 0, e^{x_t^{(j)}})} \frac{f_N(x_t^{(j)}; \tilde{\mu}_t, v_t^2)}{f_N(x_t^*; \tilde{\mu}_t, v_t^2)}\right\}$$

It has been extensively argued that this is a rather inefficient route which is bound to produce highly correlated chains and, consequently, failing to traverse the whole parameter space. The example of the simple SV (see page 51) illustrates the performance of both random-walk MH and independent MH algorithms.

Sampling states jointly
When the model belongs to (or can be approximated well by) the class of conditionally normal dynamic linear models, it is feasible to jointly sample x^n from $p(x^n \mid y^n, \theta)$ recursively sampling x_n, then x_{n-1}, and so on

$$p(x^n \mid y^n, \theta) = p(x_n \mid y^n, \theta) \prod_{t=1}^{n-1} p(x_t \mid x_{t+1}, \theta, y_t) \qquad (2.10)$$

In the well-known class of normal dynamic linear model (NDLM), where $y_t \mid x_t \sim N(F'_t x_t, \sigma_t^2)$ and $x_t \mid x_{t-1} \sim N(G_t x_{t-1}, \tau_t^2)$ (where the quadruple $\{F_t, G_t, \sigma_t^2, \tau_t^2\}$, for $t = 1, \ldots, n$ is known, F_t a vector of regressors, G_t drives the dynamic of x_t and the initial distribution $(x_0 \mid y^0) \sim N(m_0, C_0)$), it is straightforward to show that $x_t \mid y^{t-1} \sim N(a_t, R_t), y_t \mid y^{t-1} \sim N(f_t, Q_t)$ and $x_t \mid y^t \sim N(m_t, C_t)$, for $t = 1, \ldots, n$. The means and variances of the three densities are provided by the Kalman recursions: $a_t = G_t m_{t-1}$, $R_t = G_t C_{t-1} G'_t + \tau_t^2$, $f_t = F'_t a_t$, $Q_t = F'_t R_t F_t + \sigma_t^2$, $m_t = a_t + A_t e_t$ and $C_t = R_t - A_t Q_t A'_t$, where $e_t = y_t - f_t$ is the prediction error and $A_t = R_t F_t Q_t^{-1}$ is the Kalman gain. Two other useful densities are conditional and marginal smoothed densities, ie

$$x_t \mid x_{t+1}, y^t \sim N(h_t, H_t)$$
$$x_t \mid y^T \sim N(m_t^T, C_t^T)$$

where

$$h_t = m_t + B_t(x_{t+1} - a_{t+1})$$
$$H_t = C_t - B_t R_{t+1} B'_t$$
$$m_t^T = m_t + B_t(m_{t+1}^T - a_{t+1})$$
$$C_t^T = C_t - B_t^2(R_{t+1} - C_{t+1}^T)$$

for $B_t = C_t G'_{t+1} R_{t+1}^{-1}$, $C_T^T = C_t$ and $m_T^T = m_T$ (West and Harrison 1997, Chapter 4).

Kim et al (1998) introduce an MCMC scheme that approximates the distribution of $\log y_t^2$ by a carefully tuned mixture of normals with seven components. More precisely, the observation in Equation 2.4 can be rewritten as

$$\log y_t^2 = x_t + \epsilon_t \qquad (2.11)$$

where $\epsilon_t = \log \varepsilon_t^2$ follows a log χ_1^2 distribution, a parameter-free left-skewed distribution with mean -1.27 and variance 4.94. They argue that $\epsilon = \log \chi_1^2$ can be approximated well by

$$p(\epsilon_t) = \sum_{i=1}^{7} \pi_i p_N(\epsilon_t; \mu_i, v_i^2) \qquad (2.12)$$

where

$$\pi = (0.0073, 0.1056, 0.00002, 0.044, 0.34, 0.2457, 0.2575)$$
$$\mu = (-11.4, -5.24, -9.84, 1.51, -0.65, 0.53, -2.36)$$
$$v^2 = (5.8, 2.61, 5.18, 0.17, 0.64, 0.34, 1.26)$$

Therefore, a standard data augmentation argument allows the mixture of normals to be transformed into individual normals, ie, $(\epsilon_t \mid k_t) \sim N(\mu_{k_t}, v_{k_t}^2)$ and $k_t \sim$ Multinomial(q). Conditionally on k^t, the SV model for $z_t = \log y_t^2 - \mu_{k_t}$ can be rewritten as a standard first-order dynamic linear model, ie

$$(z_t \mid x_t, k_t, \theta) \sim N(x_t, v_{k_t}^2) \qquad (2.13)$$
$$(x_t \mid x_{t-1}, \theta) \sim N(\beta_0 + \beta_1 x_{t-1}, \tau^2) \qquad (2.14)$$

Then, the standard forward-filtering, backward-sampling (FFBS) scheme of Carter and Kohn (1994) and Frühwirth-Schnatter (1994) can be implemented in order to jointly sample the vector of states x^n conditional on (y^n, k^n, θ). Finally, conditionally on x^n, the indicators k_t are sampled straightforwardly from $\{1, \ldots, 7\}$ with probability $\Pr(k_t = j) \propto \pi_j p_N(z_t; x_t, v_j^2)$, for $t = 1, \ldots, n$. The example of the simple SV (see page 51) illustrates the performance of this algorithm.

Posterior inference via sequential Monte Carlo

Let us start by assuming that the vector of static parameter of the SV model, ie, $\theta = (\beta_0, \beta_1, \tau^2)$ is known. Then, particle filters (PFs) use Monte Carlo methods, mainly the sampling importance resampling (SIR), to sequentially reweigh and resample draws from the propagation density. The nonlinear Kalman filter is summarised by the predictive and smoothing steps

$$p(x_t \mid y^{t-1}) = \int f_N(x_t; \beta_0 + \beta_1 x_{t-1}, \tau^2) p(x_{t-1} \mid y^{t-1}) \, dx_{t-1} \qquad (2.15)$$
$$p(x_t \mid y^t) \propto p_N(y_t; 0, e^{x_t}) p(x_t \mid y^{t-1}) \qquad (2.16)$$

Particle filters, loosely speaking, combine the sequential estimation nature of Kalman-like filters with the modelling flexibility of MCMC samplers, while avoiding some of their shortcomings. On the one hand, like MCMC samplers and unlike Kalman-like filters, particle filters are designed to allow for more flexible observational and evolutional dynamics and distributions. On the other hand, like Kalman-like filters and unlike MCMC samplers, particle filters provide online filtering and smoothing distributions of states and parameters. The goal of most particle filters is to draw a set of iid particles $\{x_t^{(i)}\}_{i=1}^N$ that approximates $p(x_t \mid y^t)$ by starting with a set of iid particles $\{x_{t-1}^{(i)}\}_{i=1}^N$ that approximates $p(x_{t-1} \mid y^{t-1})$. The most popular filters are the bootstrap filter (BF),[3] proposed by Gordon et al (1993), and the auxiliary particle filter (APF),[4] proposed by Pitt and Shephard (1999b).

The BF of Gordon et al (1993) is based on sequential SIR steps over time (Smith and Gelfand 1992). The Kalman recursions from Equations 2.15 and 2.16 are combined in

$$p(x_t, x_{t-1} \mid y_t, y^{t-1})$$
$$\propto \underbrace{p_N(y_t; 0, e^{x_t})}_{\text{2. Resample}} \underbrace{p_N(x_t \mid \beta_0 + \beta_1 x_{t-1}, \tau^2) p(x_{t-1} \mid y^{t-1})}_{\text{1. Propagate}} \quad (2.17)$$

In other words, the BF first propagates particles from the posterior at time $t-1$ in order to generate particles from the prior at time t. Then it resamples the propagated particles with weights proportional to their likelihoods. Similarly, the APF first resamples particles from the posterior at time $t-1$ with weights taking into account the next observed data point, y_t. Then, it propagates the resampled particles. They rewrite the identity from Equation 2.17 as

$$p(x_t, x_{t-1} \mid y_t, y^{t-1})$$
$$\propto \underbrace{p(x_t \mid x_{t-1}, y^t)}_{\text{2. Propagate}} \underbrace{p(y_t \mid x_{t-1}) p_N(x_t \mid \beta_0 + \beta_1 x_{t-1}, \tau^2)}_{\text{1. Resample}} \quad (2.18)$$

The main difficulty in implementing the APF in the SV case is that $p(y_t \mid x_{t-1})$ is not available for pointwise evaluation and $p(x_t \mid x_{t-1}, y^t)$ is not available for sampling. Pitt and Shephard (1999b) suggest approximating $p(y_t \mid x_{t-1})$ and $p(x_t \mid x_{t-1}, y^t)$ by $p(y_t \mid g(x_{t-1}))$ and $p(x_t \mid x_{t-1})$, respectively, where $g(\cdot)$ is usually the expected value, median or mode of $p(x_t \mid x_{t-1})$. In this case, the weights of the propagated particles are given by

$$w_t \propto \frac{p(y_t \mid x_t)}{p(y_t \mid g(x_{t-1}))} \qquad (2.19)$$

Algorithm 2.1 (bootstrap filter for the SV model).

1. Propagate $\{x_{t-1}^{(i)}\}_{i=1}^N$ to $\{\tilde{x}_t^{(i)}\}_{i=1}^N$ via $p_N(x_t \mid \beta_0 + \beta_1 x_{t-1}, \tau^2)$.
2. Resample $\{x_t^{(i)}\}_{i=1}^N$ from $\{\tilde{x}_t^{(i)}\}_{i=1}^N$ with weights

$$w_t^{(i)} \propto p_N(y_t; 0, e^{\tilde{x}_t^{(i)}})$$

Algorithm 2.2 (auxiliary particle filter for the SV model).

1. Resample $\{\tilde{x}_{t-1}^{(i)}\}_{i=1}^N$ from $\{x_{t-1}^{(i)}\}_{i=1}^N$ with weights

$$w_t^{(i)} \propto p_N(y_t; 0, e^{\beta_0 + \beta_1 x_{t-1}^{(i)}})\ .$$

2. Propagate $\{\tilde{x}_{t-1}^{(i)}\}_{i=1}^N$ to $\{\tilde{x}_t^{(i)}\}_{i=1}^N$ via $p_N(x_t; \beta_0 + \beta_1 \tilde{x}_{t-1}, \tau^2)$.
3. Resample $\{x_t^{(i)}\}_{i=1}^N$ from $\{\tilde{x}_t^{(i)}\}_{i=1}^N$ with weights

$$w_t^{(i)} \propto \frac{p_N(y_t; 0, e^{\tilde{x}_t^{(i)}})}{p_N(y_t; 0, e^{\beta_0 + \beta_1 \tilde{x}_{t-1}^{(i)}})}$$

Pitt and Shephard (1999a) suggest local linearisation of the observation equation via an extended Kalman filter-type approximation in order to better approximate $p(x_t \mid x_{t-1}, y_t)$.[5] A more efficient approximation is based on the mixture Kalman filters of Chen and Liu (2000), when analytical integration of some components of the state vector is possible by conditioning on some other components. Such filters are commonly referred to as Rao–Blackwellised particle filters. This is also acknowledged in Pitt and Shephard (1999b) and many other references.

Parameter learning involves the sequential and joint learning of x_t and θ. The immediate idea of simply resampling θ over time is bound to fail since, in general, after a few time steps the particle set will contain only one particle. In their seminal paper, Gordon et al (1993) suggest incorporating artificial evolution noise for θ when tackling the problem of sequentially learning the static parameters of a state-space model. Here, for the sake of brevity, we derive only two well-established filters for sequentially learning both x_t and θ in the SV context: the Liu–West (LW) filter (Liu and West 2001) and the particle learning of Carvalho et al (2010) and Lopes et al (2010).

Liu–West filter

Liu and West (2001) combine the following elements:

- the APF of Pitt and Shephard (1999b);
- a kernel-smoothing approximation to $p(\theta \mid y^{t-1})$ via a mixture of multivariate normals;
- a neat shrinkage idea to incorporate artificial evolution for θ without the associated loss of information (West 1993a,b).

More specifically, let the set of iid particles $\{x_{t-1}^{(i)}, \theta_{t-1}^{(i)}\}_{i=1}^{N}$ approximate $p(x_{t-1}, \theta \mid y^{t-1})$ such that

$$p^N(\theta \mid y^{t-1}) \approx \frac{1}{N} \sum_{j=1}^{N} p_N(\theta; m^{(j)}, V) \qquad (2.20)$$

where

$$m^{(j)} = a\theta_{t-1}^{(j)} + (1-a)\bar{\theta}, \qquad \bar{\theta} = \sum_{j=1}^{N} \frac{\theta_{t-1}^{(j)}}{N}$$

and

$$V = h^2 \sum_{j=1}^{N} \frac{(\theta_{t-1}^{(j)} - \bar{\theta})(\theta_{t-1}^{(j)} - \bar{\theta})'}{N}$$

and $h^2 = 1 - a^2$. The subscript t on θ_t is used only to indicate that samples are from $p(\theta \mid y^t)$. The APF (Pitt and Shephard 1999a) of Equation 2.18 can now be written for the state vector (x_t, θ_t) as $p(x_t, x_{t-1}, \theta_t, \theta_{t-1} \mid y_t, y^{t-1})$ is decomposed into a resampling step

$$p(y_t \mid x_{t-1}, \theta_{t-1}) p(x_{t-1} \mid \theta_{t-1}, y^{t-1}) p(\theta_{t-1} \mid y^{t-1})$$

and a propagation step

$$p(x_t \mid x_{t-1}, \theta_t, y^t) p(\theta_t \mid \theta_{t-1}, y^t)$$

Again, $p(y_t \mid x_{t-1}, \theta)$ is not available for pointwise evaluation and/or $p(x_t \mid x_{t-1}, \theta_t, y^t)$ is not easy to sample from in the SV case. Liu and West (2001) follow Pitt and Shephard's (1999b) steps and resample from the proposal $p(y_t \mid g(x_{t-1}), m(\theta_{t-1}))$, where $g(\cdot)$ and $m(\cdot)$ are as described above. Then, θ_t is sampled from the artificial transition $p(\theta_t \mid \theta_{t-1})$ and x_t is sampled from the evolution density $p(x_t \mid x_{t-1}, \theta_t)$. The propagated particles (x_t, θ_t) have associated weights $\tilde{\omega}_t$ proportional to $p(y_t \mid x_t, \theta_t)/p(y_t \mid g(x_{t-1}), m(\theta_{t-1}))$.

The performance of the LW filter depends on the choice of the tuning parameter a, which drives both the shrinkage and the smoothness of the normal approximation. It is common practice to set a around 0.98 or higher. Either the components of θ can be transformed in order to accommodate the approximate local normality or the multivariate normal approximation could be replaced by a composition of, say, conditionally normal densities for location parameters and inverse-gamma densities for scale/variance parameters.[6]

Algorithm 2.3 (Liu–West filter for the SV model).

1. Resample $\{(\tilde{x}_{t-1}, \tilde{\theta}_{t-1})^{(i)}\}_{i=1}^{N}$ from $\{(x_{t-1}, \theta_{t-1})^{(i)}\}_{i=1}^{N}$ with weights
$$w_t^{(i)} \propto p_N(y_t; 0, e^{m_0^{(i)} + m_1^{(i)} x_{t-1}^{(i)}})$$
and $m_0^{(i)}$ and $m_1^{(i)}$ defined in Equation 2.20.

2. Propagate
   (a) $\{\tilde{\theta}_{t-1}^{(i)}\}_{i=1}^{N}$ to $\{\hat{\theta}_t^{(i)}\}_{i=1}^{N}$ via $N(\bar{m}^{(i)}, V)$,
   (b) $\{\tilde{x}_{t-1}^{(i)}\}_{i=1}^{N}$ to $\{\hat{x}_t^{(i)}\}_{i=1}^{N}$ via $p_N(x_t; \hat{\beta}_0^{(i)} + \hat{\beta}_1^{(i)} \tilde{x}_{t-1}^{(i)}, \hat{\tau}^{2(i)})$.

3. Resample $\{(x_t, \theta_t)^{(i)}\}_{i=1}^{N}$ from $\{(\hat{x}_t, \hat{\theta})^{(i)}\}_{i=1}^{N}$ with weights
$$w_t^{(i)} \propto \frac{p_N(y_t; 0, e^{\hat{x}_t^{(i)}})}{p_N(y_t; 0, e^{\bar{m}_0^{(i)} + \bar{m}_1^{(i)} \tilde{x}_{t-1}^{(i)}})}$$

Particle learning

Carvalho *et al* (2010) and Lopes *et al* (2010) introduce particle learning (PL) for particle filtering and parameter learning in a rather general state-space models. They extend Chen and Liu's (2000) mixture Kalman filter (MKF) methods by allowing parameter learning and utilise the resample–propagate algorithm introduced by Pitt and Shephard (1999b), also in the pure filter context, together with a particle set that includes state-sufficient statistics (Storvik 2002; Fearnhead 2002). Carvalho *et al* and Lopes *et al* empirically show that resample–propagate filters tend to outperform propagate–resample ones. They also show via several simulation studies that PL outperforms the LW filter and is comparable to MCMC samplers, even when full adaptation is considered. The advantage is even more pronounced for large values of n.

For the basic SV model, PL takes advantage of the Kalman recursions produced by Equations 2.11–2.14 and the recursive sufficient statistics (Equations 2.7–2.9) of the conditionally dynamic linear model Recall that $s_t = (b_t, B_t, c_t, d_t)$ are the parameter sufficient statistics from Equations 2.8 and 2.9 and let $s_t^x = (m_t, C_t)$ for m_t and C_t derived in the paragraph below Equation 2.10. Both s_t and s_t^x satisfy deterministic updating rules, ie, $s_t = S(s_{t-1}, x_t, y_t)$, as in the Storvik filter from the previous subsection, and $s_t^x = \mathcal{K}(s_{t-1}^x, \theta, y_t)$, for $\mathcal{K}(\cdot)$ mimicking the Kalman filter recursions. The example in the section on the simple SV (see page 51) illustrates the performance of particle filters introduced here. See Lopes and Tsay (2010) for a thorough review of particle filters via examples (and R code) for Bayesian inference in financial econometrics.

Algorithm 2.4 (particle learning for the SV model).

1. Resample $(s_{t-1}, s_{t-1}^x, \theta)$ with weights proportional to

$$p(\log y_t^2 \mid s_{t-1}^x, \theta)$$
$$= \sum_{i=1}^{7} \pi_i p_N(\log y_t^2; \mu_i + \beta_0 + \beta_1 m_{t-1}, \beta_1^2 C_{t-1} + v_i^2 + \tau^2)$$

2. Sample (x_{t-1}, x_t) from $p(x_{t-1}, x_t \mid s_{t-1}^x, \theta, y^t)$:

    (a) sample x_{t-1} from $p(x_{t-1} \mid s_{t-1}^x, \theta, y^t)$, and

    (b) sample x_t from $p(x_t \mid x_{t-1}, \theta, y^t)$.

3. Update parameter sufficient statistics: $s_t = S(\tilde{s}_{t-1}, x_t, y_t)$.

4. Sample θ from $p(\theta \mid s_t)$.

5. Update state-sufficient statistics: $s_t^x = \mathcal{K}(\tilde{s}_{t-1}^x, \theta, y_t)$.

The distributions from step 2 are

$$p(x_{t-1} \mid s_{t-1}^x, \theta, y^t) = \sum_{i=1}^{7} f_N(x_{t-1}, \hat{x}_{t-1,i}, V_{t-1,i})$$

$$p(x_t \mid x_{t-1}, \theta, y^t) = \sum_{i=1}^{7} f_N(x_t, \tilde{x}_{ti}, W_{ti})$$

where, from Equation 2.12

$$V_{t-1,i} = \left(\frac{1}{C_{t-1}} + \frac{\beta_1^2}{v_i^2 + \tau^2}\right)^{-1}$$

$$\hat{x}_{t-1,i} = V_{t-1,i}^{-1}\left(\frac{m_{t-1}}{C_{t-1}} + (\log y_t^2 - \mu_i - \beta_0)\frac{\beta_1}{v_i^2 + \tau^2}\right)$$

$$W_{ti} = \left(\frac{1}{v_i^2} + \frac{1}{\tau^2}\right)^{-1}$$

and

$$\tilde{x}_{ti} = W_{ti}^{-1}\left(\frac{\log y_t^2 - \mu_i}{v_i^2} + \frac{\beta_0 + \beta_1 x_{t-1}}{\tau^2}\right)$$

Other univariate SV models

Correlated errors

Jacquier *et al* (2004) provide an MCMC algorithm for the leverage stochastic volatility model. This extends the basic SV model to accommodate non-zero correlation ρ between ε_t and η_t from Equations 2.4 and 2.5. Now the specification becomes

$$y_t = e^{x_{t-1}/2} u_t \tag{2.21}$$

$$x_t = \beta_0 + \beta_1 x_{t-1} + \phi u_t + \omega v_t \tag{2.22}$$

$\phi = \tau\rho$ and $\omega^2 = \tau^2(1-\rho^2)$ and u_t and v_t are iid standard normal errors. The case when $\rho < 0$ characterises a leverage effect, so a negative shock in the observation y_t is associated to higher x_{t+h} for $h \geqslant 0$ and a positive shock in y_t is associated to lower x_t. They study weekly data on the equal and value weighted CRSP indexes and daily data on the Standard and Poor's 500 (S&P 500) and Deutschmark and Canadian dollar exchange rates relative to the US dollar. In their study, the posterior means of ρ range roughly between -0.48 and -0.2 for the daily data and between -0.47 and -0.41 for the weekly data.[7]

Fat-tailed, skewed and scale mixture of normals

The fat-tailed distribution for ε_t of Equation 2.4 can be obtained by a continuous scale mixture of normals (Carlin and Polson 1991; Geweke 1993; Jacquier *et al* 2004).

$$y_t = e^{x_t/2}\varepsilon_t \tag{2.23}$$

$$x_t = \beta_0 + \beta_1 x_{t-1} + \tau\eta_t \tag{2.24}$$

$$\varepsilon_t = \sqrt{\lambda_t} z_t \tag{2.25}$$

$$\lambda_t \sim \mathrm{IG}(\tfrac{1}{2}\nu, \tfrac{1}{2}\nu) \tag{2.26}$$

so that $\varepsilon_t \sim t_\nu(0,1)$, a standard Student-$t$ distribution with ν degrees of freedom. The SV model with fat-tailed error can accommodate a wide range of kurtosis and is particularly important when dealing with extreme observations or outliers. The example in the section on SV with fat-tailed errors (see Example 2.7) compares the SV model and "SV with t-errors" model for monthly log returns of GE stock from January 1926 to December 1999 for 888 observations. Additional contributions to the theme are Steel (1998), Omori *et al* (2007), Asai (2009), Nakajima and Omori (2009) and Abanto-Valle *et al* (2009a). Lopes and Polson (2010) provide a sequential analysis of this model.

Dirichlet process mixture
Jensen and Maheu (2008) use Dirichlet process mixture (DPM) prior to model semi-parametrically the observational SV-model error ε_t in the SV model given in Equation 2.4

$$\varepsilon_t \sim N(0, \lambda_t^2) \quad (2.27)$$
$$\lambda_t^2 \mid G \sim G \quad (2.28)$$
$$G \mid G_0, \alpha \sim DP(G_0, \alpha) \quad (2.29)$$
$$G_0(\lambda_t^2) \equiv IG(\tfrac{1}{2}\nu_0, \tfrac{1}{2}\nu_0 s_0^2) \quad (2.30)$$

where G_0 is the base distribution of G and $\alpha > 0$ is the scalar precision parameter. They name this class of models the SV–DPM models and show that the above representation can be rewritten as

$$y_t \mid x_t \sim \sum_{j=1}^{\infty} \pi_j p_N(y_t; 0, \lambda_j^2 \exp\{x_t\}) \quad (2.31)$$

so revealing the nonparametric nature of the DPM prior with weights π_j derived by the stick-break recursion where $\pi_1 = \omega_1$ and $\pi_j = \omega_j \prod_{s=1}^{j-1}(1-\omega_s)$, where $\omega_j \sim \text{Beta}(1, \alpha)$.[8]

Long-memory SV models
So (2002) and Jensen (2004) propose parametric and semi-parametric Bayesian inference for long-memory SV (LMSV) models where the log volatilities exhibit long-memory properties are given by

$$y_t = e^{x_t/2}\varepsilon_t \quad (2.32)$$
$$(1-L)^d x_t = \tau \eta_t \quad (2.33)$$

where the fractional differencing operator $(1-L)^d$ (L is the lag operator and $x_{t-s} = L^s x_t$) is defined by its binomial expansion. The MCMC/FFBS algorithm presented earlier (see page 33) is not available when x_t follows a long-memory process. Jensen (2004) argues that the simulation smoother for an LMSV model is computationally very expensive and memory intensive. He goes on to propose a sampling scheme that takes advantage of the properties of the long-memory process orthonormal wavelet coefficients.

SV with jumps

Similar to the previous SV model, the Euler discretisation of continuous-time jump process (the SVJ process) leads to a specification of the form

$$y_t = e^{x_t/2}\varepsilon_t + J_t z_t \qquad (2.34)$$

$$x_t = \beta_0 + \beta_1 x_{t-1} + \tau \eta_t \qquad (2.35)$$

$$J_t \sim \text{Ber}(\lambda) \qquad (2.36)$$

$$z_t \sim N(\mu_z, \sigma_z^2) \qquad (2.37)$$

where J_t is the jump indicator and Z_t is the jump size. For the jump specification, we can use the conditionally conjugate prior structure for parameters $(\lambda, \mu_z, \sigma_z^2)$, where $\lambda \sim \text{Beta}(a,b)$, $\mu_z \sim N(c,d)$ and $\sigma_z^2 \sim \text{IG}(\frac{1}{2}\nu, \frac{1}{2}\nu\bar{\sigma}_z^2)$. For instance, when $c = -3$, $d = 0.01$, $a = 2$ and $b = 100$ the prior mean and standard deviation of λ are around 0.02 and 0.014, respectively. The parameters ν and $\bar{\sigma}_z^2$ can be set, for instance, at 20 and 0.05, respectively, such that the prior mean and standard deviation of σ_z^2 are roughly 0.05 and 0.02. These prior specifications predict around five large negative jumps per year (roughly 250 business days) whose magnitudes are around an additional 3%. This structure naturally leads to conditional posterior distributions that can be easily simulated to form a Gibbs sampler (Eraker et al 2003). Example 2.8 estimates volatility with jumps for the S&P 500 Index and the Nasdaq NDX100 Index to study the early part of the 2007–8 credit crisis. In this case, jump probabilities are about 0.04 or 10 jumps per year, with the largest jump sizes around −2.14% for the S&P 500 and −1.98% for the NDX100.

Additional Bayesian literature on SV jump models, continuous-time jump diffusion models and related models includes Polson and Stroud (2003), Stroud et al (2003), Raggi (2005), Li et al (2006), Polson et al (2008), Johannes et al (2009), Li (2009) and Szerszen (2009).

Markov-switching stochastic volatility

So et al (1998) and Carvalho and Lopes (2007) propose MCMC and SMC algorithms, respectively, to estimate the Markov-switching stochastic volatility model, which is an extension of the basic SV model to allow time-varying parameters in the dynamic of the log volatilities. Thus, Equation 2.5 is replaced by Equation 2.38 and the model becomes

$$y_t = e^{x_t/2} \varepsilon_t \qquad (2.38)$$

$$x_t = \beta_{0s_t} + \beta_1 x_{t-1} + \tau \eta_t \qquad (2.39)$$

$$p_{ij} = \Pr(s_t = j \mid s_{t-1} = i) \quad \text{for } i,j = 1,\ldots,k \qquad (2.40)$$

$$\beta_{0s_t} = \gamma_1 + \sum_{j=1}^{k} \gamma_j I_{jt} \qquad (2.41)$$

with regime variables s_t following a k-state first-order Markov process, $I_{jt} = 1$ if $s_t \geq j$ and zero otherwise, γ_1 real and $\gamma_i > 0$ for $i > 1$. Carvalho and Lopes (2007) analyse the Brazilian Ibovespa stock index, from the São Paulo Stock Exchange, for daily data between 1997 and 2001. They are able to identify the major currency crises of the period, such as the Asian crisis in 1997, the Russian crisis in 1998 and the Brazilian crisis in 1999, all of which directly affected Brazil and other emerging economies.

Smooth transition SV models

Lopes and Salazar (2006a) extend the basic SV model by allowing a smoothing transition in the log volatility dynamics (Equation 2.5). The first-order logistic smooth transition autoregressive stochastic volatility (LSTAR-SV) model is

$$x_t = \beta_{01} + \beta_{11} x_{t-1} + \pi(\gamma, c, s_t)(\beta_{02} + \beta_{12} x_{t-1}) + \tau \eta_t \qquad (2.42)$$

$$\pi(\gamma, c, x_{t-d}) = \frac{1}{1 + \exp\{\gamma(x_{t-d} - c)\}} \qquad (2.43)$$

The parameter $\gamma > 0$ is responsible for the smoothness of π, while c is a location or threshold parameter and d is the delay parameter. When $\gamma \to \infty$, the LSTAR model reduces to the well-known self-exciting TAR (SETAR) model (Tong 1990), and when $\gamma = 0$ the standard AR(k) model arises. Finally, s_t is called the transition variable, with $s_t = y_{t-d}$ commonly used (Teräsvirta 1994; Lopes and Salazar 2006b). Lopes and Salazar (2006a) compare several LSTAR-SV configurations when modelling the log returns on the S&P 500

Index for roughly 3,000 daily observed data between January 1986 and December 1997.[9]

Volatility-volume models

Mahieu and Bauer (1998) were among the first to perform Bayesian inference in the modified mixture model (MMM) of Andersen (1996), which models the volatilities based on a bivariate Gaussian–Poisson system for both log returns, y_t, and trading volume, v_t

$$y_t \mid x_t, \theta \sim N(0, \exp\{x_t\}) \quad (2.44)$$

$$v_t \mid x_t, \theta \sim \text{Poi}(m_0 + m_1 \exp\{x_t\}) \quad (2.45)$$

$$x_t \mid x_{t-1}, \theta \sim N(\beta_0 + \beta_1 x_{t-1}, \tau^2) \quad (2.46)$$

where the parameter m_0 reflects the uninformed component of trading volume and is related to liquidity traders. The remaining part of trading volume that is induced by new information is represented by $m_1 \exp\{x_t\}$. Abanto-Valle *et al* (2009b) extend the model to allow for Student-t errors (Equations 2.25 and 2.26) and/or Markov-switching dynamics (Equations 2.39–2.41). They analyse daily closing prices and trading volume corrected by dividends and stock splits for the BP Company stock series listed on the London Stock Exchange, from 1999 to 2008 (around 2,400 observations).

MULTIVARIATE SV MODELS

Let y_t be a p-dimensional vector of (financial) time series. The majority of the existing multivariate stochastic volatility models assume that

$$y_t \sim N(0, \Sigma_t) \quad (2.47)$$

and focus on modelling the dynamic behaviour of the covariance matrix Σ_t. Two challenges arise in the multivariate context. Firstly, the number of distinct elements of Σ_t equals $\frac{1}{2}p(p+1)$. This quadratic growth made modelling Σ_t computationally very expensive and consequently created a practical upper bound for p.[10] The vast majority of the papers we cite illustrate their methods and models with $p < 100$. Secondly, the distinct elements of Σ_t cannot be modelled independently, since positive definiteness has to be satisfied.

There are at least three ways to decompose the covariance matrix Σ_t. In the first case

$$\Sigma_t = D_t R_t D_t \quad (2.48)$$

where D_t is a diagonal matrix of standard deviations, ie, $D_t = \text{diag}(\sigma_{1t}, \ldots, \sigma_{pt})$, and R_t is the correlation matrix. The two challenges above remain in this parameterisation, ie, the number of parameters increases with p^2 and R_t has to be positive definite. In the second case

$$\Sigma_t = A_t H_t A_t' \tag{2.49}$$

where $A_t H_t^{1/2}$ is the lower triangular Cholesky decomposition of Σ_t. H_t is a diagonal matrix, the diagonal elements of A_t are all equal to 1 and, more importantly, its lower diagonal elements are unrestricted, since positive definiteness is guaranteed by Equation 2.49. Finally, in the third case (also the most popular) a standard factor analysis structure is used

$$\Sigma_t = \beta_t H_t \beta_t' + \Psi_t \tag{2.50}$$

where β_t is the $p \times k$ matrix of factor loadings and, similar to A_t, is lower block-triangular with diagonal elements equal to 1. Ψ_t and H_t are the diagonal covariance matrices of the specific factors and common factors, respectively. One of the main reasons for the popularity of this decomposition, which became known as "factor stochastic volatility", is that usually k is much smaller than p, leading to a drastic reduction in the number of free parameters necessary to estimate Σ_t, ie, $(k+1)p$. In two fairly realistic situations we set $(p, k) = (10, 3)$ and $(p, k) = (100, 10)$. In the first case, $\frac{1}{2}p(p+1) = 45$ and $p(k+1) = 40$, so the difference in the number of parameters is not very significant. In the second example though, $\frac{1}{2}p(p+1) = 4{,}950$ and $p(k+1) = 1{,}100$, which translates to roughly 80% fewer parameters whose dynamics must be estimated. Still under the first two decompositions, $p = 1{,}000$ and $p = 5{,}000$ generate 0.5 million and 13 million parameters, respectively, against 10% under the factor decomposition. A thorough review of the multivariate stochastic volatility literature up to the middle of the first decade of the 21st Century is provided in Asai et al (2006).

Wishart random processes

Uhlig (1997) and Philipov and Glickman (2006a) proposed models for the covariance matrix based on the temporal update of the parameters of a Wishart distribution.[11] Uhlig (1997) proposed the following recursion for the Cholesky decomposition of the precision matrix in structural vector autoregressions

$$y_t = \sum_{i=1}^{q} B_i y_{t-i} + B_t \epsilon_t \qquad (2.51)$$

where $B_t = A_t H_t^{1/2}$ (see Equation 2.49), $\epsilon_t \sim N(0, I_p)$ and

$$\Sigma_t^{-1} = \frac{\nu}{\nu+1} B_{t-1}^{-1} \Theta_{t-1} (B_{t-1}^{-1})' \qquad (2.52)$$

$$\Theta_{t-1} \sim \text{Beta}(\tfrac{1}{2}(\nu + pq), \tfrac{1}{2}) \qquad (2.53)$$

with Beta denoting the multivariate Beta distribution (Uhlig 1994).[12] Triantafyllopoulos (2008) models daily/current prices per tonne of aluminium, copper, lead and zinc exchanged in the London Metal Exchange from January 4, 2005, to April 28, 2006 (334 trading days).

Philipov and Glickman's (2006a) Wishart random process is given by the observational equation 2.47 combined with Equation 2.54

$$(\Sigma_t^{-1} \mid \Sigma_{t-1}^{-1}, \theta) \sim W(\nu, S_{t-1}^{-1}) \qquad (2.54)$$

$$S_{t-1}^{-1} = \frac{1}{\nu} (A^{1/2})(\Sigma_{t-1}^{-1})^d (A^{1/2})' \qquad (2.55)$$

where $\theta = (\nu, A)$ and

$$E(\Sigma_t^{-1} \mid \Sigma_{t-1}^{-1}, \theta) = (A^{1/2})(\Sigma_t^{-1})^d (A^{1/2})' \qquad (2.56)$$

$$E(\Sigma_t \mid \Sigma_{t-1}, \theta) = \frac{\nu}{\nu - p - 1} (A^{-1/2})(\Sigma_{t-1})^d (A^{-1/2})' \qquad (2.57)$$

A constant covariance model arises when $d = 0$, so $E(\Sigma_t) = \nu A^{-1}/(\nu - p - 1)$. Then, A plays the role of a precision matrix. When $d = 1$ and $A = I_p$, it follows that $E(\Sigma_t^{-1}) = \Sigma_{t-1}^{-1}$, thus generating random-walk evolution for the covariance. They fit their model to 240 monthly return data for $p = 5$ industry portfolios, so have a relatively small dimensional problem.

Cholesky stochastic volatility

Lopes *et al* (2008) introduced the class of Cholesky stochastic volatility (CSV) models by exploring a triangular and recursive representation of the multivariate model in Equation 2.47. More precisely, they use the decomposition equation 2.49, where

$$A_t = \begin{pmatrix} 1 & 0 & \cdots & 0 \\ a_{21t} & 1 & \cdots & 0 \\ \vdots & \vdots & \ddots & \vdots \\ a_{p1t} & a_{p2t} & \cdots & 1 \end{pmatrix}, \quad \Phi_t = A_t^{-1} = \begin{pmatrix} 1 & 0 & \cdots & 0 \\ -\phi_{21t} & 1 & \cdots & 0 \\ \vdots & \vdots & \ddots & \vdots \\ -\phi_{p1t} & \phi_{p2t} & \cdots & 1 \end{pmatrix}$$

and $H_t = \text{diag}(h_{1t}, \ldots, h_{pt})$. The system $\Phi_t y_t \sim N(0, H_t)$ generates the following conditionally independent CSV recursions (for $t = 1, \ldots, n$)

$$y_{1t} = e^{h_{1t}/2} \varepsilon_{1t} \tag{2.58}$$

$$y_{it} = \phi_{i1t} y_{1t} + \cdots + \phi_{i,i-1,t} y_{i-1,t} + \exp\{h_{it}\} \varepsilon_{it}, \quad i = 2, \ldots, p \tag{2.59}$$

where $\varepsilon_t \sim N(0, I_p)$. The model is completed with standard SV structures for h_{it}, ie, $\log h_{it} \sim N(\beta_{0i} + \beta_{1i} \log h_{i,t-1}, \tau_i^2)$, $i = 1, \ldots, p$, and first-order autoregressive structures for $\phi_{ijt} \sim N(\beta_{0ij} + \beta_{1ij} \phi_{ij,t-1}, \tau_{ij}^2)$ for $i = 2, \ldots, p$ and $j = 1, \ldots, i - 1$. They show that the prior on the parameters driving the dynamics of the hs and ϕs plays an important role in producing more parsimonious models, which is particularly important when p is moderately large, say $p = 100$. In fact, there are $\frac{1}{2}p(p+1)$ dynamic linear models to be estimated and, therefore, $\frac{3}{2}p(p+1)$ static parameters. When $p = 30$ and $p = 100$, for example, there are 465 and 5,050 latent states, respectively, and 1,395 and 15,150 static parameters. Lopes et al (2008) implement their model for the 100 components of the S&P 100 Index and for the 30 components of the Dow Jones Industrial Average Index.[13]

Factor stochastic volatility

The literature on factor-based multivariate stochastic volatility models is now abundant.[14] Loosely speaking, in this literature the levels (or first differences) of a set of (financial) time series are modelled by a standard normal factor model (Lopes and West 2004) in which both the common factor variances and the specific (or idiosyncratic) time-series variances are modelled as univariate or multivariate (low-dimensional) SV processes. The main practical and computational advantage of the factor stochastic volatility (FSV) model is its parsimony, where all the variances and covariances of a vector of time series are modelled by a low-dimensional stochastic volatility structure dictated by common factors. It is fairly common to find that, for large vectors of time series, the number of common factors is usually one or two orders of magnitude smaller, which speeds up computation and estimation considerably.

The large class of FSV models, reviewed here and based on the decomposition of Equation 2.50, is written as

$$(y_t \mid f_t, \beta_t, \Sigma_t) \sim N(\beta_t f_t; \Phi_t) \qquad (2.60)$$
$$(f_t \mid H_t) \sim N(0; H_t) \qquad (2.61)$$

where, as before, H_t is a diagonal matrix and contains the variances of the common factors and Ψ_t is a diagonal matrix and contains the variances of the specific or idiosyncratic factors. The elements Ψ_t are modelled by conditionally independent univariate SV structures, while $\log h_t = (\log h_{1t}, \ldots, \log h_{kt})'$ follows a first-order vector autoregression

$$(\log h_t \mid h_{t-1}, \beta_0, \beta_1, U) \sim N(\beta_0 + \beta_1 \log h_{t-1}, U) \qquad (2.62)$$

with correlated innovations characterised by the non-diagonal matrix U (Aguilar and West 2000). When U is a diagonal matrix, the above multivariate model is reduced to p univariate conditionally independent autoregressive models (Pitt and Shephard 1999a). Both Pitt and Shephard and Aguilar and West consider $\beta_t = \beta$ for all t time periods. Lopes and co-workers[15] extend the previous works by modelling the evolution of the unconstrained loadings by univariate first-order autoregressions.[16]

Philipov and Glickman (2006b) extend the above FSV model (with $\Sigma_t = \Sigma$) and model H_t as a full covariance matrix via their Wishart random process (see Equations 2.54 and 2.55). They implement their model for 324 monthly observed returns on 88 individual companies from the S&P 500 Index and use $k = 2$ common factors. Han (2006) implements a similar FSV model to form a portfolio based on 36 stocks, 1,200 observations collected from the Center for Research in Security Prices (CRSP[17]). Chib et al (2006) introduce fat-tailed errors and jumps in the FSV model as well as an efficient and fast MCMC algorithm. They implement their extension to simulated data ($p = 50$) and real data on international weekly stock index returns where $p = 10$.[18] Finally, Lopes and Carvalho (2007) extend the FSV model to allow for Markovian regime shifts in the dynamic of the variance of the common factors and apply their model to study Latin America's main markets ($p = 5$).

Additional MSV references

Yu and Meyer (2006) compare several bivariate SV models, ie, $p = 2$, when studying weekly data on both the Australian dollar and the New Zealand dollar against the US dollar for the period from January 1994 to December 2003. They use the deviance information criterion (DIC) of Spiegelhalter *et al* (2002) and comparisons are consequently made via the Bayesian software WINBUGS.[19] In a related paper, Meyer and Yu (2000) used BUGS, which is an older version of WINBUGS, when comparing univariate SV models.

Asai *et al* (2006) review the literature on specification, estimation and evaluation of MSV models and divide the models into various categories:

- asymmetric models;
- factor models;
- time-varying correlation models;
- alternative MSV specifications.

Liesenfeld and Richard (2006) use efficient importance sampling (EIS) to perform Bayesian analysis of relatively low-dimensional ($p = 4$) multivariate SV models.

APPLICATIONS

In this section we illustrate the use of SV models in a series of different contexts. The first example compares random-walk Metropolis–Hastings, independent Metropolis–Hastings, naive normal approximation and mixture of seven normal approximation MCMC/FFBS methods via a mixture of seven normals for the SV model for simulated data. A few variants of the SV model are applied in Examples 2.6–2.8. Example 2.6 deals with SV models with smooth transition between competing regimes, while Example 2.7 models GE stock returns with normal and Student-t errors and computes sequential Bayes factors. In Example 2.8, the credit crisis of 2007–8 is analysed and monitored by particle filters. Finally, the popular and parsimonious class of factor stochastic volatility is used in Example 2.9 to model multivariate exchange rate data.

Example 2.5 (simple SV). This example illustrates the performance of four MCMC algorithms to estimate the parameters $(\beta_0, \beta_1, \tau^2)$ and states $x^n = (x_1, \ldots, x_n)$ given y^n in the SV model (see

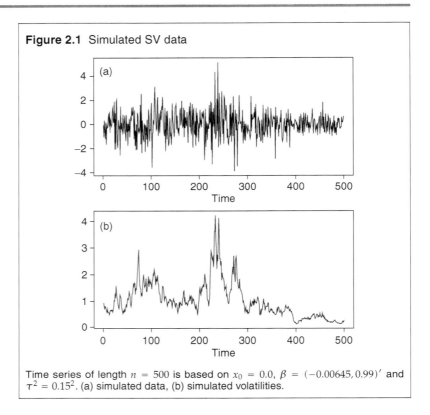

Figure 2.1 Simulated SV data

Time series of length $n = 500$ is based on $x_0 = 0.0$, $\beta = (-0.00645, 0.99)'$ and $\tau^2 = 0.15^2$. (a) simulated data, (b) simulated volatilities.

page 32 onwards). Namely, the random-walk Metropolis–Hastings, independent Metropolis–Hastings, naive normal approximation to $\log \chi_1^2$ and MCMC/FFBS via a mixture of seven normals (see page 33 onwards) and Liu–West filter and particle learning (see page 36 onwards). A time series of length $n = 500$ is simulated from $x_0 = 0.0$, $\beta = (-0.00645, 0.99)'$ and $\tau^2 = 0.15^2$. Figure 2.1 exhibits the simulated time series and volatilities. The prior hyperparameters are $m_0 = -0.8$, $C_0 = 100$, $b_0 = (-0.013, 0.962)'$, $C_0 = 100I_2$, $c_0 = 5$ and $d_0 = 0.1078$.

The MCMC schemes are based on $M = 3{,}000$ draws, after discarding the initial $M_0 = 1{,}000$ draws. Posterior inference based on the four MCMC algorithms is summarised in Figure 2.2. As expected, both random-walk and independent Metropolis–Hastings algorithms behave very similarly. In terms of mixing of the chains, both are outperformed by the FFBS scheme based on the mixture of seven normals, in terms of mixing chains. The FFBS scheme based on

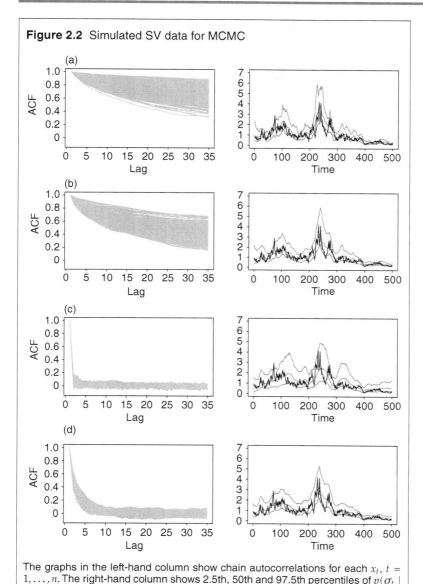

Figure 2.2 Simulated SV data for MCMC

The graphs in the left-hand column show chain autocorrelations for each x_t, $t = 1, \ldots, n$. The right-hand column shows 2.5th, 50th and 97.5th percentiles of $p(\sigma_t \mid y^n)$. (a) Random-walk Metropolis, (b) independent Metropolis, (c) normal-based FFBS and (d) mixture-normal-based FFBS.

the normal approximation produces chains with good mixing properties, but the approximation to the marginal posterior distributions of the volatilities is rather crude.

Table 2.1 The six models for Lopes and Salazar's (2006b) analysis

Model	Definition
$\mathcal{M}_1$	AR(1)
$\mathcal{M}_2$	AR(2)
$\mathcal{M}_3$	LSTAR(1) with $d = 1$
$\mathcal{M}_4$	LSTAR(1) with $d = 2$
$\mathcal{M}_5$	LSTAR(2) with $d = 1$
$\mathcal{M}_6$	LSTAR(2) with $d = 2$

Example 2.6 (SV with smooth transition). Lopes and Salazar (2006b) use LSTAR(k)-stochastic volatility models to analyse log returns on the S&P 500 Index for roughly 3,000 daily observed data between January 1986 and December 1997. They compared six SV models based on Akaike's (1974) information criterion (AIC), Schwarz's (1978) Bayesian information criterion (BIC) and Spiegelhalter *et al*'s (2002) deviance information criterion (DIC).[20] The six models are shown in Table 2.1.

Lopes and Salazar arrive at an LSTAR(1) with $d = 1$ as the best model under three criteria. It can be argued that the linear relationship prescribed by an AR(1) structure is insufficient to capture the dynamic behaviour of the log volatilities. The LSTAR structure brings more flexibility to the modelling. Table 2.2 presents the posterior mean and standard deviations of all parameters for each of the six models listed in Table 2.1.

Example 2.7 (SV with fat-tailed errors). We revisit the simple SV model with normal innovations of Example 2.6 and compute sequential Bayes factor against the alternative SV model with Student-t innovations (Chib *et al* 2002; Jacquier *et al* 2004). We assume initially that the number of degrees of freedom is known. We use monthly log returns of GE stock from January 1926 to December 1999 for 888 observations. This series was analysed in Example 6 of Tsay (2005, Chapter 12).[21] The competing models are defined by the number of degrees of freedom

$$y_t \mid (x_t, \theta) \sim t_\eta(0, \exp\{x_t\}) \quad \text{(observation equation)}$$
$$x_t \mid (x_{t-1}, \theta) \sim N(\alpha + \beta x_{t-1}, \tau^2) \quad \text{(system equation)}$$

Table 2.2 LSTAR-SV for S&P 500

Parameter	$\mathcal{M}_1$	$\mathcal{M}_2$	$\mathcal{M}_3$	$\mathcal{M}_4$	$\mathcal{M}_5$	$\mathcal{M}_6$
β_{01}	−0.060	−0.066	0.292	−0.354	−4.842	−6.081
	(0.184)	(0.241)	(0.579)	(0.126)	(0.802)	(1.282)
β_{11}	0.904	0.184	0.306	0.572	−0.713	−0.940
	(0.185)	(0.242)	(0.263)	(0.135)	(0.306)	(0.699)
β_{21}	—	0.715	—	—	−1.018	−1.099
		(0.248)			(0.118)	(0.336)
β_{02}	—	—	−0.685	0.133	4.783	6.036
			(0.593)	(0.092)	(0.801)	(1.283)
β_{12}	—	—	0.794	0.237	0.913	1.091
			(0.257)	(0.086)	(0.314)	(0.706)
β_{22}	—	—	—	—	1.748	1.892
					(0.114)	(0.356)
γ	—	—	118.18	163.54	132.60	189.51
			(16.924)	(23.912)	(10.147)	(0.000)
c	—	—	−1.589	0.022	−2.060	−2.125
			(0.022)	(0.280)	(0.046)	(0.000)
τ^2	0.135	0.234	0.316	0.552	0.214	0.166
	(0.020)	(0.044)	(0.066)	(0.218)	(0.035)	(0.026)
DIC	7,223.1	7,149.2	7,101.1	7,150.3	7,102.4	7,159.4

The table shows posterior means (with posterior standard deviations given in parentheses) for the parameters from all six models plus the deviance information criterion.

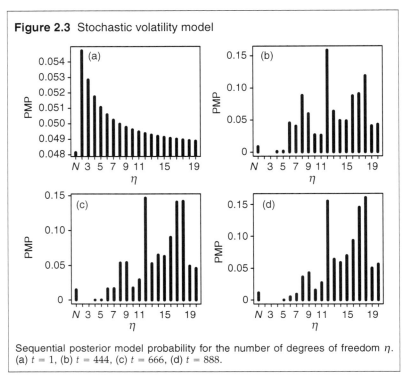

Figure 2.3 Stochastic volatility model

Sequential posterior model probability for the number of degrees of freedom η.
(a) $t = 1$, (b) $t = 444$, (c) $t = 666$, (d) $t = 888$.

where $t_\eta(\mu, \sigma^2)$ denotes the Student-t distribution with η degrees of freedom, location μ and scale σ^2. The number of degrees of freedom η is treated as known. Sequential posterior inference is based on the Liu–West filter with $N = 100{,}000$ particles. The shrinkage constant a is set at $a = 0.95$, whereas prior hyperparameters are $m_0 = 0$, $C_0 = 10$, $v_0 = 3$, $\tau_0^2 = 0.01$, $b_0 = (0, 1)'$ and $B_0 = 10I_2$. Particle approximation to the sequential posterior model probabilities, assuming uniform prior for η over models $\{t_\infty, t_2, \ldots, t_{20}\}$, appears in Figure 2.3, where t_∞ denotes normal distribution. Figure 2.3(d) shows percentiles of $p(\sigma_t \mid y^t)$ when integrating out over all competing models in $\{t_\infty, t_2, \ldots, t_{20}\}$. We can argue that the data slowly moves over time from a more t-like, heavy-tail model towards a more Gaussian, thin-tail model. Figures 2.4 and 2.5 present posterior summaries for the volatilities and parameters of a few competing models.

Example 2.8 (SV with jumps). The credit crisis of 2007–8 is analysed and monitored by particle filters in Lopes and Polson (2010).

Figure 2.4 Stochastic volatility model

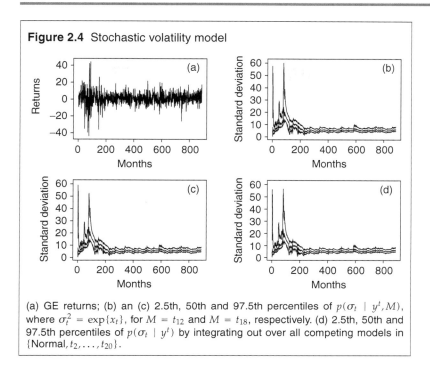

(a) GE returns; (b) an (c) 2.5th, 50th and 97.5th percentiles of $p(\sigma_t \mid y^t, M)$, where $\sigma_t^2 = \exp\{x_t\}$, for $M = t_{12}$ and $M = t_{18}$, respectively. (d) 2.5th, 50th and 97.5th percentiles of $p(\sigma_t \mid y^t)$ by integrating out over all competing models in $\{\text{Normal}, t_2, \ldots, t_{20}\}$.

They sequentially estimate the volatility and examine the volatility dynamics for three major financial time series during the early part of the crisis, namely the S&P 500 Index, the Nasdaq NDX100 Index and the financial index XLF. Sequential model choice is a natural outcome of our application and they show how the evidence in support of the SV with jumps model accumulates over time as market turbulence increases.

Figure 2.6 shows that before August 2007 the Bayes factor favours the stochastic volatility jump model. The market volatility risk premiums are effectively constant for this model over this data period, except at the very end of the period, where the implied option volatility decays quickly and the estimated volatility does not. This is also coincident with the Bayes factor decaying back in favour of the pure SV model for the NDX100 Index. By the end of 2007, the odds favour the pure SV model over the SVJ model for the NDX100 Index. For the XLF, most of the evidence for jumps is again contained in the February move. The sequential Bayes factor tends to lie in between the strong evidence for the S&P 500 and weaker evidence for the NDX100 Index. The story for the S&P 500 is different.

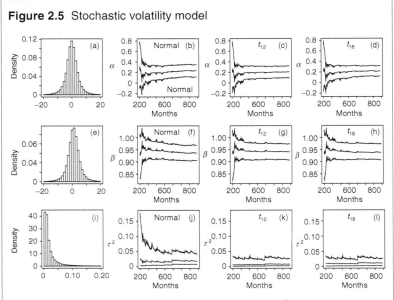

Figure 2.5 Stochastic volatility model

First column, marginal prior distributions for α, β and τ^2: (a) $p(\alpha)$, (e) $p(\beta)$, (i) $p(\tau^2)$. The second, third and fourth columns show the sequential 2.5th percentiles, 50th percentiles and 97.5th percentiles, respectively, of $p(y \mid y^t, M1)$, for y in (α, β, τ^2) and model $M \in \{\text{Normal}, t_{12}, t_{18}\}$.

The sequential Bayes factor of Figure 2.6 shows that after the February shock the SVJ model is preferred to the SV model for the whole period. When comparing with the VIX Index the jump model seems to track the option implied volatility with an appropriate market price of volatility risk.

Example 2.9 (FSV with time-varying loadings). Lopes and co-workers[22] analysed daily log returns on weekday closing spot prices for six currencies relative to the US dollar: German mark, British pound, Japanese yen, French franc, Canadian dollar and Spanish peseta. They used the factor stochastic volatility model with time-varying loadings presented in the section on the FSV (see page 49). The data analysed spans from January 1, 1992, to October 31, 1995 in order to keep the analysis somewhat comparable (Aguilar and West 2000). They consider a $k = 3$ factor model with relatively vague priors for all model parameters and run their MCMC scheme for 35,000 iterations and several initial values. All chains converged, in practical terms, after around 20,000 iterations.

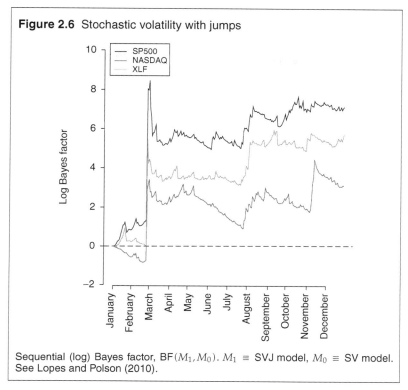

Figure 2.6 Stochastic volatility with jumps

Sequential (log) Bayes factor, BF(M_1, M_0). $M_1 \equiv$ SVJ model, $M_0 \equiv$ SV model. See Lopes and Polson (2010).

An interesting observation that highlights the importance of time-varying loadings in the context of this example is the change in the explanatory power of factor 1 (Figure 2.7), the "European factor" on the British pound. The final months of 1992 marked the withdrawal of Great Britain from the European Union exchange-rate agreement, a fact that is captured in our analysis by changes in the British loading in factor 1 and emphasised by the changes in the percentage of variation of the British pound explained by factors 1 and 2 (Figure 2.8). If temporal changes on the factor loadings were not allowed, the only way the model could capture this change in Great Britain's monetary policy would be by a "shock" on the idiosyncratic variation of the pound, reducing, in turn, the predictive ability of the latent factor structure.

FINAL REMARKS

This chapter reviews the major contributions to the literature since 1990 on Bayesian analysis of stochastic volatility models, both in the

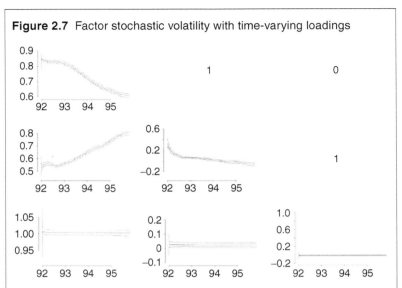

Figure 2.7 Factor stochastic volatility with time-varying loadings

Posterior 2.5th, 50th and 97.5th percentiles of the posterior distribution for the unconstrained elements of β_t, $p(\beta_t \mid y^n)$, for the first three time series for the period from January 1, 1992, to October 31, 1995. Top row, German mark; middle row, British pound; bottom row, Japanese yen. See Lopes (2000) and Lopes *et al* (2002).

univariate (Jacquier *et al* 1994) and the multivariate context (Shephard 2005; Shephard and Andersen 2009). Posterior inference for the majority of the models is performed by tailored MCMC schemes that take into account specific modelling characteristics. Jacquier *et al* (1994) and Kim *et al* (1998) are amongst the most influential contributions when dealing with univariate SV models, with Jacquier *et al* (1995), Pitt and Shephard (1999a) and Aguilar and West (2000) playing similar roles in the multivariate case.

These and other early contributions have, since 2000, played a fundamental role in helping to shape the field of financial time series and econometrics.[23] Factor and Cholesky stochastic volatility models for high-dimensional systems have also become fairly popular.[24]

Markov chain Monte Carlo methods, again since 2000, have started to share the Bayesian computational stage with efficient sequential Monte Carlo methods, with a detailed illustration in the SV context introduced on page 36 along with additional SMC references. Other successful implementation in the univariate SV literature has been carried out by Pitt and Shephard (1999b), Stroud *et al* (2004), Carvalho and Lopes (2007) and Johannes *et al* (2009), to name

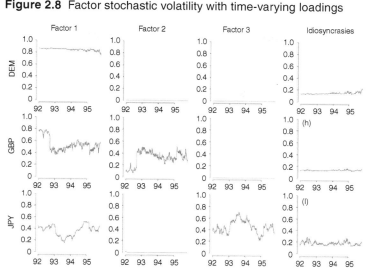

Figure 2.8 Factor stochastic volatility with time-varying loadings

Proportion of the variances of the first three time series explained by the three common factors and the idiosyncratic or specific factor for the period from January 1, 1992, to October 31, 1995. Top row, German mark; middle row, British pound; bottom row, Japanese yen. See Lopes (2000) and Lopes *et al* (2002).

but a few. Berg *et al* (2004) and Raggi and Bordignon (2006) compare the performance of several univariate SV models. In the multivariate SV case, Liu and West (2001) and Lopes (2000, Chapter 6) implement particle filter with parameter learning for two variants of the FSV model.

1 See Kalayloglu and Ghosh (2009) for Bayesian unit root tests regarding β.
2 For further details see the sections on univariate SV (page 42) and multivariate SV (page 46).
3 Also known as the sequential importance sampling with resampling (SISR) filter.
4 Also known as the auxiliary SIR (ASIR) filter.
5 See Doucet *et al* (2000) and Guo *et al* (2005), amongst others, for additional discussion on approximations based on local linearisation.
6 See, for example, Petris *et al* (2009, pp. 222–8) for an example based on the local level model, and Carvalho and Lopes (2007) for an application on Markov-switching SV models.
7 See also Omori and Watanabe (2008).
8 For more details on Bayesian nonparametric and semi-parametric models, see, amongst others, Dey *et al* (1998), Ghosh and Ramamoorthi (2003), Hjort *et al* (2010) and Carvalho *et al* (2009).
9 See Example 2.6 for more details.
10 Until the increase in computer processing power in the 1990s.

11 See also Asai and McAleer (2009).

12 See also Triantafyllopoulos (2008) for a similar derivation in the context of multivariate dynamic linear models.

13 See Dellaportas and Pourahmadi (2004) for a similar model for Garch-type dynamics and $A_t = A$ for all t.

14 See for example, Harvey et al (1994), Pitt and Shephard (1999b), Aguilar and West (2000), Lopes and Migon (2002), Chib et al (2006) and Lopes and Carvalho (2007).

15 See Lopes (2000) and Lopes et al (2002).

16 See the section on FSV with time-varying loadings (page 49) for a brief review of their exchange rate example.

17 See http://www.crsp.com.

18 See also Nardari and Scruggs (2007).

19 WINBUGS is a Bayesian software whose development started in the 1990s as part of the "Bayesian inference Using Gibbs Sampling (BUGS) project" in the MRC Biostatistics Unit. WINBUGS can be freely downloaded from http://www.mrc-bsu.cam.ac.uk/bugs. See Spiegelhalter et al (2003) and the WINBUGS web page for more details.

20 For data y and parameter θ, these criteria are defined as follows: AIC $= -2\log(p(y \mid \hat{\theta})) + 2p$ and BIC $= -2\log(p(y \mid \hat{\theta})) + p \log n$; p is the dimension of θ, n is the sample size and $\hat{\theta}$ denotes the maximum likelihood estimator. The DIC is defined as DIC $= D(\tilde{\theta}) + 2p_D = \bar{D} + p_D$, where $D(\theta) = -2\log p(y \mid \theta)$ is the deviance, $p_D = \bar{D} - D(\tilde{\theta})$ is the measure of model complexity, $\tilde{\theta} = E(\theta \mid y)$ and $\bar{D} = E(D(\theta) \mid y)$ is the measure of model fit.

21 See http://faculty.chicagobooth.edu/ruey.tsay/teaching/fts2/m-geln.txt.

22 See Lopes (2000) and Lopes et al (2002).

23 See Johannes and Polson (2010), for instance, for a thorough review of MCMC methods for continuous-time financial econometrics.

24 See, amongst others, Chib et al (2006), Lopes and Carvalho (2007) and Lopes et al (2008).

REFERENCES

Abanto-Valle, C. A., D. Bandyopadhyay, V. H. Lachos and I. Enriquez, 2009a, "Robust Bayesian Analysis of Heavy-Tailed Stochastic Volatility Models Using Scale Mixtures of Normal Distributions", *Computational Statistics and Data Analysis*, DOI:10.1016/j.csda.2009.06.011.

Abanto-Valle, C. A., H. S. Migon and H. F. Lopes, 2009b, "Bayesian Modeling of Financial Returns: A Relationship Between Volatility and Trading Volume", *Applied Stochastic Modeling in Business and Industry* 26(2), pp. 172–93.

Aguilar, O., and M. West, 2000, "Bayesian Dynamic Factor Models and Variance Matrix Discounting for Portfolio Allocation", *Journal of Business and Economic Statistics* 18, pp. 338–57.

Akaike, H., 1974, "New Look at the Statistical Model Identification", *IEEE Transactions in Automatic Control* 19, pp. 716–23.

Andersen, T., 1996, "Return Volatility and Trading Volume: An Information Flow Interpretation of Stochastic Volatility", *Journal of Finance* 51, pp. 169–204.

Asai, M., 2009, "Bayesian Analysis of Stochastic Volatility Models with Mixture-of-Normal Distributions", *Mathematics and Computers in Simulation* 79, pp. 2579–96.

Asai, M., and M. McAleer, 2009, "The Structure of Dynamic Correlations in Multivariate Stochastic Volatility Models", *Journal of Econometrics* 150, pp. 182–92.

Asai, M., M. McAleer and J. Yu, 2006, "Multivariate Stochastic Volatility: A Review", *Econometric Reviews* 25, pp. 145–75.

Berg, A., R. Meyer and J. Yu, 2004, "Deviance Information Criterion for Comparing Stochastic Volatility Models", *Journal of Business & Economic Statistics* 22, pp. 107–20.

Carlin, B. P., and N. G. Polson, 1991, "Inference for Non-Conjugate Bayesian Models Using the Gibbs Sampler", *Canadian Journal of Statistics* 19, pp. 399–405.

Carter, C. K., and R. Kohn, 1994, "On Gibbs Sampling for State Space Models", *Biometrika* 81, pp. 541–53.

Carvalho, C., and H. F. Lopes, 2007, "Simulation-Based Sequential Analysis of Markov Switching Stochastic Volatility Models", *Computational Statistics and Data Analysis* 51, pp. 4526–42.

Carvalho, C., Lopes, H. F., Polson, N. G. and M. Taddy, 2009, "Particle Learning for General Mixtures", Working Paper, University of Chicago Graduate School of Business.

Carvalho, C., M. Johannes, H. F. Lopes and N. G. Polson, 2010, "Particle Learning and Smoothing", *Statistical Science* 25, pp. 88–106.

Chen, R., and J. S. Liu, 2000, "Mixture Kalman Filter", *Journal of the Royal Statistical Society: Series B* 62, pp. 493–508.

Chib, S., F. Nardari and N. Shephard, 2002, "Markov Chain Monte Carlo Methods for Stochastic Volatility Models", *Journal of Econometrics* 108, pp. 281–316.

Chib, S., F. Nardari and N. Shephard, 2006, "Analysis of High Dimensional Multivariate Stochastic Volatility Models", *Journal of Econometrics* 134, pp. 341–71.

Dellaportas, P., and M. Pourahmadi, 2004, "Large Time-Varying Covariance Matrices with Applications to Finance", Working Paper, Department of Statistics, Athens University of Economics and Business.

Dey, D., P. Müller and D. Sinha, 1998, *Practical Nonparametric and Semiparametric Bayesian Statistics* (Springer).

Doucet, A., S. Godsill, and C. Andrieu, 2000, "On Sequential Monte Carlo Sampling Methods for Bayesian Filtering", *Statistics and Computing* 10, pp. 197–208.

Eraker, B., M. Johannes and N. G. Polson, 2003, "The Impact of Jumps in Volatility and Returns, *Journal of Finance* 59, pp. 227–60.

Fearnhead, P., 2002, "Markov Chain Monte Carlo, Sufficient Statistics and Particle Filter", *Journal of Computational and Graphical Statistics* 11, pp. 848–62.

Frühwirth-Schnatter, S., 1994, "Data Augmentation and Dynamic Linear Models", *Journal of Time Series Analysis* 15, pp. 183–202.

Gamerman, D., and H. F. Lopes, 2006, *Markov Chain Monte Carlo: Stochastic Simulation for Bayesian Inference*, Second Edition (London: Chapman & Hall/CRC).

Geweke, J., 1993, "Bayesian Treatment of the Independent Student-t Linear Model", *Journal of Applied Econometrics* 8, pp. S19–40.

Ghosh, J. K., and R. V. Ramamoorthi, 2003, *Bayesian Nonparametrics* (Springer).

Ghysels, E., A. C. Harvey and E. Renault, 1996, "Stochastic Volatility", in C. R. Rao and G. S. Maddala (eds) *Handbook of Statistics: Statistical Methods in Finance*, pp. 119–91 (Amsterdam: North-Holland).

Gordon, N., D. Salmond and A. F. M. Smith, 1993, "Novel Approach to Nonlinear/Non-Gaussian Bayesian State Estimation", *IEE Proceedings F: Radar and Signal Processing* 140, pp. 107–13.

Guo, D., X. Wang and R. Chen, 2005, "New Sequential Monte Carlo Methods for Nonlinear Dynamic Systems", *Statistics and Computing* 15, pp. 135–47.

Han, Y., 2006, "Asset Allocation with a High Dimensional Latent Factor Stochastic Volatility Model", *The Review of Financial Studies* 19, pp. 237–71.

Harvey, A. C., E. Ruiz and N. Shephard, 1994, "Multivariate Stochastic Variance Models", *Review of Economic Studies* 61, pp. 247–64.

Hjort, N. L., C., Holmes, P. Müller and S. G. Walker, 2010, *Bayesian Nonparametrics* (Cambridge University Press).

Hull, J., and A. White, 1987, "The Pricing of Options on Assets with Stochastic Volatilities", *Journal of Finance* 42, pp. 281–300.

Jacquier, E., N. G. Polson and P. E. Rossi, 1994, "Bayesian Analysis of Stochastic Volatility Models", *Journal of Business and Economic Statistics* 20, pp. 69–87.

Jacquier, E., N. G. Polson and P. E. Rossi, 1995, "Models and Priors for Multivariate Stochastic Volatility Models", Working Paper, The University of Chicago Booth School of Business.

Jacquier, E., N. G. Polson and P. E. Rossi, 2004, "Bayesian Analysis of Stochastic Volatility Models with Fat-Tails and Correlated Errors", *Journal of Econometrics* 122, pp. 185–212.

Jensen, M. J., 2004, "Semiparametric Bayesian Inference of Long-Memory Stochastic Volatility", *Journal of Time Series Analysis* 25, pp. 895–922.

Jensen, M. J., and J. M. Maheu, 2008, "Bayesian Semiparametric Stochastic Volatility Modeling", Working Paper, Federal Reserve Bank of Atlanta.

Johannes, M., and N. Polson, 2010, "MCMC Methods for Continous-Time Financial Econometrics", in Y. Aït-Sahalia and L. P. Hansen (eds), *Handbook of Financial Econometrics*, Volume 2, pp. 1–72 (Princeton, NJ: Princeton University Press).

Johannes, M. S., N. G. Polson and J. R. Stroud, 2009, "Optimal Filtering of Jump Diffusions: Extracting Latent States from Asset Prices", *Review of Financial Studies* 22, pp. 2559–99.

Kalayloglu, Z. I., and S. K. Ghosh, 2009, "Bayesian Unit-Root Tests for Stochastic Volatility Models", *Statistical Methodology* 6, pp. 189–201.

Kim, S., N. Shephard and S. Chib, 1998, "Stochastic Volatility: Likelihood Inference and Comparison with Arch Models", *Review of Economic Studies* 65, pp. 361–93.

Li, H., M. T. Wells and C. L. Yu, 2006, "A Bayesian Analysis of Return Dynamics with Lévy Jumps", *Review of Financial Studies* 21, pp. 2345–78.

Li, H., 2009, "Sequential Bayesian Analysis of Time-Changed Infinite Activity Derivatives Pricing Models", Working Paper, ESSEC Business School, Paris–Singapore.

Liesenfeld, R., and J.-F. Richard, 2006, "Classical and Bayesian Analysis of Univariate and Multivariate Stochastic Volatility Models", *Econometric Review* 25, pp. 335–60.

Liu, J., and M. West, 2001, "Combined Parameters and State Estimation in Simulation-Based Filtering", in A. Doucet, N. De Freitas and N. Gordon (eds), *Sequential Monte Carlo Methods in Practice*, pp. 197–223 (Springer).

Lopes, H. F., 2000, "Bayesian Analysis in Latent Factor and Longitudinal Models", PhD Thesis, Institute of Statistics and Decision Sciences, Duke University.

Lopes, H. F., and H. S. Migon, 2002, "Comovements and Contagion in Emergent Markets: Stock Indexes Volatilities", *Case Studies in Bayesian Statistics* 6, pp. 285–300.

Lopes, H. F., and N. G. Polson, 2010, "Extracting SP 500 and NASDAQ Volatility: The Credit Crisis of 2007–2008", in A. O'Hagan and M. West (eds), *The Oxford Handbook of Applied Bayesian Analysis*, pp. 319–42 (Oxford University Press).

Lopes, H. F., and E. Salazar, 2006a, "Time Series Mean Level and Stochastic Volatility Modeling by Smooth Transition Autoregressions: A Bayesian Approach", in T. B. Fomby (ed), *Advances in Econometrics: Econometric Analysis of Financial and Economic Time Series*, Volume 20, Part B, pp. 229–42 (Elsevier).

Lopes, H. F., and E. Salazar, 2006b, "Bayesian Model Uncertainty in Smooth Transition Autoregressions", *Journal of Time Series Analysis* 27, pp. 99–117.

Lopes, H. F., and R. S. Tsay, 2010, "Particle Filters and Bayesian Inference in Financial Econometrics", *Journal of Forecasting*, in press.

Lopes, H. F., and M. West, 2004, "Bayesian Model Assessment in Factor Analysis", *Statistica Sinica* 14, pp. 41–67.

Lopes, H. F., O. Aguilar, and M. West, 2002, "Time-Varying Covariance Structures in Currency Markets", Working Paper, Department of Statistical Methods, Federal University of Rio de Janeiro.

Lopes, H. F., and C. M. Carvalho, 2007, "Factor Stochastic Volatility with Time Varying Loadings and Markov Switching Regimes", *Journal of Statistical Planning and Inference* 137, pp. 3082–91.

Lopes, H. F., R. E. McCulloch and R. Tsay, 2008, "Choleski Multivariate Stochastic Volatility", Working Paper, The University of Chicago Booth School of Business.

Lopes, H. F., C. M. Carvalho, M. Johannes and N. G. Polson, 2010, "Particle Learning for Sequential Bayesian Computation", in J. M. Bernardo, M. J. Bayarri, J. O. Berger, A. P. Dawid, D. Heckerman, A. F. M. Smith and M. West (eds), *Bayesian Statistics*, Volume 9 (Oxford University Press).

Mahieu, R., and R. Bauer, 1998, "A Bayesian Analysis of Stock Return Volatility and Trading Volume", *Applied Financial Economics* 8, pp. 671–87.

Meyer, R., and J. Yu, 2000, "BUGS for a Bayesian Analysis of Stochastic Volatility Models", *Econometrics Journal* 3, pp. 198–215.

Migon, H. S., D. Gamerman, H. F. Lopes and M. A. R. Ferreira, 2005, "Dynamic Models", in D. Dey and C. R. Rao (eds), *Bayesian Thinking, Modeling and Computation*, Handbook of Statistics, Volume 25, pp. 553–88 (Elsevier).

Nakajima, J., and Y. Omori, 2009, "Leverage, Heavy-Tails and Correlated Jumps in Stochastic Volatility Models", *Computational Statistics and Data Analysis* 53, pp. 2335–53.

Nardari, F., and J. T. Scruggs, 2007, "Bayesian Analysis of Linear Factor Models with Latent Factors, Multivariate Stochastic Volatility, and APT Pricing Restrictions", *Journal of Financial and Quantitative Analysis* 42, pp. 857–92.

Omori, Y., and T. Watanabe, 2008, "Block Sampler and Posterior Mode Estimation for Asymmetric Stochastic Volatility Models", *Computational Statistics and Data Analysis* 52, pp. 2892–910.

Omori, Y., S. Chib, N. Shephard and J. Nakajima, 2007, "Stochastic Volatility with Leverage: Fast and Efficient Likelihood Inference", *Journal of Econometrics* 140, pp. 425–49.

Petris, G., S. Petrone and P. Campagnoli, 2009, *Dynamic Linear Models with R* (Springer).

Philipov, A., and M. E. Glickman, 2006a, "Multivariate Stochastic Volatility via Wishart Processes", *Journal of Business and Economic Statistics* 24, pp. 313–28.

Philipov, A., and M. E. Glickman, 2006b, "Factor Multivariate Stochastic Volatility Via Wishart Processes", *Econometric Reviews* 25, pp. 311–34.

Pitt, M., and N. Shephard, 1999a, "Time Varying Covariances: A Factor Stochastic Volatility Approach ", in J. M. Bernardo, J. O. Berger, A. P. Dawid and A. F. M. Smith (eds), *Bayesian Statistics*, Volume 6, pp. 547–70 (Oxford University Press).

Pitt, M., and N. Shephard, 1999b, "Filtering via Simulation: Auxiliary Particle Filters", *Journal of the American Statistical Association* 94, pp. 590–9.

Polson, N. G., and J. R. Stroud, 2003, "Bayesian Inference for Derivative Prices", in J. M. Bernardo, M. J. Bayarri, J. O. Berger, A. P. Dawid, D. Heckerman, A. F. M. Smith and M. West (eds), *Bayesian Statistics*, Volume 7, pp. 641–50 (Oxford University Press).

Polson, N. G., J. R. Stroud and P. Müller, 2008, "Practical Filtering with Sequential Parameter Learning", *Journal of the Royal Statistical Society: Series B* 70, pp. 413–28.

Raggi, D., 2005, "Adaptive MCMC Methods for Inference on Affine Stochastic Volatility Models with Jumps", *Econometrics Journal* 8, pp. 235–50.

Raggi, D., and S. Bordignon, 2006, "Comparing Stochastic Volatility Models through Monte Carlo Simulations", *Computational Statistics and Data Analysis* 50, pp. 1678–99.

Rosenberg, B., 1972, "The Behaviour of Random Variables with Nonstationary Variance and the Distribution Of Security Prices", Working Paper.

Schwarz, G., 1978, "Estimating the Dimension of a Model", *Annals of Statistics* 6, pp. 461–4.

Shephard, N., 2005, *Stochastic Volatility: Selected Readings* (Oxford University Press).

Shephard, N., and T. A. Andersen, 2009, "Stochastic Volatility: Origins and Overview", in T. G. Andersen, R. A. Davis, J.-P. Kreiss and T. Mikosch (eds), *Handbook of Financial Time Series* (Springer).

Smith, A. F. M., and A. E. Gelfand, 1992, "Bayesian Statistics Without Tears: A Sampling-Resampling Perspective", *American Statistician* 46, pp. 84–8.

So, M. K. P., 2002, "Bayesian Analysis of Long Memory Stochastic Volatility Models", *Sankhya: The Indian Journal of Statistics* 64, pp. 1–10.

So, M. K. P., K. Lam and W. K. Li, 1998, "A Stochastic Volatility Model with Markov Switching", *Journal of Business and Economic Statistics* 16, pp. 244–53.

Spiegelhalter, D. J., N. G. Best, B. P. Carlin and A. van der Linde, 2002, "Bayesian Measures Of Model Complexity and Fit", *Journal of the Royal Statistical Society: Series B* 64, p. 583–639.

Spiegelhalter, D. J., A. Thomas, N. G. Best and W. R. Gilks, 2003, "WinBUGS User Manual (Version 1.4)", MRC Biostatistics Unit, Cambridge, UK.

Steel, M. F. J., 1998, "Bayesian Analysis of Stochastic Volatility Models with Flexible Tails", *Econometric Reviews* 17, pp. 109–43.

Storvik, G., 2002, "Particle Filters for State-Space Models with the Presence of Unknown Static Parameters", *IEEE Transactions on Signal Processing* 50, pp. 281–89.

Stroud, J. R., P. Müller and N. G. Polson, 2003, "Nonlinear State-Space Models with State-Dependent Variances", *Journal of the American Statistical Association* 98, pp. 377–86.

Stroud, J. R., N. G. Polson and P. Müller, 2004, "Practical Filtering for Stochastic Volatility Models", in A. Harvey, S. J. Koopman and N. Shephard (eds), *State Space and Unobserved Components Models*, pp. 236–47 (Cambridge University Press).

Szerszen, P. J., 2009, "Bayesian Analysis of Stochastic Volatility Models with Lévy Jumps: Application to Risk Analysis", Working Paper, Divisions of Research & Statistics and Monetary Affairs, Federal Reserve Board, Washington, DC.

Taylor, S. J., 1986, *Modelling Financial Time Series* (New York: John Wiley and Sons).

Teräsvirta, T., 1994, "Specification, Estimation, and Evaluation of Smooth Transition Autoregressive Models", *Journal of the American Statistical Association* 89, pp. 208–18.

Tong, H., 1990, *Non-Linear Time Series: A Dynamical Systems Approach* (Oxford University Press).

Triantafyllopoulos, K., 2008, "Multivariate Stochastic Volatility with Bayesian Dynamic Linear Models", *Journal of Statistical Planning and Inference* 138, pp. 1021–37.

Uhlig, H., 1994, "On Singular Wishart and Singular Multivariate Beta Distributions", *The Annals of Statistics* 22, pp. 395–405.

Uhlig, H., 1997, "Bayesian Vector Autoregressions with Stochastic Volatility", *Econometrica*, 65, pp. 59–73.

West, W., 1993a, "Approximating Posterior Distributions by Mixtures", *Journal of the Royal Statistical Society: Series B* 54, pp. 553–68.

West, W., 1993b, "Mixture Models, Monte Carlo, Bayesian Updating and Dynamic Models", *Computing Science and Statistics* 24, pp. 325–33.

West, M., and J. Harrison, 1997, *Bayesian Forecasting and Dynamic Models*, Second Edition (Springer).

Yu, J., and R. Meyer, 2006, "Multivariate Stochastic Volatility Models: Bayesian Estimation and Model Comparison", *Econometric Reviews* 25, pp. 361–84.

3

Bayesian Prediction of Risk Measurements Using Copulas

Maria Concepcion Ausin;
Hedibert Freitas Lopes

Universidad Carlos III de Madrid;
University of Chicago Booth School of Business

In this chapter we use the Bayesian approach to modelling risk measures, such as the variance, value-at-risk and expected shortfall for a portfolio of assets. We argue that the Bayesian methodology offers a natural framework to introduce parameter uncertainty into predicting such risk measures, making it possible to perform full posterior inference.

Another important issue in risk management is the portfolio selection problem. Investors are mainly interested in how to allocate their investments between different assets so as to minimise the overall risk for a given expected return. The Bayesian method provides a very useful tool with which to obtain not only the optimal portfolio weights, but also a measure of the uncertainty of these weights via Bayesian credibility intervals. Analogously, Bayesian credibility regions can be obtained for the traditional mean–variance efficient frontiers which give the minimum variance for a given expected return.

Portfolio risk measurements depend on the time behaviour of the individual assets and also on the time-varying dependence structure between them. Thus, it is very important to find adequate models to describe the temporal dependence in multivariate time series. The usual assumption in most cases is that the conditional joint distribution of the returns follows a multivariate normal or multivariate t-distribution. However, it is well known that these elliptical distribution models require a very strong symmetry of the data and might not be appropriate in many circumstances. Alternatively, the dependence structure between the marginal series can be modelled through the use of copulas, which, unlike the correlation matrix, give a complete description of the joint distribution.

The chapter is organised as follows. In the next section we introduce the most common risk measures. We illustrate the necessity of jointly time-varying modelling of risk measurements via two well-known market indexes: the Dow Jones Industrial Average and DAX indexes, both derived from daily closing prices. Dependence is modelled via copula-based structures, which are introduced (see page 74) and then generalised to accommodated time-varying behaviour in (see page 76). The next section (see page 79) shows that Bayesian posterior inference is possible via Markov chain Monte Carlo (MCMC) methods. Prediction of volatilities and dependence measures, Bayesian prediction of portfolio VaR and ES and Bayesian procedure for portfolio allocation are studied in the following sections. In the final section (see page 93) we give our conclusions.

INTRODUCTION

The value-at-risk (VaR) and the expected shortfall (ES) have become important and widely used measures of the risk inherent in asset portfolios. The VaR is defined as the maximum potential loss over a given time period at a certain confidence level. Statistically speaking, the VaR is the negative value of a quantile of the conditional distribution of the portfolio return. The ES, which is also known as "conditional VaR", "mean excess loss", "mean shortfall" or "tail VaR", is defined as the conditional expectation of losses beyond the VaR level. The ES is a coherent risk measure, which means that it satisfies the properties of monotonicity, sub-additivity, homogeneity and translational invariance (see, for example, Artzner *et al* 1997). The VaR is coherent only when it is based on normal distributions.

The portfolio selection problem consists in the determination of the optimal weights assigned to each return in the portfolio. The classical portfolio optimisation approach is the mean–variance method, which follows the pioneering work of Markowitz (1952) and assigns the weights that minimise the variance subject to achieving different levels of expected returns. Markowitz optimisation makes sense for elliptical distributions, as the variance–covariance matrix is only valid for measuring linear dependence, and may be insufficient to capture other dependence structures between portfolio assets. Thus, in non-normal settings, the variance is a very restrictive measure of risk, and minimising the VaR or ES seems to be a more natural approach. The use of the VaR and ES in portfolio optimisation is a relatively novel alternative (see, for example, Gaivoronski and Pflug 2005). Using this approach, the optimal portfolio is the one which minimises the VaR or the ES, subject to achieving a specified level of expected return. The analogues to the classical mean–variance efficient frontiers are the mean–VaR and mean–ES efficient frontiers, which give the minimum VaR and minimum ES, respectively, for given expected return. Note that, for the case of elliptical distributions, the portfolio that minimises VaR and ES coincides with the Markowitz variance minimising portfolio.

The VaR and the ES of a portfolio strongly depend on the distribution of the individual assets and the dependence structure between them. In particular, the dependence in the tails of the distribution strongly influences the VaR and ES calculation. Thus, the correlation coefficient, which is not adequate to measure the dependence in the tails, may lead to inaccurate estimations of VaR and ES. An alternative approach to the study of dependence in financial data is the use of copulas (see, for example, Nelsen 2006). The main advantage of this approach is that the individual marginal densities of the returns can be defined separately from their dependence structure. Hence, first the models for the marginal distributions can be specified using the required univariate characteristics and then the dependence between the returns can be completely modelled by selecting an appropriate copula function. Using this approach, many non-elliptical and flexible multivariate distributions can be obtained.

In practice, we are mainly interested in the estimation of one-step-ahead or various-step-ahead forecasts of the VaR or ES given historical data. These quantities depend on the conditional distribution of the portfolio of assets given past data. Thus, it is important to find adequate models to describe the temporal dependence of the individual assets and the time-varying dependence structure between them. Garch models, proposed by Bollerslev (1986), have been successfully applied in modelling temporal dependence in financial time series.[1] These models allow for periods of tranquility followed by periods of high volatility frequently observed in the individual returns. The time-varying dependence between the assets can be

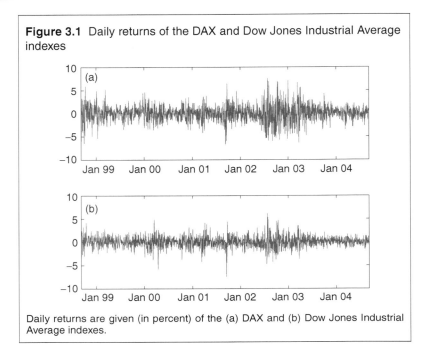

Figure 3.1 Daily returns of the DAX and Dow Jones Industrial Average indexes

Daily returns are given (in percent) of the (a) DAX and (b) Dow Jones Industrial Average indexes.

Table 3.1 Summary statistics of the daily returns of the DAX and Dow Jones Industrial Average indexes

	DAX	Dow Jones
Mean	−0.0152	0.0164
Standard deviation	1.8255	1.2177
Skewness	−0.0300	−0.0369
Kurtosis	4.5419	5.6049
Linear correlation	0.5300	

modelled using copula functions which vary through time following certain evolution equations depending on their previous values and historical data. This approach for multivariate time series has been called copula–Garch models.[2]

Assume, for example, that we are interested in the estimation of one-step-ahead or various-step-ahead forecasts of the VaR or ES of a portfolio of the Dow Jones Industrial Average and DAX indexes given a sample of the daily closing prices of the period from September 7, 1998, to September 7, 2004. Figure 3.1 shows the log return of this bivariate series, whose sample size is $T = 1{,}543$. Table 3.1 shows some summary statistics. Observe that the kurtosis of the individual series is larger than 3, indicating that the distributions have higher peaks and heavier tails than a normal distribution with the same variance. Copula–Garch models seems to be an adequate approach to describe the temporal dependence structure of these data. On the one hand, univariate Garch models can capture the usual features such that time-varying volatility, heavy-tailed distributions and large kurtosis observed in the individual series and, on the other hand, time-varying copula functions can be used to describe the temporal dependence structure between the series.

The Bayesian method provides many advantages for prediction of risk measures based on copula–Garch models. Firstly, using the Bayesian approach, we can account for the uncertainties of the parameters simultaneously. Most works on copula–Garch models are generally based on a two-stage approach where, in the first step, the marginal series are estimated assuming independence and then, in the second step, these estimations are plugged into the copula function in order to estimate the copula parameters. Although two-step approaches are usually straightforward to implement for copula models, they may produce inadequate measures of uncertainty. In fact, it can be shown that two-stage maximum likelihood estimation approaches lead to consistent but inefficient estimators (Patton 2006).

Secondly, the Bayesian perspective offers a natural way to introduce parameter uncertainty in the estimation of in-sample and out-of-sample volatilities. For example, using the Bayesian method, we can obtain the predictive distributions of the one-step-ahead volatilities allowing for the calculation of Bayesian confidence intervals which are much more helpful than simple point forecasts. Analogously, the Bayesian method accounts for the parameter uncertainty in the estimation of dependence measures, such as rank correlations and tail-dependence measures. Thus, we can obtain, for example, confidence bands for the time-varying Kendall's tau rank correlation over time.

Finally, one of the main benefits of the Bayesian perspective is that predictive distributions for the one-or-more-step-ahead risk measures, such as the variance, VaR or ES, can be obtained. The Bayesian approach provides a simple way of measuring the uncertainty in the estimations of these quantities via predictive intervals. Also, a measure of precision for the optimal portfolio weights can be obtained using Bayesian confidence intervals. This provides an important decision tool for investors who are interested not only in point estimations of portfolio weight but also in measures of the statistical accuracy of these estimations.

BASIC COPULA CONCEPTS

A p-dimensional copula $C(u_1, \ldots, u_p)$ is a multivariate distribution function in the unit hypercube $[0, 1]^p$, with uniform $U(0, 1)$ marginal distributions. It can be shown[3] that every joint distribution, $F(x_1, \ldots, x_p)$, whose marginals are given by $F_1(x_1), \ldots, F_p(x_p)$, can be written as

$$F(x_1, \ldots, x_p) = C(F_1(x_1), \ldots, F_p(x_p)) \tag{3.1}$$

for a function C that is called a copula of F. Furthermore, if the marginal distributions are continuous, then there is a unique copula associated to the joint distribution, F, that can be obtained from

$$C(u_1, \ldots, u_p) = F(F_1^{-1}(u_1), \ldots, F_p^{-1}(u_p)) \tag{3.2}$$

Conversely, given a p-dimensional copula, $C(u_1, \ldots, u_p)$, and p univariate distributions, $F_1(x_1), \ldots, F_p(x_p)$, the function in Equation 3.1 is a p-variate distribution function with margins $F_1, \ldots, F_p$, whose corresponding density function is given by

$$f(x_1, \ldots, x_p) = c(F_1(x_1), \ldots, F_p(x_p)) \prod_{i=1}^{p} f_i(x_i) \tag{3.3}$$

provided the density exists, where f_i represents the marginal density functions and c is the density function of the copula which is derived from Equation 3.2 and is given by

$$c(u_1, \ldots, u_p) = \frac{f(F_1^{-1}(u_1), \ldots, F_p^{-1}(u_p))}{\prod_{i=1}^{p} f_i(F_i^{-1}(u_i))}$$

There are a large number of parametric families of copulas in the literature.[4] The basic example is the Gaussian copula, which is obtained from the multivariate normal distribution with correlation matrix, R, and is given by

$$C_R^{Ga}(u_1,\ldots,u_p)$$
$$= \int_{-\infty}^{\Phi^{-1}(u_1)} \cdots \int_{-\infty}^{\Phi^{-1}(u_p)} \frac{1}{\sqrt{(2\pi)^p|R|}} \exp\left\{\frac{-u'R^{-1}u}{2}\right\} du$$

where $u = (u_1,\ldots,u_p)$ and Φ^{-1} is the inverse of the cumulative distribution function of the univariate standard normal distribution. The normal copula assumes that there is no dependence in the tails of the distribution. Therefore, in financial economics, it is often more useful to consider the t-copula, which is obtained from the multivariate t-distribution with η degrees of freedom and correlation matrix R, and is given by

$$C_{\eta,R}^{St}(u_1,\ldots,u_p)$$
$$= \int_{-\infty}^{(F_\eta^{St})^{-1}(u_1)} \cdots \int_{-\infty}^{(F_\eta^{St})^{-1}(u_p)} \frac{1}{\Gamma(\frac{1}{2}\eta)\sqrt{(\pi\eta)^p|R|}}$$
$$\times \Gamma\left(\frac{\eta+p}{2}\right)\left(1+\frac{u'R^{-1}u}{\eta}\right)^{-(\eta+p)/2} du \qquad (3.4)$$

where F_η^{St} denotes the cumulative distribution function of the standard univariate Student-t distribution with η degrees of freedom. Note that the Gaussian copula is obtained as a special case of the t-copula when η goes to infinity.

It is important to note that various dependence measures between two random variables depend only on their copula function. For example, an important measure of dependence is Kendall's tau rank correlation, which is defined by

$$\tau = E[\text{sgn}(X_1 - X_1')(X_2 - X_2')]$$

where (X_1, X_2) and (X_1', X_2') are two independent and identically distributed (iid) pairs of random variables. Kendall's tau is a very useful alternative to the linear correlation coefficient because it does not depend on the marginal distributions of X_1 and X_2. In fact, Kendall's tau only depends on the copula function and it can be shown that

$$\tau = 4\int_0^1\int_0^1 C(u_1,u_2)c(u_1,u_2)\,du_1\,du_2 - 1$$

Kendall's tau admits the same form for the bivariate Gaussian copula and for the bivariate t-copula with correlation coefficient ρ, and is given by

$$\tau = \frac{2}{\pi} \arcsin \rho \qquad (3.5)$$

which can be used for assessing the copula parameter ρ by expert judgement.[5]

Other useful dependence measures between two variables are the coefficients of upper tail dependence, λ_u, and lower tail dependence, λ_l, which are defined by

$$\lambda_u = \lim_{q \to 1} P(X_2 > F_{X_2}^{-1}(q) \mid X_1 > F_{X_1}^{-1}(q))$$

$$\lambda_l = \lim_{q \to 0} P(X_2 \leqslant F_{X_2}^{-1}(q) \mid X_1 \leqslant F_{X_1}^{-1}(q))$$

and can be expressed in terms of the copula as follows

$$\lambda_u = \lim_{q \to 1} \frac{1 - 2q + C(q,q)}{1 - q}, \qquad \lambda_l = \lim_{q \to 0} \frac{C(q,q)}{q}$$

As noted above, the Gaussian copula is characterised by zero tail dependence. The t-copula exhibits tail dependence which is determined by

$$\lambda_u = \lambda_l = 2 t_{\eta+1}\left(\frac{-\sqrt{\eta + 1}\sqrt{1 - \rho}}{\sqrt{1 + \rho}}\right) \qquad (3.6)$$

where $t_{\eta+1}$ denotes the cumulative distribution function of the standard univariate Student-t distribution with $\eta + 1$ degrees of freedom.

COPULA–GARCH MODELS

A p-dimensional vector of financial log returns, $y_t = (y_{1t}, \ldots, y_{pt})$, follows a copula–Garch model if the joint cumulative distribution function is given by

$$F(y_t \mid \boldsymbol{\mu}, h_t) = C_t(F_1(y_{1t} \mid \mu_1, h_{1t}), \ldots, F_p(y_{pt} \mid \mu_p, h_{pt}))$$

where $\boldsymbol{\mu} = (\mu_1, \ldots, \mu_p)$, $h_t = (h_{1t}, \ldots, h_{pt})$, C_t is a p-dimensional copula which varies through time, F_i is the conditional distribution function of the marginal series y_{it}, for $i = 1, \ldots, p$, and y_{it} follows a standard univariate Garch$(1,1)$-model

$$y_{it} = \mu_i + \sqrt{h_{it}} \epsilon_{it}$$
$$h_{it} = \omega_i + \alpha_i (y_{i,t-1} - \mu_i)^2 + \beta_i h_{i,t-1}$$

where h_{it} is the conditional variance of y_{it} given the information set $I_{i,t-1} = \{y_{i,t-1}, y_{i,t-2}, \ldots\}$, ϵ_{it} are iid random variables with zero mean. Finally, we assume that $\omega_i, \alpha_i, \beta_i > 0$ and $\alpha_i + \beta_i < 1$, to ensure positivity of h_{it} and covariance stationarity, respectively.

In order to complete the specification of the copula–Garch model, we need to define a distribution for the innovations, ϵ_{it}, and a time-varying model for the copula. Firstly, we can assume, for example, that the innovations follow the standard Student-t distribution, $\epsilon_{it} \sim t_{\nu_i}$, with ν_i degrees of freedom, zero mean and variance $\nu_i / (\nu_i - 2)$, for $i = 1, \ldots, p$, whose density is given by

$$f_{\nu_i}^t(\epsilon_{it}) = \frac{\Gamma(\frac{1}{2}(\nu_i + 1))}{\Gamma(\frac{1}{2}\nu_i)\sqrt{\nu_i \pi}} \left(1 + \frac{\epsilon_{it}^2}{\nu_i}\right)^{-(\nu_i+1)/2}$$

Then, the conditional distribution function of each marginal series is

$$F_i(y_{it} \mid \mu_i, h_{it}) = F_{\nu_i}^{St}\left(\frac{y_{it} - \mu_i}{h_{it}^{1/2}}\right) \quad (3.7)$$

for $i = 1, \ldots, p$, where $F_{\nu_i}^{St}$ is the cumulative distribution function of the standard t-distribution with ν_i degrees of freedom. The Student-t distribution is the usual choice to model fat tails in univariate time series.[6] However, many other specifications could be also used for the innovations, such as a mixture of two zero-mean Gaussian distributions as proposed in Ausin and Galeano (2007). This mixture model is known to be statistically more stable, but the number of parameters is increased by one unit for each marginal variable.

Now, it is necessary to specify a model for the copula function. One possibility is to choose a time-varying t-copula function with η degrees of freedom, as defined in Equation 3.4, whose density for each time t is given by

$$c_{\eta,R_t}^{St}(u_{1t}, \ldots, u_{pt}) = \frac{f_{\eta,R_t}^{St}((F_\eta^{St})^{-1}(u_{1t}), \ldots, (F_\eta^{St})^{-1}(u_{pt}))}{\prod_{i=1}^{p} f_\eta^{St}((F_\eta^{St})^{-1}(u_{it}))} \quad (3.8)$$

where $u_{it} = F_i(y_{it} \mid \mu_i, h_{it})$, for $i = 1, \ldots, p$; f_{η,R_t}^{St} is the joint density of the standard multivariate Student-t distribution with η degrees of freedom and correlation matrix R_t and f_η^{St} is the density of the standard univariate t-distribution with η degrees of freedom. The advantage of the t-copula is that it assumes dependence in the tails. Also, the resulting joint distribution of the multivariate series is not elliptically contoured except for the case when the degrees of freedom η of the t-copula and the degrees of freedom v_i of the marginals coincide, in which case the joint distribution corresponds to the multivariate t-distribution.

Finally, this model allows for the specification of a time-varying copula by assuming that the correlation matrix, R_t, varies through time according to the following equation

$$R_t = (1 - a - b)R + a\Psi_{t-1} + bR_{t-1} \qquad (3.9)$$

where a and b are non-negative parameters satisfying $a + b \leqslant 1$, R is a time-invariant $p \times p$ symmetric positive definite parameter matrix with unit diagonal elements and Ψ_{t-1} is a $p \times p$ matrix whose (i,j)th element is given by

$$\Psi_{ij,t-1} = \frac{\sum_{h=1}^{m} x_{it-h} x_{jt-h}}{\sqrt{\sum_{h=1}^{m} x_{it-h}^2 \sum_{h=1}^{m} x_{jt-h}^2}}$$

which gives the sample correlation of $\{x_{t-1}, \ldots, x_{t-m}\}$, with $m \geqslant 2$, where

$$x_t = (x_{1t}, \ldots, x_{pt}) = (t_\eta^{-1}(t_{v_1}(\epsilon_{1t})), \ldots, t_\eta^{-1}(t_{v_p}(\epsilon_{pt}))) \qquad (3.10)$$

Note that x_t follows a standard multivariate Student-t distribution with η degrees of freedom. Equation 3.9 is based on the dynamics for the correlation matrix proposed by Tse and Tsui (2002) in a multivariate Garch model. Note that the time-varying equation (Equation 3.9) has the advantage that the parameter matrix, R_t, is a well-defined correlation matrix, ie, positive definite with unit diagonal elements.

Thus, using Equations 3.3, 3.7 and 3.8, the joint density function of the time series can be computed by

$$f(y_t \mid \mu, h_t) = c_{\eta,R_t}^{St} \left(F_{v_1}^{St}\left(\frac{y_{1t} - \mu_1}{h_{1t}^{1/2}}\right), \ldots, F_{v_p}^{St}\left(\frac{y_{pt} - \mu_p}{h_{pt}^{1/2}}\right) \right)$$

$$\times \prod_{i=1}^{p} f_{v_i}^{St}\left(\frac{y_{it} - \mu_i}{h_{it}^{1/2}}\right) \frac{1}{h_{it}^{1/2}}$$

$$= \frac{f_{\eta,R_t}^{St}(x_{1t}, \ldots, x_{pt})}{\prod_{i=1}^{p} f_\eta^{St}(x_{it})} \prod_{i=1}^{p} f_{v_i}^{St}\left(\frac{y_{it} - \mu_i}{h_{it}^{1/2}}\right) \frac{1}{h_{it}^{1/2}}$$

where x_{it}, for $i = 1,\ldots,p$, is given in Equation 3.10. Therefore, the likelihood is given by

$$l(\boldsymbol{\theta} \mid y) = \prod_{t=1}^{T} f(\boldsymbol{y}_t \mid \boldsymbol{\mu}, \boldsymbol{h}_t)$$

$$= \prod_{t=1}^{T} \frac{\Gamma(\frac{1}{2}\eta)\Gamma(\frac{1}{2}\eta)^{p-1}}{\Gamma(\frac{1}{2}(\eta+1))^p}$$

$$\times \frac{(1 + (x_t' R_t^{-1} x_t)/\eta)^{-(\eta+p)/2}}{\sqrt{|R_t|}} \prod_{i=1}^{p} \left(1 + \frac{x_{it}^2}{\eta}\right)^{(\eta+1)/2}$$

$$\times \prod_{i=1}^{p} \frac{\Gamma(\frac{1}{2}(\nu_i+1))}{\Gamma(\frac{1}{2}\nu_i)\sqrt{\pi \nu_i h_{it}}} \left(1 + \frac{(y_{it} - \mu_i)^2}{\nu_i h_{it}}\right)^{-(\nu_i+1)/2} \qquad (3.11)$$

where $\boldsymbol{\theta} = \{(\mu_i, \omega_i, \alpha_i, \beta_i, \nu_i)_{i=1}^{p}, (a, b, R, \eta)\}$, $y = (y_1, \ldots, y_T)$ and $x_t = (x_{1t}, \ldots, x_{pt})$.

BAYESIAN INFERENCE FOR THE MODEL PARAMETERS

We want to make Bayesian inference for the model parameters, $\boldsymbol{\theta}$, constituted by the parameters of the dynamic copula function, (η, a, b, R), the parameters of the conditional variances' equations, $(\mu_i, \omega_i, \alpha_i, \beta_i)$, for $i = 1, \ldots, p$, and the degrees of freedom of each marginal series, ν_i. Firstly, we need to define prior distributions for $\boldsymbol{\theta}$. For each of the parameters $(\mu_i, \omega_i, \alpha_i, \beta_i)$, we can assume a uniform prior over their respective domains imposing the stationary condition $\alpha_i + \beta_i < 1$. For the degrees-of-freedom parameters, we cannot assume a flat prior, as it would lead to an improper posterior distribution, as shown in Bauwens and Lubrano (1998). Then, we can assume a half Cauchy prior

$$f(\nu_i) \propto \frac{1}{1 + \nu_i^2}, \quad \nu_i > 0 \qquad (3.12)$$

for $i = 1, \ldots, p$. For the time-varying copula parameters (a, b, R), we can assume a uniform prior distribution over their respective domains imposing the stationarity condition, $a + b \leq 1$, and the requirement that the parameter matrix, R, is a positive definite parameter matrix. Finally, we might assume a half-right-side Cauchy distribution as given in Equation 3.12 for the degrees of freedom η of the t-copula.

Given an observed series, $y = \{y_1, \ldots, y_T\}$, and the priors specified above, the evaluation of the joint posterior distribution $f(\theta \mid y)$ is analytically intractable. Therefore, we can make use of the MCMC sampling strategies in order to obtain a sample from the joint posterior distribution which allows us to develop Bayesian inference.[7] Initially, a Gibbs sampling scheme can be carried out by cycling repeatedly through draws of each parameter conditional on the remaining parameters (Tierney 1994). Given the prior distributions and the likelihood function in Equation 3.11, it is straightforward to see that the conditional posterior distribution of the model parameters is given by

$$f(\phi_i \mid \cdot) \propto \prod_{t=1}^{T} \frac{(1 + (x_t' R_t^{-1} x_t)/\eta)^{-(\eta+p)/2}}{\sqrt{|R_t|}(1 + x_{it}^2/\eta)^{-(\eta+1)/2}} \times \frac{(1 + (y_{it} - \mu_i)^2/\nu_i h_{it})^{-(\nu_i+1)/2}}{\sqrt{h_{it}}}$$

for $\phi_i = \mu_i, \omega_i, \alpha_i, \beta_i$, for $i = 1, \ldots p$

$$f(\nu_i \mid \cdot) \propto \frac{\Gamma(\frac{1}{2}(\nu_i + 1))^T \nu_i^{-T/2}}{\Gamma(\frac{1}{2}\nu_i)^T (1 + \nu_i)^2} \times \prod_{t=1}^{T} \frac{(1 + (x_t' R_t^{-1} x_t)/\eta)^{-(\eta+p)/2}}{\sqrt{|R_t|}(1 + x_{it}^2/\eta)^{-(\eta+1)/2}(1 + (y_{it} - \mu_i)^2/\nu_i h_{it})^{(\nu_i+1)/2}}$$

for $i = 1, 2$,

$$f(\eta \mid \cdot) \propto \frac{\Gamma(\frac{1}{2}(\eta + p))^T \Gamma(\frac{1}{2}\eta)^{T(p-1)}}{\Gamma(\frac{1}{2}(\eta + 1))^{Tp}(1 + \eta)^2} \times \prod_{t=1}^{T} \frac{(1 + x_t' R_t^{-1} x_t/\eta)^{-(\eta+p)/2}}{\sqrt{|R_t|} \prod_{i=1}^{p}(1 + x_{it}^2/\eta)^{-(\eta+1)/2}}$$

and

$$f(d \mid \cdots) \propto \prod_{t=1}^{T} \frac{1}{\sqrt{|R_t|}} \left(1 + \frac{x_t' R_t^{-1} x_t}{\eta}\right)^{-(\eta+p)/2}$$

for $d = a, b, r_{ij}$. Then, using these conditional posterior distributions, the simplest sampling approach is to update each model parameter separately in the MCMC algorithm. For example, we can consider a simple one-dimensional random-walk Metropolis for each parameter using normal candidate distributions whose variances can be calibrated to obtain good acceptance rates in a range between 25%

Table 3.2 Values of Geweke's statistic and p-values for each parameter obtained for the DAX and Dow Jones indexes

Parameter	Geweke's statistic	p-value
μ_1	1.637	0.1016
μ_2	1.798	0.0721
ω_1	1.422	0.1550
ω_2	−1.080	0.2801
α_1	1.716	0.0861
α_2	0.5189	0.6038
β_1	−1.430	0.1527
β_2	0.3344	0.7380
ν_1	−0.7018	0.4828
ν_2	0.718	0.4727
a	0.1210	0.9037
b	0.0508	0.9595
c	−0.2559	0.7980
η	1.065	0.2869

and 50%. However, in practice the mixing in the MCMC algorithm can be significantly improved and the computational cost can be drastically reduced if we use simultaneous updating of highly correlated subvectors of the model parameters $\boldsymbol{\theta}$ (block updating). More specifically, we can update simultaneously the subset of parameters $\boldsymbol{\phi}_i = (\mu_i, \omega_i, \alpha_i, \beta_i)$ by using a multivariate Metropolis step for each $i = 1, \ldots, p$, where a candidate vector is generated from a multivariate normal distribution $N(\boldsymbol{\phi}_i^{(n)}, c\Sigma)$, where $\boldsymbol{\phi}_i^{(n)}$ denotes the current value of the parameter subvector, Σ is an estimation of the variance covariance matrix associated to this subvector and c is a constant for calibrating the acceptance rate. The matrix Σ can be obtained, for example, from a moderate number of iterations from the one-dimensional random-walk Metropolis algorithm considered previously. Analogously, we can update simultaneously the subset of parameters (a, b, R) of the copula evolution equations.

Now consider the bivariate series presented in Figure 3.1. Firstly, we run the simple one-dimensional random-walk Metropolis for 2,000 iterations (discarding the first 1,000 as burn-in iterations) in order to obtain estimates of the variance covariance matrices of the subsets of parameters $\boldsymbol{\phi}_i = (\mu_i, \omega_i, \alpha_i, \beta_i)$, for each $i = 1, \ldots, p$, and

Table 3.3 Parameter estimation results for the DAX and Dow Jones indexes

Parameter	Posterior mean	Posterior STD
μ_1	0.0236	0.0364
μ_2	0.0374	0.0249
ω_1	0.0441	0.0143
ω_2	0.0204	0.0071
α_1	0.0724	0.0112
α_2	0.0508	0.0099
β_1	0.9061	0.0136
β_2	0.9181	0.0146
ν_1	157.12	1501.2
ν_2	10.549	2.4754
η	8.6929	2.5068
a	0.0225	0.0079
b	0.9684	0.0135
c	0.5806	0.1467

(a, b, R). Then, using these matrices, we run through the entire block-updating MCMC algorithm 20,000 times, discarding the first 10,000 as burn-in iterations. The resulting samples are checked for convergence using the test proposed by Geweke (1992). Table 3.2 shows the values of the Geweke's statistic for each parameter. These indicate that convergence has been achieved, because if the samples are drawn from the stationary distribution of the chain, the Geweke statistic has an asymptotically standard normal distribution.

Table 3.3 shows the posterior means and standard deviations obtained from this algorithm. We have chosen $m = 5$ in the computation of $\Psi_{ij,t-1}$ in order to approximate the short-term correlation over one week, as suggested in Jondeau and Rockinger (2006). However, we have observed that similar results are obtained using different values for m ($m = 10$ and $m = 20$). Also note the large value for the posterior mean and standard deviation of the degrees of freedom, ν_1, of the DAX returns, which indicates that the innovations, ϵ_{1t}, of this marginal series may be normally distributed, while the relatively small value for ν_2 indicates that the tails of the innovations of the Dow Jones returns are longer than the tails of the normal distribution, which is not appropriate in this case. This result is consistent with Table 3.1, where the kurtosis of the DAX is lower than that of the Dow Jones index. Then, it is clear that the multivariate normal or

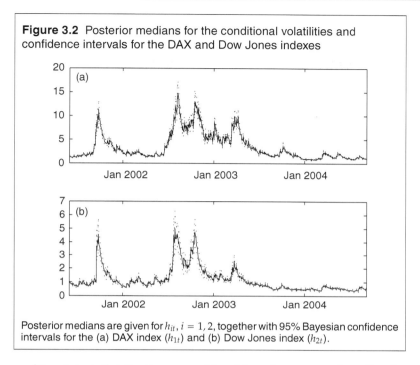

Figure 3.2 Posterior medians for the conditional volatilities and confidence intervals for the DAX and Dow Jones indexes

Posterior medians are given for h_{it}, $i = 1, 2$, together with 95% Bayesian confidence intervals for the (a) DAX index (h_{1t}) and (b) Dow Jones index (h_{2t}).

multivariate t-distributions would not be adequate to describe the multivariate distribution of the innovation process in this case.

PREDICTION OF VOLATILITIES AND DEPENDENCE MEASURES

In financial time series, we frequently observe changes in the temporal dependence during periods of high volatility. This effect is known as "financial contagion". Thus, in multivariate Garch models, it is important to estimate the dependence measures and volatilities as a function of t. Given the MCMC output and the observed y_{it}, we can obtain samples from the posterior distribution of the individual conditional volatilities, h_{it}, by averaging their values $h_{it}^{(n)}$ for each draw $\boldsymbol{\theta}^{(n)}$ of the model parameters in the MCMC sample. Then, we can approximate their posterior means using

$$E[h_{it} \mid \boldsymbol{y}] \approx \frac{1}{N} \sum_{n=1}^{N} h_{it}^{(n)}$$

Also, we can approximate the posterior median and 95% Bayesian confidence intervals for h_{it} by just calculating the median and the

0.025 and 0.975 quantiles, respectively, of the posterior sample of h_{it}. Figure 3.2 shows the posterior medians and 95% Bayesian confidence intervals for the conditional volatilities for the DAX and Dow Jones indexes since May 2001. We can observe that there is little uncertainty in the estimation of these volatilities. Also, it appears that the DAX index is, in general, more volatile than the Dow Jones index in this last period.

Analogously, we can obtain samples from the posterior distribution of the individual elements, r_{ijt}, of the parameter matrix R_t by averaging their values $r_{ijt}^{(n)}$ for each draw $\boldsymbol{\theta}^{(n)}$ of the MCMC sample. For the particular case of a bivariate times series, we can easily estimate the posterior mean of Kendall's tau correlation, given in Equation 3.5, for each time t using

$$E[\tau_t \mid y] \approx \frac{1}{N} \sum_{n=1}^{N} \frac{2}{\pi} \arcsin \rho_t^{(n)} \qquad (3.13)$$

where $\rho_t^{(n)} = r_{12t}^{(n)}$, which is the off-diagonal element of the time-varying matrix given in Equation 3.9 evaluated for each draw $\boldsymbol{\theta}^{(n)}$ of the model parameters in the MCMC sample of size N. Also, we can approximate the posterior median of τ_t and Bayesian confidence intervals as before. Analogously, we can estimate the posterior mean, median and Bayesian confidence intervals for the coefficient of tail dependence λ_t as a function of t using Equation 3.6 as follows

$$E[\lambda_t \mid y] \approx \frac{1}{N} \sum_{n=1}^{N} 2 t_{\eta^{(n)}+1} \left(\frac{-\sqrt{\eta^{(n)}+1}\sqrt{1-\rho_t^{(n)}}}{\sqrt{1+\rho_t^{(n)}}} \right) \qquad (3.14)$$

Finally, note that using this approach we can also estimate the predictive distribution and intervals for the one-step-ahead volatilities, $h_{i,T+1}$, the one-step-ahead Kendall's tau, τ_{T+1}, and the one-step-ahead coefficient of tail dependence, λ_{T+1}, which are of particular interest for prediction purposes.

Now, we examine the temporal dependence between the bivariate series on the DAX and Dow Jones indexes. Figure 3.3 illustrates the posterior means of Kendall's τ_t, the copula coefficient ρ_t and the tail dependence λ_t, as functions of time, which have been obtained as described in Equations 3.13 and 3.14. In order to assess the quality of these estimations, we compare in Figure 3.4 the posterior means of τ_t with sample estimates of Kendall's τ_t evaluated in two rolling windows of sizes 100 and 250 observations. Observe that the dynamics

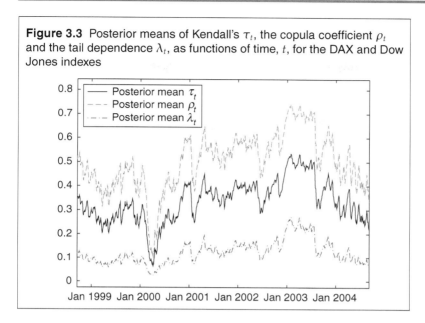

Figure 3.3 Posterior means of Kendall's τ_t, the copula coefficient ρ_t and the tail dependence λ_t, as functions of time, t, for the DAX and Dow Jones indexes

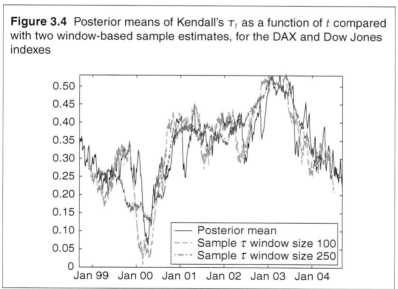

Figure 3.4 Posterior means of Kendall's τ_t as a function of t compared with two window-based sample estimates, for the DAX and Dow Jones indexes

of the Bayesian posterior means are very similar to the sample estimations. However, as opposed to our dynamic model, the moving window is not capable of forecasting ahead the quantities of interest; nor it is possible to compute credible intervals as we do in Figure 3.5.

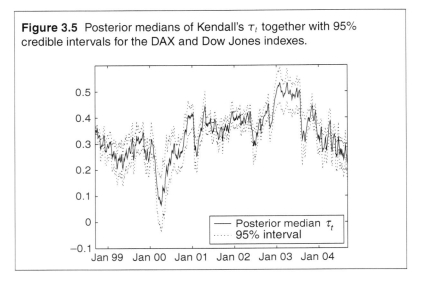

Figure 3.5 Posterior medians of Kendall's τ_t together with 95% credible intervals for the DAX and Dow Jones indexes.

BAYESIAN PREDICTION OF PORTFOLIO VAR AND ES

In this section, we consider three of the most common measures of the risk of a portfolio, namely, the portfolio variance, VaR and ES.

The VaR of a portfolio is defined as a low-order quantile of the portfolio loss in a given period of time. More specifically, given a portfolio obtained from a log-return series

$$\sum_{i=1}^{p} \delta_i y_{it}, \quad \text{where} \sum_{i=1}^{p} \delta_i = 1 \quad (3.15)$$

the $q\%$ VaR at time t is given by

$$q = \Pr\left(\sum_{i=1}^{p} \delta_i y_{it} \leqslant -\text{VaR}_t\right) \quad (3.16)$$

where q is supposed to be a small probability such as 0.01 or 0.05.

As an alternative measure of risk, the ES is known to have better properties than VaR (Artzner *et al* 1997). By definition, with respect to a specified probability level, q, the ES is the conditional expectation of losses above the $q\%$ VaR. More specifically, given the portfolio in Equation 3.15, the $q\%$ ES at time t is given by

$$\text{ES}_t = -E\left[\sum_{i=1}^{p} \delta_i y_{it} \,\bigg|\, \sum_{i=1}^{p} \delta_i y_{it} \leqslant -\text{VaR}_t\right]$$

where VaR_t is the $q\%$ VaR at time t given in Equation 3.16.

Given the observed series, $y = \{y_1, \ldots, y_T\}$, it is particularly interesting to estimate the one-step-ahead VaR and ES, that is, the $(T+1)$-period VaR and ES. We can obtain consistent estimators of these quantities using

$$E[\text{VaR}_{T+1} \mid y] \approx \frac{1}{N} \sum_{n=1}^{N} \text{VaR}_{T+1}^{(n)} \qquad (3.17)$$

and

$$E[\text{ES}_{T+1} \mid y] \approx \frac{1}{N} \sum_{n=1}^{N} \text{ES}_{T+1}^{(n)} \qquad (3.18)$$

where $\text{VaR}_{T+1}^{(n)}$ and $\text{ES}_{T+1}^{(n)}$ are the predicted one-step-ahead VaR and ES, respectively, given the model parameters $\theta^{(n)}$ of the nth MCMC iteration. Although the conditional distribution of the multivariate series $(y_{1,T+1}, \ldots, y_{p,T+1})$ is explicit given the model parameters, it is not straightforward to derive the distribution of the portfolio in Equation 3.15. Therefore, it is complicated to obtain an analytic expression for $\text{VaR}_{T+1}^{(n)}$ and $\text{ES}_{T+1}^{(n)}$ given $\theta^{(n)}$. However, these can be easily approximated by generating values from our copula–Garch model as follows. For each value of the parameters $\theta^{(n)}$, the values of $(h_{1,T+1}^{(n)}, \ldots, h_{p,T+1}^{(n)})$ and $R_{T+1}^{(n)}$ are known. Then, we can generate M replications $\{(y_{1,T+1}^{(n,m)}, \ldots, y_{p,T+1}^{(n,m)})\}_{m=1}^{M}$ from the one-step-ahead density of the series using the following two steps.

For each $m = 1, \ldots, M$:

1. simulate $(x_{1,T+1}^{(n,m)}, \ldots, x_{p,T+1}^{(n,m)})$ from a multivariate-t with parameters $\eta^{(n)}$ and $R_{T+1}^{(n)}$;

2. set

$$y_{i,T+1}^{(n,m)} = t_{\nu_i^{(n)}}^{-1}(t_{\eta^{(n)}}(x_{i,T+1}^{(n,m)}))\sqrt{h_{i,T+1}^{(n)}} + \mu_i^{(n)} \quad \text{for } i = 1, \ldots, p$$

Then, the value of $\text{VaR}_{T+1}^{(n)}$ can be approximated by the negative value of the empirical q-quantile of the sample of portfolios

$$\left\{ \sum_{i=1}^{p} \delta_i y_{i,T+1}^{(n,m)} \right\}_{m=1}^{M}$$

Also, the value of $\text{ES}_{T+1}^{(n)}$ can be approximated by the negative value of the empirical mean of the following conditional sample of portfolios

$$\left\{ \sum_{i=1}^{p} \delta_i y_{i,T+1}^{(n,m)} \text{ such that } \sum_{i=1}^{p} \delta_i y_{i,T+1}^{(n,m)} \leq -\text{VaR}_{T+1}^{(n)} \right\}_{m=1}^{M}$$

Figure 3.6 Predictive mean and 95% Bayesian confidence intervals for the VaR, ES and variance of the one-step-ahead portfolio for different values of δ and q

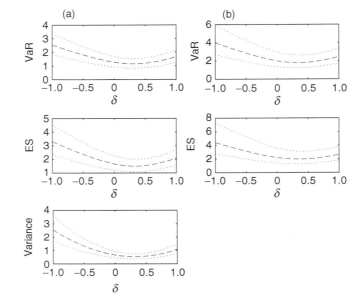

The graph shows predictive mean (dashed lines) and 95% Bayesian confidence intervals (dotted lines) for the VaR, ES and variance of the one-step-ahead portfolio, $\delta \times \text{DAX}_{T+1} + (1 - \delta) \times \text{DowJ}_{T+1}$, for different values of δ and (a) $q = 0.05$ and (b) $q = 0.01$ for the DAX and Dow Jones indexes.

Now, we can estimate the posterior means (Equations 3.17 and 3.18) and obtain 95% predictive intervals for VaR and ES using the 0.025 and 0.975 quantiles of the posterior sample of $\text{VaR}^{(n)}$ and $\text{ES}^{(n)}$, respectively, for $n = 1, \ldots, N$. A similar simulation procedure is considered in Ausin and Galeano (2007) to obtain predictive intervals for the VaR in univariate Garch models. Finally, note that using a similar approach we can also approximate the variance of the one-step-ahead portfolio using the empirical variance of the sample of portfolios

$$\left\{ \sum_{i=1}^{p} \delta_i y_{i,T+1}^{(n,m)} \right\}_{m=1}^{M} \quad \text{for } n = 1, \ldots, N$$

Assume now that we want to make Bayesian prediction for the considered risk measures in different one-step-ahead portfolios of the two indexes analysed earlier. Figure 3.6 shows the predictive means and 95% Bayesian confidence intervals for the VaR, ES and variance of the one-step-ahead portfolio, $\delta \times \text{DAX}_{T+1} + (1-\delta) \times \text{DowJ}_{T+1}$, for different values of δ in the interval $(-1,1)$ and $q = 0.05$ and $q = 0.01$. These are obtained using the simulation procedure that we have just described with $M = 100$ replications for each MCMC iteration. Observe that these predictions can be also used to choose the optimal portfolio that minimises the posterior mean of the VaR, ES or variance. The problem of selecting the optimal portfolio weights will be addressed in detail in the next section.

Finally, observe that if we were interested in the prediction of multi-step-ahead variance, VaR and ES estimation, we could not obtain samples directly from the multiple-step-ahead portfolio using the same procedure as for the one-step-ahead portfolio. This is because the values of $R_{T+s}^{(n)}$ and $h_{i,T+s}^{(n)}$ given $\boldsymbol{\theta}^{(n)}$ are unknown for $s > 1$. However, we can use a simulation procedure similar that the proposed in Ausin and Galeano (2007) as follows. For each $\boldsymbol{\theta}^{(n)}$, the values for $R_{T+1}^{(n)}$ and $h_{i,T+1}^{(n)}$ are known and a sample $y_{i,T+1}^{(n,m)}$ can be generated as before. Sequentially, given $y_{i,T+s-1}^{(n,m)}$, the values for $R_{T+s}^{(n,m)}$ and $h_{i,T+s}^{(n,m)}$ are known and a sample $y_{i,T+s}^{(n,m)}$ can be generated leading to the sample of portfolios

$$\left\{ \sum_{i=1}^{p} \delta_i y_{i,T+s}^{(n,m)} \right\}_{m=1}^{M}$$

for $n = 1,\ldots,N$, which allows us to estimate the s-step-ahead variance, VaR and ES as before.

BAYESIAN PROCEDURE FOR PORTFOLIO ALLOCATION

We have shown how to estimate the one-step-ahead variance, VaR and ES of a given portfolio. A different problem is how to choose the optimal portfolio which minimises the one-step-ahead variance, VaR or ES. Unfortunately, given the model parameters, it is not possible to obtain a closed expression for the optimal weights

$$\delta_{\text{opt},V} = \underset{\delta}{\operatorname{argmin}} \left\{ V\left(\sum_{i=1}^{p} \delta_i y_{i,T+1} \right) : \sum_{i=1}^{p} \delta_i = 1 \right\} \qquad (3.19)$$

$$\delta_{\text{opt,VaR}} = \underset{\delta}{\operatorname{argmin}} \left\{ \text{VaR}_{T+1} : \sum_{i=1}^{p} \delta_i = 1 \right\} \qquad (3.20)$$

$$\delta_{\text{opt,ES}} = \underset{\delta}{\operatorname{argmin}} \left\{ \text{ES}_{T+1} : \sum_{i=1}^{p} \delta_i = 1 \right\} \qquad (3.21)$$

Table 3.4 Predictive means and 95% predictive intervals for the optimal weight which minimises the VaR, ES and variance of the one-step-ahead portfolio

	$q = 0.05$		$q = 0.01$	
	Mean	95% interval	Mean	95% interval
VaR	0.3192	(0.1984, 0.4407)	0.3473	(0.1855, 0.5224)
ES	0.3405	(0.2147, 0.4650)	0.3736	(0.1844, 0.5737)
Variance	0.3223	(0.2395, 0.4036)		

In fact, it is well known that the solutions to Problems 3.20 and 3.21 are not analytically tractable even under the Gaussianity assumption. However, we can make use of numerical optimisation procedures to approximate the optimal weights $\delta^{(n)}_{opt,V}$, $\delta^{(n)}_{opt,VaR}$ and $\delta^{(n)}_{opt,ES}$ for each set of model parameters, $\boldsymbol{\theta}^{(n)}$, and then obtain consistent estimators of the posterior mean of the optimal weights using

$$E[\delta_{opt,V} \mid y] \approx \frac{1}{N} \sum_{n=1}^{N} \delta^{(n)}_{opt,V}$$

$$E[\delta_{opt,VaR} \mid y] \approx \frac{1}{N} \sum_{n=1}^{N} \delta^{(n)}_{opt,VaR}$$

$$E[\delta_{opt,ES} \mid y] \approx \frac{1}{N} \sum_{n=1}^{N} \delta^{(n)}_{opt,ES}$$

Also, 95% Bayesian confidence intervals can be obtained by just calculating the 0.025 and 0.975 quantiles of the posterior samples of the optimal weights.

In order to illustrate this procedure, Table 3.4 shows the posterior means and 95% Bayesian confidence intervals of the optimal weight, δ_{opt}, which minimises the ES, VaR and variance of the one-step-ahead portfolio $\delta \times DAX_{T+1} + (1 - \delta) \times DowJ_{T+1}$. Note that there are certain differences between the optimal weights obtained with the three different optimising criteria based on the VaR, the ES and the variance, respectively, but they are not statistically significant. In particular, it can be seen that for the 99% VaR ($q = 0.01$) the weights of the optimal portfolios are measured with high uncertainties, as can be seen from the credible interval. Clearly, this is a simple example of only two assets. However, it is also clear that for more complicated and realistic portfolios the situation is expected to be even worse. Hence, our findings should also be considered by bank managers who always seek an optimal risk-return strategy for their bank without accounting for uncertainty.

Note that in the definition of the portfolio given in Equation 3.15 we have not imposed that $0 \leq \delta_i$, $i = 1,\ldots,p$. However, if we wanted to impose the condition that the portfolio weights are positive in order to prevent investors from short-selling, these restrictions should be included in Equations 3.19–3.21, and imposed in the numerical optimisation procedure to approximate the optimal weights $\delta_{opt,V}^{(n)}$, $\delta_{opt,VaR}^{(n)}$ and $\delta_{opt,ES}^{(n)}$ for each set of model parameters $\boldsymbol{\theta}^{(n)}$.

Now, assume that we are interested in the portfolio which minimises the variance, the VaR or the ES subject to achieving at least some specified expected gain. The posterior mean of the portfolio expected return is given by

$$g = E\left[\sum_{i=1}^{p} \delta_i \mu_i \mid y\right] \approx \frac{1}{N} \sum_{n=1}^{N} \sum_{i=1}^{p} \delta_i \mu_i^{(n)}$$

Thus, for a given value of g, we can find the set of values for $(\delta_1,\ldots,\delta_p)$ which lead to this expected gain. Then, for each set of weights and for each set of model parameters $\boldsymbol{\theta}^{(n)}$, we can approximate the $V_{T+1}^{(n)}$, $VaR_{T+1}^{(n)}$ and $ES_{T+1}^{(n)}$ as before, and choose those which minimises the portfolio variance, VaR and ES. Repeating this procedure for a number of values for the expected gain, g, we can approximate the mean–variance, mean–VaR and mean–ES efficient frontier with associated predictive regions of credibility. This procedure is illustrated in Figure 3.7, where the Bayesian estimations for the mean–VaR, mean–ES and mean–variance efficient frontiers with the corresponding 95% Bayesian confidence regions are obtained for the DAX and Dow Jones indexes for $q = 0.05$ and $q = 0.01$. Observe that there is a large uncertainty in the estimation of efficient frontiers, in particular for $q = 0.99$. Also note that we have obtained that the estimated variance efficient frontier is less uncertain than the VaR efficient frontier.

Finally, in order to analyse the effect of assuming a time-varying copula model instead of a constant copula, Figure 3.8(a) compares the estimated VaR of the one-step-ahead portfolio

$$\delta \times DAX_{T+1} + (1 - \delta) \times DowJ_{T+1}$$

Figure 3.7 Predictive mean and 95% Bayesian confidence intervals for the mean–VaR, mean–ES and mean–variance efficient frontiers for the DAX and Dow Jones indexes for $q = 0.05$ and $q = 0.01$

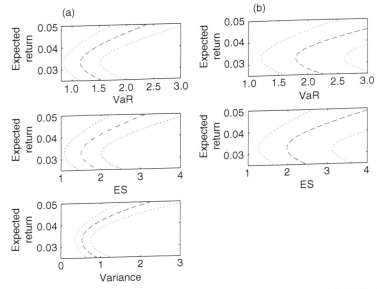

Predictive mean (dashed lines) and 95% Bayesian confidence intervals (dotted lines) for the mean–VaR, mean–ES and mean–variance efficient frontiers for the DAX and Dow Jones indexes for (a) $q = 0.05$ and (b) $q = 0.01$.

for different values of the weight δ, obtained with our time-varying copula–Garch model with those obtained assuming a constant copula model, where a and b are assumed to be equal to zero in Equation 3.9 and the resulting posterior mean and standard deviation for R are 0.5048 and 0.0217, respectively. Observe that the predictive means of the one-step-ahead VaR are quite different if we impose the condition that the copula is constant rather than assuming a time-varying copula function. Note also that our time-varying copula model predicts that the optimal portfolio should assign a weight of approximately $\delta_{opt} = 0.32$ (see also Table 3.4), while the constant copula model predicts that $\delta_{opt} = 0.28$. Figure 3.8(b) illustrates the Bayesian estimations for the mean–VaR efficient frontiers, assuming a constant and a time-varying copula model. Observe that again the predictive curves are quite different if we impose the condition that the copula is constant rather than assuming a time-varying copula function.

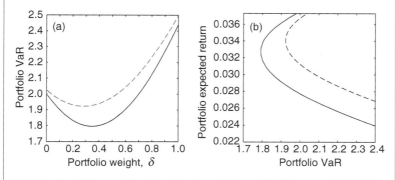

Figure 3.8 Bayesian estimations of the one-step-ahead VaR for the portfolio as a function of δ, for $q = 0.01$ and for the mean–VaR efficient frontiers assuming a constant and a time-varying copula model

Portfolio, $\delta \times \mathrm{DAX}_{T+1} + (1 - \delta) \times \mathrm{DowJ}_{T+1}$; (a) $q = 0.01$, (b) mean–VaR efficient frontiers. The dashed line denotes the constant copula and the solid line denotes the time-varying copula.

CONCLUSION

In this chapter we modelled risk measurements via time-varying copula-based dependence structures. We showed empirically the advantages of our approach by modelling the Dow Jones Industrial Average and DAX returns. For example, we observed that DAX returns have Gaussian tails, while Dow Jones Industrial Average returns have t tails, so a copula-based covariance structure is more suitable than either a bivariate normal or a bivariate t-distributions to describe their joint behaviour.

We also showed that changes in the temporal dependence during periods of high volatility were adequately captured by our copula–Garch model. This was noticed, for instance, by tracking the posterior mean of Kendall's tau correlation coefficient and the one-step-ahead coefficient of tail dependence. When compared with its constant copula version, our copula–Garch model produces more efficient portfolios with smaller variances by looking at either the one-step-ahead VaR or mean–VaR efficient frontiers.

We believe that the Bayesian paradigm, when coupled with MCMC schemes, provides overwhelming flexibility to the modelling of time-varying multivariate risk measurements.

1 See Bauwens et al (2006) for a survey on multivariate Garch models.
2 See, for example, Patton (2006) and Jondeau and Rockinger (2006).

3   See, for example, Schweizer and Sklar (1983).

4   See, for example, Nelsen (2006).

5   See Chapter 7 of Volume I.

6   See, for example, Bollerslev (1987).

7   See Chapter 2 of Volume I.

REFERENCES

Artzner, P., F. Delbaen, J. M. Eber and D. Heath, 1997, "Thinking Coherently", *Risk* 10, pp. 68–71.

Ausin, M. C., and P. Galeano, 2007, "Bayesian Estimation of the Gaussian Mixture Garch Model", *Computational Statistics and Data Analysis* 51, pp. 2636–52.

Bauwens, L., and M. Lubrano, 1998, "Bayesian Inference on Garch Models Using the Gibbs Sampler", *Econometrics Journal* 1, pp. C23–46.

Bauwens, L., S. Laurent and J. Rombouts, 2006, "Multivariate Garch Models: A Survey", *Journal of Applied Econometrics* 21, pp. 79–109.

Bollerslev, T., 1986, "Generalised Autoregressive Conditional Heteroscedasticity", *Journal of Econometrics* 51, pp. 307–27.

Bollerslev, T., 1987, "A Conditional Heteroskedastic Time Series Model for Speculative Prices and Rates of Return", *Review of Economics and Statistics* 69, 542–7.

Gaivoronski, A. A., and G. Pflug, 2005, "Value-at-Risk in Portfolio Optimization: Properties and Computational Approach", *Journal of Risk* 7, pp. 1–31.

Geweke, J., 1992, "Evaluating the Accuracy of Sampling-Based Approaches to Calculating Posterior Moments", in J. M. Bernardo, J. O. Berger, A. P. Dawid and A. F. M. Smith (eds), *Bayesian Statistics*, Volume 4 (Oxford: Clarendon Press).

Jondeau, E., and M. Rockinger, 2006, "The Copula–Garch Model of Conditional Dependencies: An International Stock-Market Application", *Journal of International Money and Finance* 25, pp. 827–53.

Markowitz, H., 1952, "Portfolio Selection", *Journal of Finance* 8, pp. 77–91.

Nelsen, R. B., 2006, *An Introduction to Copulas*, Second Edition (Springer).

Patton, A., 2006, "Estimation of Multivariate Models for Time Series of Possibly Different Lengths", *Journal of Applied Econometrics* 21, pp. 147–73.

Schweizer, B., and A. Sklar, 1983, *Probabilistic Metric Spaces* (New York: North Holland).

Tierney, L., 1994, "Markov Chains for Exploring Posterior Distributions", *Annals of Statistics* 22, pp. 1701–62.

Tse, Y. K., and A. K. C. Tsui, 2002, "A Multivariate Generalized Autoregressive Conditional Heteroscedasticity Model with Time-Varying Correlations", *Journal of Business and Economics Statistics* 20, pp. 351–62.

4
Bayesian Inference for Hedge Funds with Stable Distribution of Returns

Biliana Güner; Svetlozar T. Rachev; Daniel Edelman; Frank J. Fabozzi

Yeditepe University; FinAnalytica; UBS Alternative and Quantitative Investments LLC; Yale School of Management

The financial crisis of 2008 had a devastating effect on the hedge fund industry and reshaped the way investors, risk personnel and portfolio managers think about risk. According to Hedge Fund Research Inc,[1] total industry assets contracted by US$461 billion in 2008 and nearly 1,000 hedge funds were liquidated. Hundreds of otherwise attractive, "safe" hedge funds found themselves unable to pay panicked investors in a timely fashion. Many were compelled to throw up gates, suspend redemptions, discontinue net asset value calculations, reorganise into illiquid side-pocket tranches, make payments in-kind rather than cash or otherwise tamper with their ordinary terms and liquidity. For the investor, whether individual high net-worth, institution or fund-of-funds, 2008 led to a sober reassessment of the tools and techniques for evaluating hedge fund risk. The entire spectrum of risk forecasting – from market and credit risk to liquidity analysis, operational due diligence and fraud mitigation to diversification – saw major upheavals and rethinking over the period 2009–10.

This chapter offers a new approach to forecasting the tail risk of hedge funds. While some researchers have studied the topic of Bayesian inference for stable distributions, to the best of our knowledge no researchers have applied this analysis to the hedge fund industry. Furthermore, although numerous authors have applied Bayesian techniques to hedge fund performance, all have assumed normally distributed returns, ignoring the fat-tailed behaviour described by the family of stable distributions. Finally, while researchers have touched on the topic of stable distributions and hedge funds, to our knowledge nobody has considered the analysis within a Bayesian framework.

One of the problems in evaluating the true tail risk of hedge funds is the lack of accurate performance data. Hedge funds often drop out of commercially available databases prior to revealing large losses. Many large, institutional-quality hedge funds choose not to report to public vendors whatsoever. To mitigate such concerns, we obtained proprietary data from a leading hedge fund-of-funds, whose database is several times larger than that of the public vendors. Thus, we were able to investigate the complete and accurate performance histories of many active and dead hedge funds that were unavailable to any other researchers. In this chapter we analyse the returns of a large collection of funds through the tumultuous market meltdown surrounding the Lehman Brothers' bankruptcy in 2008, as well as the dramatic rebound of many survivors through December 2009. Consequently, our conclusions regarding the fat-tailed behaviour of hedge funds may be considerably more telling than the findings of most studies written prior to 2008–9.

The goal of the chapter is threefold. The first is illustrative: we discuss the stable density that, thanks to its heavy-tailedness and skewness, lends itself well to modelling hedge fund performance. Beginning with a frequentist overview, we proceed to describe a means of estimation of the parameters of the distribution in a Bayesian setting, in both unconditional and Arma–Garch contexts. This is followed by an example using simulated data. The second goal is to contrast the results of our risk evaluation methods with others in a broad, general context. We focus on the performance of the overall hedge fund industry as represented by a popular index, as well as the track record of an actual hedge fund with a long performance history. This comparison is more qualitative, and is meant to guide the typical hedge fund practitioner. The third goal also involves evaluating our models against alternatives, but in a more specific, rigorous vein. We assess how each model performs in forecasting value-at-risk (VaR) and conditional value-at-risk (CVaR) during the extreme market turmoil of 2008, with particular emphasis on the months of September and October of that year. We perform a battery of tests to determine whether the various approaches are properly specified, and also the degree of accuracy of each measure. Knowing now that 2008 was for most hedge funds the worst year ever experienced, we seek to determine whether our methods would have given superior forecasts well enough in advance for a risk or portfolio manager to have made meaningful preparation for the worst.

LITERATURE REVIEW

Until the mid 1990s, there was a dearth of research on Bayesian inference on stable distribution parameter estimation. Buckle (1995) was one of the earliest to implement a Markov chain Monte Carlo (MCMC) algorithm (specifically, the Gibbs sampler), to make parametric and predictive Bayesian inference for stable distributions, and to generate Bayesian posterior samples from the parameters of a stable distribution with any prior distribution. The work by Buckle was followed by a slew of articles across disparate fields: computational statistics, finance/economics, signal processing, acoustics/speech, astronomy/astrophysics, pattern recognition, pharmacology and genetics/biostatistics (gene expression profiling), among others. Qiou (1996) and Qiou and Ravishanker (1997, 1999) developed a sampling-based conditional Bayesian approach that simultaneously estimates the stable-law parameters and the parameters of a linear autoregressive moving average (Arma) model, thus extending Buckle's approach to time series and multivariate sub-Gaussian Arma problems. Ravishanker and Qiou (1998) further refined this research using Monte Carlo expectation maximisation (MCEM). Godsill and Kuruoglu (1999) employed a hybrid rejection sampling and importance sampling scheme to implement MCMC and MCEM using a general framework involving scale mixtures of normals (SMiN). They claim their approach improves upon straightforward rejection sampling and Metropolis–Hastings approaches for symmetric stable models and find use for this technique in the field of audio signal noise reduction. Tsionas (1999) likewise used a SMiN representation limited to symmetric stable distributions with applications to econometric time series. Casarin (2004) generalised existing techniques to include Bayesian inference for mixtures of stable distributions, arguing that in some cases financial data exhibits not only heavy tails and skewness but also multimodality. Salas-Gonzalez et al (2006a,b) employed a reversible-jump

MCMC algorithm for parameter estimation of stable distributions involving impulsive, asymmetric, and multimodal data from the field of digital signal processing. Lombardi (2007) developed a random walk Metropolis sampler using a fast Fourier transform (FTT) of the stable-law characteristic function to approximate the likelihood function, as explained in Rachev and Mittnik (2000).

Little has been written on stable distribution modelling of hedge fund returns. Olszewski (2005) fitted a stable distribution to Hedge Fund Research (HFR) indexes and ran simulations to generate returns; he then optimised a fund-of-funds portfolio of these assets using a mean-CVaR objective function. The result was shown to be more efficient than other naive combinations. Literature on Bayesian inference for hedge fund returns is also scarce and generally limited to the normal distribution case. Avramov *et al* (2007) and Kosowski *et al* (2007) both used Bayesian approaches to determine that hedge funds do indeed produce alphas and exhibit return persistence. These studies, however, offer limited insight into the dynamics of hedge fund return distributions, and are merely extensions of research done on mutual funds. Agarwal *et al* (2008) used a Bayesian approach to estimate alphas and factor sensitivities of hedge funds. Gibson and Wang (2009) improved upon Avramov *et al*'s Bayesian research by incorporating liquidity risk into the assessment of hedge fund returns.

DATA DESCRIPTION

Hedge fund performance data was taken from a proprietary database of Alternative Investment Solutions (AIS), a large fund-of-funds group that is part of UBS's Alternative and Quantitative Investments platform. This database is several times larger than any commercial vendor platform and in fact is a superset of most all publicly available systems. As to time of writing, the AIS database stores qualitative and quantitative information on over 20,000 programmes and 45,000 share classes of these funds; the typical vendor lists only about 10,000 classes of 5,000 funds.[2] Moreover, the database contains the histories of thousands of funds long since liquidated; among these are entities dating back over four decades. Having access to a database used by the world's largest investor in hedge funds[3] allows for industry analysis that heretofore has been unattainable by academic researchers. For example, over 30% of the collection of funds in the

AIS database are unknown to any vendor. This includes a substantial collection of the most desirable, successful, institutional-quality managers who typically do not report their results publicly. Such data has been obtained directly from primary sources including the hedge fund managers themselves, fund administrators and prime brokers. A second benefit is that the data is thoroughly cleaned. By contrast, public providers often include numerous errors in their performance histories. Quite often, reports by different vendors on the performance of the same fund share class are inconsistent. A third benefit is that the track records of funds are far more complete than those provided to commercial vendors. AIS captures the complete track record of many funds that have ceased reporting to public databases. This includes both successful funds and those that suffered dramatic losses. As commercially available databases paint only a partial, and potentially inaccurate, picture of the hedge fund landscape, it becomes evident that quite possibly much academic research heretofore has biases more serious than previously thought.

The analysis is performed on a range of hedge fund strategies. Here too, we believe we make valuable improvements over previously published studies. Quite a number of hedge funds are misclassified into incorrect strategies by the hedge fund vendors, who in turn rely on the self-description coming from a manager or marketing agent. Extensive work by a team of practitioners has helped reclassify funds into more meaningful categories. The purpose of this classification is to determine whether any of the techniques we employ in this chapter prove more valuable for certain strategies over others.

To conduct the analysis, we initially draw a random sample of just over 100 hedge funds with eight years of monthly in-sample performance data spanning January 2000 to December 2007. Using these 96 observations, we compute the expected VaR and CVaR for the following out-of-sample month and compare it with actual performance. We repeat this process by rolling forward a month for a total of 24 out-of-sample months through December 2009. (Not all funds survived to the end.)

Unlike individual equities, equity indexes, mutual funds and other traded assets where researchers can take comfort in long histories of daily observations, hedge funds prove to be highly difficult vehicles to study due to the infrequency of their performance reporting (monthly) and lack of history (many funds live short lives, and many of today's managers started only recently). While our approach afforded us a relatively thorough sample size of numerous funds with nearly 100 observations, we note several data issues. First, funds chosen for this analysis have lengthy histories and are thus not indicative of the totality of all funds (alive and defunct). Second, the object of our analysis is to test critically different risk methodologies over one of the most tumultuous years in hedge fund history, namely 2008, and the dramatic recovery experienced by many managers who survived into 2009. However, the efficacy of VaR and CVaR models is better tested over longer business cycles. Third, we are limited in our assessment of the various risk models by the lack of out-of-sample observations. For a given fund, 24 data points are rather restrictive (compared with 250 daily observations in a year for a mutual fund or stock). Tests used in VaR back-testing may thus be lacking in power.

METHODOLOGY

A desirable characteristic of the return distribution is that it is flexible enough to accommodate varying degrees of tail thickness and asymmetry. Stable distributions are distributions with very flexible features, which nests as a special case the normal (Gaussian) distribution.[4] However, with the exception of three special cases, stable distributions in general lack a closed-form density function; this has led to criticism and slow adoption of stable distributions as a mainstream distributional choice. While this criticism was valid at one time, the advances in computer power make their application increasingly accessible today. Rachev and Mittnik (2000) is a comprehensive source of information on alpha-stable distributions, their estimation and numerous applications in finance. See also Stoyanov and Racheva-Iotova (2004) for a comparison of the efficiency of various numerical stable density approximation algorithms.

In this chapter, we employ two risk models based on the stable distribution in the Bayesian setting – an unconditional one and a conditional one – to model hedge fund returns. The conditional stable model has an Arma(1, 1)–Garch(1, 1) formulation and we propose its estimation as a two-stage process. First, we estimate an Arma(1, 1)–Garch(1, 1) process with Student-t distributed innovations and then we fit an alpha-stable distribution to the standardised residuals, before computing the expected risk measures. As part of our MCMC computational algorithm for estimation of the stable distribution, we employ the fast Fourier transform approach to stable density approximation of Rachev and Mittnik (2000).

Bayesian estimation of the parameters of the alpha-stable distribution in the unconditional setting

Stable distributions are characterised by four parameters (tail parameter, α; skewness parameter, β; scale parameter, σ; location parameter, μ) and are denoted by $S_\alpha(\beta, \sigma, \mu)$. We make the following prior assumptions for the parameters of the stable distribution in the unconditional setting: α and β have uniform distributions on the intervals $(1, 2)$ and $[-1, 1]$, respectively;[5] σ is modelled with a gamma distribution, and μ with a stable distribution.[6]

Since (the stable likelihood function and therefore) the log-posterior density is not available in closed form, we employ MCMC methods to simulate it. In particular, a modification of the Gibbs sampler, called the griddy Gibbs sampler, is used.[7] Developed by Ritter and Tanner (1992), the griddy Gibbs sampler is a combination of an ordinary Gibbs sampler and a numerical routine. Each parameter's conditional posterior density is evaluated numerically, on a grid of equally spaced nodes spanning the effective support of the respective parameter. The supports of the stable parameters, α and β, are determined by the theoretical and empirical considerations that led to the choice of priors. The situation is less straightforward in the cases of σ and μ, as the definition of "effective support" changes, together with the sampler exploring the parameters' sampling space.[8] Since the number of grid nodes is fixed *a priori*, the larger the range of the grid selected, the more sparsely the grid spans that range. Then, it is possible that at a certain iteration of the sampler the value of the posterior density computed at the grid nodes is virtually zero, since most of the probability mass falls between two grid points (or outside of the grid range altogether). On the other hand, constructing a grid with a large number of grid nodes can make the numerical computations prohibitively expensive from a computational standpoint. The reason is that in a given iteration of the griddy Gibbs sampler, to compute the full conditional posterior density of a single parameter, the relatively computationally intensive FFT has to be performed (for each data point and each grid node) for a total of nm times, where n is the number of data points (hedge fund returns) and m is the number of grid nodes. We used 26-node grids for each of the four stable distribution parameters, while the length of the sample used for calibration is 96 months.

If no prior intuition exists about what the likely parameter values are, a solution is to employ a variable instead of a fixed grid. Then, at each iteration of the sampling algorithm, we analyse the distribution of the posterior mass of a parameter and adjust spacing (equivalently, range) of the grid, so that the majority of the grid nodes falls into the interval of the greatest posterior mass (that is, into the effective parameter support). Extensive fine-tuning and sometimes multiple evaluations of the posterior density are required in the process.

Once the posterior density has been evaluated numerically, we need to obtain the empirical cumulative distribution function (CDF) and draw from the parameter's posterior distribution using the CDF inversion method.

Bayesian estimation of Arma–Garch processes with stable disturbances

Our conditional modelling of hedge fund returns is based on the assumption that returns are linear functions of two components: a time-varying mean, μ_t, and an error term with a time-varying scale parameter, σ_t. Our model formulation is an Arma$(1,1)$–Garch$(1,1)$ process, which specifies the conditional mean and variance equations as[9]

$$\left.\begin{array}{l} \mu_t = \phi_0 + \phi_1 r_{t-1} + \phi_2 \epsilon_{t-1} \\ \sigma_t^2 = \omega + \alpha \sigma_{t-1}^2 + \beta \epsilon_{t-1}^2 \end{array}\right\} \quad (4.1)$$

respectively, where $\epsilon_t = \sigma_t u_t$ is a zero-mean random noise and u_t are zero-mean, unit-scale independently and identically distributed (iid) random variables.

We develop our Arma–Garch process with stable innovations in a two-stage modelling procedure. In the first stage, we assume that the innovations, ϵ_t, are distributed with the Student-t distribution with ν degrees of freedom and scale σ_t and we estimate the Arma–Garch process in Equation 4.1. This stage accounts for the volatility-clustering feature of hedge fund returns and, to some degree, for their heavy-tailedness. Nevertheless, the standardised residuals of the Arma–Garch process still exhibit leptokurtosis and, moreover, are skewed. Therefore, in the second stage, we fit a stable distribution to the standardised residuals from stage 1, where the residuals are computed using the posterior means of the Arma–Garch process parameters.

In our empirical investigation, we consider the risk prediction capabilities of three conditional models, based on Equation 4.1. The first one is an Arma(1, 1)–Garch(1, 1) model with Student-t innovations, estimated with the method of maximum likelihood. The second one is an Arma(1, 1)–Garch(1, 1) model with Student-t innovations, estimated in the Bayesian setting, using only step 1 of the procedure above. The third one is an Arma(1, 1)–Garch(1, 1) model with stable innovations, estimated in the Bayesian setting, using the complete two-stage procedure. In other words, the latter two models have a common Bayesian Arma–Garch estimation procedure. In the section on empirical results, we will label these models as models 6, 7 and 8, respectively. Below, we outline in some more detail the two estimation stages of the Arma–Garch stable process (ie, model 8).

Stage 1: Bayesian estimation of the Arma(1,1)–Garch(1,1) process with Student-t distributed innovations

Uninformative prior distributions are asserted for the Arma and Garch parameters in Equation 4.1. For the degrees-of-freedom parameter, ν, we assert an exponential prior distribution.[10] During the sampling process, we impose the stationarity, invertibility and positivity constraints of the Arma–Garch process. The (covariance) stationarity constraint which, in a Garch(1, 1) model with Student-t distributed innovations, takes the form $\alpha + \beta \nu / (\nu - 2) < 1$,[11] is not enforced. Instead, we can observe whether that constraint is violated by examining the posterior distribution of the left-hand-side quantity.

The likelihood function for the Arma(1, 1)–Garch(1, 1) model with Student-t innovations is

$$L(\boldsymbol{\theta} \mid \boldsymbol{r}, \mathfrak{I}_0)$$
$$\propto \prod_{t=1}^{T} \left[\frac{1}{\sigma_{t|t-1}^2} \left(1 + \frac{1}{\nu} \frac{(r_t - (\phi_0 + \phi_1 r_{t-1} + \phi_2 \epsilon_{t-1}))^2}{\sigma_{t|t-1}^2}\right)^{-(\nu+1)/2} \right]$$
(4.2)

where $\mathfrak{I}_0$ is the information set at the start of the process ($t = 0$). For simplicity, all information at $t = 0$ is assumed known; that is, ϵ_0 and σ_0^2 are known.[12]

The posterior density of the parameter vector

$$\boldsymbol{\theta} = (\nu, \phi_0, \phi_1, \phi_2, \omega, \alpha, \beta)$$

is then

$$p(\boldsymbol{\theta} \mid \boldsymbol{r}, \mathfrak{I}_0) \propto L(\boldsymbol{\theta} \mid \boldsymbol{r}, \mathfrak{I}_0) \pi(\nu) I_{\text{Arma}} I_{\text{Garch}} \qquad (4.3)$$

where I_{Arma} and I_{Garch} are the constraints on the Arma and Garch parameters, respectively.

When an estimation problem involving the Student-t distribution is cast in the Bayesian setting, it is convenient, from a computational point of view, to employ the scale-mixture of normals representation of the Student-t distribution, and we adopt that approach too. The conditional distribution of the additional T parameters, with which the parameter space is augmented, is simulated in the MCMC procedure, together with the posterior densities of the remaining parameters. For details on the forms of the likelihood function of the Student-t distribution, the scale-mixture representation of the Student-t distribution, and the forms of the posterior densities of the model parameters, see Chapters 10 and 11 of Rachev *et al* (2008a).[13]

Two general approaches are available for the simulation of the posterior densities of Arma and Garch parameters: simulation parameter-by-parameter and simulation *en bloc*. We found that the parameter-by-parameter simulation results in a posterior sample of the Arma parameters characterised by very high degree of autocorrelation and cross-correlation. Therefore, for both groups of parameters, we adopt the second approach and generate multivariate samples from the posterior distributions of the 3×1 vectors of Arma and Garch parameters. As proposal distributions, we use multivariate normal distributions with means given by the modes of the posterior kernels and covariance matrices given by the negative inverse Hessian matrices evaluated at the posterior modes.[14]

Stage 2: fitting stable distribution to the standardised Arma(1,1)–Garch(1,1) residuals from stage 1

Stage 2 is the step "upgrading" model 7 (the conditional Student-t Bayesian model) to model 8 (the conditional stable Bayesian

Table 4.1 Simulation results: stable iid Bayesian model case

Parameter	Simulated parameter value	Bayesian posterior mean	Maximum likelihood estimate
α	1.7	1.2464 (1.1300, 1.3662)	1.7471
β	0.2	0.2733 (0.1219, 0.4183)	−0.1626
σ	0.3	0.1653 (0.1497, 0.1813)	0.2786
μ	0.05	−0.0210 (−0.0530, 0.0110)	0.0429

The numbers in brackets are the 95% Bayesian coverage intervals based on 8,000 simulations (after burn-in) of the MCMC stable iid model estimation procedure.

model). Since we assume that the innovations, ϵ_t, of the Arma(1, 1)–Garch(1, 1) process are distributed with the Student-t distribution, the standardised residuals are given by

$$\hat{\epsilon}_t = \frac{r_t - \hat{\mu}_t}{\sqrt{\hat{\nu}/(\hat{\nu}-2)}\,\hat{\sigma}_{t|t-1}}, \qquad (4.4)$$

where $\hat{\mu}_t$ is the vector of conditional means computed at the posterior means of the Arma parameters, $\hat{\sigma}_{t|t-1}$ is the vector of conditional scales, computed at the posterior means of the Garch parameters, and $\hat{\nu}$ is the posterior mean of the degrees-of-freedom parameter of the Student-t distribution. The term $\hat{\nu}/(\hat{\nu}-2)$ in the denominator is due to the variance of the Student-t distribution. We fit a stable distribution to the standardised residuals above, using the maximum-likelihood FFT approach of Rachev and Mittnik (2000).

Illustration with simulated data

We illustrate our Bayesian approaches to unconditional and conditional estimation by simulating samples of observations from an iid variable with the stable distribution and from the Arma(1, 1)–Garch(1, 1) with Student-t innovations (given in Equation 4.1) and then comparing the true parameters to their estimated counterparts.

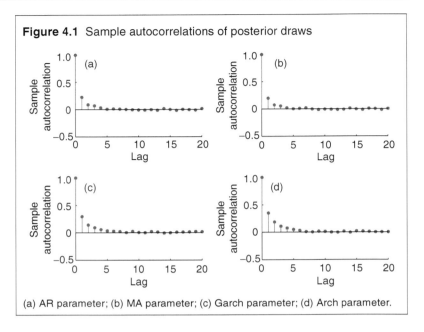

Figure 4.1 Sample autocorrelations of posterior draws

(a) AR parameter; (b) MA parameter; (c) Garch parameter; (d) Arch parameter.

Unconditional stable case

We generate a sample of 500 observations from a stable distribution and estimate its parameters using our MCMC procedure. The Markov chain is run for 10,000 iterations. The first 2,000 of the simulations are discarded as burn-in. Table 4.1 presents the comparison among the Bayesian and frequentist estimates and the true parameters. The sample autocorrelations of the stable parameter simulations decay at a comfortable rate. Therefore, a procedure whereby the posterior parameter simulations are sampled periodically from the generated Markov chain is deemed unnecessary.

Conditional Student-t case

We consider the Arma(1, 1)–Garch(1, 1) model in Equation 4.1 with Student-t distributed innovations. The generated sample consists of 3,000 observations. We estimate the conditional model using our MCMC approach, running the Markov chain for 10,000 iterations, and discarding as burn-in the first 2,000 of them. The comparison among the true and estimated parameters, together with the maximum-likelihood estimates, is shown in Table 4.2. The true parameter values fall into the 95% Bayesian credible intervals for all parameters, save for the degrees of freedom. Figure 4.1 presents the

Table 4.2 Simulation results: Arma–Garch Bayesian model case

Parameter	Simulated parameter value	Bayesian posterior mean	Maximum likelihood estimate
ϕ_0	0.01	0.0109 (0.0087, 0.0133)	0.0105
ϕ_1	0.65	0.5987 (0.5175, 0.6716)	0.6112
ϕ_2	−0.35	−0.3248 (−0.4174, −0.2286)	−0.3405
ω	0.001	0.0010 (0.0008, 0.0013)	0.0011
α	0.55	0.4477 (0.3336, 0.5593)	0.4685
β	0.2	0.2389 (0.1758, 0.3089)	0.2518
ν	4	5.2546 (4.45, 6.15)	4.1797

The numbers in brackets are the 95% Bayesian coverage intervals based on 8,000 simulations (after burn-in) of the MCMC conditional model estimation procedure.

sample autocorrelations estimated using the after-burn-in posterior simulations of the AR, MA, Garch and Arch parameters; all sample autocorrelation functions exhibit a fast decay.

Finally, we observe whether the Garch(1,1) model stationarity constraint is violated by estimating the posterior probability of the persistence quantity, $\alpha + \beta\nu/(\nu - 2)$, in the Garch (covariance) stationarity constraint. The posterior mean of this persistence quantity is 0.8334, which is below 1 and signifies a conditional process with finite variance (for comparison, the true value of the quantity is 0.95). The histogram of its posterior draws is seen in Figure 4.2. The greater part of the posterior mass is indeed below 1, as expected.

Value-at-risk and conditional value-at-risk prediction

In our empirical investigation, we estimate VaR and CVaR for a number of risk-model formulations, the first two of which are very basic standard methodologies, still used by many banks; we include them for benchmarking purposes. We label these formulations as Models 1–8, as follows:[15]

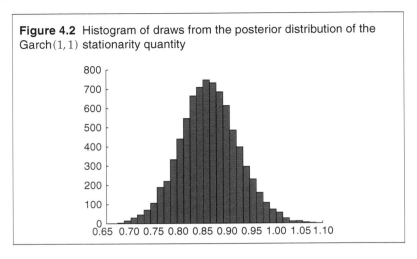

Figure 4.2 Histogram of draws from the posterior distribution of the Garch(1, 1) stationarity quantity

Model 1: unconditional (iid) normal model, estimated in a frequentist (maximum-likelihood) setting;

Model 2: historical VaR/CVaR methodology;

Model 3: unconditional (iid) stable model, estimated in a frequentist setting;

Model 4: unconditional (iid) stable model, estimated in a Bayesian setting;

Model 5: unconditional (iid) Student-t model, estimated in a frequentist setting;

Model 6: conditional (Arma(1, 1)–Garch(1, 1)) Student-t model, estimated in a frequentist setting;

Model 7: conditional (Arma(1, 1)–Garch(1, 1)) Student-t model, estimated in a Bayesian setting;

Model 8: conditional (Arma(1, 1)–Garch(1, 1)) stable model, estimated in a Bayesian setting.

Recall that models 7 and 8 have a common Bayesian Arma–Garch estimation step (described as stage 1 in the section on methodology), while model 8 is obtained via an additional step of fitting the stable distribution to the standardised residuals from the common step (described as stage 2 in the section on methodology).

In all models, VaR and CVaR estimation is based on the linear-form decomposition of returns, $R_t = \mu_t + \sigma_t u_t$, where u_t is a noise term with the respective distribution (normal in model 1, stable in models

3, 4 and 8, and Student-*t* in models 6 and 7). Based on the available information up to time *t*, and using their translation invariance and positive homogeneity properties, the VaR and CVaR estimates are expressed, respectively, as

$$\widehat{\text{VaR}}_{\kappa,t} = \hat{\sigma}_t \,\text{VaR}_\kappa(u) - \hat{\mu}_t \qquad (4.5)$$

$$\widehat{\text{CVaR}}_{\kappa,t} = \hat{\sigma}_t C_\kappa(u) - \hat{\mu}_t \qquad (4.6)$$

where $\text{VaR}_\kappa(u)$ is the value-at-risk (the κ quantile) of the innovation's (u_t's) distribution, and $C_\kappa(u)$ is a constant which depends only on the tail probability, κ.[16] (In our discussion below, we omit the "hats" on VaR and CVaR for notational simplicity.) In the unconditional model approaches (models 1–5), $\hat{\mu}_t$ and $\hat{\sigma}_t$ are constants represented by the sample estimates and hedge fund returns are assumed independent and identically distributed with the respective distributions. In the conditional modelling approaches (models 6–8), $\hat{\mu}_t$ and $\hat{\sigma}_t$ are the forecasts of the conditional mean and conditional scale from the Arma(1, 1)–Garch(1, 1) model in Equation 4.1.[17]

We now outline the explicit and semi-explicit expressions used to compute CVaR for the normal, Student-*t* and stable distributions.

The normal distribution

For a normal distribution with standard deviation σ and expected value μ, the CVaR is expressed as

$$\text{CVaR}_\kappa(R) = \frac{\sigma}{\kappa\sqrt{2\pi}} \exp\left(-\frac{(\text{VaR}_\kappa(Z))^2}{2}\right) - \mu \qquad (4.7)$$

where Z is a standard normal random variable.

The location-scale Student-*t* distribution

In the case of a location-scale Student-*t* distribution with degrees of freedom ν, scale σ, and location μ, CVaR is computed from the following explicit expression[18]

$$\text{CVaR}_\kappa(R)$$
$$= \begin{cases} \dfrac{\sigma \Gamma(\frac{1}{2}(\nu+1))}{\kappa \Gamma(\frac{1}{2}\nu)} \dfrac{\sqrt{\nu-2}}{(\nu-1)\sqrt{\pi}} \left(1 + \dfrac{(t_\nu^{-1}(\kappa))^2}{\nu-2}\right)^{-(\nu-1)/2} - \mu, & \nu > 1 \\ \infty, & \nu = 1 \end{cases}$$
$$(4.8)$$

where $\Gamma(x)$ is the gamma function and $t_\nu(\kappa)$ is the κ-quantile of a standardised (zero mean and variance equal to 1) Student-t distributed random variable with ν degrees of freedom.[19]

The stable distribution

Stoyanov *et al* (2006) derived the semi-analytical expression for the CVaR for stable distributions. The CVaR$_\kappa$ is represented as

$$\mathrm{CVaR}_\kappa(R) = \sigma A_{\kappa,\alpha,\beta} - \mu \qquad (4.9)$$

The term $A_{\kappa,\alpha,\beta}$ is given by

$$A_{\kappa,\alpha,\beta} = \frac{\alpha}{1-\alpha} \frac{|\mathrm{VaR}_\kappa(R)|}{\pi\kappa}$$
$$\times \int_{-\bar\theta_0}^{\pi/2} g(\theta) \exp(-|\mathrm{VaR}_\kappa(R)|^{\alpha/(\alpha-1)} \upsilon(\theta))\, \mathrm{d}\theta$$

where

$$g(\theta) = \frac{\sin(\alpha(\bar\theta_0 + \theta) - 2\theta)}{\sin(\alpha(\bar\theta_0 + \theta))} - \frac{\alpha \cos^2\theta}{\sin^2(\alpha(\bar\theta_0 + \theta))}$$

$$\upsilon(\theta) = (\cos\alpha\bar\theta_0)^{1/(\alpha-1)} \left(\frac{\cos\theta}{\sin(\alpha(\bar\theta_0 + \theta))}\right)^{\alpha/(\alpha-1)}$$
$$\times \frac{\cos(\alpha\bar\theta_0 + (\alpha-1)\theta)}{\cos\theta}$$

and

$$\bar\theta_0 = \frac{1}{\alpha} \arctan(\bar\beta \tan \tfrac{1}{2}\pi\alpha), \qquad \bar\beta = -\mathrm{sgn}(\mathrm{VaR}_\kappa(R))\beta$$

$\mathrm{VaR}_\kappa(R)$ is the VaR of the stable distribution at tail probability κ, and β is the stable skewness parameter. The parameters of the stable distribution are estimated in either the frequentist or the Bayesian setting.

Back-testing VaR and CVaR

We back-test the risk models using the Kupiec (1995) frequency of failures test and the Christoffersen (1998) test of independence of the VaR violations. For back-testing CVaR, we use a loss-function-based procedure.[20] Our general back-testing process consists of repeatedly estimating VaR and CVaR based on a moving estimation window and comparing the predicted risk values to the out-of-sample realisation of one-step-ahead returns. That is, the sequences of VaR and

CVaR estimates are based on the updated (revised) parameter estimates using the latest estimation window. An exceedance of the VaR occurs when the realised loss is greater than the predicted VaR for the one-step-ahead horizon. Next, we describe the CVaR back-testing procedure.

CVaR back-testing procedure

Our CVaR back-testing procedure relies on a loss function, developed in the spirit of Blanco and Ihle (1999)'s loss function for ranking models based on their VaR predictive capacity.[21] Denote the loss at time t by L_t. The loss function is defined as

$$LF_t = \begin{cases} \dfrac{L_t - CVaR_{\kappa,t}}{L_t} & \text{if } L_t > VaR_{\kappa,t} \\ 0 & \text{if } L_t \leqslant VaR_{\kappa,t} \end{cases} \quad (4.10)$$

Then, the statistic

$$S = \sqrt{\dfrac{1}{T} \sum_{t=1}^{T} LF_t^2} \quad (4.11)$$

where T is the sampling horizon, provides a summary metric for the average distance of the forecast CVaR from the realised loss, in the case of VaR exceedance. In our empirical analysis, we compute this statistic for each model and each hedge fund in our sample universe.

EMPIRICAL ANALYSIS

Our empirical analysis consists of four parts. First, we analyse and compare the models' risk forecasts using hedge fund index data. Second, we focus on the performance of a particular convertible arbitrage hedge fund that experienced a large loss in 2008 and staged a strong recovery in the following year. Third, we perform a general comparison among models' VaR and CVaR predictions across six hedge fund strategies most deeply impacted by the 2008 financial crisis: merger arbitrage, convertible bond (CB) arbitrage, directional credit (distressed debt and high-yield), long/short (LS) credit, fixed income (FI) arbitrage and mortgage-backed security (MBS) arbitrage. Finally, we focus our attention on the momentous months of September and October 2008, with the aim of comparative evaluation of models across the hedge fund strategies. In all four investigations, we use eight years of monthly data in-sample (starting in January 1990 for the hedge fund index data and in January 2000

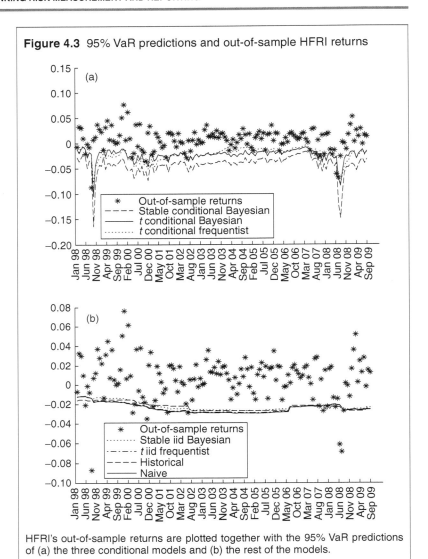

Figure 4.3 95% VaR predictions and out-of-sample HFRI returns

HFRI's out-of-sample returns are plotted together with the 95% VaR predictions of (a) the three conditional models and (b) the rest of the models.

for the individual hedge fund data) and compare methodologies on a rolling month-by-month out-of-sample basis (spanning 12 years for the hedge fund index and two years for the remaining data). Our sample universe consists of 27 funds in the merger arbitrage strategy, 17 funds in the CB arbitrage strategy, 40 funds in the directional credit strategy, 17 funds in the LS credit strategy, 16 funds in the FI arbitrage strategy and 10 funds in the MBS arbitrage strategy.

Comparisons of risk forecasts on hedge fund index data

The HFRI Fund Weighted Composite Index is widely used as an indicator of the performance of the overall hedge fund industry. Comprised of over 2,000 funds listed in the internal HFR database, the index is an equally weighted average of monthly returns net of fees starting in January 1990. As such, the index records hedge fund trends over a lengthy business cycle of busts and booms. This evaluation includes a number of major crisis periods ranging from the Long Term Capital Management/Russian default of August 1998, the terrorist attack of September 2001, the credit crunch of summer 2002, the credit correlation crisis of Spring 2005, the market meltdown of May 2006, the quant debacle of August 2007, the subprime jitters of November 2007, the market corrections of January and March 2008, and, ultimately, the Lehman Brothers' bankruptcy/market collapse of September–October 2008. In all, there were 14 monthly events in 12 years where performance, as measured by total return, was less than −2%, yet the overall average return during this period was a positive 0.66%.

As seen in Figure 4.3, the 8.7% drop in August 1998 and the back-to-back losses of 6.13% and 6.84% in September and October 2008 sent hedge fund investors into a state of panic. We observe that traditional risk models – naive, historical, and Student-t – did poor jobs not only in forecasting the severity of these downturns but also in adjusting properly afterwards. For example, after the massive LTCM shock, simple and historical models did not adjust their risk prediction much at all, and continued to forecast inadequately a VaR at the 95% level of around −2%. Worse, CVaR forecasts for August 1998 were roughly −2% for the non-Bayesian approaches at the 95% level and only −3% at the 99% level. These results are very difficult to accept for risk managers, portfolio decision-makers and investors, all of whom demand models that make meaningful forecasts when crises hit, not merely during normal market conditions!

Our first observation is that the stable models tended to do a much better job of anticipating these large-tail events than the non-stable approaches and that the Bayesian methodologies proved superior to the frequentist forecasts. The conditional stable Bayesian model anticipated the losses of August 1998 and September 1998 with predictions of −6.50% and −5.77% of the 99% VaR, while the CVaR forecasts were quite close at −12.04% and −6.58%, respectively.

Table 4.3 Kupiec test for unconditional coverage and Christoffersen joint test

	Kupiec test: model number							
	1	2	3	4	5	6	7	8
Merger arbitrage	25.9 11.1	29.6 0.0	29.6 0.0	25.9 11.1	29.6 0.0	11.1 0.0	7.4 0.0	0.0 0.0
CB arbitrage	41.2 5.9	52.9 0.0	52.9 5.9	41.2 0.0	52.9 0.0	23.5 0.0	17.6 0.0	0.0 0.0
Directional credit	45.0 12.5	50.0 0.0	55.0 2.5	50.0 15.0	52.5 0.0	15.0 0.0	12.5 0.0	0.0 0.0
Long/short credit	47.1 11.8	41.2 11.8	52.9 5.9	58.8 17.6	58.8 5.9	11.8 0.0	5.9 0.0	0.0 0.0
Fixed-income arbitrage	18.8 6.3	37.5 0.0	37.5 0.0	25.0 0.0	25.0 0.0	0.0 0.0	6.3 0.0	6.3 0.0
MBS arbitrage	20.0 10.0	30.0 0.0	30.0 10.0	40.0 20.0	30.0 0.0	20.0 0.0	10.0 0.0	0.0 0.0
	Christoffersen test: model number							
	1	2	3	4	5	6	7	8
Merger arbitrage	63.0 37.0	48.1 7.4	55.6 3.7	63.0 33.3	66.7 0.0	29.6 0.0	11.1 0.0	0.0 0.0
CB arbitrage	41.2 17.6	70.6 0.0	64.7 11.8	41.2 5.9	64.7 11.8	29.4 0.0	23.5 0.0	0.0 0.0
Directional credit	75.0 60.0	80.0 12.5	87.5 30.0	77.5 52.5	87.5 12.5	47.5 15.0	47.5 5.0	2.5 0.0
Long/short credit	58.8 47.1	64.7 17.6	64.7 29.4	64.7 47.1	70.6 23.5	41.2 11.8	29.4 5.9	5.9 0.0
Fixed-income arbitrage	31.3 18.8	50.0 6.3	43.8 18.8	31.3 18.8	37.5 6.3	31.3 6.3	25.0 6.3	12.5 0.0
MBS arbitrage	20.0 10.0	30.0 0.0	30.0 10.0	40.0 20.0	30.0 10.0	20.0 0.0	10.0 0.0	0.0 0.0

The numbers in the first (second) row for each strategy refer to the 95% (99%) VaR prediction and represent the percentage of hedge funds for which the respective test is rejected at 5% significance level.

However, our second observation is that the conditional models (and the conditional stable Bayesian solution, in particular) substantially overshot (in terms of both VaR and CVaR) the actual performance in months subsequent to the large market dislocations and the CVaR forecasts of these models took considerable time to readjust to more

Table 4.4 Loss function metric for the distance between realised losses and CVaR forecasts, conditional on VaR exceedance, for the merger arbitrage and convertible bond arbitrage strategies

| Model rank | Model number ||||||||
	1	2	3	4	5	6	7	8
Merger arbitrage: 95% VaR/CVaR								
1	0.0	18.5	3.7	0.0	3.7	14.8	22.2	33.3
2	14.8	22.2	3.7	11.1	0.0	33.3	29.6	7.4
3	14.8	14.8	7.4	37.0	7.4	18.5	25.9	3.7
4	33.3	7.4	7.4	33.3	3.7	14.8	11.1	0.0
5	18.5	11.1	18.5	3.7	7.4	11.1	3.7	14.8
6	3.7	7.4	22.2	3.7	48.1	3.7	3.7	7.4
7	3.7	14.8	22.2	3.7	18.5	0.0	0.0	0.0
8	3.7	0.0	11.1	0.0	3.7	0.0	0.0	0.0
Accurate VaR	7.4	0.0	0.0	7.4	3.7	0.0	0.0	33.3
Merger arbitrage: 99% VaR/CVaR								
	There are too many instances of accurate predictions across models. Therefore, meaningful comparison of deviation sizes across models cannot be made.							
Accurate VaR	59.3	74.1	81.5	59.3	85.2	85.2	88.9	100.0

The numbers are percentages of hedge funds for which the respective model is assigned a given rank. Higher rank, coupled with a greater percentage of hedge funds for which that rank is achieved, indicates superior model performance. Ranking should be analysed in conjunction with the accuracy of VaR prediction. The percentage of hedge funds for which VaR is predicted accurately is given in the last row of each panel.

rational levels. While the Bayesian and stable methods were suggesting the potential for worsening conditions, markets rebounded and hedge funds shook off these isolated losses.[22] Of all the CVaR risk estimates, the iid stable Bayesian, the conditional Student-*t* frequentist and conditional Student-*t* Bayesian models seemingly did best over the two-month consecutive meltdown of September–October 2008, neither dramatically under-forecasting, nor over-forecasting losses.

How well did the different risk methods perform in the overall time-frame? The Kupiec test at the 95% level suggests a non-rejection range of between 3 and 12 exceedances inclusive; the iid stable Bayesian and conditional stable Bayesian approaches both had only two exceedances and could be considered to be misspecified in

Table 4.4 Continued

Model rank	Model number							
	1	2	3	4	5	6	7	8
Convertible bond arbitrage: 95% VaR/CVaR								
1	0.0	0.0	0.0	0.0	5.9	11.8	11.8	76.5
2	0.0	0.0	5.9	0.0	0.0	35.3	58.8	11.8
3	23.5	5.9	5.9	11.8	17.6	23.5	23.5	11.8
4	29.4	23.5	23.5	47.1	17.6	17.6	5.9	0.0
5	41.2	23.5	11.8	29.4	5.9	11.8	0.0	0.0
6	5.9	23.5	29.4	11.8	23.5	0.0	0.0	0.0
7	0.0	23.5	11.8	0.0	23.5	0.0	0.0	0.0
8	0.0	0.0	11.8	0.0	5.9	0.0	0.0	0.0
Accurate VaR	0.0	0.0	0.0	0.0	0.0	0.0	0.0	0.0
Convertible bond arbitrage: 99% VaR/CVaR								
1	0.0	11.8	11.8	0.0	17.6	17.6	5.9	47.1
2	11.8	29.4	23.5	11.8	17.6	11.8	0.0	5.9
3	0.0	23.5	29.4	0.0	17.6	5.9	17.6	23.5
4	58.8	17.6	5.9	11.8	5.9	0.0	0.0	5.9
5	5.9	11.8	5.9	23.5	23.5	11.8	17.6	0.0
6	5.9	5.9	17.6	23.5	11.8	23.5	17.6	0.0
7	17.6	0.0	0.0	11.8	0.0	23.5	29.4	0.0
8	0.0	0.0	5.9	17.6	5.9	5.9	11.8	0.0
Accurate VaR	0.0	0.0	0.0	0.0	0.0	0.0	0.0	17.6

The numbers are percentages of hedge funds for which the respective model is assigned a given rank. Higher rank, coupled with a greater percentage of hedge funds for which that rank is achieved, indicates superior model performance. Ranking should be analysed in conjunction with the accuracy of VaR prediction. The percentage of hedge funds for which VaR is predicted accurately is given in the last row of each panel.

the long term (though the null hypothesis could not be rejected at the 99% level for any test). The Christoffersen test was inconclusive for all of the models. As for the comparison based on deviation size, the conditional stable Bayesian approach did the best job of explaining performance conditional upon there being an exceedance of the VaR level.

Comparison of risk forecasts on an individual hedge fund

Rather than looking at hedge fund index data, which can in many ways be artificial and misleading, we contrast the different risk models using actual hedge fund performance. We examine an interesting (CB) arbitrage fund that has been around for over 20 years, experiencing not only the market shocks described in the previous section but also the idiosyncratic busts that affected the convertibles market and the CB arbitrage strategy, especially in the period 2004–5. At its peak, this fund commanded nearly US$400 million in assets. Since its inception, the fund has produced a solid average monthly return of 0.65% with low volatility and a Sharpe ratio exceeding 1. It suffered a drawdown of 15% from May 2008 to July 2009 (in itself a remarkable feat, as many other funds lost twice that) including a single worst monthly loss of around 9% in October 2008. The fund got caught in the Mandalay Bay dividend crunch of 2003 and suffered losses in 2004 due to rising yields, lacklustre primary market issuance and low implied volatility. In 2005, the fund, like many others, was caught by surprise at General Motors's profit warning; the result was a loss of over 3% in April 2005. Amid massive investor redemptions, the fund recovered and turned strong profits in 2006 and 2009.

Over the period 2008–9, the Kupiec and Christoffersen tests could not be rejected, as the two exceedances of 2008 were not unexpected. As with the HFRI analysis in the previous section, we find that the conditional stable Bayesian model was the only model that recognised the severity of the large September–October 2008 losses. The 95% VaR forecasts were -1.5% and -8.2%, and the 95% CVaR forecasts were -3.9% and -18.4% for the months of September and October 2008, respectively, while realised losses were 3.7% and 9.4%, respectively. As also reported above, the non-Bayesian VaR models failed to budge much after the 2008 meltdown, though the Bayesian methodologies (and the conditional ones, in particular) greatly overestimated the losses in later months, when in fact the CB arbitrage manager was staging a recovery. The conditional models' VaR forecasts returned to reasonable levels as the hedge fund showed only positive gains in 2009; however, these models continued to exhibit uncharacteristically high CVaR estimates after the markets calmed.

The lesson for risk managers from the findings reported in this section and the previous sections may be that the conditional Bayesian models seem to give the best advance warning of the tail risk in hedge funds, but should be treated carefully after a large market

Table 4.5 Loss function metric for the distance between realised losses and CVaR forecasts, conditional on VaR exceedance, for the directional credit and long/short credit strategies

Model rank	Model number							
	1	2	3	4	5	6	7	8
Directional credit: 95% VaR/CVaR								
1	5.0	7.5	2.5	5.0	0.0	20.0	17.5	40.0
2	7.5	10.0	0.0	15.0	0.0	17.5	42.5	2.5
3	15.0	10.0	0.0	5.0	0.0	27.5	27.5	10.0
4	15.0	20.0	5.0	32.5	7.5	12.5	2.5	0.0
5	30.0	10.0	2.5	25.0	5.0	12.5	5.0	7.5
6	20.0	27.5	5.0	7.5	10.0	5.0	0.0	22.5
7	2.5	5.0	65.0	2.5	17.5	2.5	0.0	2.5
8	2.5	5.0	15.0	2.5	57.5	0.0	2.5	2.5
Accurate VaR	2.5	5.0	5.0	5.0	2.5	2.5	2.5	12.5
Directional credit: 99% VaR/CVaR								
1	5.0	50.0	2.5	2.5	2.5	7.5	0.0	22.5
2	40.0	22.5	10.0	0.0	5.0	2.5	5.0	5.0
3	27.5	7.5	2.5	2.5	12.5	2.5	17.5	7.5
4	10.0	5.0	25.0	5.0	15.0	22.5	5.0	2.5
5	2.5	0.0	10.0	27.5	15.0	10.0	10.0	0.0
6	0.0	0.0	10.0	7.5	5.0	30.0	22.5	0.0
7	0.0	0.0	7.5	17.5	10.0	12.5	25.0	0.0
8	0.0	0.0	2.5	20.0	2.5	7.5	5.0	0.0
Accurate VaR	15.0	15.0	30.0	17.5	32.5	5.0	10.0	62.5

The numbers are percentages of hedge funds for which the respective model is assigned a given rank. Higher rank, coupled with a greater percentage of hedge funds for which that rank is achieved, indicates superior model performance. Ranking should be analysed in conjunction with the accuracy of VaR prediction. The percentage of hedge funds for which VaR is predicted accurately is given in the last row of each panel.

dislocation; hedge funds tend to either liquidate or bounce back strongly.

Comparison of risk forecasts on a panel of many funds across different strategies

Performance according to Kupiec and Christoffersen tests

The Kupiec test for unconditional coverage and the Christoffersen joint test for unconditional coverage and independence are performed for each hedge fund within our sample universe, on the basis of the 24 out-of-sample forecasts of VaR at the 95% and 99%

Table 4.5 Continued

Model rank	Model number							
	1	2	3	4	5	6	7	8
Long/short credit: 95% VaR/CVaR								
1	0.0	5.9	5.9	0.0	5.9	11.8	23.5	47.1
2	5.9	11.8	11.8	0.0	0.0	41.2	17.6	5.9
3	11.8	5.9	0.0	11.8	0.0	23.5	23.5	17.6
4	11.8	29.4	5.9	23.5	11.8	5.9	5.9	0.0
5	29.4	17.6	0.0	29.4	0.0	0.0	5.9	5.9
6	17.6	11.8	23.5	11.8	17.6	11.8	0.0	5.9
7	5.9	5.9	23.5	11.8	29.4	0.0	11.8	0.0
8	11.8	5.9	23.5	0.0	29.4	5.9	0.0	0.0
Accurate VaR	5.9	5.9	5.9	11.8	5.9	0.0	11.8	17.6
Long/short credit: 99% VaR/CVaR								
1	5.9	58.8	5.9	0.0	0.0	0.0	0.0	23.5
2	35.3	5.9	23.5	0.0	5.9	5.9	5.9	5.9
3	23.5	0.0	23.5	0.0	29.4	5.9	5.9	0.0
4	5.9	11.8	17.6	11.8	23.5	5.9	11.8	0.0
5	11.8	5.9	5.9	23.5	11.8	11.8	5.9	5.9
6	5.9	0.0	0.0	5.9	5.9	41.2	11.8	0.0
7	0.0	5.9	5.9	17.6	0.0	5.9	35.3	0.0
8	0.0	0.0	0.0	23.5	0.0	5.9	5.9	0.0
Accurate VaR	11.8	11.8	17.6	17.6	23.5	17.6	17.6	64.7

The numbers are percentages of hedge funds for which the respective model is assigned a given rank. Higher rank, coupled with a greater percentage of hedge funds for which that rank is achieved, indicates superior model performance. Ranking should be analysed in conjunction with the accuracy of VaR prediction. The percentage of hedge funds for which VaR is predicted accurately is given in the last row of each panel.

levels. We report our results summarised by hedge fund strategy across models. The conditional stable Bayesian model seemingly performs best among the eight models in terms of overall quality of its VaR prediction: the null hypotheses of the Kupiec and Christoffersen tests for the $VaR_{0.05}$ forecast are rejected for only one hedge fund in each of the directional credit and LS credit strategies; as for FI arbitrage, the null hypothesis could only be rejected for one hedge fund under the Kupiec test and two funds under the Christoffersen test. Overall, the three conditional models – stable Bayesian, Student-t Bayesian and Student-t frequentist – demonstrate superior performance, with the Student-t Bayesian having an upper edge over

Table 4.6 Loss function metric for the distance between realised losses and CVaR forecasts, conditional on VaR exceedance, for the fixed income arbitrage and mortgage-backed securities (MBS) arbitrage strategies

Model rank	Model number							
	1	2	3	4	5	6	7	8
Fixed-income arbitrage: 95% VaR/CVaR								
1	18.8	6.3	0.0	0.0	0.0	25.0	12.5	37.5
2	0.0	12.5	0.0	25.0	6.3	12.5	37.5	0.0
3	6.3	12.5	6.3	0.0	0.0	31.3	25.0	6.3
4	18.8	6.3	0.0	31.3	18.8	6.3	6.3	0.0
5	37.5	12.5	0.0	18.8	6.3	6.3	6.3	0.0
6	0.0	12.5	25.0	12.5	18.8	12.5	0.0	6.3
7	6.3	18.8	37.5	0.0	12.5	6.3	0.0	6.3
8	0.0	12.5	18.8	0.0	25.0	0.0	0.0	6.3
Accurate VaR	12.5	6.3	12.5	12.5	12.5	0.0	12.5	37.5
Fixed-income arbitrage: 99% VaR/CVaR								
1	12.5	25.0	6.3	6.3	0.0	0.0	12.5	25.0
2	18.8	12.5	18.8	6.3	12.5	12.5	0.0	6.3
3	12.5	18.8	12.5	0.0	6.3	0.0	6.3	12.5
4	12.5	18.8	12.5	0.0	12.5	6.3	0.0	0.0
5	12.5	0.0	12.5	12.5	25.0	0.0	6.3	0.0
6	6.3	0.0	0.0	25.0	0.0	18.8	6.3	6.3
7	0.0	0.0	0.0	12.5	12.5	12.5	25.0	6.3
8	0.0	0.0	6.3	12.5	0.0	18.8	12.5	0.0
Accurate VaR	25.0	25.0	31.3	25.0	31.3	31.3	31.3	43.8

The numbers are percentages of hedge funds for which the respective model is assigned a given rank. Higher rank, coupled with a greater percentage of hedge funds for which that rank is achieved, indicates superior model performance. Ranking should be analysed in conjunction with the accuracy of VaR prediction. The percentage of hedge funds for which VaR is predicted accurately is given in the last row of each panel.

the frequentist one. The percentages of hedge funds for which the Kupiec and Christoffersen tests are rejected, summarised by model and strategy, are given in Table 4.3.

CVaR performance according to the loss function metric

As expected, based on the results from the Kupiec and Christoffersen tests, the conditional stable Bayesian model outperforms the rest in terms of accuracy of its VaR forecasts, as seen in Tables 4.4–4.6. It has the lowest incidence of VaR exceedances among the eight models for

Table 4.6 Continued

Model rank	Model number							
	1	2	3	4	5	6	7	8
MBS arbitrage: 95% VaR/CVaR								
1	0.0	0.0	10.0	0.0	0.0	10.0	20.0	40.0
2	0.0	10.0	0.0	0.0	30.0	10.0	40.0	0.0
3	10.0	10.0	0.0	0.0	0.0	30.0	10.0	20.0
4	20.0	10.0	10.0	0.0	10.0	10.0	10.0	0.0
5	20.0	20.0	10.0	20.0	0.0	0.0	10.0	0.0
6	10.0	0.0	10.0	10.0	20.0	30.0	0.0	0.0
7	0.0	10.0	30.0	30.0	0.0	0.0	0.0	10.0
8	10.0	20.0	10.0	0.0	20.0	0.0	0.0	0.0
Accurate VaR	30.0	20.0	20.0	40.0	20.0	10.0	10.0	30.0
MBS arbitrage: 99% VaR/CVaR								
1	10.0	10.0	10.0	20.0	10.0	0.0	0.0	10.0
2	10.0	20.0	0.0	0.0	10.0	10.0	0.0	20.0
3	20.0	10.0	20.0	0.0	0.0	10.0	10.0	0.0
4	10.0	10.0	10.0	0.0	10.0	10.0	10.0	0.0
5	0.0	10.0	0.0	10.0	10.0	0.0	10.0	20.0
6	20.0	0.0	0.0	0.0	10.0	10.0	20.0	0.0
7	0.0	0.0	10.0	10.0	10.0	10.0	20.0	0.0
8	0.0	0.0	10.0	20.0	0.0	20.0	0.0	0.0
Accurate VaR	30.0	40.0	40.0	40.0	40.0	30.0	30.0	50.0

The numbers are percentages of hedge funds for which the respective model is assigned a given rank. Higher rank, coupled with a greater percentage of hedge funds for which that rank is achieved, indicates superior model performance. Ranking should be analysed in conjunction with the accuracy of VaR prediction. The percentage of hedge funds for which VaR is predicted accurately is given in the last row of each panel.

the overall out-of-sample period January 2008–December 2009. It is interesting to note that, in the case of the CB arbitrage strategy, violations of the predicted VaR at 95% and 99% are much more numerous across all models, compared with other strategies (Table 4.4). CB arbitrage suffered more than other approaches not only from market losses but also as a result of larger-than-expected investor redemptions that forced funds to sell at the most inopportune times to raise cash. By contrast, most models do an adequate job in predicting VaR at 95% level in the case of the merger arbitrage strategy, while the conditional stable Bayesian approach fared best overall.

Table 4.7 Loss function metric for the distance between realised losses and VaR forecasts, conditional on VaR exceedance, for the merger arbitrage and convertible bond arbitrage strategies during September 2008

Model rank	Model number							
	1	2	3	4	5	6	7	8
Merger arbitrage: 95% VaR/CVaR								
Metric: Distance between predicted VaR and realised loss, conditional on VaR exceedance								
1	0.0	3.7	0.0	0.0	0.0	0.0	0.0	51.9
2	7.4	29.6	7.4	0.0	14.8	33.3	7.4	0.0
3	29.6	7.4	11.1	14.8	3.7	25.9	18.5	3.7
4	22.2	7.4	14.8	25.9	14.8	3.7	11.1	0.0
Accurate VaR	7.4	18.5	11.1	7.4	7.4	7.4	22.2	44.4
Merger arbitrage: 95% VaR/CVaR								
Metric: Distance between predicted CVaR and realised loss, conditional on VaR exceedance								
1	11.1	11.1	11.1	0.0	25.9	14.8	7.4	14.8
2	7.4	11.1	18.5	14.8	22.2	11.1	3.7	3.7
3	3.7	3.7	18.5	11.1	7.4	33.3	7.4	14.8
4	0.0	18.5	14.8	11.1	11.1	22.2	18.5	0.0
Accurate VaR	7.4	18.5	11.1	7.4	7.4	7.4	22.2	44.4

The numbers are percentages of hedge funds for which the respective model is assigned a given rank. Higher rank, coupled with a greater percentage of hedge funds for which that rank is achieved, indicates superior model performance. Ranking should be analysed in conjunction with the accuracy of VaR prediction. The percentage of hedge funds for which VaR is predicted accurately is given the last row of each panel. With space considerations in mind, results are provided only for the first four ranks and the 95% VaR. The complete results are available from the authors upon request.

When the predicted VaR levels are violated, analysis of the distance between the realised loss and the predicted CVaR could give an indication of whether a risk manager would have had an adequate warning signal as to the potential average loss. The eight models are ranked across strategies on the basis of the achieved distance, with higher rank signifying smaller difference between realised loss and predicted CVaR, conditional on a VaR violation. Comparison across the strategies and models unsurprisingly again singles out the three conditional models. The conditional stable Bayesian model,

Table 4.7 Continued

Model rank	Model number							
	1	2	3	4	5	6	7	8

Convertible bond arbitrage: 95% VaR/CVaR
Metric: Distance between predicted VaR and realised loss, conditional on VaR exceedance

1	5.9	0.0	0.0	0.0	5.9	0.0	0.0	88.2
2	0.0	29.4	0.0	5.9	0.0	35.3	35.3	5.9
3	11.8	11.8	29.4	11.8	23.5	23.5	29.4	0.0
4	35.3	23.5	23.5	29.4	23.5	11.8	11.8	0.0
Accurate VaR	5.9	5.9	5.9	5.9	5.9	5.9	5.9	5.9

Convertible bond arbitrage: 95% VaR/CVaR
Metric: Distance between predicted CVaR and realised loss, conditional on VaR exceedance

1	0.0	0.0	0.0	0.0	17.6	0.0	0.0	76.5
2	0.0	0.0	23.5	0.0	52.9	17.6	11.8	11.8
3	0.0	17.6	23.5	5.9	11.8	23.5	23.5	0.0
4	17.6	5.9	17.6	17.6	11.8	23.5	23.5	0.0
Accurate VaR	5.9	5.9	5.9	5.9	5.9	5.9	5.9	5.9

The numbers are percentages of hedge funds for which the respective model is assigned a given rank. Higher rank, coupled with a greater percentage of hedge funds for which that rank is achieved, indicates superior model performance. Ranking should be analysed in conjunction with the accuracy of VaR prediction. The percentage of hedge funds for which VaR is predicted accurately is given the last row of each panel. With space considerations in mind, results are provided only for the first four ranks and the 95% VaR. The complete results are available from the authors upon request.

however, is invariably ranked first for the greatest proportion of hedge funds; for example, for 33.3%, 76.5%, 40%, 47.1%, 37.5% and 40% of the funds at the 95% VaR/CVaR level for the merger arbitrage, CB arbitrage, directional credit, LS credit strategies, FI arbitrage and MBS arbitrage, respectively, when its predicted 95% VaR is exceeded. The conditional Student-t Bayesian model demonstrates an overall marginal performance advantage over the frequentist one, based on this distance metric.

Risk performance during September and October 2008

As mentioned in previous sections, a risk forecast comparison for the months of September and October 2008 is informative in view of

Table 4.8 Loss function metric for the distance between realised losses and VaR forecasts, conditional on VaR exceedance, for the directional credit and long/short credit strategies during September 2008

Model rank	Model number							
	1	2	3	4	5	6	7	8
Directional credit: 95% VaR/CVaR								
Metric: Distance between predicted VaR and realised loss,								
conditional on VaR exceedance								
1	2.5	5.0	0.0	0.0	5.0	2.5	5.0	65.0
2	7.5	25.0	15.0	0.0	2.5	10.0	22.5	0.0
3	30.0	2.5	7.5	7.5	7.5	12.5	15.0	0.0
4	17.5	10.0	7.5	20.0	15.0	10.0	2.5	0.0
Accurate VaR	20.0	20.0	17.5	20.0	17.5	20.0	17.5	32.5
Directional credit: 95% VaR/CVaR								
Metric: Distance between predicted CVaR and realised loss,								
conditional on VaR exceedance								
1	2.5	12.5	2.5	10.0	22.5	2.5	5.0	27.5
2	5.0	7.5	15.0	12.5	22.5	5.0	7.5	7.5
3	12.5	10.0	15.0	5.0	10.0	17.5	12.5	0.0
4	7.5	15.0	7.5	5.0	0.0	25.0	17.5	2.5
Accurate VaR	20.0	20.0	17.5	22.5	17.5	20.0	17.5	32.5

The numbers are percentages of hedge funds for which the respective model is assigned a given rank. Higher rank, coupled with a greater percentage of hedge funds for which that rank is achieved, indicates superior model performance. Ranking should be analysed in conjunction with the accuracy of VaR prediction. The percentage of hedge funds for which VaR is predicted accurately is given the last row of each panel. With space considerations in mind, results are provided only for the first four ranks and the 95% VaR. The complete results are available from the authors upon request.

the unusually large losses sustained by many hedge funds during this period. In order to gain more insight into the performance of the models, in this section we analyse two metrics:

- the distance between realised loss and CVaR, conditional on VaR exceedance (as above), and
- the distance between realised loss and VaR, conditional on VaR exceedance.

We perform this analysis because it is important to distinguish between models whose VaR forecast undershoots the realised loss

Table 4.8 Continued

Model rank	Model number							
	1	2	3	4	5	6	7	8

Long/short credit: 95% VaR/CVaR
Metric: Distance between predicted VaR and realised loss,
conditional on VaR exceedance

1	0.0	5.9	0.0	5.9	5.9	5.9	0.0	64.7
2	5.9	17.6	0.0	5.9	0.0	23.5	23.5	0.0
3	5.9	11.8	17.6	5.9	0.0	17.6	23.5	0.0
4	17.6	17.6	11.8	11.8	11.8	5.9	5.9	0.0
Accurate VaR	23.5	17.6	17.6	11.8	17.6	23.5	23.5	35.3

Long/short credit: 95% VaR/CVaR
Metric: Distance between predicted CVaR and realised loss,
conditional on VaR exceedance

1	0.0	11.8	17.6	5.9	17.6	5.9	0.0	23.5
2	0.0	5.9	17.6	17.6	23.5	5.9	5.9	5.9
3	11.8	5.9	17.6	0.0	11.8	5.9	17.6	11.8
4	5.9	11.8	5.9	0.0	0.0	23.5	23.5	11.8
Accurate VaR	23.5	17.6	17.6	17.6	17.6	23.5	23.5	35.3

The numbers are percentages of hedge funds for which the respective model is assigned a given rank. Higher rank, coupled with a greater percentage of hedge funds for which that rank is achieved, indicates superior model performance. Ranking should be analysed in conjunction with the accuracy of VaR prediction. The percentage of hedge funds for which VaR is predicted accurately is given the last row of each panel. With space considerations in mind, results are provided only for the first four ranks and the 95% VaR. The complete results are available from the authors upon request.

by a large amount and those whose VaR predictions are violated only marginally.

Again, we can see that the conditional stable Bayesian model comes closer than the other models in terms of accuracy of VaR predictions, with up to 44% and 96% of hedge funds having accurate VaR predictions at the 95% level in September and October 2008, respectively (for the merger arbitrage strategy).[23] When the 95% VaR is exceeded, the conditional stable Bayesian models' risk forecasts are closest to the realised losses.[24] The performance of the conditional Student-t Bayesian and frequentist models is comparable, as can be seen in Tables 4.7, 4.8, 4.10 and 4.11.

Table 4.9 Loss function metric for the distance between realised losses and VaR forecasts, conditional on VaR exceedance, for the fixed income arbitrage and mortgage-backed securities arbitrage during September 2008

Model rank	Model number							
	1	2	3	4	5	6	7	8
Fixed-income arbitrage: 95% VaR/CVaR								
Metric: Distance between predicted VaR and realised loss, conditional on VaR exceedance								
1	0.0	0.0	0.0	0.0	6.3	6.3	12.5	43.8
2	6.3	0.0	6.3	6.3	12.5	31.3	12.5	0.0
3	12.5	18.8	0.0	6.3	6.3	0.0	31.3	0.0
4	31.3	12.5	6.3	6.3	12.5	0.0	0.0	0.0
Accurate VaR	31.3	25.0	25.0	31.3	25.0	31.3	25.0	56.3
Fixed-income arbitrage: 95% VaR/CVaR								
Metric: Distance between predicted CVaR and realised loss, conditional on VaR exceedance								
1	12.5	0.0	0.0	0.0	18.8	0.0	18.8	25.0
2	6.3	0.0	6.3	12.5	18.8	25.0	0.0	6.3
3	0.0	12.5	18.8	6.3	12.5	6.3	18.8	0.0
4	0.0	12.5	18.8	12.5	6.3	6.3	12.5	6.3
Accurate VaR	31.3	25.0	25.0	31.3	25.0	31.3	25.0	56.3

The numbers are percentages of hedge funds for which the respective model is assigned a given rank. Higher rank, coupled with a greater percentage of hedge funds for which that rank is achieved, indicates superior model performance. Ranking should be analysed in conjunction with the accuracy of VaR prediction. The percentage of hedge funds for which VaR is predicted accurately is given the last row of each panel. With space considerations in mind, results are provided only for the first four ranks and the 95% VaR. The complete results are available from the authors upon request.

The difference in the models' risk performance for the CB arbitrage strategy in September 2008 compared with October 2008 is worth noting. For hedge funds in this strategy, October was by far the worse of the two months, with 15 out of the 17 funds experiencing sometimes more than twice as severe loss in October compared with September. This unprecedented tail event was not seen in other strategies. The severity of the September loss, however, led to a large forecasted risk for October by the three conditional models, with the stable Bayesian model predicting accurate VaR at the 95% level for more than 60% of the hedge funds.

Table 4.9 Continued

Model rank	Model number							
	1	2	3	4	5	6	7	8
MBS arbitrage: 95% VaR/CVaR							
Metric: Distance between predicted VaR and realised loss, conditional on VaR exceedance							
1	0.0	0.0	10.0	0.0	0.0	0.0	0.0	40.0
2	10.0	10.0	0.0	10.0	0.0	10.0	10.0	0.0
3	10.0	0.0	0.0	10.0	0.0	10.0	10.0	0.0
4	20.0	0.0	0.0	10.0	10.0	0.0	0.0	0.0
Accurate VaR	60.0	60.0	50.0	50.0	60.0	60.0	60.0	60.0
MBS arbitrage: 95% VaR/CVaR							
Metric: Distance between predicted CVaR and realised loss, conditional on VaR exceedance							
1	0.0	0.0	20.0	0.0	0.0	0.0	0.0	30.0
2	0.0	10.0	0.0	0.0	20.0	0.0	10.0	0.0
3	0.0	0.0	10.0	0.0	20.0	10.0	0.0	0.0
4	0.0	10.0	0.0	10.0	0.0	10.0	10.0	0.0
Accurate VaR	60.0	60.0	50.0	60.0	60.0	60.0	60.0	60.0

The numbers are percentages of hedge funds for which the respective model is assigned a given rank. Higher rank, coupled with a greater percentage of hedge funds for which that rank is achieved, indicates superior model performance. Ranking should be analysed in conjunction with the accuracy of VaR prediction. The percentage of hedge funds for which VaR is predicted accurately is given the last row of each panel. With space considerations in mind, results are provided only for the first four ranks and the 95% VaR. The complete results are available from the authors upon request.

CONCLUSION

In this chapter, we have applied the Bayesian methodology to analysing hedge fund risk with a conditional time series model with stable innovations. We have compared that model's out-of-sample risk forecasting performance to that of seven competing models estimated in the frequentist and Bayesian setting. Our analysis shows an advantage of the conditional stable Bayesian model in predicting both VaR and CVaR in general, and in particular, as far as the crisis months of September and October 2008, are concerned. The conditional Student-t models (estimated in the Bayesian and frequentist setting) perform better among the remaining models, with

Table 4.10 Loss function metric for the distance between realised losses and VaR forecasts, conditional on VaR exceedance, for the merger arbitrage and convertible bond arbitrage strategies during October 2008

Model rank	Model number							
	1	2	3	4	5	6	7	8
Merger arbitrage: 95% VaR/CVaR								
Metric: Distance between predicted VaR and realised loss, conditional on VaR exceedance								
1	18.5	11.1	3.7	0.0	11.1	7.4	11.1	3.7
2	11.1	7.4	3.7	14.8	3.7	7.4	11.1	0.0
3	7.4	18.5	3.7	11.1	11.1	7.4	0.0	0.0
4	7.4	3.7	33.3	11.1	0.0	3.7	0.0	0.0
Accurate VaR	40.7	48.1	40.7	40.7	37.0	74.1	77.8	96.3
Merger arbitrage: 95% VaR/CVaR								
Metric: Distance between predicted CVaR and realised loss, conditional on VaR exceedance								
1	11.1	11.1	14.8	3.7	7.4	7.4	11.1	0.0
2	7.4	0.0	3.7	25.9	14.8	3.7	0.0	3.7
3	14.8	14.8	3.7	3.7	11.1	7.4	3.7	0.0
4	0.0	3.7	22.2	3.7	14.8	7.4	7.4	0.0
Accurate VaR	40.7	48.1	40.7	40.7	37.0	74.1	77.8	96.3

The numbers are percentages of hedge funds for which the respective model is assigned a given rank. Higher rank, coupled with a greater percentage of hedge funds for which that rank is achieved, indicates superior model performance. Ranking should be analysed in conjunction with the accuracy of VaR prediction. The percentage of hedge funds for which VaR is predicted accurately is given the last row of each panel. With space considerations in mind, results are provided only for the first four ranks and the 95% VaR. The complete results are available from the authors upon request.

the Bayesian variety seemingly having a slight edge. Among the six hedge fund strategies we investigate, the convertible bond arbitrage strategy seems to pose the biggest challenge for our models, with fewest instances where the models' risk forecasts "caught" losses in September 2008. Even then, though, the conditional stable Bayesian model's forecasts are closest to the realised losses. Risk forecasts for October 2008, however, adjust and are adequate for a greater proportion of hedge funds in that strategy (with the conditional stable Bayesian model predicting risk best).

Table 4.10 Continued

Model rank	Model number							
	1	2	3	4	5	6	7	8
Convertible bond arbitrage: 95% VaR/CVaR								
Metric: Distance between predicted VaR and realised loss,								
conditional on VaR exceedance								
1	5.9	0.0	0.0	0.0	0.0	5.9	47.1	35.3
2	0.0	0.0	5.9	0.0	0.0	52.9	35.3	0.0
3	41.2	5.9	0.0	29.4	0.0	29.4	5.9	0.0
4	35.3	35.3	11.8	41.2	0.0	0.0	0.0	0.0
Accurate VaR	5.9	5.9	5.9	5.9	5.9	11.8	11.8	64.7
Convertible bond arbitrage: 95% VaR/CVaR								
Metric: Distance between predicted CVaR and realised loss,								
conditional on VaR exceedance								
1	0.0	0.0	5.9	0.0	0.0	47.1	35.3	11.8
2	0.0	11.8	0.0	0.0	11.8	17.6	47.1	11.8
3	0.0	23.5	11.8	0.0	35.3	17.6	5.9	0.0
4	0.0	17.6	29.4	17.6	29.4	5.9	0.0	0.0
Accurate VaR	5.9	5.9	5.9	5.9	5.9	11.8	11.8	64.7

The numbers are percentages of hedge funds for which the respective model is assigned a given rank. Higher rank, coupled with a greater percentage of hedge funds for which that rank is achieved, indicates superior model performance. Ranking should be analysed in conjunction with the accuracy of VaR prediction. The percentage of hedge funds for which VaR is predicted accurately is given the last row of each panel. With space considerations in mind, results are provided only for the first four ranks and the 95% VaR. The complete results are available from the authors upon request.

The fact that in periods of market rebound the three conditional models are slow to "catch on" suggests that there may be no "one model fits all" solution and risk managers may wish to employ different models in different market regimes. Additionally, even though our empirical analysis suggests that in periods of market distress the conditional stable Bayesian model offers the most adequate risk predictions across all hedge fund strategies, a longer back-testing period may reveal additional insights in terms of across-strategy and across-model comparisons.

Table 4.11 Loss function metric for the distance between realised losses and VaR forecasts, conditional on VaR exceedance, for the directional credit and long/short credit strategies during October 2008

Model rank	Model number							
	1	2	3	4	5	6	7	8

Directional credit: 95% VaR/CVaR
Metric: Distance between predicted VaR and realised loss, conditional on VaR exceedance

1	10.0	7.5	2.5	0.0	2.5	10.0	27.5	20.0
2	7.5	2.5	5.0	7.5	0.0	30.0	22.5	0.0
3	20.0	15.0	10.0	10.0	0.0	12.5	10.0	0.0
4	12.5	25.0	7.5	20.0	12.5	0.0	0.0	0.0
Accurate VaR	22.5	25.0	22.5	22.5	20.0	42.5	40.0	80.0

Directional credit: 95% VaR/CVaR
Metric: Distance between predicted CVaR and realised loss, conditional on VaR exceedance

1	7.5	5.0	12.5	0.0	12.5	12.5	22.5	7.5
2	0.0	0.0	15.0	10.0	15.0	20.0	17.5	0.0
3	2.5	17.5	7.5	0.0	20.0	17.5	10.0	2.5
4	0.0	2.5	20.0	17.5	22.5	7.5	7.5	0.0
Accurate VaR	22.5	25.0	22.5	22.5	20.0	42.5	40.0	80.0

The numbers are percentages of hedge funds for which the respective model is assigned a given rank. Higher rank, coupled with a greater percentage of hedge funds for which that rank is achieved, indicates superior model performance. Ranking should be analysed in conjunction with the accuracy of VaR prediction. The percentage of hedge funds for which VaR is predicted accurately is given the last row of each panel. With space considerations in mind, results are provided only for the first four ranks and the 95% VaR. The complete results are available from the authors upon request.

1 See http://www.hedgefundresearch.com/.

2 The convention used by many hedge fund vendors is to label each entity in their database collection a "fund". This is misleading, as many of the vehicles reported by such suppliers are actually pari-passu tranches of larger programmes; such tranches differ only by currency, fees, terms, leverage, hot issue eligibility or domicile. The practice of AIS's database is to consider these items "share classes" of a common "fund" programme. A "fund" is thus a unique trading approach or strategy taken by a manager; funds differ based on investment criteria, not accounting, financial or legal criteria. In this chapter, we select one share class per each fund as the representative class for statistical purposes. Typically, this class is the one with the longest record, and whose fees and terms are most indicative of a US-dollar-based day-one continuing investor.

3 Institutional Investor lists UBS Alternative and Quantitative Investments's multi-manager platform as the world's largest hedge fund-of-funds with US$32.286 billion in assets under management, as of January 1, 2010.

Table 4.11 Continued

Model rank	Model number							
	1	2	3	4	5	6	7	8
Long/short credit: 95% VaR/CVaR								
Metric: Distance between predicted VaR and realised loss,								
conditional on VaR exceedance								
1	11.8	0.0	0.0	5.9	5.9	23.5	0.0	35.3
2	11.8	17.6	0.0	17.6	0.0	5.9	23.5	0.0
3	0.0	5.9	23.5	11.8	11.8	17.6	5.9	0.0
4	23.5	41.2	5.9	0.0	5.9	0.0	0.0	0.0
Accurate VaR	29.4	23.5	23.5	17.6	23.5	41.2	58.8	64.7
Long/short credit: 95% VaR/CVaR								
Metric: Distance between predicted CVaR and realised loss,								
conditional on VaR exceedance								
1	5.9	11.8	11.8	5.9	11.8	5.9	5.9	17.6
2	5.9	11.8	5.9	0.0	23.5	17.6	11.8	0.0
3	0.0	11.8	17.6	17.6	5.9	17.6	5.9	0.0
4	5.9	11.8	17.6	5.9	17.6	5.9	11.8	0.0
Accurate VaR	29.4	23.5	23.5	23.5	23.5	41.2	58.8	64.7

The numbers are percentages of hedge funds for which the respective model is assigned a given rank. Higher rank, coupled with a greater percentage of hedge funds for which that rank is achieved, indicates superior model performance. Ranking should be analysed in conjunction with the accuracy of VaR prediction. The percentage of hedge funds for which VaR is predicted accurately is given the last row of each panel. With space considerations in mind, results are provided only for the first four ranks and the 95% VaR. The complete results are available from the authors upon request.

4 Stable distributions (both Gaussian and non-Gaussian) possess the property of stability (sums of stable random variables are themselves stable), which is clearly a desirable property for modelling returns. Moreover, a version of the Central Limit Theorem governs the asymptotic behaviour of sums of stable random variables. Therefore, the financial modelling framework built around the normal distribution can be extended to the more general class of stable distributions.

5 For the purposes of modelling returns, it is reasonable to assume that the tail parameter, α, takes values between 1 and 2. The characteristic function of the stable distribution is discontinuous for $\alpha = 1$. In order to avoid this problematic case and disregarding the trivial case of $\alpha = 2$ (corresponding to the normal distribution), the support of α is the open interval $(1, 2)$. The support of β is its theoretical support.

6 The stable parameters are assumed to be independently distributed, although the independence assumption may be contended in the case of α and β. The skewness and the tail parameters are not independent: β becomes unidentified for $\alpha = 2$. The evidence in Rachev *et al* (2005) corroborates this. Specifying an appropriate joint distribution, though, is indeed a challenge. Lombardi (2007) provides a possible approach to the joint modelling of α and β.

Table 4.12 Loss function metric for the distance between realised losses and VaR forecasts, conditional on VaR exceedance, for the fixed income arbitrage and mortgage-backed securities arbitrage strategies during October 2008

Model rank	Model number							
	1	2	3	4	5	6	7	8
Fixed-income arbitrage: 95% VaR/CVaR								
Metric: Distance between predicted VaR and realised loss,								
conditional on VaR exceedance								
1	6.3	0.0	0.0	0.0	0.0	6.3	25.0	18.8
2	6.3	0.0	6.3	0.0	0.0	18.8	18.8	6.3
3	18.8	0.0	0.0	6.3	6.3	18.8	6.3	0.0
4	18.8	6.3	6.3	18.8	6.3	0.0	0.0	0.0
Accurate VaR	43.8	43.8	43.8	43.8	43.8	56.3	50.0	75.0
Fixed-income arbitrage: 95% VaR/CVaR								
Metric: Distance between predicted CVaR and realised loss,								
conditional on VaR exceedance								
1	6.3	6.3	0.0	0.0	0.0	12.5	6.3	25.0
2	0.0	0.0	6.3	6.3	12.5	12.5	18.8	0.0
3	6.3	6.3	6.3	0.0	12.5	12.5	12.5	0.0
4	0.0	6.3	12.5	6.3	18.8	0.0	12.5	0.0
Accurate VaR	43.8	43.8	43.8	43.8	43.8	56.3	50.0	75.0

The numbers are percentages of hedge funds for which the respective model is assigned a given rank. Higher rank, coupled with a greater percentage of hedge funds for which that rank is achieved, indicates superior model performance. Ranking should be analysed in conjunction with the accuracy of VaR prediction. The percentage of hedge funds for which VaR is predicted accurately is given the last row of each panel. With space considerations in mind, results are provided only for the first four ranks and the 95% VaR. The complete results are available from the authors upon request.

7   More information about computational Bayesian methods and MCMC can be found in Chapter 2 of Volume I.

8   The only obvious constraint is that σ's support is the positive part of the real line.

9   See any standard textbook on time series analysis for detailed definitions of conditional mean and volatility models, as well as their properties and stationarity, invertibility, and other constraints.

10 Bauwens and Lubrano (1998) contend that if a diffuse prior on the interval $[0, \infty]$ is chosen for v, then the posterior distribution is not proper (its right tail does not decay fast enough). One prior distribution option is a uniform distribution on the interval $[0, K]$, where K is some finite number. Our choice of prior follows Geweke (1993), who advocates the use of the exponential distribution, $\pi(v) = \lambda \exp(-v\lambda)$. Prior intuition can be used to determine exponential mean, $1/\lambda$.

Table 4.12 Continued

Model rank	Model number							
	1	2	3	4	5	6	7	8
MBS arbitrage: 95% VaR/CVaR								
Metric: Distance between predicted VaR and realised loss,								
conditional on VaR exceedance								
1	0.0	0.0	0.0	0.0	0.0	10.0	20.0	20.0
2	10.0	10.0	0.0	0.0	0.0	10.0	20.0	0.0
3	10.0	0.0	0.0	10.0	10.0	20.0	0.0	0.0
4	10.0	10.0	20.0	10.0	0.0	0.0	0.0	0.0
Accurate VaR	60.0	50.0	50.0	60.0	50.0	50.0	50.0	80.0
MBS arbitrage: 95% VaR/CVaR								
Metric: Distance between predicted CVaR and realised loss,								
conditional on VaR exceedance								
1	0.0	0.0	0.0	0.0	10.0	0.0	20.0	20.0
2	0.0	0.0	20.0	0.0	0.0	20.0	10.0	0.0
3	0.0	10.0	0.0	0.0	20.0	20.0	0.0	0.0
4	0.0	10.0	20.0	0.0	10.0	0.0	10.0	0.0
Accurate VaR	60.0	50.0	50.0	60.0	50.0	50.0	50.0	80.0

The numbers are percentages of hedge funds for which the respective model is assigned a given rank. Higher rank, coupled with a greater percentage of hedge funds for which that rank is achieved, indicates superior model performance. Ranking should be analysed in conjunction with the accuracy of VaR prediction. The percentage of hedge funds for which VaR is predicted accurately is given the last row of each panel. With space considerations in mind, results are provided only for the first four ranks and the 95% VaR. The complete results are available from the authors upon request.

---

11 See, for example, Bauwens *et al* (2000).

12 It is also possible to treat ϵ_0 (and, therefore, σ_0^2) as an unknown parameter in the Arma–Garch process and simulate it together with the remaining parameters in the MCMC algorithm. See, for example, Chib and Greenberg (1994), among others.

13 See also Chapter 1.

14 The parameters of the proposal density are due to an asymptotic result from maximum-likelihood theory concerning the distribution of the maximum-likelihood estimator of the mean of the normal distribution. See Rachev *et al* (2008a) for additional details.

15 For the definitions and properties of various risk measures, in particular VaR and CVaR, as well as their applications in risk and portfolio management, see, for example, Rachev *et al* (2008b).

16 The VaR and CVaR estimates above are computed at a time horizon of one month in our empirical investigation.

17 For more details on VaR/CVaR prediction using a time-series model, see, for example, Tsay (2005).

18 See, for example, Alexander and Sheedy (2008).

19 For $v = 1$, CVaR explodes because the Student-t distribution with one degree of freedom – known as the Cauchy distribution – has an infinite expectation. In this case, we can use the median of the loss distribution, when the loss exceeds $\text{VaR}_\kappa(R)$, as a robust alternative to CVaR. See Rachev et al (2008b) for more details.

20 Back-testing CVaR is a challenging task. See Rachev et al (2008b) for a discussion.

21 Dowd (2008) provides an overview of back-testing market risk models. For a suggestion on a more rigorous approach to CVaR back-testing, see Rachev et al (2008b).

22 That the conditional stable Bayesian model suggested considerable losses subsequent to the major market events of August 1998 and September–October 2008 was not lost on many individual hedge funds which did in fact lose almost all their value and liquidate. The analysis herein involves an industry index which has some biases in that it often fails to include the performance of funds that are terminating. Since the index will continue indefinitely as an average of surviving and existing funds, it is no surprise that some risk estimators will tend to overshoot after a major market event.

23 Due to space considerations, we discuss and present only the results concerning the 95% VaR and CVaR forecasts. The 99% VaR/CVaR results for September and October 2008 per model and strategy are available from the authors upon request.

24 Notice that in certain instances (for example, the CB arbitrage October 2008 results in Table 4.10, the directional credit October 2008 results in Table 4.11 or the FI arbitrage October 2008 results in Table 4.12) model 7 (the conditional Student-t Bayesian model) has been ranked first for a greater proportion of hedge funds in the respective strategy than model 8 (the conditional stable Bayesian model). These results are produced by virtue of the fact that there are more funds for which model 7's VaR is exceeded than model 8's and should not mislead the reader into interpreting model 7 as superior to model 8. When rankings are viewed in conjunction with the results on VaR exceedances at the bottom of each table, it is evident that model 8's risk performance is better.

REFERENCES

Agarwal, V., G. Bakshi and J. Huij, 2008, "Dynamic Investment Opportunities and the Cross-Section of Hedge Fund Returns: Implications of Higher-Moment Risks for Performance", Working Paper, University of Maryland Robert H. Smith School of Business.

Alexander, C., and E. Sheedy, 2008, "Developing a Stress Framework Based on Market Risk Models", *Journal of Banking and Finance* 32, pp. 2220–36.

Avramov, D., R. Kosowski, N. Naik and M. Teo, 2007, "Investing in Hedge Funds when Returns Are Predictable", Working Paper.

Bauwens, L., and M. Lubrano, 1998, "Bayesian Inference on Garch Models Using the Gibbs Sampler", *Econometrics Journal* 1, pp. C23–46.

Bauwens, L., M. Lubrano and J. Richard, 2000, *Bayesian Inference in Dynamic Econometric Models* (Oxford University Press).

Blanco, C., and G. Ihle, 1999, "How Good Is Your VaR? Using Backtesting to Assess System Performance", *Financial Engineering News* 11, pp. 1–2.

Buckle, D., 1995, "Bayesian Inference for Stable Distributions", *Journal of the American Statistical Association* 90, pp. 605–13.

Casarin, R., 2004, "Bayesian Inference for Mixtures of Stable Distributions", Working Paper 0428, CEREMADE, Université Paris IX.

Chib, S., and E. Greenberg, 1994, "Bayes Inference in Regression Models with Arma (P, Q) Errors", *Journal of Econometrics* 64, pp. 183–206.

Christoffersen, P. F., 1998, "Evaluating Interval Forecasts", *International Economic Review* 39(4), pp. 841–62.

Dowd, K., 2008, "Backtesting Market Risk Models", in F. J. Fabozzi (ed), *Handbook of Finance*, Volume 3 (Hoboken, NJ: John Wiley & Sons).

Geweke, J., 1993, "Bayesian Treatment Of The Independent Student's t Linear Model", *Journal of Applied Econometrics* 8 (Supplement: Special Issue on Econometric Inference Using Simulation Techniques), pp. S19–40.

Gibson, R., and S. Wang, 2009, "Hedge Fund Alphas: Do They Reflect Managerial Skill or Mere Compensation for Liquidity Risk Bearing", Working Paper.

Godsill, S., and E. Kuruoglu, 1999, "Bayesian Inference for Time Series with Heavy Tailed Symmetric α-Stable Noise Processes", *Proceedings of Applications of Heavy Tailed Distributions in Economics, Engineering and Statistics Conference, Washington DC*. URL: http://www-sigproc.eng.cam.ac.uk/-sjg/.

Henneke, J., S. Rachev and F. Fabozzi, 2007, "MCMC Based Estimation of Markov-Switching Arma–Garch Models", Technical Report. Department of Statistics and Applied Probability, University of California, Santa Barbara.

Kosowski, R., N. Naik and M. Teo, 2007, "Do Hedge Funds Deliver Alpha? A Bayesian and Bootstrap Analysis", *Journal of Financial Economics* 84, pp. 229–64.

Kupiec, P., 1995, "Techniques for Verifying the Accuracy of Risk Management Models", *Journal of Derivatives* 4(3), pp. 73–84.

Lombardi, M., 2007, "Bayesian Inference for α-Stable Distributions: A Random Walk MCMC Approach", *Computational Statistics and Data Analysis* 51(5), pp. 2688–700.

Olszewski, J., 2005, "Building a Better Fund of Hedge Funds: A Fractal and α-Stable Distribution Approach", Working Paper, Maple Financial Alternative Investments.

Qiou, Z., 1996, "Bayesian Inference for Stable Processes", PhD Dissertation, University of Connecticut.

Qiou, Z., and N. Ravishanker, 1997, "Bayesian Inference for Time Series with Stable Innovations", *Journal of Time Series Analysis* 19, pp. 235–49.

Qiou, Z., and N. Ravishanker, 1999, "Bayesian Inference for Vector Arma Models with Stable Innovations", Working Paper, Palisades Research Inc and University of Connecticut.

Rachev, S., and S. Mittnik, 2000, *Stable Paretian Models in Finance* (New York: John Wiley & Sons).

Rachev, S., S. Stoyanov, A. Biglova and F. Fabozzi, 2005, "An Empirical Examination of Daily Stock Return Distributions For US Stocks", in D. Baier, R. Decker and L. Schmidt-Thieme (ed), *Data Analysis and Decision Support*, Studies in Classification, Data Analysis and Knowledge Organization (Springer).

Rachev, S., J. Hsu, B. Bagasheva and F. Fabozzi, 2008a, *Bayesian Methods in Finance* (Hoboken, NJ: John Wiley & Sons).

Rachev, S., S. Stoyanov and F. Fabozzi, 2008b, *Advanced Stochastic Models, Risk Assessment, and Portfolio Optimization: The Ideal Risk, Uncertainty, and Performance Measures* (Hoboken, NJ: John Wiley & Sons).

Ravishanker, N., and Z. Qiou, 1998, "Bayesian Inference for Time Series with Infinite Variance Stable Innovations", in R. J. Adler, R. Feldman and M. S. Taqqu (eds), *A Practical Guide to Heavy Tails: Statistical Techniques and Applications* (Boston, MA: Birkhäuser).

Ritter, C., and M. Tanner, 1992, "Facilitating the Gibbs Sampler: The Gibbs Stopper and the Griddy Gibbs Sampler", *Journal of the American Statistical Association* 87(419), pp. 861–68.

Robert, C., and J.-M. Marin, 2010, *On Computational Tools of Bayesian Data Analysis* (London, Risk Books).

Salas-Gonzales, D., E. Kuruoglu and D. Ruiz, 2006a, "Bayesian Estimation of Mixtures of Skewed Alpha Stable Distributions with an Unknown Number of Components", presented at European Signal Processing Conference, Florence.

Salas-Gonzales, D., E. Kuruoglu and D. Ruiz, 2006b, "Bayesian Inference on Mixture of Alpha-Stable Distributions", Working Paper, ISTI-CNR, Pisa.

Stoyanov S., and B. Racheva-Iotova, 2004, "Univariate Stable Laws in the Field of Finance: Parameter Estimation", Working Paper.

Stoyanov, S., G. Samorodnitsky, S. Rachev and S. Ortobelli, 2006, "Computing the Portfolio Conditional Value-at-Risk in the α-Stable Case", *Probability and Mathematical Statistics* 26, pp. 1–22.

Tsay, R., 2005, *Analysis of Financial Time Series* (Hoboken, NJ: John Wiley & Sons).

Tsionas, E., 1999, "Monte Carlo Inference in Economic Models with Symmetric Stable Distributions", *Journal of Econometrics* 88, pp. 365–401.

5

Model Uncertainty and Its Impact on Derivative Pricing

Alok Gupta, Christoph Reisinger, Alan Whitley

University of Oxford

Financial derivatives written on an underlying can normally be priced and hedged accurately only after a suitable mathematical model for the underlying has been determined. This chapter explains the difficulties in finding a (unique) realistic model: model uncertainty. If the wrong model is chosen for pricing and hedging, unexpected and unwelcome financial consequences may occur. By "wrong model" we mean either the wrong model type (specification uncertainty) or the wrong model parameter (parameter uncertainty). In both cases, the impact of model uncertainty on pricing and hedging is significant. A variety of measures are introduced to value the model uncertainty of derivatives and a numerical example again confirms that these values are a significant proportion of the derivative price.

In this introductory section, we will look at various ways in which the model selection problem may manifest itself and the consequences of this for derivative pricing.

Motivating examples

To demonstrate the prevalence of model uncertainty in derivative pricing, we look at calibrating different derivative pricing models to a set of observed prices. We consider a set of 60 European call prices for six maturities varying between one month and one year, and 10 strikes varying between 90% and 110% of the spot value. We look at two examples of trying to calibrate models to these prices. In the first we do not assume we know the model type (thus investigating specification uncertainty), and in the second we fix the model type and try to identify the model parameter (therefore considering parameter uncertainty).

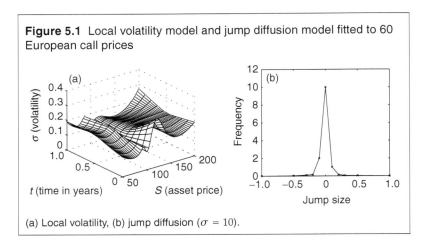

Figure 5.1 Local volatility model and jump diffusion model fitted to 60 European call prices

(a) Local volatility, (b) jump diffusion ($\sigma = 10$).

Table 5.1 Heston stochastic volatility model fitted to 60 European call prices

Parameter	Value
Rate of reversion	0.0745
Long-run variance	0.1415
Volatility of volatility	0.1038
Correlation	−0.2127
Initial variance	0.0167

Example 5.1 (specification uncertainty). To the same set of 60 observed European call prices, we fit a local volatility model (Dupire 1994), a jump-diffusion model (Cont and Tankov 2004) and a Heston stochastic volatility model (Heston 1993). The models are all very different: a one-factor continuous process, a two-factor continuous process and a discontinuous process respectively. But each model is nevertheless fitted to within an average of three basis points (bp) of the same quoted call prices. Two of the calibrated models are displayed in Figure 5.1, where part (a) shows a local volatility surface that reproduces the 60 prices to within an average of 3bp, part (b) shows the jump density (of an exponential Lévy process) that does the same. Table 5.1 gives the parameters for a Heston model that also fits the observed prices.

Example 5.2 (parameter uncertainty). For the same set of 60 European call prices, we now assume the model is known to be local

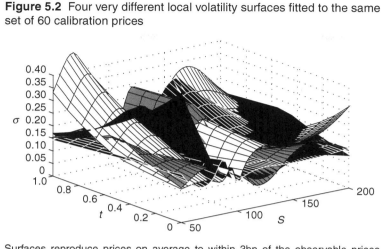

Figure 5.2 Four very different local volatility surfaces fitted to the same set of 60 calibration prices

Surfaces reproduce prices on average to within 3bp of the observable prices. European call options have maturities varying between one month and one year and strikes varying between 90% and 110% of the spot value.

volatility and try to find different local volatility surfaces that fit the prices. This is now a problem related to the uncertainty involved when fitting a pricing model. Observe in Figure 5.2 the variety of differently shaped local volatility surfaces that arise. Note that each local volatility surface reproduces all 60 prices to within an average of 3bp. We have only plotted four surfaces to demonstrate the disparity between the shapes.

Now imagine trying to price another option on the same underlying. Below are the prices given by the different models and the different model calibrations in Examples 5.1 and 5.2, respectively, for a three-month up-and-out barrier call option with strike 90% of the spot and barrier 110% of the spot.

As Table 5.2 indicates, the derivative price variation is noticeable for different local volatility surfaces – up to 26 basis points. The disparity in pricing is even larger for different model types – by up to 177 basis points.

Risk and Knightian uncertainty

The cost of selecting the wrong model is most commonly referred to as model risk, but the more accurate terminology is model uncertainty. The reason for this is as follows. Suppose the underlying S

Table 5.2 Barrier prices found by different fitted models

Model	Price	Local volatility	Price
Local volatility	7.41	A	7.51
Jump-diffusion	9.18	B	7.32
Stochastic volatility	7.77	C	7.48
		D	7.58

Barrier prices found by different fitted models according to Example 5.1 (in the two left-hand columns) and Figure 5.2 (the two right-hand columns). We price an up-and-out barrier call option with strike 90% of the spot and barrier 110% of the spot value.

takes different values $S(\omega)$ depending on the future scenario $\omega \in \Omega$ that occurs. And let $\mathbb{P}$ be the probability measure corresponding to the set of future scenarios Ω. Then risk corresponds to not knowing which future scenario $\omega \in \Omega$ will occur, whereas uncertainty corresponds to lack of knowledge of the probability measure $\mathbb{P}$.

The distinction between risk and uncertainty was highlighted by Knight (1921).[1] Although subtle, the difference between not knowing the future state and not knowing the probability of the possible future states is important, and investors and risk-managers are likely to have differing aversions to both.

It is important to also note the difference between model uncertainty and market incompleteness (Branger and Schlag 2004). In an incomplete market, the true data-generating process may be known, but not all contracts are attainable, so the pricing measure is not unique. However, under model uncertainty, we do not even know the true data-generating process.

Sources and types of model uncertainty

The investigation of model uncertainty applied to financial models is in its infancy and only began to receive attention when, for example, Derman (1996) published his research notes on model uncertainty. Derman identifies several sources of model uncertainty, which we group into three distinct classes, with examples, and give some extensions.

Incorrect model. On a fundamental level, known mathematical models might not be capable of projecting stock movements, such that brinkmanship or psychology might play a more important role. Furthermore, some factors might have been forgotten, or factors incorrectly modelled (eg, as deterministic when they are stochastic or vice versa). The model for a price process in one market may be inappropriate for another in a different market with differing levels of interest rates or volatility. A model suitable in a stable market might become inappropriate in a time of financial crisis. Once market frictions such as transaction costs and illiquidity are factored in, a model might no longer be applicable.

Incorrect solution. The model might be correct but the final analytical solution found could be wrong. For example, Li's famous copula formula (Li 2000), on which billions of dollars were invested, had an important right bracket missing. Numerical approximations may not be accurate enough. For example, Monte Carlo methods often need many simulations to converge. Software and hardware can be faulty so, because a lot of trading and pricing platforms use many thousands of lines of program code, difficult-to-detect errors can cause incorrect solutions. For example, the R2009b release of MATLAB incorrectly solved a linear system for a transposed 2×2 matrix.[2]

Incorrect calibration. Instationarity of the underlying process may cause previous calibrations to no longer be applicable. Instability of the solution might imply that the wrong model (parameter) is chosen. Furthermore, there may be a lack of robustness of the solution, ie, pricing and hedging is non-robust with respect to the modelling assumptions.

Whatever the source of model uncertainty, the consequences can be dramatic and costly. We highlight some of these effects in the following section, with a focus on the first and last points above.

Effect of uncertainty on derivative pricing

Uncertainty in the modelling of the underlying will manifest itself as risk in derivative pricing and hedging. There is a broad spectrum of model uncertainty ranging, at one extreme, from situations where very little, if anything, is known about the detailed structure of the model of the underlying (specification uncertainty), to the opposite extreme where the structure of the model is specified in detail but there is uncertainty over the parameters of the model (parameter uncertainty).

At the one extreme, even though we do not have a full specification of the model, we may still be able to draw conclusions about derivative pricing. There is a substantial body of literature that discusses the range of arbitrage-free prices for certain kinds of derivatives where only the most general properties of the model of the underlying are assumed. For example, elementary bounds on the prices of vanilla derivatives can be given that are completely model-free (Chance 2008). As a fully parameterised description of the model is not assumed in such cases, we will refer to this kind of uncertainty as specification uncertainty.

Later in this chapter, as examples of specification uncertainty we will describe two model uncertainty frameworks where the underlying follows a stochastic volatility process. Model uncertainty is present in these frameworks because we have only limited information on the volatility process driving the model; no particular form of volatility process is assumed and it remains unparameterised.

At the other extreme, model uncertainty may reduce to the complete description of a family of models in which the 'true' model is believed to lie and where each family member is fully specified as a parameterised model. For example, we may have a family of classic Black–Scholes models which differ only in the value of the (constant) volatility used to define each member; the volatility is then the parameter describing the uncertainty. We will refer to this later as parameter uncertainty. This kind of uncertainty lends itself to analysis by Bayesian methods, as we can begin by assigning a prior probability distribution to the set of parameters describing the family of models and then use observed data (such as the behaviour of the underlying or prices of derivatives on the underlying) to derive a posterior distribution for the parameters. This approach is described in detail later. Other methods of describing the uncertainty in this framework exist; for example, the uncertainty might be described using the language of fuzzy set theory, where "possibility" replaces the concept of probability, eg, as illustrated by Swishchuk *et al* (2008).

Typically, we will have some prior beliefs about the model uncertainty and, in the absence of any other information, will take these beliefs into account in pricing and hedging. For example, in the situation where we do not specify the form of the volatility, we might only begin with the prior belief that the spot volatility always lies between 0.2 and 0.3. But, in the case of parameter uncertainty, we might begin with the prior belief that the appropriate family of models consists of Black–Scholes models with (constant) volatility between 0.2 and 0.3.

Analysis of derivative pricing and hedging using only this limited prior information is likely to result in an unacceptably wide range of possible prices and hedging strategies. It is standard practice to then make use of additional data to calibrate (or "constrain") the family of possible models in order to reduce the uncertainty range. As an excellent example of this, Cox and Obłój (2008, 2009) describe price bounds for certain kinds of barrier options that make only mild assumptions about the model of the underlying, but assume knowledge of European option prices for the same maturity and all strikes.

Calibration may use data for only the underlying to reduce uncertainty about the real world measure or it may use observable prices of traded derivatives to reduce uncertainty about the risk-neutral measure. A key feature of the Bayesian framework applied to parameter uncertainty (detailed later) is that calibration yields a posterior probability distribution for the family of allowable models which can then be used to inform the pricing of other derivatives. A posterior distribution results because many models may give a "sufficient" fit to the calibration data, although some will be more probable than others.

In this chapter, the main focus will be on the problem of incorrect model choice. As described above, specification uncertainty and parameter uncertainty are two ways of describing the situation where we believe we have some (perhaps limited) prior information about the "true" model, eg, that it is a member of a particular family of models that we can describe in some way. We must acknowledge this and understand the implications for the pricing and hedging of derivatives.

MODEL-FREE PRICING

In this section we will present examples of model uncertainty where the family of models cannot or shall not be parameterised. The first example to be presented is the uncertain volatility model introduced by Avellaneda *et al* (1995) and we will follow this example with a variant of this problem as described by Mykland (2009). These examples will illustrate that, although we have a situation where the model for the underlying is uncertain and we cannot fully specify the members of the family of allowable models, we can nevertheless obtain useful information about derivative pricing and hedging. Furthermore, just as with the Bayesian techniques to be described later, it is possible to use the prices of traded financial instruments in a form of calibration that reduces the effect of the model uncertainty on the pricing and hedging of derivatives.

Bounded volatility assumptions

Avellaneda et al (1995) described a pricing problem where the model for the underlying, S_t, is taken to be the stochastic differential equation

$$dS_t = S_t(\mu_t\, dt + \sigma_t\, dZ_t)$$

where Z_t is a standard Brownian motion, μ_t is the drift and the volatility, σ_t, is a stochastic process satisfying the condition

$$\sigma_t \in [\sigma_{\min}, \sigma_{\max}] \quad \text{for all } t \in [0, T] \qquad (5.1)$$

for some non-negative constants, $\sigma_{\min}$ and $\sigma_{\max}$, over a time interval $[0, T]$. Avellaneda et al (1995) mention that the bounds could, in fact, be taken to be functions of the price of the underlying and of time. This uncertainty framework has also been studied by Lyons (1995).

Avellaneda et al consider the pricing and hedging of a European derivative with payoff $h(S_T)$ at maturity, T, in this framework (in fact, they consider the pricing and hedging of a portfolio of European claims with various maturities) and give expressions for upper and lower bounds for the derivative price, $W^+(S_t, t)$ and $W^-(S_t, t)$.

The initial upper bound, $W^+(S_0, 0) = W_0^+$, is the lowest price that can be charged for the derivative such that, by following an appropriate hedging strategy, the seller can be sure to avoid making a loss on hedging. The initial lower bound, $W^-(S_0, 0)$, is the highest price that can be paid for the derivative such that, by following an appropriate hedging strategy, the buyer can be sure to avoid making a loss on hedging.

The authors show that these price bounds satisfy two versions of a non-linear partial differential equation, the Black–Scholes–Barenblatt (BSB) equation. The BSB equation is

$$\frac{\partial W}{\partial t} + r\left(S\frac{\partial W}{\partial t} - W\right) + \tfrac{1}{2}\hat{\sigma}^2\left[\frac{\partial^2 W}{\partial S^2}\right]S^2\frac{\partial^2 W}{\partial S^2} = 0$$

In the equation for W^+, $\hat{\sigma}$ is defined by

$$\hat{\sigma}[\Gamma] = \begin{cases} \sigma_{max} & \text{if } \Gamma \geqslant 0 \\ \sigma_{min} & \text{if } \Gamma < 0 \end{cases}$$

and, in the equation for W^-, σ_{min} and σ_{max} are interchanged. This equation must be solved numerically using the portfolio payoffs as time boundary conditions.

In the case of a derivative with a convex payoff, the BSB ask price is the same as the standard Black–Scholes price with the volatility set identically equal to σ_{max} and the bid price is the standard Black–Scholes price with the volatility set identically equal to σ_{min}. For a concave payoff, these results apply with σ_{max} and σ_{min} interchanged. For payoffs of mixed convexity, the BSB ask and bid prices may lie outside the range of the standard Black–Scholes prices computed with the volatility set identically equal to σ_{max} or σ_{min}.

Under certain conditions on the stochastic volatility process, as σ_{max} tends to ∞ and σ_{min} tends to 0, the ask price is given by the smallest concave super-majorant of the payoff function, ie, the smallest concave function that is always at least as large as the payoff (Cvitanić et al 1999). So, for example, in the case of a European call option when the volatility is unbounded, the ask price is given by the spot price of the asset, which is an elementary model-free bound.

The span of prices between W^+ and W^- is a measure of the effect of model uncertainty on the price of the derivative. If the derivative were sold for a price outside this range, an arbitrage opportunity would arise for either the buyer or the seller. When the volatility range shrinks to zero, the upper and lower price bounds both equal the Black–Scholes price for the then fixed volatility, as would be expected.

The solution of the BSB equation also provides the appropriate hedging strategy to use if the derivative is sold for, say, $W^+(S_0, 0)$. The hedge ratio is then simply given by the delta of the value process, ie, $\partial W^+/\partial S$.

Frey and Sin (2001) point out that, in practice, it may not be possible to determine a finite upper bound on the volatility process to use as σ_{max} (nor may it be possible to precisely specify the lower bound σ_{min}). They suggest a practical approach in which volatility bounds are estimated such that the probability of the volatility process straying outside the bounds during the time interval $[0, T]$ is

$1 - \alpha$, ie, they define a prediction set for the volatility process where α is the probability that the conditions assumed in the calculation of the ask price do not hold. If the ask price is calculated using these bounds and the derivative is then continuously hedged using the corresponding hedge ratios, the probability of incurring a hedging error will not exceed α.

In practice, it would be convenient if the volatility bounds could be chosen so that the probability of incurring a hedging error were equal to some agreed tolerance level, β. Unfortunately, the link between the α as described above and the resulting β is rather weak and β can be much smaller than α. As a result, too high a value of α may be chosen, leading to an excessively high ask price, for example.

This behaviour is illustrated by the results of a pricing and hedging simulation carried out by the authors. In this simulation, the underlying volatility process follows a Heston model with known parameters, and σ_{max} and σ_{min} were chosen to be 0.40 and 0.10, respectively. Simulation over a period of six months showed that around 50% of the volatility paths strayed outside these limits. The BSB equation with these volatility bounds was used to calculate the ask price for a particular butterfly spread and a hedging simulation was then run using the hedge ratios from the BSB solution with the asset price trajectories being again derived from the Heston model. Analysis of the hedging errors from the simulation showed that only 5% of the paths incurred hedging errors.

Furthermore, when the volatility bounds were changed to 0.50 and 0.03, it was found that about 5% of the paths violated the constraints but none of the 50,000 paths sampled resulted in hedging errors.

In this case, if the error tolerance had been set at 5%, it would have been acceptable to set the volatility bounds at 0.40 and 0.10. However, if the bounds had been set, in a rather natural way, to ensure that the model conditions were only violated 5% of the time, the bounds could have been set at 0.50 and 0.03. This choice would have resulted in a higher, and thus less competitive, ask price, albeit with a much lower probability of incurring a hedging error.

Super-replication

In an incomplete market, the price for a claim X cannot in general be uniquely identified by no-arbitrage arguments. In this case the "super-replication" price of X is an indicator of the (maximum selling) value of the claim. Under certain conditions, the super-replication price is equal to $\sup_{\mathbb{Q}} \mathbb{E}^{\mathbb{Q}}[X]$, where $\mathbb{Q}$ belongs to the set of pricing measures.

The pricing problem in the uncertain volatility model framework is an example of super-replication. It addresses the problem of identifying an initial wealth and a self-financing trading strategy that will almost surely achieve the derivative payoff. In this case, the super-replication must be achieved whenever the volatility process satisfies the stated condition. The terminology "super-hedging" is sometimes used instead of super-replication.

The uncertain volatility model has been explicitly studied as a super-replication problem by Frey (2000), who identifies a process that super-replicates a given European claim given the conditions satisfied by the volatility process (Frey's method also works for a restricted set of path-dependent claims, eg, some special types of barrier derivatives). The super-replicating process he identifies has a value process given by the price of an American derivative where the underlying is a normalised geometric Brownian motion (ie, it has zero drift and unit volatility), the payoff is a modified version of the original derivative payoff and the volatility bounds determine the exercise window for the American derivative.

Although Frey finds a super-replicating process and hence the initial worst-case ask price, the super-replication is not necessarily minimal, ie, it may be possible to charge a lower price and hedge appropriately to guarantee hedging losses do not occur. He goes on to discuss when it is possible to formulate the problem as the solution of a partial differential equation (recovering the BSB equation) which does give a minimal super-replication and demonstrates the circumstances under which the two approaches give the same result.

Although Frey deals only with the super-replicating price, a similar method could be used to compute a lower bound on the derivative price, the sub-replication price, thus producing an uncertainty range for the derivative price.

Frey presents his results in detail for a single derivative of maturity T and his method clearly extends to a portfolio of European derivatives with the same maturity. He also describes how to calculate the super-replication price for a portfolio of European derivatives with different maturities.

Bounded total-variance assumptions

Mykland (2009) describes an uncertain volatility model which differs from the framework by Avellaneda *et al*, Lyons and Frey by placing an alternative constraint on the stochastic volatility process. Mykland assumes that the volatility process, σ_t, satisfies the following total-variance condition

$$\Xi^- \leqslant \int_0^T \sigma_t^2 \, dt \leqslant \Xi^+ \tag{5.2}$$

for two constants Ξ^- and Ξ^+. The quantity being constrained here is the quadratic variation of the log process for the underlying.

Mykland shows that the worst-case ("conservative") ask price for a European derivative with maturity T can be described as the price of a suitable American derivative in this framework. In other words, there is a starting price, A_0 and a super-replication process, V, with $V_0 = A_0$, whose value at time t, V_t, is given by an American derivative price and there is an associated hedging strategy that ensures no loss will be made as long as the volatility process satisfies the condition given above.

Given a volatility process that satisfies the volatility bounds in Equation 5.1, we will have

$$\sigma_{\min}^2 T \leqslant \int_0^T \sigma_t^2 \, dt \leqslant \sigma_{\max}^2 T$$

so the range of initial prices that results from the Mykland framework cannot be wider than the range derived from the framework by Avellaneda *et al*, Lyons and Frey, given the same volatility process.

An important feature of the Mykland model is that the hedging strategy relies on the continuous estimation of the realised variance of the underlying, ie

$$\int_0^t \sigma_u^2 \, du$$

as this quantity is used to adjust the exercise window for the American derivative being calculated. This quantity can be estimated from the history of the log returns of the underlying but the accuracy of the super-replication will depend on the accuracy with which the realised variance is estimated.

Mykland provides a further interpretation of his model where the condition satisfied by the quadratic variation is viewed as the definition of a prediction set, ie, a probability $(1 - \alpha)$ is attributed to the outcome that a realisation of the volatility process will satisfy the constraints. With this interpretation, the conservative ask price becomes the price at which the derivative can be sold, so that, by following the appropriate hedging strategy, the seller can be sure that the probability of incurring a hedging error is at most α. The idea is that the seller can choose a tolerable level for the risk of incurring hedging errors and price and hedge the derivative accordingly.

This approach can be compared to the use of a prediction set with the bounded volatility uncertainty framework as described earlier. It should again be noted that a hedging error does not necessarily result from a particular volatility path violating the total-variance bounds, Ξ^- and Ξ^+, so α may overstate the probability of a hedging error occurring.

Using calibration to reduce model uncertainty

An important property of the price found by super-replication is that the pricing mechanism is non-linear, ie, if we have two European derivatives maturing at times T_1 and T_2, with payoffs $h_1(S_{T_1})$ and $h_2(S_{T_2})$, then the super-replication price for a linear combination of these two derivatives will not in general be the same linear combination of the super-replication prices. This property of the pricing mechanism opens up the possibility of reducing the worst-case ask price for a European claim by setting up a static hedge using traded derivatives in the same underlying.

If we let the holdings in the n hedging instruments be given by $\lambda_1, \ldots, \lambda_n$, and instrument i have payoff $h_i(S_{T_i})$ and traded price p_i, then the worst-case ask price for another derivative with payoff $h(S_T)$ is given by

$$W_0^+(h + \lambda_1 h_1 + \lambda_2 h_2 + \cdots + \lambda_n h_n) - (\lambda_1 p_1 + \lambda_2 p_2 + \cdots + \lambda_n p_n)$$

ie, we calculate the worst-case "ask" price for the enlarged (statically hedged) portfolio and then subtract the initial cost of the hedge. We then find the static hedge coefficients $\lambda_1, \ldots, \lambda_n$ which minimise this price. Due to the non-linearity of the pricing mechanism, the result may be lower than the ask price in the absence of the hedge, so a reduced ask price can be charged, safe in the knowledge that hedging the enlarged portfolio will not incur a hedging loss if the volatility satisfies the assumed condition.

This method of reducing the uncertainty range of the derivative price is a form of calibration and, in the absence of a bid–ask spread for the traded derivatives, the calibration would be exact, as the value of a traded derivative calculated by this method will simply deliver the traded derivative price. In practice there will be bid–ask spreads and a simple approach might be to use the average of the bid and ask prices to represent the price of a traded derivative in the equation. However, a more sophisticated approach would be to include the bid or ask prices in the formula depending on the signs of the hedging coefficient, λ_i, which determine whether the hedges in the traded derivatives are held long or short. This will lead to a more complicated optimisation problem to determine the hedging coefficients.

For the Avellaneda *et al* uncertain volatility model, this method of static hedging can easily be applied, as the pricing mechanism described in Avellaneda *et al* (1995) can handle a portfolio of mixed maturity European derivatives. Similarly, as Frey (2000) describes how to calculate the super-replication price for a portfolio of mixed maturity European derivatives, his method could also be used for calibration against a set of mixed maturity European options.

In the case of Mykland's uncertainty volatility model, a method of determining the ask price for a mixed maturity portfolio would be required. This would probably require constraints on the quadratic variation to be specified for time intervals other than $[0, T]$.

Model uncertainty measures will be discussed in more detail later but, in passing, we can observe that one measure of model uncertainty can be defined by setting

$$\mu(X) = \text{conservative ask price}(X) - \text{conservative bid price}(X)$$

where X is a claim. In the case of both the Frey and Mykland super-replication approaches, this is because the conservative ask price can be written as

$$\bar{\pi}(X) = \sup_{P \in \mathcal{P}} \{\mathbb{E}^P[X]\}$$

where $\mathcal{P}$ is a suitable family of probability measures. Cont (2006) describes how an upper bound on price of this type can be combined with a lower bound given by

$$\underline{\pi}(X) = -\bar{\pi}(-X)$$

to give a coherent measure of model uncertainty. The lower bound on price is the conservative bid price.

Although calibration (using a static hedge with an appropriate choice of calibrating instruments) can be expected to reduce the uncertainty in the price of a derivative, the lack of a detailed specification of the underlying model may mean that the uncertainty range cannot be reduced to an acceptable level. For this reason, it may be necessary to attempt a more detailed description of the underlying model and use the Bayesian techniques described in the next section to reduce the range of prices and better quantify the model uncertainty.

However, it should be borne in mind that moving to a more precise description of the underlying model carries the risk that the family of candidate models will be made too narrow, so that uncertainty is underestimated. Consequently, selection of the family of candidate models and the associated choice of the prior distribution should be made with some care.

CALIBRATION AND PARAMETER UNCERTAINTY

If a model class has been chosen for the underlying, a decision still has to be made on how to calibrate the model for subsequent derivative pricing and hedging. The problem is non-trivial and a wrong decision can be costly for the decision maker. In this section, we focus on the problem of choosing a suitable parameter for a model, and explain why it is often difficult and unstable. We then present a robust Bayesian solution.

The inverse problem

Let the underlying asset price process be $S = (S_t)_{t \geqslant 0}$ and suppose it depends on the time t, stochastic process(es) $Z = (Z_t)_{t \geqslant 0}$ and model parameter $\theta \in \Theta$, ie

$$S_t = S(S_0, t, (Z_u)_{0 \leqslant u \leqslant t}; \theta) \tag{5.3}$$

where S_0 is the value of the underlying at time 0.

Suppose we wish to price an option on $S(\theta)$ that has maturity T and a payoff function h. Let $f_t(\theta)$ be the price of this option at t when the model parameter is θ. If we assume there is a risk-neutral pricing measure $\mathbb{Q}$, then we can explicitly write this price as

$$f_t(\theta) = \mathbb{E}^{\mathbb{Q}}[B(t,T)h(S(\theta)) \mid (S_u)_{0 \leqslant u \leqslant t}]$$

where $B(t, T)$ is a discount factor between t and T.

Now we observe many such option prices $\{f_t^{(i)}(\theta): i \in I_t\}$ at time $t \in [0, T]$, where I_t is an index set of data. Usually, prices are only observed to within bid–ask spreads so there exists a noise component $\{e_t^{(i)}: i \in I_t\}$, ie

$$V_t^{(i)} = f_t^{(i)}(\theta^*) + e_t^{(i)} \qquad (5.4)$$

for $i \in I_t$. θ^* denotes the true parameter. The calibration problem is then to select θ which best reproduces the observed prices $\{V_t^{(i)}: i \in I_t, t \in Y_n([0,T])\}$, where $Y_n([0,T]) = \{t_1, \ldots, t_n: 0 = t_1 < t_2 < \cdots < t_n \leq T\}$ is an n-partition of the interval $[0, T]$. The calibration problem is an example of an "inverse problem", since we know the forward function f_t which enables us to compute the price if we know θ, but we do not know how to explicitly recover θ if we know the price.

However, before attempting to find the solution θ, it is first necessary to ascertain whether a stable solution exists at all.

Well-posedness

We call a mathematical problem "well posed" if it satisfies Hadamard's criteria:[3]

(i) for all admissible data, a solution exists;

(ii) for all admissible data, the solution is unique;

(iii) the solution depends continuously on the data.

If, on the other hand, a mathematical problem violates one or more of the above criteria, then we call it "ill posed". Parameter identification problems are often ill posed. In the context of calibration, we start by assuming we can find a solution fitting the data to within an acceptable error tolerance, δ say, and hence satisfying (i). The classical example where this is not given is the Black–Scholes model, where a single volatility parameter cannot be chosen to simultaneously fit options with different strikes and maturities to an acceptable level. Such models would not be adequate in practice, and we assume that the class of models is sufficiently rich to contain models which fit the prices to an acceptable degree, in which case we often cannot guarantee properties (ii) and (iii). The effects of violating either of these two properties will be seen for pricing and hedging.

A good example for this is the local volatility model, which extends the Black–Scholes model by allowing the volatility to depend on both time and the spot price. Dupire's Formula (Dupire 1994) provides an explicit expression of this volatility function in terms of option values for a continuum of strikes and maturities. However, finitely many data – as are observable in practice – do not suffice to pin down the infinite-dimensional parameter.

If there is more than one possible solution, ie, more than one calibrated parameter, then we call the inverse problem "underdetermined". This happens when we do not have enough market prices to restrict the value of the calibrated parameter. In this situation, choosing the wrong calibrated parameter will lead to incorrect pricing and hedging of other options, which can result in losses for a trading agent.

Furthermore, the admissible data is almost always noisy (the values are only observed with added error as in Equation 5.4), so we assume the true values to lie within some confidence interval around the observed value. In our context, prices are never observed exactly, but only to within a bid–ask spread. So the bid–ask spread can be thought of as this error confidence interval.

If a solution does not depend continuously on the data, ie, market prices, then a small mis-pricing in the market of one of the observed prices can lead to a disproportionately large error in the chosen calibrated parameter. This is again drastically exemplified by the local volatility model, which is extremely ill conditioned with respect to noisy observations even when the surface is discretised. And again, this results in incorrect pricing and hedging of other (exotic) contracts.

Regularisation

We call the process of approximating an ill-posed problem by a well-posed problem "regularisation". A vast literature[4] exists on handling ill-posed problems and especially ill-posed inverse problems.

Let us consider a general inverse problem in which we know the forward function f and want to solve

$$f(\theta) = V, \quad \theta \in \Theta, \; V \in \mathcal{V} \qquad (5.5)$$

for finite-dimensional θ, but do not know the inverse function f^{-1}. Θ is the parameter set, eg, the set of discretised local volatility functions in the context of the previous section, and $\mathcal{V}$ is the image set, eg, the set of quoted prices for vanilla instruments. Suppose further that we can only observe an approximation V^δ for V,

$\|V^\delta - V\|_\mathcal{V} \leqslant \delta$ with some observation error norm, and are instead trying to solve $f^{-1}(V^\delta) = \theta^\delta$. Assume that f^{-1} does not satisfy Hadamard's condition (ii) and/or (iii) from the previous section.

The most widely used approach to regularisation is to replace f^{-1} by a regularisation operator f_λ^{-1} with regularisation parameter $\lambda > 0$ which depends on δ and/or V^δ. The operator and parameter are chosen so that

$$\lambda = \lambda(\delta, V^\delta) > 0$$
$$f_\lambda^{-1}: \mathcal{V} \to \Theta \text{ is bounded for all } \lambda \in (0, \lambda_0)$$
$$\limsup_{\lambda \to 0} \{\|f_\lambda^{-1}(V^\delta) - f^{-1}(V^\delta)\|_\Theta\} = 0$$

This ensures that $(f_\lambda^{-1}(V^\delta) =:)\theta_\lambda^\delta \to \theta^\delta$ as $\lambda \to 0$ (Engl *et al* 1996).

It still remains, however, to find a regularisation operator and parameter. There are several methods for doing so:[5] using the spectrum of operator f, using Fourier, Laplace and other integral transformations.[6]

A common way to address the potential non-existence of a solution is to replace Equation 5.5 by a minimisation (least-squares) problem for the calibration error

$$\|g(\theta^\delta)\|_\mathcal{V} = \|f(\theta^\delta) - V^\delta\|_\mathcal{V}$$

and to address the non-uniqueness and stability by adding a stabilising function $h: \Theta \to \mathbb{R}$. Hence, our original problem (Equation 5.5) becomes

$$\text{find the } \theta^\delta \text{ which minimises } \|g(\theta)\|_\mathcal{V}^2 + \lambda h(\theta) \qquad (5.6)$$

An appropriate choice for h varies from problem to problem, but common practice is to take a Tikhonov functional (Tikhonov *et al* 1977). The Tikhonov functional favours solutions with smaller $h(\theta)$. In the context of calibrating local volatility, different functionals, composed of (potentially higher-order) Sobolev semi-norms of the local volatility function, have been proposed by various authors, originating with Jackson *et al* (1999), and including Crepey (2003), Egger and Engl (2005) and Achdou (2005).

However, this formulation for h usually has no immediate financial meaning, but rather is taken for mathematical convenience in terms of proofing regularisation properties. A noteworthy exception in several respects is the work of Berestycki *et al* (2002), where the regularisation functional is motivated by an asymptotic analysis of the implied volatility for short time-to-maturity and far in-the-money and out-of-the-money options. The Bayesian framework, in contrast, offers a way to attach financial meaning to the regularisation term.

Bayesian framework

Bayesian theory can be used to estimate the value of an unknown parameter and to quantify its uncertainty.[7] It provides a rigorous framework for combining prior information with observations to calculate likely values. It provides a natural way of "smoothing" inverse and regression problems (Green and Silverman 1994). Suppose we wish to estimate the value of some (finite-dimensional) parameter θ. Assume we have some prior information for θ (for example, that it is positive or represents a smooth function), summarised by a prior density $p(\theta)$ for θ. And suppose we observe some noisy data $V = \{V_t : t \in Y_n\}$ (which in our case usually represents the observed option prices)

$$V_t = f_t(\theta^*) + e_t$$

for all $t \in Y_n$, where θ^* is the true parameter, e_t is some random noise, Y_n is an index set of size n and $f_t(\theta)$ is the option price at time t given model parameter θ. Note that this is a special case of Equation 5.4 with one observation per time t, ie, $|I_t| = 1$ for all t. In what follows, by abuse of notation, the function p will depend upon its argument. Then $p(V \mid \theta)$ is the probability of observing the data V given θ, and is called the likelihood function.

Now, an application of Bayes's Rule implies that the posterior density of θ is given by

$$p(\theta \mid V) = \frac{p(V \mid \theta) p(\theta)}{p(V)} \qquad (5.7)$$

where the normalising constant $p(V)$ is given by

$$p(V) = \int p(V \mid \theta) p(\theta) \, d\theta$$

and it is assumed that $\theta \in \mathbb{R}^M$ for finite M.

Definition 5.3. A function $L \colon \mathbb{R}^{2M} \to \mathbb{R}$ is a loss function if and only if

$$L(\theta, \theta') = 0 \quad \text{if } \theta' = \theta$$
$$L(\theta, \theta') > 0 \quad \text{if } \theta' \neq \theta$$

where $\theta, \theta' \in \mathbb{R}^M$.

Definition 5.4. Given data V and loss function L, a corresponding Bayes estimator $\theta_L(V)$ is a value of θ which minimises the expected loss with respect to the posterior, ie

$$\theta_L(V) = \underset{\theta'}{\operatorname{argmin}} \left\{ \int_\Theta L(\theta, \theta') p(\theta \mid V) \, d\theta \right\} \qquad (5.8)$$

Note that the minimiser $\theta_L(V)$ is not necessarily unique. However, Gupta and Reisinger (2007) show that, for a certain class of loss functions and suitable calibration options, the Bayesian estimator can be proved to be consistent; that is, as more data is observed and the estimator updated, the estimate converges to the true value.

It is worth remarking that, for particular combinations of prior and likelihood function, both Gaussian for example, and a 0-1 loss function (Lehmann and Casella 1998), the minimisation formulation of Equation 5.8 is equivalent to Equation 5.6. In this sense, the Bayesian approach can be seen as a reformatting of the regularisation framework presented in the previous section (Fitzpatrick 1991).

Example 5.5. Consider claims C_i with corresponding observations

$$V^{(i)} = \tfrac{1}{2}(V^{(i)\,\text{bid}} + V^{(i)\,\text{ask}})$$

pricing functions

$$f^{(i)}(\theta) = \mathbb{E}^{Q_\theta}[C_i]$$

noises

$$e^{(i)} \sim N\left(0, \frac{S_0^2}{10^8} \delta_i^2\right)$$

and weights

$$w_i = [\tfrac{1}{4}|V^{(i)\,\text{bid}} - V^{(i)\,\text{ask}}|^2]^{-1}$$

The likelihood function is then fixed. For the prior we use a Gaussian density $\exp\{-\tfrac{1}{2}\lambda\|\theta\|^2\}$, where $\|\cdot\|$ is some norm of the finite-dimensional parameter θ which summarises model θ (with abuse of notation to simplify it). The posterior equation (Equation 5.7) then becomes

$$p(\theta \mid V) \propto \exp\{-\tfrac{1}{2}\lambda\|\theta\|^2\}$$
$$\times k \exp\left\{-\frac{1}{2}\frac{10^8}{\delta^2 S_0^2}\sum_{i\in I}\frac{4|\mathbb{E}^{Q_\theta}[C_i] - V^{(i)}|^2}{|V^{(i)\,\text{bid}} - V^{(i)\,\text{ask}}|^2}\right\}$$
$$= k \exp\left\{-\frac{1}{2}\left[\frac{10^8}{\delta^2 S_0^2}\sum_{i\in I}\frac{4|\mathbb{E}^{Q_\theta}[C_i] - V^{(i)}|^2}{|V^{(i)\,\text{bid}} - V^{(i)\,\text{ask}}|^2} + \lambda\|\theta\|^2\right]\right\}$$

where k is a normalising constant, $\delta^2 = \sum_i w_i \delta_i^2$ and λ is a predefined constant indicating how strongly we believe in our prior assumptions. Observe that the Bayesian prior takes the role of the regularisation term and gives an interpretation for the regularisation parameter λ in Equation 5.6. Under the Bayesian framework, λ is viewed as the confidence parameter, ie, the strength of our belief in the prior assumptions.

Bayesian pricing and hedging

In the previous section, we described how to find the Bayesian posterior $p(\theta \mid V)$ and Bayesian estimator $\theta_L(V)$ for the unknown parameter θ. We now consider how these two quantities can be used to price and hedge contracts. There are three obvious approaches that can be taken, as detailed below: a naive Bayesian method, a partial Bayesian method and a full Bayesian method. Although the first is most commonly used in practice, and the second is conceptually simpler, the third method better uses the full power of the Bayesian approach and gives robust results. To clarify the three methods we reference the Black–Scholes delta hedge, but a similar method can be used for any hedge parameter.

(i) Naive Bayesian method: only the Bayesian estimator $\theta_L(V)$ is used. Examples of this method are least squares or the maximum *a posteriori* (MAP) estimator (Coleman *et al* 2001). The price of a different contract X with payoff h^X on S is taken to be

$$f_t^X(\theta_L(V)) = \mathbb{E}^{\mathbb{Q}}[B^{-1}(t,T)h^X(S(\theta_L(V))) \mid (S_u)_{0 \leqslant u \leqslant t}] \quad (5.9)$$

Similarly, the Black–Scholes delta hedge for X at time t is taken to be

$$\Delta(\theta_L(V)) = \frac{\partial f_t^X(\theta_L(V))}{\partial S_t}$$

This is a naive approach because the full information of the problem, as captured by the posterior distribution $p(\theta \mid V)$, is ignored.

(ii) Partial Bayesian method (Branger and Schlag 2004): this method uses the full Bayesian posterior $p(\theta \mid V)$ to average over the prices and deltas, so instead of finding the price in the Bayesian average model, it finds the Bayesian average model price and delta. More specifically, the price of contract X is given by

$$\int_\Theta f_t^X(\theta) p(\theta \mid V) \, d\theta \qquad (5.10)$$

and the hedge is given by

$$\int_\Theta \frac{\partial f_t^X(\theta)}{\partial S_t} p(\theta \mid V) \, d\theta$$

This is only a partial approach because the price should correspond to the strategy which most closely hedges the contract X and there is no guarantee or intuition for why the above hedge should do this.

(iii) Full Bayesian method (Gupta and Reisinger 2009): this method uses the precise formulation of Equation 5.8 with the posterior $p(\theta \mid V)$ and for a suitable choice of loss function L. Suppose that $\tilde{L}(\theta, \theta')$ corresponds to a measure of the hedging error caused by hedging contract X using parameter θ' when the correct hedge is found using parameter θ. Then

$$\theta_{\tilde{L}}(V) = \underset{\theta'}{\text{argmin}} \left\{ \int_\Theta \tilde{L}(\theta, \theta') p(\theta \mid V) \, d\theta \right\} \qquad (5.11)$$

gives the optimal parameter to use for hedging and pricing X. In particular, we would take

$$f_t^X(\theta_{\tilde{L}}(V)) = \mathbb{E}^{\mathbb{Q}}[B^{-1}(t, T) h^X(S(\theta_{\tilde{L}}(V))) \mid (S_u)_{0 \leqslant u \leqslant t}]$$

for the price of the contract X and

$$\Delta_t(\theta_{\tilde{L}}(V)) = \frac{\partial f_t^X(\theta_{\tilde{L}}(V))}{\partial S_t}$$

as the delta hedge ratio. In this way we use the full information of the Bayesian posterior and the power of the loss function. Moreover, the hedge and price we use actually corresponds to a calibrated model, unlike for the previous method.

Advantages and disadvantages of Bayesian approaches

For solving inverse problems in derivative pricing, the Bayesian framework offers some advantages over the regularisation method introduced earlier. Point estimates $\theta_L(V)$ are useful, but of limited use without some measure of their correctness. The Bayesian approach offers a formal and consistent way to attach confidence to estimates. Equally, the approach provides a rigorous way to incorporate all available information regarding the unknown parameter, clearly differentiating between the *a priori* and observed information.

With special choices for the prior and likelihood, we can actually recover the regularisation operator in Equation 5.6 and the MAP estimator is equivalent to the solution of Equation 5.6. However, the advantage of the Bayesian approach is that we also discover a natural value for the regularisation parameter λ. As remarked earlier (see page 155 onwards), λ can be thought of as the confidence in the prior beliefs. This is important because in the regularisation method λ is often found through trial and error. The choice of stabilising term is often *ad hoc* or non-rigorous and therefore unsatisfactory. In the Bayesian framework, however, each term is meaningful and non-arbitrary.

Opponents of the Bayesian approach to data analysis often argue that it is fundamentally wrong to treat an unknown model parameter as a random variable and attach a distribution to it. They argue that the model parameter is unknown but not random. However, in some cases it is as important to be able to measure the uncertainty of a model parameter as it is to find the model parameter. One method of measuring the potential error is precisely to put a distribution on the model parameter and regard it as a random variable.[8] A second argument against the use of Bayesian theory is that the prior is inappropriate and meaningless, that scientists should not analyse data with any preconceptions or bias. However, in the mathematics of this chapter, the prior is a neat method of formally incorporating underlying assumptions. For example, no-arbitrage assumptions can be incorporated into the prior by attaching zero prior probability to parameters which introduce arbitrage opportunities for calibration instruments.

Other, more practically minded, opponents of the Bayesian methodology sometimes argue that the assignment of probabilities to different parameters is too arbitrary, subjective and difficult. For example, Cont (2006) argues that assigning weights to models "requires too much probabilistic sophistication on the part of the end user". However, the view here is that, because the calibration problem is ill-posed, we must draw on additional information not reflected in the prices of calibration instruments, and a prior naturally and unavoidably arises. Whether we choose to call the regularisation adjustment a roughness penalty function or smoothing term or prior is, in the opinion of the authors, a preference more of terminology than philosophy. Moreover, it is not even important that the prior should be very accurate or very carefully deliberated over; in typical option-pricing problems, the choice of a particular prior has less impact on the result. Indeed, if the estimator is updated by new observations, Gupta and Reisinger (2007) show that this estimator is consistent.

Given a Bayesian posterior distribution has been found, a variety of useful analyses can be performed:

- **Credible sets** (also known as confidence intervals) can be generated by finding sets of the parameter space which capture a certain proportion of the distribution. For example, if θ is scalar, then taking an interval holding 95% of the distribution, with 2.5% in each tail, gives a centred confidence interval for the unknown parameter.

- **Marginal distributions** of a component of θ can be found by integrating the joint posterior with respect to the other components. Viewing the marginal distribution of each component is useful in understanding how sensitive the joint posterior is to each of the components of θ and also how much each component can vary.

- **Inferences** can be made about another quantity of interest, W say, that is a function of θ. The spread of W can be measured and hence the errors associated with using a single point estimate for θ can be calculated.

With respect to the third item, we can make inferences regarding the model uncertainty of a claim; this is the subject of the following section.

MODEL UNCERTAINTY MEASURES

Having identified how model uncertainty can arise in the parameter-estimation problem, we now study measures of valuing this uncertainty. Risk measures are used in practice to determine the amount of capital to be held in reserve to make a risky position acceptable. Market risk measures like value-at-risk (VaR) are constructed on the implicit premise that a model for the market has been identified, and a risk measure $\rho(X)$ for a contract (or future net worth) X is calculated within this model. Further examples are coherent and convex measures as introduced in Artzner *et al* (2002), Frittelli and Gianin (2002) and Föllmer and Schied (2002), which form the motivation for the following.

In market risk, the random variable X is understood to be random through its dependence on a "state of nature" $\omega \in \Omega$, ie, $X = X(\omega)$. In the context of the previous section, this would indicate the dependence on the path realised by the standard Brownian motion Z. If the model and all its parameters are known, this determines the law of X. However, the philosophy of this chapter is to acknowledge that the model/parameter $\theta \in \Theta$ is not known, and we make this explicit by writing $X(\omega, \theta)$, and ρ^{P_θ} for the corresponding market risk measure under model θ.

In this section, instead of referring to different model types and different model parameters, we simply refer to different models. This is to emphasise that the measures presented can be applied very generally to either competing model types and/or a fixed model type with competing parameters.

The approaches described in this section all propose ways of accounting for this model uncertainty, but differ in the way they aggregate market risk and model uncertainty into a combined risk measure, or conversely how they separate out a model uncertainty measure from an overall measure of risk. A further divide can be drawn between measures based on worst-case scenarios within the assumed set of models, and those incorporating distributional information on the probabilities imposed on models/parameters, inferred, eg, from Bayesian analysis.

When it comes to measuring the model uncertainty of a derivative contract, it appears both logically consistent and practically relevant to associate with X a hedging portfolio with a hedge parameter Δ, and to then apply one of the measures of the next two subsections (see pages 162 and 163). Then $X = X(\omega, \theta, \Delta)$, where θ is the true parameter and Δ is, for example, determined by hedging according to a model with parameter θ', in which case we write $X = X(\omega, \theta, \theta')$ for clarity. A simple example would be a European option which is priced and hedged under a Black–Scholes model with assumed volatility σ', when the true volatility is actually σ (so in this problem the unknown parameter "θ" is the scalar Black–Scholes volatility parameter "σ").

The measures of the final three subsections of this section are aimed at measuring the model uncertainty reflected in the spread of derivative prices more directly. Taking a view on hedging, they implicitly make the assumption that the distribution of (model) option prices $f_t(\theta)$, derived from a (posterior) distribution for the unknown parameter θ, is a good indicator for the model uncertainty present in the subsequent hedging strategy. This will be justified for vanilla options but can underestimate the uncertainty for more exotic derivatives.

Risk-averaging measures

Branger and Schlag (2004) consider Bayesian market risk measures which are close in spirit to the philosophy of this book. For a set Θ of candidate models θ, denote as above the probability of model θ by $p(\theta)$. $\mathbb{P}_\theta$ is the probability measure for the set of future scenarios corresponding to model θ and $\rho^{\mathbb{P}_\theta}(X)$ is the market risk measure of contract X under $\mathbb{P}_\theta$. Then Branger and Schlag define two different Bayesian methods of integrating market and model risk: model integration and risk integration.

In the first method, model integration, Branger and Schlag (2004) define the weighted market measure $\mathbb{P}$ and the consequent market risk measure as follows

$$\rho(X) = \rho^{\mathbb{P}}(X), \quad \text{where } \mathbb{P} = \sum_{\theta \in \Theta} p(\theta)\mathbb{P}_\theta \qquad (5.12)$$

Observe that there is a degree of symmetry in the above expression: $\mathbb{E}^{\mathbb{P}}[X]$ can be viewed as a double sum (or double integral in the infinite model and scenario case) over the different models and scenarios.

For the second method, risk integration, Branger and Schlag (2004) define the weighted market risk measure by

$$\rho(X) = \sum_{\theta \in \Theta} p(\theta)\phi(\rho^{\mathbb{P}_\theta}(X)) \qquad (5.13)$$

for some model risk aversion function ϕ. ϕ is increasing and taken as convex if the decision maker is model risk averse, linear if the decision maker is model risk neutral and concave if the decision maker is model risk preferring. $\phi(x) = x^n$ for different $n \geq 1$ are proposed as possible convex functions. Note that Branger and Schlag (2004) measure market risk and model risk together, whereas an agent might find it useful to have a value for each separately.

Risk-differencing measures

Kerkhof *et al* (2002) look to quantify model uncertainty with a view to determining how much regulatory capital should be set aside. They specify model uncertainty μ as the difference between the worst-case market risk measure ρ and some reference market risk measure corresponding to reference model $\alpha \in \Theta$

$$\mu(X) = \sup_{\theta \in \Theta} \rho^{\mathbb{P}_\theta}(X) - \rho^{\mathbb{P}_\alpha}(X) \tag{5.14}$$

where each model θ in Θ corresponds to measure $\mathbb{P}_\theta$ and so gives a different market risk $\rho^{\mathbb{P}_\theta}(X)$ for claim X.

This model uncertainty measure is interpretable as a conservative premium to be allocated in addition to the market risk measure in the assumed model α, to account for uncertainty of the true model. For the actual form of ρ, Kerkhof *et al* (2002) suggest a number of alternatives: VaR, the coherent market risk measures introduced by Artzner *et al* (2002), worst conditional expectation and tail conditional expectation.

Worst-case measures

Suppose we observe claims C_i, with corresponding observable bid–ask spreads $[V^{(i)\,\text{bid}}, V^{(i)\,\text{ask}}]$ for $i \in I$, that we use as a calibration set and a set of models Θ. As before, let $\mathbb{Q}_\theta$ represent the risk-neutral probability measure for asset price process S corresponding to the model θ for S. Now assume that

$$\text{for all } \theta \in \Theta, \quad \mathbb{E}^{\mathbb{Q}_\theta}[C_i] \in [V^{(i)\,\text{bid}}, V^{(i)\,\text{ask}}] \quad \text{for all } i \in I \tag{5.15}$$

ie, all measures $\theta \in \Theta$ reproduce benchmark options to within their bid–ask spreads.

Let $\mathcal{X} = \{X \colon \forall \theta \in \Theta,\ \mathbb{E}^{\mathbb{Q}_\theta}[|X|] < \infty\}$ be the set of all contingent claims that have a well-defined price in every model. Define Φ to be the set of admissible trading strategies ϕ such that

$$\mathbb{E}^{\mathbb{Q}_\theta}\left[\int_0^t \phi_u \,\mathrm{d}S_u\right] = 0$$

for all $\theta \in \Theta$. For simplicity, we assume the risk-free rate of growth is zero, so there is no discounting.

Cont (2006) defines a function $\mu \colon \mathcal{X} \to [0, \infty)$ to be a model uncertainty measure if it satisfies Equation 5.15 and the following four axioms.

A1. For benchmark options, the model uncertainty is no greater than the uncertainty of the market price

$$\text{for all } i \in I, \quad \mu(C_i) \leqslant |V^{(i)\,\text{bid}} - V^{(i)\,\text{ask}}|$$

A2. Model-dependent dynamic hedging with the underlying does not reduce model uncertainty, since the hedge is model dependent

$$\text{for all } \phi \in \Phi, \quad \mu\left(X + \int_0^T \phi_t \, dS_t\right) = \mu(X)$$

But if the value of a claim can be totally replicated in a model-free way using only the underlying, then the claim has zero model uncertainty

if $\exists x \in \mathbb{R}, \phi \in \Phi$ such that, for all $\theta \in \Theta$,

$$X = x + \int_0^T \phi_t \, dS_t, \quad \theta\text{-a.s., then } \mu(X) = 0$$

A3. Diversification does not increase the model uncertainty of a portfolio

for all $X_1, X_2 \in \mathcal{X}$ and for all $\lambda \in [0,1]$,

$$\mu(\lambda X_1 + (1-\lambda) X_2) \leqslant \lambda \mu(X_1) + (1-\lambda) \mu(X_2)$$

A4. Static hedging of a claim with traded options is bounded by the sum of the model uncertainty of that claim and the uncertainty in the cost of replication

for all $X \in \mathcal{X}$ and for all $a \in \mathbb{R}^d$,

$$\mu\left(X + \sum_{i=1}^d a_i C_i\right) \leqslant \mu(X) + \sum_{i=1}^d |a_i| |V^{(i)\,\text{bid}} - V^{(i)\,\text{ask}}|$$

Cont (2006) shows that the function

$$\mu_0(X) = \sup_{\theta \in \Theta} \{\mathbb{E}^{Q_\theta}[X]\} - \inf_{\theta \in \Theta} \{\mathbb{E}^{Q_\theta}[X]\} \quad (5.16)$$

is a measure of model uncertainty, ie, it satisfies Equation 5.15 and the axioms (A1)–(A4). The measure finds the difference between the highest and lowest prices in Θ. It is called the "worst-case" measure because it finds the largest difference amongst the collection of prices $\mathbb{E}^{Q_\theta}[X]$ for contract X.

Cont (2006) generalises the above to the case when not all the models θ satisfy Equation 5.15, and instead assumes only that there exists at least one model θ that satisfies Equation 5.15. Under subtle modification of the axioms (A1)–(A4), Cont proposes the function

$$\mu_0^*(X) = \sup_{\theta \in \Theta}\{\mathbb{E}^{Q_\theta}[X] - \alpha_0(\theta)\} - \inf_{\theta \in \Theta}\{\mathbb{E}^{Q_\theta}[X] + \alpha_0(\theta)\} \quad (5.17)$$

with the convex penalty functional α_0 defined by

$$\alpha_0(\theta) = \|\mathbb{E}^{Q_\theta}[C] \triangleright V\|$$

where $\|\cdot\|$ is a vector norm on $\mathbb{R}^{|I|}$ and

$$(\mathbb{E}^{Q_\theta}[C] \triangleright V)_i = \max\{V^{(i)\,\text{bid}} - \mathbb{E}^{Q_\theta}[C_i], \mathbb{E}^{Q_\theta}[C_i] - V^{(i)\,\text{ask}}, 0\}$$

as a model uncertainty measure. It is a "penalised worst-case" measure because it finds the largest difference amongst the collection of penalised prices $\mathbb{E}^{Q_\theta}[X] - \alpha_0(\theta)$ for contract X. Note the penalisation $\alpha_0(\theta)$ reflects the calibration error, ie, the difference between market prices V and corresponding model prices $\mathbb{E}^{Q_\theta}[C]$ of the benchmark options C.

Coherent measures

Motivated by the coherent model uncertainty measures introduced by Cont (2006), Gupta and Reisinger (2008) look at defining coherent model uncertainty measures which are more in spirit with the coherent market risk measures introduced by Artzner et al (2002). Gupta and Reisinger measure the distribution of $-2|\mathbb{E}^{Q_\theta}[X] - x|$ in Θ (we have already taken the expectation over the scenarios ω) for some fixed point x. The authors cite the following properties that should be expected of model uncertainty measures.

- Function of spreads: the "spread" of a claim X is the set of the prices for X found by all the different models.
- Monotonicity: if the spread of prices for Y is greater than that for X, then the model uncertainty for Y should be greater than for Y.
- Sub-additivity: claims X and Y have a combined spread less than or equal to the sum of the individual spreads so the uncertainty measure should reflect this.
- Homogeneity: the spread for X should scale linearly with the number of claims X.

An example of a coherent measure is the "average-value" coherent measure given by

$$\mu_1(X) = E^Q[2|\mathbb{E}^{Q_\theta}[X] - M^Q[\mathbb{E}^{Q_\theta}[X]]|]$$

where $M^Q[\mathbb{E}^{Q_\theta}[X]]$ is the median value of $\mathbb{E}^{Q_\theta}[X]$ with respect to some measure Q on the set of models θ and the expectation E is also taken with respect to measure Q on Θ.

Convex measures

Motivated by the convex model uncertainty measures introduced by Cont (2006), Gupta and Reisinger (2008) construct a set of axioms for convex model uncertainty measures which more closely follow those introduced by Frittelli and Gianin (2002) for convex market risk measures. Gupta and Reisinger drop the assumption that all or any models θ in the model set Θ satisfy Equation 5.15. A variety of convex model uncertainty measures is likely to be far more applicable than coherent measures, since it is atypical to find a large set of perfectly calibrated models.

Suppose $p(\theta \mid V)$ is as given in Example 5.5. Then one example of a convex measure is

$$\mu_\lambda^*(X) = \sup_{\theta \in \Theta}\{\mathbb{E}^{Q_\theta}[X] - \alpha_\lambda(\delta_\theta)\} - \inf_{\theta \in \Theta}\{\mathbb{E}^{Q_\theta}[X] + \alpha_\lambda(\delta_\theta)\}$$

where the convex penalty functional α is given by

$$\alpha_\lambda(\delta_\theta) = \frac{S_0}{10^4}\left[-2\delta^2 \log \frac{p(\theta \mid V)}{k}\right]^{1/2}$$

$$= \left[\sum_{i \in I} w_i |\mathbb{E}^\theta[C_i] - V^{(i)}|^2 + \lambda \|\theta\|^2\right]^{1/2}$$

Observe that the confidence parameter, λ, plays a crucial role in determining the size of the model uncertainty values for contract X.

Worked example

Each surface is a sample of the posterior so is equally opaque. t, time in years; σ, volatility; S, asset price.

We continue with the numerical example presented in Examples 5.1 and 5.2. Using the Markov chain Monte Carlo Metropolis sampling algorithm described in Gupta and Reisinger (2007), we can sample the Bayesian posterior $p(\theta \mid V)$ constructed in Example 5.5, where the unknown parameter θ represents a discretised

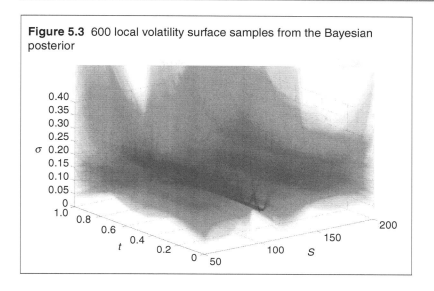

Figure 5.3 600 local volatility surface samples from the Bayesian posterior

Table 5.3 Different model uncertainty values for the barrier option

Model uncertainty measure	Value	Percentage of Bayes price
Penalised worst-case	0.80	10.6
Convex	0.77	10.3

The model uncertainty measures are calculated using the Bayesian posterior $p(\theta \mid V)$.

local volatility surface. Figure 5.3 shows a sample of 600 local volatility surfaces calibrated to an average of 3bp. Note the variety of shapes of local volatility surfaces.

With these samples, we can construct a distribution for the prices of derivatives. Recall the three-month up-and-out barrier call option we priced in Table 5.2 with strike $0.9S_0$ and barrier $1.10S_0$. The Bayesian posterior $p(\theta \mid V)$ gives the distribution of prices plotted in Figure 5.4. In this graph we have shown the MAP price 7.62, computed using Equation 5.9 and the Bayesian price 7.47, computed by Equation 5.10.

Next, using this distribution of prices, we can compute different model uncertainty measures for derivatives as described above, and we give examples for the penalised worst-case and convex measures.

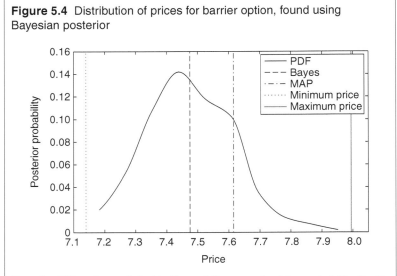

Figure 5.4 Distribution of prices for barrier option, found using Bayesian posterior

From the 600 surfaces plotted in Figure 5.3 we construct the probability density function of the price of the barrier option and display the associated MAP and Bayes price. The Bayes price is calculated by an approximation to Equation 5.10 using the 600 sample surfaces. Also shown are the minimum and maximum prices calculated from the 600 surfaces.

We use the Bayesian posterior $p(\theta \mid V)$ to construct these model uncertainty measures as follows.

1. Penalised worst-case measure: price the claim X in models $\theta \in \Theta$ and take supremums and infimums. Note that Θ is the set of parameters θ with positive posterior density.

2. Convex measure: take the Bayesian posterior $p(\theta \mid V)$ and select confidence parameter $\lambda = 1$ in order to get an even trade-off between the penalisation from the prior and the likelihood function.

The results are shown in Table 5.3.

We observe from Figure 5.4 that both these values, 0.80 and 0.77, capture the size of the interval over which the majority of the probability density function is concentrated. The convex measure is simply a generalisation of the penalised worst-case and allows the decision maker to tune the measure using λ according to their confidence in prior beliefs.

CONCLUSION

Decision rules for regulators and risk-managers

In practice, a "yes–no" rule-of-thumb for judging whether a contract X has a model uncertainty value $\mu(X)$ that is too high would be useful for regulators and risk-managers. The VaR measure for market risk is widely used to make the following kind of decision

$$\text{reject } X \text{ if } \text{VaR}_{0.01}(X) > c_\rho$$

ie, do not buy X if the smallest loss of X in the worst 1% of scenarios is greater than c_ρ. Thus we could identically construct a yes–no rule for model uncertainty measure μ, such as

$$\text{reject } X \text{ if } \mu(X) > c_\mu$$

ie, do not buy X if the model uncertainty value $\mu(X)$ is greater than c_μ. The value of c_μ should depend on the investor's risk preferences or there could be industry-standard values set by regulators. For example, c_μ could be taken as 10% of the time-0 price V_0^X of X. The obvious generalisation is to aggregate market risk and model uncertainty with a combined rule such as

$$\text{reject } X \text{ if } \text{VaR}_{0.01}(X) + \mu(X) > c$$

for some c. Then note that, if $\text{VaR}_{0.01}(X) + \mu(X) < 0$, we would always buy X, since positive returns are made in all combinations of market scenarios and models.

Summary

At the start of this chapter the distinction between (market) risk and (model) uncertainty was clarified. Possible sources of model uncertainty were detailed and explained. The model selection problem for derivative pricing was formally presented, first in the case of model-free pricing and then in the case of parameter estimation. For the second case, a robust Bayesian solution was detailed. We next studied five classes of model uncertainty measures. An example using a discretised local volatility surface was given to demonstrate the use of model uncertainty measures and the consequence on pricing derivatives. Finally, decision rules were proposed for risk-managers and regulators.

Recommended further reading

We briefly highlight a few publications of interest related to pricing and hedging under model uncertainty, measures of model uncertainty, Bayesian approaches and the topics presented in this chapter.

The application of Bayesian theory to calibration problems in mathematical finance, although not a novel idea, is something that has only gathered weight since the early 1990s; Jacquier *et al* (1994) showed that Bayes estimators for a particular class of stochastic volatility models outperform the widely used method of moments and quasi-maximum likelihood estimators. More recently, Bhar *et al* (2006) and Para and Reisinger (2007) have considered dynamic Bayesian approaches to calibrating instantaneous spot and forward interest rates respectively.

Recently, attention has turned to using the Bayesian framework to examine the implications of parameter uncertainty in financial models. Jobert *et al* (2006) consider a Bayesian approach to explain the consistently large observed excess return earned by risky securities over the return on Treasury bills. They argue that, by dropping the assumption that the parameters of the dividend process are known to an agent but instead the agent only has some prior beliefs of these parameters, the excess rates of return are a natural consequence. Similarly, Monoyios (2007) examines the effects of drift parameter uncertainty in an incomplete market in which claims on non-traded assets are optimally hedged by a correlated traded asset. Using Bayesian learning, Monoyios (2007) concludes that terminal hedging errors are often very large. Jacquier and Jarrow (2000) look at the effect on parameter uncertainty and model error in the Black–Scholes framework. They use Bayes estimators to infer values for option prices and hedge ratios and assess non-normality of the posterior distributions.

Closer to the example of the local volatility model used in this chapter are the works by Darsinos and Satchell (2007a,b). Darsinos and Satchell (2007a) formulate a joint prior for the asset price S_t and the Black–Scholes implied constant volatility σ using historical log returns of the asset price. The prior is updated using newly observed returns to give the posterior. The posterior is then transformed to a function of the asset price S_t and Black–Scholes European call price c and marginalised to give the probability density function for the option price c. Darsinos and Satchell (2007b) use this density to forecast European call option prices one day ahead and numerical experiments show substantial improvement to benchmark mean implied volatility procedures, especially in terms of hedging profits.

Green and Figlewski (1999) conduct an empirical study into the market and model risk exposures faced by an agent trading European calls and puts. They consider different volatility forecasting methods based on historical data and apply the methods to four underlyings: S&P 500 Index, three-month US dollar Libor, 10-year Treasury yield and the Deutschmark Exchange Rate. Their first finding is that the strategy of writing and holding option positions without hedging produces very large risk exposures, even over long horizons, and diversification does not significantly reduce this risk exposure. After daily delta re-hedging was added to the portfolios, Green and Figlewski (1999) found that the standard deviation, mean and worst-case returns were all reduced. However, worst-case losses were still several times the initial premium, particularly for out-of-the-money contracts. They conclude that writing options with volatility mark-ups (of up to 50%) turns a very risky trading strategy into a profitable one. By writing an option with a volatility mark-up we mean that the value of the volatility used in the calculation of the price is greater (ie, "marked up") than the volatility actually estimated from the data. This gives a price greater than would have been found with the original estimated volatility and is thus a safer price for an agent to sell the option for. This finding, Green and Figlewski conclude, indicates that the model risk from mis-estimating volatility in trading and hedging derivatives positions is very large.

In contrast, Hull and Suo (2002) look at the model risk from mis-specification of the model rather than mis-estimation. They consider the pricing errors arising from a continually recalibrated local volatility model. They price a compound option, a European call option on a European call option and a barrier option. They find that the continually recalibrated local volatility model always correctly prices European style options, where the payoff is contingent on the asset price at just one time. However, for exotic options dependent on the distribution of the asset price at two or more times, the model can perform badly.

Hull and Suo (2002) argue that this failure of the local volatility surface is to be expected. They explain that the local volatility model is designed to match European options correctly but not options dependent on the value of the underlying asset at multiple times. Let $\phi_n(t_1, \ldots, t_n)$ be the joint probability distribution of the asset price at times $t_1, \ldots, t_n$ and $\phi_1(t_1), \ldots, \phi_n(t_n)$ be the marginal distributions of the asset price at times $t_1, \ldots, t_n$, respectively. Then Hull and Suo (2002) point out that the local volatility model is designed so that all the marginals $\phi_1(t_1), \ldots, \phi_n(t_n)$ are correct but in no way correctly reproduce $\phi_n(t_1, \ldots, t_n)$ or any other joint probability distribution. And this is fundamental to why different local volatility surfaces can be fitted to the same calibration prices (marginals) as we saw in Chapter 4, but why these surfaces give very different prices for exotic and path dependent options (joint distributions). This point is further clarified by Britten-Jones and Neuberger (2000), who show how very different volatility processes can be adjusted to fit the same observed option prices exactly; hence the prevalence of high model uncertainty.

Contreras and Satchell (2003) use a Bayesian approach to construct confidence intervals for the VaR measure. They design priors for the mean μ and standard deviation σ of VaR(X) for some claim X, and update these statistics using the observed data. However, because VaR is not sub-additive or convex, it can lead to anomalous values for a portfolio of options (Artzner *et al* 2002). For example, we can easily find two options such that the VaR of the portfolio of two options is greater than the sum of the individual VaRs.

> The authors are grateful for financial support from the UK Engineering and Physical Sciences Research Council (EPSRC).

1   See also the discussion in Chapter 16 of Volume I.

2   See *NA Digest* v.09 n.48 (http://www.netlib.org/na-digest-html/09/v09n48.html) for details.

3   See, for example, Engl *et al* (1996).

4   See, for example Engl *et al* (1996) and Tikhonov *et al* (1977).

5   See Tikhonov *et al* (1977) for details.

6   Bouchouev and Isakov (1999) offer a good overview of applications in financial markets.

7   An introduction into Bayesian statistics in general and its computational methods is given in Chapters 1 and 2 of Volume I; other valuable references are Lehmann and Casella (1998) and Gelman *et al* (2004).

8   See Lindley (2006) for a very readable introduction to uncertainty.

REFERENCES

Achdou, Y., 2005, "An Inverse Problem for Parabolic Variational Inequalities in the Calibration of American Options", *SIAM Journal of Control* 43(5), pp. 1583–1615.

Artzner, P., F. Delbaen, J. M. Eber and D. Heath, 2002, "Coherent Measures of Risk", in *Risk Management: Value at Risk and Beyond*, p. 145 (Cambridge University Press).

Avellaneda, M., A. Lévy and A. Paras, 1995, "Pricing and Hedging Derivative Securities in Markets with Uncertain Volatilities", *Applied Mathematical Finance* 2, pp. 73–88.

Berestycki, H., J. Busca and I. Florent, 2002, "Asymptotics and Calibration of Local Volatility Models", *Quantitative Finance* 2(1), pp. 61–9.

Bhar, R., C. Chiarella, H. Hung and W. J. Runggaldier, 2006, "The Volatility of the Instantaneous Spot Interest Rate Implied by Arbitrage Pricing: A Dynamic Bayesian Approach", *Automatica* 42(8), pp. 1381–93.

Bouchouev, I., and V. Isakov, 1999 "Uniqueness, Stability and Numerical Methods for the Inverse Problem that Arises in Financial Markets", *Inverse Problems* 15, pp. 95–116.

Branger, N., and C. Schlag, 2004, "Model Risk: A Conceptual Framework for Risk Measurement and Hedging", Technical Report, Goethe University.

Britten-Jones, M., and A. Neuberger, 2000, "Option Prices, Implied Price Processes, and Stochastic Volatility", *The Journal of Finance* 55(2), pp. 839–66.

Chance, D. M., 2008, "Rational Rules and Boundary Conditions for Option Pricing", Teaching Note 99-05.

Coleman, T. F., Y. Li and A. Verma, 2001, "Reconstructing the Unknown Local Volatility Function", in *Quantitative Analysis in Financial Markets: Collected Papers of the New York University Mathematical Finance Seminar*, p. 192 (World Scientific).

Cont, R., 2006, "Model Uncertainty and Its Impact on the Pricing of Derivative Instruments", *Mathematical Finance* 16(3), pp. 519–47.

Cont, R., and P. Tankov, 2004, *Financial Modelling with Jump Processes* (London: Chapman & Hall/CRC Press).

Contreras, P., and S. E. Satchell, 2003, "A Bayesian Confidence Interval for Value-at-Risk", Cambridge Working Papers in Economics.

Cox, A. M. G., and J. K. Obłój, 2008, "Robust Hedging of Double Touch Barrier Options", Arxiv Preprint arXiv:0808.4012.

Cox, A. M. G., and J. K. Obłój, 2009, "Robust Pricing and Hedging of Double No-Touch Options", Arxiv Preprint arXiv:0901.0674.

Crepey, S., 2003, "Calibration of the Local Volatility in a Trinomial Tree Using Tikhonov Regularization", *Inverse Problems* 19(1), pp. 91–127.

Cvitanić, J., H. Pham and N. Touzi, 1999, "Super-Replication in Stochastic Volatility Models under Portfolio Constraints", *Journal of Applied Probability* 36(2), pp. 523–45.

Darsinos, T., and S. Satchell, 2007a, "Bayesian Analysis of the Black–Scholes Option Price", in S. Satchell (ed), *Forecasting Expected Returns in the Financial Markets*, p. 117 (Elsevier).

Darsinos, T., and S. Satchell, 2007b, "Bayesian Forecasting of Options Prices: Natural Framework for Pooling Historical and Implied Volatility Information", in S. Satchell (ed), *Forecasting Expected Returns in the Financial Markets*, p. 151 (Elsevier).

Derman, E., 1996, "Model Risk", *Risk Magazine* 9(5), pp. 34–7.

Dupire, B., 1994, "Pricing with a Smile", *Risk Magazine* 7(1), pp. 18–20.

Egger, H., and H. W. Engl, 2005, "Tikhonov Regularization Applied to the Inverse Problem of Option Pricing: Convergence Analysis and Rates", *Inverse Problems* 21(3), pp. 1027–45.

Engl, H. W., M. Hanke and A. Neubauer, 1996, *Regularization of Inverse Problems* (Kluwer Academic).

Fitzpatrick, B. G., 1991, "Bayesian Analysis in Inverse Problems", *Inverse Problems* 7(5), pp. 675–702.

Föllmer, H., and A. Schied, 2002, "Convex Measures of Risk and Trading Constraints", *Finance and Stochastics* 6(4), pp. 429–47.

Frey, R., 2000, "Superreplication in Stochastic Volatility Models and Optimal Stopping", *Finance and Stochastics* 4(2), pp. 161–87.

Frey, R., and C. A. Sin, 2001, "Bounds on European Option Prices under Stochastic Volatility", *Mathematical Finance* 9(2), pp. 97–116.

Frittelli, M., and E. R. Gianin, 2002, "Putting Order in Risk Measures", *Journal of Banking and Finance* 26(7), pp. 1473–86.

Gelman, A., J. B. Carlin, H. S. Stern and D. B. Rubin, 2004, *Bayesian Data Analysis*, Second Edition (London: Chapman & Hall/CRC).

Green, P. J., and B. W. Silverman, 1994, *Nonparametric Regression and Generalized Linear Models: A Roughness Penalty Approach* (London: Chapman & Hall/CRC).

Green, T. C., and S. Figlewski, 1999, "Market Risk and Model Risk for a Financial Institution Writing Options", *The Journal of Finance*, pp. 1465–99.

Gupta, A., and C. Reisinger, 2007, "Calibrating Financial Models Using a Consistent Bayesian Estimator", Preprint.

Gupta, A., and C. Reisinger, 2008, "Model Uncertainty Measures in Finance Using Bayesian Posteriors", Working Paper.

Gupta, A., and C. Reisinger, 2009, "Optimal Bayesian Hedging", Working Paper.

Heston, S. L., 1993, "A Closed-Form Solution for Options with Stochastic Volatility with Applications to Bond and Currency Options", *Review of Financial Studies* 6(2), pp. 327–43.

Hull, J., and W. Suo, 2002, "A Methodology for Assessing Model Risk and Its Application to the Implied Volatility Function Model", *The Journal of Financial and Quantitative Analysis* 37(2), pp. 297–318.

Jackson, N., E. Suli and S. Howison, 1999, "Computation of Deterministic Volatility Surfaces", *Journal of Computational Finance* 2(2), pp. 5–32.

Jacquier, E., and R. Jarrow, 2000, "Bayesian Analysis of Contingent Claim Model Error", *Journal of Econometrics* 94, pp. 145–80.

Jacquier, E., N. G. Polson and P. E. Rossi, 1994, "Bayesian Analysis of Stochastic Volatility Models", *Journal of Business and Economic Statistics* 12(4), pp. 371–89.

Jobert, A., A. Platania and L. C. G. Rogers, 2006 "A Bayesian Solution to the Equity Premium Puzzle", Report, Statistical Laboratory, University of Cambridge.

Kerkhof, F. L. J., B. Melenberg and J. M. Schumacher, 2002, "Model Risk and Regulatory Capital", CentER Discussion Paper 2002-27, pp. 1–57.

Knight, F. H., 1921, *Risk, Uncertainty and Profit* (New York: Houghton Mifflin).

Lehmann, E. L., and G. Casella, 1998, *Theory of Point Estimation* (Springer).

Li, D. X., 2000, "On Default Correlation: A Copula Approach", *Journal of Fixed Income* 9(4), pp. 43–54.

Lindley, D. V., 2006, *Understanding Uncertainty* (Chichester: John Wiley & Sons).

Lyons, T. J., 1995, "Uncertain Volatility and the Risk-Free Synthesis of Derivatives", *Applied Mathematical Finance* 2, pp. 117–33.

Monoyios, M., 2007, "Optimal Hedging and Parameter Uncertainty", *IMA Journal of Management Mathematics* 18(4), p. 331.

Mykland, P. A., 2009, "Option Pricing Bounds and Statistical Uncertainty: Using Econometrics to Find an Exit Strategy in Derivatives Trading", Technical Report, University of Chicago.

Para, H., and C. Reisinger, 2007, "Calibration of Instantaneous Forward Rate Volatility in a Bayesian Framework", Working Paper.

Swishchuk, A., A. Ware and H. Li, 2008, "Option Pricing with Stochastic Volatility Using Fuzzy Sets Theory", Northern Finance Association 2008 Conference Papers.

Tikhonov, A. N., V. Y. Arsenin and F. John, 1977, *Solutions of Ill-Posed Problems* (Washington, DC: VH Winston).

Part II

Credit Risk

6
Predictions Based on Certain Uncertainties: A Bayesian Credit Portfolio Approach

Christoff Gössl
UniCredit

The analysis of default probabilities and correlations within credit-risky portfolios is usually strongly affected by the scarce availability of data. High standard deviations and a fair amount of uncertainty in the derived estimates are well-known consequences of this. However, these volatilities are usually ignored when deriving predictions in a second stage and only point estimators are used, giving a false appearance of accuracy. The aim of this chapter is to show how a consideration of these uncertainties will affect this second-stage analysis. For this purpose, a credit portfolio approach is introduced in a Bayesian framework and the joint posterior distribution of default probabilities and correlation parameters is derived. Furthermore, we quantify the effects that a consideration of this distribution would have with respect to the prediction of portfolio risk figures and for the pricing of structured derivatives.

Historic default time series are a natural data source for predicting the future evolution of credit-risky instruments. In addition to the estimation of individual default rates, the estimation of potential dependencies between elements of the portfolio plays an important role in this context, particularly for the assessment of portfolio risk. In several publications approaches have been presented to quantify the default probabilities of different rating classes and the correlations within and between industries.[1]

Credit portfolio management and the structured finance sector are, for example, two areas where the findings of the above approaches are utilised. In both areas an accurate description of the risks inherent to credit portfolios is essential. In credit portfolio management and structured finance, the calculated maximum likelihood estimators for default probabilities and correlations are used to assess the future risk of a portfolio of interest, where risk is in many cases defined as a certain quantile of the portfolio loss distribution. However, in these applications the fact that parameter estimates are random variables themselves is in general not taken into account. Even though in most publications standard deviations or errors of estimators due to the limited sample size and data quality are conspicuously displayed, these uncertainties about the accuracy of the parameters used are usually ignored. Because of the supposedly complex distributions of, and dependency structures between, the parameters, in classic statistics consideration of these relationships is also far from straightforward. Furthermore, the measurement error problem in itself is the subject of a complete research area, as is obvious from the other chapters in this book.

Bayesian models in general have already been introduced for a wide range of applications. Due to its underlying idea and theoretical simplicity, hierarchical Bayesian modelling allows for the formulation and solution of a wide range of complex questions and problems. The quantification of multi-dimensional distributions and stochastic restrictions, as well as the incorporation of temporal- and spatial-dependency structures, forms the foundation of the success of the Bayesian paradigm. Moreover, the benefits of incorporating prior information in order to mitigate the consequences of sparse databases and measurement error environments are well known. In this chapter we mainly focus on the development of a credit portfolio model within the Bayesian framework. One advantage of such a Bayesian approach is the ability to easily overcome the problems mentioned above. Using adequate estimation techniques within a Bayesian framework, it is possible to derive and make available the joint distribution of a set of parameters conditional on a given set of observations, rather than a few descriptive statistics. This distribution could then be used in a second inferential stage to take into account the randomness of derived default probability and correlation estimates, and to assess the likely effects with respect to risk figures and pricing.

The aim and the structure of this chapter are as follows. The first part briefly recapitulates the basic principles of the Bayesian approach, with emphasis on its inherent fundamental paradigm switch. We present a short summary of the standard estimation approach for Bayesian models: the Markov Chain Monte Carlo (MCMC) methods. In the second part of the chapter, a simple application of the Bayesian paradigm to the credit risk sector will first be proposed to show its potential. After the formulation of a Bayesian standard one-factor credit portfolio model, estimates for individual rating-dependent probabilities of default (PDs) and the portfolio correlation are derived from rating agency data. As this could also easily be done within the classical framework, in addition the joint dependency structures between these parameters are quantified and the benefits and implications that these results will have when applied to the calculation and prediction of risk figures are shown for particular portfolios.

Throughout the chapter, all densities will be denoted by $p(\cdot)$ and all distribution functions will be denoted by $P(\cdot)$. The context should reduce potential confusion regarding the corresponding probability spaces. Finally, the focus of this chapter is on a Bayesian approach to assess the effects of parameter uncertainty in portfolio modelling; a general comparison of frequentist and Bayesian techniques is presented in Chapter 7.

THE BAYESIAN APPROACH

The fundamental idea of Bayesian statistics builds on the Bayes Theorem[2]

$$\pi(\theta \mid x) = \frac{\pi(x, \theta)}{\pi(x)}$$
$$= \frac{f(x \mid \theta)\pi(\theta)}{\int f(x \mid \theta)\pi(\theta)\,d\theta} \quad (6.1)$$

describing the relation between a set of observed data x and some unknown parameters θ. Inherent to the theorem is the basic difference between Bayesian and classical approaches in statistics: the assumption that the model parameters, though unknown, are nevertheless no longer fixed. It is supposed that these parameters also have a distribution, comparable to the observed data sample. This distribution can and must be specified. This so-called prior distribution, $\pi(\theta)$, is now combined with the information about the parameters contained in the data sample, the likelihood function $f(x \mid \theta)$, to form a posterior distribution $\pi(\theta \mid x)$ of parameters conditional on the observed data. This is sometimes also called a "learning process" or an update of the prior information with the data sample. The resulting posterior distribution finally holds all the information regarding the parameters, contributed once by the priors and once by the observed data. To calculate the posterior, one part is built by the standard likelihood function of the observed data conditional on the unknown parameters and the other part is covered by the prior of the parameters.

For the formulation of these priors, two general cases can be distinguished. The first is where substantial prior information is available. This can be in the form of specific distributions or samples from previous analyses and can be expressed as a distributional assumption, which does not necessarily have to be in an analytical or parametrical form. For example, prior knowledge can be elicited from expert opinion as described in great detail in Part 2 of Volume I of this book. This information, then, is evidently a natural choice for prior distributions. The second case is where there is very little or no prior information available. In this case this non-existent information also has to be translated into a distributional assumption. For this purpose, over-dispersed or flat priors are usually applied. This includes, for example, uniform distributions on the unit interval $\mathcal{U}(0,1)$ for probabilities, or flat normal distributions $\mathcal{N}(0,s^2)$ for metric unrestricted parameters, with a sufficiently large variance s^2 ($\gg 1,000$) to allow for a practically over-dispersed distribution on a reasonable interval. So-called "conjugate priors" can also be used to allow for an analytic solution for the posterior in fairly simple settings. For more detail on this subject see Chapter 1 of Volume I.

As a general remark, it is the formulation of the prior distributions that offers the flexibility of the Bayesian approach. Parameters which change smoothly over time can be described by autoregressive random-walk priors. Two-dimensional versions of these can also be used to introduce spatial dependencies into the estimation, where differences in the parameter values of neighbouring observations are penalised, yielding a smooth parameter surface. Robust spatial priors, using Cauchy or Student distributions, can even be used to describe edges within the surface. And, as a matter of fact, the use of latent variables with adequate prior distributions to achieve conditional independence, as also applied in the factor models for credit portfolios, is one of the most frequently used ideas in Bayesian statistics, as many examples in Gilks *et al* (1996) show.

ESTIMATION: MCMC METHODS

Even though the Bayes Theorem has been known since the 18th Century and the Bayesian paradigm of a learning process and its advantages have been widely discussed in statistics, a major drawback until the last few decades of the 20th Century was the fact that, apart from some simple and analytically tractable settings, the denominator of Equation 6.1 could not be determined. The posterior could be quantified only up to a normalising constant, making it almost impossible to analyse its characteristics because standard direct Monte Carlo methods like rejection or importance sampling could not be applied. Even though the principles of algorithms which were able to overcome this limitation had been presented by Metropolis *et al* (1953) and Hastings (1970), only the dramatic increase in computational power in the 1990s finally allowed their application to statistics. Once initiated by the publication of, for example, Besag *et al* (1991), Smith and Roberts (1993) and Gilks *et al* (1996), the MCMC techniques soon became the methods of choice in Bayesian statistics because of their flexibility, robustness and almost unlimited applicability. Chapter 2 of Volume I gives an in-depth introduction into the field of MCMC methods.

In general, the main goal of MCMC approaches is to generate a sample from the posterior distribution of the parameters, based on which estimators can be calculated and conclusions regarding higher-order dependencies between parameters can be drawn. Many Bayesian models can be implemented and estimated using freely available software packages, such as WinBUGS (Spiegelhalter *et al* 2003) or BayesX (Lang *et al* 2004). Within these packages, samples from the posterior distributions are generated using Gibbs or Metropolis–Hastings algorithms. Furthermore, advanced monitoring tools are supplied to ensure mixing properties and convergence of the Markov chains used. Sample means or medians are well-established point estimators for the unknown parameters. If over-dispersed priors are applied, taking the posterior mode as estimator would yield results comparable to the maximum-likelihood framework. However, because in practice the mode is empirically quite difficult to determine exactly, even for massive samples in high-dimensional settings, the statistics given above are usually used. The highest posterior density regions can be used as the Bayesian analogue of classical confidence intervals.

A SIMPLE BAYESIAN CREDIT PORTFOLIO MODEL

In the second part of this chapter the Bayesian idea will be applied to the credit risk sector. In the following, let us consider a portfolio of N credit-risky instruments or assets a_i, $i = 1, \ldots, N$, each comprising one unit. Each of these assets can be classified into one of a finite number of risk classes $r_i \in \{R_1, \ldots, R_K\}$, defining its risk profile completely. The risk or rating classes have individual one-year probabilities of default p_{R_j}, $j = 1, \ldots, K$, with the asset PDs $p_i = p_{R_j}$ for $r_i = R_j$. Further, let us suppose the respective instruments follow a one-factor asset-value model, as introduced by Merton (1974) and Vasicek (1991). In this framework it is assumed that an instrument or firm defaults when its asset-value process X_i falls below the firm's liabilities or a certain default frontier. The corresponding default frontier or threshold is determined by its individual risk profile or risk class r_i. In its discrete version on a one-year horizon, the underlying asset return process is defined as

$$\left. \begin{array}{l} X_i = \sqrt{\rho} Y + \sqrt{1-\rho} Z_i, \quad i = 1, \ldots, N \\ \rho \in [0,1], \quad Y \sim \mathcal{N}(0,1), \quad Z_i \sim \mathcal{N}(0,1) \text{ iid} \end{array} \right\} \quad (6.2)$$

The process is the sum of a common systematic risk factor Y, which is invariant throughout the portfolio, and an idiosyncratic component Z_i resembling the independent individual contribution of asset i to its evolution over time. These two components are weighted by a correlation parameter, ρ, which determines the intra-portfolio dependencies within the whole portfolio.[3] This model also corresponds to the restrictions R1 and R3 of Gordy and Heitfield (2003). Even though there may be criticisms about the adequacy of this simplifying approach, it is perfectly well suited for the ideas to be shown in this chapter. Potential generalisations to more flexible multi-factor approaches should be obvious. With the above default probabilities, we can write the following relation

$$P(\text{asset } i \text{ defaults}) = P(X_i < k_i) = p_i \implies k_i = \Phi^{-1}(p_i) \quad (6.3)$$

Further, conditional on the systematic risk factor Y, this equation becomes

$$P(\text{asset } i \text{ defaults} \mid Y = y) = P(X_i < k_i \mid Y = y) = p_{i|y}$$

$$\Longrightarrow p_{i|y} = \Phi\left(\frac{\Phi^{-1}(p_i) - \sqrt{\rho}y}{\sqrt{1-\rho}}\right) \quad (6.4)$$

completing a generalised linear model for Bernoulli data with a probit link function. Using the conditional independence of the elements on the factor Y and the grouping into homogeneous risk classes further allows us to specify the joint probability distribution of observing a certain number l_{R_j} of defaults in the respective risk classes of the portfolio comprising n_{R_j} assets

$$L_{j|Y=y} = \sum_{r_i=R_j} \mathbf{1}_{D_i|Y=y}, \quad j = 1, \ldots, K,$$

$$P(L_1 = l_1, \ldots, L_K = l_K \mid Y = y) = \prod_{j=1}^{K} \mathcal{B}(n_{R_j}, p_{j|y}, l_{R_j})$$

with $\mathcal{B}(n,p,k)$ the standard binomial distribution. This model is referred to as the binomial mixture model. Without loss of generality, and for simplicity, at this point it is supposed that, in the case of default, every obligor suffers the same loss of one unit, ie, their loss given default is 100%. General concepts of loss severity or loss given defaults should not be too difficult to incorporate. The complete conditional likelihood function for period t and for a one-year horizon can be rewritten in a concise form, defining

$$L_t = (L_{t,1}, \ldots, L_{t,K})$$
$$n_t = (n_{t,1}, \ldots, n_{t,K})$$
$$p = (p_{R_1}, \ldots, p_{R_K})'$$

and considering the unknown parameters, namely the latent factor variables and the asset correlation

$$P(L_t = l_t \mid n_t, p, \rho, y_t) = \prod_{j=1}^{K} \mathcal{B}(n_{t,R_j}, p_{j|y_t}, l_{t,R_j}) \quad (6.5)$$

As pointed out in the section on the Bayesian approach (see page 181), to complete the Bayesian portfolio model it remains only to specify the prior distributions in addition to the likelihood function. Let us assume a case with no substantial prior information and therefore flat priors for the parameters p_{R_j} and ρ. For the systematic risk factors of each year y_t a normal prior is applied in accordance with the model assumptions (Equation 6.2). Then, exploiting the serial independence of observations, this yields the complete Bayesian credit portfolio approach and the corresponding posterior distribution of the unknown parameters (p, ρ, y) conditional on the observations (n, l)

$$P(p, \rho, y \mid n, l) = \frac{\prod_{t=1}^{T} P(L_t = l_t \mid n_t, p_{y_t}, \rho, y_t) p(p) p(\rho) p(y)}{P(L = l \mid n)}$$

$$p_{y_t} = (p_{1|y_t}, \ldots, p_{K|y_t})'$$

$$p_{j|y} = \Phi\left(\frac{\Phi^{-1}(p_{R_j}) - \sqrt{\rho} y}{\sqrt{1-\rho}}\right)$$

$$p_{R_j} \sim \mathcal{U}(0,1), \text{ iid}, \quad j = 1, \ldots, K, \quad \rho \sim \mathcal{U}(0,1),$$

$$y = (y_1, \ldots, y_T)', \quad y_t \sim N(0,1), \text{ iid}, \quad t = 1, \ldots, T$$

(6.6)

with $\mathcal{U}(0,1)$ as the uniform distribution in the unit interval. In general, the denominator $P(L = l \mid n)$ can be calculated by integrating the numerator of Equation 6.6 with respect to the parameters p, ρ and y. Indicated by the priors above, in this chapter the correlation between instruments is assumed to be positive, even though this is known to be the subject of a lively discussion. The above model is easily estimated using the WINBUGS package and in the remainder of the chapter its application to historic Standard & Poor's rating agency default data will be discussed in detail.

APPLICATION: ANALYSIS OF HISTORIC DATA

The data which we use to illustrate the Bayesian approach was published in Standard & Poor's default report (Standard & Poor's 2005). In this report, beginning in 1981, the numbers of rated companies and also the fraction defaulting are listed according to their respective rating categories. Even though agency data is also available for AAA and AA rated classes, the analysis is restricted to the lower-rated grades, beginning with the A class. By doing this we can avoid the difficult question of whether the lack of observing a significant number of defaults in these higher classes is the result of a very conservative classification, or whether it is the actual consequence

Table 6.1 Descriptive statistics for the marginal posterior distributions of the asset correlation and the default probabilities per rating class

	Rating class					
	A	BBB	BB	B	CCC	ρ
Historical mean	0.0004	0.0023	0.0107	0.0561	0.2813	
Mean	0.0006	0.0029	0.0123	0.0591	0.2789	0.0941
Standard deviation	0.0003	0.0010	0.0031	0.0095	0.0257	0.0357
2.5%	0.0002	0.0016	0.0079	0.0445	0.2328	0.0449
25%	0.0004	0.0022	0.0102	0.0526	0.2613	0.0690
Median	0.0005	0.0027	0.0118	0.0578	0.2772	0.0873
75%	0.0007	0.0034	0.0137	0.0642	0.2949	0.1115
97.5%	0.0014	0.0055	0.0198	0.0817	0.3341	0.1826

The table shows mean, standard deviation, median and certain quantiles for the marginal posterior distributions of the asset correlation and the default probabilities per rating class according to model Equation 6.6.

or manifestation of correlation. It should also be pointed out that the real data examples in this chapter are used for illustrative purposes only and should be understood as such. No efforts were undertaken to validate the data beforehand, but the published default data was assumed to be suitable for the model presented, ie, to fulfil the assumptions made in the previous section. With this data, our initial aim is to derive

- the joint posterior distribution of average default frequencies of the rating classes,
- the portfolio correlation,
- the systematic risk-factor time series.

We generated joint posterior distribution samples of 25,000 observations using Markov chains with a length of 2,200,000 and taking every 80th state of the chains, with a burn-in phase of 200,000 iterations. By using this strategy, autocorrelations and convergence diagnostics of the algorithm reached sufficiently low levels. Table 6.1 shows a number of descriptive statistics of the marginal posterior distributions of the asset correlation and the default probabilities

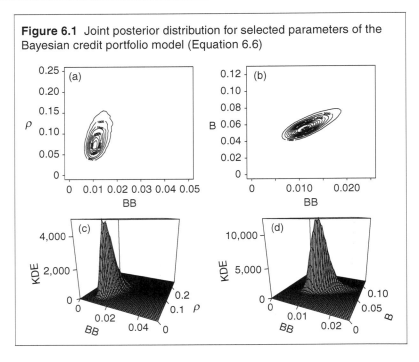

Figure 6.1 Joint posterior distribution for selected parameters of the Bayesian credit portfolio model (Equation 6.6)

per rating class. Figure 6.1 displays two-dimensional contour plots, as well as kernel density estimates for selected two-dimensional marginal distributions. In addition, in Figure 6.2 the posterior mean of the systematic risk-factor time series is shown together with its 97.5% and 2.5% quantiles.

It can easily be verified that for rating classes A to B the results for the average PDs are slightly higher than the average number of defaults over time. The use of the arithmetic mean as a Bayesian point estimator should be the most likely reason for these differences. Especially for skewed distributions such as the observed (see, for example, parts (c) and (d) of Figure 6.1), shifts of the arithmetic mean towards the heavier tails are to be expected in comparison to the posterior mode, which would be more similar to the classic likelihood estimator. Furthermore, the estimate for the correlation factor is roughly at the same level compared to the results of Gordy and Heitfield (2003) for restrictions R1 and R3, and the results of Servigny and Renault (2003). Besides the explanations already mentioned, changes in the underlying data and the sensitivity of this parameter even to slight data changes should contribute most to the

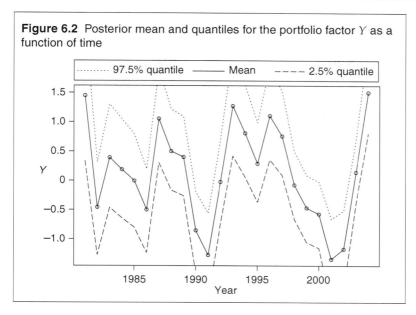

Figure 6.2 Posterior mean and quantiles for the portfolio factor Y as a function of time

differences. As a back-test, the approximate Bayesian posterior mode has been also derived for the data used by Servigny and Renault (2003), with similar results compared with their estimated portfolio correlation of 6.3%. For these numbers, due to the highly skewed correlation distribution, the posterior mean was at 7.9%. However, particularly notable are the high standard deviations, particularly for the higher rating classes and also for the correlation parameter, which indicates a fair amount of uncertainty in these estimates. The time series of the systematic risk factors themselves are not remarkably different from the results when solving Equation 6.4 for the variable Y, using frequentistic estimates for the correlation and, for example, the PD estimate for class CCC. Nevertheless, at least one important difference exists between classical solutions for this problem and the Bayesian results. For all the parameters mentioned, a sample of their joint posterior distribution exists. Particularly with respect to the systematic risk factors, parameters do not have to be estimated using a back-fitting algorithm or a two-step approach; they can be derived simultaneously. Instead of being confined to the Hessian or information matrix, the above sample allows us to additionally derive a whole variety of characteristics of their joint dependence structure, such as joint exceedance probabilities, etc, or simply to resample from it. For the remainder or this chapter, the

Table 6.2 Predictions of risk class-dependent loss distributions for infinitely granular homogeneous portfolios using the classical approach

	Rating class				
	A	BBB	BB	B	CCC
Mean	0.0006	0.0029	0.0123	0.0591	0.2790
Standard deviation	0.0008	0.0032	0.0110	0.0381	0.1039
1%	0.0000	0.0001	0.0009	0.0084	0.0860
5%	0.0000	0.0003	0.0019	0.0149	0.1259
10%	0.0001	0.0005	0.0028	0.0199	0.1519
25%	0.0001	0.0009	0.0049	0.0316	0.2025
Median	0.0003	0.0019	0.0091	0.0504	0.2694
75%	0.0007	0.0037	0.0160	0.0773	0.3452
90%	0.0014	0.0064	0.0256	0.1096	0.4193
95%	0.0020	0.0089	0.0333	0.1329	0.4662
99%	0.0039	0.0158	0.0534	0.1858	0.5532

The table shows predictions of risk class-dependent loss distributions as percentage loss of the portfolio for infinitely granular homogeneous portfolios using Equation 6.8.

latter aspect is of special interest. The problem of how to account for the estimators' uncertainties in the prediction simplifies dramatically with the joint distribution available. It reduces to a simple resampling problem.

APPLICATION: PREDICTIONS

One of the most important applications of the above results is the prediction of risk measures such as credit value-at-risk for particular portfolios. In classical approaches, unfortunately, only point estimators derived from historical data are used to assess this risk, in general neglecting any measurement problem. As pointed out, in the Bayesian framework this could be easily overcome because of the direct availability of a posterior distribution sample for the parameters. To show the remarkable effects an incorporation of the above-mentioned uncertainties can have, the default/loss distribution will be derived for homogeneous portfolios for all rating classes $r_i \in \{R_1, \ldots, R_K\}$, consisting of an infinite number of identical assets. To calculate the fraction of defaulting assets, in one case the historical point estimators are used and in the other case random samples are drawn from the joint posterior distribution. It is well known that

Table 6.3 Predictions of risk class-dependent loss distributions for infinitely granular homogeneous portfolios using the Bayesian approach

	Rating class				
	A	BBB	BB	B	CCC
Mean	0.0006	0.0029	0.0123	0.0591	0.2790
Standard deviation	0.0011	0.0039	0.0125	0.0408	0.1074
1%	0.0000	0.0001	0.0008	0.0072	0.0786
5%	0.0000	0.0003	0.0018	0.0144	0.1230
10%	0.0001	0.0004	0.0027	0.0196	0.1507
25%	0.0001	0.0009	0.0048	0.0314	0.2026
Median	0.0003	0.0018	0.0088	0.0497	0.2679
75%	0.0006	0.0035	0.0154	0.0758	0.3433
90%	0.0013	0.0063	0.0253	0.1092	0.4205
95%	0.0020	0.0090	0.0340	0.1354	0.4733
99%	0.0047	0.0182	0.0602	0.2029	0.5805

The table shows predictions of risk class-dependent loss distributions as percentage loss of the portfolio for infinitely granular homogeneous portfolios using Equation 6.9.

for an infinite uniform portfolio the default quote of the portfolio equals almost surely the conditional default probability $p_{i|y}$ given in Equation 6.4.[4] Hence, for the fraction l_{R_k} of defaulting assets in a portfolio of assets from risk class R_k, Equation 6.4 can be applied in the following context

$$l_{R_k}(p^*, \rho^*, y) = \Phi\left(\frac{\Phi^{-1}(p^*) - \sqrt{\rho^*}y}{\sqrt{1-\rho^*}}\right), \quad y \sim N(0,1) \quad (6.7)$$

I: classical approach $\quad p^* = \hat{p}, \quad \rho^* = \hat{\rho}$ \quad (6.8)

II: Bayesian approach $\quad (p^*, \rho^*) \sim P(p_{R_k}, \rho \mid n, l, y)$ \quad (6.9)

Thereby, the p^* and ρ^* are drawn from their posterior distribution. The arithmetic means from the same distribution are used as point estimators $\hat{p}$ and $\hat{\rho}$, to result in identical expected losses for the portfolios. Samples of 100,000 realisations have been generated. Tables 6.2 and 6.3 show some descriptive statistics of the default distributions; Figure 6.3 displays the corresponding kernel density estimates. In Figure 6.4 the differences in the quantiles, which are also observable in the tables, are illustrated by normalising them to the quantiles for approach I. In the tables and in the quantile plot, considerable increases of up to 20% in the 95% and 99% quantile

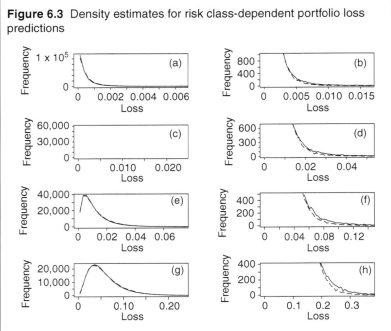

Figure 6.3 Density estimates for risk class-dependent portfolio loss predictions

Predictions are given as percentage loss of the portfolio. (a) Rating A; (b) tails for rating A; (c) rating BBB; (d) tails for rating BBB; (e) rating BB; (f) tails for rating BB; (g) rating B; (h) tails for rating B. The solid line denotes the Bayesian approach; the dashed line denotes classical approach.

values can be observed, moving from the classical to the Bayesian approach. This observation should be a direct consequence of the variation of the underlying parameters in the Bayesian approach and of the dependence between PDs and correlation parameter ρ, as can also be seen in Figure 6.1.

Two conclusions can be drawn from the above results for credit portfolio modelling: incorporating parameter uncertainties generally inherent in point estimators into a portfolio model in a second stage yields significantly increased quantiles and therefore increased risk figures in the predictions; this effect varies with the amount (or lack) of information available. In other words, the more reliable the point estimators are, the less additional risk is introduced in the predictions when accounting for their randomness. The effect is largest for the A rated class and decreases when going down the rating scale. Where there are only few defaults observable for a rating class, the estimated PD's standard deviation or uncertainty is quite a bit

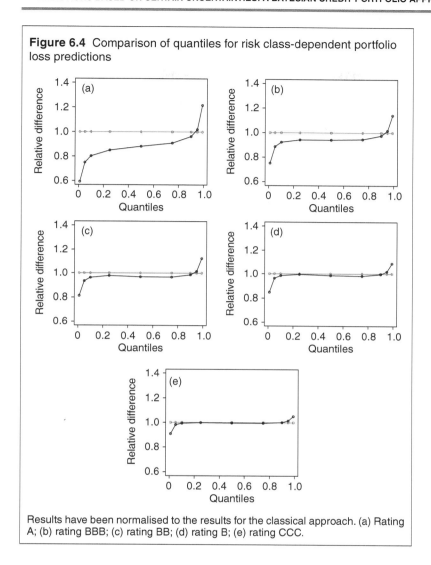

Figure 6.4 Comparison of quantiles for risk class-dependent portfolio loss predictions

Results have been normalised to the results for the classical approach. (a) Rating A; (b) rating BBB; (c) rating BB; (d) rating B; (e) rating CCC.

higher than for rating classes with very frequent defaults like the CCCs. Accordingly, the risk or unexpected number of defaults also increases. It should further be emphasised that we used the posterior mean in the point estimates for $\hat{p}$ and $\hat{\rho}$ in the classical approach to derive the above numbers. The increases in the quantiles should be even more prominent when applying the posterior mode, which is more comparable with the likelihood estimates. Due to the skewed posterior distributions, the posterior mode should be smaller than

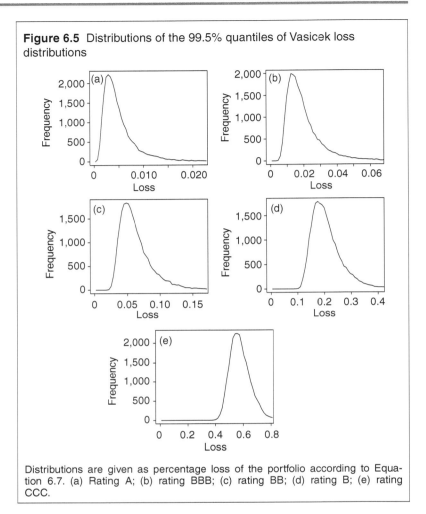

Figure 6.5 Distributions of the 99.5% quantiles of Vasicek loss distributions

Distributions are given as percentage loss of the portfolio according to Equation 6.7. (a) Rating A; (b) rating BBB; (c) rating BB; (d) rating B; (e) rating CCC.

the posterior mean and the quantiles in the classic approach should also be smaller. In this context, we can furthermore use the posterior samples to derive a distribution for a given function of the parameters p and ρ, eg, a certain quantile of a Vasicek portfolio loss distribution as defined by Equation 6.7. For each sample pair (p^*, ρ^*), any loss quantile for Equation 6.7 can be calculated directly. Consequently, for each rating class we obtain a distribution for the quantile of the Vasicek loss distribution, eg, the 99.5% quantile as displayed in Figure 6.5. However, it should be noted that these "quantile distributions" have a more illustrative character and give only an idea of how the uncertainty in the default probability and correlation estimates would translate into volatility in predictive parameters. It is important to note that for portfolio risk management purposes we would only use the Bayesian posterior loss distribution as derived in the previous paragraph. And for this loss distribution there exists only one 99.5% quantile which already takes into account all uncertainty regarding the underlying parameters.

Are the above results interesting from a portfolio manager perspective: what are the effects with respect to structured products, which also heavily depend on accurate portfolio modelling? Let us consider an arguably hypothetical transaction based on one of the above infinitely granular portfolios, eg, comprising BB assets. For simplicity and to avoid any complexities regarding multi-year PDs, we want to sell protection for one year on a tranche with an attachment point of 1.90% and a 1% thickness. The attachment point of 1.90% is chosen for mathematical convenience, as it coincides with the 99.5% quantile of the classic prediction's loss distribution. Furthermore, we are only concerned about the credit risk in this transaction. What would be the adequate price of this transaction? In other words, we want to calculate the probability of default and the expected loss for both scenarios

$$\text{PD} = P(l_{R_k}(p^*, \rho^*) > 0.019)$$

and

$$\text{EL} = \int_{0.019}^{0.029} l_{R_k}(p^*, \rho^*) - 0.019 \, dP(l_{R_k}(p^*, \rho^*))$$

By definition, in the standard setting we have a hitting probability of 50 basis points (bp) and the expected loss can be quantified with 23bp, resulting in a loss given default of 46%. Deriving these quantities for the Bayesian approach, the PD of this tranche turns out to be at 88bp, the expected loss increases to 50bp, thus yielding a loss given default of 57%. In other words, the incorporation of some "doubts" about the accuracy of the underlying parameters more than doubles the adequate price at which this protection should be sold. The effects on the rating of this tranche are evident and need not be mentioned.

DISCUSSION

The aim of this chapter was to introduce a Bayesian approach to the modelling of credit-risky portfolios. A Bayesian portfolio model was formulated, which allows us to describe default frequencies and intra-portfolio correlations. Furthermore, we have shown the implications that a consideration of the randomness of derived parameter estimates would have in a second stage when assessing portfolio risk. Those effects were analysed from a portfolio management point of view as well as for the purpose of pricing and rating credit portfolio derivatives.

Since 2000, publicly available models like the S&P "CDO Evaluator" or Fitch's "VECTOR" model have became more and more popular, particularly in the area of pricing and rating credit derivatives, and can without doubt be regarded as a commonly accepted industry standard. However, even though they are undoubtedly based on more sophisticated underlying factor models, they exemplify exactly the classic approach discussed in the previous section (see page 190). For ratings as well as for correlations, fixed estimates or parameters are used without any consideration of any sampling error or the dependence structure between them. Additionally, the fact that many predictions are made not only for the next year, as in the above example, but usually for time periods of between five and seven years makes the situation even more precarious. With an increasing number of parameters to estimate or calibrate, the effects of the small sample sizes usually present in this area should become increasingly important. This holds for multi-year PDs as well as for, say, industry-specific correlation levels. The latter might possibly be derived from the broader data basis of equity data. Nevertheless, due to the transfer from equity to asset or default correlations, this too would not solve the problem completely. When looking at the results of the portfolio model in Table 6.1, as pointed out, an interesting detail is the relation between the sample means and the corresponding standard deviations. For the higher rating classes and the correlation parameter, the standard error amounts to 30–50% of the mean. Comparable results can also be seen in Servigny and Renault (2003). The results are also in agreement with a general study on confidence intervals for default probabilities of Hanson and Schuermann (2005) and the findings in Chapter 7. An effect of this relation surfaces when omitting one or two years from the analysis. In general, it is assumed that the default data is serially independent, so this should pose no problem. However, changes of 5–10%, especially in the correlation parameter, are not unusual. This again raises the question of whether the use of relatively volatile point estimators is a sensible choice for deriving quantities down to basis-point precision. In Bayesian approaches as well as classical measurement error models, these problems surely do not vanish, but at least they are accounted for.

Models with latent variables are only one of a variety of Bayesian applications in statistics. Autoregressive hierarchical Bayesian models have already been applied in econometrics to macroeconomic problems such as unemployment durations or flat rent data. In addition, the use of substantial prior information for credit scoring has been analysed. As presented in the previous sections, Bayesian techniques also proved to be useful in the portfolio credit risk sector. Prospects for the future may therefore be a more thorough investigation of how more advantages of these approaches can be exploited, particularly in the area of credit risk. For example, the extension towards a multi-factor approach is obviously within reach. Furthermore, the use of time-series techniques to describe the temporal evolution of underlying systematic risk and portfolio factors is conceivable. For example, moving from a copula-induced single-period-factor model to temporal dependencies seems to be a reasonable idea.

1   See, for example, Demey *et al* (2004), Servigny and Renault (2003) and Gordy and Heitfield (2003).

2   For a general introduction on Bayesian methods, see Chapter 1 of Volume I.

3   An example where different correlations ρ_i, $i = 1, \ldots, K$, are assumed for different rating classes is given in Chapter 7.

4   See, for example, Bluhm *et al* (2003, Proposition 2.5.4).

REFERENCES

Besag, J., J. York and A. Mollie, 1991, "Bayesian Image Restoration with Two Applications in Spatial Statistics", *Annals of the Institute of Statistical Mathematics* 43(1), pp. 1–59.

Bluhm, C., L. Overbeck and C. Wagner, 2003, *An Introduction to Credit Risk Modeling* (Boca Raton, FL: Chapman & Hall/CRC).

Demey, P., J.-F. Jouanin, C. Roget and T. Roncalli, 2004, "Maximum Likelihood Estimate of Default Correlations", *Risk Magazine*, November, pp. 104–8.

Gilks, W. R., S. Richardson and D. J. Spiegelhalter, 1996, *Markov Chain Monte Carlo in Practice* (London: Chapman & Hall).

Gordy, M., and E. Heitfield, 2003, "Estimating Default Correlations from Short Panels of Credit Rating Performance Data", Working Paper, Federal Reserve Board.

Hanson, S., and T. Schuermann, 2005, "Confidence Intervals for Probabilities of Default", Technical Report, Federal Reserve Bank of New York.

Hastings, W. K., 1970, "Monte Carlo Sampling Methods Using Markov Chains and Their Applications", *Biometrika* 57, pp. 97–109.

Lang, S., A. Brezger and T. Kneib, 2004, "BayesX: Software for Bayesian Inference", Department of Statistics, University of Munich, URL: http://www.stat.uni-muenchen.de/~bayesx.

Merton, R. C., 1974, "On the Pricing of Corporate Debt: The Risk Structure of Interest Rates", *Journal of Finance* 29, pp. 449–70.

Metropolis, N., A. W. Rosenbluth, M. N. Rosenbluth, A. H. Teller and E. Teller, 1953, "Equations of State Calculations by Fast Computing Machines", *Journal of Chemical Physics* 21, pp. 1087–91.

Servigny, A. D., and O. Renault, 2003, "Correlation Evidence", *Risk Magazine* July, pp. 90–4.

Smith, A. F. M., and G. O. Roberts, 1993, "Bayesian Computation via the Gibbs Sampler and Related Markov Chain Monte Carlo Methods", *Journal of the Royal Statistical Society: Series B* 55, pp. 3–23.

Spiegelhalter, D. J., A. Thomas, N. Best and D. Lunn, 2003, "BUGS Software", MRC Biostatistics Unit, Institute of Public Health, Cambridge, UK, URL: http://www.mrc-bsu.cam.ac.uk/bugs.

Standard & Poor's, 2005, "Annual Global Corporate Default Study: Corporate Defaults Poised to Rise in 2005", Technical Report, Global Fixed Income Research.

Vasicek, O. A., 1991, "The Loan Loss Distribution", Technical Report, KMV Corporation.

7

Uncertainty in Credit Risk Parameters and Its Implication on Risk Figures

Christina R. Bender; Ludger Overbeck

d-fine GmbH; University of Giessen

In credit risk the derivation of the capital needed to support the riskiness of the business is usually based on expected loss and unexpected loss. The most important parameters driving these potential loss figures are default probabilities and correlations. Calibration and estimation of these parameters is usually obtained by statistical procedures which can be addressed as point estimation. This means that, as an output of the statistical analysis of the data, only a single value for each parameter is reported. For example, in order to estimate the default probability in a homogeneous cohort, we just take the empirical average loss observed in the cohort, ie, the empirical mean, as an estimator for the default probability. A major problem with such classical point-estimation techniques in credit risk is the large estimation errors caused by a very small number of observations (here 28 periods from 1981 to 2008). Errors in the parameter estimation are carried forward to estimation errors of the analysed risk figures, such as value-at-risk (VaR) or expected shortfall (ES), inducing model risk or, more precisely, parameter uncertainty. The consequences of such a mismeasurement by neglecting estimation risk might be purely financial (eg, additional costs, incorrect pricing or faulty loan loss reserves), but may also include cognitive and decision theoretical aspects as pointed out in Chapter 15 of Volume I. We therefore build frequentistic confidence and Bayesian credible regions of the parameters, which in turn imply confidence and credible intervals for our risk figures in order to quantify the amount of parameter uncertainty.

On the one hand, these intervals are established by deriving the (asymptotic) distribution of the parameters. We show that our parameters are asymptotically normal, ie, the parameter distributions are normal if the number of time periods is very large. The confidence intervals obtained are therefore called "asymptotic". Van der Vaart (1998) serves as a good reference for the necessary background in mathematical statistics. On the other hand, we apply Bayesian Monte Carlo methods to derive credible intervals of parameters and risk figures.

Specifically, Bayesian credible intervals are easy to interpret because they are based directly on a probability distribution for the parameter and not on the empirical data.[1] To show that these intervals are more realistic in comparison with the asymptotic approach, we focus on the simple but commonly used Gaussian Copula model with a large number of obligors. In this case, an analytical, non-asymptotic distribution of the parameters, and therefore non-asymptotic intervals, can be derived by common frequentist methods. Moreover, if we assume that no prior information about the parameters is available (corresponding to uniform prior distributions; see below), the Bayesian Monte Carlo approach yields the same intervals (up to a Monte Carlo error). The Bayesian method is therefore verified and can be applied to more complex model eg, in the case of smaller number of obligors. Chapter 6 presents an empirical study in this case.

In detail, our analysis utilises the one-factor Gaussian credit portfolio model, yielding a mixed binomial distribution for the number of losses. Assuming an "infinite" (or very large) number of obligors implies its infinite granular limit, the so-called Vasicek or Gordy distribution for the loss rate in a portfolio, which is often referred as the asymptotic single-risk-factor (ASRF) model. Note that, in both model variants (the mixed binomial and the ASRF) the losses in different years are assumed to be independent and identically distributed (iid) with default probability and correlation parameter (p, ρ). We thus work in the context of a through-the-cycle (TTC) calibration of both the default probability and the correlation.

Based on historical loss data provided by S&P's default study (2009) we consider, for both model variants, the frequentistic moment estimator (ME) and the maximum-likelihood (ML) principle to estimate default probabilities and correlations jointly.[2] Note that the maximum-likelihood estimator can also be derived as the mode of a Markov chain Monte Carlo (MCMC) sample of the corresponding stationary Bayesian posterior distribution, if prior distributions are chosen to be uniform on $[0,1]$. Credible intervals are naturally implied from the sampled Markov chain obtained by Gibbs sampling, whereas for the frequentist approach a more complex partially asymptotic theory has to be used, which is only analytically tractable in the ASRF setting.

In our simulation study, it turns out that the ME is valid in both model variants and meets parameters best, ie, the recovered estimated parameters are fairly close to the original parameters. However, in the ASRF model, asymptotic confidence intervals seem to be too small for good rating classes. Via an adjustment of the ML estimator, quite reliable confidence intervals can be presented. Yet, the credible intervals of the Bayesian approach and their analytical non-asymptotic equivalents turn out to be much larger in the simulation study as well as for the real data provided by Standard and Poor's (S&P). The difference from the asymptotic approach makes it clear that the approximation, which to some extent goes along with linearisation, underestimates the true uncertainty of the parameter estimation. The Bayesian approach shows that parameter uncertainty must not be neglected in risk management.

Similar estimation analyses of correlation in the context of credit portfolio management can be found in Demey *et al* (2004), Duellmann *et al* (2008) and Tarashev and Zhu (2007). The latter also considers potential errors (more precisely, model selection and calibration errors), but neither different estimators in the same statistical model nor explicit or asymptotic confidence and credible intervals (the main aim of this chapter) are derived.

The chapter is organised as follows. In the first section we explain the considered model and estimators as well as the necessary concept of asymptotic normality by means of techniques presented in Le Cam and Yang (1990) and Van der Vaart (1998). Then we use this property to derive the (asymptotic) confidence intervals for the considered point estimators for the parameters p and ρ. In the next section, comparable Bayesian techniques are introduced. In addition, we show asymptotic normality of the risk figures, which are functionals of those parameters, again yielding confidence intervals for the risk figures. We then contrast those results with the comparable results based on the Bayesian approach. In the last section, the different frequentist (asymptotic) approaches are compared within a simulation study and an empirical study based on S&P's default study (2009).

This chapter is based on earlier preprints by the authors (Niethammer 2008; Niethammer and Overbeck 2008), but many new aspects and extension are given.

MODELS, ESTIMATORS AND ASYMPTOTIC NORMALITY

In this section we introduce the tools and concepts we need for our empirical examination later in this chapter. We describe two different models: the binomial mixed model, and its limit case, the ASRF model. For both models we will discuss possible estimators for the default probability and the correlation. However, to describe the parameter uncertainty isolated from other numerical effects coming from numerical integration or Monte Carlo simulations, in the remainder of the chapter we base our empirical study on the ASRF.[3] In this simpler setting, we are able to derive asymptotic intervals for all estimators and we can also establish an analytical confidence interval for the ML estimator of the asset correlation without the asymptotic assumption of a large number of periods. A simulation comparison later in this chapter shows that this non-asymptotic interval is very close to the Bayesian credible interval in the case of a uniform prior distribution, whereas the asymptotic one is a lot smaller. We will thus establish below that the Bayesian Monte Carlo approach is superior to the asymptotic one in the AFRS model. Therefore, finally, if an analytical confidence interval cannot be derived in more complex models as (in the binomial model), the Bayesian Monte Carlo method still leads to a realistic estimation of the uncertainty.

Mixed binomial

The mixed binomial model is a general and basic approach for modelling credit portfolio risk. Here, we recap some of its main properties, followed by some estimators for the correlation and default probabilities.

Model

The Gaussian one-factor model was introduced into finance by Vasicek (1991) as a multivariate extension of a stylised asset value model. The univariate asset value model is given in Merton (1974). We formulate the model introduced by Vasicek slightly more generally. As usual, on a one-year horizon, the asset value of firm i at t is given by

$$X_{i,t} = \sqrt{\rho} Y_t + \sqrt{1-\rho} Z_{i,t}, \quad i = 1,\ldots,N_t, \; t = 1,\ldots,n$$

where $\rho \in (0,1)$, is the asset correlation, $Y_t \overset{iid}{\sim} F$ and $Z_{i,t} \overset{iid}{\sim} G$ with distribution functions F and G.

If we denote by $\tilde{F}_\rho$ the distribution of $X_{i,t}$ and consider an obligor i in a rating class R_k, we have

$$D_{i,t} = \tilde{F}_{\rho_k}^{-1}(p_{i,t}) = \tilde{F}_{\rho_k}^{-1}(p_k) =: D_k \tag{7.1}$$

where p_k is the constant default probability and ρ_k is the correlation in rating class R_k. Furthermore, it follows from our assumptions that the conditional default probability is

$$P(\text{asset } i \text{ defaults at } t \mid Y_t) = P(X_{i,t} \leq D_{i,t} \mid Y_t) = p_{k|Y_t}$$

$$\implies p_{k|Y_t} = G\left(\frac{D_k - \sqrt{\rho_k} Y_t}{\sqrt{1-\rho_k}}\right)$$

The portfolio loss in rating class R_k is

$$L_{k,t} = \sum_{i:\, k_{i,t}=R_k}^{N_t} \mathbf{1}_{(X_{i,t} \leq D_k)}$$

where $\mathbf{1}$ is the indicator function, N_t is the number of all obligors at the beginning of time period t and $k_{i,t}$ is the rating of obligor i. The corresponding conditional loss distribution encompassing all rating classes is therefore given by

$$P_{p,\rho}(L_{1,t} = l_{1,t}, \ldots, L_{K,t} = l_{K,t} \mid Y_t) = \prod_{k=1}^{K} \text{Binom}(N_{R_k,t}, p_{k|Y_t}, l_{R_k,t})$$

from which we obtain by integration the unconditional loss distribution

$$P_{p,\rho}(L_{1,t} = l_{1,t}, \ldots, L_{K,t} = l_{K,t}) = \int \prod_{k=1}^{K} \text{Binom}(N_{R_k,t}, p_{k|y_t}, l_{R_k,t}) \, dF(y_t) \tag{7.2}$$

where $(N_{1,t}, \ldots, N_{K,t})$ represents the numbers of companies and $l_t := (l_{1,t}, \ldots, l_{K,t})$ denotes the number of defaults in rating classes 1 to K. The observed losses in each year in rating class k are then viewed as realisations of $L_{k,t}$. $N_{k,t}$ is known and the distribution of the number of defaults in period t in rating class k, $L_{k,t}$, is supposed to be modelled: parametrized by the default probability p_k and asset correlation ρ_k in rating class k. The loss rate is defined as

$$\tilde{L}_{k,t} := \frac{L_{k,t}}{N_{k,t}}$$

Estimators

Let us consider one rating class k_0 and assume we have an iid sample $(l_{k_0,1}, \ldots, l_{k_0,n})$ of defaults collected over n time periods. By plugging these observations into the product over the considered time periods of expressions like Equation 7.2 and maximising it with respect to p_{k_0} and ρ_{k_0}, we obtain the ML estimator within rating k_0. In general, for all rating classes k, the default probability $P(X_{k,t} \leqslant D_{k,t})$ itself might also depend on ρ_k, since the distribution of X_i does. But, as usual, assuming that $F = G = \Phi$, where Φ denotes the standard normal distribution function, yields that $P(X_{k,t} \leqslant D_{k,t}) = p_k$ does not depend on ρ_k, which makes the maximisation of the likelihood function considerably easier. In all cases, numerical integration or an MCMC method is necessary (the latter means that the mode of a sample of the Bayesian posterior distribution with the uniform prior distribution of p and ρ is taken, as explained later in this chapter). However, numerical errors arise in both cases such that we cannot precisely distinguish numerical errors from parameter uncertainty. We therefore do not discuss the ML estimator for the mixed binomial model any further.

Instead, we consider the following moment-based estimators as reasonable estimators for the mean and the variance of $\tilde{L}_{k,t}$, $t = 1, \ldots, n$

$$\hat{p}_k := m_{\tilde{L}(k)} = \frac{1}{n} \sum_{t=1}^{n} \tilde{L}_{t,k}, \quad s^2_{\tilde{L}(k)} = \frac{1}{n-1} \sum_{t=1}^{n} (\tilde{L}_{t,k} - \hat{p}_k)^2 \quad (7.3)$$

A moment estimator for p_k is easily found by calculating the above time average of $\tilde{L}_{k,t}$, ie, $\hat{p}_k$, since $E[\hat{p}_k] = p_k$. In order to estimate ρ_k we again calculate the variance of $\tilde{L}_{k,t}$ and equate it with the sample variance of the observations. This gives an implicit estimate for ρ_k; ie, we can implicitly estimate ρ_k by the moment estimator $s^2_{\tilde{L}(k)}$ of the variance of $\tilde{L}_{k,t}$, $t = 1, \ldots, n$ (also with $F = G = \Phi$)

$$\begin{aligned}
\operatorname{var}(\tilde{L}_k) &= \operatorname{var}\left(\frac{1}{N_k} \sum_{i=1}^{N_k} \mathbf{1}_{X_i \leqslant D_k}\right) \\
&= \frac{1}{N_k^2} \sum_{i=1}^{N_k} \sum_{j=1}^{N_k} \operatorname{cov}(\mathbf{1}_{X_i \leqslant D_k}, \mathbf{1}_{X_j \leqslant D_k}) \\
&= \frac{1}{N_k^2} \sum_{i=1}^{N_k} \sum_{j=1}^{N_k} (P(X_i \leqslant D_k, X_j \leqslant D_k) - p_k^2) \\
&= \Phi_2(\Phi^{-1}(p_k), \Phi^{-1}(p_k), \rho_k) - p_k^2
\end{aligned} \quad (7.4)$$

An estimator of ρ_k is obtained by replacing $\operatorname{var}(\tilde{L}_k)$ by $s^2_{\tilde{L}(k)}$ and inverting the above equality.[4] The question of whether a solution exists, and further details are discussed later (see page 208).

Asymptotic single-risk-factor model

We again start with the model and describe two different estimators: the moment and the maximum likelihood estimator.

Model

The Law of Large Numbers conditioned on the economic state at t, Y_t, motivates the infinite granular assumption for the loss rates in a portfolio of a large number of equal obligors within a rating class k (Bluhm *et al* 2002), where we again set $F = G = \Phi$.

Assumption 7.1 (ASRF). The loss rate $\tilde{L}_{t,k}$ in rating class k in period t possesses the form

$$\tilde{L}_{t,k} = g_k(Y_t) = \Phi\left(\frac{\Phi^{-1}(p_k) - \sqrt{\rho_k} Y_t}{\sqrt{1-\rho_k}}\right), \quad Y_t \stackrel{\text{iid}}{\sim} \mathcal{N}(0,1) \quad (7.5)$$

where $p_k := p_{R_k}$ is the one-period default probability in rating class R_k and ρ_k denotes the asset correlation within the obligors in rating class k for $k = 1, \ldots, K$.

Basically, $\tilde{L}_{t,k}$ is a monotone decreasing function of the state of economy Y_t. Therefore the distribution of $\tilde{L}_{t,k}$ can easily be derived. Under Assumption 7.1 the loss rate $\tilde{L}_{t,k}$ has the following (Vasicek) distribution

$$\tilde{L}_{t,k} \sim F_\infty = F_{L,p_k,\rho_k} \quad \text{with density } f_{\tilde{L},p_k,\rho_k}(\cdot) := \frac{n_{\mu_k,\sigma_k^2}(\Phi^{-1}(\cdot))}{\phi(\Phi^{-1}(\cdot))} \quad (7.6)$$

where $\tilde{L}$ indicates that we consider percentage loss

$$\mu_k = \frac{\Phi^{-1}(p_k)}{\sqrt{1-\rho_k}}, \qquad \sigma_k = \frac{\sqrt{\rho_k}}{\sqrt{1-\rho_k}}$$

$n_{\mu,\sigma}$ is the Gaussian density with mean μ and variance σ^2, $\phi = n_{0,1}$ and $p_k := p_{R_k}$ is the one-period default probability in rating class R_k, $k = 1, \ldots, K$. Motivated by the binomial model and assuming a large number of obligors, we have specified the distribution of the loss rate as a function of the probability of default p_k and the asset correlation ρ_k. The information regarding how many obligors are in one rating class can be ignored under the additional assumption that $N_{t,k}$ tends to infinity. The model is based and fully specified by the distribution of $\tilde{L}_{t,k}$ instead of $L_{t,k}$ in the mixed binomial model. This model is widely used in the context of collateralised debt obligation (CDO) modelling.[5]

Estimators

The moment estimator under the ASRF stays the same as under the binomial model. The maximum likelihood estimator can be calculated analytically now that we have the following.

- A maximum likelihood (ML) ($\hat{p}_{ML}, \hat{\rho}_{ML}$) estimate can be calculated as the maximiser of

$$\max_{p_k, \rho_k} \prod_{t=1}^{N} f_{\tilde{L}_{t,k}, p_k, \rho_k}(\tilde{L})$$

(see below for the calculation).

- The moment estimator (ME) ($m_{\tilde{L}}, \hat{\rho}_{ME}$) from the binomial model (see page 204) based on $\hat{p}_k := m_{\tilde{L}(k)}$, and ρ_{ME} as the solution of Equation 7.4 is still a possible estimator. This moment estimator is robust to both model variants. To calculate confidence intervals of the estimator of ρ_{ME}, we will, however, need the ASRF assumption.

The ML estimator will again coincide with the mode of a Bayesian posterior distribution, if the prior distributions of p and ρ are uniform.

Both the ML and ME methods describe how to estimate default probability and asset correlation jointly within one rating class. Every approach coincides for every rating class. As we have no structural information driving correlation, we stick to the grouping in rating classes. Another approach is to set the correlation equal over all rating classes (see Chapter 6) or additionally relate the estimated intra-rating-class correlations (Bluhm and Overbeck 2003). In fact, the Bayesian approach by MCMC then becomes somehow more stable if there is just one correlation for all rating classes. However, the above techniques are more complicated; analytical solutions are not feasible. As we want to discuss estimation errors and isolate the influence on risk figures, we stick to the analytical case. Under the assumption that every rating class is one large homogeneous portfolio (ASRF), the ML estimator and ME are reasonable and can be calculated for every rating class separately. We skip the index k and write $p_k = p$, $\tilde{L}_{t,k} = \tilde{L}_t$.

Estimation errors based on asymptotic normality

In this section, we sketch the first main issue of this chapter. We discuss implications of (point) estimation errors on risk figures by asymptotic considerations (the frequentist approach), ie, we assume that the number of observed periods n is very large.[6]

Suppose we have already obtained estimators $(\hat{p}, \hat{\rho})$ in the Gaussian one-factor model, eg, moment or maximum likelihood estimation as discussed above. If the (asymptotic; see Definition 7.2) distribution of the estimators is known, we can also obtain the (asymptotic) distribution of our risk figures provided that there are continuously differentiable functions of the true values p and ρ. This directly follows from the so-called delta method.[7] Confidence intervals can be calculated. In our case, both estimators of the considered parameters are even asymptotically normal as long as the true parameters do not lie on the boundary $\rho, p \notin \{0, 1\}$.

We start with the definition of asymptotic normality.

Definition 7.2. A sequence of (multivariate) random variables (eg, a sequence of estimators) U_n is asymptotically normal with mean μ_n and covariance matrix Σ, denoted by $U_n \sim A\mathcal{N}(\mu_n, \delta_n^2 \Sigma)$ if Σ is positive definite and there exists a sequence $\delta_n \to 0$ such that

$$\frac{U_n - \mu_n}{\delta_n} \xrightarrow{d} \mathcal{N}(0, \Sigma)$$

We now provide a special case of the delta method sufficient in our case.[8]

Theorem 7.3. Let Σ be a covariance matrix and let

$$U_n = (U_{n1}, \ldots, U_{nk}) \sim \mathcal{AN}(\mu, \delta_n^2 \Sigma)$$

ie, U_n is asymptotically normal with respect to the sequence $\delta_n \to 0$. Further suppose that $f(u)$ is a real-valued function having a non-zero differential at $u = \mu$. Then $f(U_n)$ is asymptotically normal with respect to the same sequence δ_n and

$$f(U_n) \sim \mathcal{AN}\left(f(\mu), \delta_n^2 \sum_{i=1}^{k}\sum_{j=1}^{k} \sigma_{ij} \frac{\partial f}{\partial u_i}\bigg|_{u=\mu} \frac{\partial f}{\partial u_j}\bigg|_{u=\mu}\right) \quad (7.7)$$

Suppose we consider a risk figure that can be described by a continuously differentiable function f of the true parameters p and ρ. Let us assume that the estimators $\hat{p}$ and $\hat{\rho}$ are asymptotically normal with δ_n. Then, by applying Theorem 7.3 we get an asymptotic confidence interval with level $\alpha \in (0,1)$ for the considered risk figure $f(p, \rho)$

$$(f(\hat{p}, \hat{\rho}) - \sigma_n \delta_n \Phi^{-1}(1 - \tfrac{1}{2}\alpha), f(\hat{p}, \hat{\rho}) + \sigma_n \delta_n \Phi^{-1}(1 - \tfrac{1}{2}\alpha)) \quad (7.8)$$

where

$$\sigma_n^2 = \sigma_{11}^2 \left(\frac{\partial f}{\partial p}\right)^2 + \sigma_{22}\left(\frac{\partial f}{\partial \rho}\right)^2 + 2\sigma_{12} \frac{\partial f}{\partial \rho}\frac{\partial f}{\partial p}$$

and δ_n comes from the norming sequence stated in the asymptotic normality of $\hat{p}$ and $\hat{\rho}$; it will be made explicit later in this chapter.

FREQUENTIST APPROACH: UNCERTAINTY OF POINT ESTIMATORS

In this section, we describe in further detail the maximum likelihood and the moment estimators for the default probabilities and correlations in the ASRF model. Asymptotic normality of both estimators is proven.

Moment estimator in an ASRF model

We start with the consistency and asymptotic normality of m_L and s_L^2. We then continue by showing that Equation 7.4 has a solution and prove asymptotic normality of its estimator under mild assumptions.

Asymptotic normality of $m_{\tilde{L}}$ and $s_{\tilde{L}}^2$

Let n be the number of observed periods and let $\tilde{L}_t$ ($t = 1, \ldots, n$) be the loss rate under Assumption 7.1 (ASRF), ie, $\tilde{L}_t$ is a function of Y_t

$$g(Y_t) := p_{|Y_t} = \tilde{L}_t \qquad (7.9)$$

Since the Y_t are iid and $g(Y_t)$ is bounded in the unit interval, we have by the Law of Large Numbers that

$$\overline{g^n(Y)} := \frac{1}{n} \sum_{t=1}^n g(Y_t) \xrightarrow{\text{almost surely}} E(g(Y)) = p \qquad (7.10)$$

$$\frac{1}{n-1} \sum_{t=1}^n (g(Y_t) - \overline{g^n(Y)})^2 \xrightarrow{\text{almost surely}} \text{var}(g(Y)) \qquad (7.11)$$

and in addition by the Central Limit Theorem

$$\sqrt{n}\left(\frac{1}{n} \sum_{t=1}^n \tilde{L}_t^j - E(g^j(Y))\right) \xrightarrow{d} \mathcal{N}(0, \text{var}(g^j(Y))), \quad j = 1, 2 \qquad (7.12)$$

As we consider iid random variables, we have joint asymptotic normality with covariance matrix $\sigma_{ij} = E(\tilde{L}^{i+j}) - E(\tilde{L}^i)E(\tilde{L}^j)$, $i = 1$, $j = 2$.[9] The moment estimators $m_{\tilde{L}}$ and $s_{\tilde{L}}^2$ are consistent and asymptotically normal and therefore reasonable estimates for $E(g(Y))$ and $\text{var}(g(Y))$. It remains to prove that ρ_{ME}, the solution of Equation 7.4, exists and its estimator possesses the same properties as a function of $m_{\tilde{L}}$ and $s_{\tilde{L}}^2$.

Existence of $\hat{\rho}_{\text{ME}}$

To estimate ρ, we use the relation in Equation 7.4 and replace p and $\text{var}(g(Y))$ by their sample moments $m_{\tilde{L}}$ and $s_{\tilde{L}}^2$. The estimate is then supposed to be a function h of $m_{\tilde{L}}$ and $s_{\tilde{L}}^2$

$$\hat{\rho}_{\text{ME}} := h(m_{\tilde{L}}, s_{\tilde{L}}^2) \qquad (7.13)$$

To find this function and to show asymptotic normality, we apply the Implicit Function Theorem: let $\rho \in (0,1)$ and define $f: (0,1) \times (0, \infty) \times (0,1) \to \mathbb{R}$ with

$$f(p, s, \rho) = \Phi_2(\Phi^{-1}(p), \Phi^{-1}(p), \rho) - p^2 - s \qquad (7.14)$$

$(0,1) \times (0, \infty) \times (0,1)$ is open in itself. Furthermore, we know that f is continuously differentiable infinitely often, ie, $f \in C^q$, $q \in \mathbb{N}$.

Finally, if

$$\frac{\partial f}{\partial \rho}(E(g(Y)), \mathrm{var}(g(Y)), h(E(g(Y)), \mathrm{var}(g(Y)))) \neq 0 \qquad (7.15)$$

$$f(E(g(Y)), \mathrm{var}(g(Y)), h(E(g(Y)), \mathrm{var}(g(Y)))) = 0 \qquad (7.16)$$

then there exists a neighbourhood $U \subset (0,1) \times (0,\infty)$ and an $h \in C^q(U,(0,1))$, $q \in \mathbb{N}$, such that, for all $u = (p,s) \in U: f(u,h(u)) = 0$

$$\nabla h(u) = -\left(\frac{\partial f}{\partial \rho}\right)^{-1} \begin{pmatrix} \frac{\partial f}{\partial p} \\ \frac{\partial f}{\partial s} \end{pmatrix}(u)$$

To show Equation 7.15, we start by deriving $\partial f / \partial \rho$. By Vasicek (1998)

$$\frac{\partial}{\partial \rho}\Phi_2(z_1,z_2,\rho) = \phi_2(z_1,z_2,\rho)$$

$$= (2\pi)^{-1}(1-\rho^2)^{-1/2}\exp\left\{-\frac{1}{2}\frac{z_1^2 - 2\rho z_1 z_2 + z_2^2}{1-\rho^2}\right\}$$

Hence,

$$\frac{\partial f}{\partial \rho}(p,s,\rho) = (2\pi)^{-1}(1-\rho^2)^{-1/2}\exp\left\{-\frac{(\Phi^{-1}(p))^2}{1+\rho}\right\} > 0 \qquad (7.17)$$

We next prove Equation 7.16. As f is continuous, $f(p,s,0) = -s < 0$, and $f(p,s,1) = p(1-p) - s$, it remains to ensure that $p(1-p) \geq s$. This is the case for $\rho \in [0,1)$, $p = E(g(Y))$ and $s = \mathrm{var}(g(Y))$ as $f(E(g(Y)), \mathrm{var}(g(Y)), 1) = E(g(Y) - g^2(Y)) = \mathrm{var}(g(Y)) > 0$ for all $E(g(Y)) =: p \in (0,1)$, because $g(Y) \in (0,1)$, P-almost surely. The solution of Equation 7.4 therefore uniquely exists by Equation 7.17. Also a unique solution exists if p and s are replaced by the (sample) mean and variance of a random variable X (here $\tilde{L}$) with observations between $[0,1)$ with $P(X > 0) > 0$ (since then the relation $E(X)(1-E(X)) > \mathrm{var}(X)$ holds). This is valid for the empirical distribution of the default rates as well as the true distribution of $g(Y)$. We summarise as follows.

Lemma 7.4. For $p = E(g(Y)) \in (0,1)$ with $s := \mathrm{var}(g(Y)) > 0$ the following equation has a unique solution $\rho \in (0,1)$

$$\Phi_2(\Phi^{-1}(p), \Phi^{-1}(p), \rho) - p^2 = s$$

In particular, replacing the theoretical distribution of $g(Y)$ by the observed empirical distribution, the estimator $\hat{\rho}_{\mathrm{ME}}$ is uniquely defined and Equations 7.15 and 7.16 hold.

The last assertion of Lemma 7.4 is obvious when replacing $n-1$ by n in $s_{\tilde{L}}^2$ as defined in Equation 7.3. For reasonable n this replacement can be neglected.

Asymptotic normality of $\hat{\rho}_{ME}$

We are not able to determine ρ_{ME} (respectively, the function h from Equation 7.13) more explicit, but we already know from the last section that h is continuously differentiable. That means, at first, as h is continuous and $m_{\tilde{L}}$ and $s_{\tilde{L}}^2$ are consistent, that $\hat{\rho}_{ME} = h(m_{\tilde{L}}, s_{\tilde{L}}^2)$ is shown to be consistent as well. Secondly, for our analysis (to derive asymptotic normality), it remains to calculate its first derivative at $p = E(g(Y))$ and $s = \text{var}(g(Y))$.

In addition to Lemma 7.4, we have $\partial f/\partial s = -1$. To obtain ∇h, it remains to derive $\partial f/\partial p$. As

$$\frac{\partial \Phi^{-1}(p)}{\partial p} = \frac{1}{\phi(\Phi^{-1}(p))}$$

$$\frac{\partial \tilde{f}}{\partial v} = \int_{-\infty}^{w} \phi_2(z_1, v, \rho)\, dz_1$$

and

$$\frac{\partial \tilde{f}}{\partial w} = \int_{-\infty}^{v} \phi_2(w, z_2, \rho)\, dz_2$$

where $\tilde{f}(w,v) = \Phi_2(w,v,\rho)$, by applying the chain rule we obtain

$$\frac{\partial f}{\partial p}(p,s,\rho) = 2\mathcal{N}_{\rho\Phi^{-1}(p),1-\rho^2}(\Phi^{-1}(p)) - 2p \quad (7.18)$$

where $\mathcal{N}_{\rho\Phi^{-1}(p),1-\rho^2}$ is the cumulative Gaussian distribution with variance $1-\rho^2$ and mean $\rho\Phi^{-1}(p)$. Finally with $\rho = h(p,s)$, we have

$$\nabla h(p,s) = -\left(\frac{1}{2\pi\sqrt{1-\rho^2}}\exp\left\{-\frac{(\Phi^{-1}(p))^2}{1+\rho}\right\}\right)^{-1}$$
$$\times \begin{pmatrix} 2\mathcal{N}_{\rho\Phi^{-1}(p),1-\rho^2}(\Phi^{-1}(p)) - 2p \\ -1 \end{pmatrix}$$

To show asymptotic normality of $\hat{\rho}_{ME}$, according to Theorem 7.3 we need joint asymptotic normality of $s_{\tilde{L}}^2$ and $m_{\tilde{L}}$. This is shown as follows: the joint asymptotic normality of $m_{\tilde{L}}$ and

$$\frac{1}{n}\sum_t \tilde{L}_t^2$$

holds by (Serfling 1980, Theorem 2.2.1B) as shown above (see Equation 7.12). By multiplication with $n/(n-1)$, we obtain the same result for

$$\frac{1}{n-1}\sum_{s=1}^{n}\tilde{L}_s^2 \quad \text{as} \quad \frac{n}{n-1} \to 1$$

We then define

$$\tilde{h}(z_1, z_2) = z_1 - z_2^2, \quad z_1 = \frac{1}{n}\sum_{s=1}^{n}\tilde{L}_s^2, \quad z_2 = m_{\tilde{L}}$$

Hence, by Theorem 7.3 and because

$$\frac{1}{n}\sum_{s=1}^{n}\tilde{L}_s \quad \text{and} \quad \frac{1}{n-1}\sum_{s=1}^{n}\tilde{L}_s^2$$

are asymptotically equal, we get

$$s_{\tilde{L}}^2 \sim A\mathcal{N}(\text{var}(g(Y)), n^{-1}\sigma_{\tilde{s}}^2) \tag{7.19}$$

where

$$\sigma_{\tilde{s}}^2 = \text{var}(g(Y))4E^2(g(Y)) + \text{var}(g^2(Y)) \times 1 \\ - 4(E(g(Y)^3) - E(g(Y)^2)E(g(Y)))E(g(Y)) \tag{7.20}$$

We further calculate the covariance between $m_{\tilde{L}}$ and $s_{\tilde{L}}^2$, again since $g(Y_t)$ are iid (Niethammer and Overbeck 2008)

$$\text{cov}\left(m_{\tilde{L}}, \frac{n-1}{n}s_{\tilde{L}}^2\right) = \frac{E(g^3(Y)) - pE(g^2(Y))}{n} - \frac{p\,\text{var}(g(Y))}{n} + \mathcal{O}(n^{-2})$$

where $\mathcal{O}(n^{-2})$ is an expression which converges to a positive constant if it is multiplied by n^2.

Finally, note that

$$f\left(m_{\tilde{L}}, \frac{1}{n}\sum_{s=1}^{n}\tilde{L}_s^2 - m_{\tilde{L}}^2, 1\right) = m_{\tilde{L}} > 0$$

We conclude that $(m_{\tilde{L}}, s_{\tilde{L}}^2)$ is asymptotically normal with covariance matrix in Equation 7.20 and thus by Theorem 7.3 and Lemma 7.4 we can determine the asymptotic distribution of $\hat{\rho}_{\text{ME}}$.

Theorem 7.5. For $p := E(g(Y)) \in (0,1)$ with $\text{var}(g(Y)) > 0$ we have

$$\hat{\rho}_{\text{ME}} = h(m_{\tilde{L}}, s_{\tilde{L}}^2) \sim A\mathcal{N}(h(p, \text{var}(g(Y))), n^{-1}\sigma_{\rho,\text{ME}}^2) \tag{7.21}$$

where

$$\sigma^2_{\rho,ME} = \text{var}(g(Y))\left(\frac{\partial h}{\partial p}(p, \text{var}(g(Y)))\right)^2 + \sigma^2_s\left(\frac{\partial h}{\partial s}(p, \text{var}(g(Y)))\right)^2$$
$$+ 2\sigma_{ms}\frac{\partial h}{\partial p}(p, \text{var}(g(Y)))\frac{\partial h}{\partial s}(p, \text{var}(g(Y))) \quad (7.22)$$

and

$$\sigma_{ms} = (E(g^3(Y)) - pE(g^2(Y))) - p\,\text{var}(g(Y)) \quad (7.23)$$

In practical applications, we replace $h(p, \text{var}(g(Y)))$ by $h(m_{\tilde{L}}, s^2_{\tilde{L}})$ and $E(g^j(Y))$ by

$$\frac{1}{n}\sum_t \tilde{L}^j_t, \quad j = 2, 3$$

According to Theorem 7.3, as $m_{\tilde{L}}$ and $\hat{\rho}_{ME}$ are asymptotically normal, the distribution of interesting risk figures can be derived (see the section starting on page 221). In summary, we can say that the asymptotic normal distribution for p and ρ_{ME} are given in Equations 7.12 and 7.21 and that later in this chapter we will use this result to obtain asymptotic confidence intervals for our risk measures. We continue with the maximum likelihood estimator.

Maximum likelihood estimate in an ASRF model

We next derive the ML estimator and its asymptotic normality in an ASRF model (see Equation 7.5).

Estimator

Recall that $\tilde{L}_t \sim F_{\tilde{L},p,\rho}$, where

$$f_{\tilde{L},p,\rho} = \phi_{\mu,\sigma^2}(\Phi^{-1}(\cdot))\frac{1}{\phi(\Phi^{-1}(\cdot))}, \quad \mu = \frac{\Phi^{-1}(p)}{\sqrt{1-\rho}}, \quad \sigma^2 = \frac{\rho}{1-\rho}$$

ie, we consider the following log-likelihood function

$$L_a(p, \rho \mid \tilde{L}) = \log f_{\tilde{L},p,\rho}(\tilde{L})$$

Using this information we are able to derive the exact form of the ML estimator in the ASRF model

$$\frac{\partial L_a}{\partial p} = \frac{\sqrt{1-\rho}}{\rho\phi(\Phi^{-1}(p))}\sum\left(\Phi^{-1}(\tilde{L}_t) - \frac{\Phi^{-1}(p)}{\sqrt{1-\rho}}\right) \stackrel{!}{=} 0$$
$$\Rightarrow \hat{p}^\rho_{ML} = \Phi\left(\frac{\sqrt{1-\rho}}{n}\sum_t \Phi^{-1}(\tilde{L}_t)\right)$$

and

$$\frac{\partial L_a}{\partial \rho} = \frac{1}{2} \sum \left(\frac{1}{\rho^2} \left(\left(\Phi^{-1}(\tilde{L}_t) - \frac{\Phi^{-1}(p)}{\sqrt{1-\rho}} \right)^2 \right) \right.$$
$$+ \frac{1}{\rho\sqrt{1-\rho}} \Phi^{-1}(p) \left(\Phi^{-1}(\tilde{L}_t) - \frac{\Phi^{-1}(p)}{\sqrt{1-\rho}} \right) \right)$$
$$- \frac{1}{2} n \left(\frac{1}{1-\rho} + \frac{1}{\rho} \right) \quad (7.24)$$

The last term in the sum of Equation 7.24 is zero if $\partial L_a / \partial p = 0$. Thus, plugging $\hat{p}_{\mathrm{ML}}^{\hat{\rho}_{\mathrm{ML}}}$ into Equation 7.24 yields that $\partial L_a(\hat{p}_{\mathrm{ML}}^{\hat{\rho}_{\mathrm{ML}}}, \hat{\rho}_{\mathrm{ML}})/\partial \rho = 0$ is equivalent to

$$-\hat{\rho}_{\mathrm{ML}}^2 + \frac{1}{n} \sum \left(\Phi^{-1}(\tilde{L}_t) - \frac{\Phi^{-1}(\hat{p}_{\mathrm{ML}})}{\sqrt{1-\hat{\rho}_{\mathrm{ML}}}} \right)^2 (1 - \hat{\rho}_{\mathrm{ML}}) - \hat{\rho}_{\mathrm{ML}}(1 - \hat{\rho}_{\mathrm{ML}}) = 0$$
$$\iff \frac{1}{n} \sum \left(\Phi^{-1}(\tilde{L}_t) - \frac{1}{n} \sum_t \Phi^{-1}(\tilde{L}_t) \right)^2 (1 - \hat{\rho}_{\mathrm{ML}}) - \hat{\rho}_{\mathrm{ML}} = 0$$

which is further equivalent to

$$\hat{\rho}_{\mathrm{ML}} = \frac{(1/n) \sum (\Phi^{-1}(\tilde{L}_t) - (1/n) \sum_t \Phi^{-1}(\tilde{L}_t))^2}{1 + (1/n) \sum (\Phi^{-1}(\tilde{L}_t) - (1/n) \sum_t \Phi^{-1}(\tilde{L}_t))^2}$$

In short

$$\hat{p}_{\mathrm{ML}} = \Phi\left(\frac{\bar{\Lambda}}{\sqrt{1 + \bar{\Lambda}_2 - \bar{\Lambda}^2}} \right), \qquad \hat{\rho}_{\mathrm{ML}} = \frac{\bar{\Lambda}_2 - \bar{\Lambda}^2}{1 + \bar{\Lambda}_2 - \bar{\Lambda}^2} \quad (7.25)$$

where

$$\bar{\Lambda} = \frac{1}{n} \sum_t \Phi^{-1}(\tilde{L}_t), \qquad \bar{\Lambda}_2 = \frac{1}{n} \sum_t (\Phi^{-1}(\tilde{L}_t))^2$$

Remark 7.6.

- In practice, we do not have an infinite number of obligors. Nevertheless we interpret the relative default frequency in year t as a realisation of the random variable $\tilde{L}_t$. However, sometimes the empirical default frequency is zero. Then an adjustment has to be made. Different choices are discussed in the empirical study (see page 225 onwards).

- A similar estimator which only needs the median of $\tilde{L}$ to be non-zero is the following: we know that

$$\sqrt{1-\rho} \frac{1}{n} \sum_t \Phi^{-1}(\tilde{L}_t)$$

is Gaussian with expectation and median $\Phi^{-1}(p)$ (see Assumption 7.1). As the median is invariant with respect to monotonic transformations, the median of

$$p_{ML} = \Phi\left(\sqrt{1-\rho}\frac{1}{n}\sum_t \Phi^{-1}(\tilde{L})\right)$$

is p.

If the median of the loss rates is non-zero, we get

$$\text{median}(\tilde{L}_t) = \Phi\left(\frac{\Phi^{-1}(p)}{\sqrt{1-\rho}}\right)$$

since

$$\text{median}(\sqrt{1-\rho}\Phi^{-1}(\tilde{L}_t)) = \Phi^{-1}(p)$$

So, finally, we achieve quite good results by replacing p by $m_{\tilde{L}}$ and setting

$$\rho = 1 - \left(\frac{\Phi^{-1}(m_{\tilde{L}})}{\Phi^{-1}(\text{median}(\tilde{L}))}\right)^2$$

Empirical results are not displayed here as the moment estimator yields good results and confidence intervals have not been derived for this new estimator.[10] Moreover, it does not work for a zero median of $\tilde{L}$.

Asymptotic normality

We next wish to prove that the ML estimator is actually asymptotically normal. This is done by establishing typical regularity conditions as in Van der Vaart (1998, Theorem 5.41). We essentially face Gaussian distributed random variables. L_a is three times continuously differentiable with first derivative $\dot{L}_a$. Furthermore, $\Phi^{-1}(\tilde{L}_t)$ is Gaussian and therefore possesses all moments. So by setting the parameter space equal to $\Theta = (0,1) \times (0,1)$ we always find for all $\vartheta_0 \in \Theta$ a sphere such that the third derivative of L_a at $\vartheta_0 = (p_0, \rho_0)$ is dominated by an integrable function in this sphere around ϑ_0. The Fisher information $I_\vartheta = E(\dot{L}'_a \dot{L}_a)$ is well defined and invertible, as the determinant of I_ϑ can be easily calculated and shown to be positive. So, finally, all regularity conditions of the ML estimator are satisfied. We have established that $(\hat{p}_{ML}, \hat{\rho}_{ML})$ is asymptotically normal with variance equal to the inverse of the Fisher information. The Fisher information is easily calculated, such that the asymptotic variance of p (that is $\sigma^2_{p,\text{ML}}$) and ρ (that is $\sigma^2_{\rho,\text{ML}}$) and the covariance $\sigma_{p\rho,\text{ML}}$ between both have the following form

$$\left. \begin{aligned} \sigma^2_{p,\text{ML}} &= \frac{\phi^2(\Phi^{-1}(p))\rho^2}{n}\left(\frac{1}{\rho} + \frac{(\Phi^{-1}(p))^2}{2}\right) \\ \sigma^2_{\rho,\text{ML}} &= \frac{2(1-\rho)^2\rho^3}{n} \\ \sigma_{p\rho,\text{ML}} &= \frac{(\Phi^{-1}(p))^2(1-\rho)\rho^2\phi(\Phi^{-1}(p))}{n} \end{aligned} \right\} \quad (7.26)$$

Finally, asymptotic confidence intervals for our risk figures can be derived as described above in the section on estimation errors based on asymptotic normality (see page 207). An empirical analysis is presented later in this chapter.

In fact we can derive exact (non-asymptotic) confidence intervals. As $\Phi^{-1}(\tilde{L}_t), t = 1, \ldots, n$, are iid normally distributed with mean $\Phi^{-1}(p)/\sqrt{1-\rho}$ and variance $\rho/(1-\rho)$, we have

$$\frac{1-\rho}{\rho}\bar{\Lambda}_v := \frac{1-\rho}{\rho}\sum_{t=1}^{n}(\Phi^{-1}(\tilde{L}_t) - \bar{\Lambda})^2 \sim \chi^2_{n-1}$$

where $\bar{\Lambda}$ is defined in Equation 7.25. This implies that the interval

$$\rho \in \left(\frac{\bar{\Lambda}_v}{\bar{\Lambda}_v + \chi^{-1}_{n-1}(\tilde{\alpha}_1)}, \frac{\bar{\Lambda}_v}{\bar{\Lambda}_v + \chi^{-1}_{n-1}(\tilde{\alpha}_2)}\right) \quad (7.27)$$

has a probability of $\tilde{\alpha}_1 - \tilde{\alpha}_2$ to cover ρ. n is again the number of periods and $\chi^{-1}_{n-1}(\tilde{\alpha})$ is the $\tilde{\alpha}$-quantile of the χ^2_{n-1}-distribution.

In the empirical study we compare credible intervals derived by MCMC (which under our settings are the non-asymptotic ones[11] for the ML estimator) and the asymptotic ones.

Finally, note that we could start to examine the variation and bias of the estimators. The less variation is determined, the more efficient an estimator is supposed to be, provided all estimators possess the expectation of the parameter (otherwise a bias is included in the notion of efficiency). As shown in Niethammer and Overbeck (2008), the ML estimator is the most efficient estimator under ASRF (strictly in comparison to the moment estimator). It can be expected that for a large number of periods the intervals for the risk figures will be smallest when using the ML estimator.

Asymptotic confidence intervals

In the empirical and simulation study we will work with the asymptotic confidence intervals for the ME and ML estimators for p and

ρ as given by the asymptotic normality or, more precisely, by the covariance matrix, in Theorem 7.5 and Formula 7.26. For the moment estimator, we get, for example

$$\left(m_{\tilde{L}}(k) - \frac{\sqrt{s_{\tilde{L}}^2(k)}\tilde{K}_{1-\alpha/2}}{\sqrt{n}}, m_{\tilde{L}}(k) + \frac{\sqrt{s_{\tilde{L}}^2(k)}\tilde{K}_{1-\alpha/2}}{\sqrt{n}}\right) \quad (7.28)$$

where $\tilde{K}_{1-\alpha/2} = \Phi^{-1}(1 - \alpha/2)$. For ρ_k, by Theorem 7.5, we obtain

$$\left(\hat{\rho}_{\text{ME}}(k) - \frac{\hat{\sigma}_{\rho,\text{ME},k}\tilde{K}_{1-\alpha/2}}{\sqrt{n}}, \hat{\rho}_{\text{ME}}(k) + \frac{\hat{\sigma}_{\rho,\text{ME},k}\tilde{K}_{1-\alpha/2}}{\sqrt{n}}\right) \quad (7.29)$$

where $\hat{\sigma}_{\rho,k}^2$ is an estimator of $\sigma_{\rho,\text{ME},k}^2$. Replacing $\hat{\rho}_{\text{ME}}$ by $\hat{\rho}_{\text{ML}}$ and $\sigma_{\rho,\text{ME},k}$ by $\sigma_{\rho,\text{ML},k}$ yields the asymptotic confidence interval of the ML estimator of the asset correlation ρ obtained just above.

BAYESIAN ESTIMATION

The advantage of the Bayesian approach is that it can easily be extended to more general distributions, whereas the above moment estimator and, in particular, the ML estimator heavily depend on the model. Estimators thus have to be re-established if model assumptions change slightly. In the Bayesian approach, a new derivation of the estimators is not necessary; however, if the model becomes too complex, the algorithm used (usually MCMC) might become unstable. We use the software BUGS to generate Markov chains from the desired (stationary) posterior distribution. Moreover, Bayesian credible intervals are easy to interpret because they are based on the probability distribution of the parameter itself. More about Bayesian statistics can be found in Chapter 1 of Volume I.

Mixed binomial model

An empirical study to obtain the ML estimator as the mode of a sample of the Bayesian posterior distribution in the mixed binomial is presented in Chapter 6. As we cannot calculate the ML estimator analytically, we focus on ASRF in the empirical study for a comparison with the frequentist approach. The algorithm is similar to that of the ASRF as presented in the next section. (In addition, the common factor Y_t is simulated for every time period.)

Asymptotic single risk factor

In this section, we roughly sketch how parameter estimation in a Bayesian set-up works.[12]

We consider $\pi(p, \rho \mid \tilde{L})$ as posterior distribution for every rating class separately. Prior distributions of p_k and ρ_k are set on $[0, 1]$ for all rating classes k. As $(\tilde{L}_{t,k})$ are iid (see also Equation 7.6), the posterior distribution[13] has the following form with the likelihood function from Equation 7.6

$$\pi(p, \rho \mid \tilde{L}) = \frac{\prod_{t=1}^{n} \prod_{k=1}^{K} f_{\tilde{L}_{t,k}, p_k, \rho_k}(p_k, \rho_k) f_{p_k}(p_k) f_{\rho_k}(\rho_k)}{\int \prod_{t=1}^{n} \prod_{k=1}^{K} f_{\tilde{L}_{t,k}, p_k, \rho_k}(p_k, \rho_k) f_{p_k}(p_k) f_{\rho_k}(\rho_k) \, \mathrm{d}(p, \rho)} \quad (7.30)$$

where $f_x(x)$, $x = p, \rho$ are the prior distributions of p and ρ. Then, samples $(p^{(i)}, \rho^{(i)}) \sim \pi(p, \rho \mid \tilde{L})$ are generated by an MCMC algorithm (see, for example, Gibbs sampling in the section below). For a large enough burn-in[14] $\bar{b}$, approximately the $(I - \bar{b}) \times (2K)$-matrix $(p^{(i)}, \rho^{(i)})_i$, are then $(I - \bar{b})$ samples of $\pi(p, \rho \mid l, N)$.[15] Taking the mode of $(p^{(i)}, \rho^{(i)})_i$ yields a point estimator. If the priors of p_k and ρ_k are set to be uniform on $[0, 1]$, $f_{p_k}(p_k) f_{\rho_k}(\rho_k) = 1$ for all rating classes k and the denominator of Equation 7.30 is 1. Hence, the mode is by definition a good approximation of the ML estimator,[16] ie, the solution of

$$\max_{p, \rho} \prod_{t=1}^{n} \prod_{k=1}^{K} f_{\tilde{L}_{t,k}, p_k, \rho_k}$$

Therefore, the MCMC provides a numerical method to approximate the ML estimator (see page 213 onwards). More on the relation between ML estimators and posterior analysis can be found in Chapter 1 of Volume I.

Roughly speaking, priors leading to an ML estimate are called "uninformative priors". In fact, we have no idea where the parameter might be in the parameter space. The probability of the parameter ρ or p_{R_j} is set to be uniform over the parameter space $(0, 1)$. We know, however, that p_{R_j} should be bigger than p_{R_k} when R_k is the better rating. So, bearing in mind that modes of the resulting Markov chains are no longer ML estimates, Bayesian methodology further gives the possibility to include an "informative" prior belief into the estimation, ie, specifying the parameters in the Beta distribution by an appropriate "pre-information" as, for example, KMV-EDFs[17] (see, for example, Niethammer 2008). As a matter of fact, the possibility to include prior knowledge in addition to empirical data is a major advantage of Bayesian analysis.[18]

Bayesian estimation: Gibbs sampler

For a better understanding of the algorithm, we present a simple example: how estimation works. Instead of sampling the probability of default directly, we observed that sampling the threshold $D = \Phi^{-1}(p)$ yields better results. The following scheme shows the algorithm for two rating classes.

1. Let $\vartheta = (D_A, D_{BB}, \rho_A, \rho_{BB})$. Set $i = 0$.
2. Give starting values, eg, set $D^{(0)} = (0.5, 0.5)', \rho^{(0)} = (0.2, 0.2)$.
3. Simulate full conditional distributions

$$D_A^{(i+1)} \text{ from } \pi(D_A \mid D_{BB}^{(i)}, \rho_A^{(i)}, \rho_B^{(i)}, \tilde{L})$$
$$D_{BB}^{(i+1)} \text{ from } \pi(D_{BB} \mid D_A^{(i+1)}, \rho_A^{(i)}, \rho_B^{(i)}, \tilde{L})$$
$$\vdots$$
$$\rho_{BB}^{(i+1)} \text{ from } \pi(\rho_{BB} \mid D_A^{(i+1)}, D_{BB}^{(i+1)}, \rho_A^{(i+1)}, \tilde{L})$$

4. Set $i = i + 1$. If $i + 1 < I$, go to step 3, where I is the number of iterations.

For i large enough ($i \geqslant \bar{b}$ = burn in), $\vartheta^{(i)}$ is approximately a sample of the posterior function $\pi(D, \rho \mid \tilde{L})$. Full conditional distributions of π are given as a function of D_k, (eg, D_A) given $D_{BB}, \rho_A, \rho_{BB}, \tilde{L}$

$$\pi(D_A \mid D_{BB}, \rho_A, \rho_{BB}, \tilde{L}) \propto \prod_{t=1}^{n} \prod_{j=1}^{K} \mathcal{N}(\Phi^{-1}(\tilde{L}_{k,t})\sqrt{1-\rho_k}, \rho_k) \quad (7.31)$$

where $\mathcal{N}$ denotes the normal distribution with parameter (μ, σ^2). Analogous derivations yield full conditionals for D_{BB}. This means that the full conditionals for the thresholds are standard distributions from which sampling is easily possible. In contrast, the full conditionals for the correlations are non-standard distributions. However, samples from the density $\pi(\rho_A \mid D, \rho_{BB}, \tilde{L})$ can be drawn by the ARMS algorithm.[19]

UNCERTAINTY OF RISK FIGURES UNDER ASRF

In this section we describe the effect of estimation errors on risk figures. Firstly, we define the risk figures and continue by deriving the corresponding confidence intervals. Since a specific risk figure is a specific function of the parameters p and ρ, an estimator of the considered risk figures is then always given by replacing p and ρ in that specific function by the moment $(m_L, h(m_L, s_L^2))$ or the ML estimator $(\hat{p}_{ML}, \hat{\rho}_{ML})$. Since the risk figures are all functions of the parameter p and ρ, the calculations (especially of the derivatives) are easier for the ML estimator. Since for the ME the correlation is a function of p and s^2, namely $\rho(p, s^2) = h(p, s^2)$ (cf Equation 7.13), we then have to additionally derive the derivatives of the correlation as a function of p and s^2. We will describe this in detail for the quantile of the Vasicek distribution. In the last section, we explain the Bayesian approach to obtain credible intervals of risk figures.

Considered risk figures

We consider the following risk figures: the quantile, economic capital and the expected shortfall of Vasicek's loss distribution.

We start with the inverse function of the Vasicek distribution: the quantile of loss or the VaR to the level θ

$$q_\theta(F_{\infty,\rho}) = F_{\infty,\rho}^{-1}(\theta)$$
$$= \Phi\left(\frac{\sqrt{\rho}\Phi^{-1}(\theta) + \Phi^{-1}(p)}{\sqrt{1-\rho}}\right)$$
$$=: Q_\theta(p, \rho)$$

$Q_\theta(m_L, h(m_L, s_L^2))$ is then the moment estimator of the VaR; the moment estimators of the other risk factors can be derived analogously. The economic capital is the quantile minus the expected loss, which is here just p. An analysis is therefore omitted.

To derive the confidence intervals of the expected shortfall, we start with the expected loss of a CDO tranche. At a fixed point in time the expected loss of a CDO tranche with attachment point $K_1\%$ and detachment point $K_2\%$ (at one single payment date, see below) is

$$\mathrm{EL}_{K_1,K_2} = \int_{K_1}^1 (x - K_1)\, dF(x) - \int_{K_2}^1 (x - K_2)\, dF(x) \qquad (7.32)$$

where F is the distribution function of the accumulated losses up to this fixed time point. Under Assumption 7.1, we have (Kalemanova et al 2005)

$$\mathrm{EL}_{K_1,K_2} = \bar{r}(p, \rho, K_1, K_2)$$

where

$$\bar{r}(p, \rho, K_1, K_2) = \Phi_2(-\Phi^{-1}(K_1), D, -\sqrt{1-\rho}) - \Phi_2(-\Phi^{-1}(K_2), D, -\sqrt{1-\rho})$$

with $D = \Phi^{-1}(p)$. The excess expected shortfall above level θ is then

$$EX_\theta = E[L - q_\theta | L > q_\theta] = \frac{EL_{q_\theta,1}}{1 - F(q_\theta)} = \frac{EL_{q_\theta,1}}{1 - \theta}$$

and can be written as a function of p and ρ

$$\begin{aligned} EX_\theta(p, \rho) &= \frac{\bar{r}(p, \rho, Q_\theta(p, \rho), 1)}{1 - \theta} \\ &= \frac{\Phi_2(-\Phi^{-1}(Q_\theta(p, \rho)), \Phi^{-1}(p), -\sqrt{1-\rho})}{1 - \theta} \\ &= \frac{\Phi_2(-(\sqrt{\rho}\Phi^{-1}(\theta) + \Phi^{-1}(p))/\sqrt{1-\rho}, \Phi^{-1}(p), -\sqrt{1-\rho})}{1 - \theta} \end{aligned}$$

The excess expected shortfall describes the excess risk, in case the VaR is reached. In total, the expected shortfall can be expressed as

$$ES_\theta(p, \rho) = Q_\theta(p, \rho) + EX_\theta(p, \rho, Q_\theta(p, \rho), 1)$$

The total amount EX above the VaR is (given p and ρ) independent of the VaR.

Moment and maximum likelihood estimation

We next derive confidence intervals for all considered risk figures as functions $\bar{h}$ of p and ρ. To obtain the moment estimators of the risk figures, ρ is again replaced by the function of the time average and empirical variance, ie, $\hat{\rho}_{ME} = h(m_{\bar{L}}, s_{\bar{L}}^2)$ as defined in Equation 7.13. To obtain the ML-estimator of the risk figures ρ is replaced by ρ_{ML}. According to Theorem 7.3, it remains to calculate the derivatives of these functions $\bar{h}$ with respect to p and ρ (in the case of the ME, further adjusted by $\partial h/\partial p$ and $\partial h/\partial s$) and to show that the gradient of $\bar{h}$ is non-zero. For all risk figures, we obtain asymptotic normality.

Theorem 7.7. Suppose the assumptions of Lemma 7.4 hold. Then for $\bar{h} = Q_\theta$, EL_{K_1,K_2}, EX_θ, ES_θ and $\tilde{h}(p,s) = \bar{h}(p, h(p,s))$ we have that the corresponding estimators are asymptotic normal at rate $\delta_n = n^{-1/2}$, ie,

$$\tilde{h}(m_{\bar{L}}, s_{\bar{L}}^2) \sim AN(\tilde{h}(p, \text{var}(g(Y))), n^{-1}\sigma_{\tilde{h},ME}^2) \qquad (7.33)$$

where

$$\sigma_{\tilde{h},\text{ME}}^2 = \text{var}(g(Y))\left(\frac{\partial \tilde{h}}{\partial p}(p,\text{var}(g(Y)))\right)^2 + \sigma_{\tilde{s}}^2\left(\frac{\partial \tilde{h}}{\partial s}(p,\text{var}(g(Y)))\right)^2$$
$$+ 2\sigma_{ms}\frac{\partial \tilde{h}}{\partial p}(p,\text{var}(g(Y)))\frac{\partial \tilde{h}}{\partial s}(p,\text{var}(g(Y))) \quad (7.34)$$

and $\sigma_{\tilde{s}}^2, \sigma_{ms}$ are given in Equations 7.20 and 7.23. For the ML estimator, we have

$$\bar{h}(\hat{p}_{\text{ML}},\hat{\rho}_{\text{ML}}) \sim \mathcal{AN}(\bar{h}(p,\rho), n^{-1}\sigma_{\bar{h},\text{ML}}^2) \quad (7.35)$$

where

$$\sigma_{\bar{h},\text{ML}}^2 = \sigma_{p,\text{ML}}^2\left(\frac{\partial \bar{h}}{\partial p}(p,\rho)\right)^2 + \sigma_{\rho,\text{ML}}^2\left(\frac{\partial \bar{h}}{\partial \rho}(p,\rho)\right)^2$$
$$+ 2\sigma_{p\rho,\text{ML}}\frac{\partial \bar{h}}{\partial p}(p,\rho)\frac{\partial \bar{h}}{\partial \rho}(p,\rho) \quad (7.36)$$

where $\sigma_{p,\text{ML}}, \sigma_{\rho,\text{ML}}$ and $\sigma_{p\rho,\text{ML}}$ are defined in Equation 7.26.

Confidence intervals can be derived as described in Equation 7.8. To do so, we need to calculate the above gradients for the different risk figures next.

Asymptotic normality of VaR

We calculate the partial derivatives of $\bar{h} = Q_\theta$ with respect to p and ρ and $\tilde{Q}_\theta(p,s) = \bar{h}(p,h(p,s))$ with respect to p and s. We further show that the gradient vector is non-zero

$$\frac{\partial \tilde{Q}_\theta}{\partial p}(p,s)$$
$$= \phi\left(\frac{\sqrt{h(p,s)}\Phi^{-1}(\theta) + \Phi^{-1}(p)}{\sqrt{1-h(p,s)}}\right)$$
$$\times \left(\tfrac{1}{2}(1-h(p,s))^{-3/2}\frac{\partial h}{\partial p}(p,s)(\sqrt{h(p,s)}\Phi^{-1}(\theta) + \Phi^{-1}(p))\right.$$
$$\left. + \frac{1}{\sqrt{1-h(p,s)}}\left(\tfrac{1}{2}\frac{\partial h}{\partial p}(p,s)h(p,s)^{-1/2}\Phi^{-1}(\theta) + \frac{1}{\phi(\Phi^{-1}(p))}\right)\right)$$

and

$$\frac{\partial \tilde{Q}_\theta}{\partial s}(p,s)$$
$$= \phi\left(\frac{\sqrt{h(p,s)}\Phi^{-1}(\theta) + \Phi^{-1}(p)}{\sqrt{1-h(p,s)}}\right)$$
$$\times \left(\frac{1}{2}(1-h(p,s))^{-3/2}\frac{\partial h}{\partial s}(p,s)(\sqrt{h(p,s)}\Phi^{-1}(\theta) + \Phi^{-1}(p))\right.$$
$$\left. + (1-h(p,s))^{-1/2}\frac{1}{2}\frac{\partial h}{\partial s}(p,s)(h(p,s))^{-1/2}\Phi^{-1}(\theta)\right)$$

Finally, if $\partial \tilde{Q}_\theta(p,s)/\partial s = 0$ then $\partial \tilde{Q}_\theta(p,s)/\partial p \neq 0$, because $\partial h/\partial s \neq 0$.

For the ML estimator, we just need the derivative with respect to ρ and the derivatives of h do not appear

$$\frac{\partial Q_\theta}{\partial p}(p,\rho) = \phi\left(\frac{\sqrt{\rho}\Phi^{-1}(\theta) + \Phi^{-1}(p)}{\sqrt{1-\rho}}\right)\frac{1}{\phi(\Phi^{-1}(p))\sqrt{1-\rho}}$$

and

$$\frac{\partial Q_\theta}{\partial \rho}(p,\rho) = \phi\left(\frac{\sqrt{\rho}\Phi^{-1}(\theta) + \Phi^{-1}(p)}{\sqrt{1-\rho}}\right)$$
$$\times \left(\frac{1}{2}(1-\rho)^{-3/2}(\sqrt{\rho}\Phi^{-1}(\theta) + \Phi^{-1}(p)) + \frac{\Phi^{-1}(\theta)}{2\sqrt{(1-\rho)\rho}}\right)$$

Obviously, $\partial Q_\theta/\partial p$ is non-zero. Hence, Theorem 7.7 holds for $\bar{h} = Q_\theta$.

Asymptotic normality of the expected loss of a CDO-tranche

We start by calculating the derivatives for the expected loss (EL) of a CDO tranche. The excess risk is then a special case.

Again, we calculate the gradient of $\tilde{r}(p,s) = \bar{r}(p,h(p,s))$ with

$$\frac{\partial(-\sqrt{1-h(s,p)})}{\partial p} = \frac{1}{2}(1-h(s,p))^{-1/2}\frac{\partial h}{\partial p}$$
$$\frac{\partial \Phi_2(w,v,\rho)}{\partial \rho} = \phi_2(w,v,\rho)$$
$$\frac{\partial \Phi_2(w,v,\rho)}{\partial v} = \int_{-\infty}^{w}\phi_2(u,v,\rho)\,du$$

and by applying the chain rule we get with $\tilde{f}(u,w) := \Phi_2(u,w,\rho)$

$$\frac{\partial \tilde{r}}{\partial p}(p,s) = \bar{r}(p,s,K_1) - \bar{r}(p,s,K_2)$$

where

$$\tilde{r}(p,s,K) := \left(\frac{\partial \tilde{f}_w}{\partial v}(\Phi^{-1}(p), -\sqrt{1-\rho})\frac{\partial \tilde{f}_w}{\partial \rho}(\Phi^{-1}(p), -\sqrt{1-\rho})\right)$$

$$\times \begin{pmatrix} \frac{\partial \Phi^{-1}(p)}{\partial p} \\ \frac{\partial - \sqrt{1-\rho}}{\partial p} \end{pmatrix}$$

$$= \mathcal{N}_{-\sqrt{1-\rho}\Phi^{-1}(p), \rho}(-\Phi^{-1}(K))$$

$$+ \phi_2(-\Phi^{-1}(K), \Phi^{-1}(p), -\sqrt{1-\rho})\tfrac{1}{2}(1-\rho)^{-1/2}\frac{\partial h}{\partial p}$$

with $\rho = h(p,s)$ and $w = -\Phi^{-1}(K)$. For the derivative of $\tilde{r}$ with respect to p the second term of $\tilde{r}$ vanishes as we do not have to calculate the derivative of ρ with respect to p. The derivative of $\tilde{r}$ with respect to s is as follows

$$\frac{\partial \tilde{r}}{\partial s}(p,s) = \frac{1}{2\sqrt{(1-\rho)}}\left(\frac{\partial h}{\partial s}(\phi_2(-\Phi^{-1}(K_1), D, -\sqrt{1-\rho})\right.$$

$$\left. - \phi_2(-\Phi^{-1}(K_2), D, -\sqrt{1-\rho}))\right)$$

where $D = \Phi^{-1}(p)$ and $\rho = h(p,s)$. For the derivative of $\tilde{r}$ with respect to ρ the derivative of h with respect to s is 1. Again if $\partial \tilde{r}/\partial s = 0$ and $K_1 \neq K_2$, then $\partial \tilde{r}/\partial p \neq 0$, as $\partial h/\partial s \neq 0$. Theorem 7.7 follows.

Asymptotic normality of expected shortfall
Recall that

$$\tilde{r}(p,s,K,1) = \Phi_2(-\Phi^{-1}(K), \Phi^{-1}(p), -\sqrt{1-h(p,s)})$$

The excess risk is then

$$\tilde{\text{EX}}(p,s) = \frac{\tilde{r}_\theta(p,s,\tilde{Q}_\theta(p,s),1)}{1-\theta}$$

To determine the total risk $\tilde{\text{ES}}_\theta(p,s) = \text{ES}_\theta(p,h(p,s))$, with $x = p,s$ we have

$$\frac{\partial \tilde{\text{ES}}_\theta}{\partial x} = \frac{\partial \tilde{Q}_\theta}{\partial x} + \frac{\partial \tilde{\text{EX}}_\theta}{\partial x}, \quad \frac{\partial \tilde{r}}{\partial K} = \frac{-\phi_2(-\Phi^{-1}(K), D, -\sqrt{1-\rho})}{\phi(\Phi^{-1}(K))}$$

and

$$\frac{\partial \tilde{EX}_\theta}{\partial p} = (1-\theta)^{-1}\left(\tilde{r}(p,s,\tilde{Q}_\theta(p,s)) + \frac{\partial \tilde{r}}{\partial K}\frac{\partial \tilde{Q}_\theta}{\partial p}(p,s)\right)$$

$$\frac{\partial \tilde{EX}_\theta}{\partial s} = \frac{1}{1-\theta}\left(\frac{1}{2\sqrt{(1-h(p,s))}}\right.$$
$$\times \left(\frac{\partial h}{\partial s}\phi_2(-\Phi^{-1}(\tilde{Q}_\theta(p,s)),\Phi^{-1}(p),-\sqrt{1-\rho})\right)$$
$$\left.+ \frac{\partial \tilde{r}}{\partial K}\frac{\partial \tilde{Q}_\theta}{\partial s}(p,s)\right)$$

For the derivatives of ES and EX, again just the derivatives of h with respect to p and s vanish, only the first term of $\tilde{r}$ is relevant and $\tilde{Q}$ is replaced by Q.

Bayesian approach with MCMC

For Bayesian credible intervals no asymptotic theory is necessary. The same formulas for the risk figures obtained in the last section are valid. So every sample point of p and ρ from the MCMC algorithm can be plugged into the formulas. This yields a new chain of different samples of the risk figure and therefore a simulated distribution. Quantiles of this risk figure distribution can then easily be calculated. Suppose for example within in the MCMC algorithm 50,000 samples of $p(i), \rho(i), i = 1,\ldots,50{,}000$ have been drawn, this yields 50,000 samples of the expected shortfall: $ES_\theta(p(i),\rho(i)), i = 1,\ldots,50{,}000$.

EMPIRICAL STUDY

To guarantee that our method actually delivers correct results, we perform a simulation study with fixed parameters p and ρ for all rating classes and try to recover those with our estimators. Afterwards we analyse the effect of estimation errors on risk figures by real loss data provided by S&P. The different estimators and the implied risk figures are shown together with their confidence (credible) intervals, where "a" corresponds to the 2.5% quantile and "b" to the 97.5% quantile. The theoretical foundation is presented in Theorem 7.3, Equation 7.8 and Theorem 7.7.

The two studies are described in the next two subsections, followed by a discussion.

Simulation study

For the simulation study, we consider five different rating classes CCC, B, BB, BBB and A. The associated default probabilities are summarised by the vector

$$p = (0.2292, 0.0521, 0.0117, 0.0027, 0.0004)$$

For the asset correlation ρ, we consider two cases, one with low correlations for better ratings (already considered in Niethammer and Overbeck (2008))

$$\rho = (0.1683, 0.0763, 0.1032, 0.0744, 0.0747) \qquad \text{(Case 1)}$$

and one with the Basel II correlations (implying higher correlations for smaller default probabilities)

$$\rho_{\text{Basel C}}(p) = 0.12 \frac{1 - \exp(-50p)}{1 - \exp(-50)} + 0.24 \frac{1 - (1 - \exp(-50p))}{1 - \exp(-50)}$$
(Case 2)

resulting with the above default probabilities p in

$$\rho_{\text{Basel C}}(p) = (0.12, 0.1289, 0.1869, 0.2248, 0.2376)$$

The common factor Y_t and the idiosyncratic components $Z_{i,t}$ are sampled independently from a standard normal distribution. The number of obligors is drawn from a Poisson distribution with intensity 2,000 for every period and rating class.

All results are reported in Figure 7.1 and Tables 7.1–7.6.

S&P default study

For the empirical investigation we use the results from S&P's default study (2009). The different estimators and the implied risk figures are again shown together with their confidence and credible intervals.

All results are reported in Figure 7.2 and Tables 7.7–7.11.

Discussion of the results

We compare all estimators of the default probability and the asset correlation including their effect on the implied risk figures. We consider VaR and ES with respect to a confidence level of $\theta = 99\%$. Recall, we display estimates together with their confidence/credible intervals $(a, b) = (q_{2.5\%}, q_{97.5\%})$. As far as the Bayesian credible intervals are concerned, we can say that, under the assumptions made,

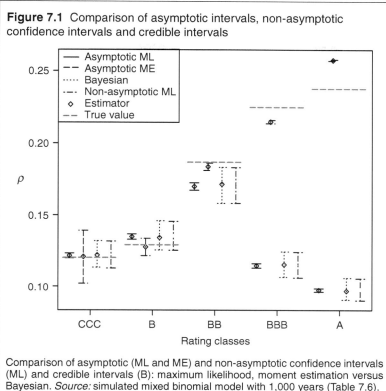

Figure 7.1 Comparison of asymptotic intervals, non-asymptotic confidence intervals and credible intervals

Comparison of asymptotic (ML and ME) and non-asymptotic confidence intervals (ML) and credible intervals (B): maximum likelihood, moment estimation versus Bayesian. *Source:* simulated mixed binomial model with 1,000 years (Table 7.6).

estimates of VaR(99%) or ES(99%) lie in this interval with a probability of $1 - \alpha$, where $\alpha = 5\%$. The correct interpretation of frequentistic confidence intervals is usually more involved. All estimators and their confidence/credible intervals shown in this empirical study are based on the ASRF model. We start with the moment estimator.

The moment estimator is valid in the mixed binomial and in the ASRF model (see Equations 7.3 and 7.13). To derive asymptotic confidence intervals, however, we need the ASRF assumption.

For rating classes BBB and A, a problem of the ME becomes apparent when looking at the results of the simulation study described above. The confidence boundaries of ρ, (cf Equation 7.29) are too low (Figure 7.2 and Table 7.4). Even increasing the number of periods n does not greatly improve the problem (Figure 7.1 and Table 7.6).

In fact, the number of obligors in the better rating classes is too low to judge the ASRF model (although the average number of obligors is

Table 7.1 Simulated binomial model with 25 years

	p	$p_{ml} \in [a_{p(ml,a)}, b_{p(ml,a)}]$
CCC	0.2292	$0.23764 \in [0.21196, 0.26332]$
B	0.0521	$0.05487 \in [0.04893, 0.06081]$
BB	0.0117	$0.01235 \in [0.01022, 0.01448]$
BBB	0.0027	$0.00303 \in [0.00251, 0.00355]$
A	0.0004	$0.00045 \in [0.00036, 0.00054]$
	p	$p_{me} \in [a_{p(me,a)}, b_{p(me,a)}]$
CCC	0.2292	$0.23921 \in [0.18970, 0.28871]$
B	0.0521	$0.05466 \in [0.04366, 0.06565]$
BB	0.0117	$0.01206 \in [0.00833, 0.01580]$
BBB	0.0027	$0.00288 \in [0.00185, 0.00391]$
A	0.0004	$0.00042 \in [0.00020, 0.00064]$
	p	$p_B \in [a_{p(B)}, b_{p(B)}]$
CCC	0.2292	$0.26119 \in [0.21510, 0.32660]$
B	0.0521	$0.06213 \in [0.05110, 0.08755]$
BB	0.0117	$0.01795 \in [0.01263, 0.03632]$
BBB	0.0027	$0.00446 \in [0.00313, 0.00999]$
A	0.0004	$0.00076 \in [0.00050, 0.00256]$

Comparison of the Bayesian, the moment and the maximum likelihood estimator of the default probability under the assumption of an asymptotic single risk factor (Case 1, 20% adjustment on $m_{\tilde{L}}$).

already 2,000). There is too large a number of periods (years) where the loss rate has the same value of zero. The variation in the loss rates $s_{\tilde{L}}^2$ is too small (see Equation 7.3). This does not cause a problem for the estimated default probability, as it becomes smaller for better ratings, but ρ stays around the same quantity over all rating classes. Asymptotic confidence intervals of ρ derived from the moment estimator are therefore questionable.

The problem that loss rates can be zero is more severe for the ML estimator and the Bayesian estimator[20] in the ASRF model as the calculation becomes infeasible because $\Phi^{-1}(0) = -\infty$ cannot be a sample of Equation 7.6 (see also Equation 7.24). Zero loss rates therefore have to be adjusted to a substitute value $\min(\tilde{L}) > 0$. Clearly, the question is what we should actually choose for $\min(\tilde{L})$. The sensitivity to this adjustment is higher the more zeros are observed in the data set and thus especially for the basket A. The lower the substitute

Table 7.2 Simulated binomial model with 25 years

	ρ	$\rho_{ml} \in [a_{\rho(ml,a)}, b_{\rho(ml,a)}]$
CCC	0.1683	$0.1710 \in [0.1545, 0.1876]$
B	0.0763	$0.0716 \in [0.0665, 0.0766]$
BB	0.1032	$0.1104 \in [0.1012, 0.1196]$
BBB	0.0744	$0.0790 \in [0.0732, 0.0848]$
A	0.0747	$0.0785 \in [0.0728, 0.0842]$
	ρ	$\rho_{me} \in [a_{\rho(me,a)}, b_{\rho(me,a)}]$
CCC	0.1683	$0.1590 \in [0.0407, 0.2774]$
B	0.0763	$0.0596 \in [0.0235, 0.0956]$
BB	0.1032	$0.0763 \in [0.0633, 0.0893]$
BBB	0.0744	$0.0684 \in [0.0636, 0.0732]$
A	0.0747	$0.0868 \in [0.0853, 0.0882]$
	ρ	$\rho_B \in [a_{\rho(B)}, b_{\rho(B)}]$
CCC	0.1683	$0.1726 \in [0.1204, 0.3012]$
B	0.0763	$0.0756 \in [0.0496, 0.1470]$
BB	0.1032	$0.1182 \in [0.0787, 0.2235]$
BBB	0.0744	$0.0845 \in [0.0561, 0.1699]$
A	0.0747	$0.0872 \in [0.0569, 0.1775]$
	ρ	$[a_{\rho(ml,non-a)}, b_{\rho(ml,non-a)}]$
CCC	0.1683	$[0.1159, 0.2938]$
B	0.0763	$[0.0467, 0.1345]$
BB	0.1032	$[0.0730, 0.2001]$
BBB	0.0744	$[0.0517, 0.1474]$
A	0.0747	$[0.0513, 0.1465]$

Comparison of the Bayesian, the moment, and the maximum likelihood estimator of the asset correlation under the assumption of an asymptotic single risk factor (Case 1, 20% adjustment on $m_{\tilde{L}}$).

value, the higher the correlation will be (see Formula 7.25). Setting the substitute value $\min(\tilde{L})$ equal to 1bp leads to very high correlations, although the original correlations used in the simulation study are low (Niethammer and Overbeck 2008). In this study, correlations (for classes A and BBB) have not been recovered with this adjustment of $\min(\tilde{L}) = 1$bp. In the present simulation study, the adjustment dependent on the average loss rate $m_{\tilde{L}}(k)$ of each rating is set as follows: $\min(\tilde{L})(k) = 20\% m_{\tilde{L}}(k)$, $k = $ CCC, ..., A. This

Table 7.3 Simulated binomial model with 28 years

	p	$p_{ml} \in [a_{p(ml,a)}, b_{p(ml,a)}]$
CCC	0.2292	$0.2253 \in [0.2048, 0.2457]$
B	0.0521	$0.0514 \in [0.0440, 0.0588]$
BB	0.0117	$0.0108 \in [0.0087, 0.0130]$
BBB	0.0027	$0.0027 \in [0.0022, 0.0033]$
A	0.0004	$0.0003 \in [0.0002, 0.0004]$
	p	$p_{me} \in [a_{p(me,a)}, b_{p(me,a)}]$
CCC	0.2292	$0.2244 \in [0.1798, 0.2690]$
B	0.0521	$0.0524 \in [0.0335, 0.0713]$
BB	0.0117	$0.0123 \in [0.0040, 0.0206]$
BBB	0.0027	$0.0035 \in [0.0002, 0.0067]$
A	0.0004	$0.0004 \in [0.0000, 0.0008]$
	p	$p_B \in [a_{p(B)}, b_{p(B)}]$
CCC	0.2292	$0.2421 \in [0.2048, 0.2961]$
B	0.0521	$0.0648 \in [0.0507, 0.1043]$
BB	0.0117	$0.0190 \in [0.0124, 0.0421]$
BBB	0.0027	$0.0053 \in [0.0033, 0.0165]$
A	0.0004	$0.0006 \in [0.0004, 0.0024]$

Comparison of the Bayesian, the moment, and the maximum likelihood estimator of the default probability under the assumption of an asymptotic single risk factor (Case 2, 20% adjustment on $m_{\tilde{L}}$).

seemed to perform better; however, this will only be true if the correlations in the simulation study are set small (Case 1); see Table 7.2. If correlations are set equal to the Basel II correlation formula, these correlations are not met (for A and BBB) again by the ML estimates (see Figure 7.1 or Tables 7.4 and 7.6 (Case 2)). In fact, correlations for better ratings can be manipulated almost arbitrarily by shifting the substitute value for zero loss rates. This becomes worse the more loss rates are zero. Hence, we should refrain from using the ML estimator and the Bayesian estimator for the asset correlation in case of zero loss rates at least for the buckets A and BBB.[21] Still, a trick will enable us to use the Bayesian approach to obtain realistic credible intervals (see later in this section). Furthermore, note that the problem of zero loss rates does not exist in the binomial mixed model; the cost in this case is the numerical method to obtain estimates (see the above section about the binomial model on page 202 and Chapter 6).

Table 7.4 Simulated binomial model with 28 years

	ρ	$\rho_{ml} \in [a_{\rho(ml,a)}, b_{\rho(ml,a)}]$
CCC	0.1200	$0.1295 \in [0.1186, 0.1403]$
B	0.1289	$0.1372 \in [0.1255, 0.1489]$
BB	0.1869	$0.1630 \in [0.1483, 0.1777]$
BBB	0.2248	$0.1400 \in [0.1279, 0.1520]$
A	0.2376	$0.0988 \in [0.0913, 0.1063]$
	ρ	$\rho_{me} \in [a_{\rho(me,a)}, b_{\rho(me,a)}]$
CCC	0.1200	$0.1545 \in [0.0417, 0.2673]$
B	0.1289	$0.1812 \in [0.1415, 0.2208]$
BB	0.1869	$0.2618 \in [0.2434, 0.2801]$
BBB	0.2248	$0.2699 \in [0.2610, 0.2789]$
A	0.2376	$0.1973 \in [0.1953, 0.1993]$
	ρ	$\rho_B \in [a_{\rho(B)}, b_{\rho(B)}]$
CCC	0.1200	$0.1350 \in [0.0921, 0.2313]$
B	0.1289	$0.1498 \in [0.0990, 0.2494]$
BB	0.1869	$0.1776 \in [0.1200, 0.2924]$
BBB	0.2248	$0.1498 \in [0.1040, 0.2753]$
A	0.2376	$0.1073 \in [0.0732, 0.2052]$
	ρ	$[a_{\rho(ml,non-a)}, b_{\rho(ml,non-a)}]$
CCC	0.1200	$[0.0879, 0.2223]$
B	0.1289	$[0.0935, 0.2341]$
BB	0.1869	$[0.1121, 0.2723]$
BBB	0.2248	$[0.0954, 0.2382]$
A	0.2376	$[0.0663, 0.1740]$

Comparison of the Bayesian, the moment, and the maximum likelihood estimator of the asset correlation under the assumption of an asymptotic single risk factor (Case 2, 20% adjustment on $m_{\underline{L}}$).

We conclude, that in the ASRF model the moment estimator gives more reliable results for rating buckets A and BBB than the maximum likelihood and the Bayesian estimators for both the default probability and the asset correlation. However, the ML and Bayesian estimators seem to give more stable results for the confidence bounds of ρ for better ratings than the moment estimator.[22] As the ML estimator is theoretically more efficient than the moment estimator (yielding smaller confidence intervals, see page 216), confidence intervals of

Table 7.5 Simulated binomial model with 1,000 years

	p	$p_{ml} \in [a_{p(ml,a)}, b_{p(ml,a)}]$
CCC	0.2292	0.2301 ∈ [0.2267, 0.2334]
B	0.0521	0.0526 ∈ [0.0513, 0.0538]
BB	0.0117	0.0117 ∈ [0.0113, 0.0121]
BBB	0.0027	0.0024 ∈ [0.0023, 0.0025]
A	0.0004	0.0003 ∈ [0.0003, 0.0003]
	p	$p_{me} \in [a_{p(me,a)}, b_{p(me,a)}]$
CCC	0.2292	0.2302 ∈ [0.2235, 0.2368]
B	0.0521	0.0524 ∈ [0.0498, 0.0550]
BB	0.0117	0.0119 ∈ [0.0109, 0.0129]
BBB	0.0027	0.0027 ∈ [0.0023, 0.0030]
A	0.0004	0.0004 ∈ [0.0003, 0.0005]
	p	$p_B \in [a_{p(B)}, b_{p(B)}]$
CCC	0.2292	0.2448 ∈ [0.2380, 0.2513]
B	0.0521	0.0660 ∈ [0.0627, 0.0697]
BB	0.0117	0.0193 ∈ [0.0178, 0.0215]
BBB	0.0027	0.0040 ∈ [0.0037, 0.0044]
A	0.0004	0.0006 ∈ [0.0005, 0.0007]

Comparison of the Bayesian, the moment, and the maximum likelihood estimator of the default probability under the assumption of an asymptotic single risk factor (Case 2, 20% adjustment on $m_{\tilde{L}}$).

the ML estimator can be considered as a lower bound for those of the moment estimator (if the point estimates are similar). We therefore modify zero loss rates in such a way that the adjusted ML estimator (and therefore also the Bayesian estimator) almost equates the moment estimator $\hat{\rho}_{ML}(k) \approx \hat{\rho}_{ME}(k)$ for all rating classes k

$$\min(\tilde{L}) = (0.044813, 0.010537, 0.002353, 0.000524, 0.000025)$$
(7.37)

As $\hat{\rho}_{ML}(k) \approx \hat{\rho}_{ME}(k)$ for the rating buckets with many zero loss rates, we then use the confidence intervals of the ML estimator for the moment estimator as a lower bound. We have still assumed a very large number of periods to obtain these confidence intervals. The Bayesian analysis does not need this assumption; the implied credible intervals are a much more conservative alternative and an

Table 7.6 Simulated binomial model with 1,000 years

	ρ	$\rho_{ml} \in [a_{\rho(ml,a)}, b_{\rho(ml,a)}]$
CCC	0.1200	$0.1214 \in [0.1197, 0.1230]$
B	0.1289	$0.1347 \in [0.1328, 0.1366]$
BB	0.1869	$0.1699 \in [0.1673, 0.1725]$
BBB	0.2248	$0.1144 \in [0.1129, 0.1159]$
A	0.2376	$0.0973 \in [0.0961, 0.0985]$

	ρ	$\rho_{me} \in [a_{\rho(me,a)}, b_{\rho(me,a)}]$
CCC	0.1200	$0.1206 \in [0.1021, 0.1392]$
B	0.1289	$0.1274 \in [0.1213, 0.1335]$
BB	0.1869	$0.1837 \in [0.1811, 0.1862]$
BBB	0.2248	$0.2147 \in [0.2136, 0.2158]$
A	0.2376	$0.2574 \in [0.2570, 0.2579]$

	ρ	$\rho_B \in [a_{\rho(B)}, b_{\rho(B)}]$	$[a_{\rho(ml,non-a)}, b_{\rho(ml,non-a)}]$
CCC	0.1200	$0.1217 \in [0.1132, 0.1317]$	$[0.1126, 0.1314]$
B	0.1289	$0.1340 \in [0.1253, 0.1460]$	$[0.1251, 0.1456]$
BB	0.1869	$0.1715 \in [0.1583, 0.1833]$	$[0.1583, 0.1831]$
BBB	0.2248	$0.1152 \in [0.1066, 0.1242]$	$[0.1061, 0.1239]$
A	0.2376	$0.0967 \in [0.0906, 0.1060]$	$[0.0901, 0.1056]$

Comparison of the Bayesian, the moment, and the maximum likelihood estimator of the asset correlation under the assumption of an asymptotic single risk factor (Case 2, 20% adjustment on $m_{\tilde{L}}$)

extensive discussion is given below. First, we highlight an intriguing effect observed in the real data of Standard & Poor's, which is closely related to the 2007–9 financial crisis.

For the old adjustment $\min(\tilde{L}) = 20\% m_{\tilde{L}}$ the estimated correlation by the ML and Bayesian estimators of basket A was much too low in S&P's default study (2009) (see Table 7.8). With the new adjustment, the ME, Bayesian estimator and ML estimator of the asset correlation are very close (see Table 7.10 or Figure 7.2). From the simulation study we know that the moment estimator is reliable. We can therefore conclude that in comparison to the default study from 2006 (Niethammer and Overbeck 2008) this can be interpreted as an almost doubled correlation for basket A, which can be explained by the upcoming financial crisis. With the first adjustment this would not have become visible.

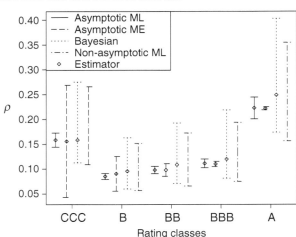

Figure 7.2 Comparison of asymptotic intervals, non-asymptotic confidence intervals and credible intervals

Comparison of asymptotic (ML and ME) and non-asymptotic confidence intervals (ML) and credible intervals (B): maximum likelihood, moment estimation versus Bayesian. *Source:* S&P's default study (2009) (Table 7.10).

As promised, we next try to judge the goodness of the asymptotic approximation of the confidence intervals by a comparison with a Bayesian MCMC method and the analytical non-asymptotic confidence interval in Equation 7.27. The latter are denoted by $a_{\text{ml, non-a}}$ and $b_{\text{ml, non-a}}$ in the tables. The MCMC samples of the posterior distribution (with uniform priors for p and ρ) were sampled by the MCMC algorithm implemented in the software BUGS.[23] The mode of the chain is denoted by p_B, the corresponding intervals are indexed by "B". The same adjusted data as for the analytical ML estimator was used in both cases. Consequently, the mode of the MCMC sample should approximately coincide with analytical ML estimator.[24] Moreover, the lengths of the credible intervals of the posterior distribution can be compared with the asymptotic ones. In Tables 7.2, 7.4 and 7.6, we observe that the intervals obtained by MCMC are a lot larger than the asymptotic intervals of the ML estimator, particularly the upper bound. On the other hand, except for numerical errors, intervals obtained from the Monte Carlo method are very similar to the analytical non-asymptotic ones in Equation 7.27 (Figure 7.1). Bayesian techniques are therefore confirmed to be a good tool to display uncertainty in the parameters. We conclude

Table 7.7 S&P's default study (2009) (1981–2008)

	$p_{ml} \in [a_{p(ml,a)}, b_{p(ml,a)}]$	$p_{me} \in [a_{p(me,a)}, b_{p(me,a)}]$
CCC	0.2248 ∈ [0.2022, 0.2474]	0.2241 ∈ [0.1793, 0.2688]
B	0.0525 ∈ [0.0466, 0.0584]	0.0527 ∈ [0.0400, 0.0654]
BB	0.0118 ∈ [0.0100, 0.0137]	0.0118 ∈ [0.0077, 0.0158]
BBB	0.0031 ∈ [0.0025, 0.0037]	0.0029 ∈ [0.0016, 0.0043]
A	0.0006 ∈ [0.0005, 0.0008]	0.0007 ∈ [0.0000, 0.0015]

	$p_B \in [a_{p(B)}, b_{p(B)}]$
CCC	0.2404 ∈ [0.2058, 0.3042]
B	0.0613 ∈ [0.0499, 0.0865]
BB	0.0166 ∈ [0.0120, 0.0298]
BBB	0.0051 ∈ [0.0034, 0.0120]
A	0.0012 ∈ [0.0008, 0.0042]

Comparison of the Bayesian, the moment and the maximum likelihood estimator of the default probability under the assumption of an asymptotic single risk factor (20% adjustment on $m_{\tilde{L}}$).

Table 7.8 S&P's default study (2009) (1981–2008)

	$\rho_{ml} \in [a_{\rho(ml,a)}, b_{\rho(ml,a)}]$	$\rho_{me} \in [a_{\rho(me,a)}, b_{\rho(me,a)}]$
CCC	0.1586 ∈ [0.1444, 0.1728]	0.1560 ∈ [0.0431, 0.2689]
B	0.0851 ∈ [0.0791, 0.0912]	0.0905 ∈ [0.0556, 0.1253]
BB	0.0963 ∈ [0.0890, 0.1035]	0.0980 ∈ [0.0853, 0.1106]
BBB	0.1045 ∈ [0.0964, 0.1126]	0.1100 ∈ [0.1048, 0.1152]
A	0.1066 ∈ [0.0983, 0.1150]	0.2217 ∈ [0.2185, 0.2249]

	$\rho_B \in [a_{\rho(B)}, b_{\rho(B)}]$	$[a_{\rho(ml,non-a)}, b_{\rho(ml,non-a)}]$
CCC	0.1623 ∈ [0.1137, 0.2700]	[0.1089, 0.2659]
B	0.0899 ∈ [0.0601, 0.1662]	[0.0569, 0.1517]
BB	0.0998 ∈ [0.0700, 0.1872]	[0.0646, 0.1699]
BBB	0.1120 ∈ [0.0757, 0.2067]	[0.0703, 0.1831]
A	0.1109 ∈ [0.0795, 0.2171]	[0.0718, 0.1866]

Comparison of the Bayesian, the moment and the maximum likelihood estimator of the asset correlation under the assumption of an asymptotic single risk factor (20% adjustment on $m_{\tilde{L}}$).

that the asymptotic intervals underestimate the uncertainty in the parameters and therefore the model risk of the implied risk figures, which are described next.

Table 7.9 S&P's default study (2009) (1981–2008)

	$p_{ml} \in [a_{p(ml,a)}, b_{p(ml,a)}]$	$p_{me} \in [a_{p(me,a)}, b_{p(me,a)}]$
CCC	0.2248 ∈ [0.2022, 0.2474]	0.2241 ∈ [0.1793, 0.2688]
B	0.0525 ∈ [0.0466, 0.0584]	0.0527 ∈ [0.0400, 0.0654]
BB	0.0118 ∈ [0.0100, 0.0137]	0.0118 ∈ [0.0077, 0.0158]
BBB	0.0031 ∈ [0.0025, 0.0037]	0.0029 ∈ [0.0016, 0.0043]
A	0.0005 ∈ [0.0003, 0.0007]	0.0007 ∈ [0.0000, 0.0015]

	$p_B \in [a_{p(B)}, b_{p(B)}]$
CCC	0.2431 ∈ [0.2067, 0.3050]
B	0.0612 ∈ [0.0498, 0.0869]
BB	0.0158 ∈ [0.0120, 0.0301]
BBB	0.0051 ∈ [0.0034, 0.0131]
A	0.0021 ∈ [0.0009, 0.0142]

Comparison of the Bayesian, the moment and the maximum likelihood estimator of the default probability under the assumption of an asymptotic single risk factor (optimised adjustment according to Equation 7.37).

Table 7.10 S&P's default study (2009) (1981–2008)

	$\rho_{ml} \in [a_{\rho(ml,a)}, b_{\rho(ml,a)}]$	$\rho_{me} \in [a_{\rho(me,a)}, b_{\rho(me,a)}]$
CCC	0.15864 ∈ [0.14443, 0.17285]	0.15599 ∈ [0.04309, 0.26889]
B	0.08513 ∈ [0.07906, 0.09121]	0.09046 ∈ [0.05558, 0.12534]
BB	0.09807 ∈ [0.09066, 0.10547]	0.09798 ∈ [0.08533, 0.11063]
BBB	0.11125 ∈ [0.10244, 0.12007]	0.11004 ∈ [0.10483, 0.11524]
A	0.22257 ∈ [0.20075, 0.24439]	0.22171 ∈ [0.21850, 0.22491]

	$\rho_B \in [a_{\rho(B)}, b_{\rho(B)}]$	$[a_{\rho(ml,non-a)}, b_{\rho(ml,non-a)}]$
CCC	0.1586 ∈ [0.1126, 0.2753]	[0.1089, 0.2659]
B	0.0957 ∈ [0.0600, 0.1634]	[0.0569, 0.1517]
BB	0.1086 ∈ [0.0708, 0.1927]	[0.0658, 0.1728]
BBB	0.1198 ∈ [0.0814, 0.2188]	[0.0751, 0.1939]
A	0.2489 ∈ [0.1741, 0.4028]	[0.1565, 0.3549]

Comparison of the Bayesian (B), the moment (ME) and the maximum likelihood (ML) estimator of the asset correlation under the assumption of an asymptotic single risk factor (optimised adjustment according to Equation 7.37).

In Table 7.11 implied risk figures (the VaR and the expected shortfall at a level of 99%) are considered. We observe that the asymptotic confidence intervals of the risk figures are significantly smaller in comparison to the Bayesian approach.

Table 7.11 S&P's default study (2009) (1981–2008)

	$Q_{ml} \in [a_{ml}, b_{ml}]$	$Q_{me} \in [a_{me}, b_{me}]$	$Q_B \in [a_B, b_B]$
CCC	$0.574 \in [0.558, 0.590]$	$0.569 \in [0.402, 0.737]$	$0.6300 \in [0.509, 0.781]$
B	$0.162 \in [0.154, 0.171]$	$0.167 \in [0.122, 0.212]$	$0.1900 \in [0.140, 0.312]$
BB	$0.053 \in [0.048, 0.058]$	$0.053 \in [0.037, 0.068]$	$0.0710 \in [0.047, 0.166]$
BBB	$0.019 \in [0.016, 0.021]$	$0.018 \in [0.011, 0.025]$	$0.0300 \in [0.018, 0.097]$
A	$0.006 \in [0.005, 0.008]$	$0.009 \in [0.001, 0.018]$	$0.0236 \in [0.009, 0.175]$

	$ES_{ml} \in [a_{ml}, b_{ml}]$	$ES_{me} \in [a_{me}, b_{me}]$	$ES_B \in [a_B, b_B]$
CCC	$0.629 \in [0.554, 0.704]$	$0.624 \in [0.402, 1.000]$	$0.682 \in [0.558, 0.832]$
B	$0.190 \in [0.132, 0.249]$	$0.197 \in [0.122, 0.496]$	$0.220 \in [0.161, 0.366]$
BB	$0.067 \in [0.038, 0.097]$	$0.067 \in [0.037, 0.165]$	$0.089 \in [0.059, 0.212]$
BBB	$0.026 \in [0.012, 0.039]$	$0.024 \in [0.011, 0.064]$	$0.040 \in [0.023, 0.134]$
A	$0.012 \in [0.008, 0.015]$	$0.016 \in [0.001, 0.042]$	$0.039 \in [0.015, 0.262]$

A comparison of the VaR and the expected shortfall implied by the Bayesian, the moment and the maximum likelihood estimator under the assumption of an asymptotic single risk factor (optimised adjustment according to Equation 7.37).

In summary, if the simple ASRF model is adequate, which is the case when (almost) no zero loss rates are observed or after making the adjustment in Equation 7.37, the ML estimator and the Bayesian estimator yield realistic non-asymptotic confidence and credible intervals, respectively, ie, they are reliable tools to estimate the uncertainty of the asset correlation and the risk figures. However, in more complex models such as the binomial mixed model, such intervals for the ML estimator in Equation 7.27 are hard to obtain. The Bayesian approach is the only method to gain realistic information about uncertainty in the parameters as well as in the risk figures, and the reader is referred to Chapter 6 for a readable analysis; note, however, that in Chapter 6 only one homogeneous correlation is used for all rating classes.

CONCLUSION

In this chapter we have derived different (frequentist and Bayesian) estimation techniques and methods to quantify the effect of estimation errors within the large pool approximation of the Gaussian copula model. We obtained the following results: the simulation study shows that for all rating buckets the initial parameters are fitted well by the moment estimator in the binomial mixed model and its limit case (the ASRF model). However, asymptotic confidence intervals of the correlation parameter are not stable. In fact, if zero loss rates are observed in the data (mostly in rating buckets A and BBB), these rates have to be adjusted such that the ASRF model makes sense, and that the ML estimator and the Bayesian estimator in this model can be applied. The ML estimator and the Bayesian estimator for the asset correlation are in fact adjusted such that they almost coincide with the moment estimator. Intervals of the ML estimator for the probability of default and the asset correlation can then be obtained by two non-asymptotic approaches (Equation 7.27 and the Bayesian one). As both intervals have approximately the same length (Figures 7.1 and 7.2), we conclude that Bayesian credible intervals yield the best guess for such intervals and conclude that Bayesian methods yield a reliable tool to estimate uncertainty. In fact, in the binomial mixed model, the Bayesian methodology by the MCMC is the only way to derive such intervals.

Although the asymptotic confidence intervals of the risk figures are already quite large, the comparison with the Bayesian approach shows that the latter are even higher, implying higher costs of model risk. This underestimation by the asymptotic confidence interval might also be caused by the implicit linearisation within the asymptotic normality approach and the need for unrealistically long time series to efficiently estimate one correlation for every rating class. An approach with just one correlation is presented in Chapter 6.

Finally, note that all of the results presented here are gained under very restrictive but common assumptions. Nevertheless, our findings show a clear qualitative direction: in our empirical study we can clearly observe a very high implied model risk that must not be neglected.

> The opinions expressed in this article are those of the authors, and do not necessarily reflect those of the authors' employers.

1   See Chapter 1 of Volume I for more details on this.
2   See also Bluhm and Overbeck (2003).
3   This means that we assume that the number of obligors is large; therefore, this assumption is also called a "large pool" or "infinite granular" assumption.
4   See also Bluhm and Overbeck (2003).
5   See Chapter 8.

6   Note, for the ASRF assumption, that it has been already assumed that the number of obligors N is very large.

7   See, for example, Van der Vaart (1998, Theorem 3.8).

8   See also Serfling (1980, p. 124).

9   See, for example, Serfling (1980, Theorem 2.2.1B).

10 As the new estimator is a function of m_L, Theorem 7.3 can be applied as in the section on the frequentist approach (see page 208). A detailed derivation is left for future research.

11 n does not have to be assumed to be very large.

12 For further details on MCMC simulation techniques see Chib and Greenberg (1996) or Chapter 2 of Volume I. In the context of credit risk modelling, the reader is referred to Chapter 6.

13 As p_k and ρ_k are not dependent on other rating classes, the algorithm can be performed for every rating class separately.

14 To make sure that the Markov chain generated has approximately the posterior distribution as stationary distribution.

15 I is the number of iterations and K is the number of rating classes.

16 In the binomial model this works similarly by additionally sampling y from a Gaussian prior if $F = G = \Phi$.

17 EDFs (expected default frequencies) are trademarks owned by MIS Quality Management Corp and are used under license by Moody's KMV Company.

18 Again see Chapter 1 of Volume I for more details on this.

19 See also McNeil and Wendin (2006), Wendin (2006) and Gilks *et al* (1995).

20 Here, the Bayesian estimator is the mode of the generated Markov chain of Equation 7.30 with uniform priors; it is by definition equal to the ML estimator up to a Monte Carlo error. To sample from Equation 7.30 the adjustment described in the text is also needed such that the Vasicek approximation (Equation 7.6) makes sense.

21 It is worth repeating here the quote from Gelman as given in Chapter 1 of Volume I, namely that Bayesian statistics is "a method for… making … predictions using probability statements conditional on observed data and an assumed model." In the case of A and BBB rating classes, roughly speaking, there are no observations and, as a natural consequence of the Bayesian method, there is nothing to predict.

22 Confidence intervals are too small for the ME; the true correlation value in the simulation study does not lie in the interval (see Tables 7.2, 7.4 and 7.6).

23 See www.mrc-bsu.cam.ac.uk/bugs/.

24 However, probably because the algorithm is very generic and not specifically programmed for the asymptotic single risk factor model, small differences arise. For 1,000 periods the difference is already negligible. A deep analysis by implementing an own MCMC algorithm is left for future research.

REFERENCES

Bluhm, C., and L. Overbeck, 2003, "Estimating Systematic Risk in Uniform Credit Portfolios", in G. Bol *et al* (eds), *Credit Risk: Measurement, Evaluation and Management* (Heidelberg: Physica).

Bluhm, C., L. Overbeck and C. K. J. Wagner, 2002, *An Introduction to Credit Risk Modeling* (London: Chapman & Hall/CRC).

Chib, S., and E. Greenberg, 1996, "Markov Chain Monte Carlo in Econometrics", *Econometric Theory* 12, pp. 409–31.

Demey, P., J.-F. Jouanin, C. Roget and T. Roncalli, 2004, "Maximum Likelihood Estimate of Default Correlations", *Risk Magazine*, November.

Duellmann, K., J. Küll, and M. Kunisch, 2008, "Estimating Asset Correlation from Stock Proces or Default Rates: Which Method Is Superior?" Discussion Paper 04/2008, Series 2, Deutsche Bundesbank.

Gilks, W. R., N. G. Best and K. K. C. Tan, 1995, "Adaptive Rejection Metropolis Sampling with Gibbs Sampling", *Applied Statistics* 4, pp. 455–75.

Kalemanova, A., B. Schmid and R. Werner, 2007, "The Normal Inverse Gaussian Distribution for Synthetic CDO Pricing", *Journal of Derivatives* 14(3), pp. 80–93.

Le Cam, L., and G. L. Yang, 1990, *Asymptotics in Statistics: Some Basic Concepts* (Springer).

McNeil, A., and J. P. Wendin, 2007, "Bayesian Inference for Generalized Linear Mixed Models of Portfolio Credit Risk", *Journal of Empirical Finance* 14(2), pp. 134–49.

Merton, R. C., 1974, "On the Pricing of Corporate Debt: The Risk Structure of Interest Rates", *Journal of Finance* 29, pp. 449–70.

Niethammer, C. R., 2008, "Are Default Correlations Time-Dependent? A Bayesian Approach", Working Paper.

Niethammer, C. R., and L. Overbeck, 2008, "Default Correlations and the Effect of Estimation Errors on Risk Figures", Working Paper, URL: http://www.defaultrisk.com.

Serfling, R. J., 1980, *Approximation Theorems of Mathematical Statistics* (Chichester: John Wiley & Sons).

Standard & Poor's, 2009, "Annual 2009 Global Corporate Default Study and Rating Transitions", Standard & Poor's.

Tarashev, N., and H. Zhu, 2007, "Modeling and Calibration Errors in Measures of Portfolio Credit Risk", Working Paper 230, Bank for International Settlements.

Van der Vaart, A. W., 1998, *Asymptotic Statistics* (Cambridge University Press).

Vasicek, O. A., 1991, "The Loan Loss Distribution", Technical Report, KMV Corporation.

Vasicek, O. A., 1998, "A Series Expansion for the Bivariate Normal Integral", Technical Report, KMV Corporation.

Wendin, J. E. P., "Bayesian Methods in Portfolio Credit Risk Management", Dissertation No. 16481, ETH Zurich.

8

Lessons from the Crisis in Mortgage-Backed Structured Securities: Where Did Credit Ratings Go Wrong?

Erik Heitfield
Federal Reserve Board

Unexpected deterioration in the credit quality of structured residential mortgage-backed securities (RMBSs) and collateralised debt obligations (CDOs) backed by mortgage securities played a central role in the 2008–9 financial crisis. As investors became increasingly concerned about the credit risk embedded in RMBSs and CDOs, demand for these and other credit products plummeted, creating severe liquidity and credit challenges for many financial institutions. After a brief overview of the crisis in mortgage securities, we use a simple normal copula model of portfolio credit risk to illustrate how the process of pooling assets and tranching liabilities inherent in asset securitisation filters out idiosyncratic risk but concentrates those risks that cannot be diversified away. We argue that credit ratings for structured products including RMBS and CDOs invested in RMBS did not provide investors with clear signals about the risks embedded in these securities because

- one-dimensional bond credit ratings are not designed to differentiate among exposures' sensitivity to systematic risk, and
- credit ratings do not adequately reflect the uncertainty associated with forecasting tail credit-loss events.

Structured securities are debt instruments backed by large pools of loans or bonds. Holders of structured securities are particularly vulnerable to systematic risk, which leads to correlation in the performance of assets, and model uncertainty, which can cause investors to poorly forecast the performance of large numbers of assets. It is precisely because systematic risk and model uncertainty are not diversifiable in a cross-section of credit exposures that they are difficult to measure when historical data is limited. Credit rating processes designed to rank credit exposures in terms of relative risk at a point in time, or which do not fully account for the effects of systematic risk and model uncertainty, provide an incomplete and potentially misleading picture of the credit quality of structured securities.

THE CRISIS IN MORTGAGE SECURITISATION

Securitisation is a means of funding a large number of small, heterogeneous and/or illiquid assets by issuing liabilities whose payouts depend on the aggregate performance of those assets. In the simplest type of cash-funded structured finance deal, a financial institution wishing to move a pool of loans or bonds off its balance sheet sets up a bankruptcy remote special purpose vehicle (SPV), which issues several classes of debt and an equity tranche. The proceeds from the SPV's liability issues are used to purchase the assets in question from the financial institution and investors in the SPV are repaid from principal and interest flowing from those assets. In this way, the financial institution is able to transform a pool of loans or bonds into ready cash. Because of scale and scope economies associated with underwriting and servicing and because the aggregate cashflows from a large pool of assets are easier to forecast than those of individual assets, securities issued by the SPV are typically more liquid and may be purchased by a broader base of investors than the individual loans or bonds backing those securities. Furthermore, the risk–return characteristics of the deal's liabilities can be tailored to meet market demand by adjusting the SPV's capital structure.[1] Junior investors who are first in line to bear losses in the event that the SPV's assets perform poorly receive higher contractual spreads than more senior investors who are partially protected from credit losses.

Securitisation has provided an important source of funding for a diverse array of credit products including credit cards, vehicle loans and leases, student loans, corporate loans and bonds and commercial and residential mortgages. Until recently, securitisation was

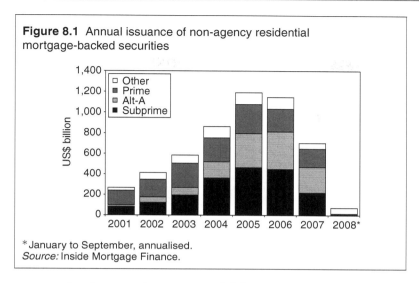

Figure 8.1 Annual issuance of non-agency residential mortgage-backed securities

*January to September, annualised.
Source: Inside Mortgage Finance.

even used to finance other structured debt instruments. For example, under a so-called CDO-squared structure, an SPV would issue liabilities backed by a pool of investments in other CDOs. Though nearly all classes of private debt have performed poorly during the financial crisis, problems in structured finance markets can be traced most directly to unexpectedly high default rates among US residential mortgages issued from 2005 to 2007.

While the pooling and resale of mortgage assets has been a fixture of US residential housing markets since the 1970s, issuance of "non-agency" RMBSs expanded dramatically in the first half of this decade. "Agency" RMBSs are pass-through instruments guaranteed by a government sponsored enterprise (typically the Federal Home Loan Mortgage Corporation or the Federal National Mortgage Association) and backed by pools of smaller, prime loans that conform to government-sponsored enterprise (GSE) underwriting guidelines. In contrast, non-agency RMBSs are structured securities backed by pools of mortgages that are either too large (jumbo loans) or too risky (Alt-A and subprime loans) to receive a GSE guarantee. As shown in Figure 8.1, annual issuance of non-agency RMBSs grew fourfold from just shy of US$300 billion in 2001 to US$1.2 trillion in 2006.

The rapid growth in RMBS issuance, along with the development of standardised documentation for credit default swaps that reference RMBSs and other asset-backed securities, bolstered the issuance ABS CDOs, which reached a peak of US$308 billion globally in 2006

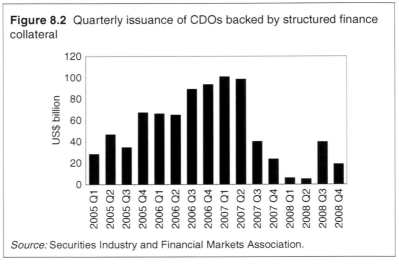

Figure 8.2 Quarterly issuance of CDOs backed by structured finance collateral

Source: Securities Industry and Financial Markets Association.

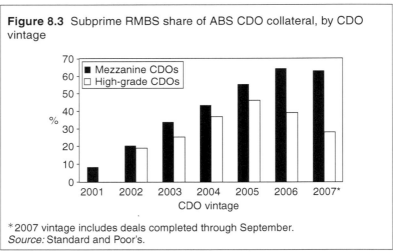

Figure 8.3 Subprime RMBS share of ABS CDO collateral, by CDO vintage

*2007 vintage includes deals completed through September.
Source: Standard and Poor's.

(see Figure 8.2); ABS CDOs are structured securities backed by pools of asset-backed securities (ABSs) including residential and commercial mortgage-backed securities and tranches of other CDOs. A typical ABS CDO may hold cash or synthetic investments in 100 or more asset-backed securities. ABS CDOs are described as "high grade" or "mezzanine" depending on the rating of the collateral held by the CDO. High-grade ABS CDOs generally hold securities rated A− and higher, while mezzanine ABS CDOs are backed by lower-rated securities. RMBS collateral held by high-grade CDOs may have higher

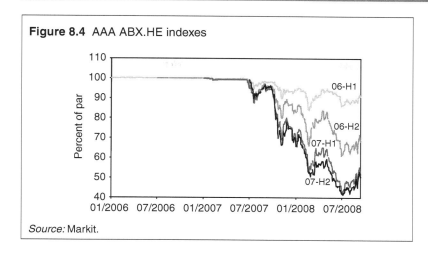

Figure 8.4 AAA ABX.HE indexes

Source: Markit.

ratings because it is backed by higher quality mortgages (eg, Alt-A rather than subprime), or because it has better credit enhancement (eg, higher seniority in the RMBS deal structure), or both. As shown in Figure 8.3, ABS CDOs in general, and mezzanine ABS CDOs in particular, issued from 2005 to 2007 were heavily invested in RMBSs backed by subprime mortgages.[2]

In 2007, falling house prices and rising default rates led to a dramatic reappraisal of the value of even the most highly rated structured securities backed by residential mortgages. Figure 8.4 shows the market value (as a percentage of par) for various vintages of the AAA ABX.HE index, which covers the most important AAA-rated RMBS tranches issued over a given half-year interval. By the middle of 2008 AAA RMBS tranches issued in 2007 were trading at half their face value.[3]

As Figure 8.5 shows, all classes of mortgage-backed structured securities suffered ratings downgrades. Downgrades of AAA-rated securities are particularly significant because these highly rated notes comprise the largest share of total RMBS and CDO issuance by value and because investors in these securities expect them to be almost risk free. Standard and Poor's (2009) has downgraded US$660 billion of the US$2.5 trillion (27%) worth of 2005–7 vintage US RMBS tranches it originally rated AAA. Because of their implicit leverage and their concentrated exposure to subprime and other non-agency RMBS, 2005–7 vintages of ABS CDOs experienced even more dramatic rating downgrades. Grouping US RMBS, ABS

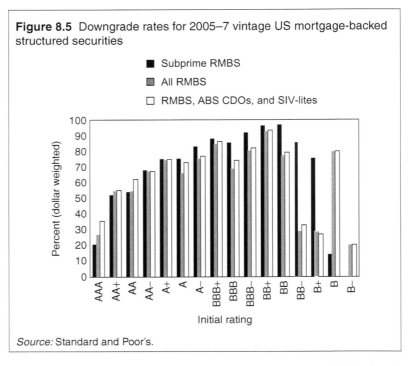

Figure 8.5 Downgrade rates for 2005–7 vintage US mortgage-backed structured securities

Source: Standard and Poor's.

CDOs and the liabilities of structured investment vehicle (SIV)-lites[4] together, S&P reports that it has downgraded US$1 trillion of US$2.9 trillion (35%) in AAA-rated structured securities issued from 2005 to 2007 that were directly or indirectly backed by US mortgages. The other major credit rating agencies have taken similar actions.

It is difficult to overstate the consequences of the collapse of the market for mortgage-backed structured credit products. It forced tiny pension funds and global investment banks alike to take huge losses, precipitated the failure of some of the world's largest and most venerable financial institutions and would surely be included on any shortlist of the most important factors contributing to the 2007–9 global financial crisis. Policymakers and regulators have been highly critical of credit rating agencies. According to the President's Working Group on Financial Markets (2008), a committee of financial regulators chaired by the Secretary of the US Treasury,

> [c]redit rating agencies contributed significantly to the recent market turmoil by underestimating the credit risk of subprime residential-mortgage-backed securities and other structured credit products, notably asset-backed-security CDOs.

Although much attention has focused on the inadequacies of public ratings assigned to the liabilities of structured finance deals, problems were not limited to institutions that relied on these ratings directly. A study commissioned by the Committee on the Global Financial System (2008) reports that

> [w]hile many relatively sophisticated investors... are unlikely to have relied on credit rating agencies to assess the risk of CDO *tranches*, they appear, nonetheless, to have relied on them to assess the risk of the underlying RMBS *collateral*.

SECURITISATION CONCENTRATES EXPOSURE TO SYSTEMATIC RISK

Why did so many structured credit products perform so poorly relative to expectations? To a great extent, the potential for significant, contemporaneous drops in the market value and credit quality of large numbers of highly rated structured securities is a foreseeable consequence of the pooling and tranching of credit risk inherent in securitisation. The securitisation process tends to filter out idiosyncratic credit risk while concentrating systematic risk. Highly rated structured securities are designed to perform well under a wide range of economic circumstances; however, unlike more traditional fixed income securities such as corporate bonds, these securities are also very sensitive to systematic risk. In the parlance of finance, structured credit products are "high beta" instruments.

Credit ratings are typically designed to reflect a credit obligation's probability of default or expected loss, not its exposure to systematic risk. Thus, a bond issued by a strong company in a not particularly cyclical industry might receive the same AAA credit rating as the senior tranche of an RMBS deal backed by subprime mortgages. Both ratings may be "accurate" in the sense that both securities might share the same very low unconditional default probability. Nonetheless, under conditions of severe systematic stress, the structured credit product can be expected to perform much more poorly than the corporate debt obligation.[5]

A simple normal copula model

To illustrate how securitisation leverages exposure to systematic risk, we will use a very simple version of a normal copula model.

Normal copula models are ubiquitous in risk management applications. Industry standard portfolio evaluation tools developed by The RiskMetrics Group (Gupton *et al* 1997) and Moody's/KMV (Kealhofer 1998) can be interpreted as variants of normal copula models (Li 2000). Normal copula models are used to compute risk-based regulatory capital requirements under the Basel II Bank Capital Accord (Basel Committee on Banking Supervision 2004). Moody's, S&P's and Fitch, the three largest bond-rating agencies, rely on normal copula models to develop credit ratings for CDOs and normal copula models are commonly used to price CDO notes (Andersen and Sidenius 2005). Because the model presented here is intended for pedagogical purposes, I will make simplifying assumptions wherever helpful, though it should be noted that the models used in more applied settings are considerably richer than the one presented in this chapter.

Under the simplest normal copula model of loss dependence, the default status of credit obligation i at a one-year-ahead assessment horizon depends on the realisation of a continuous index of the obligor's credit quality, denoted Y_i. For corporate loan obligations this variable is commonly interpreted as a measure of the firm's return on assets over the assessment horizon. If the realised value of Y_i lies below a critical default threshold then the obligation defaults. For simplicity we assume that the loss-given-default (LGD) per dollar exposure (LGD_i) is non-random. The unconditional probability of default of obligation i (PD_i) is simply the probability that the realised value of Y_i lies below the default threshold. So, if Y_i is a standard normal random variable, then the loss per dollar exposure associated with the obligation is

$$L_i = 1\{Y_i \leqslant \phi^{-1}(\mathrm{PD}_i)\} \cdot \mathrm{LGD}_i \tag{8.1}$$

where $1\{A\}$ is an indicator function that is equal to 1 if A is true and 0 if A is false and $\phi^{-1}(p)$ is the inverse of the standard normal cumulative distribution function.

In normal copula models of this sort, dependence in losses across obligors is modelled by assuming that Y_i depends on a number of underlying risk factors, some of which are shared by groups of obligors and some of which are unique to individual obligors. The presence of common factors that influence groups of obligors leads to correlations in losses across portfolio exposures. Under the simplest possible specification, Y_i is the weighted sum of two independent standard normal factors: a systematic risk factor X that affects all obligations and an idiosyncratic factor U_i that is unique to obligation i

$$Y_i = X\sqrt{\rho} + U_i\sqrt{1-\rho} \qquad (8.2)$$

The factor loading, ρ, is a parameter that lies between 0 and 1 and describes the sensitivity of Y_i to the systematic factor X.

By construction, the unconditional default probability for obligation i is PD_i. One way of thinking about this unconditional default probability is that it is our assessment of the likelihood that obligation i will default, assuming we know nothing about the realised value of the systematic factor X. If X were observed, the credit assessment could be refined. The conditional default probability of obligation i given X is

$$CPD_i(X) = \phi\left(\frac{\phi^{-1}(PD_i) - X\sqrt{\rho}}{\sqrt{1-\rho}}\right) \qquad (8.3)$$

If we think about a large number of obligations that share the same PD and factor loading, $CPD(X)$ should closely approximate the realised default rate over a one-year horizon. This default rate will change from year to year. While the long-run average annualised default rate for a pool of loans should be equal to their common PD, the realised default rate in any given year could be substantially higher or lower depending on the realised value of X. The higher the value of ρ, the greater the volatility of annual default rates relative to the long-run average.

Given this simple framework, it is straightforward to compute the probability that a credit obligation will default under adverse systematic stress conditions. Since a lower value of X implies a higher conditional default probability, an intuitive adverse systematic stress scenario is one in which the systematic risk factor takes on a value less than some low percentile $\phi^{-1}(1-q)$. We call this the qth percentile or worse stress scenario. It is easy to show that under this stress scenario a credit exposure with an unconditional default probability of PD will default with probability

$$PD^q = \frac{\phi_2(\phi^{-1}(PD), \phi^{-1}(1-q); \sqrt{\rho})}{1-q} \qquad (8.4)$$

where $\phi_2(v_1, v_2; r)$ is bivariate cumulative distribution function for a standard normal random double with correlation parameter r.

Pooling assets does not mitigate systematic risk

Structured credit products depend on the performance of large pools of credit obligations. Commercial mortgage-backed securities may reference several dozen loans, while traditional CDOs may reference hundreds of bonds. Securitisations of retail loans such as residential mortgages, credit cards or automobile loans commonly reference several thousand individual credit obligations. Resecuritisations, such as ABS CDOs, might directly reference a hundred structured securities, but since each of these securities is itself backed by hundreds or thousands of loans, resecuritisations can indirectly reference many thousands of credit obligations.

Basic probability theory predicts that, under stress conditions, a large pool of loans will perform differently from an individual loan, even if all loans in the pool have similar unconditional default probabilities and expected losses. Pooling reduces uncertainty about future losses, but pools of loans are actually more sensitive to systematic risk. To see this, consider a pool of N loans that are homogeneous in the sense that each has the same unconditional probability of default, LGD and factor loading. Let

$$\bar{L} = \frac{1}{N} \sum_i L_i$$

denote the loss rate for the pool of loans. The expected loss for one loan is $E[L_i] = PD \cdot LGD$ and, likewise, the expected loss rate for the loan pool is $E[\bar{L}] = PD \cdot LGD$. Thus, if we were rating investments to an expected loss standard, we would assign a single loan the same credit rating as a pool of N such loans even though the distribution of losses for the two investments are obviously quite different.

Suppose we ask "what is the likelihood that losses on an investment will exceed some critical threshold?" For a single loan, this probability is simply its PD. For a pool of loans, realised losses are drawn from a normal–binomial mixture distribution and loss exceedance probabilities must be computed numerically (Frey and McNeil 2003). The top panel of Table 8.1 reports loss exceedance probabilities for hypothetical loan pools of different sizes, assuming each loan has a PD of 10%, an LGD of 45%, and a factor loading of 0.2. Observe that the larger the pool, the lower its tail loss exceedance probabilities. In this sense, diversification reduces uncertainty.

Table 8.1 Loss rate exceedance probabilities for less diversified and more diversified loan pools

	Number of loans	Loss exceedance probability (%)		
		$\bar{L} > 10\%$	$\bar{L} > 15\%$	$\bar{L} > 20\%$
Unconditional	1	10.0	10.0	10.0
	25	12.1	3.4	0.8
	50	9.7	3.1	0.7
	100	9.5	2.5	0.6
	∞	9.1	2.3	0.5
Conditional on 98th percentile or worse systematic shock	1	41.2	41.2	41.2
	25	96.2	72.2	32.3
	50	98.8	81.1	31.2
	100	99.9	84.6	29.4
	∞	100.0	100.0	24.3

Each pool contains N loans, each of which has a default probability of 10%, a loss given default of 45 % and a factor loading of 0.20. Diversification reduces unconditional tail exceedance probabilities. Under systematic stress conditions, all exceedance probabilities increase and diversification does not reduce the likelihood of tail losses.

But now suppose we ask "what is the likelihood that losses on an investment will exceed some critical threshold under severe systematic stress conditions?" The lower panel of Table 8.1 documents loss exceedance probabilities for pools of loans, conditional on a 98th percentile or worse adverse draw of the systematic risk factor X. Obviously, all loss exceedance probabilities increase under stress conditions, but what is most striking is that exceedance probabilities for diversified investments are not particularly smaller, and are often much larger, than those for undiversified investments. Pooling loans can reduce the overall likelihood of tail loss events, but diversification offers little protection against tail loss events that are driven by adverse systematic shocks.

Tranching liabilities leverages exposure to systematic risk

Senior tranches of structured finance deals only default when the losses on deal collateral exceed the value of all subordinated tranches.[6] As a result, senior tranches are highly sensitive to the tail of the distribution of collateral losses. Consider a hypothetical

Table 8.2 Default probabilities for a whole loan and four hypothetical CDOs

No. of loans	C	PD_C	$PD_C^{0.98}$
Whole loan	—	0.90	7.86
25	20.0	0.85	32.25
50	19.0	0.89	38.88
100	18.5	0.90	42.95
∞	18.0	0.92	45.82

"No. of loans", number of loans in collateral pool; "C", senior tranche attachment point; "PD_C", unconditional senior tranche default probability; "$PD_C^{0.98}$", stress condition senior tranche default probability. Each credit exposure is constructed to have roughly the same 90bp unconditional default probability. The structured credit products are likely to perform much worse than the whole loan under systematic stress conditions and senior tranches backed by better diversified collateral pools are likely to perform worse than those backed by more concentrated pools. The stress condition is defined as a 98th percentile or worse systematic shock.

structured finance deal in which N homogeneous loans are funded by two debt tranches: a junior tranche which funds proportion C of deal assets and a senior tranche which funds the remaining $1 - C$ of assets. The probability that the senior tranche will incur a credit loss is simply the unconditional probability that the pool loss rate $\bar{L}$ exceeds the attachment point C. As we have just shown, diversification can lower this unconditional exceedance probability without substantially reducing the likelihood that the senior tranche will default under systematic stress conditions.

Table 8.2 compares conditional default probabilities and expected losses under stress conditions for four hypothetical senior structured finance securities and a whole loan. Collateral loans backing the structured securities are assumed to have the same PDs, LGDs and factor loading as those described in Table 8.1. Structured securities that reference better diversified collateral pools are given less credit enhancement, so that all four securities have an unconditional default probability of about 90 basis points (bp).[7] The whole loan is assumed to have a 90bp default probability and a factor loading of 0.2. All the credit exposures in Table 8.2 would receive the same PD-based credit ratings despite their very different performance under systematic stress conditions.

Although greater credit enhancement provides added protection for structured finance investors both on average and in times of severe systematic stress, the benefits of greater seniority are attenuated under stress conditions. If the collateral backing a structured finance deal consists of a very large number of homogeneous credit exposures,[8] the realised pool loss rate is approximated well by $\bar{L} = \text{CPD}(X) \cdot \text{LGD}$. In this case, the unconditional default probability for a senior tranche with attachment point C is

$$\text{PD}_C = \phi(H) \tag{8.5}$$

where

$$H = \phi^{-1}(\text{PD})\frac{1}{\sqrt{\rho}} - \phi^{-1}\left(\frac{C}{\text{LGD}}\right)\sqrt{\frac{1-\rho}{\rho}}$$

Under a qth percentile or worse stress scenario, the tranche default probability is

$$\text{PD}_C^q = \begin{cases} \dfrac{1}{1-q}\phi(H) & \text{if } H < \phi^{-1}(1-q) \\ 1 & \text{if } H \geqslant \phi^{-1}(1-q) \end{cases} \tag{8.6}$$

The three panels in Figure 8.6 show how tranche seniority affects unconditional and stress scenario tranche default probabilities given low-, medium- and high-quality collateral. The solid and dotted lines show that increasing the tranche attachment point lowers both the unconditional tranche default probability defined by Equation 8.5 and the stress scenario tranche default probability defined by Equation 8.6. The dashed line in the figure shows the stress condition default probability for a whole loan whose unconditional default probability is set to match the unconditional tranche default probability.[9] Comparing the dotted and dashed lines reveals that senior structured securities have much higher default probabilities under severe stress conditions than whole loans with the same unconditional default probabilities.

Ratings designed to reflect unconditional default probabilities or expected losses can fail to predict credit performance under severe stress conditions. Furthermore, the liabilities of a structured finance deal are usually finely tuned to achieve the best possible distribution of credit ratings given the collateral backing them. If a deal is backed by higher quality or better diversified collateral, the deal's senior tranche can garner a high credit rating with less credit enhancement

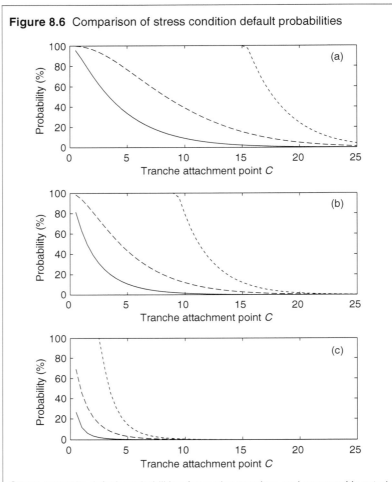

Figure 8.6 Comparison of stress condition default probabilities

Stress scenario default probabilities for senior tranches and comparably rated whole loans. Collateral PD is equal to: (a) 10.0%; (b) 5.0%; (c) 1.0%. Solid line shows tranche and whole loan default probability, dotted line shows tranche stress default probability and dashed line shows whole loan stress default probability.

(ie, a lower attachment point) than would otherwise be the case. As a result, higher quality or better diversified collateral does not necessarily imply less risk for investors in AAA-rated structured securities and may actually expose these investors to higher losses under stress conditions. In light of this analysis, it is perhaps not surprising that so many highly rated structured securities performed so poorly when subjected to a nationwide fall in house prices and escalating mortgage default rates.

Table 8.3 Distribution of the minimum variance unbiased PD estimator for a mezzanine-grade whole loan

T	Mean	Standard deviation	5th percentile	95th percentile
5	10.01	3.56	5.02	16.57
10	10.01	2.52	6.30	14.51
30	10.00	1.44	7.78	12.49

This table summarises the distribution of the minimum variance unbiased estimator of the default rate for an arbitrarily large collection of homogeneous credit obligations assuming that T years of historical cohort performance data are available. Each credit exposure has a true default probability of 10% and a factor loading of 0.20. Even though the cohorts are arbitrarily large, there is considerable dispersion in estimates of unconditional default rates, particularly when T is small.

MEASUREMENT UNCERTAINTY: MODEST ERRORS IN RATING COLLATERAL IMPLY LARGE ERRORS IN RATING STRUCTURED SECURITIES

Because credit losses on structured securities can be highly sensitive to systematic shocks, a great deal of historical data on the performance of collateral is needed to accurately rate them. Moreover, it is not sufficient that such data cover a large number of individual collateral exposures; it must also cover a broad range of macroeconomic conditions. This section uses a simple Monte Carlo simulation and the preceding copula model to illustrate how modest errors in measuring the default rates of collateral assets can translate into large errors in the measured default rates for senior structured securities.

If the senior tranche of a structured finance deal is backed by a well-diversified pool of homogeneous credit exposures and the PD, LGD and ρ of the deal collateral are known, the tranche default probability can be computed directly using Equation 8.6. But what if some of these parameters must be estimated? To keep things simple, let us make the heroic assumption that both LGD and ρ are known and that only PD must be estimated from historical data. Assume we observe T annual cohorts of data on the credit performance of an effectively infinite number of homogeneous loans. In the appendix, we show that under these assumptions it is possible to construct a unique minimum variance unbiased estimator (MVUE) of the loans' unconditional PD and any tranche default probability (PD_C).

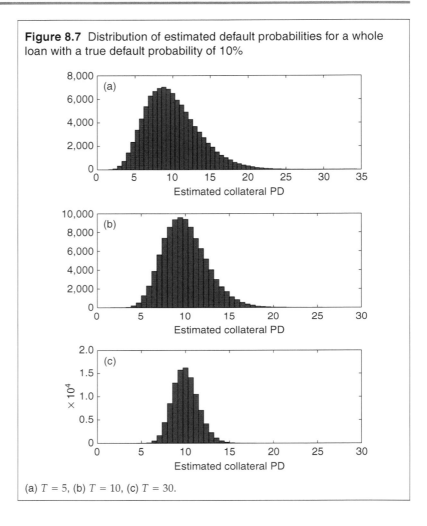

Figure 8.7 Distribution of estimated default probabilities for a whole loan with a true default probability of 10%

(a) $T = 5$, (b) $T = 10$, (c) $T = 30$.

Table 8.3 and Figure 8.7 describe the distribution of MVUE PD estimates given five-year, 10-year and 30-year simulated data histories, assuming that the true collateral default probability is 10%.[10] Notice that there is significant dispersion among these estimated default probabilities even though we have assumed that the number of exposures in each cohort is so large that the observed default rate for a cohort is arbitrarily close to its conditional expectation given X. Because systematic risk leads to correlation in defaults across obligors, a long time series of data – not a large cross-section – is needed to accurately estimate the unconditional default probability.

Table 8.4 Distribution of the minimum variance unbiased PD estimator for a senior structured security

T	Mean	Standard deviation	5th percentile	95th percentile
5	0.92	1.43	0.03	3.50
10	0.92	0.91	0.12	2.66
30	0.92	0.47	0.34	1.81

This table summarises the distribution of the minimum variance unbiased estimator of the default probability for a senior structured tranche backed by a well-diversified collateral pool assuming that T years of collateral performance data are available. Loans in the collateral pool have a 10% default probability, a 45% LGD and a factor loading of 0.20. The senior tranche has an attachment point of 20% and a true default probability of 91 basis points. The dispersion in estimated tranche default probabilities is extremely large compared to the true parameter, even when 30 years of historical data are available.

Table 8.4 and Figure 8.8 show the distribution of MVUE PD_C estimates for a senior tranche with a true default probability of 91 basis points (this is the same tranche described in the last row of Table 8.2). Even if 30 years of data on a very large number of credit exposures are available for estimating the collateral default probability, the dispersion in estimated default probabilities for senior structured securities is exceptionally large. A 90% confidence interval would cover a range from about one-third to double the true default probability. When fewer years of data are available, the sampling error is even larger.

To put these results in perspective, Table 8.5 and Figure 8.9 describe the distribution of PD estimates for a whole loan whose true default probability matches that of the senior structured security. Notice that the third line of Table 8.4 is similar to the first line of Table 8.5. In other words, about six times as much historical data is required to rate the structured security with the same precision as a whole loan with the same true default probability.

The results illustrated in this simple Monte Carlo exercise are quite general. The appendix provides analytic expressions for the sampling variances of best unbiased PD and PD_C estimators given any configuration of model parameters. Figure 8.10 compares the standard deviation of the MVUE of a tranche default probability with that of the MVUE of a whole loan default probability with the same actual PD as the tranche.[11] In all cases, the standard deviation of

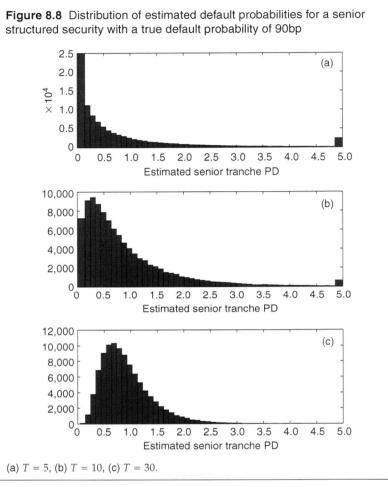

Figure 8.8 Distribution of estimated default probabilities for a senior structured security with a true default probability of 90bp

(a) $T = 5$, (b) $T = 10$, (c) $T = 30$.

the tranche default probability estimator is more than double that of the whole loan default probability estimator. The difference is greatest for tranches with more credit enhancement (higher attachment points) or backed by higher-quality (lower-PD) collateral. Evidently, the safest structured securities are the hardest to rate relative to whole loans of comparable quality.

This analysis illustrates how relatively modest uncertainty about the credit quality of collateral assets can translate into very large uncertainty about the credit quality of structured liabilities backed by those assets.[12] Note that, if anything, the simplifying assumptions used in this analysis tend to minimise the uncertainty associated

Table 8.5 Distribution of the minimum variance unbiased PD estimator for a high-grade whole loan

T	Mean	Standard deviation	5th percentile	95th percentile
5	0.92	0.52	0.31	1.92
10	0.92	0.36	0.44	1.59
30	0.92	0.20	0.62	1.28

This table summarises the distribution of the minimum variance unbiased estimator of the default rate for an arbitrarily large collection of homogeneous credit obligations assuming that T years of historical cohort performance data are available. Each credit exposure has a default probability of 92bp and a factor loading of 0.20. Comparing these results with those of Table 8.4, we see that the dispersion in the estimated default probabilities for a whole loan is substantially lower than that for a senior structured security with the same true default probability.

with evaluating structured credit products. Factor loadings and LGDs are notoriously difficult to pin down and ample empirical research finds that much more flexible copula models are needed to capture observable features of real-world data.[13]

LOOKING FORWARD

Moody's, Standard and Poor's and Fitch use the same ordinal rating scales to rank traditional corporate debt securities and structured securities. Even as the crisis in mortgage-backed structured securities was unfolding, the agencies argued that their ratings should be treated as comparable across debt classes. For example, S&P (2007b) asserted:

> Our ratings represent a uniform measure of credit quality globally and across all types of debt instruments. In other words, an "AAA" rated corporate bond should exhibit the same degree of credit quality as an "AAA" rated securitized debt issue.

The analysis presented here suggests that the uncertainty associated with ratings for high quality structured products is likely to be much greater than that associated with high-quality corporate debt securities. Ratings designed to capture a credit exposure's unconditional default probability or expected loss provide little insight into how a structured security might perform under systematic stress conditions. Furthermore, estimated default probabilities and expected

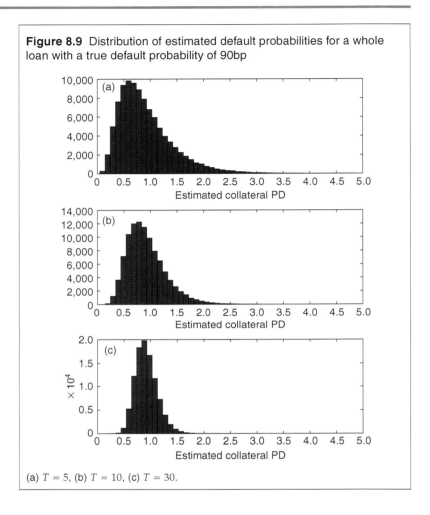

Figure 8.9 Distribution of estimated default probabilities for a whole loan with a true default probability of 90bp

(a) $T = 5$, (b) $T = 10$, (c) $T = 30$.

losses for senior structured securities are likely to be highly sensitive to modest and foreseeable errors in assessing the credit quality of underlying collateral.

Financial regulators (President's Working Group on Financial Markets 2008) have urged rating agencies to "make changes to the credit rating process that could clearly differentiate ratings for structured products from ratings for corporate and municipal securities" and "work with investors to provide the information investors need to make informed decisions about risk, including measures of the uncertainty associated with ratings and of potential ratings volatility." In response, rating agencies have taken steps to better convey

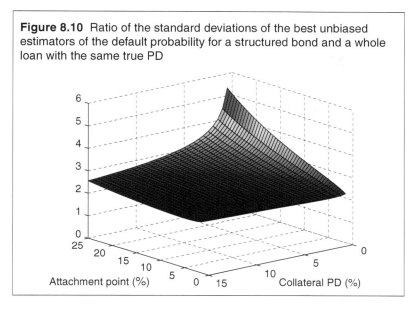

Figure 8.10 Ratio of the standard deviations of the best unbiased estimators of the default probability for a structured bond and a whole loan with the same true PD

the uncertainty associated with structured finance ratings. At the time of writing in 2010, Moody's has started to provide sensitivity scores alongside its structured finance ratings; these are designed to provide users with better information about how ratings are affected by model assumptions and the credit quality of underlying collateral. S&P publishes regular forecasts of the performance of structured credit products under a range of systematic stress scenarios. Disclosures such as these may help to increase market confidence in the agencies' structured finance rating processes.

However, ultimate responsibility for risk management rests not with rating agencies, but with those institutions that elect to invest in structured securities. Even in the absence of model uncertainty, similarly rated credit exposures may perform very differently under systematic stress conditions, so one-dimensional credit ratings cannot be treated as sufficient summaries for credit quality. To the extent that securitisation is used to fund retail and corporate debt going forward, risk management systems designed primarily with loan-level underwriting in mind need to be adapted to better reflect undiversifiable risks.

> The views expressed here those of the author and do not necessarily reflect the opinions of the Federal Reserve Board of Governors or its staff.

APPENDIX: MINIMUM VARIANCE UNBIASED ESTIMATORS FOR DEFAULT PROBABILITIES WHEN THE NUMBER OF BONDS IN A COHORT IS VERY LARGE BUT THE NUMBER OF COHORTS IS FIXED

The PD estimators used in this chapter are derived under the following assumptions.

- Individual whole loan defaults are described by a one-factor normal copula model. All whole loans are homogeneous in the sense that they share the same unconditional default probability (PD) and factor loading (ρ). The loss rate per default (LGD) is non-random and constant across loans.

- Realised default rates ($F_1, \ldots, F_T$) are observed for T cohorts of whole loans. Each cohort is arbitrarily large, so that

$$F_t = \phi\left(\frac{\phi^{-1}(\text{PD}) - X_t\sqrt{\rho}}{\sqrt{1-\rho}}\right)$$

where ($X_1, \ldots, X_t$) are independent, identically distributed (iid) standard normal random variables.

- PD is not directly observable, but ρ and LGD are known.

Estimating the default probability for a whole loan

We shall first construct the unique minimum variance unbiased estimator for PD. Observe that $E[F_1] = \text{PD}$ so a single observed default rate is an unbiased (though very inefficient) estimator of PD. The Lehmann–Scheffe Theorem (Bickel and Doksum 1977, p. 122) provides a means of constructing a unique minimum variance unbiased estimator (MVUE) for a function of a model parameters. To apply this result, we need to find a complete sufficient statistic for the unknown parameter of the model.

Let

$$Z_t = \phi^{-1}(F_t)\sqrt{\frac{1-\rho}{\rho}}.$$

Note that since we have assumed that ρ is known, Z_t can be computed directly from the observed default rate for cohort t. By construction, each Z_t is a standard normal random variable with mean

$$\mu = \frac{\phi^{-1}(\text{PD})}{\sqrt{\rho}}$$

and unit variance, and all Z_t are independent of one another. It is well known that the sample average of a vector of iid normal random variables is a complete sufficient statistic for the population mean when the variance is known, so

$$\bar{Z} = \frac{1}{T}\sum_t Z_t$$

is a complete sufficient statistic for μ. Since $PD = \phi(\mu\sqrt{\rho})$ and F_1 is an unbiased estimator of PD the Lehmann–Scheffe Theorem implies that the minimum variance unbiased estimator for PD is $E[F_1 \mid \bar{Z}]$. We can derive an explicit expression for this conditional expectation. Let W be a standard normal random variable that is independent of all Z_t. Then

$$E[F_1 \mid \bar{Z}] = E\left[\phi\left(Z_1\sqrt{\frac{\rho}{1-\rho}}\right) \mid \bar{Z}\right]$$

$$= E\left[1\left\{W < Z_1\sqrt{\frac{\rho}{1-\rho}}\right\} \mid \bar{Z}\right]$$

$$= \Pr\left[W - Z_1\sqrt{\frac{\rho}{1-\rho}} \leqslant 0 \mid \bar{Z}\right]$$

Using the fact that

$$Z_1 \mid \bar{Z} \sim N\left(\bar{Z}, \frac{T-1}{T}\right)$$

it follows immediately that the unique MVUE for PD is

$$\hat{P}(\bar{Z}) = \phi\left(\bar{Z}\sqrt{\frac{\rho}{1-\rho/T}}\right)$$

The variance of this estimator has a closed-form expression. Observe that $\bar{Z} \sim N(\mu, 1/T)$ and let W_1 and W_2 be two independent standard normal random variables.

$$\mathrm{var}[\hat{P}(\bar{Z})]$$

$$= E\left[\phi\left(\bar{Z}\sqrt{\frac{\rho}{1-\rho/T}}\right)^2\right] - PD^2$$

$$= E\left[1\left\{W_1 \leqslant \bar{Z}\sqrt{\frac{\rho}{1-\rho/T}}\right\} \cdot 1\left\{W_2 \leqslant \bar{Z}\sqrt{\frac{\rho}{1-\rho/T}}\right\}\right] - PD^2$$

$$= \Pr\left[\left(W_1 - \bar{Z}\sqrt{\frac{\rho}{1-\rho/T}}\right)\sqrt{\frac{T-\rho}{T}} \leq 0,\right.$$
$$\left.\left(W_2 - \bar{Z}\sqrt{\frac{\rho}{1-\rho/T}}\right)\sqrt{\frac{T-\rho}{T}} \leq 0\right] - \text{PD}^2$$
$$= \phi_2\left(\phi^{-1}(\text{PD}), \phi^{-1}(\text{PD}); \frac{\rho}{T}\right) - \text{PD}^2.$$

A consistent estimator for the sampling variance of $\hat{P}(\bar{Z})$ can be computed by plugging the estimated PD into the right-hand expression.

Estimating the default probability for a tranche backed by a large number of homogeneous bonds

A corollary to the Lehmann–Scheffe Theorem (Patil and Wani 1964) provides a method of constructing the MVUE of a distribution function when complete sufficient statistics for the parameters of that distribution are available. Adapting this result to the current application provides the unique MVUE of PD_C. The loss rate for an arbitrarily large pool of homogeneous bonds is

$$F_t \cdot \text{LGD} = \phi\left(Z_t \sqrt{\frac{\rho}{1-\rho}}\right) \cdot \text{LGD}.$$

Substituting this expression for the collateral loss rate into the definition of PD_C (see Equation 8.5) and rearranging terms yields

$$\text{PD}_C = \Pr\left[Z_t > \phi^{-1}\left(\frac{C}{\text{LGD}}\right)\sqrt{\frac{1-\rho}{\rho}}\right].$$

We have already shown that $\bar{Z}$ is a complete sufficient statistic for the distribution of Z_t and that

$$Z_t \mid \bar{Z} \sim N\left(\bar{Z}, \frac{T-1}{T}\right)$$

By Patil and Wani's corollary, the MVUE of PD_C is

$$\hat{P}_C(\bar{Z}) = \Pr\left[Z_t > \phi^{-1}\left(\frac{C}{\text{LGD}}\right)\sqrt{\frac{1-\rho}{\rho}} \mid \bar{Z}\right]$$
$$= \phi\left(\left(\bar{Z} - \phi^{-1}\left(\frac{C}{\text{LGD}}\right)\sqrt{\frac{1-\rho}{\rho}}\right)\sqrt{\frac{T}{T-1}}\right)$$

As with a whole loan, we can derive an analytic expression for sampling variance of the MVUE of the tranche default probability

$$\operatorname{var}[\hat{P}_C(\bar{Z})]$$

$$= E\left[\phi\left(\left(\bar{Z} - \phi^{-1}\left(\frac{C}{\mathrm{LGD}}\right)\sqrt{\frac{1-\rho}{\rho}}\right)\sqrt{\frac{T}{T-1}}\right)^2\right] - (\mathrm{PD}_C)^2$$

$$= E\left[1\left\{W_1 \leqslant \left(\bar{Z} - \phi^{-1}\left(\frac{C}{\mathrm{LGD}}\right)\sqrt{\frac{1-\rho}{\rho}}\right)\sqrt{\frac{T}{T-1}}\right\}\right.$$

$$\left. \cdot 1\left\{W_2 \leqslant \left(\bar{Z} - \phi^{-1}\left(\frac{C}{\mathrm{LGD}}\right)\sqrt{\frac{1-\rho}{\rho}}\right)\sqrt{\frac{T}{T-1}}\right\}\right] - (\mathrm{PD}_C)^2$$

$$= \Pr\left[W_1\sqrt{\frac{T-1}{T}} - \bar{Z} \leqslant -\phi^{-1}\left(\frac{C}{\mathrm{LGD}}\right)\sqrt{\frac{1-\rho}{\rho}},\right.$$

$$\left. W_2\sqrt{\frac{T-1}{T}} - \bar{Z} \leqslant -\phi^{-1}\left(\frac{C}{\mathrm{LGD}}\right)\sqrt{\frac{1-\rho}{\rho}}\right] - (\mathrm{PD}_C)^2$$

$$= \phi_2\left(\phi^{-1}(\mathrm{PD})\sqrt{\frac{1}{\rho}} - \phi^{-1}\left(\frac{C}{\mathrm{LGD}}\right)\sqrt{\frac{1-\rho}{\rho}},\right.$$

$$\left.\phi^{-1}(\mathrm{PD})\sqrt{\frac{1}{\rho}} - \phi^{-1}\left(\frac{C}{\mathrm{LGD}}\right)\sqrt{\frac{1-\rho}{\rho}}; \frac{1}{T}\right) - (\mathrm{PD}_C)^2.$$

1 The return distribution for a cash structured security can often be replicated synthetically by constructing a derivative instrument whose payouts depend on the performance of a pool of credit default swaps. Hybrid structured securities are backed by a mix of cash and synthetic assets. Synthetic and hybrid securities became popular as investor demand for exposure to structured credit risk outstripped the supply of cash instruments available for inclusion in new structured finance deals.

2 The data in Figure 8.3 is reported by Standard and Poor's (2007a). While this data only reflects deals rated by Standard and Poor's, similar information published by other rating agencies confirms that recent ABS CDOs are heavily concentrated in subprime RMBSs. See also Moody's (2007) and Fitch (2007).

3 Of course, not all of the change in RMBS market values should be attributed to increases in expected losses. Market-wide liquidity problems and rising risk premiums also contributed to adverse valuation changes.

4 Similar to CDOs, structured investment vehicles issued structured short term liabilities to fund longer duration investments in fixed income securities including structured securities. While SIVs were managed as ongoing concerns, SIV-lites were set up as one-off, self-liquidating investment vehicles.

5 The converse is also true. Under benign macroeconomic conditions the corporate debt obligation would be more likely to default than the structured security.

6 This is a bit of an over-simplification since, depending on the details of the a deal's cashflow waterfall, some interest and principal payments may be directed to junior tranches before senior tranches are fully paid off. Typically, this is only permitted when realised credit losses on collateral assets fall below pre-specified benchmarks so that senior tranches are protected.

7 Some minor variation in the unconditional default probability arises from the fact that for finite N and non-random LGD, $\hat{L}$ is a discrete random variable.

8   For more formal treatments of asymptotically fine grained portfolios in a single systematic factor model, see Gordy (2003) and Vasicek (1991).

9   This conditional default probability is computed by substituting PD_C produced by Equation 8.5 for the PD parameter that appears in the right-hand side of Equation 8.4.

10 In each simulation, T pseudo-random realisations of X were drawn and used to compute T values of $CPD(X)$ using Equation 8.3. One hundred thousand Monte Carlo iterations were run. To the best of the author's knowledge, the MVUE PD estimators used in these simulations have not been applied in practice. In assessing the credit quality of whole loans, practitioners commonly use long-run averages of rating-cohort default rates. These estimators are unbiased under standard assumptions, but they are not efficient (in a mean-squared-error sense) when systematic risk is present.

11 This analysis assumes a factor loading of 0.2, an LGD of 45% and 10 years of historical data. Similar results obtain under alternative parameter configurations.

12 This chapter examines parameter uncertainty from a classical perspective. As discussed in Chapter 6 a Bayesian approach yields similar results.

13 Heitfield (2009) examines the effects of errors in estimating factor loadings and loss-given default on CDO risk metrics.

REFERENCES

Andersen, L., and J. Sidenius, 2005, "CDO Pricing with Factor Models: Survey and Comments", *Journal of Credit Risk* 1(3), pp. 71–88.

Basel Committee on Banking Supervision, 2004, *International Convergence of Capital Measurement and Capital Standards: A Revised Framework* (Basel: Bank for International Settlements).

Bickel, P., and K. Doksum, 1977, *Mathematical Statistics: Basic Ideas and Selected Topics* (Oakland, CA: Holden-Day).

Committee on the Global Financial System, 2008, "Ratings in Structure Finance: What Went Wrong and What Can Be Done to Address Shortcomings?", CGFS Paper 32.

Fitch, 2007, "Rating Stability of Fitch-Rated Global Cash Mezzanine Structured Finance CDOs with Exposure to US Subprime RMBS", Special Report, DerivativeFitch Structured Credit.

Frey, R., and A. McNeil, 2003, "Dependent Defaults in Models of Portfolio Credit Risk", *Journal of Risk* 6(1), pp. 59–92.

Gordy, M., 2003, "A Risk Factor Model Foundation for Ratings-Based Bank Capital Rules", *Journal of Financial Intermediation* 12, pp. 199–232.

Gupton, G., C. Finger and M. Bhatia, 1997, *CreditMetrics Technical Document* (New York: JP Morgan).

Heitfield, E., 2009, "Parameter Uncertainty and the Credit Risk of Collateralised Debt Obligations", Working Paper, URL: http://ssrn.com/abstract=1190362.

Kealhofer, S., 1998, "Portfolio Management of Default Risk", Discussion Paper, KMV Corporation.

Li, D. X., 2000, "On Default Correlations: A Copula Function Approach", *Journal of Fixed Income* 9, pp. 43–54.

Moody's, 2007, "The Impact of Subprime Residential Mortgage-Backed Securities on Moody's-Rated Structured Finance CDOs: A Preliminary Review", Special Comment, Moody's Structured Finance.

Patil, G., and J. Wani, 1964, "Minimum Variance Unbiased Estimation of the Distribution Function Admitting a Sufficient Statistic", *Annals of the Institute of Statistical Mathematics* 18(1), pp. 39–47.

President's Working Group on Financial Markets, 2008, "Policy Statement on Financial Market Developments", Policy Statement.

Standard and Poor's, 2007a, "The Effect of Mortgage Market Stress on US CDO Ratings in Third-Quarter 2007", Report, Standard and Poor's CDO Spotlight.

Standard and Poor's, 2007b, "Principles-Based Rating Methodology For Global Structured Finance Securities", Discussion Paper, Standard and Poor's.

Standard and Poor's, 2009, "Transition Study: Structured Finance Rating Transition and Default Update as of February 27, 2009", Report, Standard and Poor's RatingsDirect.

Vasicek, O. A., 1991, "Limiting Loan Loss Probability Distributions", Discussion Paper, KMV Corporation.

9
Rethinking Credit Risk Modelling

Christian Bluhm; Christoph Wagner
Technische Universität München; Allianz Risk Transfer

The financial crisis which started in the first half of 2007 as a consequence of the collapsed subprime mortgage market in the United States (with its peak in September 2008, when Lehman Brothers filed for Chapter 11) led to a lot of criticism of modelling approaches to credit risk and financial products. Very soon afterwards, when it became clear that the bulk of complex structured credit derivatives, such as multi-leveraged collateralised debt obligations (CDOs), accelerated the downturn in financial markets, various press articles started to fire against "quants".[1] One reason for blaming the quants in such press articles was the following chain of arguments. Structured finance rests on financial engineering techniques. But such techniques rely on the work of quants. Therefore, the alleged malfunction of structured credit instruments relates to the failure of quant models in one way or another. So, does financial crisis also mean model crisis? Our answer to this question is a clear "no" but it would be foolish not to use the opportunity to take a deep breath and rethink credit risk modelling approaches as they are applied in the financial industry today. Questions we ask and discuss are the following.

- What is the role of credit risk models in the context of the financial crisis? What should be done better or differently in the future?
- Are there obvious or less obvious problems with credit risk models in the way they are applied in financial institutions today?
- Is the "model universe" sufficiently rich to provide adequate models?
- Are current risk management practices still a match for today's complexity of products and markets?

DOES "FINANCIAL CRISIS" MEAN "MODEL CRISIS"?

In order to open the discussion we start with a reference to the article by Shreve (2008), which contains comments on the role of quants in the recent crisis. In short, Shreve says the following:

- it is true that complex financial derivatives were not possible without the help of quants and their financial engineering techniques;
- but, underlying drivers of the crisis were an increased appetite for higher returns and the strong wish to outperform markets without counterbalancing risk management practices;
- quants knew about the steady increase in risks and in many banks they warned that a scenario like the 2007–9 crisis is within reach if euphoria in booming markets does not swing back to reasonable levels. But usually quants are not the decision makers and it is generally difficult to play the role of the pessimist in an euphoric market. Another complicating circumstance is a certain lack of appropriate communication channels between analytics and management.

Later in his article Shreve (2008) makes the following comparison:

> When a bridge collapses, no one demands the abolition of civil engineering. One first determines if faulty engineering or shoddy construction caused the collapse. If engineering is to blame, the solution is better – not less – engineering. Furthermore, it would be preposterous to replace the bridge with a slower, less efficient ferry rather than to rebuild the bridge and overcome the obstacle.

We principally agree with Shreve's point of view. However, we should not underestimate the influence quantitative models had during the first decade of the 21st Century. In contrast to the insurance side of the financial industry, where regulators require certified quantitative people ("actuaries") to ensure a prudent reserve estimate, it seems that the risk-management side of financial institutions gets away with lower standards, although models have evolved and started to dominate large parts of the financial scene. Proof of evidence for this statement is easy: already a glimpse into the Basel II documentation (Basel Committee on Banking Supervision 2004) will reveal that large parts of the document are basically unreadable for the typical executive manager in a bank because formulas and complex expressions are all over the place. In the early days of Basel II, quants wrote whole articles (for a quant audience!) explaining the formulas underneath the current regulatory capital framework. The wish for a sound quantification of risks as a basis for decisions and management is a good trend, which supplements business understanding and economic reasoning and mitigates the risk of being vague and imprecise in decision making. It prevents bankers from committing the economic fortune of their institutions to their "gut feeling" only.

But, as Föllmer (2009) points out, the quantitative part of decision making requires special prudence and diligence and is not without risks. Among other things he argues as follows.

- Quantitative models bear the risk of being misunderstood. The general mode of operation of a quantitative risk model is that it sheds some light on a certain aspect but might mask or neglect some other aspects. Föllmer (2009), very much to the point, speaks of partial analyses when it comes to financial modelling.
- He also brings the argument that models bear the danger of making people believe that risks and uncertainties are fully tamed and under control. But financial markets are complex; systemic risks are not always visible and not all factors and drivers which should be part of the equation are really taken into consideration in quantitative models.
- Another problem he touches on are assumptions and conditions necessary for the application of mathematical theorems. Conclusions in probability and finance rely on preconditions and if such conditions are not fulfilled, theorems and results tend to be no longer true. Practitioners tend to forget about preconditions and work with any formula they can find as long as it seemingly solves their problem. Such behaviour can lead to wrong conclusions and then trigger unfortunate decisions.

Föllmer concludes that there is not just one and only one true and right mathematical model for financial markets. Instead, quant groups in banks should allow themselves to work with various models, always looking at a problem from different angles, trying to reveal worst cases. An important aspect of both Shreve's and Föllmer's discussions is transparent and addressee-adequate communication. Model uncertainties need to be made transparent and should be part of the cover story in any presentation of a quantitative result to executives. In the academic literature, we typically find a clear description of preconditions and shortcomings of model results as well as intense discussions on model uncertainties. But, in their daily work, practitioners tend to present the solution to their superiors without mentioning the potential weaknesses of their approach and the concluded results. Often such a habit is combined with a certain impatience of executives to listen to their quants until the very end of the story. In this way, misunderstandings and misplaced faith in sometimes weak model results is preprogrammed. Another difficulty indicated by speaking of model uncertainty instead of model risk is that potential variations of model components are not necessarily quantifiable under all circumstances.

For our discussion of the questions at the beginning of this chapter, we start with a very general formula for the (random) loss of a credit portfolio. We then discuss in detail a general mixture-model framework which can serve as an explicit implementation of the aforementioned credit portfolio loss formula and sketch market-typical submodels and their pros and cons. We also briefly address questions of parameterisation, model uncertainty and communication of outcomes.

An excellent paper in this context is Donnelly and Embrechts (2010), which contains a very interesting discussion as a reply to the aforementioned press articles blaming quants and mathematics for the financial debacle of the 2007–9 financial crisis. Moreover, by means of the example of the Gaussian copula model, the paper explains in detail the problems caused by the application of Gaussian dependence to market instruments in the derivative sector. We return to this point in our discussion later in this chapter.

Limited space here does not allow for more than an indication of problems and restricts our discussion to mixture models as one example for a popular model framework. A more comprehensive discussion with a special focus on structured credit products addressing also intensity-based and first-passage time models can be found in Bluhm and Wagner (Forthcoming).

DIFFERENT LEVELS OF VALUATION MAKE A DIFFERENCE

Let us start with a brief look at the origin of the 2007–9 crisis. The crisis goes back to a combination of an increased risk appetite, euphoric markets and a fatal disregard for concentrations and steadily increasing risks in certain market segments. To be more explicit, low lending standards in the US subprime market and euphoric betting on ever-increasing house prices and low interest rates triggered the US subprime debacle. Global infection then came as a consequence of the fact that US residential mortgages found their way into mortgage-backed securities over a course of many years, such that so-called structured finance collateralised debt obligations (SFCDOs) and, in general, the whole CDO and asset-backed securities (ABS) market started to suffer from the US subprime mortgage crisis. As an additional difficulty, it is worthwhile mentioning that SFCDOs were often based on multi-leverage, so that their structural description could easily be of the type "CDO of CDOs of CDOs of ABS". This means that asset pooling as a tool for improving diversification was applied several times, so that resulting instruments were bearing systemic risk in, say, its purest form (see also Chapter 8). In the synthetic part of the structured credit market there was another systemic risk pusher: due to a limited number of liquid assets[2] grouped into many CDOs over and over again, cross-references[3] became a strong driver of risk. The consequences of cross-references were already observable when Enron collapsed. Enron was used as a reference name in so many transactions that the whole CDO market suffered from its default.

Altogether, we can say that the systemic risk inherent in the CDO market is tremendous. So it does not come much as a surprise that the US subprime mortgage crisis triggered huge value drops in the mark-to-market valuation of CDOs and ABS. Of course, if markets bounce back over time, we see that valuation goes up and profits will be back. At the time of writing in 2010, some "bounce back" effects are observable in some so-called "bad banks" (restructuring units), which have reported nice profits in some cases. But there is also a certain segment of products in the CDO and ABS market which will not recover from the crisis, namely, all those assets which had fundamentally spoilt assets in their reference portfolios: for instance, residential mortgage-backed securities (RMBS) referenced to US subprime mortgages which defaulted on payment obligations in one way or another.

So much for the economic story of the crisis. What have quantitative models to do with it? Well, as indicated by Shreve (2008)

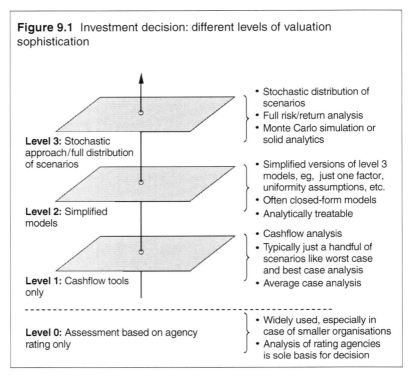

Figure 9.1 Investment decision: different levels of valuation sophistication

and Föllmer (2009), quantitative models are the bread-and-butter of structuring units, investment boutiques and banks in their investment units as well as in their securitisation units, not forgetting that quantitative models are also used by rating agencies and regulators. Today, the whole financial industry relies more or less on quantitative models. But, and here is our first point, the way various market participants deal with models is very heterogeneous and at very different levels of understanding.

Let us consider this point in greater detail. In the market we find a wide range of model cultures, from using no own models at all to using highly sophisticated stochastic models. Figure 9.1 illustrates the different levels found in the market when it comes to, eg, the valuation of investments in structured credit products. We distinguish four levels where the level of sophistication is increasing in an upward direction.

Level 0 is the purely ratings-based approach, where an investment decision is made based on the assessment of rating agencies only. Typical level-0 investors are smaller institutions as well as individuals like private banking clients with a large-scale investment capacity.[4] level-0 investors buy a credit instrument, eg, a senior tranche of a CDO, based on the information that rating agencies like Standard & Poor's, Moody's or Fitch provide by assigning a rating to the tranche, eg, a AA/Aa or AAA/Aaa rating. In the course of the 2007–9 financial crisis, market participants experienced downgrades of CDO tranches often by more than just one or two notches. This led to a lot of confusion among investors who relied on agency analysis in their investment process. In addition, various articles appeared in the press with a lot of criticism of rating agencies and their rating processes. Voices spoke up loudly saying that agencies are not sufficiently independent from issuers because agencies get paid by issuers for the assignment and publication of ratings. In fact, without a rating from at least two of the three large rating agencies it was difficult, if not impossible, to get a CDO tranche successfully sold in the public market. As a consequence, issuers and arrangers of structured credit products asked rating agencies to assess their products and assign a rating to them. Agencies did their analysis, attached a rating to the considered CDO tranche and in turn collected a fee for their rating-assignment service. There are three important issues we want to mention in this context.

First, it seems that tranche ratings are not as stable as they are supposed to be. So maybe the analysis made by rating agencies is indeed not as sustainable as claimed. In fact, if we consider downgrade statistics, it seems that senior tranches are more vulnerable to multi-notch downgrades than lower-rated tranches. This could be evidence that agency models do not take tail dependence (see Example 9.20 as well as Figure 9.5) into account in appropriate ways. As we will see later, ignorance with respect to tail dependence is a common phenomenon which concerns the whole industry and not just the rating agencies.

Second, if we forget about tranche rating downgrades for a moment and focus solely on CDO mark-to-market value changes, then we stumble across an example dealing with communication challenges (Example 9.1), which shows that level-0 investors really have a hard time understanding the approach of rating agencies, independent of the question of whether the agency analysis is appropriate or not.

Third, Example 9.1 can be used to formulate an important cautionary recommendation.

Example 9.1. CDO investors relying mainly on rating agency analysis only (Level 0) and complaining about mark-to-market drops of tranches with high credit quality might not have taken into account the fact that, by definition, a CDO tranche rating addresses timely and full payment of interest and principal but does not say much about potential value fluctuations of the tranche in the time between issuance and maturity.

In the situation of Example 9.1 something went wrong in the communication of the meaning of the rating and the purpose of the underlying rating model, namely, that the model focuses not on mark-to-market fluctuations but on payment stability. In fact, there are many CDO tranches in the market which experienced significant drops in value but still have very stable and reliable payments. The "gap" level-0 investors have is the lack of their own analysis of a CDO tranche: they just received the rating of the tranche from external sources and do not have their own opinion on the tranche, its credit quality and its potential mark-to-market behaviour in the case of certain scenarios. This gives rise to the following recommendation.

Recommendation 9.2. In the same way as banks should rely on their internal rating of borrowers and not just use public ratings in their credit assessment it is not sufficient to rely on agency ratings when investing in structured credit. In fact, investors without internal quant capacity should perhaps not invest in structured credit products.

Level-0 investors were caught by surprise during the crisis because many products assumed to AAA quality got in trouble and will take time to recover (with respect to their mark-to-market) or might not recover at all if underlying credit assets are "toxic". The surprise of such investors came from a lack of understanding of both the purchased product itself and the rating agency model, and their analysis and the outcome (rating) of such analysis.

It is interesting to note that the number of level-0 investors in the private sector but also institutional sector is still shockingly large. In the private sector the burden also is on the private bankers who sold

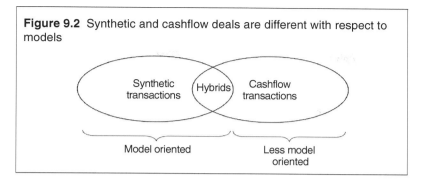

Figure 9.2 Synthetic and cashflow deals are different with respect to models

such complex products to private investors without fully revealing the risks to their clients. Let us now move on to the next level in Figure 9.1.

Level-1 investors are market participants who believe it is sufficient to analyse structured credit products with in-house or off-the-shelf (purchased) deterministic cashflow tools. Such tools calculate the return of an investment based on discounted future cashflows of the considered instrument. Typically, such cashflow analysis incorporates a feature to test certain scenarios like worst case, best case or expected case. Instead of a loss simulation model, assumptions are made regarding realised losses over the lifetime of the deal as well as regarding the timing of defaults and losses. Deterministic cashflow tools do not model the stochastics underlying the credit risk of reference assets in the reference portfolio.

Large parts of the classical asset-backed securities (ABSs) market are still driven by cashflow tools lacking a sound credit portfolio model as an underlying driver. In the case of large banks and sophisticated investment boutiques, level-2 and level-3 approaches (which we describe in a moment) are increasingly dominating the scene, but level-1 investment behaviour is still very common even, in the large institutional sector.

At this point we should make an important distinction. Players in synthetic transactions tend to be much more model-driven than players in the traditional cashflow deal market. One reason is that the synthetics market is a derivatives market which is highly model-driven (cf Black–Scholes for option markets). Figure 9.2 illustrates the difference between synthetics and cash-deal markets. In fact, it is interesting to note that the synthetics market performed much better, even during the crisis, than the cash-deal market. The same observation applies to the recovery of markets in 2009–10: synthetics have it easier. There is one segment in between: so-called "hybrid" deals, which have cashflow elements as well as synthetics characteristics. In Bluhm and Overbeck (2007b) a typical hybrid transaction is used as a case study and it turns out that the deal relies heavily on quantitative modelling. So we can count hybrids in the segment of synthetics when it comes to the use of quantitative models.

Recommendation 9.3. Level 1 valuation misses the point that cashflows are actually stochastic, driven by random defaults and losses of reference assets in the underlying reference portfolio. Analysing a CDO tranche at level 1 is comparable with an attempt to analyse a financial time series on just a handful of price observations. Nobody seriously investing in the stock or index market would do that, but it seems that there is a significant number of investors in structured credit transactions, in particular in the cashflow deal segment, who think it is sufficient to judge a cashflow ABS based on a handful (or less) of cashflow scenarios.

We now move on to the next two levels, which will keep us busy for the rest of this chapter.

Level-2 and level-3 investors have an understanding that cashflow modelling is part of the assessment but is not the whole story. They know that cashflow scenarios of the considered credit product are driven by the outcome of stochastic variables associated with the underlying reference portfolio.

The mechanism is illustrated in Figure 9.3. The principle of structured credit products referenced to a certain credit portfolio is always the same: performance of the underlying credit assets (the left-hand side in Figure 9.3) determines the cashflows at the liability side of the credit product (the right-hand side of Figure 9.3). Hereby, interest and repayments are paid ("distributed" in cashflow deals) to tranche investors in order of their seniority, ie, higher seniority tranches receive payments before lower seniority tranches, whereas losses in the underlying reference portfolio eat up into tranches from the bottom up. In this way, lower seniority securities suffer from losses before higher seniority securities experience a hit. Therefore, lower tranches provide a capital cushion or loss buffer in order to protect tranches which are more senior. Without going further into detail it becomes immediately clear that cashflows at the right-hand

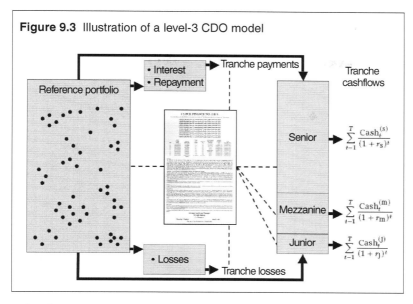

Figure 9.3 Illustration of a level-3 CDO model

side of Figure 9.3 are determined by the credit quality and payment behaviour of underlying reference assets on the left-hand side of the figure.

Recommendation 9.4. In order to capture the full width of potential outcomes, the reference portfolio's uncertainty needs to be modelled by an appropriate probability space $(\Omega, \mathcal{F}, \mathbb{P})$. Then, for each portfolio scenario $\omega \in \Omega$ from the left-hand side of Figure 9.3 we can determine a cashflow scenario at the right-hand side of the figure for each tranche or security of the considered product. In more mathematical terms, the cashflow of a tranche is represented by a random variable or, if considered as a function of time, a stochastic process defined on the underlying reference portfolio's probability space $(\Omega, \mathcal{F}, \mathbb{P})$.

The difference between level-2 and level-3 assessment is that level-2 assessment works with shortcuts and significant simplifications, whereas level-3 assessment always works at the level of detail required for a full coverage of reference portfolio properties and structural details of the product. We will come back to level-2 and level-3 differences later, when we shall discuss mixture models and their implementations.

The structured credit market is one of the most complex markets in the world. Therefore, it is crucial that players in that market have sufficient knowhow for valuation of the products they invest in. So, to be successful in the structured credit market it is indispensable to have good quants to hand for doing the mathematics of the transactions. However, having good quants in place is not sufficient, and is no guarantee for surviving a crisis, as we recently experienced it in the market. As a supporting argument let us consider the following example.

Example 9.5. Lehman Brothers had excellent quant teams. If we look up the number of quantitative articles published by Lehman quants over the last decade, then it immediately becomes clear that Lehman had one of the best developed quant groups in the world. Nevertheless, Lehman crashed in the financial crisis. So there must be essential reasons for failure which are related not to the work of quants but to an institution's risk appetite, risk culture, willingness to listen to risk people and risk quants, etc.

Example 9.5 illustrates that good quant teams are no guarantee for success. But good quant teams are an important driver of success, although there are various other factors like risk culture, risk appetite, etc, which might dominate the positive effects of good quantitative capabilities of an institution.

In an ideal world, in which institutions always base their investment decisions on a sound combination of quantitative and qualitative assessments, the following conclusions can be drawn.

- Level-0 assessments rely on the quality of rating agency analysis. The responsibility for the problem of "correctness" of the valuation is shifted to the rating agencies. If rating agencies do well in their analysis, then the assessment is appropriate. However, level-0 institutions have no chance to develop their own opinion on investments. They rely completely on external opinions. They will never fully understand their investments. They will be caught by surprise if external opinions turn out not to be sustainable.

- Level-1 assessments have rating agency analysis plus internal cashflow analysis at their disposal. However, deterministic cashflow tools do not allow for more than a brief glance at the true nature of the problem. In accordance with Figure 9.3, level-1 analysis calculates cashflow scenarios at the right-hand side based on a few manually picked scenarios. In our opinion, this hardly helps us to understand a transaction. Such an approach misses the important link between the probability space of the underlying portfolio and the CDO tranche performance.

- Level-2 and level-3 assessments have good chances to reveal the true nature of the structured product, but, depending on the degree of simplification and the chosen shortcuts, level-2 assessments bear the risk of overlooking or misunderstanding certain aspects and risks of the product. Analysing certain details can be critical in the valuation process of a complex structured credit product.

The following recommendation is a direct answer to the post-crisis question "What can be done to make the structured credit market a safer place?"

Recommendation 9.6. It can be safely assumed that level-3 assessment, if combined with investment and market experience, decent risk culture, appropriate risk practices and economic reasoning, has the best chances of revealing the true risk-return profile of a structured credit product. We strongly believe that markets would be a safer place if level-0 and level-1 investors would upgrade their assessment capabilities to level 2 or, even better, level 3. In addition, level-2 investors should reconsider their applied assumptions, shortcuts and model simplifications. Model level upgrades and a sound risk culture have the potential to improve market stability in the long run.

An additional inherent message is the given below.

Recommendation 9.7.

- Instead of asking for new models, it would make a big difference if market participants exploited the existing model universe. Moreover, it is highly recommendable to transfer various good ideas and modelling approaches offered by academia into the banking and insurance world.

- Another requirement is that decision makers in financial institutions show more responsibility in what kind of structuring they support or even push. The cashflow-deal market suffered a lot from opacity, caused by multi-leverage, and complexity such that even very capable quant teams had no chance to analyse (say, four-times leveraged) transactions via a so-called "look-through" approach, where deals are evaluated bottom-up (asset-wise) as well as top-down (structure-wise).

- A golden rule for the structured credit market should be that transactions which are too complex to be modelled and evaluated in an intellectually honest way should not find acceptance in the market.

For the remainder of this chapter we indicate a few thoughts on credit risk modelling by means of the example of mixture models. We will introduce such models in a very general way and then discuss typical level-3 and level-2 implementations. As mentioned earlier, approaches serving as alternatives to mixture models are discussed in Bluhm and Wagner (Forthcoming) with a special focus on structured credit portfolios and related products.

A VERY GENERAL CREDIT RISK FORMULA

We start at time $t = 0$ and assume we are given a credit portfolio with m credit-risky assets. Figure 9.3 illustrates that the probability space $(\Omega, \mathcal{F}, \mathbb{P})$ generated by the credit portfolio underlying a CDO is what we really need to be concerned about. If we have that probability space under control, the modelling of the CDO on the liability side is just tedious routine work: studying the term sheet and the offering circular of the deal and programming the Monte Carlo simulation-based translation of portfolio scenarios into CDO tranche scenarios. So we concentrate our efforts on modelling portfolio loss scenarios.

The portfolio loss $L^{(t)}$ at any time $t > 0$ is driven by exactly two effects, namely,

- the assets which are in default before the time horizon t and
- the amount of money, denoted by η_i, lost with a defaulted asset i.

Denoting the time of default of an asset i by τ_i, where $i \in \{1, \ldots, m\}$, the portfolio loss $L^{(t)}$ with respect to the time horizon t can be written as follows

$$L^{(t)} = \sum_{i=1}^{m} \eta_i(\tau_i) \mathbf{1}_{\{\tau_i \leqslant t\}} \quad (9.1)$$

This is a very general and assumption-free way to denote a credit portfolio loss because at this point no assumptions have been made

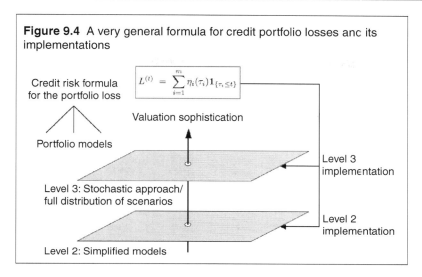

Figure 9.4 A very general formula for credit portfolio losses and its implementations

about underlying models or parameterisations. Whenever we think about credit portfolio loss, we necessarily arrive at Equation 9.1. Let us briefly describe the constituents of the formula. The Bernoulli variable[5]

$$1_{\{\tau_i \leq t\}} = \begin{cases} 0 & \text{if asset } i \text{ does not default before or at time } t \\ 1 & \text{if asset } i \text{ defaults before or at time } t \end{cases}$$

is simply used as a default indicator. The random variable $\eta(s)$, where s is a parameter denoting "time", refers to the amount of money effectively lost with asset i in the portfolio in the case when the asset defaults. The effective loss given default often depends on the particular timing of default such that we need to set $s = \tau_i$ in order to make explicit that the time of default of asset i has a certain impact on the effective realised loss of asset i. It is not difficult to find realistic examples illustrating this dependence (see, for example, Example 9.22).

We now want to discuss level-2 and level-3 implementations of the portfolio loss formula (Equation 9.1), as they are now industry standard. For this purpose we introduce mixture models in a very general set-up as the basis for all further discussions.[6] We first focus on level-3 implementations and then discuss market-common simplification pushing down solutions from level 3 to level 2. The result of such model downgrades can be meaningful but also wrong and misleading, and we will reconsider many questions we have already touched upon. In this context we will also come to the questions of parameterisation and communication. For clarity, we provide all references and suggestions for further reading at the end of the chapter.

A GENERAL MIXTURE MODEL FRAMEWORK

Mixture models are a major tool in credit risk modelling. Their functionality can be summarised as follows: random variables representing defaults and losses are coupled with each other by means of common underlying influences which are also random effects. The formal mathematical way to encode such models is via probability spaces and random variables and that is our starting point in this section. For readers not familiar with the theory underlying probability spaces and random variables, the following ideas can be found in various books on probability theory.

Let $(\Omega, \mathcal{F}, \mathbb{P})$ be a suitable probability space on which all random variables will be defined. Let q be a positive integer. We choose some random vector

$$\boldsymbol{\Phi} = (\Phi_1, \ldots, \Phi_q) : (\Omega, \mathcal{F}, \mathbb{P}) \to \mathbb{R}^q$$

for which we do not yet specify the distribution. Later in this chapter we will use $\boldsymbol{\Phi}$ as a vector of systematic indices which does exactly what we described at the beginning of this section, namely, defining a coupling between different single-name credit risks. In addition, we shall need a family of functions, later to be used for the assignment of default probabilities

$$F_i \colon \mathbb{R}^q \times [0, \infty) \to [0, 1], \quad (z; t) \mapsto F_i(z; t), \quad i = 1, \ldots, m$$

such that the following conditions are satisfied.

Condition 9.8.

- F_i is $(\mathcal{B}(\mathbb{R}^q) \otimes \mathcal{B}([0, \infty))) - \mathcal{B}([0, 1])$-measurable for all $i = 1, \ldots, m$, where $\mathcal{B}(E)$ denotes the Borel σ-field with respect to the usual topology on the spaces $E = \mathbb{R}^q$, $E = [0, \infty)$ and $E = [0, 1]$.
- $F_i(z; \cdot) : [0, \infty) \to [0, 1]$, $t \mapsto F_i(z; t)$, is a continuous and strictly increasing probability distribution function on $[0, \infty)$ for all $z = (z_1, \ldots, z_q) \in \mathbb{R}^q$ and $i = 1, \ldots, m$.

For readers not familiar with probability theory we should mention that Condition 9.8 is a technical condition which is stated in order to allow some mathematical formalism in the following.

We will later pick $z \in \mathbb{R}^q$ at random with respect to the distribution $\mathbb{P}_\Phi$ of Φ and in this way randomise (or, as we later call it, "mix") the distribution functions $F_i(z, \cdot)$. Condition 9.8 could be formulated in weaker terms and is more than we need in the following but things get less complicated if we formulate the conditions as we have above. Another (slightly more complex) approach would be to define each F_i as a random distribution function

$$F_i : (\mathbb{R}^q, \mathcal{B}(\mathbb{R}^q), \mathbb{P}_\Phi) \to \Delta([0, \infty)), \quad z = (z_1, \ldots, z_q) \mapsto (F_i(z; t))_{t \geq 0}$$

where $\Delta([0, \infty))$ denotes a suitable subspace of the space of probability distribution functions on $[0, \infty)$ and F_i is assumed to be measurable with respect to the usual topology[7] on the function space $\Delta([0, \infty))$. However, Condition 9.8 is appropriate for our purposes and an overly complex set-up can be avoided.

For each realisation $z = (z_1, \ldots, z_q)$ of $\Phi = (\Phi_1, \ldots, \Phi_q)$ we choose a vector of default times

$$\left.\begin{aligned}(\tau_1^{(z)}, \ldots, \tau_m^{(z)}) : (\Omega, \mathcal{F}, \mathbb{P}) &\to [0, \infty)^m \\ \omega &\mapsto (\tau_1^{(z)}(\omega), \ldots, \tau_m^{(z)}(\omega))\end{aligned}\right\} \quad (9.2)$$

such that the following conditions are satisfied.

Condition 9.9.

- For each $i = 1, \ldots, m$ and fixed $z = (z_1, \ldots, z_q) \in \mathbb{R}^q$ we have

$$\mathbb{P}[\tau_i^{(z)} \leq t] = F_i(z; t) \quad \text{for all } t \geq 0$$

which means that the default time $\tau_i^{(z)}$ is $F_i(z; \cdot)$-distributed.

- Given $z = (z_1, \ldots, z_q)$, the joint distribution of default times $\tau_1^{(z)}, \ldots, \tau_m^{(z)}$ satisfies

$$\mathbb{P}[\tau_1^{(z)} \leq t_1, \ldots, \tau_m^{(z)} \leq t_m] = F_1(z; t_1) \cdots F_m(z; t_m),$$
$$t_1, \ldots, t_m \geq 0$$

which means that $\tau_1^{(z)}, \ldots, \tau_m^{(z)}$ are independent for $z \in \mathbb{R}^q$ chosen and fixed.

As indicated earlier, when we later interpret z as "state" of a vector of systematic indexes Φ, we obtain from Condition 9.9 that, conditional on such states, the default times of credit assets are independent.

Having made all these definitions it is natural to ask if default times obeying Condition 9.9 exist for arbitrarily given functions $(F_1, \ldots, F_m)$ satisfying Condition 9.8. The following proposition answers this question positively, given the conditions we assumed before.

Proposition 9.10. Let functions $F_1, \ldots, F_m$ satisfy Condition 9.8 and let $z = (z_1, \ldots, z_q) \in \mathbb{R}^q$ be given. Choose independent random variables $U_1, \ldots, U_m$ uniformly distributed in $[0, 1]$. Then

$$\tau_i^{(z)} := F_i^{-1}(z; U_i), \quad i = 1, \ldots, m$$

defines a vector of default times $(\tau_1^{(z)}, \ldots, \tau_m^{(z)})$ satisfying Condition 9.9. Here, $u \mapsto F_i^{-1}(z; u)$ denotes the inverse function for $t \mapsto F_i(z; t)$, ie, $F_i^{-1}(z; F_i(z; t)) = t$ for all $t \geqslant 0$.

Proof Let $U_1, \ldots, U_m$ be independent random variables on a probability space $(\Omega, \mathcal{F}, \mathbb{P})$ such that U_i is uniformly distributed in $[0, 1]$ (ie, $U_i \sim U([0, 1])$) for each $i = 1, \ldots, m$. Due to Condition 9.8 the distribution functions $F_i(z; \cdot)$ are continuous and strictly increasing, so we can calculate the inverse[8] functions $F_i^{-1}(z; u)$. The range of the random variables $F_i^{-1}(z; U_i)$ is the space where "time t lives", namely, $[0, \infty)$. The first part of Condition 9.9 is obvious

$$\mathbb{P}[\tau_i^{(z)} \leqslant t] = \mathbb{P}[F_i^{-1}(z; U_i) \leqslant t] = \mathbb{P}[U_i \leqslant F_i(z; t)] = F_i(z; t)$$

Combining this with the independence of $U_1, \ldots, U_m$, the joint distribution of $\tau_1^{(z)}, \ldots, \tau_m^{(z)}$ reads

$$\mathbb{P}[\tau_1^{(z)} \leqslant t_1, \ldots, \tau_m^{(z)} \leqslant t_m]$$
$$= \mathbb{P}[F_1^{-1}(z; U_1) \leqslant t_1, \ldots, F_m^{-1}(z; U_m) \leqslant t_m]$$
$$= \mathbb{P}[U_1 \leqslant F_1(z; t_1), \ldots, U_m \leqslant F_m(z; t_m)]$$
$$= \mathbb{P}[U_1 \leqslant F_1(z; t_1)] \cdots \mathbb{P}[U_m \leqslant F_m(z; t_m)]$$
$$= F_1(z; t_1) \cdots F_m(z; t_m)$$

which is the second part of Condition 9.9, so that the assertion of the proposition follows. □

Proposition 9.10 shows that we can construct z-depending default times $(\tau_1^{(z)}(\omega), \ldots, \tau_m^{(z)}(\omega))$ such that Condition 9.9 is satisfied. However, the following construction goes much further.

Construction 9.11. Let $U_1, \ldots, U_m \sim U([0,1])$ be independent random variables on a probability space $(\Omega', \mathcal{F}', \mathbb{P}')$ and let $\boldsymbol{\Phi} = (\Phi_1, \ldots, \Phi_q)$ be a vector of continuous random variables on another probability space $(\Omega'', \mathcal{F}'', \mathbb{P}'')$. We define a new probability space

$$(\Omega, \mathcal{F}, \mathbb{P}) = (\Omega' \times \Omega'', \mathcal{F}' \otimes \mathcal{F}'', \mathbb{P}' \otimes \mathbb{P}'')$$

and a vector of functions

$$(\tau_1, \ldots, \tau_m): (\Omega, \mathcal{F}, \mathbb{P}) \to [0, \infty)^m, \qquad \omega \mapsto (\tau_1(\omega), \ldots, \tau_m(\omega))$$

via the relations

$$\tau_i(\omega) = \tau_i(\omega', \omega'') = F_i^{-1}(\boldsymbol{\Phi}(\omega''); U_i(\omega'))$$

for all $\omega = (\omega', \omega'') \in \Omega = \Omega' \times \Omega''$ and all $i = 1, \ldots, m$, where the inverse of F_i in the definition of τ_i again (as in Proposition 9.10) refers to the mapping $u \mapsto F_i^{-1}(z; u)$ for $u \in [0,1]$ and $z \in \mathbb{R}^q$ and the functions F_i are assumed to satisfy Condition 9.8.

Note that Construction 9.11 includes that $\boldsymbol{\Phi} = (\Phi_1, \ldots, \Phi_q)$ and $U_1, \ldots, U_m$ can (and will in the following) be considered as random variables on $(\Omega, \mathcal{F}, \mathbb{P})$ via the projection mappings

$$\pi': (\Omega, \mathcal{F}, \mathbb{P}) \to (\Omega', \mathcal{F}'), \quad \omega = (\omega', \omega'') \mapsto \pi'(\omega) = \omega'$$

$$\pi'': (\Omega, \mathcal{F}, \mathbb{P}) \to (\Omega'', \mathcal{F}''), \quad \omega = (\omega', \omega'') \mapsto \pi''(\omega) = \omega''$$

which are clearly measurable such that

$$U_i(\omega') = U_i \circ \pi'(\omega)$$

for all $\omega = (\omega', \omega'') \in \Omega$ and all $i = 1, \ldots, m$ as well as

$$(\Phi_1(\omega''), \ldots, \Phi_q(\omega'')) = (\Phi_1 \circ \pi''(\omega), \ldots, \Phi_q \circ \pi''(\omega))$$

for all $\omega = (\omega', \omega'') \in \Omega$, are measurable. In the following, for convenience we write $\boldsymbol{\Phi}(\omega)$ and $U_i(\omega)$ instead of $\boldsymbol{\Phi} \circ \pi''(\omega)$ and $U_i \circ \pi'(\omega)$. Construction 9.11 also yields independence of $\boldsymbol{\Phi}$ and $U_1, \ldots, U_m$ based on the trivial observation

$$\mathbb{P}_{\pi' \otimes \pi''} = \mathbb{P}_{\text{id}} = \mathbb{P}' \otimes \mathbb{P}'' = \mathbb{P}_{\pi'} \otimes \mathbb{P}_{\pi''}$$

where id denotes the identity mapping on Ω.

Proposition 9.12. For $(\tau_1, \ldots, \tau_m)$ defined on $(\Omega, \mathcal{F}, \mathbb{P})$ as in Construction 9.11 the following hold.

- For every $i = 1, \ldots, m$ the function
$$\tau_i \colon (\Omega, \mathcal{F}, \mathbb{P}) \to ([0, \infty), \mathcal{B}([0, \infty)))$$
is measurable and, therefore, is a random variable which can be interpreted as the default time of an asset or obligor.
- Fix $z \in \mathbb{R}^q$. Conditional on $\boldsymbol{\Phi} = z$ we can identify $(\tau_1, \ldots, \tau_m)$ with $(\tau_1^{(z)}, \ldots, \tau_m^{(z)})$ as in Equation 9.2 such that Condition 9.9 is satisfied for $(\tau_1, \ldots, \tau_m)|_{\boldsymbol{\Phi}=z}$.
- Due to $\boldsymbol{\Phi}$-conditional independence of $(\tau_1^{(z)}, \ldots, \tau_m^{(z)})$, the following "mixture formula" holds
$$\mathbb{P}[\tau_1 \leqslant t_1, \ldots, \tau_m \leqslant t_m] = \int_{\mathbb{R}^q} F_1(z; t_1) \cdots F_m(z; t_m) \, d\mathbb{P}_{\boldsymbol{\Phi}}(z)$$

The mixture formula says that the unconditional joint distribution of default times can be obtained by integration of the conditional default times distributions over all "states" z drawn at random with respect to $\mathbb{P}_{\boldsymbol{\Phi}}$.

Proof To show that $\tau_i(\omega) = F_i^{-1}(\boldsymbol{\Phi}(\omega); U_i(\omega))$ is measurable, we consider
$$\{\omega \in \Omega \colon \tau_i(\omega) \leqslant t\} = \{\omega \in \Omega \colon F_i^{-1}(\boldsymbol{\Phi}(\omega); U_i(\omega)) \leqslant t\}$$
$$= \{\omega \in \Omega \colon U_i(\omega) \leqslant F_i(\boldsymbol{\Phi}(\omega); t)\} \quad (9.3)$$

which is an event in $\mathcal{F}$ because of the measurability of F_i (Condition 9.8), U_i and $\boldsymbol{\Phi}$. For Equation 9.3 note again that the inversion of F_i as we apply it refers to the mapping $u \mapsto F_i^{-1}(z; u)$. Thus, we obtain $\{\tau_i \leqslant t\} = \{U_i \leqslant F_i(\boldsymbol{\Phi}; t)\} \in \mathcal{F}$ for all $t \geqslant 0$, which proves $\mathcal{F}$-$\mathcal{B}([0, \infty))$-measurability of τ_i.

Next, we look at $\tau_1, \ldots, \tau_m$ conditional on $\boldsymbol{\Phi} = z$. The first part of Condition 9.9 is obvious. Now
$$\mathbb{P}[\tau_1 \leqslant t_1, \ldots, \tau_m \leqslant t_m \mid \boldsymbol{\Phi} = z]$$
$$= \mathbb{P}[F_1^{-1}(\boldsymbol{\Phi}; U_1) \leqslant t_1, \ldots, F_m^{-1}(\boldsymbol{\Phi}; U_m) \leqslant t_m \mid \boldsymbol{\Phi} = z]$$
$$= \mathbb{P}[U_1 \leqslant F_1(z; t_1), \ldots, U_m \leqslant F_m(z; t_m)]$$
$$= \mathbb{P}[U_1 \leqslant F_1(z; t_1)] \cdots \mathbb{P}[U_m \leqslant F_m(z; t_m)]$$
$$= F_1(z; t_1) \cdots F_m(z; t_m) \quad (9.4)$$

which proves the second part of Condition 9.9. Note that independence of $U_1, \ldots, U_m$ and, in general, the assumptions inherent in Construction 9.11 are crucial for the proof.

RETHINKING CREDIT RISK MODELLING

Finally, the mixture formula follows directly from Equation 9.4 via integration over $\mathbb{R}^q$ with respect to $\mathbb{P}_\Phi$. □

In Proposition 9.12, the random variables

$$F_i(\Phi, t), \quad i = 1, \ldots, m; \ t \geq 0$$

can be interpreted as (conditional) random default probabilities due to the equation

$$\mathbb{P}[\tau_i \leq t \mid \Phi = z] = F_i(z, t) \quad z \in \mathbb{R}^q \tag{9.5}$$

which says that the likelihood of default occurring before or at time t is (conditional on the scenario $\Phi = z$) given by $F_i(z, t)$. Thus, $F_i(\Phi, t)$ is a random default probability for asset i.

We did cover quite some ground with Construction 9.11 and Proposition 9.12 because we now have access to a very general default times mixture model. It can be translated into a Bernoulli mixture model, as shown in Proposition 9.13. We denote the Bernoulli distribution with parameter p by $B(1; p)$.

Proposition 9.13. Let $(\tau_1, \ldots, \tau_m)$ on $(\Omega, \mathcal{F}, \mathbb{P})$ be given as in Construction 9.11. Fix $t > 0$. Then,

$$(\mathbf{1}_{\{\tau_1 \leq t\}}, \ldots, \mathbf{1}_{\{\tau_m \leq t\}})$$

defines a Bernoulli mixture model with respect to the valuation horizon t, ie,

- $\mathbf{1}_{\{\tau_i \leq t\}} \mid \Phi = z \sim B(1; F_i(z; t))$ for $i = 1, \ldots, m$;

- $(\mathbf{1}_{\{\tau_i \leq t\}} \mid \Phi = z)_{i=1,\ldots,m}$ is independent for every fixed $z \in \mathbb{R}^q$.

- The joint default distribution of the Bernoulli mixture is given by

$$\mathbb{P}[\mathbf{1}_{\{\tau_1 \leq t\}} = \delta_1, \ldots, \mathbf{1}_{\{\tau_m \leq t\}} = \delta_m]$$
$$= \int_{[0,1]^m} \left(\prod_{i=1}^m \chi_i^{\delta_i} (1 - \chi_i)^{1-\delta_i} \right) d\mathbb{P}_{(X_1^{(t)}, \ldots, X_m^{(t)})}(\chi_1, \ldots, \chi_m)$$

where $\delta_1, \ldots, \delta_m \in \{0, 1\}$ and $(X_1^{(t)}, \ldots, X_m^{(t)}) : (\Omega, \mathcal{F}, \mathbb{P}) \to [0, 1]^m$ is a vector of random default probabilities defined by $X_i^{(t)} = F_i(\Phi, t)$ for $i = 1, \ldots, m$.

Proof It is clear that $\mathbf{1}_{\{\tau_i \leqslant t\}}$ as an indicator variable is Bernoulli distributed. As in Equation 9.5 we obtain

$$\mathbb{P}[\mathbf{1}_{\{\tau_i \leqslant t\}} | _{\Phi=z} = 1] = \mathbb{P}[\tau_i \leqslant t \mid \Phi = z] = F_i(z, t)$$

from Proposition 9.12 such that the first assertion is shown. The second assertion also follows immediately from Proposition 9.12 (cf Condition 9.9 for $\tau_1^{(z)}, \ldots, \tau_m^{(z)}$). The third assertion is a straightforward consequence of the mixture formula in Proposition 9.12. □

This concludes our introduction of a general mixture-model framework. We are now prepared for a discussion of level-3 and level-2 implementations of Equation 9.1.

LEVEL-3 IMPLEMENTATION OF THE CREDIT RISK FORMULA (EQUATION 9.4)

The formula we need to implement and specify, based on a mixture-model approach, is

$$L^{(t)} = \sum_{i=1}^{m} \eta_i(\tau_i) \mathbf{1}_{\{\tau_i \leqslant t\}}$$

So we need to specify how the random default times $\tau_1, \ldots, \tau_m$ from Construction 9.11 are typically modelled in applied portfolio models in banks. Thus, we follow a common approach whose variations are used in many institutions and also in various off-the-shelf industry models.

For the implementation it makes sense to start with its less disputable elements. In the case of credit risk modelling, the less disputable part is the modelling of probabilities of default (PDs). The reason why we consider PDs as less disputable is that all large banks today have a sufficiently long history of default frequencies which yields stable estimates of default likelihoods. There are exceptions to the rule, such as the so-called low-default portfolios,[9] but in general PD modelling is a rather mature and developed field in mathematical finance. This is also true for the PDs of traded assets, where spreads are the main ingredient of the model. Summarising, we feel quite comfortable regarding the modelling of PDs, be it based on rating systems and fundamental analysis of balance sheet data or on spreads and market data. Note that we do not state that there is no work to do in the area of PDs; there can be many challenges in PD modelling and the area of PDs is still a wide open field for research and calibration techniques. But, compared with dependence modelling, we can consider the field of PD modelling to be established and standardised in many aspects. We will soon see that our statement about PDs is a statement about marginal distributions, meaning that financial institutions are more comfortable regarding the marginal distributions than regarding the dependence underlying portfolio losses (Equation 9.1). So let us now as a first step consider PDs and their role in Construction 9.11 and then move on to the more disputable topic of dependencies.

Implementation step 1: credit curves $t \mapsto \int_{\mathbb{R}^q} F_i(z;t) \, d\mathbb{P}_{\Phi}(z)$

Based on the remarks just made on the undisputability of PDs, we choose them as starting point for the definition of functions F_i satisfying Condition 9.8. For this, we start with the specification of their unconditional version, namely, a term structure of default probabilities also called a credit curve for every asset $i = 1, \ldots, m$ in the portfolio. We denote the credit curve for asset i in Construction 9.11 by $(p_i^{(t)})_{t \geq 0}$ and note that, based on Equation 9.5, credit curves in our mixture approach look like

$$t \mapsto p_i^{(t)} = \int_{\mathbb{R}^q} F_i(z;t) \, d\mathbb{P}_{\Phi}(z) \qquad (9.6)$$

We now forget about F_i and Φ for a moment and focus on the direct specification of $t \mapsto p_i^{(t)}$ based on empirical migration data. What we need (in order to satisfy Condition 9.8 later on) for each $i = 1, \ldots, m$ is a family

$$(p_i^{(t)})_{t \geq 0} \in [0,1]^{\mathbb{R}_+}$$

of PDs such that $t \mapsto p_i^{(t)}$ is a continuous and strictly increasing distribution function on $[0, \infty)$, which we denote in the following by

$$\varphi_i : [0, \infty) \to [0,1], \quad t \mapsto \varphi_i(t) = p_i^{(t)} \qquad (9.7)$$

for $i = 1, \ldots, m$. $p_i^{(t)} = \varphi_i(t)$ represents the probability that asset i defaults in the time interval $[0, t]$. As pointed out above, we consider the calibration of such credit curves (functions φ_i) as doable in satisfactory ways by most large financial institutions. In the final section we mention literature on credit curves. Here, we present just the following example, which is elaborated on in Bluhm and Overbeck (2007a).

Example 9.14. A common approach to derive $(\varphi_i)_{i=1,\ldots,m}$ is via homogeneous (HCTMC) or non-homogeneous continuous-time Markov chains (NHCTMCs) as follows.

- HCTMC approach: calibrate a generator or Q-matrix, Q, based on a given one-year migration matrix M obtained by statistical analysis of internal and/or external rating migration data. Assume the bank works with N rating classes such that $M, Q \in \mathbb{R}^{N \times N}$. Denote by $R(i)$ the mapping which assigns to asset i in the portfolio its credit rating. Then we can set

$$\varphi_i(t) = p_i^{(t)} = (\exp(tQ))_{\text{row}(R(i)), N}, \quad t \geq 0$$

where row(R) denotes the row in the matrices M and Q referring to rating R and N addresses the default column of migration matrices in $\mathbb{R}^{N \times N}$.

- NHCTMC approach: calibrate time-dependent generators or Q-matrices $(Q_t)_{t \geq 0}$ based on internal and/or external migration data and histories of observed default frequencies. In analogy to the HCTMC approach, we derive credit curves for assets $i = 1, \ldots, m$ via

$$\varphi_i(t) = p_i^{(t)} = (\exp(tQ_t))_{\text{row}(R(i)), N}, \quad t \geq 0$$

If we define the functions φ_i in this way, the underlying Markov chain is non-homogeneous in time, driven by the time dependence of the generator $Q(t) = Q_t, t \geq 0$.

It turns out that the NHCTMC approach is particularly well suited to generating credit curves that fit empirical data nicely (Bluhm and Overbeck 2007a). Therefore, we can safely assume in the following that the functions $\varphi_i, i = 1, \ldots, m$, are at our disposal in to work with.

The distribution functions φ_i can be interpreted as distribution functions of default times τ_i

$$\mathbb{P}[\tau_i \leq t] = p_i^{(t)} = \varphi_i(t)$$

because, by definition, $p_i^{(t)}$ is the default probability of asset i with respect to the valuation horizon t, which equals the likelihood that τ_i falls into the time interval $[0, t]$. As in Equation 9.6, we next construct a random vector $\boldsymbol{\Phi}$ in $\mathbb{R}^q$ and functions F_i in line with Condition 9.8 such that

$$\varphi_i(t) = \int_{\mathbb{R}^q} F_i(z; t) \, d\mathbb{P}_{\boldsymbol{\Phi}}(z) \tag{9.8}$$

for $i = 1, \ldots, m$, which is the PD of asset i for the time interval $[0, t]$.

Implementation step 2: mixing variables $\Phi = (\Phi_i)_{i=1,\ldots,q}$

So far we have derived default times in their unconditional version. But we are looking for mixed default times, where the mixing is based on latent mixing variables $\Phi = (\Phi_1, \ldots, \Phi_q)$. Because the mixing procedure steers the dependence between different default times, we arrive here (in contrast to the definition of credit curves in the previous section) at a very much disputable component of Construction 9.11. There are many uncertainties involved in the definition of Φ and there is also much confusion in this context. We will later indicate some of the problems by means of Example 9.20.

A common approach for the definition of $\Phi = (\Phi_1, \ldots, \Phi_q)$ is to work with a generalisation of an imitation of the well-known capital asset pricing model (CAPM) but in a credit risk context. For doing so, each asset i gets assigned a latent variable

$$Y_i = \beta_i \sum_{j=1}^{q} w_{ij}\Phi_j + w_i\varepsilon_i \qquad (9.9)$$

such that for its constituents the following conditions are satisfied:

- $\varepsilon_1, \ldots, \varepsilon_m, \Phi$ are independent;
- $\varepsilon_1, \ldots, \varepsilon_m \sim N(0,1)$, where $N(\mu, \sigma^2)$ denotes the normal distribution with mean μ and variance σ^2;
- $\Phi = (\Phi_1, \ldots, \Phi_q)$ is centred multivariate Gaussian;
- $w_i = (1 - \beta_i^2 \mathbb{V}[w_{i1}\Phi_1 + \cdots + w_{iq}\Phi_q])^{1/2}$.

Based on these conditions it follows that

$$Y_i \sim N(0,1), \quad i = 1, \ldots, m$$

The weighted sums

$$\Psi_i = \sum_{j=1}^{q} w_{ij}\Phi_j$$

are often called systemic factors and its summands Φ_j typically represent market and/or macroeconomic indexes based on market and macroeconomic data (for example, MSCI indexes, GDP, unemployment rate, mortgage indexes, price indexes, regional or sectorial performance indexes). Note that dependence between latent variables Y_i is exclusively driven by the vector $\Phi = (\Phi_1, \ldots, \Phi_q)$.

Depending on the underlying data, it makes sense to design latent variables $Y = (Y_1, \ldots, Y_m)$ in a way matching a certain dependence structure which often is expressed by means of the so-called copula function of Y. Copulas were used by statisticians long before finance specialists rediscovered the concept. The basic underlying idea is to separate the stochastic dependence from the marginal behaviour of multivariate distribution functions. In the final section we mention some literature explaining the concept and working with it in a finance context. Here, we briefly define the notion and then apply it in the course of our discussion.

Remark 9.15. A copula function $C : [0,1]^m \to [0,1]$ is a multivariate distribution function whose marginal distributions are uniform in $[0,1]$. A famous theorem by Sklar says that for any distribution function F on $\mathbb{R}^m$ with marginal distribution functions $F_1, \ldots, F_m$ we can find a copula function C such that

$$F(x_1, \ldots, x_m) = C(F_1(x_1), \ldots, F_m(x_m)), \quad x_1, \ldots, x_m \in \mathbb{R}^q \quad (9.10)$$

In Sklar's proof it turns out that

$$C(u_1, \ldots, u_m) = F(F_1^{-1}(u_1), \ldots, F_m^{-1}(u_m))$$

defines such a copula. Conversely, given a copula function C and distribution functions $F_1, \ldots, F_m$ on $\mathbb{R}$, the function F defined by Equation 9.10 is a multivariate distribution function on $\mathbb{R}^m$ with marginal distributions $F_1, \ldots, F_m$. An important supplement is that the copula function C for given F is unique if the marginal distributions $F_1, \ldots, F_m$ of F are continuous.

In our mixed-default-times model the marginal distributions stem from the conditional credit curves $F_i(\Phi, t)$, whereas the copula function is defined by the multivariate distribution of Y.

The two most commonly applied copula functions in a credit risk context are the Gaussian copula and the Student-t copula. These two copulas are a kind of "close relatives" because Student-t copulas can be parameterised[10] in a way which brings it arbitrarily close to the Gaussian copula. However, the difference between the two copulas becomes very significant if we choose degrees of freedom for the Student-t copula below, say, $n = 10$. The basis of the choice of copula and of the parameterisation must be empirical evidence based on economic rationale. We later point out that we have great doubts whether the Gaussian copula is a meaningful choice in a credit risk context because it has a real deficit, which more or less disqualifies it for the application to credit portfolios. We come to that point in Example 9.20 and Figure 9.5.

Proposition 9.16. We consider two common cases for latent variables $Y = (Y_1, \ldots, Y_m)$.

The Gaussian copula case. Let $Y_1, \ldots, Y_m$ be defined as in Equation 9.9. Then $Y = (Y_1, \ldots, Y_m)$ has the Gaussian copula

$$C(u_1, \ldots, u_m) = N_{m,\Gamma}[N^{-1}[u_1], \ldots, N^{-1}[u_m]]$$

where $N_{m,\Gamma}[\cdot]$ denotes the m-dimensional Gaussian distribution function with correlation matrix Γ and $N^{-1}[\cdot]$ denotes the inverse standard normal distribution function. We have

$$\Gamma = (\gamma_{ij})_{1 \leq i,j \leq m} \quad \text{with } \gamma_{ij} = \begin{cases} \beta_i \beta_j \, \text{Corr}[\Psi_i, \Psi_j] & \text{if } i \neq j \\ 1 & \text{if } i = j \end{cases} \quad (9.11)$$

with

$$\Psi_i = \sum_{j=1}^{q} w_{ij} \Phi_j$$

according to Equation 9.9 and in line with the conditions corresponding to Equation 9.9.

The Student-t copula case. Choose a $\chi^2(d)$-distributed random variable X with d degrees of freedom such that X is independent of $\Phi = (\Phi_1, \ldots, \Phi_q)$, $\varepsilon_1, \ldots, \varepsilon_m$ from Equation 9.9 and replace the definition (Equation 9.9) of $Y_1, \ldots, Y_m$ by

$$Y_i = \sqrt{\frac{d}{X}} \left(\beta_i \sum_{j=1}^{q} w_{ij} \Phi_j + w_i \varepsilon_i \right) \quad (9.12)$$

with the same conditions satisfied as required for Equation 9.9 (and listed right below it). Then, the vector $Y = (Y_1, \ldots, Y_m)$ has the Student-t copula

$$C(u_1, \ldots, u_m) = \Theta_{m,\Gamma,d}[\Theta_d^{-1}[u_1], \ldots, \Theta_d^{-1}[u_m]]$$

where $\Theta_{m,\Gamma,d}$ denotes the m-dimensional Student-t distribution function with $d > 2$ degrees of freedom and correlation matrix Γ where Γ is as in Equation 9.11. Further, Θ_d denotes the distribution function of a Student-t distributed random variable in $\mathbb{R}$ with $d > 2$ degrees[11] of freedom and Θ_d^{-1} is its inverse.

Proof The proof of the proposition is straightforward, but for the convenience of the reader we include it here.

1. If we leave $Y_1, \ldots, Y_m$ untouched as in Equation 9.9, then the marginal distribution functions F_{Y_i} of Y are standard normal by construction. Applying Equations 9.9 and 9.10, we get

$$\mathbb{P}[Y_1 \leqslant c_1, \ldots, Y_m \leqslant c_m] = N_{m,\Gamma}[c_1, \ldots, c_m]$$
$$= N_{m,\Gamma}[N^{-1}[N[c_1]], \ldots, N^{-1}[N[c_m]]]$$
$$= N_{m,\Gamma}[N^{-1}[F_{Y_1}(c_1)], \ldots, N^{-1}[F_{Y_m}(c_m)]]$$
$$= C(F_{Y_1}(c_1), \ldots, F_{Y_m}(c_m)) \qquad (9.13)$$

with $C(u_1, \ldots, u_m) = N_{m,\Gamma}[N^{-1}[u_1], \ldots, N^{-1}[u_m]]$. Based on the conditions corresponding to Equation 9.9, the only contribution to $\text{Corr}[Y_i, Y_j]$ comes from the systemic factors Ψ_i, Ψ_j and β_i, β_j such that Equation 9.11 also follows.

2. If we define $Y_1, \ldots, Y_m$ as in Equation 9.12, then the marginal distribution functions F_{Y_i} of Y are Student-t distributed with d degrees of freedom. In analogy to the Gaussian case we obtain

$$\mathbb{P}[Y_1 \leqslant c_1, \ldots, Y_m \leqslant c_m] = \Theta_{m,\Gamma,d}[\Theta_d^{-1}[\Theta_d[c_1]], \ldots, \Theta_d^{-1}[\Theta_d[c_m]]]$$
$$= C(F_{Y_1}(c_1), \ldots, F_{Y_m}(c_m)) \qquad (9.14)$$

with $C(u_1, \ldots, u_m) = \Theta_{m,\Gamma,d}[\Theta_d^{-1}[u_1], \ldots, \Theta_d^{-1}[u_m]]$ and Γ as in Equation 9.11. □

At this point it is interesting to remark that many institutions restrict their analysis to the Gaussian copula case. It is also interesting to note that the use of copula functions other than Gaussian or Student t is rare. There are other copulas appearing in the finance literature (for instance, the large class of Archimedean copulas), but it is seldom that we see such copulas applied in a portfolio model in real life.

For the conclusion recall again that, based on Equation 9.9, we find that dependence of latent variables $Y = (Y_1, \ldots, Y_m)$ is driven by the dependence structure of $\Phi = (\Phi_1, \ldots, \Phi_q)$ and by the order of magnitude of common weights[12] w_{ij} of assets i in factors Φ_j. Therefore, if we use the coordinate variables of Y as latent variables in a mixture model, we find that in our construction the essential mixing influence comes from Φ, so that we now proceed as follows: we translate the special copula form of Y as in Proposition 9.16 into parametric functions (see the functions g_i in the next section) and reduce the mixing component to the random vector Φ as variable in the functions F_i as constructed in the following section. Note that in our special approach here we generate the time dynamics of the mixture model only via the time dynamics of the credit curves φ_i and its conditional relatives $F_i(z, \cdot)$. Modifications and generalisations of our approach are thinkable and meaningful.

Implementation step 3: conditional credit curves
$F_i : \mathbb{R}^q \times [0, \infty) \to [0, 1]$

We now finally come to the point where we define functions F_i, $i = 1, \ldots, m$, in line with Condition 9.8. A typical special form of F_i based on Proposition 9.16 can be derived as follows.

Let $Y = (Y_1, \ldots, Y_m)$ be a random vector as in Proposition 9.16. Depending on whether we are in the Gaussian or Student-t copula cases we define functions based on Equation 9.9 and by

$$g_i : \mathbb{R}^q \times \mathbb{R} \to \mathbb{R} \quad \text{or} \quad g_i : \mathbb{R}^q \times \mathbb{R} \times \mathbb{R}_+ \to \mathbb{R}$$

by

$$g_i(z, \epsilon) := N\left[\beta_i\left(\sum_{j=1}^q w_{ij} z_j\right) + w_i \epsilon\right] \tag{9.15a}$$

or

$$g_i(z, \epsilon, x) := \Theta_d\left[\sqrt{\frac{d}{x}}\left(\beta_i\left(\sum_{j=1}^q w_{ij} z_j\right) + w_i \epsilon\right)\right] \tag{9.15b}$$

for $i = 1, \ldots, m$ and $z = (z_1, \ldots, z_q)$, where the first definition of g_i refers to the Gaussian copula case and the second definition of g_i refers to the Student-t copula. For $i = 1, \ldots, m$ let φ_i be the distribution function defined in Equation 9.7 in step 1 of the implementation. Recall that the definition of φ_i rests on a construction of credit curves $(p_i^{(t)})_{t \geq 0}$ for which Example 9.14 provided explicit guidance on how to derive such functions.

Lemma 9.17. For the Gaussian copula case in Proposition 9.16 set

$$F_i(z, t) := \mathbb{P}[g_i(z, \varepsilon_i) \leq \varphi_i(t)]$$

and for the Student-t copula case in Proposition 9.16 set

$$F_i(z, t) := \mathbb{P}[g_i(z, \varepsilon_i, X) \leq \varphi_i(t)]$$

where $z \in \mathbb{R}^q$, g_i is as in Equation 9.15, $X \sim \chi^2(d)$ and $\boldsymbol{\varepsilon} = (\varepsilon_1, \ldots, \varepsilon_m)$ with $\varepsilon_i \sim N(0,1)$ as in Proposition 9.16. Then, the functions $F_i : \mathbb{R}^q \times [0, \infty) \to [0,1]$, $i = 1, \ldots, m$, satisfy Condition 9.8.

Proof For $i = 1, \ldots, m$, F_i clearly is $(\mathcal{B}(\mathbb{R}^q) \otimes \mathcal{B}([0, \infty))) - \mathcal{B}([0,1])$-measurable based on the assumptions we made when constructing g_i in Equation 9.15 and defining the distribution functions φ_i.

The distribution functions φ_i are continuous and strictly increasing and all random variables involved in Proposition 9.16 as well as the functions g_i are also continuous. This implies that

$$F_i(z; \cdot) : [0, \infty) \to [0,1], \quad t \mapsto F_i(z;t)$$

is continuous and strictly increasing for fixed $z \in \mathbb{R}^q$.

The last condition we need to check is whether $F_i(z; \cdot)$ is a distribution function on $[0, \infty)$. For this just recall that we can invert the functions φ_i and rewrite $F_i(z; \cdot)$ as

$$F_i(z;t) = \mathbb{P}[\varphi_i^{-1}(g_i(z, \varepsilon_i)) \leq t]$$

or

$$F_i(z;t) = \mathbb{P}[\varphi_i^{-1}(g_i(z, \varepsilon_i, X)) \leq t]$$

which shows that $F_i(z; \cdot)$ is the distribution function of the random variable

$$\tau_i^{(z)} := \varphi_i^{-1}(g_i(z, \varepsilon_i)) \quad \text{or} \quad \tau_i^{(z)} := \varphi_i^{-1}(g_i(z, \varepsilon_i, X)) \quad (9.16)$$

in $[0, \infty)$ for any fixed $z \in \mathbb{R}^q$. This concludes the proof of the proposition. $\square$

Proposition 9.17 could be generalised to the case of individual (asset-i-specific) non-uniform marginal distributions in Proposition 9.16 as is obvious from the proof of Proposition 9.17.

In Equation 9.16 we recognise the conditional default times from Proposition 9.12. However, to compute credit risk by means of Equation 9.1 we need to simulate unconditional default times τ_i for each obligor. The following corollary shows how this can be achieved and is an almost immediate consequence of Proposition 9.17 and Construction 9.11.

Corollary 9.18. Let $\boldsymbol{\Phi} = (\Phi_1, \ldots, \Phi_q)$ be the systemic indexes as in Equation 9.9. Define $\tau_1, \ldots, \tau_m$ on $(\Omega, \mathcal{F}, \mathbb{P})$ as in Construction 9.11

(see also the comment on $\boldsymbol{\Phi}$ and $U_1, \ldots, U_m$ immediately below it) by

$$\tau_i(\omega) := F_i^{-1}(\boldsymbol{\Phi}(\omega); U_i(\omega)), \quad \omega \in \Omega$$

with F_i as in Lemma 9.17 and the inverse of F_i referring to the function $u \mapsto F_i^{-1}(z; u)$ as in Construction 9.11. Then, depending on the two copula choices in Proposition 9.16

$$\tau_i \stackrel{d}{=} \varphi_i^{-1}(g_i(\boldsymbol{\Phi}, \varepsilon_i)) \quad \text{or} \quad \tau_i \stackrel{d}{=} \varphi_i^{-1}(g_i(\boldsymbol{\Phi}, \varepsilon_i, X)) \qquad (9.17)$$

where $\stackrel{d}{=}$ denotes "equality in distribution". Moreover, Equation 9.8 holds for $t \geqslant 0$ and we have $\mathbb{P}[\tau_i \leqslant t] = \varphi_i(t)$ for all $i = 1, \ldots, m$ and $t \geqslant 0$.

Proof Let τ_i be as in Construction 9.11 and F_i be as in Lemma 9.17. Then

$$\begin{aligned}
\mathbb{P}[\tau_i \leqslant t] &= \mathbb{P}[F_i^{-1}(\boldsymbol{\Phi}; U_i) \leqslant t] \\
&= \mathbb{P}[U_i \leqslant F_i(\boldsymbol{\Phi}, t)] \\
&= \mathbb{P}[U_i \leqslant \mathbb{P}[g_i(\boldsymbol{\Phi}, \varepsilon_i) \leqslant \varphi_i(t)]] \\
&= \mathbb{P}[\varphi_i^{-1}(g_i(\boldsymbol{\Phi}, \varepsilon_i)) \leqslant t]
\end{aligned}$$

for the Gaussian copula in Proposition 9.16 and an analogous calculation holds for the Student-t copula. Therefore, the distribution functions of τ_i and $\varphi_i^{-1}(g_i(\boldsymbol{\Phi}, \varepsilon_i))$ coincide, which means that they are equal in distribution.

Now let us look how we can recover φ_i from F_i via integration over all scenarios z of $\boldsymbol{\Phi}$. Again, we consider only the Gaussian copula case in Proposition 9.16. The Student-t copula works analogously. By the construction in Equation 9.15, $g_i(\boldsymbol{\Phi}, \varepsilon_i)$ is uniformly distributed in $[0, 1]$. Therefore, we obtain

$$\begin{aligned}
\varphi_i(t) &= \mathbb{P}[g_i(\boldsymbol{\Phi}, \varepsilon_i) \leqslant \varphi_i(t)] \\
&= \int_{\mathbb{R}^q} \mathbb{P}[g_i(z, \varepsilon_i) \leqslant \varphi_i(t)] \, d\mathbb{P}_{\boldsymbol{\Phi}}(z) \\
&= \int_{\mathbb{R}^q} F_i(z; t) \, d\mathbb{P}_{\boldsymbol{\Phi}}(z)
\end{aligned}$$

because $F_i(z,t) = \mathbb{P}[g_i(z,\varepsilon_i) \leqslant \varphi_i(t)]$ and due to Lemma 9.17. This proves Formula 9.8. Moreover

$$\begin{aligned}\mathbb{P}[\tau_i \leqslant t] &= \mathbb{P}[\varphi_i^{-1}(g_i(\Phi,\varepsilon_i)) \leqslant t] \\ &= \mathbb{P}[g_i(\Phi,\varepsilon_i) \leqslant \varphi_i(t)] \\ &= \varphi_i(t)\end{aligned}$$

by construction for all $t \geqslant 0$. This concludes our proof. □

Corollary 9.18 is an important result. Equation 9.17 can now be used to generate dependent random variates of the unconditional default times based on random realisations of the dependent systemic factor vector Φ. In case of the Student-t copula, we additionally need random draws of the χ^2-distribution.

The only missing piece now is η_i in Formula 9.1, but before we come to that we want to pick up the aforementioned discussion on economic reasoning and empirical evidence for copula functions. Economic arguments are important when it comes to the choice of a copula function for the implementation of Formula 9.1. In the following brief discussion we want to make the point explicitly that in a credit risk context the Gaussian copula is hardly an empirically justifiable choice.

Remark 9.19. Let X, Y be continuous random variables on a probability space $(\Omega, \mathcal{F}, \mathbb{P})$ and let $C: [0,1]^2 \to [0,1]$ denote the unique copula function of the random vector (X, Y) in line with Remark 9.15. Denote by $\mathbb{F}_X, \mathbb{F}_Y$ the distribution functions of X, Y. Define the lower and upper tail dependence of X, Y by

$$\begin{aligned}\lambda_L(X,Y) &:= \lim_{y \to 0^+} \mathbb{P}[Y \leqslant \mathbb{F}_Y^{-1}(y) \mid X \leqslant \mathbb{F}_X^{-1}(y)] \\ &= \lim_{y \to 0^+} \frac{C(y,y)}{y}\end{aligned} \qquad (9.18)$$

$$\begin{aligned}\lambda_U(X,Y) &:= \lim_{y \to 1^-} \mathbb{P}[Y > \mathbb{F}_Y^{-1}(y) \mid X > \mathbb{F}_X^{-1}(y)] \\ &= \lim_{y \to 1^-} \frac{1 - 2y + C(y,y)}{1 - y}\end{aligned} \qquad (9.19)$$

Example 9.20. Let (X, Y) be bivariate Gaussian. Then

$$\lambda_U(X,Y) = \lambda_L(X,Y) = 2\lim_{x \to \infty}\left(1 - N\left[x\frac{\sqrt{1 - \operatorname{Corr}[X,Y]}}{\sqrt{1 + \operatorname{Corr}[X,Y]}}\right]\right) = 0$$

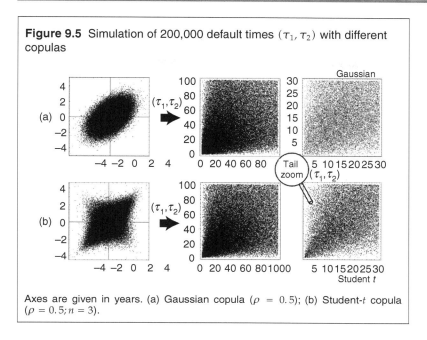

Figure 9.5 Simulation of 200,000 default times (τ_1, τ_2) with different copulas

Axes are given in years. (a) Gaussian copula ($\rho = 0.5$); (b) Student-t copula ($\rho = 0.5; n = 3$).

Let (X, Y) be bivariate Student-t with n degrees of freedom. Then

$$\lambda_U(X, Y) = \lambda_L(X, Y) = 2\left(1 - \Theta_{n+1}\left[\sqrt{n+1}\frac{\sqrt{1 - \text{Corr}[X, Y]}}{\sqrt{1 + \text{Corr}[X, Y]}}\right]\right) > 0$$

So the Student-t copula exhibits positive tail dependence, whereas the Gaussian copula has tail dependence zero so that X, Y are asymptotically independent if (X, Y) has a Gauss copula.

Figure 9.5 illustrates the different tail behaviour of the Gaussian and the Student-t copula (with $n = 3$ degrees of freedom) functions. At left-hand side of the figure the bivariate scatter plot of the respective latent variables (Y_1, Y_2) (see Proposition 9.16) is shown. Next to it, a bivariate default time vector (τ_1, τ_2) (in the form of 200,000 scenarios) is simulated (based on a simple credit curve). On the right-hand side we zoom in to tail scenarios which correspond to a zoom into the cloud of (τ_1, τ_2) (the lower left corner of the default time scatter plots). We then nicely see that in the case of the Gaussian copula the "coordinated default timing" is no longer visible, whereas in case of the Student-t copula "coordinated default timing" is still very much recognisable. Figure 9.5 is an illustration of asymptotic independence of (τ_1, τ_2) in the case of the Gaussian copula.

Example 9.20 and Figure 9.5 create a huge problem for believers in the Gaussian copula because if this were the right choice as a dependence model for credit portfolios then we should observe that in heavy crisis scenarios (tail scenarios) credit risks start to move in uncoordinated ways. Unfortunately, the opposite is the case. In fact, historically there is clear evidence that tail scenarios in credit risk tend to amplify dependencies. We could go even further and generalise this statement to the overall market: during the financial crisis there was no safe haven. Equity did not really diversify debt, Asia did not diversify Europe, CDOs did not diversify mortgages, and so on. Markets exhibited a behaviour which was not asymptotically independent at all. So, based on empirical evidence, the Gaussian copula cannot be the right choice as a dependence model.

Remark 9.21. The Gaussian copula model is widespread in credit risk models but, based on economic reasoning, cannot be the right copula choice, because if it were the right choice, then credit risks would exhibit asymptotic independence. Real crisis scenarios show the opposite: credit risks behave in a rather more coordinated way in extreme (heavy-tail) scenarios.

In general, copula techniques can be very useful for stress testing different parts of the loss distribution of a credit portfolio. For instance, tails can be stress tested by the use of copulas with high tail dependence.

We now stop the discussion on tail behaviour and consider the variables η_i in Formula 9.1.

Implementation step 4: $\eta_i : (\Omega, \mathcal{F}, \mathbb{P}) \times [0, \infty) \to \mathbb{R}_+$

We will only briefly touch on the implementation part belonging to η_i because it is not in our primary focus in this chapter. However, a few remarks might be helpful. The role of η_i is to quantify the realised loss in monetary amounts in case of default of asset i. In realistic cases, the realised loss is dependent on the time profile of exposures, the workout process and as such on the timing of default.

Example 9.22. Consider a regularly amortising loan like a mortgage. The later in time the borrower defaults, the lower the realised loss because in the case where default occurs later there was more time for the bank to collect amortisation amounts which reduce the outstanding exposure.

RETHINKING CREDIT RISK MODELLING

Remark 9.23. Models for the loss amount η_i or realised loss fraction (if η_i is considered in percentage terms) have to be time-dynamic in general. In many cases the realised loss depends on the point in time when default occurs.

The ideal set-up for implementing default timing dependent η_i is Monte Carlo simulation. Assuming a model for $\tau_1, \ldots, \tau_m$ as in Corollary 9.18 we can simulate n independent scenarios

$$(\tau_1^{(\nu)}, \ldots, \tau_m^{(\nu)}), \quad \nu = 1, \ldots, n$$

with a sufficiently high number of scenarios n. Variance reduction techniques like importance sampling can help to improve simulation accuracy even with moderate n but practitioners know that stable simulation results for large portfolios might need n to be in the order of magnitude of millions. This also depends on the underlying model of systemic indexes according to Formula 9.9.

Example 9.24. It is interesting to note that even in the case of professional companies in the analyst business one was able to observe very "lightheaded" modelling attempts not too long ago where people implemented factor models via Monte Carlo simulation in EXCEL based on its internal random number generator for which it is known that cycles appear very quickly so that scenarios start to occur repeatedly very soon. The best mathematical model does no good if the implementation from technical perspective is sloppily carried out.

The simulation of $(\tau_1^{(\nu)}, \ldots, \tau_m^{(\nu)})$ is straightforward if taking Proposition 9.16 for the mixing variables and, for instance, Example 9.14 for the distribution functions φ_i into account. Then, for each asset i in the portfolio we need to predict the outstanding exposure at risk reduced by loss mitigating effects arising from collateral securities and insights regarding expected recovery proceeds if assets end up in the workout portfolio of the bank. We can then put the pieces together in line with Formula 9.1 and simulate loss scenarios

$$L^{(1)}, \ldots, L^{(n)}$$

Based on the generated n portfolio loss scenarios, we can then analyse the distribution of portfolio losses, eg,

- drawing the histogram of the loss distribution,

- calculating risk measures like expected shortfall or quantile-based measures,
- tranching the portfolio for structuring reasons, etc.

Besides the challenge of time dynamics of realised losses as, eg, in Example 9.22, there is another challenge for η_i, namely, non-deterministic (stochastic) exposures and, therefore, stochastic realised loss rates. We cannot go into details here but introduce two brief cases as examples for "challenging modelling questions" in this context. We also indicate potential solutions.

Example 9.25. Let an asset in the portfolio refer to an unsecured loan. This means that in the default case, the lending institution has no pledged collateral from the borrower at hand which can be liquidated for mitigating the realised loss arising from a default of the obligor. But, nevertheless, the bank will work together with the client or the client's insolvency administrator to find ways to mitigate the realised loss arising from the client's default.

Loss mitigators in Example 9.25 can be achieved via restructuring and collecting future proceeds or via liquidating the property of the firm and receiving all or part of the proceeds. If the default refers to a private client, then the client's personal belongings can be distrained and sold, and proceeds can be transferred to the lending institution. Now, here is a rule of thumb.

Empirical analysis of sub-portfolios collecting unsecured exposures of certain client categories[13] reveals that the distribution of realised losses is close to "all or nothing", which means that recovery proceeds for unsecured exposures are very often close to full recovery or full loss.

Doing experiments with such data sets and drawing a histogram of realised losses of a portfolio of unsecured exposures shows that it exhibits much similarity with the arcsine distribution. To be more explicit, let us briefly describe a potential modelling approach. We do not describe a real data set in this chapter; our presentation is only illustrative.

We change our set-up slightly for the following and consider η as realised loss fraction in percent. A random variable η_i is said to follow an arcsine distribution if it has a probability density

$$f_{\beta(1/2,1/2)}(x) = \frac{1}{\pi\sqrt{x(1-x)}}, \quad 0 < x < 1$$

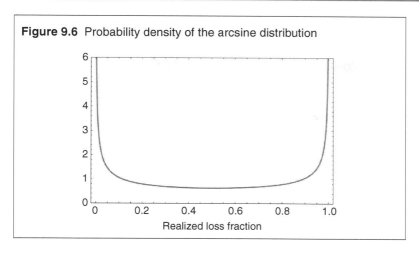

Figure 9.6 Probability density of the arcsine distribution

The arcsine distribution is a special case of the Beta distribution $\beta(a,b)$ with $a = b = \frac{1}{2}$. Figure 9.6 shows the density $f_{\beta(1/2,1/2)}$. The point of argument now could be along the following lines.

In contrast to the "early days" of credit risk modelling when people would have argued that without any information on the realised loss fraction η_i we should choose 50% as the best estimate for the realised loss,[14] we could argue based on the aforementioned rule of thumb for unsecured exposures that 50% might be the mean of η_i, but that extreme realisations of η_i are much more likely than a medium loss. A reasonable approach could be to include η_i in the case of unsecured exposures in the portfolio $\{1,\ldots,m\}$ as a random variable in the Monte Carlo simulation. We could choose η_i for unsecured exposures in each scenario at random with respect to the arcsine distribution. The expectation and variance of η_i would then be equal to

$$\mathbb{E}[\eta_i] = \tfrac{1}{2} \quad \text{and} \quad \mathbb{V}[\eta_i] = \tfrac{1}{8}$$

such that the medium loss indeed would be 50% but loss fractions in the extremes would be much more likely. In fact, the medium loss scenario would be the most unlikely (see Figure 9.6).

Example 9.25 and our brief discussion thereafter illustrates how we can find a probabilistic mechanism reflecting a practitioner's rule of thumb based on empirical evidence in data.

Recommendation 9.26. If exposures or realised loss rates are uncertain, as in Example 9.25, then it does not make sense to feed the Monte Carlo simulation with a best-guess point estimate. Instead,

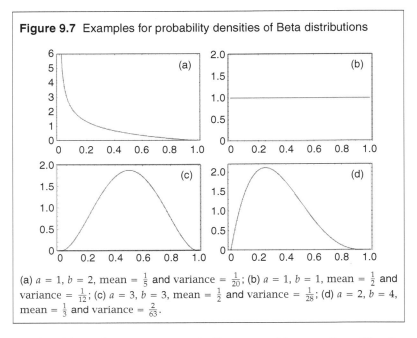

Figure 9.7 Examples for probability densities of Beta distributions

(a) $a = 1$, $b = 2$, mean $= \frac{1}{3}$ and variance $= \frac{1}{20}$; (b) $a = 1$, $b = 1$, mean $= \frac{1}{2}$ and variance $= \frac{1}{12}$; (c) $a = 3$, $b = 3$, mean $= \frac{1}{2}$ and variance $= \frac{1}{28}$; (d) $a = 2$, $b = 4$, mean $= \frac{1}{3}$ and variance $= \frac{2}{63}$.

we should work on an economically reasonable paradigm like the aforementioned rule of thumb, trying to find evidence in observed data histories and then come up with a robust stochastic approach (like the arcsine distribution for unsecured exposures). Of course, the effect of such an approach will be visible only if applied in combination with Remark 9.28.

The Beta distribution $\beta(a, b)$ for which the arcsine distribution is a special case is, in general, a useful distribution family for modelling η_i. Its probability density $f_{\beta(a,b)}$ is given by

$$f_{\beta(a,b)}(x) = \frac{\Gamma(a+b)}{\Gamma(a)\Gamma(b)} x^{a-1}(1-x)^{b-1}, \quad 0 \leqslant x \leqslant 1, a > 0, b > 0$$

and its expectation and variance are equal to

$$\mathbb{E}[\eta_i] = \frac{a}{a+b} \quad \text{and} \quad \mathbb{V}[\eta_i] = \frac{ab}{(a+b)^2(a+b+1)}$$

Figure 9.7 shows a few examples of probability densities of Beta distributions. Important for the application of random effects to η_i is empirical evidence and, again, economic reasoning which, in combination, often needs to insights like the aforementioned "rule of thumb".

Another challenge with η_i is that there can be dependencies between recovery proceeds and the random effects driving $\tau_1, \ldots, \tau_m$. In the final section we mention some references dealing with this issue. We mentioned before that the criteria for judging whether some random mechanism is reasonably applied to η are empirical evidence and economic reasoning. Let us start with the latter. The most fundamental principle underlying market behaviour is the principle of supply and demand. Based on this, we easily find economic reasoning for positive dependence between defaults and realised loss rates.

Example 9.27. Consider a market scenario corresponding to a crisis in residential mortgages just as we observed it in the 2007–8 US subprime mortgage market: as a consequence of default peaking, many private houses are offered for sale. Economically speaking, supply goes up and demand goes down. A consequence of this trend is a drop in house prices (which is a phenomenon we could observe closely during the US subprime mortgage crisis). Declining house prices and decreased demand leads to lower recovery proceeds for lending institutions, who try to sell the houses of defaulted clients in the house market. But lower recovery proceeds mean higher realised loss quotes on defaulted mortgage-backed loans.

Example 9.27 illustrates a situation where a scenario with default rates significantly higher than usual leads to higher realised loss rates on defaulted loans. So here we could again formulate a rule of thumb and combine it with empirical evidence based on default as well as loss data.

Remark 9.28. Recovery proceeds tend to be driven by the same effects as default events, possibly with a certain time-lagging and different sensitivity. We have to be careful not to underestimate credit portfolio losses when deciding for leaving this effect outside of Equation 9.1.

How can we embed such insights into Formula 9.1? Admittedly, the model approach to do this is not so easy and needs good data and good economic understanding. It needs intense analysis of empirical evidence in the form of loss rates, defaults and systemic risk drivers. Without going into details, we can describe the procedure as follows:

- find systemic indexes explaining defaults as well as loss rates in the segment considered;

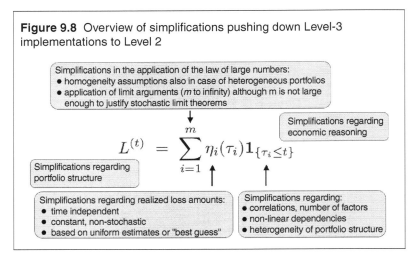

Figure 9.8 Overview of simplifications pushing down Level-3 implementations to Level 2

- use such indexes in Formula 9.9, which decomposes the systemic factors of assets with respect to market or macroeconomic indexes (see also the discussion around Formula 9.9);
- define a probabilistic model for η_i ($i = 1, \ldots, m$), eg, mixed Beta distributed, and connect it to the indexes;
- base the model-implied sensitivity of outcomes (defaults, realised loss rates) on statistical estimates like, for instance, the R-squared of variables with respect to explaining indexes;
- implement Formula 9.1 via Monte Carlo simulation.

As already indicated in Remark 9.28, one difficulty in the statistical analysis underlying this procedure is time lagging, because the effect of lower recovery rates will be visible some time after the occurrence of default peaking and are not synchronous.

We close the discussion here with the remark that the modelling of η_i still is a wide-open field. In the past decade we did not see much research dealing with it in form of explicit suggestions on how to model η_i in the way we just described. This last remark concludes our discussion on level-3 implementations of Formula 9.1.

LEVEL-2 SIMPLIFICATIONS

The purpose of this section is to briefly indicate typical common shortcuts and simplifications of the previously introduced Level-3 mixture-model implementations. Figure 9.8 illustrates five broad categories of model simplifications as they are common in the financial industry.

Application of Stochastic Limit Theorems ($m \to \infty$)

It is not difficult to show[15] that under certain homogeneity assumptions the distribution of the portfolio loss

$$L_m^{(t)} = \sum_{i=1}^{m} \eta_i(\tau_i) \mathbf{1}_{\{\tau_i \leq t\}}$$

converges to a limit distribution. The proof is based on a Law-of-Large-Numbers-type argument and a conditioning argument. The problem is that such limit theorems only hold under certain conditions concerning, for instance,

- the exposure distribution which, in our set-up, is the collection of variables $(\eta_i(s))_{i=1,\ldots,m; s \geq 0}$, or
- the structure of the portfolio, eg, with respect to homogeneity assumptions, and so on.

Most importantly, the limit theorem takes the limit $m \to \infty$, which means it assumes m to be very large. In some application cases such conditions are fulfilled but in some they are not. Here are two examples.

Example 9.29. Assume a portfolio of thousands of residential mortgage-backed loans. For such a portfolio we have a good chance of finding a limit portfolio which is a satisfactory approximation of the original portfolio.

Example 9.30. In the synthetic CDO world, people calculated so-called base correlations.[16] One popular approach common in the markets is to apply the so-called homogeneous large pool Gaussian copula (HLPGC) model to index[17] tranches based on 125 credit default swaps. Besides the fact that it is good that such trades are at all model based, it is nevertheless clearly recognisable in the name that such base correlations rely on the assumption that the reference portfolio is a large pool. Now, 125 names is not really what we should call a large pool for the application of limit theorems. There are situations where the limit approach nevertheless yields a good fit of the situation, but we can easily run into difficulties in real-life situations.

In fact, during the crisis we could observe that implied correlations scratched the 100% mark, which is due to various reasons, not just the fact that the underlying calculation model leaves room for criticism.

Correlation structure and non-linear dependencies

In Example 9.30 we mentioned implied correlations via the HLPGC approach. The last two letters in the name of the approach make it clear that the Gaussian copula is the chosen underlying dependence model of implied correlations. But in the context of Remark 9.21 we pointed out that empirical evidence actually rejects the Gaussian copula as a dependence model for credit risks. Instead, we should use a dependence model (such as Student-t with lower degrees of freedom) where tail dependence is possible such that the economic reality observed in typical crisis scenarios has a chance to be captured.

However, for linear dependence quantified by correlations much can go wrong. For instance, correlation modelling for portfolios often relies on market indexes, like MSCI or other stock-market related indexes. If quants measure correlations in such samples, eg, two-year weekly returns, than we have roughly 100 correlation observations at our disposal. The problem is that such correlation estimates are still on quite shaky ground, and hence imprecise.

Example 9.31. Assume a random pair (X, Y) with bivariate Gaussian distribution with correlation $\varrho > 0$ to be given. Taking a sample of n realisations of (X, Y), we can calculate the empirical correlation coefficient of (X, Y). The probability density f_{corr} of the correlation coefficient (considered as a random variable) equals[18]

$$f_{\text{corr}}(r) = \frac{(n-2)(1-r^2)^{(n-4)/2}(1-\varrho^2)^{(n-1)/2}}{\sqrt{2\pi}(1-\varrho r)^{n-3/2}} \frac{\Gamma(n-1)}{\Gamma(n-\frac{1}{2})}$$

$$\times {}_2F_1\left[\frac{1}{2}, \frac{1}{2}; \frac{2n-1}{2}; \frac{\varrho r + 1}{2}\right] \quad (9.20)$$

where

$${}_2F_1(a_1, a_2; b_1; x) = \sum_{k=0}^{\infty} \frac{(a_1)_k (a_2)_k}{(b_1)_k} \frac{x^k}{k!} \quad \text{and} \quad (a)_k = \frac{\Gamma(a+k)}{\Gamma(a)}$$

The function ${}_2F_1$ is a so-called Gaussian hypergeometric function. Calculating (and/or plotting) the density of f_{corr}, we find that correlation estimates can be quite noisy. Figure 9.9 shows four examples

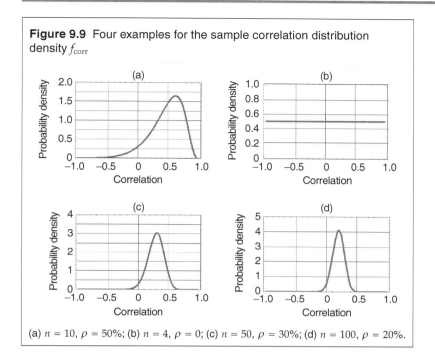

Figure 9.9 Four examples for the sample correlation distribution density f_{corr}

(a) $n = 10$, $\rho = 50\%$; (b) $n = 4$, $\rho = 0$; (c) $n = 50$, $\rho = 30\%$; (d) $n = 100$, $\rho = 20\%$.

for f_{corr}. It becomes clear that even 100 sample pairs will not yield stable estimates for the true underlying correlation.

It is rather questionable to work with correlation estimates which are based on a comparably short time series of observations. We cannot ignore the variation of estimates in such cases. Part of the problem is that deviations in estimates are hard to communicate to decision makers. People outside of the quant world have a hard time understanding why calculations sometimes are unstable. In order to cut a long story short, quants tend to just not mention the problem of variance of results and uncertainties in risk quantity estimates. This causes a lot of confusion and misunderstanding. It is strongly recommended that such misunderstandings, misinterpretations and lack of clarity come to an end. The need for clear communication of results goes hand in hand with the need to develop the best possible models. Developing a good model is just the first half of the way to success: the second half is communication, interpretation and, for the sake of clarity, a documentation of capabilities as well as model uncertainties.

Another typical source of simplifications is hidden in Formula 9.9. Because it is much simpler to work with a one-factor model, many level-2 implementations of mixture models follow that path. The most prominent example is the regulatory capital framework of Basel II Basel Committee on Banking Supervision (2004), where the one-factor-simplification has been pushed too far. The capital accord neither rewards diversification nor penalises concentrations. Thus, regulators give no incentive at all to institutions to diversify their portfolio. Admittedly, "soft" criteria in other than the quantitative pillar of Basel II carry the burden of making sure that bank portfolios are not too concentrated, but, at the heart of the system, in the quantitative pillar, diversification is not part of the equation.

Recommendation 9.32. The dependence model underlying a portfolio model (see Formula 9.9 and Proposition 9.16) should reflect economic reality. It is reasonable to work with a one-factor or one-sector model in the case of a simple portfolio. But it is questionable to simplify a level-3 model down to level 2 in terms of the dependence model when the portfolio structure requires a more complex treatment.

There is much ground to cover here in the financial industry. The way different banks model their credit risks when it comes to dependence modelling is very heterogeneous. There are large institutions with very sophisticated approaches allowing for positive tail dependence and including a series of systemic factors reflecting the economic situation of the portfolio. But there are also market-significant institutions with no meaningful dependence model at all. The poor arguments given in support of such simplified approaches are typically robustness and easy intelligibility of results. But if a portfolio is complex then it deserves a more complex mechanism (see, for instance, Chapter 7) of modelling and the robustness and "easy to communicate" arguments are very weak excuses.

We covered two areas of simplifications from Figure 9.8. We summarise the other three in the next section.

Other areas of simplification

Very common areas where simplifications take place are assumptions regarding the structure of a portfolio, eg, making uniformity assumptions in cases where the portfolio is heterogeneous, simplifying assumptions regarding the nature of exposures converting into realised losses when it comes to defaults and a certain ignorance of economic reasoning in modelling approaches. We have already discussed the problem of stochastic exposures and realised loss variables η_i in Formula 9.1. We have also provided examples where economic reasoning helped to model a certain effect and where ignoring such economic reasoning would lead us in the wrong direction. An area we did not cover is the assumptions of uniformity or homogeneity which makes modelling much easier. The answer to such level-2 modelling attempts is easy: if the portfolio is simple and allows for an approximation by a uniform portfolio then why should we not use it? But if the portfolio is complex, it needs a complex model.

SUMMARY

In this chapter we have discussed many issues in the area of credit risk modelling. We focused particularly on structured credit products but, based on Figure 9.3, we concentrated on the modelling of the portfolio loss according to Formula 9.1. We provided a very general modelling framework based on mixed default times and indicated how such a model could be implemented. We also briefly indicated simplifications which push the model down from level 3 to level 2 in Figure 9.1. Such simplifications can be meaningful but can also be misleading for complex portfolios.

Our motivation for writing this chapter was the 2007–9 financial crisis, when models experienced a lot of criticism. We do not agree with the statement of some press articles that model failure was one reason for the financial debacle. We do also not think that financial institutions need new models. Instead, we believe the following.

- The universe of credit risk models is rich enough to quantify the risk of credit portfolios.
- The financial industry does not sufficiently exploit the options at hand when it comes to modelling; many good stimulations from the academic world never found their way into banking practice although silently everyone in the field knows that such impulses would bring modelling much closer to reality.
- Quant teams should not rely on one model only; they should use many models and try different parameterisations, because credit risk (in particular, structured credit risk) is complex and each model sheds light on only some aspects of the problem.

- Communication of quantitative results to executive management really is an issue which needs more attention in the future: model weaknesses have to be made more transparent; executives should take more time to listen to their quants, should incentivise the careful and not just the quick solution.
- Sufficient quantitative understanding reflecting the complexity of the financial business should be an expertise represented in any relevant decision body in a financial institution.
- Level-0 and level-1 players in Figure 9.1 should upgrade their model capabilities to levels 2 or 3, depending on the nature of the problem. Level-2 approaches need to be revisited if shortcuts and simplifications are mathematically and economically adequate; if they are not, such models need a revision.

The word "crisis" comes from the ancient Greek noun $\kappa\rho\acute{\iota}\sigma\iota\varsigma$, which in turn is related to the verb $\kappa\rho\acute{\iota}\nu\omega$, which can mean "separating", "differentiating", "deciding", "selecting", "judging", etc. The original meaning of "crisis" can be nicely applied to the area of credit risk modelling. Although we reject the charge that models were at the root of the financial debacle, the crisis did separate good models from poor models, to differentiate between meaningful and less meaningful simplifications of models, to decide on economically reasonable approaches, to select dependence models better suited for capturing tail effects in a crisis scenario and to judge what can be done better in the future regarding communication of models as well as embedding models in financial institutions as a self-evident part of the business.

SUGGESTED REFERENCES AND FURTHER READING

As general literature on credit risk modelling and valuation, risk measures, mixture and factor models we refer the reader to Ammann (2002), Artzner *et al* (1999), Bluhm *et al* (2010), Duffie *et al* (2003), McNeil *et al* (2005), Schönbucher (2001) and Tasche (2002). As an example of a paper dealing with an interesting approach to recoveries (which influences η_i in Formula 9.1) we refer to Frye (2000). Background on the derivation of credit curves (the functions φ_i in this chapter) can be found, for example, in Bluhm and Overbeck (2007a), Bluhm *et al* (2010) and Trueck and Rachev (2009). New approaches from a slightly different angle are given in Schuermann and Jafry

(2003a,b). The Markov chain approaches to credit curves all more or less stem from the seminal paper by Jarrow *et al* (1997). For the Basel II accord see the original source (Basel Committee on Banking Supervision 2004) as well as Van Deventer and Imai (2003) and a nice paper (Wilde 2001) written by a quant for quants as an audience explaining the mathematics underlying the capital accord at an early stage of the Basel II development process (Basel Committee on Banking Supervision 2004). This is an example supporting our statement in this chapter that the capital accord is so complicated that even quants found it necessary to explain it to their colleagues. The typical non-quantitative senior manager in a bank has few chances to understand the Basel II document (Basel Committee on Banking Supervision 2004). For structured credit products, derivatives and CDOs we refer to Benvegnú *et al* (2008), Bluhm and Overbeck (2007b), Bluhm and Wagner (Forthcoming) and Schönbucher (2003). References for dependence modelling include Bluhm and Overbeck (2007b), Cherubini *et al* (2004), Joe (1997), McNeil *et al* (2005), Nelsen (1999), Rank (2006) and Schönbucher (2001). At the beginning of this chapter we mentioned the paper by Donnelly and Embrechts (2010), which nicely illustrates the deficits of the Gaussian copula. It is interesting to note that Embrechts *et al* (2002) were already warning of the shortcomings of common market dependence models more than 10 years ago.

1 See, for example, Jones (2009), Lohr (2009) and Salmon (2009). "Quant" is the nickname for a quantitative analyst working in the financial industry.

2 There are not more than a few hundred liquid (traded) single names in the market.

3 If the same asset is underlying two different structured products, we speak of a "cross-reference". The consequence of cross-references is that a single-name default, namely, default of the cross-referenced asset, triggers problems in various structured products, namely, in all products referencing the aforementioned reference asset.

4 For instance, so-called "ultra-high-net-worth" individuals.

5 We will later find that the modelling of dependencies between different Bernoulli variables is a major challenge here.

6 Mixture models are just one popular group of models. For a discussion of other popular model types in the context of structured credit products we refer to the Ammann (2002), Bluhm and Overbeck (2007b), Bluhm and Wagner (Forthcoming), Duffie (2003); Duffie *et al* (2003), McNeil *et al* (2005) and Schönbucher (2003).

7 Which, typically, is the so-called weak*-topology.

8 If we did not assume strictly increasing continuous distribution functions in Condition 9.8, we would have to work with the generalised inverse $F_i^-(z,u) = \inf\{x \geqslant 0 : F_i(z,x) \geqslant u\}$ for $u \in [0,1]$ and overcome some technical difficulties.

9 See Wilde and Lee (2006) for guidance with respect to this topic.

10 By letting the degrees of freedom go to infinity.

11 Note that the condition $d > 2$ guarantees the existence of variance for a Θ_d-random variable.

12 As well as from the order of magnitude of common weights.

13 In such an analysis we would, for example, not mix different client types like private and corporate clients.

14 Assuming losses are between "all" (100%) and "nothing" (0%).

15 References are given in the final section.

16 See the final section.

17 Such indexes are, for example, iTraxx Europe or CDX North America Investment Grade.

18 We refer the reader to Hotelling (1953) for a discussion of the formula.

REFERENCES

Ammann, M., 2002, *Credit Risk Valuation* (Springer).

Artzner, P., F. Delbaen, J. Eber and D. Heath, 1999, "Coherent Measures of Risk", *Mathematical Finance* 9(3), pp. 203–28.

Basel Committee on Banking Supervision, 2004, *International Convergence of Capital Measurement and Capital Standards* (Basel: Bank for International Settlements).

Benvegnú, S., C. Bluhm and C. Müller, 2008, *A Guide to Active Credit Portfolio Management: Spotlight on Illiquid Credit Risks* (London: Risk Books).

Bluhm, C., and L. Overbeck, 2007a, "PD Term Structures: To Be Markov or Not To Be", *Risk Magazine* 20, November.

Bluhm, C., and L Overbeck, 2007b, *Structured Credit Portfolio Analysis: Baskets and CDOs* (London: Chapman & Hall/CRC).

Bluhm, C., L. Overbeck and C. Wagner, 2010, *An Introduction to Credit Risk Modeling*, Second Edition (London: Chapman & Hall/CRC).

Bluhm, C., and C. Wagner, 2011, "Evaluation and Risk Management of Securitizations, CDOs and Related Instruments", Preprint, to appear in *American Review of Financial Economics*, Volume 3.

Cherubini, U., E. Luciano and W. Vecciato, 2004, *Copula Methods in Finance* (Chichester: John Wiley & Sons).

Donnelly, C., and P. Embrechts, 2010, "The Devil Is in the Tails: Actuarial Mathematics and the Subprime Mortgage Crisis", Working Paper, RiskLab, ETH Zurich.

Duffie, D., 2003, *Credit Risk Modelling: Pricing, Measurement and Management* (Princeton University Press).

Duffie, D., D. Filipović and W. Schachermayer, 2003, "Affine Processes and Applications in Finance", *Annals of Applied Probability* 13(3), pp. 984–1053.

Embrechts, P., A. McNeil and D. Straumann, 2002, "Correlation and Dependence in Risk Management: Properties and Pitfalls", In M. A. H. Dempster (ed), *Risk Management: Value at Risk and Beyond* (Cambridge University Press).

Föllmer, H., 2009, "Alles Richtig und Trotzdem Falsch? Anmerkungen zur Finanzkrise und zur Finanzmathematik", *Mitteilungen der Deutsche Mathematiker-Vereinigung* 17, pp. 148–54.

Frye, J., 2000, "Collateral Damage", *Risk Magazine* 13(4), pp. 91–4.

Hotelling, H., 1953, "New Light on the Correlation Coefficient and Its Transform", *Journal of the Royal Statistical Society: Series B* 15, pp. 193–32.

Jarrow, R. A., D. Lando and S. M. Turnbull, 1997, "A Markov Model for the Term Structure of Credit Risk Spreads", *Review of Financial Studies* 10, pp. 481–523.

Joe, H., 1997, *Multivariate Models and Dependence Concepts* (London: Chapman & Hall).

Jones, S., 2009, "The Formula that Felled Wall Street", *Financial Times*, April 24, URL: http://www.ft.com.

Lohr, S., 2009, "Wall Street's Math Wizards Forgot a Few Variables", *New York Times*, September 12.

McNeil, A. J., R. Frey and P. Embrechts, 2005, *Quantitative Risk Management: Concepts, Techniques and Tools* (Princeton University Press).

Nelsen, R., 1999, *An Introduction to Copulas* (Springer).

Rank, J., 2006, *Copulas: From Theory to Application in Finance* (London: Risk Books).

Salmon, F., 2009, "Recipe for Disaster: The Formula that Killed Wall Street", *Wired Magazine*, February 23.

Schönbucher, P., 2001, "Factor Models for Portfolio Credit Risk". Preprint, University of Bonn.

Schönbucher, P., 2003, *Credit Derivatives Pricing Models* (Chichester: John Wiley & Sons).

Schuermann, T., and Y. Jafry, 2003a, "Measurement and Estimation of Credit Migration Matrices", Working Paper, Wharton School Center for Financial Institutions, University of Pennsylvania.

Schuermann, T., and Y. Jafry, 2003b, "Metrics for Comparing Credit Migration Matrices", Working Paper, Wharton School Center for Financial Institutions, University of Pennsylvania.

Shreve, S., 2008, "Don't Blame the Quants", Article, URL: www.forbes.com/2008/10/07/securities-quants-models-oped-cx_ss_1008shreve.html.

Tasche, D., 2002, "Expected Shortfall and Beyond", *Journal of Banking and Finance* 26, pp. 1519–33.

Trueck, S., and S. T. Rachev, 2009, *Rating Based Modeling of Credit Risk* (New York: Academic Press).

Van Deventer, D., and K. Imai, 2003, *Credit Risk Models and the Basel Accords: The Theory and Practice of the Merton Credit Model* (Chichester: John Wiley & Sons).

Wilde, T., 2001, "IRB Approach Explained" *Risk Magazine* 14(5), pp. 87–90.

Wilde, T., and J. Lee, 2006, "Low-Default Portfolios without Simulation", *Operational Risk & Regulation* August, Technical Paper.

10

The Bayesian Approach to Default Risk: A Guide

Michael Jacobs Jr; Nicholas M. Kiefer

US Department of the Treasury, Office of the Comptroller of the Currency; Cornell University

All competent statistical analyses involve a subjective or judgmental component. Sometimes the importance of this input is minimised in a quest for objectivity. Nevertheless, it is clear that specification of a model, definition of parameters or quantities of interest, specification of the parameter space and identification of relevant data all require judgment and are subject to criticism and require justification. Indeed, this justification is an important part of the validation procedure expected of financial institutions (OCC 2000). However, estimation of parameters after these judgments are made typically proceeds without regard for potential non-data information about the parameters, again in an attempt to appear completely objective. But subject-matter experts typically have information about parameter values, as well as about model specification, etc. For example, a default rate should lie between 0 and 1 (definition of the parameter space), but if we are considering a default rate for a particular portfolio bucket, we in fact have a better idea of the location of the rate. The Bayesian approach allows formal incorporation of this information, formal combination of the data and non-data information using the rules of probability. A simple example in the case of estimating default rates is sketched in Kiefer (2007).

The Bayesian approach is most powerful and useful when used to combine data and non-data information. There is also an advantage in that powerful computational techniques such as the Markov Chain Monte Carlo (MCMC) and related techniques are available. These are widely discussed in the economics literature and have been applied in the default estimation setting. These applications invariably specify a "prior" which is convenient and adds minimal information (there is no such thing as an uninformative prior), allowing computationally efficient data analysis. This approach, while valuable, misses the true power of the Bayesian approach: the coherent incorporation of expert information.

The difficulty in Bayesian analysis is the elicitation and representation of expert information in the form of a probability distribution. This requires thought and effort, rather than mere computational power, and is therefore not commonly done. Further, in "large" samples, data information will typically overwhelm non-dogmatic prior information, so the prior is irrelevant asymptotically, and economists often justify ignoring prior information on this basis. However, there are many settings in which expert information is extremely valuable: in particular, cases in which data may be scarce, costly or of questionable reliability. These issues come up in default estimation, where data may not be available in quantity for low-default assets or for new products, or where structural economic changes may raise doubts about the relevance of historical data.

We go through the steps in a Bayesian analysis of a default rate. Estimation of long-run default rates for groups of homogeneous assets is essential for determining adequate capital. The Basel II (B2) framework (Basel Committee on Banking Supervision 2006) for calculating minimum regulatory capital requirements provides for banks to use models to assess credit (and other) risks. In response to the 2007–9 credit crisis, in a document for comment the Basel Committee has stressed the continuing importance of quantitative risk management (Basel Committee on Banking Supervision 2009a,b). Our emphasis is on the incorporation of non-data information, so we focus on elicitation and representation of expert information and then on the Bayesian approach to inference in the context of a simple model of defaults. Uncertainty about the default probability should be modelled the same way as uncertainty about defaults: represented in a probability distribution. A future default either does or does not occur, given the definition. Since we do not know in advance whether default occurs or not, we model this uncertain event with a probability distribution. Similarly, the default probability is unknown. But there is information available about the default rate in addition to the data information. The simple fact that loans are made shows that some risk assessment is occurring. This information should be organised and incorporated in the analysis in a sensible way, specifically represented in a probability distribution. We discuss elicitation generally in the next section. Then we run through the steps of a formal Bayesian analysis in a particular example. Definition of a parameter of interest requires a model, so we next turn to specification of a sequence of simple models (each generating a likelihood function). The first two models are consistent with the asymptotic single-factor model underlying B2. The third adds temporal correlation in asset values, generalising B2 and is perhaps in line with the validation expectations of Basel Committee on Banking Supervision (2009b), in that accounting for autocorrelation in the systematic factor speaks to how a model should be forward looking. The next section goes through the actual elicitation and representation for a particular expert. We then sketch the MCMC approach to calculating the posterior distribution (the distribution resulting from combining data and expert information coherently using the rules of probability) and illustrate all of the steps using Moody's data on corporate defaults. In the final section we give our conclusions.

To summarise: the steps in a Bayesian analysis are as follows.

1. Specify an economic model precisely defining the quantity of interest and generating a likelihood function for well-defined data (see page 327 onwards).

2. Identify a qualified expert and elicit information about the quantity of interest (see page 330).

3. Quantify this information in a probability distribution (see page 330).

4. Use the rules of probability to combine coherently the likelihood and the prior distribution, generating the posterior distribution of the quantity of interest (see page 334).

5. Analyse the posterior distribution using MCMC (see page 334).

ELICITATION OF EXPERT INFORMATION

A general definition of elicitation that we may offer in this context is a structured process or algorithm for transforming an expert's beliefs regarding an uncertain phenomenon into a probability distribution. In deploying Bayesian statistical technology in the domain of credit risk, elicitation arises as a method for specifying a prior distribution for one or more unknown parameters governing a model of credit risk (ie, a probability of default (PD)), where the expert may be an experienced statistician or a non-quantitatively oriented risk specialist (eg, a loan officer). In this setting, the prior distribution will be combined with a data likelihood through Bayes's Theorem, to derive the posterior distribution of the measure of risk (ie, the distribution of the default rate). While our focus is on formulating a probability distribution for uncertain quantities for the purpose of inference about a parameter, especially when there is no or very limited data, we note here that this is not the only context in which elicitation is important. This situation also arises in decision making where uncertainty about "states of nature" needs to be expressed as a probability distribution in order to derive and maximise expected utility. Similarly, this methodology arises in the application of mechanistic models built in almost all areas of science and technology to describe, understand, and predict the behaviour of complex physical processes. In that application a model developer will typically propose sensible model parameters in order to obtain outputs in cases where in general there is uncertainty about the inputs' true values. As in our application, this highlights the importance of having a coherent approach to represent that uncertainty.

A useful way to frame the elicitation is to identify the model developer or econometrician as a facilitator, who helps the expert transform the "soft data" (ie, experience or opinion) into a form amenable to statistical inference, which is the process of crafting expert's knowledge into probabilistic form. Elicitation is a complex process that, if done well, calls for a facilitator to be skilled and multi-faceted, as the role of the facilitator is central to the process of elicitation. Therefore, an econometrician not only is the facilitator but should also have knowledge of the business of making loans and issues in managing credit risk as well as be a strong communicator.

We may be able to set criteria for the quality of an elicitation. In doing so, we might believe that a meaningful distinction exists between the quality of an expert's knowledge, on the one hand, and the accuracy with which that knowledge is translated into probabilistic form, on the other. Therefore, we say that an elicitation is done well under the condition that the distribution so derived is an accurate representation of the expert's knowledge, no matter what the quality of that knowledge. A good facilitator asking probing questions may also be able to determine whether the expert really does have valuable information. We do not pursue this line here.

We may conclude that accurate elicitation of expert knowledge is by no means a straightforward task. This remains the case even if all we wish to elicit is expert's beliefs regarding only a single of event or hypothesis, an example in credit risk being the proportion of defaulted obligors in a particular rating class (or segment) over a given horizon. Here we seek an assessment of probabilities, but it is entirely possible that the expert may be unfamiliar with the meaning of probabilities, or if he can think intuitively in these terms then it still may be hard for him to articulate precise statements about probabilities. Even in the case where the expert is comfortable with probabilities and their meaning, it is still challenging to accurately assess numerical probabilities with respect to a relatively rare event such as that of default for a set of obligors, especially if they are highly rated and there is a lack of historical performance data on a portfolio of similar credits.

Let us now consider the task of eliciting a distribution for a continuous parameter θ, the proportion of customers in a given rating class defaulting. How may we proceed with this? One direct approach, which is impractical, involves implicitly eliciting an infinite collection of probabilities regarding this uncertain proportion (itself a probability), which we may write in terms of the distribution function for all of the possible values of θ. Note the symmetry here, as we characterise the uncertainty regarding the unknown probability governing the distribution of the default rate PD itself in terms of probabilities. However, we realise rather early on in this process that it is clearly impossible to do this, as in practice an expert can make only a finite number (and usually a rather limited number) of statements of belief about θ. It is likely that the best that we could hope for is that such statements might take the form of a small set of either individual probabilities, or a few quantiles of the distribution of θ; or possibly this might involve other summaries of the distribution, such as modes. In the case of a joint distribution for a collection of random quantities, for example, default rates in conjunction with loss severities, the elicitation task is much more complex.

Given the apparent formidable difficulties involved in the elicitation process, a reasonable observer may question if it is worth the effort to even attempt this. The answer to why this is a worthy endeavour lies in the use of elicitations as part of business decision making. We often find that a sensible objective for elicitation is to measure salient features of the expert's opinion, so that exact details may not be of the highest relevance with respect to the decision to be reached. For example, in forming a prior for the distribution of the default rate, a general sense of where it is centred (5 basis points, 1% or 10%?), and degree to which the tail is elongated, may be enough to inform the data at hand. Note the similarity to the issue of specification of the likelihood function, where typically an infinity (for continuous data) of probabilities are specified as a function of a small number of parameters. The point is made strongly in the normal case, when the whole set of probabilities are specified as functions of a mean and variance. This can hardly be credible as an exact description of a real data distribution, but nevertheless its usefulness has been proven in countless applications. Similarly, we specify a prior distribution on the basis of a small number of elicited properties. Even for cases in which the decision is somewhat sensitive to the exact shape of the elicited distribution, it may not be the decision but another metric that is of paramount importance, for example, the regulatory capital impact or the expected utility of the supervisor, which in many cases may quite often be robust to details of the expert's opinion.

Another use that supports the importance of elicitation is in statistical inference, particularly in the estimation of posterior distributions or predictive densities. This is a case in which elicitation promotes a careful consideration on the part of both the expert and the facilitator regarding the meaning of the parameters being elicited. This process results in two beneficial effects. First, it results in an analysis that is closer to the application, through requiring attention to the subject of the modelling exercise; in our application, this ensures that the focus is upon a set of plausible observed default rates, over a set horizon, with respect to obligors of a particular credit quality. Second, this discipline is useful in giving rise to a posterior distribution that, when finally calculated, is a meaningful object. By way of illustration, this process produces not only a PD estimate that can be used in a compliance exercise, but a complete predictive distribution of the default rate that is potentially useful in other risk management contexts, such as credit decision making, account management or portfolio stress testing.

A natural interpretation of elicitation is to conceive of it as part of the process of statistical modelling. When statisticians write down a likelihood function for an applied problem, this is nothing more than an informed (we hope) opinion regarding a data-generation process, which is conditional on a parameter set. In hierarchical frameworks (examples being random-effects models or models incorporating latent variables), we have distributions on a sub-set of parameters that are conditional on another set of parameters. Therefore, what we term "elicitation" in this context can be interpreted as nothing more than the final step in such a hierarchy: the statement of the form of the probability distribution of the highest-level parameters. This highlights that we should not lose sight of the fact that all of the usual principles of statistical modelling also apply to elicitation.

A stylised representation of the elicitation process consists of four separate stages. First, in the set-up stage, we prepare for the elicitation by identifying the expert, training the expert and identifying what aspects of the problem to elicit. The second step, clearly the heart of the process, is to elicit specific summaries of the experts' distributions for those aspects. This is followed by the fitting of a probability distribution to those summaries elicited in the second step. Note that in practice there may be overlap between this and the previous phase of the process, in the sense that the choice of what data to elicit often follows from the choice of distributional form that the facilitator prefers to fit. For example, if we prefer a simple parametric distribution such as a beta to describe the prior of the PD, then a few quantiles may suffice, whereas the more data intensive choice of a non-parametric kernel density may require other pieces of information. Finally, we note that elicitation is in almost all cases an iterative process, so that the final stage is an assessment of the adequacy of the elicitation, which leaves open the possibility of an iterative return to earlier stages in order to gather more summaries from the expert. For example, the fitted prior distribution of the PD parameter may be presented to the expert, and if the expert is not comfortable with the shape for whatever reason, we may try to gather more quantiles, re-fit and return later to make further assessments.

Thus far, we have framed the process of conducting an elicitation as that of formulating in probabilistic terms the beliefs regarding uncertainty from an expert, which we argue is the appropriate way to think about credit risk. However, in this context, who is the expert? There are two aspects here: the qualification of the expert and the basis of their information. For the first, we look at education and experience, particularly at experience in related risk-management situations. For the second, we evaluate the quality of the arguments: would they be convincing to other experts? Are they based on reasoning from particular similar portfolios or configurations of economic conditions? In practice, the choice of expert or experts must be justified. In our context, the experts are not that difficult to identify: they are the individuals who are making risk-management decisions for the relevant portfolio in a successful financial institution.

In summary, we outline suggested criteria for the conduct of elicitations, in the context of formulating beliefs regarding parameters governing default risk. While some of these aspects may be ignored in an informal elicitation, they become considerations of the utmost importance wherever substantive decisions or inferences may depend on the expert's knowledge, such as deriving a distribution of the default rate for either risk management or regulatory capital purposes. First, we should keep in mind that the objective is elicitation of a PD rate distribution, which represents the credit expert's current knowledge on the risk inherent in a portfolio, and it is very useful in this regard to have a summary of what that knowledge is based on (eg, state of the credit cycle, industry condition of the obligors or average features of the portfolio that are drivers of default risk). Second, we must be wary of any financial or personal interest that the credit expert may possess, and any inferences or decisions that will depend on the expert's distribution so elicited should be declared up front (eg, if the credit executive's bonus is a function of the regulatory capital charge on their portfolio). Next, it is also paramount that training should be offered in order to familiarise the expert with the interpretation of probability, as well as whatever other concepts and properties of probability will be required in the elicitation. It may be helpful in this regard to perform a "dry run" through an elicitation exercise with a view toward providing practice in the protocol that the facilitator proposes to use. Finally, the elicitation should be well documented. Ideally, this should set out all the questions asked by the facilitator, the expert's responses to those, and the process by which a probability distribution was fitted to those responses (eg, details of any moment matching or smoothing performed, such as well-commented computer code). These documentation requirements for expert elicitation fit well in the supervisory expectations for the documentation of developmental evidence.

STATISTICAL MODELS FOR DEFAULTS

Before elicitation can proceed, the quantities of interest need to be defined precisely. This requires a model. The simplest probability model for defaults of assets in a homogeneous segment of a portfolio is the binomial, in which the defaults are assumed independent across assets and over time, and occur with common probability $\theta \in [0, 1]$. The Basel requirements demand an annual default probability, estimated over a sample long enough to cover a full cycle of economic conditions. Thus, the probability should be marginal with respect to external conditions. Perhaps this marginalisation can be achieved within the binomial specification by averaging over the sample period; thus, many discussions of the inference issue have focused on the binomial model and the associated frequency estimator. Suppose the value of the ith asset in time t is

$$v_{it} = \varepsilon_{it}$$

where ε_{it} is the time- and asset-specific shock (idiosyncratic risk) and default occurs if $v_{it} < T^*$, a default threshold value. A mean of zero is attainable through translation without loss of generality. We assume the shock is standard normal with distribution function $\Phi(\cdot)$. Let d_i indicate whether the ith observation was a default ($d_i = 1$) or not ($d_i = 0$). The distribution of d_i is $p(d_i \mid \theta) = \theta^{d_i}(1-\theta)^{1-d_i}$, where $\theta = \Phi(T^*)$, our binomial parameter. Let $D = \{d_i, i = 1, \ldots, n\}$, let $n \in I^+$ denote the whole data set and let

$$r = r(D) = \sum_i d_i$$

denote the count of defaults. Then the joint distribution of the data is

$$p(D \mid \theta) = \prod_{i=1}^{n} \theta^{d_i}(1-\theta)^{1-d_i}$$
$$= \theta^r (1-\theta)^{n-r} \qquad (10.1)$$

Since this distribution depends on the data D only through r (n is regarded as fixed), the sufficiency principle implies that we can concentrate our attention on the distribution of r

$$p(r \mid \theta) = \binom{n}{r} \theta^r (1 - \theta)^{n-r} \tag{10.2}$$

a $\text{Binom}(n, \theta)$ distribution. This is model I. Model I underlies what the ratings agencies assume in their PD estimation.

The Basel II guidance suggests there may be heterogeneity due to systematic temporal changes in asset characteristics or to changing macroeconomic conditions. There is some evidence from other markets that default probabilities vary over the cycle (Das et al 2007; Nickell et al 2000). The B2 capital requirements are based on a one-factor model due to Gordy (2003) that accommodates systematic temporal variation in asset values and hence in default probabilities. This model can be used as the basis of a model that allows temporal variation in the default probabilities, and hence correlated defaults within years. The value of the ith asset in time t is modelled as

$$v_{it} = \rho^{1/2} x_t + (1 - \rho)^{1/2} \varepsilon_{it} \tag{10.3}$$

where ε_{it} is the time- and asset-specific shock (as above) and x_t is a common time shock, inducing correlation $\rho \in [0, 1]$ across asset values within a period. The random variables x_t are assumed to be standard normal and independent of each other and of the ε_{it}. The overall or marginal default rate we are interested in is $\theta = \Phi(T^*)$. However, in each period the default rate θ_t depends on the systematic factor x_t. The model implies a distribution for θ_t. Specifically, the distribution of v_{it} conditional on x_t is $N(\rho^{1/2} x_t, 1 - \rho)$. Hence, the period t default probability (also referred to as the conditional default probability) is

$$\theta_t = \Phi\left[\frac{T^* - \rho^{1/2} x_t}{(1 - \rho)^{1/2}} \right] \tag{10.4}$$

Thus, for $\rho \neq 0$ there is random variation in the default probability over time. The distribution function for $A \in [0, 1]$ is given by

$$\begin{aligned} \Pr(\theta_t \leqslant A) &= \Pr\left(\Phi\left[\frac{T^* - \rho^{1/2} x_t}{(1 - \rho)^{1/2}} \right] \leqslant A \right) \\ &= \Phi\left[\frac{(1 - \rho)^{1/2} \Phi^{-1}[A] - \Phi^{-1}[\theta]}{\rho^{1/2}} \right] \end{aligned} \tag{10.5}$$

using the standard normal distribution of x_t and $\theta = \Phi(T^*)$. Differentiating gives the density $p(\theta_t \mid \theta, \rho)$. This is the Vasicek distribution.[1] The parameters are θ, the marginal or mean default probability and the asset correlation ρ. The conditional distribution of the number of defaults in each period is (from Equation 10.2)

$$p(r_t \mid \theta_t) = \binom{n_t}{r_t} \theta_t^{r_t} (1 - \theta_t)^{n_t - r_t} \qquad (10.6)$$

from which we obtain the distribution conditional on the underlying parameters

$$p(r_t \mid \theta, \rho) = \int p(r_t \mid \theta_t) p(\theta_t \mid \theta, \rho) \, d\theta_t$$

Since different time periods are independent, the distribution for $R = (r_1, \ldots, r_T)$ is

$$p(R \mid \theta, \rho) = \prod_{t=1}^{T} p(r_t \mid \theta, \rho) \qquad (10.7)$$

where we condition on $(n_1, \ldots, n_T)$, ie, they are considered to be known. Regarded as a function of (θ, ρ) for fixed R, Equation 10.7 is the likelihood function. This is model II.

Model II allows clumping of defaults within time periods but not correlation across time periods. This is the next natural extension. Specifically, let the systematic risk factor x_t follow an AR(1) process

$$x_t = \tau x_{t-1} + \eta_t$$

with η_t independent and identically distributed (iid) standard normal and $\tau \in [-1, 1]$. Now the formula for θ_t (Equation 10.4) still holds but the likelihood calculation is different and cannot be broken up into the period-by-period calculation (cf Equation 10.7). Using Equation 10.6 we write

$$p(R \mid \theta_1, \ldots, \theta_T) = \prod_{t=1}^{T} p(r_t \mid \theta_t(x_t, \theta, \rho))$$

emphasising the functional dependence of θ_t on x_t as well as θ and ρ. Now we can calculate the desired unconditional distribution $p(R \mid \theta, \rho, \tau)$

$$= \int \cdots \int \prod_{t=1}^{T} p(r_t \mid \theta_t(x_t, \theta, \rho)) p(x_1, \ldots, x_T \mid \tau) \, dx_1 \cdots dx_T \qquad (10.8)$$

where $p(x_1, \ldots, x_T \mid \tau)$ is the density of a zero-mean random variable following an AR(1) process with parameter τ. Regarded as a function of (θ, ρ, τ) for fixed R, Equation 10.8 is the likelihood function. This is Model III.

Model I is a very simple example of a generalised linear model (GLM) (McCullagh and Nelder 1989). Models II and III are in the form of the general linear mixed model (GLMM), a parametric mixture generalisation of the popular GLM class. These models were analysed using MCMC in the default application by McNeil and Wendin (2007) using convenience priors and focusing on default rate estimation, and by Kiefer (2009) using an elicited prior and focusing on predictability of default rates.

ELICITATION: EXAMPLE

We asked an expert to consider a portfolio bucket consisting of loans that might be in the middle of a bank's portfolio. These are typically commercial loans to unrated companies. If rated, these might be about Moody's Ba–Baa or Standard & Poor's BB–BBB. The elicitation method included a specification of the problem and some specific questions over email, followed by a discussion. Elicitation of prior distributions is an area that has attracted attention. General discussions of the elicitation of prior distributions are given in Part 2 of Volume I and also by Garthwaite *et al* (2005), O'Hagan *et al* (2006) and Kadane and Wolfson (1998). Our expert is an experienced industry (banking) professional with responsibilities in risk management and other aspects of business analytics. They have seen many portfolios of this type in different institutions. The elicitation took place in 2006. The expert found it easier to think in terms of the probabilities directly than in terms of defaults in a hypothetical sample. This is not uncommon in this technical area, as practitioners are accustomed to working with probabilities. The mean value was 0.01. The minimum value for the default probability was 0.0001 (one basis point). The expert reported that a value above 0.035 would occur with probability less than 10%, and an absolute upper bound was 0.3. The upper bound was discussed: the expert thought probabilities in the upper tail of his distribution were extremely unlikely, but they did not want to rule out the possibility that the rates were much higher than anticipated (prudence?). Quartiles were assessed by asking the expert to consider the value at which larger or smaller values would be equiprobable given the value was less than the median, then given the value was more than the median. The median value was 0.01. The former, the 0.25 quartile, was 0.0075. The latter, the 0.75 quartile, was assessed at 0.0125. The expert, who has long experience with this category of assets, seemed to be thinking of a distribution with a long and thin upper tail but otherwise symmetric. After reviewing the implications, the expert added a 0.99 quantile at 0.02, splitting up the long upper tail.

At this point a choice must be made on the representation of the elicited information. Of course, without further assumptions, we do not have enough information to specify a probability distribution. In principle that would require an infinity of elicitations. However, choosing a parametric form for a statistical distribution allows determination of the parameters on the basis of the assessed information (assuming standard identification properties; we cannot assess a median alone and uniquely determine a $k > 1$ parameter distribution). This is the most common approach in practice and parallels the usual practice in specifying the data distribution: a parametric form based (we hope) on an economic model, allowing an infinity (or large number in the discrete case) of probabilities to be determined by finitely many parameters. This approach is illustrated in Kiefer (2010), where the elicited information was used to fit a truncated Beta distribution. The disadvantage of this approach is that there is rarely good guidance beyond convenience on the choice of functional form. Thus, this choice can insert information not elicited from the expert nor really intended by the analyst. Based on experience, we prefer a non-parametric approach (really, less parametric): the maximum entropy approach (Kiefer Forthcoming).

The maximum entropy approach provides a method to specify the distribution that meets the expert specifications and imposes as little additional information as possible. Thus, we maximise the entropy (minimise the information) in the distribution subject to the constraints indexed by k given by the assessments. Entropy is

$$H(p) = -\int \log(p(x))\,dP$$

Entropy is a widely used measure of the information in an observation (or an experiment). Further discussion from the information theory viewpoint can be found in Cover and Thomas (1991). The

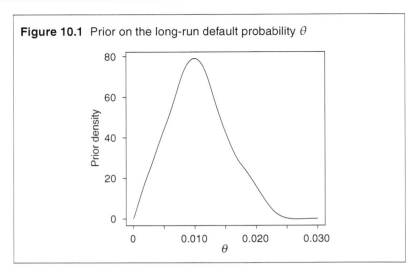

Figure 10.1 Prior on the long-run default probability θ

general framework is to solve for the distribution p

$$\max_{p} \left\{ - \int p \ln(p(x)) \, dx \right\} \qquad (10.9)$$

such that

$$\int p(x) c_k(x) \, dx = 0 \quad \text{for } k = 1, \ldots, K$$

and

$$\int p(x) \, dx = 1$$

In our application, the assessed information consists of quantiles. The constraints are written in terms of indicator functions for the α_k quantiles q_k; for example, the median constraint corresponds to $c(x) = \mathbf{1}_{\{x<\text{median}\}} - 0.5$. To solve this maximisation problem, form the Lagrangian with multipliers λ_k and μ and differentiate with respect to $p(x)$ for each x. Solving the resulting first-order conditions gives

$$p_{\text{ME}}(\theta) = \kappa \exp \left\{ \sum_{k} \lambda_k (\mathbf{1}_{\{\theta < q_k\}} - \alpha_k) \right\} \qquad (10.10)$$

The multipliers are chosen so that the constraints are satisfied.[2]

This gives a piecewise uniform distribution for θ. It can be argued that the discontinuities in $p_{\text{ME}}(\theta)$ are unlikely to reflect characteristics of expert information, and indeed this was the view of the expert. Smoothing was accomplished using the Epanechnikov kernel with several bandwidths h chosen to offer the expert choices on

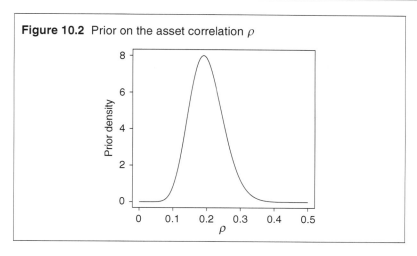

Figure 10.2 Prior on the asset correlation ρ

smoothing level (including no smoothing). Specifically, with $p_S(\theta)$ the smoothed distribution with bandwidth h we have

$$p_S(\theta) = \int_{-1}^{1} K(u) p_{ME}\left(\theta + \frac{u}{h}\right) du \qquad (10.11)$$

with $K(u) = \frac{3}{4}(1 - u^2)$ for $-1 < u < 1$. Since the density $p_{ME}(\theta)$ is defined on bounded support, there is an end-point or boundary "problem" in calculating the kernel-smoothed density estimator. Specifically, $p_S(\theta)$ as defined in Equation 10.11 has larger support than $p_{ME}(\theta)$, moving both end points out by a distance $1/h$. We adjust for this using reflection

$$p_{SM}(\theta) = \begin{cases} p_S(\theta) + p_S(a - \theta) & \text{for } a \leqslant \theta < a + 1/h \\ p_S(\theta) & \text{for } a + 1/h \leqslant \theta < b - 1/h \\ p_S(\theta) + p_S(2b - \theta) & \text{for } b - 1/h \leqslant \theta \leqslant b \end{cases}$$

The resulting smoothed density has support on $[a, b]$ and integrates to 1 (Schuster 1985). The prior distribution for θ is shown in Figure 10.1.

Model II requires a prior on the asset correlation ρ. Here B2 provides guidance. For this portfolio bucket, B2 recommends a value of approximately 0.20. We did not assess further details from an expert on this parameter. There appears to be little experience with correlation, relative to expert information available on default rates. There is agreement that the correlation is positive (as it has to be asymptotically if there are many assets). Consequently, we choose a beta prior with mean equal to 0.20 for ρ. Since the B2 procedure is to fix ρ at that value, any weakening of this constraint is a generalisation of the model. We choose a Beta(12.6, 50.4) distribution, with a standard deviation of 0.05. This prior is illustrated in Figure 10.2. Thus, the prior specifications on the parameters for which we have no expert information beyond that given in the B2 guidelines reflect the guidelines as means and little else. The joint prior for θ and ρ is obtained as the product, which is the maximum-entropy combination of the given marginals. Here, it does not seem to make sense to impose correlation structure in the absence of expert information.

As to τ, here we have little guidance. We take the prior to be uniform on $[-1, 1]$. It might be argued that τ is more likely to be positive than negative, and this could be accomplished by restricting τ to the real interval $[0, 1]$. Further, some guidance might be obtained from the literature on asset prices, though this usually considers less homogeneous portfolios. Here we choose a specification that has the standard B2 model at its mean value, so that allowing for non-zero τ is a strict generalisation of existing practice.

INFERENCE

Writing the likelihood function generically as $p(R \mid \phi)$ with $\phi \in \{\theta, (\theta, \rho), (\theta, \rho, \tau)\}$ depending on whether we are referring to the likelihood function (from Equations 10.2, 10.7 or 10.8, respectively), and the corresponding prior $p(\phi)$, inference is a straightforward application of Bayes rule. The joint distribution of the data R and the parameter ϕ is

$$p(R, \phi) = p(R \mid \phi) p(\phi)$$

from which we obtain the marginal (predictive) distribution of R

$$p(R) = \int p(R, \phi) \, d\phi \qquad (10.12)$$

and divide to obtain the conditional (posterior) distribution of the parameter ϕ

$$p(\phi \mid R) = \frac{p(R \mid \phi) p(\phi)}{p(R)} \qquad (10.13)$$

Given the distribution $p(\phi \mid R)$, we might ask for a summary statistic, a suitable estimator for plugging into the required capital formulas as envisioned by the Basel Committee on Banking Supervision (2006). A natural value to use is the posterior expectation,

$\bar{\phi} = E(\phi \mid R)$. The expectation is an optimal estimator under quadratic loss and is asymptotically an optimal estimator under bowl-shaped loss functions.

In many applications the distribution $p(\phi \mid R)$ can be difficult to calculate due to the potential difficulty of calculating $p(R)$, which requires an integration over a possibly high-dimensional parameter. Here, the dimensions in models I–III are 1, 2 and 3, respectively. The first model can be reliably integrated by direct numerical integration, as can model II (requiring rather more time). Model III becomes very difficult and simulation methods are more efficient. Since many applications will require simulation, and efficient simulation methods are available, and since these methods can replace direct numerical integration in the simpler models as well, we describe the simulation approach. Here we describe the MCMC concept briefly and give details specific to our application. For a thorough and wide-ranging description see Chapter 2 of Volume I (in particular, page 50) and Robert and Casella (2004).

MCMC methods are a wide class of procedures for calculating posterior distributions, or more generally sampling from a distribution when the normalising constant is unknown. We consider here a simple case, the Metropolis method. The idea is to construct a sampling method generating a sample of draws $\phi^0, \phi^1, \ldots, \phi^N$ from $p(\phi \mid R)$, when $p(\phi \mid R)$ is only known up to a constant. The key insight is to note that it is easy to construct a Markov chain whose equilibrium (invariant, stationary) distribution is $p(\phi \mid R)$. We begin with a proposal distribution $q(\phi' \mid \phi)$ giving a new value of ϕ depending stochastically on the current value. Assume (for simplicity; this assumption is easily dropped) that $q(\phi' \mid \phi) = q(\phi \mid \phi')$. This distribution should be easy to sample from and in fact is often taken to be normal: $\phi' = \phi + \varepsilon$, where ε is normally distributed with mean zero and covariance matrix diagonal with elements chosen shrewdly to make the algorithm work. Then, construct a sample in which ϕ^{n+1} is calculated from ϕ^n by first drawing ϕ' from $q(\phi' \mid \phi^n)$, then defining

$$\alpha(\phi', \phi^n) = p(R, \phi')/p(R, \phi^n) \wedge 1$$

and defining $\phi^{n+1} = \phi'$ with probability $\alpha(\phi', \phi^n)$ or ϕ^n with probability $(1 - \alpha(\phi', \phi^n))$. Note that $p(R, \phi)$ is easy to calculate (the product of the likelihood and prior). Further, the ratio

$$p(R, \phi')/p(R, \phi^n) = p(\phi' \mid R)/p(\phi^n \mid R)$$

since the normalising constant $p(R)$ cancels. The resulting sample $\phi^0, \phi^1, \ldots, \phi^N$ is a sample from a Markov chain with equilibrium distribution $p(\phi \mid R)$. Eventually (in N) the chain will settle down and the sequence will approximate a sequence of draws from $p(\phi \mid R)$. Thus, the posterior distribution can be plotted, moments calculated and expectations of functions of ϕ can be easily calculated by sample means. Calculation of standard errors should take into account that the data are not independent draws. Software to do these calculations with a user-supplied $p(R, \phi)$ exists. We use the MCMC package (Geyer 2009) used in "R" (R Development Core Team 2009). Some experimentation with these methods is useful to gain understanding. Valuable guidance and associated warnings are available on the website noted in the package documentation. Generally, an acceptance ratio of about 25% is good (Roberts *et al* 1997). The acceptance rate is tuned by adjusting the variances of ε. Long runs are better than short ones. There is essentially no way to prove that convergence has occurred, though non-convergence is often obvious from time-series plots. For our illustrative application, M samples from the joint posterior distribution were taken after a 5,000-sample burn-in. Scaling of the proposal distribution allowed an acceptance rate of between 22% and 25%. This procedure was used for Model II ($M = 10,000$) and for Model III ($M = 40,000$). Calculation of posterior distributions of the parameters and the functions of parameters considered below are based on these samples.

We construct a segment of upper tier high-yield corporate bonds, from firms rated Ba by Moody's Investors Service, in the Moody's Default Risk Service (DRS) database (release date January 8, 2010). These are restricted to US domiciled, non-financial and non-sovereign entities. Default rates were computed for annual cohorts of firms starting in January 1999 and running through to January 2009. In total there are 2,642 firm/years of data and 24 defaults, for an overall empirical rate of 0.00908. The data is shown in Figure 10.3.

The analysis of the binomial model is straightforward using direct calculations involving numerical integration to calculate the predictive distribution and various moments (recall we are not in a conjugate-updating framework due to the flexible form of the prior representation).

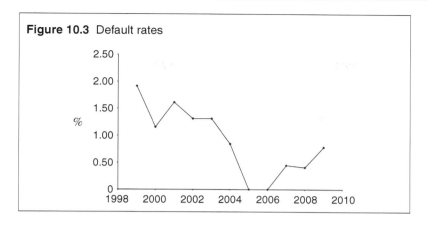

Figure 10.3 Default rates

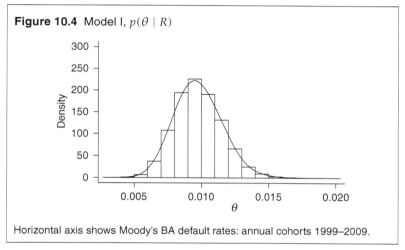

Figure 10.4 Model I, $p(\theta \mid R)$

Horizontal axis shows Moody's BA default rates: annual cohorts 1999–2009.

The posterior distribution for the binomial model is shown in Figure 10.4.

This density has $E(\theta \mid R = r = 24) = 0.0098$ and $\sigma_\theta = 0.00174$.

Note that this is higher than the empirical default rate of 0.0091. The right-skewness of the distribution is evident, which has flowed through from the prior distribution. The 95% credible interval for θ is $(0.00662, 0.0134)$, which corresponds to a relative uncertainty of about 68% for the estimated PD.

Model II has asset value correlation within periods, allowing for heterogeneity in the default rate over time (but not correlated over time) and clumping of defaults. The marginal posterior distributions are shown in Figures 10.5 and 10.6.

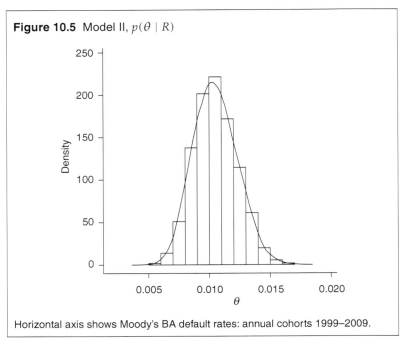

Figure 10.5 Model II, $p(\theta \mid R)$

Horizontal axis shows Moody's BA default rates: annual cohorts 1999–2009.

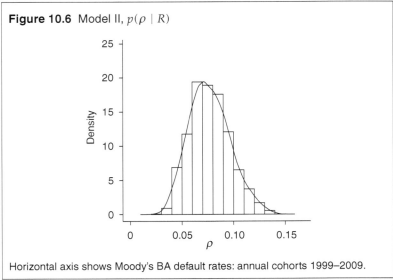

Figure 10.6 Model II, $p(\rho \mid R)$

Horizontal axis shows Moody's BA default rates: annual cohorts 1999–2009.

We observe that the estimate of the probability of default in this model is higher than in the one-parameter model, this density having $E(\theta \mid R) = 0.0105$ and $\sigma_\theta = 0.00175$. The 95% credible interval

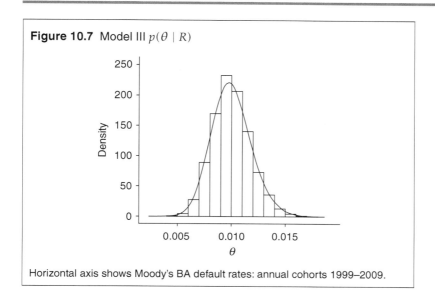

Figure 10.7 Model III $p(\theta \mid R)$

Horizontal axis shows Moody's BA default rates: annual cohorts 1999–2009.

for θ is $(0.0073, 0.0140)$. This density has $E(\rho \mid R) = 0.0770$ and $\sigma_\rho = 0.0194$, so that there is a higher degree of variability relative to the mean in the estimated distribution of the asset value correlation compared with the PD parameter. The 95% credible interval for ρ is $(0.0435, 0.119)$. Note that the prior mean (0.2) is well outside the posterior 95% confidence interval for ρ. Analysis of the Vasicek distribution shows that the data information on ρ comes through the year-to-year variation in the default rates. At $\theta = 0.01$ and $\rho = 0.2$ the Vasicek distribution implies an intertemporal standard deviation in default rates of 0.015. With $\rho = 0.077$, the posterior mean, the implied standard deviation is 0.008. In our sample, the sample standard deviation is 0.0063. This is the aspect of the data which is moving the posterior to the left of the prior.

The marginal posterior distributions for Model III are shown in Figures 10.7–10.9.

We observe that the estimate of the probability of default in this model is slightly higher than in the one-parameter model, this density having $E(\theta \mid R) = 0.0100$ and $\sigma_\theta = 0.00176$. This density has $E(\rho \mid R) = 0.0812$ and $\sigma_\rho = 0.0185$ with a 95% credible interval of $(0.043, 0.132)$. The density of the autocorrelation parameter in the latent systematic factor has $E(\tau \mid R) = 0.162$ and $\sigma_\tau = 0.0732$. The 95% credible interval is $(-0.006, 0.293)$.

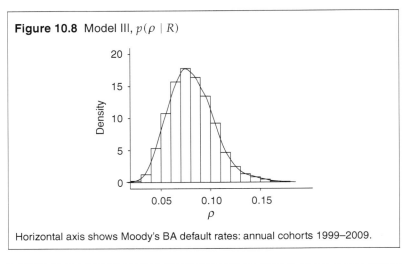

Figure 10.8 Model III, $p(\rho \mid R)$

Horizontal axis shows Moody's BA default rates: annual cohorts 1999–2009.

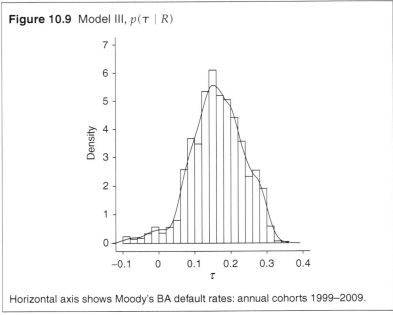

Figure 10.9 Model III, $p(\tau \mid R)$

Horizontal axis shows Moody's BA default rates: annual cohorts 1999–2009.

In summary, the picture on the default probability is pretty clear: it is around 0.01 in all models. The asset value correlation is around 0.08, estimated to be slightly higher in model III than in model II. This is substantially less than the value specified in B2. The temporal correlation in the systematic factor is only present in model III. The evidence is sparse here (recall that there are only 11 years of data and the prior information was as uninformative as possible) but it appears to be slightly positive.

CONCLUSION

In this and related applications the econometrician faces the dual chore of modelling the data distribution with a specification of a statistical distribution and modelling expert information with a statistical distribution. Adding the latter task substantially increases the range of applicability of econometric methods. This is clearly an area for further research. Our application has gone through the steps of a formal Bayesian analysis, focusing on the default probability, a key parameter which is required to be estimated under B2 by a large number of institutions worldwide. We concluded our analysis by generating the posterior distributions for the parameters of a nested sequence of models and calculating summary statistics. The mean default probability would be a natural estimator to use for calculating minimum regulatory capital requirements using the formulas provided by B2. In practice, these distributions have many uses, and the analysis would be ongoing. For example, institutions might want to use the entire distribution of the default probability in pricing credit and in setting in-house capital levels. Having an entire distribution for the PD could also be useful in stressing of Basel II Internal Rating Based models, ie, plugging in a high quantile of PD into the capital formula to model an adverse scenario. The more general models provide insight into the extent to which default rates over time are predictable, and to the extent to which risk calculations should look ahead over a number of years. An analysis of loss given default (LGD) using Bayesian methods would be useful: here there is substantial experience and a joint analysis of LGD and the default probability is likely to be extremely interesting. These and many other possible analyses build on the methods illustrated here.

> The statements made and views expressed herein are solely those of the authors, and do not necessarily represent official policies, statements or views of the Office of the Comptroller of the Currency or its staff.

1 See, for example, Bluhm *et al* (2003, Section 2.5) for details.

2 For details, see Cover and Thomas (1991) or, for an approach not using the Lagrangian, Csiszar (1975).

REFERENCES

Basel Committee on Banking Supervision, 2006, *International Convergence of Capital Measurement and Capital Standards* (Basel: Bank for International Settlements).

Basel Committee on Banking Supervision, 2009, "Proposed Enhancements to the Basel II Framework: Consultative Document", Discussion Paper, Bank for International Settlements.

Basel Committee on Banking Supervision, 2009, ""Range of Practices and Issues in Economic Capital Frameworks", Discussion Paper, Bank for International Settlements.

Bluhm, C., L. Overbeck and C. K. J. Wagner, 2003 *An Introduction to Credit Risk Modeling*, Financial Mathematics Series (London: Chapman & Hall/CRC).

Cover, T. M., and J. A. Thomas, 1991, *Elements of Information Theory* (Chichester: John Wiley & Sons).

Csiszar, I., 1975, "I-divergence Geometry of Probability Distributions and Minimization Problems", *The Annals of Probability* 3, pp. 146–58.

Das, S. R., D. Duffie, N. Kapadia and L. Saita, 2007, "Common Failings: How Corporate Defaults Are Correlated", *Journal of Finance* 62, pp. 93–117.

Garthwaite, P. H., J. B. Kadane and A. O'Hagan, 2005, "Statistical Methods for Eliciting Probability Distributions", *Journal of the American Statistical Association* 100, pp. 680–700.

Geyer, C. J., 2009, *MCMC: Markov Chain Monte Carlo, R package version 0.6*.

Gordy, M. B., 2003, "A Risk-Factor Model Foundation for Ratings-Based Bank Capital Rules", *Journal of Financial Intermediation* 12, pp. 199–232.

Kadane, J. B., and L. J. Wolfson, 1998, "Experiences in Elicitation", *The Statistician* 47(1), pp. 3–19.

Kiefer, N. M., 2007, "The Probability Approach to Default Probabilities", *Risk Magazine* July, pp. 146–50.

Kiefer, N. M., 2009, "Correlated Defaults, Temporal Correlation, Expert Information and Predictability of Default Rates", Discussion Paper, Cornell University.

Kiefer, N. M., 2010, "Default Estimation and Expert Information", *Journal of Business and Economic Statistics* 28(2), pp. 320–28.

Kiefer, N. M., Forthcoming, "Default Estimation, Correlated Defaults and Expert Information", *Journal of Applied Econometrics*.

McCullagh, P., and J. Nelder, 1989, *Generalized Linear Models*, Second Edition (London: Chapman & Hall).

McNeil, A. J., and J. P. Wendin, 2007, "Bayesian Inference for Generalized Linear Mixed Models of Portfolio Credit Risk", *Journal of Empirical Finance* 14, pp. 131–49.

Nickell, P., W. Perraudin and S. Varotto, 2000, "Stability of Rating Transitions", *Journal of Banking and Finance* 24, pp. 203–27.

Office of the Comptroller of the Currency, 2000, "Risk Modeling: Model Validation", Discussion Paper 2000-16, Office of the Comptroller of the Currency.

O'Hagan, A., C. E. Buck, A. Daneshkhah, J. R. Eiser, P. Garthwaite, D. J. Jenkinson, J. E. Oakley and T. Rakow, 2006, *Uncertain Judgements: Eliciting Experts' Probabilities* (Chichester: John Wiley & Sons).

R Development Core Team, 2009, *R: A Language and Environment for Statistical Computing* (Vienna: R Foundation for Statistical Computing).

Robert, C., and G. Casella, 2004, *Monte Carlo Statistical Methods*, Second Edition (Springer).

Roberts, G. O., A. Gelman and W. R. Gilks, 1997, "Weak Convergence and Optimal Scaling of Random Walk Metropolis Algorithms", *Annals of Applied Probability* 7(1), pp. 110–20.

Schuster, E. F., 1985, "Incorporating Support Constraints into Nonparametric Estimators of Densities", *Communications in Statistical Theory and Methods* 14, pp. 1123–36.

11

Bayesian Modelling of Small and Medium-Sized Companies' Defaults

**Mathilde Wilhelmsen, Xeni K. Dimakos;
Tore Anders Husebø, Marit Fiskaaen**
Norwegian Computing Center; Centre of Excellence Credit Risk Modelling, Sparebank 1

For many financial institutions, credit risk is by far the most important risk type. Estimation of default probabilities is fundamental in both credit scoring and credit risk models. As the Basel II Capital Accord (Bank for International Settlements 2006) allows banks to use their own default probability estimations, the calculation of regulatory capital is also influenced by the strategy applied for estimating default probabilities.

The study of bankruptcy prediction goes back to Beaver (1966) and Altman (1968). Two classes of models dominate the literature. The market models (or structural models) are based on the value of the firm as set by a market, and often approximated by stock prices. The KMV model (Crosbie and Bohn 2002) which is widely used in industry is an example of a structural model. Accounting-based models, on the other hand, use available financial indicators such as annual financial statements.

This chapter focuses on the accounting-based models, and in particular on the logistic regression model (McCullagh and Nelder 1989). The literature includes applications of neural networks, linear discriminant models and general additive models for the same purpose.[1] Studies that compare these models for the purpose of default prediction show, not surprisingly, that the behaviour and suitability depend on the data to hand. For many practitioners the logistic regression model remains the benchmark, as it is easy to interpret and available on many software platforms.

Defaults are rare and the data sets of recorded defaults tend to be moderate, particularly for smaller banks. Moreover, additional information on the risks will often be available through expert risk assessments, credit ratings from other sources, regulators or publicly available data. Hence, it makes sense to combine the data available with the additional information that can be gathered, meaning that the Bayesian approach might be particularly useful for default probability estimation.

The Bayesian approach to credit risk modelling is not new. Löffler *et al* (2005) proposed an empirical Bayes approach for banks with small credit default data sets and suggested that prior information may be retrieved from academic literature or regulators. Other applications of Bayesian models to credit risk modelling are given by McNeil and Wedin (2007), Ando (2006) and of course the other chapters in Part II of this book.

Inference in the Bayesian logistic regression model is done using the Markov chain Monte Carlo (MCMC) method (Gilks *et al* 1996). With software such as OPENBUGS (Spiegelhalter *et al* 2007) and MCMCPACK (Martin *et al* 2008), MCMC algorithms are available to everyone in user-friendly environments. However, the fundamental challenge applying MCMC in practice remains: to determine convergence! The practitioner faces the task of choosing between several different measures of convergence, which might give contradictive answers to the question of convergence. Closely related is the issue of computational speed. Many applications require that the MCMC algorithm is run for hours or even days to obtain satisfactory convergence. Mira and Tenconi (2004) showed how to speed up the convergence in a credit risk application. However, this requires implementation outside the scope of the above-mentioned packages.

The main aim of this chapter is to introduce integrated nested Laplace approximation (INLA) as an alternative to MCMC for Bayesian credit risk modelling, and to show that INLA can be used to analyse the uncertainties involved with the estimation of the regression coefficients and thus of the probabilities of defaults (PDs). INLA was developed by Rue *et al* (2009) as an efficient method for inference in complex models where the problems of convergence and computational time make MCMC unsuitable, or even infeasible. In this chapter we present the first step in a Bayesian logistic regression model, where we use fixed hyperparameters for the regression coefficients. A natural extension, which is a subject for future work, is to let the hyperparameters be stochastic, in which case we get a hierarchical model. Finally, the inclusion of random effects for both individual customers and groups of customers will constitute a more complete credit risk model. When in the future we consider the hierarchical model, possibly with some random effects, the advantages of INLA will become more apparent.

In the case of a hierarchical model, the INLA approach for approximating the posterior marginals is computed in three steps. The first step approximates the posterior marginal distribution of the so-called hyperparameters, that is the parameters of the prior distribution. The second step computes an approximation of the posterior distribution of the model parameters, given the observed response variables and the hyperparameters. The third step combines the previous two steps using numerical integration to obtain the posterior distribution of the regression parameters. In our case, with fixed hyperparameters, the INLA approach only consists of one step: to approximate the posterior marginal distribution of the model parameters, given the observed response variables and the hyperparameters.

Applying the Bayesian approach requires a method for articulating our prior information. The Bayesian logistic regression model usually has a prior distribution on the regression coefficients. For regulators and risk managers it is inherently easier to express opinions in terms of default probabilities than in terms of regression coefficients. The second aim of this chapter is to demonstrate a simple simulation-based method to convert Beta-distributed priors on default probabilities to priors on the regression coefficients.

In our case, with fixed hyperparameters, we find that INLA and MCMC give approximately the same posterior results for approximately the same CPU time. Hence, it is not obvious that INLA is the best choice for this relatively simple model.

The data set used in this chapter is collected from four SpareBank 1 banks in Norway. All four banks use the internal ratings-based (IRB) approach for calculating the capital requirements for credit risk. The data set consists of 7,080 small and medium-sized firms. For each firm a set of financial and non-financial variables are used to estimate the probability of default.

Table 11.1 Overview of the explanatory variables

Variable	Name	Values	Category
Profit	Operating profit/Financial costs	[0,10]	Income
Loss	Operating loss	[0,10]	Income
Cpinv	Circulation pace on inventory	[0,10]	Income
Dp	Degree of profit	[0,10]	Income
Eqper	Equity percent	[0,10]	Solidity
Mpay	Means of payment	[0,10]	Solidity
Dliq	Degree of liquidity	[0,10]	Solidity
Odfac	Overdraft facility	[0,10]	Solidity
Rephist	History of company's reprimands	[0,10]	Behaviour
Repkf	Reprimands of payment for key figures	[0,10]	Behaviour
Repac	Reprimands from accountants	[0,10]	Behaviour
Ad	Submitted accounts delayed	[0,10]	Behaviour
Age	Age	[0,10]	Age

The remainder of this chapter is organised as follows: after introducing the data set we present the Bayesian logistic regression model for credit risk and the latent Gaussian models for which INLA was developed. Then we give a brief introduction to the general INLA and the software used in this work. Finally, numerical results are presented before a conclusion summarises the main points of our analysis.

DATA

In this chapter we consider a Sparebank 1 portfolio from 2006/2007 which consists of 7,080 customers and their associated accounting variables.[2] The portfolio consists of non-financial firms from many industries, including manufacturing, building and construction, fishery, trade, etc. Firms in the industries shipping, shipyards and property development are not included in the portfolio considered here.

There are 126 recorded defaults in the data set, which corresponds to an average default probability of 1.8%. Table 11.1 shows the 13 explanatory variables Sparebank 1 considers to be the most important in describing defaults among customers. All variables are transformed into values between 0 and 10, where 10 is considered to be the best value a customer can get. In other words, high values are associated with behaviour that reduces the probability of default. The variables can be divided into four groups: income, solidity, behaviour

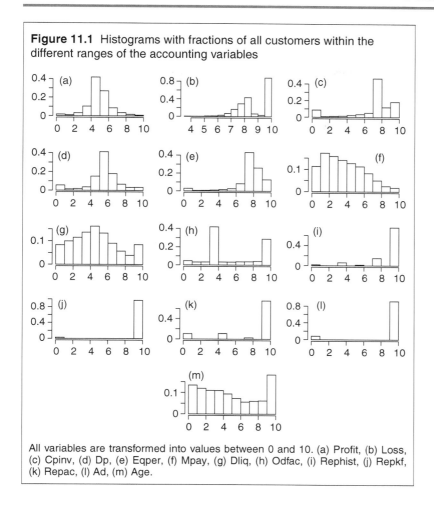

Figure 11.1 Histograms with fractions of all customers within the different ranges of the accounting variables

All variables are transformed into values between 0 and 10. (a) Profit, (b) Loss, (c) Cpinv, (d) Dp, (e) Eqper, (f) Mpay, (g) Dliq, (h) Odfac, (i) Rephist, (j) Repkf, (k) Repac, (l) Ad, (m) Age.

and age. Figure 11.1 shows the histograms of all the explanatory variables in the data set.

MODEL

Logistic regression

The logistic regression model belongs to the class of generalised linear models (GLMs) (McCullagh and Nelder 1989). The response variable in a logistic regression model is binomial and the expectation is related to the linear predictor through the logit function. We introduce an indicator of default. Let $Y_i = 1$ if customer i defaults, and $Y_i = 0$ otherwise. Then

$$Y_i \sim \text{Binom}(p_i), \quad i = 1, \ldots, N$$

and the linear predictor

$$\eta_i = \beta_0 + \sum_{j=1}^{M} \beta_j x_{ij} \tag{11.1}$$

is linked to the default probability through the logit function

$$\text{logit}(p_i) = \log\left(\frac{p_i}{1 - p_i}\right) = \eta_i$$

In our case, $N = 7{,}080$, $M = 13$ and the explanatory variables x_{ij} are customer characteristics. It follows that the probability of default is given by

$$p_i = \frac{\exp(\beta_0 + \sum_{j=1}^{M} \beta_j x_{ij})}{1 + \exp(\beta_0 + \sum_{j=1}^{M} \beta_j x_{ij})} \tag{11.2}$$

Bayesian formulation

In principle we have an $M + 1$-dimensional prior on the regression coefficients because there are $M + 1$ coefficients. As we will discuss below, we assume that the regression coefficients β_j are uncorrelated *a priori* and focus on the marginal priors for each β_j, $j = 0, \ldots, M$. Our Bayesian model is formulated by specifying prior distributions on the regression coefficients in Equation 11.1

$$\beta_j \sim \pi(\beta_j \mid \boldsymbol{\theta}_j), \quad j = 0, \ldots, M$$

The prior distribution $\pi(\cdot \mid \boldsymbol{\theta}_j)$ may be any proper probability density function and the hyperparameter $\boldsymbol{\theta}_j$ may be a scalar or a vector. The interpretation of the hyperparameters depends on the choice of the distribution, but may, for instance, include a measure of the centre and spread of the prior. By specifying different values of $\boldsymbol{\theta}_j$, the regression coefficients may have very different distributional shapes even if the function $\pi(\cdot)$ is the same. Thus, different values for $\boldsymbol{\theta}_j$ reflect different states of expert knowledge about the default probability p_i.

The hyperparameters may also be assigned priors, $\boldsymbol{\theta}_j \sim \pi_0(\boldsymbol{\theta}_j)$, in which case we obtain a hierarchical Bayesian model. The INLA methodology has been developed for such hierarchical models (see also Chapter 1 of Volume I). However, we assume here that the hyperparameters $\boldsymbol{\theta} = (\theta_0, \ldots, \theta_M)$ are non-stochastic, fixed values set by the risk manager or regulators. In future work, stochastic hyperparameters will be taken into account.

Bayesian inference is based on the posterior distribution. The posterior is the distribution of the regression coefficient β_j given the observed defaults y, that is

$$\pi(\beta_j \mid y) = \frac{\pi(\beta_j, y)}{\pi(y)} \propto f(y \mid \beta_j)\pi(\beta_j) \qquad (11.3)$$

which follows from Bayes's Theorem. As the default probabilities are given by Equation 11.2, their distributions are easily obtained from the posterior values of the regression coefficients. The posterior distribution can be found by INLA (which is described in more detail later in this chapter) or MCMC methods.

Choice of prior

In standard normal linear regression analysis it is often assumed that the coefficient vector is multivariate normally distributed with some specific mean and a (generally) non-diagonal covariance matrix. Such a prior can also be used for the logit model.[3] However, as described in Chapter 7 of Volume I, the elicitation of the prior correlation structure is a difficult task and thus it is frequently assumed that the coefficients are mutually independent. Having said that, we consider univariate, normally distributed priors $\mathcal{N}(\mu_j, \sigma_j^2)$.

In principle, any proper probability density function may be used as a prior for the regression coefficients. However, using other distributions, such as skewed or fat-tailed distributions, requires specific knowledge or opinions about the distribution of the regression coefficients. In our opinion, this kind of information will rarely be available. Also, the INLA method only allows Gaussian priors.

Prior of the default probabilities

The task of eliciting prior information about the regression coefficients can be extremely difficult, in particular because the interpretation of the coefficients depends on the choice of link function. Expert elicitation of a linear regression model is discussed in Chapter 7 of Volume I.

A cardinal rule of expert judgement is to only ask questions about variables that the expert is familiar with. Hence, rather than defining a prior distribution on the regression coefficients, we suggest the construction of prior distributions on the default probabilities. Then we can translate prior information about the default probabilities into prior information about the regression coefficients. We assume that the expected values and standard deviations of the default probabilities have been elicited by expert judgement, and that the default probability p is assumed to be Beta distributed. We then have that the relationship between the parameters a and b of the Beta distribution and its expected value and variance is given by

$$E[p] = \frac{a}{a+b} \quad \text{and} \quad \text{var}[p] = \frac{ab}{(a+b)^2(a+b+1)}$$

where $a > 0$ and $b > 0$. For each company $i, i = 1, \ldots, N$, we can sample a default probability p_i from the Beta distribution and thereafter an observation $Y_i \sim \text{Binom}(p_i)$. Further, we can do a GLM regression with the drawn Y_i variables and the observed account variables x_{ij} for all $i = 1, \ldots, N$, which gives a set of regression parameters $\beta_0, \ldots, \beta_M$. This procedure is repeated many times to obtain random samples of $\beta_0, \ldots, \beta_M$ which are related to $p_i, i = 1, \ldots, N$.

The *a priori* regression coefficients obtained will now be correlated. Hence, this approach would work to specify a covariance structure of the prior distribution of the regression coefficients. However, as already pointed out, it is common practice to assume that the regression coefficients are uncorrelated *a priori*, which we also assume in the rest of this chapter. The prior distributions for each β_j can be approximated with a Gaussian distribution where the mean and standard deviation are estimated from the generated samples of the β_j.

To illustrate the algorithm, we have used the empirical means and standard deviations of the customers' PDs, which are achieved from the posterior regression coefficients using the informative prior given by Sparebank 1 (see Table 11.2) and used these as prior information about all customers' PDs. Figure 11.2 shows the histogram of the corresponding prior distribution of the regression coefficient of CPINV, after converting prior distributions for all customers' PDs using the above described algorithm with 1,000 simulations. By studying the histogram we see that the Gaussian distribution fits well enough.

One apparent drawback with this method is that there are many default probabilities if the credit portfolio is large, which makes manual expert judgements difficult. However, we may have access to

Table 11.2 Prior means and standard deviations of the regression coefficients of the explanatory variables, assuming univariate Gaussian distributions

Variable	Prior mean	Standard deviation
(Intercept)	0	$\sqrt{1000}$
Profit	−0.096	0.042
Loss	−0.127	0.104
Cpinv	−0.045	0.022
Dp	−0.069	0.024
Eqper	−0.102	0.023
Mpay	−0.103	0.023
Dliq	−0.032	0.019
Odfac	−0.078	0.048
Rephist	−0.268	0.021
Repkf	−0.102	0.017
Repac	−0.105	0.017
Ad	−0.068	0.015
Age	−0.062	0.017

Figure 11.2 Prior density of the regression coefficient for Cpinv

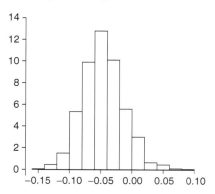

This is achieved by converting prior information about all customers' PDs to prior distributions for the regression coefficients.

previous analyses such as in the example above, or just a basic GLM regression on historic data, which can be utilised in a future specification of the prior on the PDs (the so-called empirical Bayes approach). In any case, an automated routine for generating prior means and standard deviations on the PDs is highly necessary.

Our approach is a special case of the general conditional means priors framework for GLMs proposed by Bedrik *et al* (1996). However, rather than using simulation to convert a prior on the default probabilities, they derive the induced prior analytically.

Latent Gaussian models

In the class of structured additive regression models, the response variables are, as in GLM, assumed to belong to an exponential family. The linear predictor takes the more general form

$$\eta_i = \beta_0 + \sum_{k=1}^{K} f^{(k)}(u_{ik}) + \sum_{j=1}^{M} \beta_j x_{ij} \qquad (11.4)$$

The $\{f^{(k)}(\cdot)\}$ are unknown finite-dimensional functions of a set of covariates u. As in the GLM equation (Equation 11.1) the $\{\beta_j\}$ represent the linear effect of the covariates x. The latent Gaussian model is a subset of Bayesian additive models with the linear predictor of the form in Equation 11.4 which have Gaussian priors for the regression functions and parameters, $\{f^{(k)}(\cdot)\}$ and $\{\beta_j\}$, respectively. Hence, the Bayesian logistic regression model is a special case of the latent Gaussian model (Equation 11.4) with only linear terms in the linear predictor, that is, without the terms $\{f^{(k)}(\cdot)\}$. INLA deals with models of the type given in Equation 11.4.

METHODS

Integrated nested Laplace approximation

Throughout this chapter we present the first step in a Bayesian logistic regression model, where we assume that the hyperparameters, ie, the means and the variances of the normal priors for β_j, are fixed. In a future extension of our work, the hyperparameters will be stochastic. INLA was developed to handle such hierarchical models. We will now briefly outline the INLA method, starting with the general case of a hierarchical model, before we show the special case with fixed hyperparameters. Readers who wish to go into the details of the approximations and numerical issues of INLA are referred to Rue *et al* (2009).

The key feature of INLA is to make some clever closed-form approximations of the posterior distribution so that we can bypass MCMC. In the general case of a hierarchical model, INLA utilises the nested expression of the posterior marginal distributions of β_j

$$\pi(\beta_j \mid y) = \int \pi(\beta_j, \boldsymbol{\theta} \mid y) \, d\boldsymbol{\theta} = \int \pi(\beta_j \mid \boldsymbol{\theta}, y) \pi(\boldsymbol{\theta} \mid y) \, d\boldsymbol{\theta}$$

which is equal to Equation 11.3, and approximates it with numerical integration

$$\tilde{\pi}(\beta_j \mid y) = \sum_r \tilde{\pi}(\beta_j \mid \boldsymbol{\theta}_r, y) \tilde{\pi}(\boldsymbol{\theta}_r \mid y) \Delta_r \qquad (11.5)$$

The approximation of the posterior is possible as the dimension of $\boldsymbol{\theta}$ is small, and it is computed in three steps. The first step finds the approximation $\tilde{\pi}(\boldsymbol{\theta} \mid y)$, which is described in detail by Rue et al (2009). The second step is to compute the approximation $\tilde{\pi}(\beta_j \mid \boldsymbol{\theta}, y)$ (which we come back to in Equation 11.6). The last step combines the previous two steps using the numerical integration with respect to $\boldsymbol{\theta}$.

However, we have fixed hyperparameters $\boldsymbol{\theta}$ here. Then, we only need to approximate the posterior

$$\pi(\beta_j \mid \boldsymbol{\theta}, y) = \frac{\pi(\boldsymbol{\beta}, \boldsymbol{\theta}, y)}{\pi(\boldsymbol{\beta}_{-j} \mid \beta_j, \boldsymbol{\theta}, y) \pi(\boldsymbol{\theta}, y)}$$

Rue et al (2009) discuss different approximations of this posterior, including the Laplace approximation

$$\tilde{\pi}(\beta_j \mid \boldsymbol{\theta}, y) \propto \left. \frac{\pi(\beta_j, \boldsymbol{\beta}_{-j}, \boldsymbol{\theta}, y)}{\tilde{\pi}_{GG}(\boldsymbol{\beta}_{-j} \mid \beta_j, \boldsymbol{\theta}, y)} \right|_{\boldsymbol{\beta}_{-j} = \boldsymbol{\beta}^*_{-j}(\beta_j, \boldsymbol{\theta})} \qquad (11.6)$$

Here, $\tilde{\pi}_{GG}$ is the Gaussian approximation (given by a mean and variance) to $\pi(\boldsymbol{\beta}_{-j} \mid \beta_j, \boldsymbol{\theta}, y)$, and $\boldsymbol{\beta}^*_{-j}(\beta_j, \boldsymbol{\theta})$ is the modal configuration. Finding the approximation $\tilde{\pi}_{GG}$ requires numerical optimisation, and some modifications and implementation details described in Rue et al (2009) make it computationally feasible. There are even other, less accurate, approximations of the posterior, which are faster to compute when the dimension increases.

INLA approximation error

Rue et al (2009) provide several examples of applications of the INLA approach and comparisons with results obtained from intensive MCMC runs. The examples include simulated data, a generalised linear mixed model for longitudinal data, a stochastic volatility model and two spatial models.

The approximation error of INLA is inherited from the error of the two approximations involved and the error of the numerical integration. The only way to assess the error with absolute certainty is to run an MCMC for infinite time. Rue *et al* (2009) propose two strategies to assess the approximation error. For each of the approximations, they follow Spiegelhalter *et al* (2002) and compare the effective number of parameters with the size of the data set. In addition, they compare the difference between the approximations and their Taylor expansions to the size of the data set. The second strategy is to compute increasingly accurate approximations, that is, use the other, less accurate posterior approximations and the Laplace approximation described in Equation 11.6, and compare the corresponding symmetric Kullback–Leibler divergences (Kullback 1987; Kullback and Leibler 1951). A small divergence is taken as a sign of acceptable approximation error, otherwise the approximation is labelled "problematic". Rue *et al* (2009) state that they have yet not come across examples of the latter.

The examples of Rue *et al* (2009) confirm that INLA provides fast and accurate inference compared with MCMC. In our case, we compare the INLA results with MCMC runs. We focus on an MCMC run with an appropriate number of simulations, but we have also run MCMC for a very long time.

The approximation error of INLA is the same no matter where in the posterior distribution we are focusing on, whereas the error of MCMC increases into the tails. Hence, if we, for instance, were interested in the extremes in the posterior distribution of a customer's PD, INLA would have been favoured, as it requires many iterations for MCMC to be accurate.

Markov chain Monte Carlo

It is not the purpose of this chapter to provide a deep understanding of MCMC.[4] Applied to the Bayesian logistic model described earlier, the idea of MCMC is to run an ergodic Markov chain which has Equation 11.3 as stationary distribution. Starting from a set of given initial values, in our case the parameter estimates obtained from standard (non-Bayesian) GLM, the chain is run until it is believed to have reached equilibrium. Thereafter, the chain produces a sequence of samples from the posterior distribution.

RESULTS

Here we will present the first posterior results in a Bayesian logistic regression, where we assume that the hyperparameters, ie, the means and the variances of the normal priors for β_j, are fixed. We have used the data described earlier (see Table 11.1 and Figure 11.1).

We start to present the posterior regression coefficients obtained with a non-informative or vague prior, before we present the posterior regression coefficients obtained with an informative prior given by Sparebank 1.

By using a Bayesian method such as the one described in this chapter, risk managers can incorporate expert knowledge in their analyses of customers, and it is an intuitive way of taking into account the uncertainties in the estimates, for both the regression coefficients and the customers' PDs. Even though our main focus is on the posterior distributions of the regression coefficients, it is an easy task to find the corresponding posterior distributions of the customers' PDs. Hence, it is possible to determine not only a point estimate, but also a credibility interval for each customer's PD. A fictional customer example will be presented.

All our computations were performed in the "R" environment for statistical computations and graphics.[5] The INLA software developed by Rue and Martino is now released as a package of R.[6] We ran MCMC using MCMCPACK[7] and the function MCMCLOGIT, and evaluated the MCMC results using the CODA package (Cowles and Carlin 1996; Plummer et al 2006). The sampling engine of MCMCPACK is a random walk Metropolis–Hastings algorithm (Metropolis et al 1953). The MCMC results are obtained using the 10,000 iterations after a burn-in period of 1,000 iterations. The MCMC run with an infinite number of simulations represents the "true" posterior. We ran MCMC with 10^6 iterations. The posterior obtained from this run did not differ significantly from the result obtained using 10,000 iterations.

The results obtained are shown in Figures 11.3–11.6.

Results with a vague prior

In order to study the impact of having prior information on the default probabilities, we first present the results obtained when no prior is incorporated (or in the Bayesian framework; when the prior

Table 11.3 The means, standard deviations and 95% credibility intervals obtained using INLA and MCMC

Variable	Mean		SD		95% CI	
	INLA	MCMC	INLA	MCMC	INLA	MCMC
(Intercept)	3.9263	3.9594	0.6606	0.6142	[2.6238, 5.2318]	[2.6644, 5.0837]
Profit	−0.0539	−0.0490	0.0907	0.0959	[−0.2302, 0.1284]	[−0.2315, 0.1295]
Loss	−0.1696	−0.1733	0.0974	0.0924	[−0.3628, 0.0218]	[−0.3534, 0.0149]
Cpinv	−0.0798	−0.0804	0.0307	0.0314	[−0.1396, −0.0181]	[−0.1362, −0.0174]
Dp	−0.1167	−0.1124	0.0499	0.0487	[−0.2145, −0.0174]	[−0.2065, −0.0101]
Eqper	−0.0504	−0.0500	0.0476	0.0471	[−0.1432, 0.0448]	[−0.1355, 0.0433]
Mpay	0.0626	0.0624	0.0474	0.0464	[−0.0319, 0.1552]	[−0.0276, 0.1528]
Dliq	−0.0771	−0.0798	0.0457	0.0459	[−0.1694, 0.0111]	[−0.1715, 0.0254]
Odfac	−0.2195	−0.2241	0.0441	0.0460	[−0.3086, −0.1342]	[−0.3270, −0.1301]
Rephist	−0.2277	−0.2251	0.0298	0.0299	[−0.2863, −0.1686]	[−0.2851, −0.1677]
Repkf	−0.1252	−0.1284	0.0268	0.0264	[−0.1770, −0.0709]	[−0.1789, −0.0671]
Repac	−0.0028	−0.0002	0.0264	0.0256	[−0.0545, 0.0498]	[−0.0507, 0.0513]
Ad	−0.0615	−0.0579	0.0247	0.0255	[−0.1095, −0.0118]	[−0.1117, −0.0088]
Age	−0.0882	−0.0945	0.0357	0.0387	[−0.1603, −0.0190]	[−0.1709, −0.0207]

The table shows the means, standard deviations (SD) and 95% credibility intervals (CI) (given by the 2.5% and 97.5% quantiles) for the posterior of the regression coefficients, obtained using INLA and MCMC. Results assume a vague prior with mean 0 and variance 1,000, $\beta_j \sim \mathcal{N}(0, 1,000)$ for $j = 0, \ldots, M$.

is vague or non-informative). Table 11.3 shows the regression coefficients obtained with INLA and MCMC, using a univariate Gaussian prior distribution for the regression coefficients with mean 0 and variance 1,000. We observe that the coefficients obtained with the two methods are practically the same.

Results with an informative prior

Now we use prior information given by Sparebank 1, based on customer information in the period 1994–2000. The prior knowledge was elicited using a logistic regression on this data, together with expert judgements. Alternatively, the more sophisticated method described earlier, converting priors on the default probabilities into priors on the regression coefficients, could have been used instead. The prior information given by Sparebank 1 consists of prior means and standard deviations of the regression coefficients, which are shown in Table 11.2 for all explanatory variables. INLA does not let the user specify any prior on the intercept β_0, so in order to compare the MCMC results with INLA we use the same prior for the intercept in the MCMC algorithm as the default prior for the intercept in INLA, namely the Gaussian distribution with mean 0 and standard deviation $\sqrt{1,000}$. It is often difficult for risk managers to interpret and give expert opinions on the intercept, so applying a vague prior on the intercept makes sense.

Table 11.4 gives the posterior means, standard deviations and 95% credibility intervals for the regression coefficients obtained with INLA and MCMC, using univariate Gaussian prior distributions for the regression coefficients with means and standard deviations as given in Table 11.2. We see that MCMC and INLA give very similar results. Compared with the vague prior results in Table 11.3, we also see that the informative prior given in Table 11.2 influences both the INLA and the MCMC results significantly.

Figure 11.3 shows the prior and the posterior distributions of the regression coefficients obtained using MCMC. It is easy to compare the different posterior distributions with each other. For instance, we see that the posterior means of the regression coefficients for the explanatory variables LOSS and EQPER are very similar, whereas the standard deviation, and hence the width of the posterior distribution, of the former is much larger than of the latter. Be aware of the different scales on the axes.

Table 11.4 The means, standard deviations (SD) and 95% credibility intervals obtained using INLA and MCMC

Variable	Mean		SD		95% CI	
	INLA	MCMC	INLA	MCMC	INLA	MCMC
(Intercept)	3.6248	3.5773	0.4996	0.4951	[2.6366, 4.6089]	[2.5888, 4.4994]
Profit	−0.0847	−0.0775	0.0371	0.0369	[−0.1581, −0.0114]	[−0.1555, −0.0077]
Loss	−0.0945	−0.0930	0.0617	0.0625	[−0.2166, 0.0271]	[−0.2087, 0.0344]
Cpinv	−0.0593	−0.0590	0.0179	0.0178	[−0.0945, −0.0240]	[−0.0945, −0.0284]
Dp	−0.0799	−0.0817	0.0211	0.0203	[−0.1216, −0.0384]	[−0.1245, −0.0459]
Eqper	−0.0903	−0.0903	0.0199	0.0188	[−0.1297, −0.0510]	[−0.1241, −0.0515]
Mpay	−0.0730	−0.0721	0.0207	0.0220	[−0.1139, −0.0322]	[−0.1152, −0.0258]
Dliq	−0.0307	−0.0322	0.0171	0.0175	[−0.0646, 0.0029]	[−0.0664, −0.0008]
Odfac	−0.1369	−0.1362	0.0308	0.0339	[−0.1983, −0.0768]	[−0.1992, −0.0696]
Rephist	−0.2445	−0.2442	0.0167	0.0174	[−0.2775, −0.2115]	[−0.2789, −0.2121]
Repkf	−0.1039	−0.1047	0.0143	0.0140	[−0.1320, −0.0757]	[−0.1292, −0.0772]
Repac	−0.0686	−0.0673	0.0137	0.0151	[−0.0957, −0.0415]	[−0.0943, −0.0356]
Ad	−0.0598	−0.0600	0.0125	0.0126	[−0.0844, −0.0352]	[−0.0860, −0.0341]
Age	−0.0705	−0.0683	0.0152	0.0150	[−0.1005, −0.0405]	[−0.0964, −0.0421]

The table shows the means, standard deviations (SD) and 95% credibility intervals (CI) (given by the 2.5% and 97.5% quantiles) for the posterior of the regression coefficients, obtained using INLA and MCMC. Results assume an informative prior $\beta_j \sim \mathcal{N}(\mu, \sigma^2)$ for $j = 0, \ldots, M$, where μ and σ are given in Table 11.2.

Figure 11.3 Prior and posterior distributions of the regression coefficients for all explanatory variables using MCMC

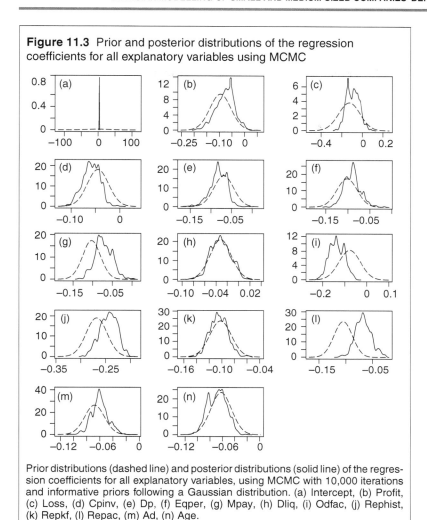

Prior distributions (dashed line) and posterior distributions (solid line) of the regression coefficients for all explanatory variables, using MCMC with 10,000 iterations and informative priors following a Gaussian distribution. (a) Intercept, (b) Profit, (c) Loss, (d) Cpinv, (e) Dp, (f) Eqper, (g) Mpay, (h) Dliq, (i) Odfac, (j) Rephist, (k) Repkf, (l) Repac, (m) Ad, (n) Age.

In general, the posterior distributions will be affected by the logistic regression model, the data and the prior distribution, as well as the dependence between the regression coefficients. If the regression coefficients are subjected to a vague prior like the one described earlier, the data will dominate the posterior distribution. If two other prior distributions are considered, both with the same means but with different variances, the posterior distribution will generally be more narrow when the prior with the smallest variance is considered.

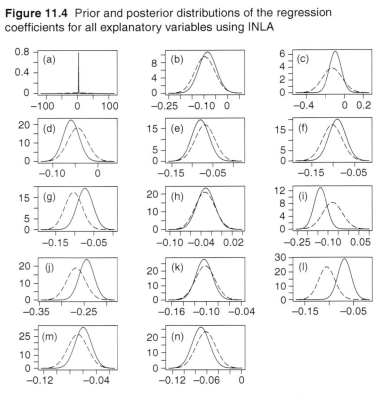

Figure 11.4 Prior and posterior distributions of the regression coefficients for all explanatory variables using INLA

Prior distributions (dashed line) and posterior distributions (solid line) of the regression coefficients for all explanatory variables, using INLA with informative priors following a Gaussian distribution. (a) Intercept, (b) Profit, (c) Loss, (d) Cpinv, (e) Dp, (f) Eqper, (g) Mpay, (h) Dliq, (i) Odfac, (j) Rephist, (k) Repkf, (l) Repac, (m) Ad, (n) Age.

Figure 11.4 shows the prior and the posterior distributions of the regression coefficients obtained using INLA. The posterior density distributions are drawn from the Gaussian distribution with the achieved approximations of the posterior means and standard deviations.

In order to better compare the MCMC and INLA results, the posterior distributions of the regression coefficients obtained using informative Gaussian distributed priors are plotted together in Figure 11.5. Figure 11.6 also compares the posterior distributions obtained with INLA and MCMC, but also includes the posterior distributions obtained using a vague prior. We see that the posterior

Figure 11.5 Posterior distributions of the regression coefficients for all explanatory variables, obtained with informative priors following a Gaussian distribution, using INLA and MCMC

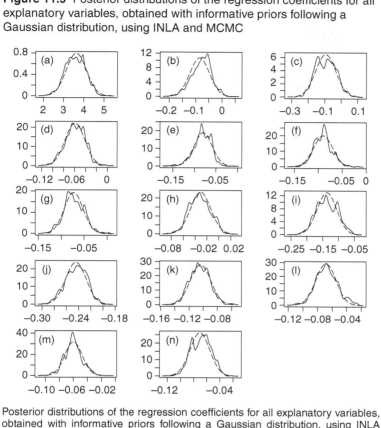

Posterior distributions of the regression coefficients for all explanatory variables, obtained with informative priors following a Gaussian distribution, using INLA (dashed line) and MCMC with 10,000 iterations (solid line). (a) Intercept, (b) Profit, (c) Loss, (d) Cpinv, (e) Dp, (f) Eqper, (g) Mpay, (h) Dliq, (i) Odfac, (j) Rephist, (k) Repkf, (l) Repac, (m) Ad, (n) Age.

distributions of MCMC and INLA are similar. Since the posterior distributions of MCMC are presented as density plots of all 10,000 realisations from the posteriors, they are rugged. The more iterations we have, the smoother the density plots will be. The results obtained with informative and vague priors differ considerably for most of the variables. When the prior and the empirical data have diverging information, the posterior is mixture of the two, as given by the Bayesian approach.

With the size of our data set, running the MCMC simulation with 10,000 iterations is done in a short amount of time. There are many

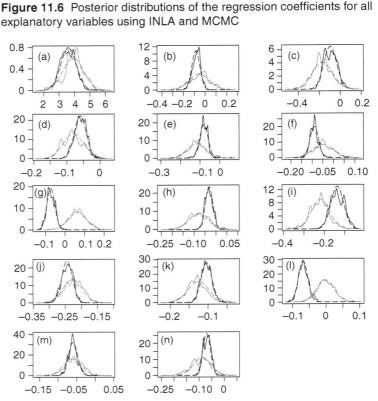

Figure 11.6 Posterior distributions of the regression coefficients for all explanatory variables using INLA and MCMC

The dashed lines show the results obtained with INLA, using informative and vague priors (black and grey dashed lines, respectively). The solid lines show the results obtained using MCMC with 10,000 iterations, using informative and vague priors (black and grey solid lines, respectively). (a) Intercept, (b) Profit, (c) Loss, (d) Cpinv, (e) Dp, (f) Eqper, (g) Mpay, (h) Dliq, (i) Odfac, (j) Rephist, (k) Repkf, (l) Repac, (m) Ad, (n) Age.

methods to check for convergence of an MCMC chain. We have focused on the methods of Geweke (1992) and Raftery and Lewis (1992). According to the convergence methods some of the coefficients have not converged after 10,000 iterations, even though it looks like they have converged from the trace plots of the MCMC run. This illustrates how difficult it is to determine when an MCMC run has converged. Overall, MCMC and INLA give approximately the same results during approximately the same amount of time.

If the prior information, unlike the case in our study, differs dramatically from what the data alone implies, MCMC will converge

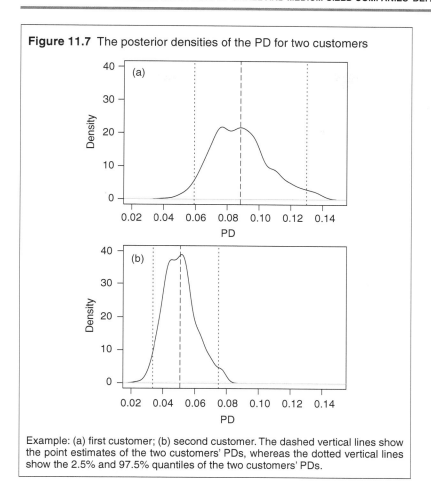

Figure 11.7 The posterior densities of the PD for two customers

Example: (a) first customer; (b) second customer. The dashed vertical lines show the point estimates of the two customers' PDs, whereas the dotted vertical lines show the 2.5% and 97.5% quantiles of the two customers' PDs.

very slowly. In such cases, INLA is favoured, as it will be computationally faster. Also, a great advantage of INLA is that the user does not have to worry much about the issue of convergence.

A customer example

We have so far only focused on the posterior distributions of the regression coefficients. As the default probabilities are given by Equation 11.2, their posterior distributions are easily obtained from the posterior values of the regression coefficients. We now consider two customers with fictional explanatory variables. For simplicity, we assume that the 13 explanatory variables for the first customer are all equal to 5, whereas for the second customer they are all equal to 5.5. As mentioned earlier, high values of the explanatory variables are associated with behaviour that reduces the probability of default, so we expect that the second customer will get a smaller PD than the first customer. Parts (a) and (b) of Figure 11.7 show the posterior distributions of the PD obtained for the first and second customers, respectively. The dashed vertical lines show the point estimates of the two customers' PDs (given as the sample mean of all 10,000 posterior realisations), whereas the dotted vertical lines show the 2.5% and 97.5% quantiles of the two customers' PDs. Hence, for each customer's PD, we have found not only a point estimate, but also a credibility interval. This analysis makes it clear that such a thing as the "true" PD cannot be estimated. Instead, we should use credible intervals for the PDs as depicted in Figure 11.7. Finally, we remark that the uncertainty involved in PD estimates translates into an uncertainty of risk figures like credit VaR. Risk management should take this into account.

CONCLUSIONS

We have introduced INLA as an alternative to MCMC for Bayesian credit risk modelling, and showed that both INLA and MCMC can be used to analyse the uncertainties involved with the estimation of the regression coefficients and thus of the customers' default probabilities. We have compared the two methods in a Bayesian logistic regression setting, for now assuming fixed hyperparameters. This work is a first step towards a more complete, hierarchical model. We have modelled the credit default risk of a data set of real default data provided by Sparebank 1.

The Bayesian approach makes is possible to incorporate prior knowledge on the regression coefficients. In our case, specific prior information on the regression coefficients was supplied by Sparebank 1, which is based on previous regression analyses on historic customers data, together with expert knowledge.

We find that INLA and MCMC give approximately the same posterior results in approximately the same amount of time. The hyperparameters are fixed, and hence the MCMC algorithm converges quickly. Therefore, it is not obvious that INLA is the best choice. However, the main advantage with INLA for this purpose is that the user does not have to worry about convergence issues. INLA is simulation-error free, although not free from approximation error.

In the future extension of our work, the consideration of stochastic hyperparameters will be more computationally demanding for MCMC, and the advantages of INLA may become more clear.

Having said that, INLA is only designed for a subclass of structured additive regression models, named latent Gaussian models, whereas MCMC is more general and can be used to make Bayesian inferences on many classes of models.

This work was supported by the Research Council of Norway, through Grant number 186951 (I30, Modern Application-driven Statistical Challenges). The authors thank Sara Martino and Håvard Rue for providing the INLA software and guidance on using it. We thank Sparebank 1, KFK (Centre of Excellence Credit Risk Modelling) for kindly providing credit default data.

1 See, for instance, Atiya (2001) and Berg (2007).
2 Accounting variables from 2006; default occurrences during 2007.
3 See, for example, Chapter 2 of Volume I.
4 For a review of MCMC methods, see Chapter 2 of Volume I or Gilks *et al* (1996).
5 See http://www.r-project.org.
6 See http://www.r-inla.org.
7 See http://mcmcpack.wustl.edu.

REFERENCES

Altman, E. I., 1968, "Financial Rations, Discriminant Analysis and the Prediction of Corporate Bankruptcy", *Journal of Finance* 23(4), pp. 589–609.

Ando, T., 2006, "Bayesian Credit Rating Analysis Based on Ordered Probit Model with Functional Predictor", In M. Holder (ed), *Proceedings of the Third IASTED International Conference on Financial Engineering and Applications, October 9–11, 2006, Cambridge, USA*, pp. 69–76 (Calgary: ACTA Press).

Atiya, A. F., 2001, "Bankruptcy Prediction for Neural Networks: A survey and New Results", *IEEE Transactions on Neural Networks* 12(4), pp. 929–35.

Bank for International Settlements, 2006, "Basel II: International Convergence of Capital Measurements and Capital Standards: A Revised Framework – Comprehensive Version", Technical Report, Bank for International Settlements.

Beaver, W. H., 1966, "Financial Rations as Predictors of Failure", *Journal of Accounting Research* 4, pp. 71–111.

Bedrik, E. J., R. Christensen and W. Johnson, 1996, "A New Perspective on Priors for Generalized Linear Models", *Journal of the American Statistical Association* 91(436), pp. 1450–60.

Berg, D., 2007, "Bankrupcty Prediction by Generalized Additive Models", *Applied Stochastic Models in Business and Industry* 23(2) pp. 129–43.

Cowles, M. K., and B. P. Carlin, 1996, "Markov Chain Monte Carlo Diagnostics: A Comparative Review", *Journal of the American Statistical Association* 91, pp. 883–904.

Crosbie, P. J., and J. R. Bohn, 2002, "Modeling Default Risk", Working Paper, KMV.

Geweke, J., 1992, "Evaluating the Accuracy of Sampling-Based Approaches to Calculating Posterior Moments", in J. M. Bernardo, J. O. Berger, A. P. Dawid and A. F. M. Smith (eds), *Bayesian Statistics 4: Proceedings of the Fourth Valencia International Meeting* (Oxford University Press).

Gilks, W. R., S. Richardson and D. J. Spiegelhalter, 1996, *Markov Chain Monte Carlo in Practice* (London: Chapman & Hall).

Kullback, S., 1987, "The Kullback–Leibler Distance", *American Statistician* 41, pp. 340–1.

Kullback, S., and R. A. Leibler, 1951, "On Information and Sufficiency", *Annals of Mathematical Statistics* 22, pp. 79–86.

Löffler, G., P. N. Prosch and C. Schöne, 2005, "Bayesian Methods for Improving Credit Scoring Models", Technical Report, Department of Finance, University of Ulm, Germany.

Martin, A. D., K. M. Quinn and J. H. Park, 2008, "Package MCMCPACK", Technical Report, Washington University in St Louis.

McNeil, A. J., and J. P. Wedin, 2007, "Bayesian Inference for Generalized Linear Mixed Models of Portfolio Credit Risk", *Journal of Empricial Finance* 14(2), pp. 131–49.

McCullagh, P., and J. A. Nelder, 1989, *Generalized Linear Models*, Second Edition (London: Chapman & Hall).

Metropolis, N., A. W. Rosenbluth, M. N. Rosenbluth, A. H. Teller and E. Teller, 1953, "Equations of State Calculations by Fast Computing Machines", *Journal of Chemical Physics* 21, pp. 1087–91.

Mira, A., and P. Tenconi, 2004, "Bayesian Estimate of Credit Risk via MCMC with Delayed Rejection", in R. C. Dalang, M. Dozzi and F. Russo (eds), *Seminar on Stochastic Analysis, Random Fields and Applications IV, Centro Stefano Franscini, Ascona, May 2002*, pp. 277–91 (Basel: Birkhäuser).

Plummer, M., N. Best, K. Cowles and K. Vines, 2006, "CODA: Convergence Diagnosis and Output Analysis for MCMC", *R News* 6(1), pp. 7–11.

Raftery, A., and S. Lewis, 1992, "One Long Run with Diagnostics: Implementation Strategies for Markov Chain Monte Carlo", *Statistical Science* 7, pp. 493–7.

Rue, H., S. Martino and N. Chopin, 2009, "Approximate Bayesian Inference for Latent Gaussian Models Using Integrated Nested Laplace Approximations", *Journal of the Royal Statistical Society: Series B* 71(2), pp. 1–35.

Spiegelhalter, D., A. Thomas, N. Best and D. Lunn, 2007, "OPENBUGS User Manual", MRC Biostatistics Unit, URL: http://mathstat.helsinki.fi/openbugs/Manuals/Manual.html.

Spiegelhalter, D. J., N. G. Best, B. P. Carlin, and A. van der Linde, 2002, "Bayesian Measures of Model Compexity and Fit", *Journal of the Royal Statistical Society: Series B* 64(2), pp. 583–639.

Part III

Operational Risk

12
Measuring Operational Risk in a Bayesian Framework

Luciana Dalla Valle
University of Milan

The last few years of the first decade of the 21st Century have seen a rapid and widespread development of statistical models aiming at managing operational risk. This is due mainly to the intervention of financial regulators, the Basel Committee on Banking Supervision (BCBS), which on behalf of the Bank of International Settlements (BIS), issued the Basel II Accord on Capital Adequacy (Basel Committee on Banking Supervision 2001, 2003). The ultimate purpose of this framework is to formulate broad supervisory standards, guidelines and statements of best practice to ensure the stability and soundness of financial systems.

Operational risk (OR), as defined by the Basel Committee, "is the risk of loss resulting from inadequate or failed internal processes, people and systems or from external events" (Risk Management Group 2003). In order to prescribe capital adequacy standards for OR for all internationally active banks, an evaluation of risk measures is needed. This is gauged through different statistical models that can be grouped according to their level of sophistication. The main categories are "top-down" and "bottom-up" methods. In the former, risk estimation is based on macro data, using measures such as the gross income as broad indicators of operational risk (Pezier 2002). "Bottom-up" techniques, on the other hand, use more sophisticated statistical methods that measure risks at local level and then calculate aggregate risk measures. Methods in this second class are grouped into advanced measurement approaches (AMAs).[1]

This work focuses on a model belonging to the AMA, called the loss-distribution approach. This method shows great improvements over simpler approaches, in that it takes into account the characteristics of the bank and calculates the capital charge on the basis of the standardised classification of operational losses into eight business lines (BLs) and seven event types (ETs), as stated by regulators. Hence, depending on the bank's operations, up to 56 separate operational risk capital requirement estimates are aggregated in order to obtain a total regulatory capital charge for the whole bank. However, the LDA does have some limitations. On the one hand, the lack of OR data, basically due to the relatively recent definition and management of operational risk, often makes it hard to measure the capital requirement. On the other hand, it is difficult to correctly consider the dependence structure among the intersections of BLs/ETs in the aggregating process. However, with the use of Bayesian methods we are able to integrate the scarce and (sometimes) inaccurate quantitative data collected by the bank with prior information brought in by experts and we are allowed to introduce parameter uncertainty into the model construction. Moreover, simulation methods and, in particular, Markov chain Monte Carlo (MCMC) methods are able to take advantage of the information available in the data and to handle complex Bayesian models, employed for OR modelling. In addition, copula functions allow us to compute the distribution of the total loss from the distributions of individual losses, by considering their dependency composition. Therefore, following the approach of Bayesian copulas, which combines the use of Bayesian models and copula functions, operational risks can be evaluated in a more adequate way (Dalla Valle 2009; Pitt *et al* 2006). Finally, the uncertainty of model parameters can be accounted for, which implies also the possibility of reporting credible intervals for risk capital charges based on value-at-risk (VaR) or expected shortfall (ES).

THE MODEL

The LDA is characterised by the categorisation of the losses in terms of "frequency" (the number of loss events during a certain time period) and "severity" (the impact of the event in terms of financial loss). Such categorisation is applied to each of the seven ETs in each of the eight BLs. Considering a matrix with BLs on the rows and ETs on the columns, the total number of cells is thus 56. Formally, for each intersection $i, i = 1, \ldots, I$, and for a given time period T, the total operational loss could be defined as a sum of a random number N_t of losses

$$L_{it} = X_{i1} + X_{i2} + \cdots + X_{iN_t}$$

where L_{it} denotes the total operational loss for the time period t, $X_1,\ldots,X_{N_t}$ denote the individual loss severities and N_t denotes the frequency, for $t = 1,\ldots,T$, with T representing the number of time periods. For instance, given monthly time buckets, $t = 1,2,\ldots,T$ represents the first, second,...,Tth month observed. Assuming that individual losses $X_1,\ldots,X_{N_t}$ are mutually independent and identically distributed random variables, each independent of N_t, then L_{it}, for $t = 1,\ldots,T$, are independent and identically distributed random variables (Dalla Valle 2009).

Indicating the severity distribution with $f(x_j \mid \boldsymbol{\eta})$ and the frequency distribution with $f(n_t \mid \boldsymbol{\theta})$, where $\boldsymbol{\eta}$ denotes the parameter vector of the severity distribution and $\boldsymbol{\theta}$ denotes the parameter vector of the frequency distribution, the likelihood function for each intersection is expressed in a general way

$$L(x,n \mid \boldsymbol{\theta},\boldsymbol{\eta}) = \prod_{t=1}^{T}\left[\prod_{j=1}^{N_t} f(x_j \mid \boldsymbol{\eta})\right] f(n_t \mid \boldsymbol{\theta}) \qquad (12.1)$$

In order to describe the functional form of the frequency $f(n_t \mid \boldsymbol{\theta})$ the most appropriate choices are the Poisson and the negative binomial and, for the distribution of the severity $f(x_j \mid \boldsymbol{\eta})$, the exponential, the Gamma and the Pareto are suitable choices as well. Then, the total number of frequency–severity combinations is six, corresponding to six different frequency–severity models yielding six different total loss distributions for operational risk (Dalla Valle and Giudici 2008).

Marginal parameter estimates

The first step is to estimate, on the basis of data, the parameters of the frequency and severity distributions, denoted by $\boldsymbol{\theta}$ and $\boldsymbol{\eta}$, respectively, in Equation 12.1. The classical approach suggests the employment of the method of moments or the method of maximum likelihood (ML), as described, for example, by Gourieroux and Monfort (1995). An alternative approach, which has only rarely been applied to OR (Shevchenko and Wüthrich 2006) is the Bayesian method, which allows the introduction of parameter uncertainty into the model.[2] Here the frequency and severity coefficients are estimated through both the ML method and the Bayesian method. All the estimates are computed for each of the six combinations of frequency and severity distributions.

The Bayesian parameter estimation for the Poisson–Gamma combination is presented in the following.[3] For each intersection the probability distribution functions of frequency and severity are, for $t = 1, \ldots, T$

$$N_t \sim \text{Poisson}(\lambda) \quad \text{and} \quad X_1, \ldots, X_{N_t} \sim \text{Gamma}(\alpha, \beta)$$

Substituting into Equation 12.1 the Poisson density for $f(n_t \mid \boldsymbol{\theta})$ and the Gamma density for $f(x_j \mid \boldsymbol{\eta})$, the likelihood function is therefore

$$L(x, n \mid \lambda, \alpha, \eta) = \prod_{t=1}^{T} \left[\prod_{j=1}^{n_t} \frac{\beta^\alpha}{\Gamma(\alpha)} x_j^{\alpha-1} \exp(-\beta x_j) \right] \frac{\exp(-\lambda)\lambda^{n_t}}{n_t!}$$

Independent conjugate priors are chosen for the parameters λ, α and β, in order to obtain a posterior belonging to the same class of distributions as the prior (Bernardo and Smith 1994). Therefore

$$\lambda \sim \text{Gamma}(a,b), \quad \beta \sim \text{Gamma}(c,d) \quad \text{and} \quad \alpha \sim \text{Gamma}(e,f)$$

where $a, b, \ldots, f$ are the hyperparameters to be estimated. In this framework, we assume that there is no relevant prior knowledge about the parameters available. Therefore, we use vague priors, first introduced by Ernest Lhoste in 1923 (Broemeling and Broemeling 2003), which both are proper and have a large variance. In doing so, hyperparameters for the prior distributions are computed by equating the expected values of the priors to the maximum likelihood estimates (MLEs) and by setting prior variances to be very large (for instance, equal to 1,000).[4] In the case that there is prior knowledge available, it must be elicited by expert judgement. Part 2 of Volume I gives detailed information about expert elicitation. A specific application to operational risk can be found in Liang (2009).

The conditional posteriors of the λ, α and β parameters are calculated according to Bayes's Theorem. Parameters λ and β have a posterior Gamma form, suggesting the implementation of the Gibbs Sampler Algorithm, while the Metropolis–Hastings (MH) algorithm is employed for α, which is non-standard form. Gibbs sampling is a special case of the MH algorithm, easier to implement and most efficient when the conditional posterior distribution of the considered parameter (named full conditional) is known to be a standard distribution. The Gibbs Sampler Algorithm generates observations from the posterior of the parameter, conditional on the current values of other parameters. The MH algorithm, on the other hand, must be employed when the explicit form of the full conditional is not known and an introduction of a proposal density is required.[5] The posterior mean of each parameter is the Bayesian estimate calculated as the mean value of the samples generated via the MCMC simulation. The posterior mean is the Bayesian estimate that will be used in the following application.

Risk measures

After estimating the parameters, the marginals are defined and the operational loss distribution has to be determined. Since its analytical form is often impossible to calculate, a convolution of the frequency and severity loss distributions via Monte Carlo simulation is required (Ripley 1987). Operational risk capital is then usually based on a risk measure like VaR or ES for that particular intersection i, $i = 1, \ldots, I$. VaR measures the worst loss over a specific time interval that is only exceeded with a small probability α (confidence level $1 - \alpha$). For example, the 99% VaR is defined as the 99th percentile of the loss distribution. Formally

$$\text{VaR}(L_{it}; \alpha): \Pr(L_{it} \geqslant \text{VaR}) \leqslant \alpha$$

This is the most famous and popular risk measure in practice. Alternatively, ES at the $1 - \alpha$ confidence level for a given time horizon represents the expected value of the losses that have exceeded the correspondent quantile given by the VaR

$$\text{ES}(L_{it}; \alpha) = E[L_{it} \mid L_{it} \geqslant \text{VaR}(L_{it}; \alpha)]$$

For example, the ES at the 1% confidence level is defined as the portfolio average loss, conditional on the fact that losses have exceeded the 99th percentile of the loss distribution, given by the 99% VaR. However, note that for very heavy tailed loss distributions, ES may not exist. Moreover, Brunner *et al* (2009) pointed out that Monte Carlo methods can have extremely bad convergence properties for heavy tailed distributions when applied to ES measures.

Once the risk measures for each intersection i are estimated, the global VaR is usually computed as the simple sum of these individual measures, thus assuming perfect dependence among the different losses.[6] An alternative is given by copulas that can be used to describe the dependence structure among these losses (Fantazzini *et al* 2008). A scheme that better describes the methodology followed here is displayed in Figure 12.1. As shown in the figure, risk measures

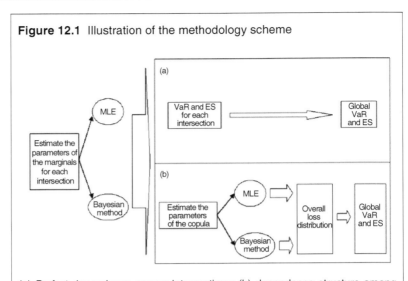

Figure 12.1 Illustration of the methodology scheme

(a) Perfect dependence among intersections; (b) dependence structure among intersections (copulas). In the first step of the analysis the parameters of the marginals are estimated. In the second step, risk measures are calculated, firstly assuming perfect dependence among intersections and secondly considering their dependence through the copula, following the IFM approach.

are calculated by firstly assuming perfect dependence among intersections and secondly considering their dependence through the copula. In the latter case the inference for margins (IFM) approach is employed, following a sequential two-step method in which the marginals are estimated in the first step and the dependence parameter is estimated in the second step using the copula after the estimated marginal distributions have been substituted into it (Trivedi and Zimmer 2007).

Copula functions

The copula is a statistical tool widely used, especially in the financial field, that allows to express the real correlation structure of a system of variables.

For continuous multivariate distributions, the univariate marginals and the multivariate or dependence structure can be separated, and the multivariate configuration can be represented by a copula (Joe 1997).

Consider $X_1, \ldots, X_I$ to be random variables and H their joint distribution function. Then we have the following definition.

Definition 12.1 (copula). The copula associated with H is a distribution function, $C: [0,1]^I \to [0,1]$, of random variables $X_1, \ldots, X_I$ with standard uniform marginal distributions $F_1, \ldots, F_I$ with the following properties:

- for all $(u_1, \ldots, u_I) \in [0,1]^I$, $C(u_1, \ldots, u_I) = 0$ if at least one coordinate of $(u_1, \ldots, u_I)$ is 0;
- $C(1, \ldots, 1, u_i, 1, \ldots, 1) = u_i$ for all $u_i \in [0,1]$, $i = 1, \ldots, I$.

Hence, if C is a copula, then it is the distribution of a multivariate uniform random vector, as stated in Sklar's Theorem (Sklar 1959).

Theorem 12.2 (Sklar's Theorem). Let H denote an I-dimensional distribution function with margins $F_1, \ldots, F_I$. Then there exists an I-copula C such that for all $(x_1, \ldots, x_I)$

$$H(x_1, \ldots, x_I) = C(F_1(x_1), \ldots, F_I(x_I))$$

If $F_1, \ldots, F_I$ are all continuous, then the copula is unique; otherwise C is uniquely determined. Conversely, if C is a copula and $F_1, \ldots, F_I$ are distribution functions, then the function H is a joint distribution with margins $F_1, \ldots, F_I$.

From Sklar's Theorem, Nelsen (1999) derives the following corollary.

Corollary 12.3. If H is a continuous I-variate distribution function with univariate marginals $F_1, \ldots, F_I$ and generalised inverse $F_1^{-1}, \ldots, F_I^{-1}$, then for every $(u_1, \ldots, u_I)$ there exists a unique copula C such that

$$C(u_1, \ldots, u_I) = H(F_1^{-1}(u_1), \ldots, F_I^{-1}(u_I))$$

A copula is thus a function that, when applied to univariate marginals, results in a proper multivariate probability distribution function. Since this probability density function embodies all the information about the random vector, it contains all the information about the dependence structure of its components. Hence, by implementing this technique, the distribution of a random vector is split into individual components (marginals) with a dependence structure (the copula) without losing any information.

In this application, two types of copulas belonging to the class of elliptical copulas are employed: the normal and the Student-t copula.

Normal copula

The normal (or Gaussian) copula is the copula of the multivariate normal distribution

$$C_G(u_1,\ldots,u_I) = \Phi_I(\Phi^{-1}(u_1),\ldots,\Phi^{-1}(u_I)) \quad (12.2)$$

where C_G denotes the normal copula, Φ_I denotes the joint distribution function of the I-variate standard normal distribution and Φ^{-1} denotes the inverse of the distribution function of the univariate standard normal distribution (Romano 2001).

Let $x' = (\Phi^{-1}(u_1),\ldots,\Phi^{-1}(u_I))$ denote the row vector of univariate normal inverse distribution functions, where $u_i = \Phi(x_i)$ for $i = 1,\ldots,I$, and let R_G denote the correlation matrix. Then the normal copula probability density function is expressed in the following form

$$c_G(\Phi(x_1),\ldots,\Phi(x_I)) = \frac{1}{|R_G|^{1/2}}\exp(-\tfrac{1}{2}x'(R_G^{-1}-I_I)x) \quad (12.3)$$

Additional information for the interested reader can be found in Cherubini *et al* (2004, p. 155).

The most common approach to generate a random variate from the normal copula C_G is the Cholesky method (Ripley 1987). However, in order to generate the copula it is firstly necessary to estimate the correlation matrix. Two methods are used here to estimate R_G: the classical and the Bayesian approach. The former employs the ML method, while the latter develops a new method, based on MCMC.

Note that, to obtain the estimator for R_G, a convenient choice in terms of calculation is to obtain the estimator of the variance–covariance matrix first, and then to derive the estimator of the correlation matrix (Liu 2008; Zhang *et al* 2008). Therefore, we need to apply to the likelihood function derived by Equation 12.3 a change of variables, where the transformation equations are the following

$$x_t = S^{-1}y_t \quad (12.4)$$
$$R_G = S^{-1}\Sigma_G S^{-1} \quad (12.5)$$

where $S^{-1} = \text{diag}(\sigma_i^{-1})$, for $i = 1,\ldots,I$ and σ_i is the sample standard deviation of the ith intersection. This change of variables allows us to express the likelihood as a function of y_t and Σ_G and then to compute the estimator of the variance–covariance matrix. Finally, Σ_G can be translated back to the correlation matrix R_G in order to simulate the joint distribution trough the copula, since

$$R_{G_{[p,q]}} = \frac{\Sigma_{G_{[p,q]}}}{\sqrt{\Sigma_{G_{[p,p]}} \Sigma_{G_{[q,q]}}}}$$

p denoting the pth row and q denoting the qth column of the matrix (Hoff 2007).

The ML method is a classical approach to estimate the normal copula parameter. After maximising the log-likelihood function, we obtain the MLE of the covariance matrix for the Gaussian copula, which is the following

$$\hat{\Sigma}_G = \frac{1}{T} \sum_{t=1}^{T} y_t y_t' \qquad (12.6)$$

(Cherubini *et al* 2004, p. 155).

The Bayesian approach instead requires the definition of an appropriate prior distribution for the parameter matrix. Here, we chose a conjugate prior for the variance–covariance matrix Σ_G, which is given by the inverse Wishart distribution (Kotz *et al* 2000)

$$\Sigma_G \sim \text{inverse Wishart}(\alpha, B)$$

where $\alpha > I - 1$ is the degrees-of-freedom parameter, B is the inverse scale matrix parameter (assumed to be positive definite). Due to lack of information *a priori*, vague priors are used to define hyperparameters, with the aim of getting uninformative distributions. Therefore α, the degrees of freedom, is set to be a fixed constant equal to $I + 1$, the dimension of the matrix (the number of intersections) plus one, as in Dellaportas and Papageorgiou (2006). Furthermore, the precision matrix B is set to be a diagonal matrix, where

$$B = \text{diag}(y_i) \quad \text{with } y_i \sim \text{Gamma}(0.001, 0.001), \quad i = 1, \ldots, I$$

In this way the expected value of y_i is equal to 1 and the variance is very large (1,000), yielding a flat distribution.[7] An alternative method for directly modelling a correlation matrix in the case of substantial prior knowledge is presented in Chapter 12 of Volume I.

The posterior distribution calculated according to Bayes's Theorem is thus another inverse Wishart and the variance–covariance matrix estimate can be calculated with the application of the Gibbs

Sampler Algorithm

$$\pi(\Sigma_G \mid y) \propto |\Sigma_G|^{-(T/2+\alpha)+(I+1)/2} \exp\left\{-\operatorname{tr}\left[\left(\frac{1}{2}\sum_{t=1}^{T} y_t y_t' + B\right)\Sigma_G^{-1}\right]\right\}$$

where $y_t = Sx_t$ and $S = \operatorname{diag}(\sigma_i)$, $i = 1, \ldots, I$.

The Gibbs Sampler Algorithm was implemented considering as the starting point of the chain, which in this case is a matrix, the MLE of the variance–covariance matrix of the normal copula, as suggested by Brooks (1998).

Finally, in order to generate the I-dimensional normal copula, the Bayesian estimate of the correlation matrix $\hat{R}_G$ is computed from the estimate of the covariance matrix $\hat{\Sigma}_G$.

Student-*t* copula

The Student-*t* copula is the copula of the multivariate Student-*t* distribution and it can be represented in the following way

$$C_T(u_1, \ldots, u_I) = t_{I,\nu}(t_\nu^{-1}(u_1), \ldots, t_\nu^{-1}(u_I)) \qquad (12.7)$$

where C_T denotes the Student-*t* copula, ν are the degrees of freedom, $t_{I,\nu}$ denotes the joint distribution function of the I-variate Student-*t* distribution function and t_ν^{-1} denotes the inverse of the distribution function of the univariate Student-*t* distribution.

If $x' = (t_\nu^{-1}(u_1), \ldots, t_\nu^{-1}(u_I))$ denotes the vector of the univariate Student-*t* inverse-distribution functions, where $u_i = t_\nu(x_i)$ for $i = 1, \ldots, I$, and R_T is the correlation matrix, then the Student-*t* copula probability density function is expressed in the following form

$$\begin{aligned}
&c_T(t_\nu(x_1), \ldots, t_\nu(x_I)) \\
&= |R_T|^{-1/2} \frac{\Gamma(\frac{1}{2}(\nu+I))}{\Gamma(\frac{1}{2}\nu)} \left[\frac{\Gamma(\frac{1}{2}\nu)}{\Gamma(\frac{1}{2}(\nu+1))}\right]^I \frac{(1+(x'R_T^{-1}x)/\nu)^{-(\nu+I)/2}}{\prod_{i=1}^{I}(1+x_i^2/\nu)^{-(\nu+1)/2}}
\end{aligned}$$
(12.8)

In order to generate a random variate from the *t*-copula C_T, first the degrees of freedom ν and the correlation matrix R_T have to be estimated, then an algorithm to simulate from the Student-*t* copula has to be implemented. However, as explained in the previous section, a change of variable is needed first, in order to express the likelihood, calculated from the probability density function

(Equation 12.8), in terms of the covariance matrix Σ_T. The applied transformation is the following

$$x_t = S^{-1} y_t, \qquad R_T = S^{-1} \Sigma_T S^{-1}$$

where $S^{-1} = \text{diag}(\sigma_i^{-1})$, for $i = 1, \ldots, I$ and σ_i is the sample standard deviation of the ith intersection. Then, in order to simulate from the t-copula, R_T can easily be derived as

$$R_{T_{[p,q]}} = \frac{\Sigma_{T_{[p,q]}}}{\sqrt{\Sigma_{T_{[p,p]}} \Sigma_{T_{[q,q]}}}}$$

where p denotes the pth row and q denotes the qth column of the matrix.

Now, let us illustrate the two estimation method employed here.

In the case of ML estimation, an analytical formula for the estimator is not available and a numerical maximisation of the likelihood is required. In the approach proposed by Chen et al (2004), first the ν parameter (the degrees of freedom) is estimated, using the MLE of the covariance matrix of the Gaussian copula, $\hat{\Sigma}_G$, in the maximisation of the log-likelihood function of the Student-t copula density. Then, $\hat{\Sigma}_T$ is derived as the MLE of the covariance matrix of the Student-t copula, given the previous estimate of the degrees-of-freedom parameter.[8]

The Bayesian method applied to the Student-t copula needs the definition of the prior distributions for the parameters Σ_T (the covariance matrix) and ν (the degrees of freedom). For the covariance matrix Σ_T we follow the approach used previously in the case of the Gaussian copula, ie, we set

$$\Sigma_T \sim \text{inverse Wishart}(\alpha, B)$$

where $a > I - 1$ is the degrees-of-freedom parameter and B is the inverse scale matrix parameter.

The B and α hyperparameters are chosen as described for the Bayesian normal copula

$$\alpha = I + 1 \quad \text{and} \quad B = \text{diag}(y_i)$$

$$\text{with } y_i \sim \text{Gamma}(0.001, 0.001), \ i = 1, \ldots, I$$

Since ν models the degrees of freedom, it is typically a positive integer and must also satisfy the constraint $\nu > \frac{1}{2}(I-1)$ (Kotz et al 2000). For this reason a suitable prior is

$$\nu \sim \text{truncated Poisson}(h)$$

where the h parameter is determined by equating the expected value of the prior to the MLE. Other choices of priors for discrete random variables like the degrees of freedom include the discrete uniform distribution (Gilks *et al* 1996). The full conditionals for the two parameters of interest are both non-standard forms, requiring the implementation of the MH algorithm, with an inverse Wishart as proposal distribution for Σ_T.[9]

APPLICATION

The data

The data set contains the operational losses of an anonymous bank, from January 1999 to December 2004, for a total of 72 monthly observations: 407 loss events, distributed in eight intersections only (two business lines and four event types), since the bank did not collect data for the remaining 48 intersections. We remark that for privacy purposes the bank assigned a random code to BLs and ETs in order to hide their identity. However, the direct association between these codes and the real ones is preserved.

The overall average monthly loss was equal to €202,158, the minimum was equal to 0 (for September 2001), while the maximum was equal to €4,570,852 (which took place on July 2003). Tables 12.1 and 12.2 respectively report parts of the frequency and loss data sets used for the empirical analysis. Table 12.1 shows the number of losses as they occurred within a specific time period for all eight intersections. Table 12.2 shows the loss amounts as they occurred within a specific time period for all eight intersections. For example, for intersection 1 in January 1999, two loss events occurred, for a total amount of €35,753, which is the sum of the two losses that took place in January 1999.

Perfect dependence risk measure results

As illustrated above, the parameter estimates of the marginals are computed according both to the classical and to the Bayesian method. As explained above, we employed the Poisson and negative binomial to describe the frequency distribution, and we used the exponential, Gamma and Pareto to describe the severity distribution. Distributions with corresponding parameters take the forms listed in Table 12.3.

Table 12.1 The frequency data set

	Jan 1999	Feb 1999	Mar 1999	Apr 1999	...	Nov 2004	Dec 2004
1	2	0	0	0	...	5	0
2	6	1	1	1	...	3	1
3	0	2	0	0	...	0	0
4	0	1	0	0	...	0	0
5	0	0	0	0	...	0	1
6	0	0	0	0	...	2	4
7	0	0	0	0	...	1	0
8	0	0	0	0	...	0	0

The table shows the number of losses as they occurred within a specific time period for all eight intersections given in the first column.

Table 12.2 The loss data set

	Jan 1999	Feb 1999	Mar 1999	Apr 1999	...	Nov 2004	Dec 2004
1	35,753	0	0	0	...	27,538	0
2	121,999	1,550	3,457	5,297	...	61,026	6,666
3	0	33,495	0	0	...	0	0
4	0	6,637	0	0	...	0	0
5	0	0	0	0	...	0	11,280
6	0	0	0	0	...	57,113	11,039
7	0	0	0	0	...	2,336	0
8	0	0	0	0	...	0	0

The table shows the loss amounts as they occurred within a specific time period for all eight intersections given in the first column.

Tables 12.4 and 12.5 list the Bayesian parameter estimates (posterior means) and the 95% credible intervals for the frequency and severity distributions, respectively. Credible bounds are a useful tool to express the variability of Bayesian parameters which, according to this approach, are not fixed (as in the classical approach) but rather are random variables. For example, regarding intersection 1, the Poisson parameter estimate is equal to about 1.4, but it can vary between 1.14 and 1.69.

Figure 12.2 shows the box plots of the simulated operational loss distribution L_{it} of the combination Poisson–Gamma for intersection 1. The distribution simulated with ML marginal estimates is displayed in part (a), while the distribution simulated with Bayesian

Table 12.3 Analytic forms of the frequency and severity distributions with corresponding parameters, and range of the parameters

Distribution	Analytic form	Parameters
$N_t \sim \text{Poisson}(\lambda)$	$f(n_t) = \dfrac{\exp(-\lambda)\lambda^{n_t}}{n_t!}$	$\lambda \in \mathbb{R}^+$
$N_t \sim \text{Negative binomial}(\theta, r)$	$f(n_t) = \theta^r \dbinom{r + n_t - 1}{r - 1} \cdot (1-\theta)^{n_t}$	$\theta \in (0,1),\ r \in \mathbb{Z}^+$
$X_1, \ldots, X_{N_t} \sim \text{Exponential}(\theta)$	$f(x_j) = \theta \exp(-\theta x_j)$	$\theta \in \mathbb{R}^+$
$X_1, \ldots, X_{N_t} \sim \text{Gamma}(\alpha, \beta)$	$f(x_j) = \dfrac{\beta^\alpha}{\Gamma(\alpha)} x_j^{\alpha-1} \exp(-\beta x_j)$	$\alpha \in \mathbb{R}^+,\ \beta \in \mathbb{R}^+$
$X_1, \ldots, X_{N_t} \sim \text{Pareto}(\alpha, \beta)$	$f(x_j) = \alpha \beta^\alpha x_j^{-(\alpha+1)} \mathbb{I}_{[\beta, \infty)}(x_j)$	$\alpha \in \mathbb{R}^+,\ \beta \in \mathbb{R}^+$

Table 12.4 Parameters and 95% credible intervals of the frequency distributions estimated with the Bayesian method

	Frequency distributions		
	Poisson	Negative binomial	
	λ	θ	r
1	1.4034 [1.1441; 1.6884]	0.5857 [0.3706; 0.7722]	2 [1; 5]
2	2.1955 [1.8662; 2.5511]	0.4672 [0.2794; 0.6306]	2 [1; 4]
3	0.0833 [0.0308; 0.1619]	0.9289 [0.8579; 0.9787]	1 [1; 2]
4	0.4581 [0.3157; 0.6278]	0.9097 [0.7908; 0.9602]	5 [2; 10]
5	0.0970 [0.0388; 0.1811]	0.9233 [0.8456; 0.9773]	1 [1; 3]
6	0.6249 [0.4550; 0.8203]	0.6164 [0.5261; 0.7062]	1 [1; 1]
7	0.6805 [0.5031; 0.8846]	0.5966 [0.5070; 0.6888]	1 [1; 1]
8	0.1113 [0.0481; 0.2002]	0.9209 [0.8358; 0.9769]	1 [1; 3]

Intersection numbers are given in the first column.

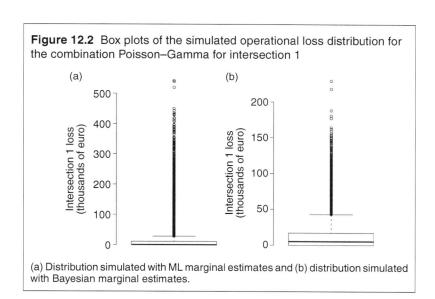

Figure 12.2 Box plots of the simulated operational loss distribution for the combination Poisson–Gamma for intersection 1

(a) Distribution simulated with ML marginal estimates and (b) distribution simulated with Bayesian marginal estimates.

marginal estimates is displayed in part (b). These plots are drawn based on the quantiles of the distribution. The lower side of the box corresponds to the first quartile, the upper side of the box corresponds to the third quartile, the black horizontal line in the box corresponds to the median and the points outside the box are outliers. The y-axis shows the loss values taken by quartiles and extreme

Table 12.5 Parameters and 95% credible intervals of the three severity distributions estimated with the Bayesian method

	Exponential θ
1	1.20×10^{-4} [9.80×10^{-5}; 1.45×10^{-4}]
2	5.49×10^{-5} [4.67×10^{-5}; 6.39×10^{-5}]
3	4.28×10^{-6} [1.58×10^{-6}; 8.34×10^{-6}]
4	4.55×10^{-6} [3.14×10^{-6}; 6.24×10^{-6}]
5	6.41×10^{-6} [2.59×10^{-6}; 1.19×10^{-6}]
6	2.24×10^{-4} [1.63×10^{-4}; 2.95×10^{-4}]
7	7.92×10^{-5} [5.87×10^{-5}; 1.03×10^{-4}]
8	2.80×10^{-5} [1.22×10^{-5}; 5.06×10^{-5}]

	Gamma	
	α	β
1	0.6267 [0.4899; 0.7826]	7.53×10^{-5} [5.16×10^{-5}; 1.03×10^{-4}]
2	0.3773 [0.3132; 0.4474]	2.07×10^{-5} [1.48×10^{-5}; 2.75×10^{-5}]
3	0.3617 [0.1072; 0.7832]	1.55×10^{-6} [5.37×10^{-8}; 4.81×10^{-6}]
4	0.3384 [0.2216; 0.4822]	1.54×10^{-6} [6.35×10^{-7}; 2.78×10^{-6}]
5	0.4425 [0.1445; 0.9325]	2.83×10^{-6} [2.13×10^{-7}; 7.98×10^{-6}]
6	1.2686 [0.8346; 1.7989]	2.85×10^{-4} [1.68×10^{-4}; 4.29×10^{-4}]
7	0.4336 [0.3059; 0.5856]	3.43×10^{-5} [1.83×10^{-5}; 5.48×10^{-5}]
8	0.4803 [0.1734; 0.9537]	1.35×10^{-5} [1.51×10^{-6}; 3.52×10^{-5}]

	Pareto	
	α	β
1	1.0966 [0.8834; 1.3326]	1,262.844 [1196.475; 1331.059]
2	0.3341 [0.2774; 0.3967]	159.287 [120.458; 202.951]
3	0.4935 [0.1809; 0.9489]	6,034.454 [5972.616; 6096.712]
4	0.3087 [0.2121; 0.4231]	1,216.396 [1154.984; 1279.085]
5	0.3189 [0.1275; 0.5984]	1,827.211 [1765.995; 1889.815]
6	1.1522 [0.8354; 1.5223]	1,212.377 [1149.101; 1278.265]
7	1.1656 [0.8602; 1.5246]	1,220.646 [1156.297; 1286.311]
8	0.5021 [0.2176; 0.9082]	1,449.648 [1387.945; 1512.401]

Intersection numbers are given in the first column.

observations. You have information about the symmetry of the distribution from the position of the median and the first and third quartiles. If the median is closer to the first quartile, the distribution

Table 12.6 Total operational risk in the case of MLE perfect dependence

	MLE perfect dependence	
	99% VaR	99% ES
Poisson/exponential	1,931,074	2,548,268
Poisson/Gamma	2,993,355	4,472,861
Poisson/Pareto	4.1×10^{13}	—
Negative binomial/exponential	2,111,538	2,820,846
Negative binomial/Gamma	3,142,903	4,708,293
Negative binomial/Pareto	3.5×10^{13}	—

Total operational risk (99% VaR and 99% ES) are given in the case of perfect dependence. Results (in €) are calculated using the MLE for all parameters.

is right-skewed, the mass is concentrated on the left and the right tail is longer. On the other hand, if the median is closer to the third quartile, the distribution is left-skewed, the mass is concentrated on the right and the left tail is longer. As is clear form the box plots in Figure 12.2, the distributions are both right-skewed, with long right tails. However, in the MLE box plot, the median and the first quartile overlap, indicating a highly skewed distribution.

Once we have estimated the parameters, the overall risk measures are calculated assuming perfect dependence among intersections. Firstly, VaR and ES are computed for each intersection BL/ET. Secondly, because of perfect dependence, risk measures are simply summed for the eight intersections considered. Risk measures are computed for each frequency–severity combination and for each intersection firstly according to the classical Monte Carlo method and secondly according to the MCMC method. Following the first approach, random extractions are generated from the frequency and severity distributions defined by the MLEs of the parameters. Alternatively, following the second method, posterior means are used as parameter estimates and then draws from the loss distributions are generated.

Table 12.6 lists perfect dependence results (VaR and ES at confidence level 99%) calculated with MLEs. Note that, for some intersection, the estimate of the Pareto tail parameter is smaller than one and then the expected value of the Pareto distribution (and also the ES) is not defined. Moreover, the combinations involving the

Table 12.7 Total operational risk in the case of Bayesian perfect dependence

	Bayesian perfect dependence 99% VaR
Poisson/exponential	2,242,805 [2,169,958; 2,320,981]
Poisson/Gamma	3,027,133 [2,876,359; 3,182,261]
Poisson/Pareto	1.96×10^9 [1.17×10^9; 3.16×10^9]
Negative binomial/exponential	2,338,374 [2,258,134; 2,416,164]
Negative binomial/Gamma	3,075,791 [2,919,898; 3,236,063]
Negative binomial/Pareto	2.24×10^9 [1.40×10^9; 3.57×10^9]
	Bayesian perfect dependence 99% ES
Poisson/exponential	3,011,717 [2,908,190; 3,118,229]
Poisson/Gamma	4,573,240 [4,337,670; 4,813,331]
Poisson/Pareto	—
Negative binomial/exponential	3,162,479 [3,052,066; 3,275,135]
Negative binomial/Gamma	4,661,401 [4,413,245; 4,904,002]
Negative binomial/Pareto	—

Total operational risk (99% VaR and 99% ES) are given in the case of perfect dependence. Results (in €) are the posterior means (with corresponding credible intervals at 95% level) calculated using Bayesian estimates for all parameters.

Pareto provide very high risk measures due to the heavy tail of this distribution. This choice of density function can be useful to better describe extreme events, such as low frequency high impact (LFHI) events (ie, catastrophes or calamities), having great effect for financial institutions, but being difficult to collect by banks as time series data.

Table 12.7 shows the 99% VaR and ES calculated using Bayesian estimates for the definition of marginals, assuming perfect dependence among intersections BLs/ETs. The Bayesian method allows us to calculate not only risk measures, but also credible intervals for VaR and ES estimates, providing information about the uncertainty of risk measures. Indeed, through credible bounds we can see how our estimate can vary in a certain range explicitly showing the "error" associated to this estimate. This is very useful when we are measuring risks, because we have an idea of the possible fluctuations of risk measures. For example, looking at Table 12.7, the

99% VaR is equal to €2,242,805, but this value can vary between €2,169,958 and €2,320,981, with a 95% confidence level, choosing the Poisson/exponential combination.

Comparing Tables 12.6 and 12.7, it is clear that risk measure results depend above all on the choice of the severity distribution. Risk measures are higher when we choose the Gamma as severity distribution, compared with the exponential, for the heavier tails of the Gamma. Pareto results are generally much higher than the other severity distributions.

Normal copula risk measure results

Now the normal copula outcomes are illustrated, making some comparisons.

In the classical approach, the following correlation matrix R_G of the normal copula is estimated through the maximum likelihood method. Estimates for the matrix components r_{pq}, with marginals described by the Poisson–Gamma combination, are

$$\begin{pmatrix} 1 & 0.129 & -0.068 & -0.209 & -0.103 & 0.386 & -0.305 & -0.123 \\ 0.129 & 1 & -0.115 & -0.028 & -0.114 & 0.143 & -0.059 & -0.106 \\ -0.068 & -0.115 & 1 & 0.543 & 0.956 & 0.206 & 0.328 & 0.941 \\ -0.209 & -0.028 & 0.543 & 1 & 0.599 & -0.243 & 0.689 & 0.640 \\ -0.103 & -0.114 & 0.956 & 0.599 & 1 & 0.163 & 0.401 & 0.947 \\ 0.386 & 0.143 & 0.206 & -0.243 & 0.163 & 1 & -0.397 & 0.122 \\ -0.305 & -0.059 & 0.328 & 0.689 & 0.401 & -0.397 & 1 & 0.440 \\ -0.123 & -0.106 & 0.941 & 0.640 & 0.947 & 0.122 & 0.440 & 1 \end{pmatrix}$$

ML results show low correlations for many intersections BLs/ETs, but intersections 3, 5 and 8 are highly correlated with $r_{35} = 0.956$, $r_{38} = 0.941$ and $r_{58} = 0.947$.

Table 12.8 lists the 99% VaR and ES calculated with the MLE of the correlation matrix of the normal copula. As in the perfect dependence case, it is clear that results involving the same severity distribution are very similar. Copulas allow us to take into account different dependence levels between intersections. Therefore, measures calculated with the classical normal copula are generally lower than the corresponding outcomes obtained assuming perfect dependence among intersections (for both the classical and the Bayesian approaches).

In the dependent Bayesian approach, the correlation matrix R_G is instead estimated via the MCMC method. Figure 12.3 shows the

Table 12.8 Total operational risk calculated with the MLE normal copula

	MLE normal copula	
	99% VaR	99% ES
Poisson/exponential	1,332,331	1,703,948
Poisson/Gamma	2,082,782	2,963,358
Poisson/Pareto	6.24×10^{13}	—
Negative binomial/exponential	1,505,331	1,927,227
Negative binomial/Gamma	2,001,456	2,849,364
Negative binomial/Pareto	3.44×10^{13}	—

Total operational risk (99% VaR and 99% ES) is calculated with the normal copula. Results (in €) are computed using MLE for all parameters.

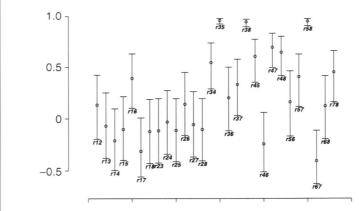

Figure 12.3 Posterior medians and credible intervals (at 95% level) for the correlation matrix components of the Bayesian normal copula

Matrix components are denoted by r_{pq}, where p is the pth row and q is the qth column.

posterior medians and credible intervals (at 95% level) for the correlation matrix components of the normal copula, with Poisson–Gamma marginals. Results are close to the classical normal copula results, with high correlations for the components r_{35}, r_{38} and r_{58}, and indicate that a perfect dependence approach is completely unrealistic. Moreover, Bayesian credible intervals allow us to take into account parameter uncertainty. For instance, the first credible interval depicted in Figure 12.3 is about the r_{12} component of the

Table 12.9 Total operational risk calculated with the Bayesian normal copula

	Bayesian normal copula 99% VaR
Poisson/exponential	1,360,907 [1,289,127; 1,438,184]
Poisson/Gamma	2,048,542 [1,901,960; 2,211,386]
Poisson/Pareto	3.83×10^{13} [1.28×10^{13}; 9.17×10^{13}]
Negative binomial/exponential	1,504,441 [1,419,032; 1,594,879]
Negative binomial/Gamma	2,035,196 [1,879,948; 2,186,469]
Negative binomial/Pareto	1.74×10^{13} [0.00; 7.51×10^{13}]

	Bayesian normal copula 99% ES
Poisson/exponential	1,755,892 [1,658,332; 1,859,158]
Poisson/Gamma	2,922,751 [2,697,973; 3,169,639]
Poisson/Pareto	—
Negative binomial/exponential	1,938,729 [1,820,598; 2,060,302]
Negative binomial/Gamma	2,794,672 [2,591,057; 3,002,441]
Negative binomial/Pareto	—

Total operational risk (99% VaR and 99% ES) is calculated with the normal copula. Results (in €) are the posterior means (with corresponding credible intervals at 95% level) calculated using Bayesian estimates for all parameters.

estimated correlation matrix R_G. The point estimate value is 0.126, but the credible interval goes from about −0.2 to 0.45, denoting variability in the parameter estimates.

Table 12.9 illustrates the 99% VaR and ES calculated with the Bayesian estimate (posterior means) of the correlation matrix of the normal copula. Outcomes show lower values than the perfect dependence case, as we have already seen for the MLE normal copula. The Bayesian approach allows us also to build credible intervals for risk measures, which are induced by the posterior distributions of the model parameters. In our case, considering the Poisson/exponential combination, VaR is equal to €1,360,907, with lower bound equal to €1,289,127 and upper bound equal to €1,438,184, showing the possible variations of this risk measure. The upper bound could, for instance, be used for computing conservative risk figures in order not to overestimate the diversification effect.

Table 12.10 Total operational risk calculated with the MLE Student-t copula

	MLE Student-t copula	
	99% VaR	99% ES
Poisson/exponential	1,242,789	1,686,827
Poisson/Gamma	2,103,169	3,147,776
Poisson/Pareto	8.74×10^{13}	—
NegativeBinomial/exponential	1,539,708	2,062,251
NegativeBinomial/Gamma	2,210,314	3,438,989
NegativeBinomial/Pareto	2.89×10^{13}	—

Total operational risk (99% VaR and 99% ES) are calculated with the Student-t copula. Results (in €) are computed using MLE for all parameters.

Student-t copula risk measure results

The main problem encountered with the t-copula is the estimation of the degrees-of-freedom parameter ν. According to the classical approach, first the MLE of ν (degrees of freedom) is computed, considering as the correlation matrix the normal copula estimate R_G. Then ν is fixed and the Student-t copula estimate of R_T is calculated. However, the log-likelihood function of the t-copula is an increasing function that grows with ν and does not reach any maximum. Therefore, we set $\nu = 30$, because it represents a good parsimonious approximation. With ν fixed at 30, we then calculate the MLE of the correlation matrix.

Since the degrees of freedom are set to the large value of 30, the behaviour of the Student-t copula is expected to be very similar to that of the normal copula. This result is straightforward since the normal copula is a particular case of the Student-t copula when the number of degrees of freedom tends to infinity. Student-t copula results (Table 12.10) are in fact very similar to those of the normal copula. This means that in this particular case the normal copula is a better choice than the Student-t copula, since it is computationally easier to manipulate and gives similar results.

In the Bayesian approach, as starting points of the chains we chose the MLE for the classical Student-t copula covariance matrix. Thus, once the parameters are estimated, the I-dimensional Student-t copula is generated.

Figure 12.4 Degrees-of-freedom trace plot for the Student-t copula and the mean of v as a function of the sample length

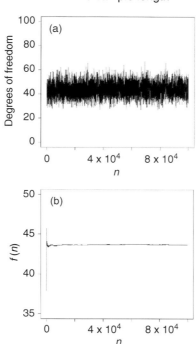

(a) The degrees-of-freedom trace plot for the Student-t copula and (b) the mean of v as a function of the sample length. The plots display the random variable being generated and the mean of v, respectively (y-axis), versus the number of iterations (x-axis). Both parts show the Poisson–Gamma combination.

Here the degrees-of-freedom variable v can be estimated, but the value is quite high (about 40).

Focusing on the Poisson–Gamma combination, part (a) of Figure 12.4 shows the chain of the degrees-of-freedom parameter and part (b) shows the mean of the draws of v as a function of the sample length. Figure 12.4(a) plots the random variable being generated versus the number of iterations. This plot is helpful not only to understand if the chain can move around the state space, but also to assess the convergence to the target distribution. As we can see from the figure, the parameter chain is mixing well, since there are no flat periods and the jumps are not too close together. Flat periods indicate that the proposal generates candidate observations that are too often rejected, while very close jumps denote that candidate observations are too often accepted, suggesting in both cases that the proposal is not suitable to describe the target distribution and that there is not convergence to the target itself. However, in our case the chain mixes very well, freely exploring the parameter space and being centred in correspondence to the parameter estimate, showing in this way convergence to the target distribution. We ran 10,000 iterations, after discarding 1,000 values as a burn-in period, considering in this way only the elements approaching to the chain's stationarity. In order to assess the convergence to the target distribution, we included Figure 12.4(b) as well; this depicts the following function

$$f(n) = \frac{1}{n}\sum_{i=1}^{n} v_i$$

where v_i are the draws of the degrees-of-freedom parameter obtained through the implementation of the MCMC algorithm and n is the sample length. Plotting $f(n)$ on the y-axis and n on the x-axis, we note that the posterior mean indeed moves quickly toward the Bayesian estimate. Therefore, our chain converges to the target distribution.

Final values of risk measure are higher than the outcomes obtained with other methods, in particular the Bayesian normal copula (Table 12.11). In the Bayesian t-copula case, in fact, both the correlation matrix and the degrees-of-freedom parameters vary across iterations, introducing much more variability.

Figure 12.5 displays credible intervals of the 99% VaR and ES calculated according to the Bayesian approach for the combination Poisson/Gamma. Bayesian Student-t outcomes show the highest risk measure results, while the Bayesian normal copula has the lowest result values. However, the credible intervals of perfect dependence and Student-t copula overlap, while the normal copula is clearly distinct from the other two outcomes.

CONCLUDING REMARKS

This application illustrates a methodology which is able to take into account the parameter uncertainty in operational risk management as well as the specification of the dependence among different business lines and event types.

The statistical methodology introduced applies the Bayesian method to distributional copula functions, yielding the Bayesian

Table 12.11 Total operational risk calculated with the Bayesian Student-t copula

	Bayesian Student-t copula 99% VaR
Poisson/exponential	2,452,805 [2,363,958; 2,590,981]
Poisson/Gamma	3,271,363 [3,056,359; 3,482,243]
Poisson/Pareto	3.96×10^{13} [3.87×10^{13}; 4.16×10^{13}]
NegativeBinomial/exponential	2,831,774 [2,258,134; 2,416,164]
NegativeBinomial/Gamma	3,207,2791 [3,119,801; 3,360,637]
NegativeBinomial/Pareto	4.14×10^{13} [4.10×10^{13}; 4.26×10^{13}]

	Bayesian Student-t copula 99% ES
Poisson/exponential	3,312,391 [3,258,190; 3,418,669]
Poisson/Gamma	4,671,914 [4,370,670; 4,953,031]
Poisson/Pareto	—
NegativeBinomial/exponential	3,200,479 [3,158,561; 3,377,435]
NegativeBinomial/Gamma	4,768,791 [4,681,328; 4,901,114]
NegativeBinomial/Pareto	—

Total operational risk (99% VaR and 99% ES) is calculated with the Student-t copula. Results (in €) are the posterior means (with corresponding credible intervals at 95% level) calculated using Bayesian estimates for all parameters.

normal copula and the Bayesian Student-t copula. We combined these copulas with different marginal loss distributions that were constructed by different combinations of the loss frequency and loss severity.

In order to evaluate the performance of this method, risk measures were computed and compared with the classical approach using MLE.

When applied to the data set, the Student-t copula showed some problems in the degrees-of-freedom estimation. In the classical case, this variable tends to grow to infinity, while in the Bayesian context the degrees-of-freedom estimates are rather stable but still very high.

Observing the final risk measures, we need to distinguish between ML and Bayesian results. In the ML case, there exists a similarity between the normal and the t-copula outcomes, due to the high value of the degrees of freedom. In the Bayesian case, on the other hand, the normal copula outcomes are lower than the t-copula outcomes,

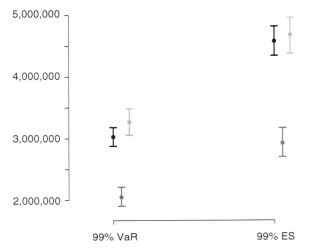

Figure 12.5 Credible Intervals of the 99% VaR and ES for the combination Poisson/Gamma using different approaches to model the dependence structure

The black line shows Bayesian perfect dependence, the dark-grey line shows the Bayesian normal copula and the light-grey line shows the Bayesian Student-t copula.

due to the variability induced by both the degrees of freedom and the correlation matrix parameter in the estimation algorithm of the Student-t copula.

Indeed, the introduction of Bayesian estimation techniques allows us to consider the variability of parameter estimates that are not fixed values, but rather are treated as random variables. It is thus possible to calculate credible intervals associated with VaR and ES. The consideration of this uncertainty is very important in order to achieve sound and reliable financial risk management, since it allows us to interpret operational risk measures correctly.

Moreover, the Bayesian method can be used to select which model best fits the data, through Bayes factors. A further step for our study would be to use Bayesian model selection to choose among the different models we employed both for the marginals and the copulas.

> The author is grateful to Klaus Böcker for his insightful comments and suggestions, which significantly improved the presentation of this work.

1   For more details, the reader should consult, for example, Frachot *et al* (2001), Kuhn and Neu (2003), Alexander (2003), Aue and Kalkbrener (2006) and Böcker and Klüppelberg (2008).

2   See Berger (1985) or Bernardo and Smith (1994) for an introduction to Bayesian methods.

3   For more details about the other combinations see Dalla Valle and Giudici (2008).

4   For more details see Dalla Valle and Giudici (2008).

5   For more details about the algorithms, see Metropolis *et al* (1953), Hastings (1970), Robert and Casella (1999) and Chapter 2 of Volume I.

6   As shown in Alexander (2003).

7   See Giudici and Green (1999) and Dellaportas and Papageorgiou (2005) in the definition of their non-hierarchical models.

8   This proposal is contained in Fantazzini *et al* (2008).

9   For more details, see Dalla Valle (2009).

REFERENCES

Acerbi, C., and D. Tasche, 2002, "On the Coherence of Expected Shortfall", *Journal of Banking and Finance* 26, pp. 1487–503.

Alexander, C. (ed), 2003, *Operational Risk: Regulation, Analysis and Management* (London: Financial Times/Prentice Hall.).

Aue, F., and M. Kalkbrener, 2006, "LDA at Work: Deutsche Bank's Approach to Quantifying Operational Risk, *The Journal of Operational Risk* 1(4), pp. 48–98.

Basel Committee on Banking Supervision, 2001, "Basel II: The New Basel Capital Accord – Second Consultantive Paper", Report to the Bank for International Settlements, URL: http://www.bis.org.

Basel Committee on Banking Supervision, 2003, "Basel II: the New Basel Capital Accord – Third Consultantive Paper", Report to the Bank for International Settlements, URL: http://www.bis.org.

Berger, J. O., 1985, *Statistical Decision Theory and Bayesian Analysis*, Second Edition (Springer).

Bernardo, J. M., and A. F. M. Smith, 1994, *Bayesian Theory* (Chichester: John Wiley & Sons).

Böcker, K., and C. Klüppelberg, 2008, "Modelling and Measuring Multivariate Operational Risk with Lévy Copulas", *The Journal of Operational Risk* 3(2), pp. 3–27.

Broemeling, L., and A. Broemeling, 2003, "Studies in the History of Probability and Statistics XLVIII the Bayesian Contributions of Ernest Lhoste", *Biometrika* 90(3), pp. 728–31.

Brooks, S. P., 1998, "Markov Chain Monte Carlo Method and Its Application", *The Statistician* 47(1), pp. 69–100.

Brunner, M., F. Piacenza, F. Monti and D. Bazzarello, 2009, "Fat tails, Expected Shortfall and the Monte Carlo Method: A Note", *The Journal of Operational Risk* 4(1), pp. 81–8.

Chen, X., Y. Fan and A. J. Patton, 2004, "Simple Tests for Models of Dependence between Multiple Financial Time Series, with Applications to US Equity Returns and Exchange Rates", Discussion Paper 483, Financial Markets Group, London School of Economics.

Cherubini, U., E. Luciano and W. Vecchiato, 2004, *Copula Methods in Finance* (Chichester: John Wiley & Sons).

Dalla Valle, L., 2009, "Bayesian Copulae Distributions, with Application to Operational Risk Management", *Methodology and Computing in Applied Probability* 11(1), pp. 95–115.

Dalla Valle, L., and P. Giudici, 2008, "A Bayesian Approach to Estimate the Marginal Loss Distributions in Operational Risk Management", *Computational Statistics and Data Analysis* 52(6), pp. 3107–27.

Dellaportas, P., and I. Papageorgiou, 2006, "Multivariate Mixtures of Normals with Unknown Number of Components", *Statistics and Computing* 16(1), pp. 57–68.

Fantazzini, D., L. Dalla Valle and P. Giudici, 2008, "Copulae and Operational Risks", *International Journal of Risk Assessment and Management* 9(3), pp. 238–57.

Frachot, A., P. Georges and T. Roncalli, 2001, "Loss Distribution Approach for Operational Risk", Working Paper, Groupe de Recherche Opérationnelle du Crédit Lyonnais.

Gilks, W. R., S. Richardson and D. J. Spiegelhalter, 1996, *Markov Chain Monte Carlo in Practice* (London: Chapman & Hall).

Giudici, P., and P. J. Green, 1999, "Decomposable Graphical Gaussian Model Determination", *Biometrica* 86(4), pp. 785–801.

Gourieroux, C., and A. Monfort, 1995, *Statistics and Econometric Models* (Cambridge University Press).

Hastings, W. K., 1970, "Monte Carlo Sampling Methods Using Markov Chains and Their Applications", *Biometrika* 57, pp. 97–109.

Hoff, P. D., 2007, "Extending the Rank Likelihood for Semiparametric Copula Estimation", *Annals of Applied Statistics* 1(1), pp. 265–83.

Joe, H., 1997, *Multivariate Models and Dependence Concepts* (London: Chapman & Hall).

Kotz, S., N. Balakrishnan and N. L. Johnson, 2000, *Continuous Multivariate Distributions, Volume 1: Models and Applications*, Second Edition (New York: John Wiley & Sons).

Kuhn, R., and P. Neu, 2003, "Functional Correlation Approach to Operational Risk in Banking Organizations", *Physica A* 322, pp. 650–66.

Liang, C. L., 2009, "Bayesian Analysis of Extreme Operational Losses", *The Journal of Operational Risk* 4(3), pp. 27–43.

Liu, X., 2008, "Parameter Expansion for Sampling a Correlation Matrix: An Efficient GPX-RPMH Algorithm", *Journal of Statistical Computation and Simulation* 78(11), pp. 1065–76.

Metropolis, N., A. N. Rosenbluth, M. N. Rosenbluth, A. H. Teller and E. Teller, 1953, "Equation of State Calculation by Fast Computing Machine", *Journal of Chemical Physics* 21(6), pp. 1087–92.

Nelsen, R. B., 1999, *An Introduction to Copulas* (New York: Springer).

Pezier, J., 2002, "A Constructive Review of the Basel Proposals on Operational Risk", ISMA Discussion Papers in Finance, University of Reading, URL: http://www.icmacentre.ac.uk/pdf/discussion/DP2002-20.pdf.

Pitt, M., D. Chan and R. Kohn, 2006, "Efficient Bayesian Inference for Gaussian Copula Regression Models", *Biometrika* 93(3), pp. 537–54.

Ripley, B. D., 1987, *Stochastic Simulation* (London: John Wiley & Sons).

Risk Management Group, 2003, "The 2002 Loss Data Collection Exercise for Operational Risk: Summary of the Data Collected", Report to the Bank for International Settlements, URL: http://www.bis.org.

Robert, C. P., and G. Casella, 1999, *Monte Carlo Statistical Methods* (Springer).

Romano, C., 2001, "Applying Copula Functions to Risk Management", Working Paper, University of Rome "La Sapienza".

Shevchenko, P. V., and M. V. Wüthrich, 2006, "The Structural Modeling of Operational Risk via Bayesian Inference: Combining Loss Data with Expert Opinions", *Journal of Operational Risk* 1(3), pp. 3–26.

Sklar, A., 1959, "Fonctions de répartition à n dimensions et leurs marges", *Publications de l'Institut de Statistique de l'Université de Paris* 8, pp. 229–31

Trivedi, P. K., and D. M. Zimmer, 2007, "Copula Modeling: An Introduction for Practitioners", *Foundations and Trends in Econometrics* 1(1), pp. 1–111.

Zhang, X., W. J. Boscardin and T. R. Belin, 2008, "Bayesian Analysis of Multivariate Nominal Measures Using Multivariate Multinomial Probit Models", *Computational Statistics and Data Analysis* 52, pp. 3697–708.

13

Operational Risk: Combining Internal Data, External Data and Expert Opinions

Pavel V. Shevchenko; Mario V. Wüthrich

CSIRO Mathematics, Informatics and Statistics;
RiskLab ETH Zurich

Under the loss distribution approach (LDA) for the Basel II Advanced Measurement Approaches (AMAs), banks should quantify the distribution of operational risk losses for each risk cell (business line/event type) over a one-year time horizon. The commonly used LDA model for the annual loss is a compound-loss process for loss frequencies and severities.[1] We consider a single risk cell (business line/event type), where the annual loss is the sum of individual losses and is given by

$$Z = \sum_{i=1}^{N} X_i \qquad (13.1)$$

Here, N is the annual number of events modelled as a random variable from some discrete distribution (typically Poisson) and X_i are the severities of the events modelled as independent random variables from a continuous distribution. Frequency N and severities X_i are assumed to be independent. Note that the independence assumed here will be conditional on parameters of the distributions.

Estimation of the frequency and severity distributions of operational risk is a challenging task for low-frequency high-impact losses due to limited data. To improve the estimation, the actual data is supplemented with expert opinions and external data. In fact, it is mandatory to include these data sources into the model estimation to meet the regulatory requirements. In particular, Basel II AMA requires (Basel Committee on Banking Supervision 2006, p.152) that

Any operational risk measurement system must have certain key features to meet the supervisory soundness standard set out in this section. These elements must include the use of internal data, relevant external data, scenario analysis and factors reflecting the business environment and internal control systems.

Combining these different data sources for model estimation is certainly one of the main challenges in operational risk. Bayesian inference is a statistical technique well suited to incorporating expert opinions into data analysis. There is a broad literature covering Bayesian inference and its applications to the insurance industry as well as to other areas. For a brief introduction to Bayesian statistics, see Chapter 1 of Volume I. Good textbook overviews on Bayesian inference are Berger (1985) and Robert (2001). The methods allow for structural modelling where external data and expert opinions are incorporated into the analysis via specifying distributions (so-called "prior distributions") for model parameters. These are updated by the internal data as it becomes available.

Bayesian methods, in the context of operational risk, have been mentioned briefly in the early literature.[2] However, Bayesian methods did not really merge into operational risk developments until the first decade of the 21st Century. One of the first detailed and illustrative publications of the Bayesian inference methodology for the estimation of operational risk was Shevchenko and Wüthrich (2006). Then, an example of a "toy" model for operational risk, based on the closely related credibility theory, was presented in Bühlmann *et al* (2007). The Bayesian methodology was extended to combine three data sources (expert opinion, internal and external data) in Lambrigger *et al* (2007), and developed further in Peters *et al* (2009) for a multivariate case with dependence modelling between risks. Moreover, it is the main topic of the book by Shevchenko (Forthcoming). Bayesian methods for operational risk is an active research area, as can be seen in recent papers in *The Journal of Operational Risk*.[3] In this chapter, we describe Bayesian techniques within the context of operational risk and provide several examples of its application for operational risk quantification. We demonstrate how three data sources (internal data, external data and expert opinions) can be combined simultaneously.

The organisation of this chapter is as follows. The next section lists several ad hoc approaches used to combine internal data, external data and expert opinions. The third section describes the Bayesian inference framework in the operational risk context. Bayesian model estimation is then reviewed. In the next section we then consider an example of modelling loss frequencies using a standard Bayesian framework combining two data sources. The framework is then extended to combine three data sources (internal data, external data and expert opinions). Estimation of the bank capital against operational risk is described in the penultimate section. Finally, discussions and conclusions are presented.

COMBINING DATA USING HEURISTIC APPROACHES

Often in practice, accounting for factors reflecting the business environment and internal control systems is achieved via scaling of data. Then ad hoc procedures are used to combine internal data, external data and expert opinions. For example:

- fit the severity distribution to the combined samples of internal and external data and fit the frequency distribution using only internal data;

- estimate the Poisson annual intensity for the frequency distribution as $w\lambda_{int} + (1-w)\lambda_{ext}$, where the intensities λ_{ext} and λ_{int} are implied by the external and internal data, respectively, using the expert-specified weight w;

- estimate the severity distribution as a mixture $w_1 F_{SA}(x) + w_2 F_I(x) + w_3 F_E(x)$, where $F_{SA}(x)$, $F_I(x)$ and $F_E(x)$ are the distributions identified by scenario analysis, internal data and external data respectively, using expert specified weights w_1, w_2, $w_3 = 1 - w_1 - w_2 \in [0,1]$;

- use the minimum variance principle – the combined estimator is a linear combination of the individual estimators obtained from internal data, external data and expert opinion separately with the weights chosen to minimise the variance of the combined estimator.

An easy procedure is the minimum variance principle. The rationale behind this principle is as follows. Consider unbiased independent estimators $\hat{\Theta}^{(k)}$ for the parameter θ, ie, $E[\hat{\Theta}^{(k)}] = \theta$ and $\text{var}[\hat{\Theta}^{(k)}] = \sigma_k^2$, $k = 1, \ldots, K$. Then, the combined unbiased linear minimum variance estimator is

$$\hat{\Theta}_{\text{tot}} = w_1 \hat{\Theta}^{(1)} + \cdots + w_K \hat{\Theta}^{(K)}, \quad w_1 + \cdots + w_K = 1 \quad (13.2)$$

and the weights are found by minimising $\text{var}[\hat{\Theta}_{\text{tot}}]$. The explicit expressions for the weights are given by the following theorem (Wüthrich and Merz 2008, Lemma 3.4).

Theorem 13.1 (minimum variance estimator). Assume that we have $\hat{\Theta}^{(1)}, \ldots, \hat{\Theta}^{(K)}$ unbiased and independent estimators of θ with variances $\sigma_k^2 = \text{var}[\Theta^{(k)}]$. Then the unbiased linear estimator Equation 13.2 minimising the variance has weights

$$w_k = \frac{1/\sigma_k^2}{\sum_{i=1}^{K}(1/\sigma_i^2)}. \quad (13.3)$$

Moreover, it has variance

$$\text{var}[\hat{\Theta}_{\text{tot}}] = \left(\sum_{k=1}^{K} \frac{1}{\sigma_k^2} \right)^{-1}$$

The weights behave as expected in practice. In particular, $w_k \to 1$ for $\sigma_k^2 \to 0$. Heuristically, the minimum variance principle can be applied to almost any quantity, eg, distribution parameters or distribution characteristics such as mean, variance, etc. The assumption that the estimators are unbiased for θ is probably reasonable when combining estimators from different experts (or from experts and internal data). However, it is certainly questionable if applied to combine estimators from external and internal data. Below, we focus on Bayesian inference methods that can be used to combine these data sources in a consistent statistical framework.

COMBINING DATA USING THE BAYESIAN APPROACH

In this section we describe the Bayesian inference framework and introduce some notation used throughout this chapter. Consider a random vector of data $X = (X_1, X_2, \ldots, X_K)'$, whose joint density for a given vector of parameters Θ is $f(x \mid \theta)$. In the context of operational risk, X may represent the loss frequencies or severities. We shall use upper-case symbols to represent random variables, lower-case symbols for their realisations and bold symbols for vectors; for example, θ is the realisation of a random variable Θ. In the Bayesian approach, both observations X and parameters Θ are considered to be random. Then, Bayes's Theorem can be formulated as follows

$$f(x, \theta) = f(x \mid \theta)\pi(\theta) = \pi(\theta \mid x)f(x) \quad (13.4)$$

where we have the following notation.

- $f(x, \theta)$ is the joint density of the data X and parameters Θ.
- $f(x \mid \theta)$ is the density of the observations for given parameters Θ.
- $\pi(\theta)$ is the probability density of the parameters Θ, the so-called "prior density function". Typically, $\pi(\theta)$ depends on a set of further parameters, called hyperparameters, which are omitted here for simplicity of notation.
- $\pi(\theta \mid x)$ is the density of parameters given the data X, the so-called "posterior distribution".
- the marginal density of X is given by

$$f(x) = \int f(x \mid \theta)\pi(\theta)\,d\theta$$

Predictive distribution.

The objective is to estimate the predictive distribution of a future observation X_{K+1}, conditional on all available information $X = (X_1, X_2, \ldots, X_K)$. Assume that, conditionally, given $\Theta = \theta$, X_{K+1} and X are independent and X_{K+1} has conditional density $f(x_{K+1} \mid \theta)$. Then, the conditional density of X_{K+1}, given $X = x$, is

$$f(x_{K+1} \mid x) = \int f(x_{K+1} \mid \theta)\pi(\theta \mid x)\,d\theta \quad (13.5)$$

Posterior distribution.

Using Equation 13.4, the posterior density of the parameters Θ can be written as

$$\pi(\theta \mid x) = \frac{f(x \mid \theta)\pi(\theta)}{f(x)} \propto \pi(\theta)f(x \mid \theta) \quad (13.6)$$

Here, the density $f(x \mid \theta)$ is a likelihood function of observations, and $f(x)$ plays the role of the normalising constant. Thus, the posterior distribution can be viewed as a product of a prior knowledge $\pi(\theta)$ with a likelihood function of observed data $f(x \mid \theta)$.

In the context of operational risk, we can go through the following three logical steps.

1. The prior distribution $\pi(\boldsymbol{\theta})$ should be estimated subjectively by expert opinions (the pure Bayesian approach, see page 407) or using external data (the empirical Bayesian approach, see page 408).

2. Then, the prior distribution should be updated with the observed data X using Formula 13.6 to get a posterior density $\pi(\boldsymbol{\theta} \mid x)$.

3. Formula 13.5 is used to calculate the predictive distribution of X_{K+1}, given the data X.

The iterative update procedure for priors.
If the data $X = (X_1, X_2, \ldots, X_K)$ is conditional given $\Theta = \boldsymbol{\theta}$, independent and X_k is distributed with density $f_k(\cdot \mid \boldsymbol{\theta})$, then the likelihood function of X can be written as

$$f(x \mid \boldsymbol{\theta}) = \prod_{i=1}^{K} f_i(x_i \mid \boldsymbol{\theta})$$

Denote the posterior density calculated after k observations as $\pi_k(\boldsymbol{\theta} \mid x_1, \ldots, x_k)$. Then, using Equation 13.6 we have

$$\pi_k(\boldsymbol{\theta} \mid x_1, \ldots, x_k) \propto \pi(\boldsymbol{\theta}) \prod_{i=1}^{k} f_i(x_i \mid \boldsymbol{\theta})$$
$$\propto \pi_{k-1}(\boldsymbol{\theta} \mid x_1, \ldots, x_{k-1}) f_k(x_k \mid \boldsymbol{\theta}) \qquad (13.7)$$

Thus, we obtain an iterative update procedure. Only the posterior distribution calculated after $k-1$ observations and the kth observation are needed to calculate the posterior distribution after k observations. Thus, the entire loss history over many years is not required, making the model easier to understand and manage, and allowing experts to adjust the priors after a new loss has occurred. Formally, the posterior distribution calculated after $k-1$ observations can be treated as a prior distribution for the kth observation. In practice, initially, we start with the prior distribution $\pi(\boldsymbol{\theta})$ identified by expert opinions and external data only. Then, the posterior distribution $\pi(\boldsymbol{\theta} \mid x)$ is calculated, using Equation 13.6, when actual data arrive. If there is a necessity (for example, a new control policy introduced in a bank), then this posterior distribution can be adjusted by an expert and treated as the prior distribution for subsequent observations.

Conjugate prior distributions.
Sometimes the posterior density (Equation 13.6) can be calculated in closed form, which is useful in practice when Bayesian inference is applied. This is the case for so-called conjugate prior distributions, where the prior and posterior distributions are of the same type.

Definition 13.2 (conjugate prior). Let F denote the class of density functions $f(x \mid \boldsymbol{\theta})$, indexed by $\boldsymbol{\theta}$. A class U of prior densities $\pi(\boldsymbol{\theta})$ is said to be a conjugate family for F if the posterior density $\pi(\boldsymbol{\theta} \mid x)$ is in the class U for all $f \in F$ and $\pi \in U$.

Formally, if the family U contains all distribution functions, then it is conjugate to any family F. However, to make a model useful in practice it is important that U should be as small as possible while containing realistic distributions. Below we present the Poisson–Gamma pair. Several other pairs (Binomial–Beta, Gamma–Gamma, exponential–Gamma) can be found, for example, in Bühlmann and Gisler (2005).

ESTIMATING PRIOR PARAMETERS

In general, the parameters of the prior distributions (hyperparameters) can be estimated subjectively using expert opinions (the pure Bayesian approach) or using data (the empirical Bayesian approach).

Pure Bayesian approach

In a pure Bayesian approach, the prior distribution is specified subjectively (that is, in the context of operational risk, using expert opinions only). Part 2 of Volume I is solely devoted to expert judgement and elicitation of subjective probabilities. Moreover, Berger (1985) lists several methods.

- **Histogram approach**: split the parameter space of Θ into cubes and specify the subjective probability for each cube. From this, a smooth density of the prior distribution can be determined.
- **Relative likelihood approach**: compare the intuitive likelihoods of the different values of Θ. Again, the smooth density of prior distribution can be determined. It is difficult to apply this method in the case of unbounded parameters.
- **CDF determinations**: subjectively construct the distribution function for the prior and sketch a smooth curve.

- **Matching a given functional form**: assume some functional form for the prior distribution to match prior beliefs (on the moments, quantiles, etc) as close as possible.

Below, using the method of matching a given function form, we consider the estimation of the prior distribution parameters for the Poisson–Gamma pair. The use of a particular method is determined by a specific problem and expert experience. Usually, if the expected values for the quantiles (or mean) and their uncertainties are estimated by the expert, then it is possible to fit the priors.

Empirical Bayesian approach

Instead of the subjective approach above, the prior distribution can also be estimated empirically from industry data, collective data in the bank, etc. For example, consider a specific risk cell (event type/business line) in J banks with frequency or severity data $X = \{X_{j,k},\ k = 1, \ldots, K_j,\ j = 1, \ldots, J\}$. Here, K_j is the number of observations in bank j. Assume that $X_{j,k}, k = 1, \ldots, K_j$, are conditionally independent and identically distributed (iid) from $f(\cdot \mid \boldsymbol{\theta}_j)$, for given $\boldsymbol{\Theta}_j = \boldsymbol{\theta}_j$. That is, data from different banks are modelled by the same parametric distribution, but with different bank-specific parameter $\boldsymbol{\theta}_j$. Assume now that $\boldsymbol{\Theta}_j, j = 1, \ldots, J$, are iid from $\pi(\cdot)$, that is, we assume that the risk cells of different banks are the same *a priori* (before we have any observations). Then, the likelihood of all observations can be written as

$$\ell(x) = \prod_{j=1}^{J} \int \left[\prod_{k=1}^{K_j} f(x_{j,k} \mid \boldsymbol{\theta}_j) \right] \pi(\boldsymbol{\theta}_j) \, d\boldsymbol{\theta}_j \qquad (13.8)$$

The hyperparameters of $\pi(\cdot)$ can now be estimated by maximising the above likelihood.

EXAMPLE: POISSON–GAMMA CASE

For illustrative purposes we now consider the case of Poisson distributed loss frequencies combined with a Gamma prior distribution. Operational risk severities can be modelled in a similar fashion. For the lognormal–normal–inverse-chi-squared model we refer the reader to Shevchenko and Wüthrich (2006, Appendix A) and for the Pareto–Gamma model we refer the reader to Shevchenko and Wüthrich (2006, Section 3.3).

OPERATIONAL RISK: COMBINING INTERNAL DATA, EXTERNAL DATA AND EXPERT OPINIONS

Model
Consider the following model assumptions.

Assumption 13.3.

- Suppose that, given $\Lambda = \lambda > 0$, frequencies $N_1, \ldots, N_{K+1}$ are independent random variables from a Poisson distribution Poisson(λ), ie, for $k = 1, \ldots, K+1$

$$f(n \mid \lambda) = \Pr[N_k = n \mid \Lambda = \lambda] = e^{-\lambda} \frac{\lambda^n}{n!}, \quad n \in \mathbb{N} \quad (13.9)$$

- The prior distribution for Λ is a Gamma distribution Gamma(α, β) with density

$$\pi(\lambda, \alpha, \beta) = \frac{(\lambda/\beta)^{\alpha-1}}{\Gamma(\alpha)\beta} e^{-\lambda/\beta}, \quad \lambda > 0, \; \alpha > 0, \; \beta > 0 \quad (13.10)$$

where Γ is the Gamma function.

Posterior.
Define $\mathbf{N} = (N_1, \ldots, N_K)$. Given $\Lambda = \lambda$, under Assumption 13.3, $N_1, \ldots, N_K$ are independent and their likelihood is given by

$$h(\mathbf{n} \mid \lambda) = \prod_{i=1}^{K} e^{-\lambda} \frac{\lambda^{n_i}}{n_i!} \quad (13.11)$$

Thus, using Formula 13.6, the posterior density is

$$\pi(\lambda \mid \mathbf{n}) \propto \frac{(\lambda/\beta)^{\alpha-1}}{\Gamma(\alpha)\beta} e^{-\lambda/\beta} \prod_{i=1}^{K} e^{-\lambda} \frac{\lambda^{n_i}}{n_i!} \propto \lambda^{\alpha_K - 1} e^{-\lambda/\beta_K} \quad (13.12)$$

which is Gamma(α_K, β_K) with updated parameters α_K and β_K given by

$$\alpha \to \alpha_K = \alpha + \sum_{i=1}^{K} n_i, \quad \beta \to \beta_K = \frac{\beta}{1 + K\beta} \quad (13.13)$$

Improper constant prior.
It is easy to see that if the prior is improper constant,[4] ie, $\pi(\lambda \mid \mathbf{n}) \propto h(\mathbf{n} \mid \lambda)$, then the posterior is Gamma(α_K, β_K) with

$$\alpha_K = 1 + \sum_{i=1}^{K} n_i, \quad \beta_K = \frac{1}{K} \quad (13.14)$$

In this case, the mode of the posterior density $\pi(\lambda \mid n)$, referred to as the maximum *a posteriori* (MAP) estimate, is

$$\hat{\lambda}_K^{\text{MAP}} = (\alpha_K - 1)\beta_K = \frac{1}{K}\sum_{i=1}^{K} n_i \qquad (13.15)$$

which is the same as the maximum likelihood estimate (MLE) $\hat{\lambda}_K^{\text{MLE}}$ of λ.

Full predictive distribution.
Now we can calculate the predictive distribution of the loss frequency of the next period, eg, the forthcoming year, given the observed loss frequencies N and the prior information. Given $N = (N_1, \ldots, N_K)$, the full predictive distribution for N_{K+1} is negative binomial, $\text{NegBin}(\alpha_K, 1/(1+\beta_K))^5$

$$\Pr[N_{K+1} = m \mid N = n]$$
$$= \int f(m \mid \lambda)\pi(\lambda \mid n)\,d\lambda$$
$$= \frac{\Gamma(\alpha_K + m)}{\Gamma(\alpha_K)m!}\left(\frac{1}{1+\beta_K}\right)^{\alpha_K}\left(\frac{\beta_K}{1+\beta_K}\right)^m \qquad (13.16)$$

This is valid for both Gamma and improper constant priors. The following gives an intuitive interpretation

$$E[N_{K+1} \mid N = n] = E[\Lambda \mid N = n] = \alpha_K \beta_K = w_K \hat{\lambda}_K^{\text{MLE}} + (1 - w_K)\lambda_0 \qquad (13.17)$$

where

- $\hat{\lambda}_K^{\text{MLE}} = (1/K)\sum_{i=1}^{K} n_i$ is the MLE estimate of λ using the observations only;
- $\lambda_0 = \alpha\beta$ is the estimate of λ using a prior knowledge only (eg, specified by expert);
- $w_K = \beta K/(1 + \beta K)$ is the credibility weight used to combine λ_0 and $\hat{\lambda}_K^{\text{MLE}}$.

Remark 13.4.

- As the number of years K increases, the credibility weight w_K increases and vice versa. That is, the more observations we have, the larger the credibility weight we assign to the estimator based on the observed counts, while the lesser credibility weight is attached to the expert opinion estimate. Also, the larger the volatility of the expert opinion (larger β), the larger the credibility weight assigned to the observations.

- Recursive calculation of the posterior distribution is very simple. The update of information from $n_1, n_2, \ldots, n_{k-1}$ to $n_1, n_2, \ldots, n_k$ is given by

$$\alpha_k = \alpha_{k-1} + n_k, \qquad \beta_k = \frac{\beta_{k-1}}{1 + \beta_{k-1}} \qquad (13.18)$$

This leads to an efficient recursive scheme, where the calculation of posterior distribution parameters is based on the most recent observation and parameters of posterior distribution calculated just before this observation.

Pure Bayesian approach

We now have to determine the hyperparameters α and β of the prior distribution used in Assumption 13.3. The expert may estimate the expected number of events $E[\Lambda] = \lambda_0 = \alpha\beta$ but cannot have full confidence in the estimate. If the expert specifies $E[\Lambda]$ and an uncertainty that the "true" λ for next year is within the interval $[a, b]$ with probability $\Pr[a \leqslant \Lambda \leqslant b] = p$, then the equations

$$\left.\begin{array}{l} E[\Lambda] = \alpha\beta \\ \Pr[a \leqslant \Lambda \leqslant b] = p = \displaystyle\int_a^b \pi(\lambda)\, d\lambda = F^{(\Gamma)}_{\alpha,\beta}(b) - F^{(\Gamma)}_{\alpha,\beta}(a) \end{array}\right\} \qquad (13.19)$$

can be solved numerically to estimate the hyperparameters α and β. Here, $F^{(\Gamma)}_{\alpha,\beta}(\cdot)$ is the Gamma distribution $\text{Gamma}(\alpha, \beta)$.

This is not the only way to assess the hyperparameters. For instance, in the insurance industry, the uncertainty for the "true" λ is often measured in terms of the coefficient of variation

$$\text{Vco}[\Lambda] = \sqrt{\text{var}(\Lambda)}/E[\Lambda]$$

Hence, instead of using Equation 13.19, the hyperparameters α and β can alternatively be computed given the expert estimates for $E[\Lambda] = \alpha\beta$ and $\text{Vco}[\Lambda] = 1/\sqrt{\alpha}$.

Example 13.5 (numerical illustration). If the expert specifies $E[\Lambda] = 0.5$ and $\Pr[0.25 \leqslant \Lambda \leqslant 0.75] = \frac{2}{3}$, then we can fit a prior distribution, $\text{Gamma}(\alpha = 3.407, \beta = 0.147)$ by solving Equation 13.19. Assume now that the bank experienced no losses over the first year (after the prior distribution was estimated). Then, using Equation 13.18, the

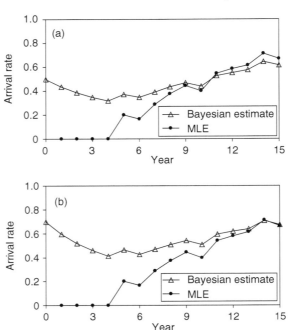

Figure 13.1 The Bayesian and the standard maximum likelihood estimates of the arrival rate versus the observation year

The Bayesian estimate is a mean of the posterior distribution when the prior distribution is Gamma with (a) $E[\Lambda] = 0.5$ and $\Pr[0.25 \leqslant \Lambda \leqslant 0.75] = \frac{2}{3}$, (b) $E[\Lambda] = 0.7$ and $\text{Vco}[\Lambda] = 0.5$. The annual counts were sampled from Poisson(0.6) and are given in Table 13.1. See Example 13.5 for details.

posterior distribution parameters are $\hat{\alpha}_1 = 3.407 + 0 = 3.407$, $\hat{\beta}_1 = 0.147/(1 + 0.147) = 0.128$ and the estimated arrival rate using the posterior distribution is $\hat{\lambda}_1 = \hat{\alpha}_1 \hat{\beta}_1 = 0.436$. If during the next year no losses are observed again, then the posterior distribution parameters are $\hat{\alpha}_2 = \hat{\alpha}_1 + 0 = 3.407$, $\hat{\beta}_2 = \hat{\beta}_1/(1 + \hat{\beta}_1) = 0.113$ and $\hat{\lambda}_2 = \hat{\alpha}_2 \hat{\beta}_2 = 0.385$. Subsequent observations will update the arrival rate estimator correspondingly using Equation 13.18. Thus, starting from the expert specified prior, observations regularly update (refine) the posterior distribution.

In Figure 13.1, we compare the Bayesian method for estimating the arrival rate of the losses (using two different prior distributions) with the classical maximum likelihood approach. In Figure 13.1(a), we show the posterior mean for the arrival rate $\hat{\lambda}_k = \hat{\alpha}_k \hat{\beta}_k$, $k = 1, \ldots, 15$

Table 13.1 The annual number of losses simulated from Poisson(0.6)

i	n_i	i	n_i
1	0	9	1
2	0	10	0
3	0	11	2
4	0	12	1
5	1	13	1
6	0	14	2
7	1	15	0
8	1		

(with the prior distribution as specified in the above example), when the annual number of events N_k, $k = 1, \ldots, 15$, is simulated from Poisson($\lambda = 0.6$) and given in Table 13.1.

In the same figure, we show the standard MLE of the arrival rate as a function of the year k

$$\hat{\lambda}_k^{MLE} = \frac{1}{k} \sum_{i=1}^{k} n_i$$

After approximately eight years, the estimators are very close to each other. However, for a small number of observed years, the Bayesian estimate is more accurate, as it takes the prior information into account. After 12 years, both estimators are close to the true value of 0.6. Note that for this example we assumed the prior distribution with a mean equal to 0.5, which is different from the true arrival rate, 0.6. Thus, this example shows that an initially incorrect prior estimator is corrected by the observations as they become available. It is interesting to observe that, in year 14, the estimators become slightly different again. This is because the bank unluckily experienced event counts 1, 1 and 2 in years 12, 13 and 14, respectively. As a result, the MLE becomes higher than the true value, while the Bayesian estimate is more stable (smooth) in respect to the unlucky years. If this example is repeated with different sequences of random numbers, then we would observe quite different MLEs (for small k) and more stable Bayesian estimates. For comparison, Figure 13.1(b) shows the example where the expert specifies $E[\Lambda] = 0.7$ and $Vco[\Lambda] = 0.5$, which gives the prior parameters $\alpha = 4$ and $\beta = 0.175$.

Empirical Bayesian approach

It is not difficult to include *a priori* known differences (for example, exposure indicators, expert opinions on the differences, etc) between the risk cells from the different banks. As an example, we consider the case when the annual frequency of the events is modelled by the Poisson distribution with the Gamma prior and estimate the hyperparameters, α and β, using the industry data with differences between the banks taken into account.

Assumption 13.6. Consider a risk cell in J banks with the annual frequencies $N_{j,k}$, $k = 1, \ldots, K_j + 1$, $j = 1, \ldots, J$, where $K_j + 1$ refers to the next year. Set $\mathbf{N}_j = (N_{j,1}, \ldots, N_{j,K_j+1})$ and assume the following.

- Given bank-specific intensities $\Lambda_j = \lambda_j$, $\mathbf{N}_j$ satisfies Assumption 13.3 with $N_{j,k}$ from $\mathrm{Poisson}(\lambda_j V_{j,k})$, where $V_{j,k} > 0$ is a fixed volume measure, which can be used to account for *a priori* known inhomogeneities of the loss frequencies between different years as well as different banks.

- $\Lambda_1, \ldots, \Lambda_J$ are assumed to be iid from $\mathrm{Gamma}(\alpha, \beta)$ (see Equation 13.10) and $(\Lambda_1, \mathbf{N}_1), \ldots, (\Lambda_J, \mathbf{N}_J)$ are independent.

Set
$$N_j = \sum_{k=1}^{K_j} N_{j,k}, \qquad V_j = \sum_{k=1}^{K_j} V_{j,k}$$

Then, the likelihood of all available data (over all J banks), $\mathbf{N} = \{N_{j,k} : j = 1, \ldots, J;\ k = 1, \ldots, K_j\}$, can be written as

$$\ell(n) = \prod_{j=1}^{J} \int \left[\prod_{k=1}^{K_j} f(n_{j,k} \mid \lambda_j) \right] \pi(\lambda_j)\, d\lambda_j$$

$$\propto \prod_{j=1}^{J} \frac{\Gamma(\alpha + n_j)}{\Gamma(\alpha)\beta^{\alpha}(V_j + 1/\beta)^{\alpha+n_j}} \qquad (13.20)$$

The hyperparameters, α and β, can now be estimated by maximising the log-likelihood

$$\ln \ell \propto \sum_{j=1}^{J} \left\{ \ln \Gamma(\alpha + n_j) - \ln \Gamma(\alpha) \right.$$
$$\left. - \alpha \ln \beta - (\alpha + n_j) \ln\left(\frac{1}{\beta} + V_j\right) \right\} \qquad (13.21)$$

To fit the parameters but avoid the use of numerical optimisation required for maximising Equation 13.21, we could also use a method of moments using the following proposition.

Proposition 13.7 (method of moments). Given Assumption 13.6, define $\lambda_0 = E[\Lambda_j] = \alpha\beta$, $\sigma_0^2 = \text{var}[\Lambda_j] = \alpha\beta^2$. Then estimates $\hat{\lambda}_0$ and $\hat{\sigma}_0^2$ for λ_0 and σ_0^2, respectively, are

$$\hat{\lambda}_0 = \frac{1}{J}\sum_{j=1}^{J}\hat{\lambda}_j, \quad \hat{\lambda}_j = \frac{1}{K_j}\sum_{k=1}^{K_j}\frac{n_{j,k}}{V_{j,k}}, \quad j = 1,\ldots,J$$

$$\hat{\sigma}_0^2 = \max\left\{\frac{1}{J-1}\sum_{j=1}^{J}(\hat{\lambda}_j - \hat{\lambda}_0)^2 - \frac{\hat{\lambda}_0}{J}\sum_{j=1}^{J}\frac{1}{K_j^2}\sum_{k=1}^{K_j}\frac{1}{V_{j,k}}, 0\right\}$$

The above proposition can easily be used to estimate α and β as $\hat{\alpha} = \hat{\lambda}_0/\hat{\beta}$ and $\hat{\beta} = \hat{\sigma}_0^2/\hat{\lambda}_0$, correspondingly. For a proof, see Shevchenko and Wüthrich (2006). Alternative unbiased moment estimators are given in Bühlmann and Gisler (2005, Section 4.10).

Once the prior distribution parameters α and β are estimated, then the posterior distributions of λ_j of the different banks are Gamma($\hat{\alpha}_j, \hat{\beta}_j$), calculated similarly to Equation 13.12 with parameters

$$\hat{\alpha}_j = \alpha + \sum_{k=1}^{K_j} n_{j,k}, \quad \hat{\beta}_j = \beta\left(1 + \beta\sum_{k=1}^{K_j} V_{j,k}\right)^{-1} \quad (13.22)$$

The predictive distributions of the annual frequency N_{j,K_j+1} for the next year are negative binomial

$$\text{NegBin}\left(\hat{\alpha}_j, \hat{p}_j = \frac{1}{1 + V_{j,K_j+1}\hat{\beta}_j}\right)$$

(see Equation 13.16). Here, V_{j,K_j+1} is a volume measure for the next year in the jth bank.

Remark 13.8. Observe that in Assumption 13.6 we have scaled the parameters λ_j by $V_{j,k}$ for considering *a priori* differences. This leads to a linear volume relation for the variance function. To obtain different functional relations, it might be better to scale the actual observations. For example, given observations $X_{j,k}, j = 1,\ldots,J$, $k = 1,\ldots,K_j$ (these could be frequencies or severities), consider variables $Y_{j,k} = X_{j,k}/V_{j,k}$. Assume that, for given θ_j, $Y_{j,k}, k = 1,\ldots,K_j$, are iid from $f(\cdot \mid \theta_j)$. Also, assume that $\Theta_1,\ldots,\Theta_J$ are iid from $\pi(\cdot)$. Then we can construct the likelihood of $Y_{j,k}$ using Equation 13.8 to fit parameters of $\pi(\cdot)$ or try to use the method of moments.

COMBINING EXPERT OPINIONS, EXTERNAL AND INTERNAL DATA

In order to estimate the risk capital of a bank to fulfil the Basel II requirements, risk managers have to take into account internal data, relevant external data (industry data) and expert opinions. It was shown in previous sections how to combine two data sources: internal data and the prior information (obtained from either external data or expert opinions), using the classical Bayesian approach. The aim of this section is to provide an example of Bayesian methodology that can be used to combine three sources of information: internal data, external data and expert opinions. Here, we follow the approach suggested in Lambrigger *et al* (2007). As in the previous section, we consider one risk cell only. From the methodological side we go through the following steps.

1. In any risk cell, we model the loss frequency and the loss severity by a parametric distribution (eg, Poisson distribution for the frequency and Pareto distribution for the severity). For the bank considered, the unknown parameters $\boldsymbol{\theta}_0$ (eg, the Poisson parameter or the Pareto tail index) of these distributions have to be quantified.

2. *A priori*, before we have any company specific information, only industry data is available. Hence, the best estimate of our bank-specific parameter $\boldsymbol{\theta}_0$ is given by the belief in the available industry data. The unknown parameter of interest is modelled by a prior distribution corresponding to a random vector $\boldsymbol{\Theta}$. The parameters of the prior distribution are estimated using industry data by, eg, maximum likelihood estimation, as described in the section on the empirical Bayesian approach (see page 408). If no industry data is available, the prior distribution could come from a "super expert" that has an overview over all banks or we choose a non-informative prior distribution with high variance.

3. In our terminology, we treat the true bank-specific parameter $\boldsymbol{\theta}_0$ as a realisation of $\boldsymbol{\Theta}$. The prior distribution of a random vector $\boldsymbol{\Theta}$ corresponds to the whole banking industry sector, whereas $\boldsymbol{\theta}_0$ stands for the unknown underlying parameter set of the bank being considered. Due to the variability amongst banks, it is natural to model $\boldsymbol{\Theta}$ by a probability distribution.

OPERATIONAL RISK: COMBINING INTERNAL DATA, EXTERNAL DATA AND EXPERT OPINIONS

Note that Θ is random with known distribution, whereas θ_0 is deterministic but unknown.

4. Over time, internal data $X = (X_1, \ldots, X_K)$ as well as expert opinions $\Delta = (\Delta_1, \ldots, \Delta_M)$ about the underlying parameter θ_0 become available. This affects our belief in the distribution of Θ coming from external data only and adjusts the prediction of θ_0. The more information X and Δ we have, the better we are able to predict θ_0. That is, we replace the prior density $\pi(\theta)$ by a conditional density of Θ given $X = x$ and $\Delta = \delta$, denoted by $\pi(\theta \mid x, \delta)$, which is also called the posterior density.

In order to determine the posterior density $\pi(\theta \mid x, \delta)$ we have to introduce some notation. The joint conditional density of observations and expert opinions given the parameter vector θ is denoted by

$$h(x, \delta \mid \theta) = h_1(x \mid \theta) h_2(\delta \mid \theta) \qquad (13.23)$$

where h_1 and h_2 are the conditional densities (given $\Theta = \theta$) of X and Δ, respectively. Thus, X and Δ are assumed to be conditionally independent given θ.

Remark 13.9.

- Notice that, in this way, we naturally combine external data information $\pi(\theta)$ with internal data X and expert opinion Δ.

- Formula 13.23 is quite a reasonable assumption: we assume that the true bank-specific parameter is θ_0. Then Equation 13.23 says that the experts in this bank estimate θ_0 (by their opinion δ) independently of the internal observations. This makes sense if the experts specify their opinions regardless of the data observed. Otherwise we should work with the joint distribution $h(x, \delta \mid \theta)$.

We further assume that different observations as well as expert opinions are conditionally iid, given $\Theta = \theta$, so that

$$h_1(x \mid \theta) = \prod_{k=1}^{K} f_1(x_k \mid \theta) \qquad (13.24)$$

$$h_2(\delta \mid \theta) = \prod_{m=1}^{M} f_2(\delta_m \mid \theta) \qquad (13.25)$$

where f_1 and f_2 are the marginal densities of a single observation and a single expert opinion, respectively. We have assumed that all expert opinions are iid, but this can be generalised easily to expert opinions having different distributions or experts whose opinions are dependent.

Let $h(x, \delta)$ denote the unconditional joint density of the data X and expert opinions Δ. Then it follows from Bayes's Theorem that

$$h(x, \delta \mid \theta)\pi(\theta) = \pi(\theta \mid x, \delta) h(x, \delta) \quad (13.26)$$

Note that the unconditional density $h(x, \delta)$ does not depend on θ. Thus, using Equations 13.23–13.25, the posterior density is given by

$$\pi(\theta \mid x, \delta) \propto \pi(\theta) \prod_{k=1}^{K} f_1(x_k \mid \theta) \prod_{m=1}^{M} f_2(\delta_m \mid \theta) \quad (13.27)$$

For the purposes of operational risk, it is used to estimate the full predictive distribution of future losses. Hereafter, we assume that the parameters of the prior $\pi(\cdot)$ are known and we look at a single risk cell in one bank.

Conjugate prior extension

Equation 13.27 can be used in a general set-up, but it is convenient to find conjugate prior distributions such that the prior and the posterior distribution have a similar type, or where, at least, the posterior distribution can be calculated analytically. For the case of Equation 13.27, the standard definition of the conjugate prior distributions can be extended as follows.

Definition 13.10 (conjugate prior distribution). Let F denote the class of density functions $h(x, \delta \mid \theta)$, indexed by θ. A class U of prior densities $\pi(\theta)$ is said to be a "conjugate family" for F if the posterior density $\pi(\theta \mid x, \delta) \propto \pi(\theta) h(x, \delta \mid \theta)$ also belongs to the class U for all $h \in F$ and $\pi \in U$.

Remark 13.11. We work with conjugate priors because in such situations the posterior distribution can be calculated analytically. In general, this is not the case and we apply simulation methods, such as the Markov chain Monte Carlo (MCMC), Gibbs and Importance Sampling methods (Gilks et al 1996).[6]

OPERATIONAL RISK: COMBINING INTERNAL DATA, EXTERNAL DATA AND EXPERT OPINIONS

Modelling loss frequency: Poisson model

To model the loss frequency for operational risk in a risk cell, consider the following model.

Assumption 13.12 (Poisson–Gamma–Gamma). Assume that a risk cell in a bank has a volume factor V for the frequency in a specified risk cell.

(a) Assume that the prior distribution for the loss frequency is given by a Gamma distribution $\Lambda \sim \text{Gamma}(\alpha_0, \beta_0)$ with shape parameter $\alpha_0 > 0$ and scale parameter $\beta_0 > 0$.

(b) The number of losses N_k in year k, $1 \leqslant k \leqslant K+1$, are assumed to be conditionally, given $\Lambda = \lambda$, iid Poisson distributed with intensity $V\lambda$, ie, $N_k \mid \Lambda \sim \text{Poisson}(V\lambda)$.

(c) The financial company has M expert opinions Δ_m, $1 \leqslant m \leqslant M$. Given $\Lambda = \lambda$, $\Delta_m \mid \Lambda \stackrel{\text{iid}}{\sim} \text{Gamma}(\xi, \lambda/\xi)$, for $\xi > 0$ fixed.

(d) Given Λ, frequencies $N_1, \ldots, N_{K+1}$ and expert opinions $\Delta_1, \ldots, \Delta_M$ are independent.

Remark 13.13.

- The hyperparameters α_0 and β_0 in Assumption 13.12(a) can be estimated using the maximum likelihood method or the method of moments from external data (see page 414).

- In Assumption 13.12(c) we assume

$$E[\Delta_m \mid \Lambda] = \Lambda, \quad 1 \leqslant m \leqslant M \quad (13.28)$$

that is, expert opinions are unbiased. A possible bias might be recognised by the regulator, as they alone have an overview of the whole market.

- Note that

$$\text{Vco}[\Delta_m \mid \Lambda] = \frac{(\text{var}[\Delta_m \mid \Lambda])^{1/2}}{E[\Delta_m \mid \Lambda]} = \frac{1}{\sqrt{\xi}}$$

is independent of Λ. Therefore, ξ is the parameter for the relative expert opinion uncertainty, which can be estimated from the observed sample of expert opinions by

$$\hat{\xi} = \left(\frac{\hat{\mu}}{\hat{\sigma}}\right)^2 \quad (13.29)$$

where

$$\hat{\mu} = \frac{1}{M}\sum_{m=1}^{M} \delta_m \quad \text{and} \quad \hat{\sigma}^2 = \frac{1}{M-1}\sum_{m=1}^{M}(\delta_m - \hat{\mu})^2, \quad M \geq 2$$

In the insurance practice ξ is often specified by the regulator denoting a lower bound for expert opinion uncertainty (eg, the Swiss Solvency Test[7]).

We now calculate the posterior density of Λ, given two types of information, namely the losses up to year K and the expert opinion of M experts. We introduce the following notation for the loss database and the experts

$$\mathbf{N} = (N_1, \ldots, N_K), \qquad \mathbf{\Delta} = (\Delta_1, \ldots, \Delta_M)$$

Here and in what follows, we denote arithmetic means by

$$\bar{n} = \frac{1}{K}\sum_{k=1}^{K} n_k, \qquad \bar{\delta} = \frac{1}{M}\sum_{m=1}^{M} \delta_m \qquad (13.30)$$

etc. The posterior density is given by the following theorem.

Theorem 13.14. Under Assumption 13.12, given loss information $\mathbf{N} = \mathbf{n}$ and expert opinion $\mathbf{\Delta} = \mathbf{\delta}$, the posterior density of Λ is

$$\pi(\lambda \mid \mathbf{n}, \mathbf{\delta}) = \frac{(\omega/\phi)^{(\nu+1)/2}}{2K_{\nu+1}(2\sqrt{\omega\phi})}\lambda^\nu e^{-\lambda\omega - \lambda^{-1}\phi} \qquad (13.31)$$

with

$$\left.\begin{array}{l} \nu = \alpha_0 - 1 - M\xi + K\bar{n} \\ \omega = VK + \dfrac{1}{\beta_0} \\ \phi = \xi M\bar{\delta} \end{array}\right\} \qquad (13.32)$$

and

$$K_{\nu+1}(z) = \frac{1}{2}\int_0^\infty u^\nu e^{-z(u+1/u)/2}\,du \qquad (13.33)$$

$K_\nu(z)$ is called a modified Bessel function of the third kind.[8]

Proof Set $\alpha = \xi$ and $\beta = \lambda/\xi$. Assumptions 13.12 applied to Equation 13.27 yield

$$\pi(\lambda \mid \boldsymbol{n}, \boldsymbol{\delta}) \propto \lambda^{\alpha_0-1} e^{-\lambda/\beta_0} \prod_{k=1}^{K} e^{-V\lambda} \frac{(V\lambda)^{n_k}}{n_k!} \prod_{m=1}^{M} \frac{\delta_m^{\alpha-1}}{\beta^\alpha} e^{-\delta_m/\beta}$$

$$\propto \lambda^{\alpha_0-1} e^{-\lambda/\beta_0} \prod_{k=1}^{K} e^{-V\lambda} \lambda^{n_k} \prod_{m=1}^{M} (\xi/\lambda)^\xi e^{-\delta_m \xi/\lambda}$$

$$\propto \lambda^{\alpha_0-1-M\xi+K\bar{n}} \exp\left(-\lambda\left(VK + \frac{1}{\beta_0}\right) - \frac{1}{\lambda}\xi M \bar{\delta}\right)$$
(13.34)

□

Remark 13.15.

- A distribution with the density given by Equation 13.31 is referred to as the generalised inverse Gaussian distribution $GIG(\omega, \phi, \nu)$. This is a well-known distribution with many applications in finance and risk management (McNeil *et al* 2005, pp. 75 and 497). The GIG has been analysed by many authors. A discussion is found, for example, in Jørgensen (1982). The algorithm for generating realisations from a GIG is provided in Dagpunar (1989).[9]

- In comparison with the classical Poisson–Gamma case of combining two sources of information (considered on page 408 onwards), where the posterior is a Gamma distribution, the posterior $\pi(\lambda \mid \cdot)$ in Equation 13.34 is more complicated. In the exponent, it involves both λ and $1/\lambda$.

- Observe that the classical exponential dispersion family with associated conjugate priors (Bühlmann and Gisler 2005, Chapter 2.5) allows for a natural extension to GIG-like distributions. In this sense, the GIG distributions enlarge the classical Bayesian inference theory on the exponential dispersion family.

It is interesting to observe how the posterior density transforms when new data from a newly observed year arrives. Let ν_k, ω_k and ϕ_k denote the parameters for the data $(N_1, \ldots, N_k)$ after k accounting years. Implementation of the update processes is then given by the following equalities (assuming that expert opinions do not change).

Information update process.
Year $k \to$ year $k+1$

$$v_{k+1} = v_k + n_{k+1}$$
$$\omega_{k+1} = \omega_k + V$$
$$\phi_{k+1} = \phi_k$$

Obviously, the information update process has a very simple form and only the parameter v is affected by the new observation N_{k+1}. The posterior density (Equation 13.34) does not change its type every time new data arrives and, hence, is easily calculated.

The moments of a GIG are not available in a closed form through elementary functions but can be expressed in terms of Bessel functions. In particular, the posterior expected number of losses is

$$E[\Lambda \mid N = n, \Delta = \delta] = \sqrt{\frac{\phi}{\omega} \frac{K_{v+2}(2\sqrt{\omega\phi})}{K_{v+1}(2\sqrt{\omega\phi})}} \qquad (13.35)$$

The mode of a GIG has a simple expression

$$\text{mode}(\Lambda \mid N = n, \Delta = \delta) = \frac{1}{2\omega}(v + \sqrt{v^2 + 4\omega\phi}) \qquad (13.36)$$

It can be used as an alternative point estimator instead of the mean. Also, the mode of a GIG differs only slightly from the expected value for large $|v|$.

We are clearly interested in a robust estimator of the bank-specific Poisson parameter Λ and thus the Bayesian estimator (Equation 13.35) is a promising candidate. The examples below show that, in practice, Equation 13.35 outperforms other classical estimators. To interpret Equation 13.35 in more detail, we make use of asymptotic properties. Using properties of Bessel functions, we can show that

$$R_{v^2}(2v) \to v, \quad \text{as } v \to \infty$$

where $R_v(z) = K_{v+1}(z)/K_v(z)$.[10] Using this result, a full asymptotic interpretation of the Bayesian estimator (Equation 13.35) can be found as follows.

Theorem 13.16 (Lambrigger *et al* 2007, Theorem 3.6). Under Assumption 13.12, the following asymptotic relations hold, *P*-almost surely.

(a) For $K \to \infty$: $E[\Lambda \mid N, \Delta] \to E[N_k \mid \Lambda = \lambda]/V = \lambda$.
(b) For $\text{Vco}[\Delta_m \mid \Lambda] \to 0$: $E[\Lambda \mid N, \Delta] \to \Delta_m, m = 1, \ldots, M$.

(c) For $M \to \infty$: $E[\Lambda \mid N, \Delta] \to E[\Delta_m \mid \Lambda = \lambda] = \lambda$.

(d) For $\text{Vco}[\Delta_m \mid \Lambda] \to \infty$, $m = 1, \ldots, M$

$$E[\Lambda \mid N, \Delta] \to \frac{1}{VK\beta_0 + 1} E[\Lambda] + \frac{1}{V}\left(1 - \frac{1}{VK\beta_0 + 1}\right)\overline{N}$$

(e) For $E[\Lambda] = $ constant and $\text{Vco}[\Lambda] \to 0$: $E[\Lambda \mid N, \Delta] \to E[\Lambda]$.

Remark 13.17. The GIG mode and mean are asymptotically the same for $\nu \to \infty$; also $4\omega\phi/\nu^2 \to 0$ for $K \to \infty$, $M \to \infty$, $M \to 0$ or $\xi \to 0$. Then we can approximate the posterior mode as

$$\text{mode}(\Lambda \mid N = n, \Delta = \delta) \approx \frac{\nu}{2\omega} \mathbf{1}_{\{\nu \geq 0\}} + \frac{\phi}{|\nu|} \quad (13.37)$$

and obtain the results of Theorem 13.16 in an elementary manner avoiding Bessel functions.

Theorem 13.16 shows that the model behaves as we would expect and require in practice, namely that credibility is given to reliable sources of information. Thus, there are good reasons to believe that it provides an adequate model to combine internal observations with relevant external data and expert opinions, as required by many risk managers. We may even go further and generalise the results from this section in a natural way to a Poisson–Gamma–GIG model, ie, where the prior distribution is a GIG. Then the posterior distribution is again a GIG (see also Remarks 13.23).

Example 13.18. A simple example, taken from Lambrigger et al (2007, Example 3.7) illustrates the above methodology for combining three data sources. It also extends Example 13.5 as shown in Figure 13.1, where two data sources are combined using the classical Bayesian inference approach. Assume the following.

- External data (eg, provided by an external database or the regulator) are used to estimate the intensity of the loss frequency by a prior Gamma distribution $\Lambda \sim \text{Gamma}(\alpha_0, \beta_0)$, as $E[\Lambda] = \alpha_0 \beta_0 = 0.5$ and $\Pr[0.25 \leq \Lambda \leq 0.75] = \frac{2}{3}$. Then, the parameters of the prior are $\alpha_0 = 3.407$ and $\beta_0 = 0.147$ (see Example 13.5).

- One expert gives an estimate of the intensity as $\delta = 0.7$. For simplicity, we consider in this example a single expert only and, hence, the coefficient of variation is given *a priori* (eg, by the regulator) by

$$\mathrm{Vco}[\Delta \mid \Lambda] = \frac{\sqrt{\mathrm{var}[\Delta \mid \Lambda]}}{E[\Delta \mid \Lambda]} = 0.5$$

ie, $\xi = 4$.

- The observations of the annual number of losses, $N_1, N_2, \ldots$, are sampled from Poisson(0.6) and are the same as in Example 13.5, ie, those given in Table 13.1.

This means that *a priori* we have a frequency parameter Λ distributed with mean $\alpha_0 \beta_0 = 0.5$. The true value of the parameter λ for this risk in our bank is 0.6, ie, it does worse than the average institution. However, our expert has an even worse opinion of their institution, namely $\delta = 0.7$. Now, we compare the following.

- The pure MLE

$$\hat{\lambda}_k^{\mathrm{MLE}} = \frac{1}{k} \sum_{i=1}^{k} n_i$$

- The Bayesian estimate (Equation 13.17)

$$\hat{\lambda}_k^{(2)} = E[\Lambda \mid N_1 = n_1, \ldots, N_k = n_k] \qquad (13.38)$$

which combines internal data with the prior distribution. The latter in this example is assumed to be estimated from external data or provided by the regulator. Note that in Example 13.5, the prior was assumed to be determined from expert opinion only.

- The Bayesian estimate derived in Formula 13.35

$$\hat{\lambda}_k^{(3)} = E[\Lambda \mid N_1 = n_1, \ldots, N_k = n_k, \Delta = \delta] \qquad (13.39)$$

which combines internal data and expert opinions with the prior.

The results are plotted in Figure 13.2(a). The estimator $\hat{\lambda}_k^{(3)}$ shows a much more stable behaviour around the true value $\lambda = 0.6$, due to the use of the prior information (market data) and the expert opinions. Given adequate expert opinions, $\hat{\lambda}_k^{(3)}$ clearly outperforms the other estimators, particularly if only a few data points are available.

We may think that this is only the case when the experts' estimates are appropriate. However, even if experts fairly underestimate (or

Figure 13.2 Bayesian and the standard maximum likelihood estimates of the arrival rate versus the observation year

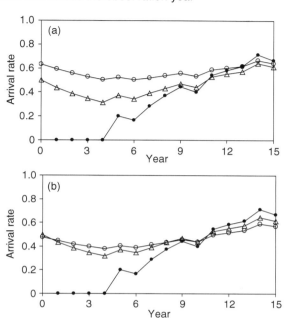

Open circles denote the Bayes estimate $\hat{\lambda}_k^{(3)}$, $k = 1, \ldots, 15$, combining the internal data simulated from $\mathrm{Poisson}(0.6)$, external data giving $E[\Lambda] = 0.5$ and expert opinion δ. Triangles denote the Bayes estimate $\hat{\lambda}_k^{(2)}$ that combines external data and internal data and closed circles denote the classical maximum likelihood estimate $\hat{\lambda}_k^{\mathrm{MLE}}$. The expert opinions are (a) $\delta = 0.7$ and (b) $\delta = 0.4$. See Example 13.18 for details.

overestimate) the true parameter λ, the method presented here performs better for our data set than the other methods mentioned when little data is available. Figure 13.2(b) displays the same estimators, but here the expert's opinion is $\delta = 0.4$, which clearly underestimates the true expected value 0.6.

The above example yields a typical picture observed in numerical experiments that demonstrates that the Bayes estimator (Equation 13.35) is often more suitable and stable than maximum likelihood estimators based only on internal data.

Remark 13.19. Note that in this example both the prior distribution and the expert opinion do not change over time. However, as soon as new information is available or when new risk management tools are in place, the corresponding parameters of $\pi(\lambda \mid N, \Delta)$ may easily be adjusted.

Remark 13.20 (Poisson with stochastic intensity). It is more realistic to assume that the Poisson intensity is not only different for different banks and different risks but also changes from year to year for the same risk in the same bank. Consider the annual number of events for a risk in one bank in year t modelled as random variable from a Poisson distribution Poisson$(\Lambda_t = \lambda_t)$. Conditional on Λ_t, the expected number of events per year is Λ_t. In general, $(\Lambda_t)_{t \geqslant 0}$ is a stochastic process that can be modelled having deterministic (trend, seasonality) and stochastic components. A simple case when $(\Lambda_t)_{t \geqslant 0}$ is purely stochastic and distributed according to a Gamma distribution was considered in Peters *et al* (2009).

Modelling loss severities: Pareto model

We now turn to the quantification of the severity distribution for operational risk. In general, we can use the methodology summarised by Equation 13.27 to develop a model combining external data, internal data and expert opinion for the estimation of the severity. Here we consider the Pareto severity example studied in Lambrigger *et al* (2007).

Consider modelling severities $X_1, \ldots, X_K$ using a Pareto distribution Pareto(θ, L) with threshold $L > 0$, tail parameter $\theta > 0$ and density

$$f(x) = \frac{\theta}{L}\left(\frac{x}{L}\right)^{-\theta-1}, \quad x \geqslant L \quad (13.40)$$

Note that if $\theta > 1$, the mean is $L\theta/(\theta-1)$; otherwise the mean does not exist. Here, we take an approach where θ is unknown and the threshold L is known. The unknown θ is treated under the Bayesian approach as a random variable Θ. Then, the combination of external data, internal data and expert opinions can be accomplished using the following model.

Assumption 13.21 (Pareto–Gamma–Gamma). Assume that for a risk cell in one bank the following hold.

(a) Let the tail parameter of the Pareto distribution

$$\Theta \sim \text{Gamma}(\alpha_0, \beta_0)$$

be a Gamma distributed random variable with hyperparameters α_0, β_0.

(b) Given $\Theta = \theta$, the losses $k = 1, \ldots, K+1$ in the risk cell are assumed to be conditionally iid Pareto(θ, L) distributed, where the threshold $L > 0$ is assumed to be non-random and given.

(c) We assume that the bank has M experts with opinions Δ_m, $1 \leq m \leq M$. Given $\Theta = \theta$, $\Delta_m \overset{iid}{\sim}$ Gamma$(\xi, \theta/\xi)$, for $\xi > 0$ fixed.

(d) Given Θ, $(X_1, \ldots, X_{K+1})$ and $(\Delta_1, \ldots, \Delta_M)$ are independent.

Set $X = (X_1, \ldots, X_K)$ and $\Delta = (\Delta_1, \ldots, \Delta_M)$.

Theorem 13.22 (Lambrigger et al 2007, Theorem 4.5). Under Assumption 13.21, given loss severities $X = x$ and expert opinions $\Delta = \delta$, the posterior distribution of Θ is GIG(ω, ϕ, ν) with the density

$$\pi(\theta \mid x, \delta) = \frac{(\omega/\phi)^{(\nu+1)/2}}{2K_{\nu+1}(2\sqrt{\omega\phi})} \theta^\nu e^{-\theta\omega - \theta^{-1}\phi} \qquad (13.41)$$

where

$$\left. \begin{array}{l} \nu = \alpha_0 - 1 - M\xi + K \\[4pt] \omega = \dfrac{1}{\beta_0} + \displaystyle\sum_{k=1}^{K} \ln \dfrac{x_k}{L} \\[4pt] \phi = \xi M \bar{\delta} \end{array} \right\} \qquad (13.42)$$

Theorems 13.14 and 13.22 show that frequencies and severities can be handled similarly under our model assumptions. Remarks similar to the case for frequencies apply.[11]

Remark 13.23. It seems natural to generalise this result to the case of the GIG prior distribution. In particular, changing the Assumption 13.21(a) to $\Theta \sim$ GIG$(\omega_0, \phi_0, \nu_0)$, with the parameters ν_0, ω_0, ϕ_0, the posterior $\pi(\theta \mid x, \delta)$ is again GIG(ω, ϕ, ν) with

$$\left. \begin{array}{l} \nu = \nu_0 - M\xi + K \\[4pt] \omega = \omega_0 + \displaystyle\sum_{k=1}^{K} \ln \dfrac{x_k}{L} \\[4pt] \phi = \phi_0 + \xi M \bar{\delta} \end{array} \right\} \qquad (13.43)$$

Note that, for $\phi_0 = 0$, the prior GIG is a Gamma distribution and hence we are in the Pareto–Gamma–Gamma situation of Assumption 13.21.

Table 13.2 Loss severities X_i, $i = 1, 2, \ldots, 15$, sampled from a Pareto(4,1) distribution

i	n_i	i	n_i
1	1.089	9	1.753
2	1.181	10	1.383
3	1.145	11	2.167
4	1.105	12	1.180
5	1.007	13	1.334
6	1.451	14	1.272
7	1.187	15	1.123
8	1.116		

Remark 13.24. The mean of the Pareto distributed severities is infinite for $\theta \leqslant 1$ (see Equation 13.40). Thus, in the case of Assumption 13.21 or assumptions in Remarks 13.23, the mean of the predictive distribution of X_{K+1} is infinite because the Pareto parameter Θ can be less than 1 with positive probability. For finite mean models, the range of possible θ has to be restricted to $\theta > 1$.[12]

The update processes of Equations 13.42 and 13.43 again have a simple linear iterative form.

Information update process.
Loss $k \to$ loss $k + 1$

$$\left.\begin{aligned} v_{k+1} &= v_k + 1 \\ \omega_{k+1} &= \omega_k + \ln \frac{x_{k+1}}{L} \\ \phi_{k+1} &= \phi_k \end{aligned}\right\} \tag{13.44}$$

Example 13.25. To illustrate the simplicity and robustness of the posterior mean estimator, consider the following example. Assume that a bank would like to model its risk severity by a Pareto distribution with tail index Θ. Also assume that the prior distribution is identified from external data (or provided by the regulator) as $\Theta \sim \text{Gamma}(\alpha_0, \beta_0)$ with $\alpha_0 = 4$ and $\beta_0 = \frac{9}{8}$, ie, $E[\Theta] = 4.5$ and $\text{Vco}[\Theta] = 0.5$. The bank has one expert opinion δ with $\text{Vco}[\Delta \mid \Theta = \theta] = 0.5$, ie, $\xi = 4$. We then observe the losses given in Table 13.2 (sampled from a Pareto(4, 1) distribution).

In Figure 13.3 we compare the following.

- The classical MLE

$$\hat{\theta}_k^{\text{MLE}} = \frac{k}{\sum_{i=1}^{k} \ln(x_i/L)} \quad (13.45)$$

- The Bayesian posterior mean estimate

$$\hat{\theta}_k^{(2)} = E[\Theta \mid X_1 = x_1, \ldots, X_k = x_k] \quad (13.46)$$

which combines the internal loss data with the prior distribution, where the latter is assumed to be identified from external data or provided by the regulator.

- The Bayesian posterior mean estimate

$$\hat{\theta}_k^{(3)} = E[\Theta \mid X_1 = x_1, \ldots, X_k = x_k, \Delta = \delta] \quad (13.47)$$

which combines the internal loss data with expert opinions and the prior distribution.

Figure 13.3 shows the high volatility of the maximum likelihood estimator, for small numbers k. It is very sensitive to newly arriving losses. The estimator $\hat{\theta}_k^{(3)}$ shows a much more stable behaviour around the true value, most notably when a few data points are available. This example also shows that consideration of the relevant external data and well-specified expert opinions stabilises and smoothes the estimator in an appropriate way.

CAPITAL CHARGE ACCOUNTING FOR PARAMETER UNCERTAINTY

According to the Basel II requirements (Basel Committee on Banking Supervision 2006) the final bank capital should be calculated as a sum of the risk measures in the risk cells if the bank's model cannot account for correlations between risks accurately. If this is the case, then we need to calculate value-at-risk (VaR) for each risk cell separately and sum the VaRs over the risk cells to estimate the total bank risk capital. It is equivalent to the assumption of perfect dependence between risks. In this section we consider one risk cell but note that adding quantiles over the risk cells to find the quantile of the total loss distribution is not necessarily conservative. In fact, it can underestimate the capital in the case of heavy tailed distribution as discussed in Embrechts *et al* (2009) and Böcker and Klüppelberg (2010).

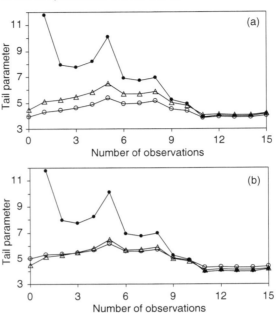

Figure 13.3 Comparison of the Bayesian and maximum likelihood estimates of the tail parameter versus the number of observations

Open circles denote the Bayes estimate $\hat{\theta}_k^{(3)}$, $k = 1, \ldots, 15$, combining the internal data simulated from Pareto(4,1), external data giving $E[\Theta] = 4.5$ and expert opinion δ. Closed circles denote the classical maximum likelihood estimate $\hat{\theta}_k^{\mathrm{MLE}}$. Triangles denote the Bayes estimate $\hat{\theta}_k^{(2)}$, which combines external data and internal data. Expert opinions are (a) $\delta = 3$ and (b) $\delta = 5$. See Example 13.25 for details.

Consider the annual loss in a bank (or the annual loss in a risk cell where the 0.999 quantile is quantified) over the next year, Z_{T+1}. Denote the density of the annual loss, conditional on parameters θ, as $f(z \mid \theta)$. Typically, given observations, the MLEs $\hat{\theta}$ are used as the "best fit" point estimators for θ. Then, the annual loss distribution for the next year is estimated as $f(z \mid \hat{\theta})$ and its 0.999 quantile, $Q_{0.999}(\hat{\theta})$, is used for the capital charge calculation.

However, the parameters θ are unknown and it is important to account for this uncertainty when the capital charge is estimated, especially for small data sets. As discussed in Shevchenko (2008), Bayesian methods are particularly useful and convenient for quantifying this uncertainty because model parameters are modelled by the random variable Θ following the posterior density $\pi(\theta \mid y)$, where $Y = y$ are all the available data (empirical frequencies and severities, expert opinions). In this case, the full predictive density (accounting for parameter uncertainty) of Z_{T+1}, given all data Y used in the estimation procedure, is

$$f(z \mid y) = \int f(z \mid \boldsymbol{\theta}) \pi(\boldsymbol{\theta} \mid y) \, d\boldsymbol{\theta} \qquad (13.48)$$

(see also Equation 13.5). Here, it is assumed that, given $\boldsymbol{\Theta}$, Z_{T+1} and Y are independent. The quantile of the full predictive distribution (Equation 13.48) given by

$$Q_q^P = \inf\{z \colon \Pr[Z_{T+1} > z \mid Y] \leqslant 1 - q\} \qquad (13.49)$$

at the level $q = 0.999$ can be used as a risk measure for capital calculations. Here, the suffix "P" is used to emphasise that this is a quantile of the full predictive distribution. Another approach under a Bayesian framework to account for parameter uncertainty is to consider a quantile $Q_{0.999}(\boldsymbol{\Theta})$ of the conditional annual loss density $f(\cdot \mid \boldsymbol{\Theta})$

$$Q_q(\boldsymbol{\Theta}) = \inf\{z \colon \Pr[Z_{T+1} > z \mid \boldsymbol{\Theta}] \leqslant 1 - q\} \qquad (13.50)$$

Then, given that $\boldsymbol{\Theta}$ is distributed as $\pi(\boldsymbol{\theta} \mid y)$, we can find the associated distribution of $Q_{0.999}(\boldsymbol{\Theta})$ and form a predictive interval to contain the true quantile value with some probability. Under this approach, we can argue that the conservative estimate of the capital charge accounting for parameter uncertainty should be based on the upper bound of the constructed predictive interval. Note that a specification of the confidence level for the predictive interval is required and it might be difficult to argue that the commonly used confidence level 0.95 is good enough for the estimation of the 0.999 quantile.

In operational risk, it seems that the objective should be to estimate the full predictive distribution (Equation 13.48) for the annual loss Z_{T+1} over the next year, conditional on all available information, and then estimate the capital charge as a quantile $Q_{0.999}^P$ of this distribution given in Equation 13.49.

Consider a risk cell in the bank. Assume that the frequency $p(\cdot \mid \boldsymbol{\alpha})$ and severity $f(\cdot \mid \boldsymbol{\beta})$ densities are chosen. Also, suppose that the posterior density $\pi(\boldsymbol{\theta} \mid y)$, $\boldsymbol{\theta} = (\boldsymbol{\alpha}, \boldsymbol{\beta})$ is estimated. Then, the full predictive annual loss distribution Equation 13.48 in the cell can be calculated using the Monte Carlo (MC) procedure with the following logical steps, under the assumption of having a compound annual loss model for given $\boldsymbol{\Theta}$.

Algorithm 13.26 (full predictive loss distribution via MC).

1. For $s = 1, \ldots, S$:

    (a) for a given risk cell simulate the risk parameters $\boldsymbol{\theta}_s = (\boldsymbol{\alpha}_s, \boldsymbol{\beta}_s)$ from the posterior $\pi(\boldsymbol{\theta} \mid y)$; if the posterior is not known in closed form then this simulation can be done using MCMC, Gibbs and Importance Sampling methods;[13]

    (b) given $\boldsymbol{\theta}_s = (\boldsymbol{\alpha}_s, \boldsymbol{\beta}_s)$, simulate the annual number of events N_s from $p(\cdot \mid \boldsymbol{\alpha}_s)$ and severities $X_1^{(s)}, \ldots, X_{N_s}^{(s)}$ from $f(\cdot \mid \boldsymbol{\beta}_s)$ and calculate the annual loss $Z^{(s)} = \sum_{n=1}^{N_s} X_n^{(s)}$.

2. Next s.

The annual losses $Z^{(1)}, \ldots, Z^{(S)}$ obtained are samples from the full predictive density (Equation 13.48) and provide an empirical approximation. Extending the above procedure to the case of many risk cells is easy but requires specification of the dependence model (Peters *et al* 2009). In general, all the model parameters (including the dependence parameters) should be simulated from their joint posterior in step (a). Then, given these parameters, step (b) should simulate all risks with a chosen dependence structure. In general, sampling from the joint posterior of all model parameters can be accomplished via MCMC methods.[14] The 0.999 quantile $Q_{0.999}^P$ and other distribution characteristics can be estimated using the empirical distribution $(Z^{(s)})_{s=1,\ldots,S}$.

Remark 13.27. Note that in the above MC procedure the risk profile $\boldsymbol{\theta}$ is simulated from its posterior distribution for each simulation. Thus, we model both the process uncertainty, which comes from the fact that frequencies and severities are random variables, and the parameter risk (parameter uncertainty), which comes from the fact that we do not know the true values of $\boldsymbol{\theta}$. The parameter uncertainty is ignored by the estimator $Q_{0.999}(\hat{\boldsymbol{\theta}})$ but is taken into account by $Q_{0.999}^P$. For high-frequency low-impact risks, where a large amount of data is available, the impact is certainly expected to be small. However, for low-frequency high-impact risks, where the data is very limited, the impact can be significant (Shevchenko 2008).

Also, in step (b) of Algorithm 13.26, we can calculate the quantile $Q_{0.999}(\boldsymbol{\theta})$ of the conditional density $f(z \mid \boldsymbol{\theta})$ using MC or more numerically efficient methods such as fast Fourier transform (FFT) or Panjer recursion. Then, the S samples of the quantile obtained can be used to estimate the distribution of $Q_{0.999}(\boldsymbol{\theta})$ implied by the posterior $\pi(\boldsymbol{\theta} \mid y)$ (see also Equation 13.50).

Algorithm 13.28 (posterior distribution of quantile via MC).

1. For $s = 1, \ldots, S$:

    (a) for a given risk simulate the risk parameters $\boldsymbol{\theta}_s = (\boldsymbol{\alpha}_s, \boldsymbol{\beta}_s)$ from the posterior $\pi(\boldsymbol{\theta} \mid y)$;

    (b) given $\boldsymbol{\theta}_s = (\boldsymbol{\alpha}_s, \boldsymbol{\beta}_s)$, calculate the quantile $Q_q^{(s)} = Q_q(\boldsymbol{\theta}_s)$ of $f(z \mid \boldsymbol{\theta}_s)$, eg, by MC, FFT or Panjer recursion.

2. Next s.

The $Q_q^{(1)}, \ldots, Q_q^{(S)}$ obtained provide an empirical approximation for the distribution of $Q_q(\boldsymbol{\Theta})$ defined in Equation 13.50. Chapter 12 provides some numerical examples and some graphical illustrations of this approach in the case of several risk cells.

GENERAL REMARKS

In this chapter we have described how the parameters of the frequency and severity distributions are estimated using internal data, external data and expert opinion. Then, calculation of VaR (accounting for parameter uncertainty) for each risk cell can easily be done using a simulation approach as described in the section on capital charge (see page 429 onwards).

The main motivation for the use of the Bayesian approach is that, typically, the bank's internal data for the large losses in risk cells is limited, so that the standard MLEs are not reliable. Overall, the use of Bayesian inference methods for the quantification of the frequency and severity distributions of operational risk is very promising. The method is based on specifying the prior distributions for the parameters of the frequency and severity distributions using industry data. Then, the prior distributions are weighted with the actual observations in the bank and internal expert opinions to estimate the posterior distributions of the model parameters. These are used to estimate the predictive annual loss distribution for the next accounting year. The estimation of low-frequency risks using this method has several appealing features, such as stable estimators, simple calculations (in the case of conjugate priors) and the ability to take into account expert opinions and industry data. The approach allows for combination of all three data sources: internal data, external data and expert opinions required by Basel II.

The models presented in this chapter give illustrative examples that can be extended to a full-scale application. The approach has a simple structure which is beneficial for practical use and can engage the banks' risk managers, statisticians and regulators in productive model development and risk assessment.

Several observations on the Bayesian method for operational risk described here are worth mentioning.

- Validation of the models in the case of small data sets is problematic. Formally, justification of the model assumptions (such as conditional independence between the losses or common distribution for the risk profiles across the risks) can be based on the analysis of the unconditional properties (eg, unconditional means, covariances) of the losses and should be addressed during model implementation.

- The examples presented have a simplistic dependence on time but can be extended to the case of more realistic time components.

- Adding extra levels to the considered hierarchical structure may be required for modelling the actual risk cell structure in a bank.

- One of the features of the method described is that the variance of the posterior distribution $\pi(\theta \mid \cdot)$ will converge to zero for a large number of observations. This means that the true value of the risk profile will be known exactly. However, there are many factors (for example, political, economical, legal) which change over time and thus do not allow precise knowledge of the risk profiles. We can model this by limiting the variance of the posterior distribution by some lower level (eg, 5%). This has been done in many solvency approaches for the insurance industry, eg, in the Swiss Solvency Test.[15]

- For convenience, we have assumed that expert opinions are iid, but all formulas can be generalised to the case of expert opinions modelled by other distributions and dependence structures.

- It would be ideal if the industry risk profiles (prior distributions for frequency and severity parameters in risk cells) are calculated and provided by the regulator to ensure consistency across the banks. Unfortunately, this may not be realistic at the time of writing. Banks might thus estimate the industry risk profiles using industry data available through external databases from vendors and consortiums of banks. The data quality, reporting and survival biases in external databases are the issues that should be considered in practice.

Finally, in this chapter we consider modelling operational risk, but the use of similar Bayesian models is also useful in other areas (such as credit risk, insurance risk, environmental risk, ecology) where, mainly due to lack of internal observations, a combination of internal data with external data and expert opinions is required.

1 For a review of quantitative methods suggested for implementation of the LDA, see Shevchenko (2010).
2 See, for example, King (2001, Chapter 12), Cruz (2002, Chapter 10) and Panjer (2006, Section 10.5).
3 Available at http://www.journalofoperationalrisk.com.
4 For more about the improper prior, see Chapter 1 of Volume I.
5 See Shevchenko and Wüthrich (2006).
6 See also Chapter 2 of Volume I.
7 See Swiss Financial Market Supervisory Authority (2006, Appendix 8.4).
8 See, for instance, Abramowitz and Stegun (1965, p. 375).
9 See also Lambrigger et al (2007, Appendix A).
10 See, for example, Lambrigger et al (2007, Lemma B.1 in Appendix B).
11 See Remarks 13.15, 13.17, 13.19 and 13.20, and Theorem 13.16.
12 See Shevchenko and Wüthrich (2006, Sections 3.4 and 4.3).
13 See Chapter 2 of Volume I.
14 See, for example, Peters et al (2009) and Chapter 12.
15 See Swiss Financial Market Supervisory Authority (2006, Formulas (25) and (26)).

REFERENCES

Abramowitz, M., and I. A. Stegun, 1965, *Handbook of Mathematical Functions* (New York: Dover).

Basel Committee on Banking Supervision, 2006, *International Convergence of Capital Measurement and Capital Standards: A Revised Framework* (Basel: Bank for International Settlements).

Berger, J. O., 1985, *Statistical Decision Theory and Bayesian Analysis*, Second Edition (Springer).

Böcker, K., and C. Klüppelberg, 2010, "Multivariate Models for Operational Risk". *Quantitative Finance*, DOI:10.1080/14697680903358222.

Bühlmann, H., and A. Gisler, 2005, *A Course in Credibility Theory and Its Applications* (Springer).

Bühlmann, H., P. V. Shevchenko and M. V. Wüthrich, 2007, "A 'Toy' Model for Operational Risk Quantification Using Credibility Theory", *The Journal of Operational Risk* 2(1), pp. 3–19.

Cruz, M. G., 2002, *Modeling, Measuring and Hedging Operational Risk* (Chichester: John Wiley & Sons).

Dagpunar, J. S., 1989, "An Easily Implemented Generalised Inverse Gaussian Generator", *Communications in Statistics, Simulation and Computation* 18, pp. 703–10.

Embrechts, P., D. D. Lambrigger and M. V. Wüthrich, 2009, "Multivariate Extremes and the Aggregation of Dependent Risks: Examples and Counter-Examples", *Extremes* 12(2), pp. 107–27.

Gilks, W. R., S. Richardson and D. J. Spiegelhalter, 1996, *Markov Chain Monte Carlo in Practice* (London: Chapman & Hall).

Jørgensen, B., 1982, *Statistical Properties of the Generalized Inverse Gaussian Distribution* (Springer).

King, J. L., 2001, *Operational Risk: Measurements and Modelling* (Chichester: John Wiley & Sons).

Lambrigger, D. D., P. V. Shevchenko and M. V. Wüthrich, 2007, "The Quantification of Operational Risk Using Internal Data, Relevant External Data and Expert Opinions", *The Journal of Operational Risk* 2(3), pp. 3–27.

McNeil, A. J., R. Frey and P. Embrechts, 2005, *Quantitative Risk Management: Concepts, Techniques and Tools* (Princeton University Press).

Panjer, H. H., 2006, *Operational Risk: Modeling Analytics* (Chichester: John Wiley & Sons).

Peters, G. W., P. V. Shevchenko and M. V. Wüthrich, 2009, "Dynamic Operational Risk: Modeling Dependence and Combining Different Data Sources of Information", *The Journal of Operational Risk* 4(2), pp. 69–104.

Robert, C. P., 2001, *The Bayesian Choice* (Springer).

Shevchenko, P. V., 2008, "Estimation of Operational Risk Capital Charge under Parameter Uncertainty", *The Journal of Operational Risk* 3(1), pp. 51–63.

Shevchenko, P. V., 2010, "Implementing Loss Distribution Approach for Operational Risk", *Applied Stochastic Models in Business and Industry* 26(3), pp. 277–307.

Shevchenko, P. V., Forthcoming, *Modelling Operational Risk Using Bayesian Inference* (Springer).

Shevchenko, P. V., and M. V. Wüthrich, 2006, "The Structural Modeling of Operational Risk via Bayesian Inference: Combining Loss Data with Expert Opinions", *The Journal of Operational Risk* 1(3), pp. 3–26.

Swiss Financial Market Supervisory Authority, 2006, "Swiss Solvency Test", Technical Document, FINMA, Bern, Switzerland.

Wüthrich, M. V., and M. Merz, 2008, *Stochastic Claims Reserving Methods in Insurance* (Chichester: John Wiley & Sons).

14

Bayesian Estimation of Lévy Copulas for Multivariate Operational Risks

Philipp Gebhard, Gernot Müller; Klaus Böcker
Technische Universität München; UniCredit Group

Among the advanced measurement approaches (AMAs) of Basel II (Basel Committee on Banking Supervision 2004) for calculating capital charges for operational risks, perhaps the most popular in the financial service industry is the loss distribution approach (LDA).

Let us briefly focus on one-dimensional operational risk modelling before we move on to the multivariate problem. Consider a single cell (business line/loss-event type) for which the total operational loss up to time horizon t is given by the aggregate loss process

$$S(t) = \sum_{k=1}^{N(t)} X_k, \quad t \geq 0 \qquad (14.1)$$

where $(X_k)_{k \in \mathbb{N}}$ is a sequence of independent and identically distributed (iid) positive random variables and $(N(t))_{t \geq 0}$ is a counting process in the time interval $[0, t]$, independent of $(X_k)_{k \in \mathbb{N}}$. The success of LDA models is, at least partially, due to the fact that they allow for a very intuitive interpretation. Basically, a bank's total operational loss, eg, within a given year, is simply the sum of all loss events observed during the year where, of course, both the number of losses and the loss severity of a single loss event are random. Hence, Equation 14.1 can be considered as a structural model for univariate operational risk, since it provides insight about how a yearly loss arises, here, by the accumulation of several random iid loss events.[1] For most practical applications, Equation 14.1 is even too general because in most cases the number of losses (or the loss frequency) is described by a homogeneous Poisson process with intensity $\lambda > 0$, so that Equation 14.1 becomes a compound Poisson process (CPP). Interestingly, as pointed out by Böcker and Klüppelberg (2005), the choice of the frequency process $(N(t))_{t \geqslant 0}$ has only a very small impact on operational value-at-risk (VaR) as long as we are interested in extreme losses and high confidence levels (as is typically the case). Therefore, we can correctly assume that univariate operational VaR figures calculated via models like Equation 14.1 are effectually all equivalent to a one-dimensional compound Poisson model.

However, the world is more complex. According to Basel II, banks should distinguish between business lines (usually eight) and loss-event types (usually seven), and this is exactly where the trouble comes in. For each cell $i = 1, \ldots, d$, the cumulated operational loss $S_i(\cdot)$ is described by a model of the form of Equation 14.1 with frequency and severity processes $N_i(\cdot)$ and $(X_k^i)_{k \in \mathbb{N}}$, respectively. Then these univariate losses $S_i(\cdot)$ have to be combined to compute the total operational risk, thereby trying to take the dependence structure between different cells into consideration. It is exactly this step – the modelling of the dependence structure – where most LDA approaches lose their appeal. The reason for this is not that there is no possibility of how the dependence structure can be introduced in principle; quite the opposite is true: there are (too) many ways for doing this, eg, by modelling the association between the number of losses occurring in different cells, between the severity distributions of different cells or between the different cells' yearly aggregate loss distributions.[2] In most of these models the complexity (and thus the number of parameters to be estimated, which is particularly problematic when data are scarce) increases dramatically, thereby destroying, or at least reducing, the benefits of the structural compound Poisson model presented in Equation 14.1. The reason for this is that in such models dependence is understood as a measure of association between the severity and/or loss numbers and/or total-loss random variables. For instance, by coupling (for a fixed $t \geqslant 0$, eg, one year) the aggregated loss distributions $S_i(t)$ and $S_j(t)$ of two different cells by means of a distributional copula, we may describe the statistical phenomenon of their association. However, such an approach does not provide any information that helps to explain the observed dependence.

In order to generalise the structural LDA model (Equation 14.1) and all its benefits to several dimensions, we have to switch from the usual distributional dependence model (no matter whether the number of losses, severities or aggregate losses is considered) to the frequency domain. This leads to the concept of Lévy copulas.[3]

MODELLING MULTIVARIATE OPERATIONAL RISK WITH LÉVY COPULAS

In this section we recall some definitions and properties of the multivariate operational risk model using Lévy copulas.[4] We assume that the cumulated operational loss $S_i(\cdot)$ in each cell $i = 1, \ldots, d$ is described by a CPP

$$S_i(t) = \sum_{k=1}^{N_i(t)} X_k^i, \quad t \geq 0 \qquad (14.2)$$

where $(X_k^i)_{k \in \mathbb{N}}$ for all i are iid and $(N_i(t))_{t \geq 0}$ are independent of $(X_k^i)_{k \in \mathbb{N}}$ with

$$P(N_i(t) = n) = e^{-\lambda_i t} \frac{(\lambda_i t)^n}{n!}, \quad n \in \mathbb{N}_0$$

where the rate $\lambda_i > 0$ is also referred to as frequency parameter. We further assume that $S(t) := (S_1(t), \ldots, S_d(t))_{t \geq 0}$ constitutes a d-dimensional compound Poisson process, which implies that also the bank's total operational risk

$$S^+(t) := S_1(t) + S_2(t) + \cdots + S_d(t), \quad t \geq 0 \qquad (14.3)$$

constitutes a one-dimensional CPP. CPPs belong to a class of more general stochastic processes, the so-called Lévy processes, which are processes in $\mathbb{R}^d$ with independent and stationary increments. If a Lévy process has only positive jumps, it is called a spectrally positive Lévy process. Since operational losses are assumed to be positive, our CPP $S(\cdot)$ is a special spectrally positive Lévy process.

The dependence structure between spectrally positive Lévy processes can be modelled by means of Lévy copulas. In contrast to distributional copulas, which are defined in the domain of probability measures, Lévy copulas are defined in the domain of Lévy measures and tail integrals. Basically, a Lévy measure controls the jump behaviour of a Lévy process. For instance, the Lévy measure

Π_i of a univariate CPP $S_i(\cdot)$ can be written in terms of the rate (frequency) $\lambda_i > 0$ and the jump size distribution function (loss severity), namely $\Pi_i([0,x)) := \lambda_i P(X^i \leq x) = \lambda_i F_i(x)$ for $x \in [0,\infty)$. Hence, the Lévy measure of a single operational risk cell measures the expected number of losses per unit time with a loss amount in a pre-specified interval. Related to the concept of a Lévy measure is that of a tail integral. A one-dimensional tail integral is simply the expected number of losses, per unit time, that are above a given threshold x

$$\bar{\Pi}_i(x) := \Pi_i([x,\infty)) = \lambda_i P(X^i > x) = \lambda_i \bar{F}_i(x), \quad x \in [0,\infty) \quad (14.4)$$

Similarly, the multivariate Lévy measure controls the joint jump behaviour (per unit time) of all univariate components and contains all information of dependence between the components. Finally, the multivariate tail integral is basically given by

$$\bar{\Pi}(x_1,\ldots,x_d) = \Pi([x_1,\infty) \times \cdots \times [x_d,\infty)), \quad (x_1,\ldots,x_d) \in [0,\infty]^d \quad (14.5)$$

As a multivariate distribution can be built from marginal distributions via a distributional copula, a multivariate tail integral (Equation 14.5) can be constructed from the marginal tail integrals (Equation 14.4) by means of a Lévy copula. This is the content of Sklar's Theorem for Lévy processes with positive jumps, which basically says that every multivariate tail integral $\bar{\Pi}$ can be decomposed into its marginal tail integrals and a Lévy copula $\mathfrak{C}$ according to

$$\bar{\Pi}(x_1,\ldots,x_d) = \mathfrak{C}(\bar{\Pi}_1(x_1),\ldots,\bar{\Pi}_d(x_d)), \quad (x_1,\ldots,x_d) \in [0,\infty]^d \quad (14.6)$$

For a precise formulation of this theorem we refer the reader to Cont and Tankov (2004, Theorem 5.6).

We can therefore conclude that the multivariate compound Poisson model based on Lévy copulas is a very natural and straightforward extension of the well-known univariate CPP model (Equation 14.1) to several dimensions. The loss frequency and the severity (both encoded in the tail integral of the CPP) between different cells are modelled by the same concept, namely that of a Lévy copula. This results in a model with comparably few parameters, making it particularly advantageous in the case where only very few data exist. Furthermore, we want to stress that Lévy copulas allow for an intuitive and structural explanation of what "dependence" in operational risk actually means, namely that losses in different cells occur at the same time. More precisely, independence means that losses in different cells never occur at the same time and that their loss severity variables are also independent. Complete positive dependence, on the other hand, means that losses always occur at the same points in time and that the loss severity variables also have a perfect positive dependence structure (co-monotonicity).

Finally, we should remark that Lévy copulas give a dynamic description of the dependence structure of a Lévy process $S(\cdot)$ in contrast to static models where the distributional dependence between the marginals of $S(\cdot)$ for a predetermined and fixed $t \geqslant 0$ is considered. Since operational losses occur in time, a statical dependence model can never reflect coincidence of losses in different cells caused, eg, by the same catastrophic event, such as Hurricane Katrina or the breakdown of a bank-wide computer system. This is also acknowledged by the regulators, who, by assuming a statical dependence model, demand that losses which affect different cells but which are caused by one and the same event are counted not as several small losses (simultaneously happening in different cells) but rather as one single big loss impacting on only a single cell. The reason is that a statical model would "forget" that these losses actually have the same origin, and it would falsely treat them as independent events instead of one single, perhaps disastrous, incident. Of course, in the framework of Lévy copulas suggested here, this artificial correction is not necessary, because coincident losses are properly reflected in the dependence model itself.

THE BIVARIATE CLAYTON MODEL

A bivariate model is particularly useful to illustrate how Bayesian statistics can be used to estimate the parameters of CPPs, especially those of the Lévy copula. Therefore, we now focus on two operational risk cells (index $i = 1, 2$) with frequency parameters λ_i and severity distributions F_i, so that the marginal tail integrals are given by $\bar{\Pi}_i(\cdot) = \lambda_i \bar{F}_i(\cdot)$ as explained in Equation 14.4.

The general Clayton model

In principle, the functions F_i, $i = 1, 2$, can be any parametric distribution function that is considered as an appropriate choice for modelling loss severities. In operational risk these are typically (one-sided) heavy-tailed distributions that can handle big losses.

In the following, we model the dependence structure between the two processes $S_1(\cdot)$ and $S_2(\cdot)$ using the Clayton–Lévy copula with parameter $\delta > 0$

$$\mathfrak{C}(u,v) = (u^{-\delta} + v^{-\delta})^{-1/\delta}, \quad u, v > 0 \qquad (14.7)$$

This copula covers the whole range of positive dependence: for $\delta \to 0$ we obtain independence of the marginal processes given by

$$\mathfrak{C}_\perp(u,v) = u\mathbf{1}_{v=\infty} + v\mathbf{1}_{u=\infty}$$

and losses in different cells never occur at the same time. For $\delta \to \infty$ we get the complete positive dependence Lévy copula given by $\mathfrak{C}_\|(u,v) = \min(u,v)$, and losses always occur at the same points in time. By varying δ, the cell dependence changes smoothly between these two extremes.

For a Clayton model where the jump sizes are described by the distributions F_1 and F_2, we will write "F_1–F_2-Clayton model" in the following. If $F_1 = F_2 = F$, we will use the notation "$(F)^2$-Clayton model".

Our goal is to determine the likelihood function for a bivariate CCP $(S_1(\cdot), S_2(\cdot))$ based on the observed loss times and loss severities in both components. In doing so, it is useful to decompose the marginal components S_i (representing the cells' aggregate loss processes) into a jump-dependent part and an independent part[5]

$$S_1 = \sum_{i=1}^{N_1} X_i = S_1^\perp + S_1^\| = \sum_{k=1}^{N_1^\perp} X_k^\perp + \sum_{m=1}^{N^\|} X_m^\| \qquad (14.8)$$

$$S_2 = \sum_{j=1}^{N_2} Y_j = S_2^\perp + S_2^\| = \sum_{l=1}^{N_2^\perp} Y_l^\perp + \sum_{m=1}^{N^\|} Y_m^\| \qquad (14.9)$$

where $S_1^\perp$ and $S_2^\perp$ are independent (no joint losses) and $(S_1^\|, S_2^\|)$ describe aggregate losses of both cells that are caused by the same event and thus always happen together. Moreover, $N_1^\perp(\cdot)$, $N_2^\perp(\cdot)$ and $N^\|(\cdot)$ are Poisson processes with intensities $\lambda_1^\perp$, $\lambda_2^\perp$ and $\lambda^\| > 0$, respectively, for which it can be shown that

$$\lambda^\| = \mathfrak{C}(\lambda_1, \lambda_2), \quad \lambda_i^\perp = \lambda_i - \lambda^\|, \quad i = 1, 2$$

In particular, we obtain for the Clayton–Lévy copula

$$\lambda^{\|} = (\lambda_1^{-\delta} + \lambda_2^{-\delta})^{-1/\delta} \tag{14.10}$$

ie, the frequency of simultaneous losses is a simple function of the Clayton copula parameter δ. This could be used for expert judgement about δ by eliciting $\lambda^{\|}$, or to compute an empirical estimate for δ based on observations of λ_1, λ_2 and $\lambda^{\|}$.

Due to Equations 14.8 and 14.9 we can write the likelihood function for the bivariate process (S_1, S_2) as the product of the likelihoods for the processes $S_1^\perp, S_2^\perp$ and $(S_1^{\|}, S_2^{\|})$. For the convenience of the reader, we briefly describe the likelihood of a univariate CPP. Assume that within the time interval $0 < t < T$ we observe n jumps at times $t_1, \ldots, t_n$, each with jump size $x_i \sim f(\cdot \mid \boldsymbol{\theta})$, where $\boldsymbol{\theta}$ is a parameter vector. Defining the inter-arrival times $T_i = t_i - t_{i-1}$ for $i = 1, \ldots, n$ with $t_0 = 0$ and recalling that the T_i are iid exponential random variables with parameter λ, we can write the likelihood as

$$f(x_i, n \mid \lambda, \boldsymbol{\theta}) = e^{-\lambda(T - t_n)} \prod_{i=1}^{n} \lambda e^{-\lambda T_i} \prod_{i=1}^{n} f(x_i \mid \boldsymbol{\theta}) \tag{14.11}$$

$$= \lambda^n e^{-\lambda T} \prod_{i=1}^{n} f(x_i \mid \boldsymbol{\theta})$$

The last term in Equation 14.11 is the likelihood for the observed jump sizes, the part in the middle is the likelihood for the observed inter-arrival times, and the first factor is simply the probability that there are no jumps within $[t_n, T]$. Note that the jump size density for the jump-dependent process $(S_1^{\|}, S_2^{\|})$ not only depends on the marginal jump size densities f_1 and f_2 but also on the Lévy copula and its parameterisation. Having said that, the entire likelihood for the bivariate CPP can be set-up straightforwardly. Let $\boldsymbol{\theta}_1$ be the parameter vector of the marginal density f_1 and $\boldsymbol{\theta}_2$ the parameter vector of the marginal density f_2, then the general result is given in Esmaeili and Klüppelberg (2010)

$$f(\tilde{x}, \tilde{y}, x, y, n_1^\perp, n_2^\perp, n^{\|} \mid \lambda_1, \boldsymbol{\theta}_1, \lambda_2, \boldsymbol{\theta}_2, \delta)$$

$$= (\lambda_1)^{n_1^\perp} e^{-\lambda_1^\perp T} \prod_{i=1}^{n_1^\perp} \left[f_1(\tilde{x}_i; \boldsymbol{\theta}_1) \left(1 - \frac{\partial}{\partial u} \mathfrak{C}(u, \lambda_2; \delta) \Big|_{u = \lambda_1 \bar{F}_1(\tilde{x}_i; \boldsymbol{\theta}_1)} \right) \right]$$

$$\times (\lambda_2)^{n_2^\perp} e^{-\lambda_2^\perp T} \prod_{i=1}^{n_2^\perp} \left[f_2(\tilde{y}_i; \boldsymbol{\theta}_2) \left(1 - \frac{\partial}{\partial v} \mathfrak{C}(\lambda_1, v; \delta) \Big|_{u = \lambda_2 \bar{F}_2(\tilde{y}_i; \boldsymbol{\theta}_2)} \right) \right]$$

$$\times (\lambda_1\lambda_2)^{n^{\|}} e^{-\lambda^{\|}T} \prod_{i=1}^{n^{\|}} \left[f_1(x_i; \boldsymbol{\theta}_1) f_2(y_i; \boldsymbol{\theta}_2) \right.$$

$$\left. \times \frac{\partial^2}{\partial u \partial v} \mathfrak{C}(u,v;\delta) \bigg|_{u=\lambda_1 \bar{F}_1(x_i;\boldsymbol{\theta}_1), v=\lambda_2 \bar{F}_2(y_i;\boldsymbol{\theta}_2)} \right] \quad (14.12)$$

where $\tilde{x}, \tilde{y}$ are the observed independent jump sizes of S_1, S_2, respectively, and (x,y) are the joint jump sizes of $(S_1^{\|}, S_2^{\|})$. Furthermore, $n_1^{\perp}$, $n_2^{\perp}$ are the number of the independent jumps in S_1, S_2, respectively, and $n^{\|}$ is the number of joint jumps of $(S_1^{\|}, S_2^{\|})$.

In the case of the Clayton–Lévy copula we can further specify

$$\left. \begin{array}{l} \dfrac{\partial}{\partial u} \mathfrak{C}(u,v) = \left(1 + \left(\dfrac{u}{v}\right)^{\delta}\right)^{-1/\delta - 1} \\[2ex] \dfrac{\partial^2}{\partial u \partial v} \mathfrak{C}(u,v) = (\delta + 1)(uv)^{\delta}(u^{\delta} + v^{\delta})^{-1/\delta - 2}, \quad u,v > 0 \end{array} \right\} \quad (14.13)$$

For notational convenience we set

$$z := (\tilde{x}, \tilde{y}, x, y, n_1^{\perp}, n_2^{\perp}, n^{\|}) \quad \text{and} \quad \boldsymbol{\psi} := (\lambda_1, \boldsymbol{\theta}_1, \lambda_2, \boldsymbol{\theta}_2, \delta)$$

Given the likelihood function $f(z \mid \boldsymbol{\psi})$ for a realization z of the process, it is straightforward to compute maximum likelihood estimates of the parameters $\boldsymbol{\psi}$.[6] In the following, however, we use a Bayesian setting, which enables us to derive uncertainty bounds for the estimates in a very natural way. A brief introduction to Bayesian statistics is given in Chapter 1 of Volume I.

The (Burr/GPD)²-Clayton model

To find a Clayton model that appropriately describes the fire insurance data, which we will analyse later in this chapter, we need to select suitable classes of distributions for the jump sizes in the bivariate process. Since the losses are naturally bounded below by zero and since there are several big losses in both components, heavy right-tailed distributions seem to be a reasonable choice. After having fitted several Clayton models to the data set (including Burr, Gamma, log-Gamma, lognormal, truncated normal, Pareto and Weibull models as well as combinations of them) it turned out that, following a Bayes factor analysis described at the end of this chapter, the (Burr/GPD)²-Clayton model is the best choice. According to the notation introduced in the previous subsection, the (Burr/GPD)²-Clayton model is a bivariate Clayton model where the jump sizes of both components are each modelled by a sliced Burr/GPD distribution. For $i = 1, 2$, it is composed by a truncated Burr distribution with parameters $c_i, k_i > 0$ and density

$$f(z_i) \propto c_i k_i z_i^{c_i-1} (1 + z_i^{c_i})^{-(k_i+1)}, \quad 0 < z_i \leqslant u_i$$

and a truncated generalised Pareto distribution (GPD) with parameters $h_i, \beta_i, \xi_i > 0$ and density

$$f(z_i) \propto \frac{1}{\beta_i} \left(1 + \xi_i \frac{z_i + h_i - u_i}{\beta_i}\right)^{-1/\xi_i - 1}, \quad z_i > u_i$$

for a fixed $u_i > 0$. For $z_i > 0$, the sliced density is then given by

$$f_i(z_i; \boldsymbol{\theta}_i) = A_i \Bigg(\mathbf{1}_{(0, u_i]}(z_i) c_i k_i z_i^{c_i-1} (1 + z_i^{c_i})^{-(k_i+1)}$$
$$+ \mathbf{1}_{(u_i, \infty)}(z_i) \frac{1}{\beta_i} \left(1 + \xi_i \frac{z_i + h_i - u_i}{\beta_i}\right)^{-1/\xi_i - 1} \Bigg)$$

where $\boldsymbol{\theta}_i = (c_i, k_i, h_i, \beta_i, \xi_i)$ and the normalisation constant can be calculated as

$$A_i := \left(1 - (1 + u_i^{c_i})^{-k_i} + \left(1 + \xi_i \frac{h_i}{\beta_i}\right)^{-1/\xi_i}\right)^{-1}$$

due to the truncation.

We see that the transition between the distributions is executed at the fixed thresholds $u_i > 0$, $i = 1, 2$. That is to say, we apply the Burr distribution for $z_i \leqslant u_i$, whereas for $z_i > u_i$ the GPD is used. We choose these transition values to be the empirical 90% quantiles (eg, for the Danish fire insurance data we have $u_1 = 3.96$ and $u_2 = 3.90$). More details on how to determine these thresholds appropriately can be found in Embrechts *et al* (1997, Section 6.5).

Given the densities from above, the tail distribution for $z_i > 0$, $i = 1, 2$, can be calculated as

$$\bar{F}_i(z_i; \boldsymbol{\theta}_i) = A_i \Bigg(\mathbf{1}_{(0, u_i]}(z_i) (A_i^{-1} - 1 + (1 + z_i^{c_i})^{-k_i})$$
$$+ \mathbf{1}_{(u_i, \infty)}(z_i) \left(1 + \xi_i \frac{z_i + h_i - u_i}{\beta_i}\right)^{-1/\xi_i} \Bigg)$$

Together with Equations 14.13, the corresponding likelihood function for the bivariate CPP can now be written as in Equation 14.12.

According to the Bayesian method, this likelihood function $f(z \mid \boldsymbol{\psi})$ has then to be combined with an appropriate prior distribution

$\pi(\boldsymbol{\psi})$ to obtain the posterior distribution

$$f(\boldsymbol{\psi} \mid z) \propto f(z \mid \boldsymbol{\psi})\pi(\boldsymbol{\psi})$$

The prior distribution may reflect available prior knowledge about the model parameters and we will give more details about their specification later in this chapter, when we analyse the empirical data set. In the following we describe the Markov chain Monte Carlo (MCMC) method used for sampling from the posterior distribution $f(\boldsymbol{\psi} \mid z)$.

THE MCMC ALGORITHM

In this section we develop an MCMC method to fit the Clayton models (particularly the (Burr/GPD)^2-Clayton model) to an empirical data set, which will enable us to approximate the marginal posterior distributions for the 13 parameters of interest.

Gibbs sampling

MCMC algorithms can achieve higher levels of efficiency when they take into account the specifics of the target density. Often this can be done more precisely when determining multiple one-dimensional proposal densities instead of one multi-dimensional proposal density.

Denoting by I the total number of iterations, the structure of our MCMC sampler is classical, using 13 univariate updates from the full conditional distributions.

1. Specify initial values $\lambda_1^{(0)}, \boldsymbol{\theta}_1^{(0)}, \lambda_2^{(0)}, \boldsymbol{\theta}_2^{(0)}, \delta^{(0)}$.
2. Repeat for $i = 1, \ldots, I$:

    - sample $\lambda_1^{(i)}$ from $f(\lambda_1 \mid z, \boldsymbol{\theta}_1, \lambda_2, \boldsymbol{\theta}_2, \delta)$;
    - sample $c_1^{(i)}$ from $f(c_1 \mid z, \lambda_1, k_1, h_1, \beta_1, \xi_1, \lambda_2, \boldsymbol{\theta}_2, \delta)$;
    - sample $k_1^{(i)}$ from $f(k_1 \mid z, \lambda_1, c_1, h_1, \beta_1, \xi_1, \lambda_2, \boldsymbol{\theta}_2, \delta)$;

    $\vdots$

    - sample $\xi_2^{(i)}$ from $f(\xi_2 \mid z, \lambda_1, \boldsymbol{\theta}_1, \lambda_2, c_2, k_2, h_2, \beta_2, \delta)$;
    - sample $\delta^{(i)}$ from $f(\delta \mid z, \lambda_1, \boldsymbol{\theta}_1, \lambda_2, \boldsymbol{\theta}_2)$.

The vectors $\boldsymbol{\psi}^{(i)} := (\lambda_1^{(i)}, \boldsymbol{\theta}_1^{(i)}, \lambda_2^{(i)}, \boldsymbol{\theta}_2^{(i)}, \delta^{(i)})$ are then considered to be samples from the posterior distribution. Looking at Equation 14.12, it immediately becomes clear that all the full conditional distributions appearing above are non-standard. Hence, Metropolis–Hastings (MH) steps have to be used and the question arises of how to choose the required proposal densities. Further information about useful computational methods in the context of Bayesian statistics can be found in Chapter 2 of Volume I.

Choice of the proposal densities

As usual, the selection of good proposal densities for the MH steps is one of the most important choices we have to make in the set-up of an MCMC procedure. The better a proposal density mimics the target density, the better the mixing of the produced MCMC chains will be.

Since we use 13 univariate updates, we have to select 13 proposal densities for the full conditionals $f(\psi_k \mid \boldsymbol{\psi}_{-k}, z), k = 1, \ldots, 13$. To get an idea of the shape of the full conditionals, it is useful to simulate data from the model and to plot the likelihood function (Equation 14.12) given the data, where 12 of the 13 parameters are fixed to the known values from the simulation. For various parameter sets and simulations, these marginal densities looked unimodal and quite symmetric, so that for all 13 parameters we used normal proposals with different means μ_k and variances $\sigma_k^2, k = 1, \ldots, 13$.

To achieve good acceptance rates for the MH steps, μ_k and σ_k^2 are adapted several times during the sampling procedure. The parameters $\mu_k, k = 1, \ldots, 13$, are set to the values which maximise the corresponding full conditionals $f(\psi_k \mid \boldsymbol{\psi}_{-k}, z)$ each. Finding one of these maxima is a univariate optimisation problem and requires only a short computation time. The standard deviations $\sigma_k, k = 1, \ldots, 13$, are specified using a special property of the normal distribution. Denoting by $g(x; \mu, \sigma^2)$ the density of the normal distribution with mean μ and variance σ^2 evaluated at x, we easily derive that

$$g''(x; \mu, \sigma^2) = \frac{1}{\sigma^2}\left(\frac{1}{\sigma^2}(x-\mu)^2 - 1\right) g(x; \mu, \sigma^2)$$

Hence, $\sigma^2 = -g(\mu; \mu, \sigma^2)/g''(\mu; \mu, \sigma^2)$, and a sensible choice for the variance of the proposal density is

$$\sigma_k^2 = -\frac{f(\psi_k \mid \boldsymbol{\psi}_{-k}, z)|_{\mu_k}}{f''(\psi_k \mid \boldsymbol{\psi}_{-k}, z)|_{\mu_k}}$$

which can be evaluated easily using numerical approximations of the second derivative of $f(\cdot \mid \boldsymbol{\psi}_{-k}, z)$ at μ_k.

It is not necessary to adapt μ_k and σ_k^2 in each iteration of the MCMC sampler, except during the burn-in phase, where adaption in each iteration improves the mixing of the sampler significantly.

Initial values, burn-in, number of iterations, subsampling

In addition to the choice of the proposal densities, the choice of good starting values plays an important role. In our case, we can use maximum likelihood (ML) estimates, since the maximisation of the likelihood given in Equation 14.12 is a 13-dimensional problem which can usually be handled by suitable software. Therefore, we will always use ML estimates as initial values, if not stated otherwise.

From several simulation studies we found that the convergence behaviour of the sampler is very satisfying. Even if the initial values are chosen quite far away from the parameters used as an input for simulation, the chain converges quickly and a burn-in period of 1,000 iterations is always sufficient.

The last aspect we want to address is the subsampling of simulated values. As we will see in the next section, the Markov chains produced for the 13 parameters of interest show a significant autocorrelation over several time lags. One reason for this is obviously the MH algorithm itself, which allows us to replicate the current value when the proposed value is rejected. To reduce the dependence between the samples from the MCMC algorithm, we use subsampling. Since the computation time in our examples is only a few minutes for 1,000 iterations, we will use only every 10th iteration. Therefore, in order to get 2,000 samples from the posterior distribution we always run the algorithm for 21,000 iterations (including the burn-in period) and then use iterations 1,010, 1,020, ..., 21,000.

SIMULATION STUDY

We now assess the mixing and convergence behaviour of the chains and the quality of the posterior mean estimates using simulated data. To simulate paths of the CPP from the (Burr/GPD)^2-Clayton model, we employ the algorithm proposed by Esmaeili and Klüppelberg (2010), which simulates the jump times and the jump sizes independently.

Throughout, we always use the parameters $\lambda_1 = 34$, $c_1 = 4.1$, $k_1 = 0.42$, $h_1 = 7.3$, $\beta_1 = 3.8$, $\xi_1 = 0.42$, $\lambda_2 = 26$, $c_2 = 1.2$, $k_2 = 1.9$, $h_2 = 16$, $\beta_2 = 8.4$, $\xi_2 = 0.18$ and $\delta = 1.8$ for simulation. These values

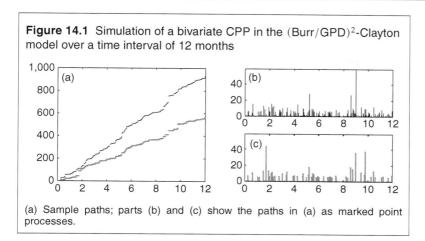

Figure 14.1 Simulation of a bivariate CPP in the (Burr/GPD)^2-Clayton model over a time interval of 12 months
(a) Sample paths; parts (b) and (c) show the paths in (a) as marked point processes.

are motivated by the analysis of the fire insurance data in the next section. Similarly, we set $T = 12$, where a time unit corresponds to one month. In general, the observed number of jumps in these simulations is random, but it is always around 480.

For all 13 parameters we choose independent Gamma[7] prior distributions $\Gamma(p_k, b_k)$, $k = 1, \ldots, 13$. Note that we always use the parameterisation where the Gamma density is given by

$$f_\Gamma(x; p, b) = \frac{b^p}{\Gamma(p)} x^{p-1} e^{-bx} 1_{[0,\infty)}(x), \quad p, b > 0$$

with mean p/b and variance p/b^2. In our analysis, the hyperparameters p_k and b_k are chosen in such a way that the prior means correspond to the initial ML estimates and the standard deviations are about one-quarter of the means. It should be mentioned, however, that in a pure Bayesian approach the hyperparameters would typically be specified by means of expert elicitation, as is described in Part 2 of Volume I.

Illustrative example

In this section we illustrate the MCMC algorithm using the simulated data set shown in Figure 14.1. Observable are the single jump sizes $\tilde{x}$ and $\tilde{y}$ of both components, the jump sizes x and y of the joint jumps, the numbers $n_1^\perp$ and $n_2^\perp$ of single jumps in both components and the number $n^\|$ of joint jumps.

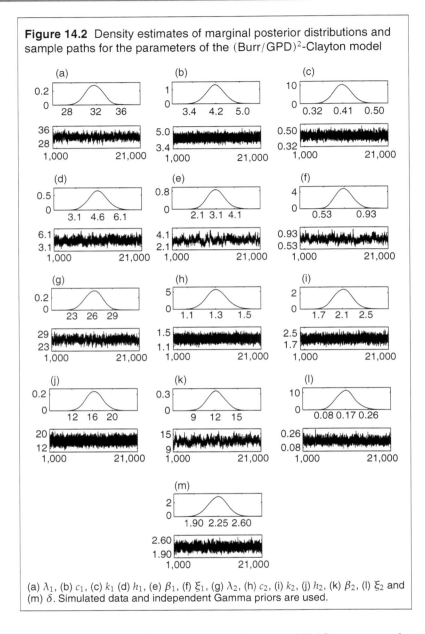

Figure 14.2 Density estimates of marginal posterior distributions and sample paths for the parameters of the (Burr/GPD)^2-Clayton model

(a) λ_1, (b) c_1, (c) k_1 (d) h_1, (e) β_1, (f) ξ_1, (g) λ_2, (h) c_2, (i) k_2, (j) h_2, (k) β_2, (l) ξ_2 and (m) δ. Simulated data and independent Gamma priors are used.

Now we apply the Bayesian method using MCMC to recover the marginal posterior distributions of all parameters used for simulation. As stated above the ML estimates are a convenient choice for starting values; they help to shorten the burn-in period.

The means of the independent Gamma priors are calculated as 32, 4.2, 0.41, 4.7, 3.2, 0.72, 26, 1.3, 2.1, 16, 12, 0.17 and 2.3, respectively, for the parameters $\lambda_1, c_1, k_1, h_1, \beta_1, \xi_1, \lambda_2, c_2, k_2, h_2, \beta_2, \xi_2$ and δ. The standard deviations are chosen to be 8.0, 1.0, 0.10, 1.2, 0.80, 0.18, 6.5, 0.33, 0.53, 4.1, 3.0, 0.043 and 0.57, respectively. Figure 14.2 shows, for each parameter of the (Burr/GPD)^2-Clayton model, the marginal posterior distribution and the produced sample path.

The marginal posterior distributions are all unimodal with peaks which are very close to the ML estimates and the distributions are all quite symmetric. Considering the sample paths, we see that the mixing behaviour of our MCMC sampler is very satisfying. We notice that there are small differences in the evolution of the paths for the different parameters. Particularly for $\beta_i, \xi_i, i = 1, 2$, which determine the tails of the distributions, the chain does not mix as fast as it does for the other parameters; in consequence the autocorrelations are higher. Hence, we decided to use subsampling and to take only every 10th iteration in order to reduce the autocorrelations.

Repeating the analysis with different initial values, also very poor ones, has shown that the produced Markov chains converge very fast, usually within 500 iterations. Thus, a burn-in period of 1,000 iterations is sufficient, and we use iterations 1,010, 1,020, 1,030, ... to derive samples from the posterior distribution.

Quality of the posterior mean estimates

To assess the quality of the posterior mean estimates we repeat the analysis of the previous section 100 times for uniform priors. More precisely, we simulate 100 data sets, using always the same fixed parameter set as before. We fit the (Burr/GPD)^2-Clayton model to these 100 data sets by MCMC to get posterior mean estimates for the parameters for all 100 data sets.

Table 14.1 gives the means and the standard deviations of the posterior mean estimates for these 100 data sets, for all 13 parameters. It shows that on average the posterior mean estimates match the simulation values very well and that the standard deviations are reasonably small, except for the GPD parameters ($h_i, \beta_i, \xi_i, i = 1, 2$). Of course, this is due to the small number of observations in the tail. If we just consider larger data sets, the posterior mean estimates would become more precise. Overall, however, we can conclude that the performance of our sampler is very satisfying.

Table 14.1 Means and standard deviations of the posterior mean estimates in the $(\text{Burr}/\text{GPD})^2$-Clayton model for 100 simulations

	λ_1	c_1	k_1	h_1	β_1	ξ_1	
True value	34	4.1	0.42	7.3	3.8	0.42	
Mean	34.2	4.08	0.409	7.38	3.93	0.438	
Std	1.72	0.320	0.0313	1.84	1.08	0.143	
	λ_2	c_2	k_2	h_2	β_2	ξ_2	δ
True value	26	1.2	1.9	16	8.4	0.18	1.8
Mean	26.1	1.26	1.97	16.5	8.68	0.173	1.88
Std	1.79	0.0726	0.150	3.18	1.99	0.0475	0.211

ANALYSIS OF FIRE INSURANCE DATA

To further exemplify our approach, we now analyse the Danish fire insurance data. We choose this specific data set because appropriate bank internal operational risk loss data was not available for us when we performed this investigation. However, analysing a data set from operational risk could be performed exactly as it is done here.

The data was collected at Copenhagen Reinsurance; an aggregated form appears, for example, in Embrechts *et al* (1997). The losses of profit, which are contained in this set, are not considered, ie, we restrict the data to the bivariate data set consisting of losses of buildings and losses of contents. The claims are reported in millions of Danish kroner. Our analysis is composed of, in total, 474 observations collected in the year 2002.

Figure 14.3 shows the observed sample paths of the accumulated losses for buildings and contents as well as their representation as marked point processes. Table 14.2 summarises some important features.

Working with sliced distributions provides quite a flexibility in modelling data sets. Whereas for the tails (of both the building and the content component) a GPD seems to be a reasonable choice, it is not so clear *a priori* which distribution could be appropriate for the smaller losses. Hence, Figure 14.4 shows histograms of the small losses in the building and the content component, respectively. Ignoring all losses greater than DKr4 million and DKr2 million, respectively, we now fit several standard distributions (Burr,

Figure 14.3 The Danish fire insurance data

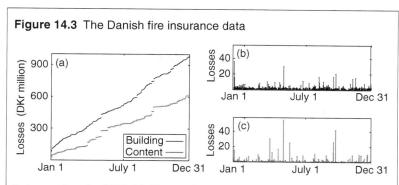

Data are given for 2002. (a) Observed sample paths of the accumulated losses for buildings and contents; parts (b) and (c) show the paths in (a) as marked point processes; (b) losses of building; (c) losses of content.

Table 14.2 Summary of the Danish fire insurance data

	\multicolumn{5}{c}{January to December 2002}
	Single jumps	Common jumps	Minimal loss	Maximal loss	Average loss
Building	131	308	70,000	36,000,000	2,076,335
Content	35	308	9,000	55,000,000	1,286,908

	\multicolumn{5}{c}{July to December 2002}
	Single jumps	Common jumps	Minimal loss	Maximal loss	Average loss
Building	71	147	70,000	20,500,000	2,257,215
Content	18	147	11,000	41,502,000	1,708,442

The table shows the number of single and common jumps and minimal, maximal and average losses in Danish kroner for insured buildings and contents.

Gamma, log-Gamma, lognormal) to these smaller losses, by maximum likelihood. As we can see from Figure 14.4, the fit both of the Burr distribution and the log-Gamma distribution is quite satisfying. Hence, in the following, we concentrate on these two families to model the body of the loss distributions. Note that this initial investigation is not linked to Bayesian analysis. It just helps to select appropriate distributions. Of course, later on, the chosen models

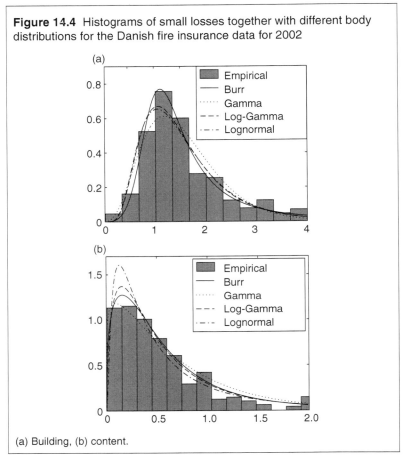

Figure 14.4 Histograms of small losses together with different body distributions for the Danish fire insurance data for 2002

(a) Building, (b) content.

should be compared using formal model selection criteria, such as Bayes factors.

Fitting the (Burr/GPD)²-Clayton model to the data

Motivated by our initial analysis, we now fit the (Burr/GPD)²-Clayton model to the data using our MCMC algorithm. As initial values we choose ML estimates for the different parameters, and then we run the sampler for 21,000 iterations and discard the first 1,000 for burn-in. Furthermore, we thin out the samples to reduce the autocorrelation and take only every 10th sample into account, as in the simulation study.

Figure 14.5 shows estimated marginal posterior densities for the parameters $\lambda_1, \theta_1, \lambda_2, \theta_2, \delta$ of the (Burr/GPD)²-Clayton model for

Figure 14.5 Density estimates of marginal posterior distributions for the parameters of the (Burr/GPD)^2-Clayton model

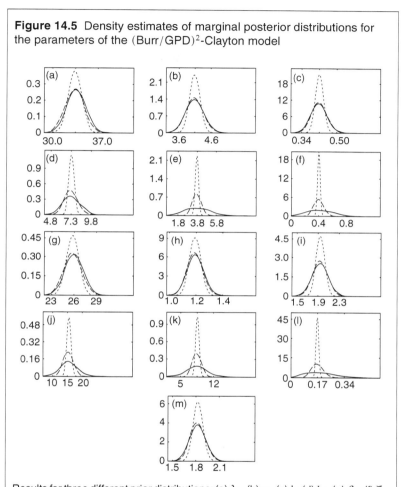

Results for three different prior distributions: (a) λ_1, (b) c_1, (c) k_1 (d) h_1, (e) β_1, (f) ξ_1, (g) λ_2, (h) c_2, (i) k_2, (j) h_2, (k) β_2, (l) ξ_2 and (m) δ. Solid lines indicate uniform prior; dashed lines indicate prior with large standard deviation; dotted lines indicate prior with small standard deviation.

the Danish fire insurance data between January and December 2002. Three different prior distributions for the parameters are used: uniform (non-informative) priors, independent Gamma priors with large standard deviations (denoted by Γ_1) and independent Gamma priors with smaller standard deviations (denoted by Γ_2). In the first case the prior standard deviations are taken as the corresponding mean divided by 4, in the second case they are taken as the corresponding mean divided by 20, hence are a factor 5 smaller.

Table 14.3 Posterior mean estimates together with 95% credible intervals and maximum likelihood estimates for comparison

	λ_1	c_1	k_1
MLE	33.49	4.094	0.4202
Uniform prior	33.66 [30.90, 36.47]	4.096 [3.578, 4.658]	0.4178 [0.3507, 0.4926]
Γ_1 prior	33.37 [30.52, 36.25]	4.095 [3.568, 4.637]	0.4202 [0.3541, 0.4895]
Γ_2 prior	33.44 [31.44, 35.39]	4.091 [3.791, 4.396]	0.4200 [0.3865, 0.4558]

	h_1	β_1	ξ_1
MLE	7.325	3.776	0.4027
Uniform prior	7.319 [5.506, 9.235]	3.846 [1.597, 6.356]	0.4170 [0.0885, 0.7748]
Γ_1 prior	7.291 [5.830, 8.973]	3.776 [2.928, 4.744]	0.4007 [0.2718, 0.5489]
Γ_2 prior	7.338 [6.707, 7.984]	3.778 [3.457, 4.116]	0.4023 [0.3646, 0.4412]

	λ_2	c_2	k_2
MLE	25.85	1.193	1.946
Uniform prior	26.02 [23.69, 28.39]	1.196 [1.081, 1.318]	1.940 [1.647, 2.251]
Γ_1 prior	25.82 [23.49, 28.16]	1.191 [1.084, 1.306]	1.941 [1.680, 2.209]
Γ_2 prior	25.80 [24.14, 27.39]	1.192 [1.113, 1.273]	1.943 [1.790, 2.102]

	h_2	β_2	ξ_2	δ
MLE	15.51	8.566	0.1690	1.829
uniform prior	15.60 [9.67, 22.23]	8.424 [3.629, 13.32]	0.1830 [0.0499, 0.4152]	1.824 [1.630, 2.025]
Γ_1 prior	15.29 [12.16, 18.73]	8.460 [6.616, 10.33]	0.1700 [0.1049, 0.2504]	1.822 [1.650, 2.016]
Γ_2 prior	15.52 [14.22, 16.93]	8.578 [7.840, 9.32]	0.1689 [0.1528, 0.1863]	1.826 [1.704, 1.950]

The 95% credible intervals are based on the empirical 2.5% and 97.5% quantiles. Results for three different prior distributions: uniform, independent Gamma with large standard deviations (Γ_1), independent Gamma with small standard deviations (Γ_2). MLE is the maximum likelihood estimate.

We clearly see the impact of the prior distributions on the uncertainty in the parameters. Whereas for the uniform prior and the Γ_1 priors the results are quite similar, the marginal densities are much more concentrated for the more informative Γ_2 priors. In particular, the estimates for the parameters of the GPD distribution used to model the tails of the sliced distributions show significant uncertainties for the uniform and the Γ_1 prior. Recalling that we have only about 40 observations available to model both tails, this behaviour is not a surprise and can be expected.

Table 14.3 reports the posterior mean estimates together with 95% credible intervals for all parameters, given the three different priors. Summarising the plots and the credible intervals, it becomes apparent that the choice of the standard deviations in the prior distributions has a major impact on the simulated values and the estimated posterior distributions. When choosing large values there is no significant difference compared to a uniform prior. Maybe informative expert judgment from experienced risk managers could justify the usage of small standard deviations in the priors and, hence, make them quite informative. From Figure 14.5, however, we can see that along with this comes the risk of underestimating the uncertainty about the parameter estimates.

In Table 14.4 we see how the estimates change when the shorter time period of six months ($T = 6$) is considered instead of the one-year period ($T = 12$). As expected, the 95% credible intervals for the shorter data set are bigger, since fewer observations are available. However, the posterior mean estimates are not significantly different.

In Figure 14.6 we finally plot the density of the fitted (Burr/GPD)^2-Clayton model together with histograms of the original data set, for both the building and the content component. Note that the estimated densities are based on the uniform prior distributions. Using the posterior mean estimates as parameters for the marginal jump size distributions in both components yields the following explicit densities for $x, y > 0$

$$f_1(x) = \mathbf{1}_{(0,3.96]} 1.49\, x^{3.10}(1 + x^{4.10})^{-1.42}$$
$$\quad + \mathbf{1}_{(3.96,\infty)} 0.226(1 + 0.108(x + 3.36))^{-3.40}$$
$$f_2(y) = \mathbf{1}_{(0,3.90]} 1.98\, y^{0.196}(1 + y^{1.20})^{-2.94}$$
$$\quad + \mathbf{1}_{(3.90,\infty)} 0.101(1 + 0.0217(y + 11.7))^{-6.47}$$

Table 14.4 Comparison of posterior mean estimates for January–December 2002 and July–December 2002

T	λ_1	c_1	k_1
12	33.37 [30.52, 36.25]	4.095 [3.568, 4.637]	0.4202 [0.3541, 0.4895]
6	33.20 [29.55, 37.07]	4.113 [3.441, 4.799]	0.4092 [0.3258, 0.4957]

T	h_1	β_1	ξ_1
12	7.291 [5.830, 8.973]	3.776 [2.928, 4.744]	0.4007 [0.2718, 0.5489]
6	7.210 [5.424, 9.277]	3.839 [2.838, 4.961]	0.3900 [0.2447, 0.5597]

T	λ_2	c_2	k_2
12	25.82 [23.49, 28.16]	1.191 [1.084 , 1.306]	1.941 [1.680, 2.209]
6	25.17 [22.00, 28.47]	1.132 [0.9830, 1.288]	1.881 [1.504, 2.301]

T	h_2	β_2	ξ_2	δ
12	15.29 [12.16, 18.73]	8.460 [6.616, 10.33]	0.1700 [0.1049 , 0.2504]	1.822 [1.650, 2.016]
6	14.40 [10.56, 18.56]	7.645 [5.689, 9.789]	0.1630 [0.09763, 0.2462]	1.778 [1.529, 2.044]

The table shows comparison of posterior mean estimates (for Γ_1 prior) for the periods January–December 2002 with the estimates for the period July–December 2002. The estimates are given with 95% credible intervals.

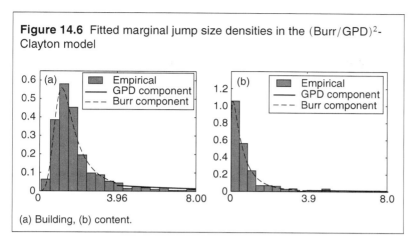

Figure 14.6 Fitted marginal jump size densities in the (Burr/GPD)^2-Clayton model

(a) Building, (b) content.

Bayes factors

So far we have just stated that the (Burr/GPD)^2-Clayton model is best (at least among the models which we tried) for fitting the Danish fire insurance data with the MCMC method. As an example, we now want to compare this model to two other Clayton models, namely the (log-Gamma/GPD)^2-Clayton model and the (Burr)^2-Clayton model. To compare these three competing models, we employ the Bayes factors, which are a powerful tool in Bayesian model selection.

Each of the models is described by a model-specific parameter vector $\boldsymbol{\psi}_l \in \Psi_l \subset \mathbb{R}^l$, $l = 1, 2, 3$. In particular we have

$$\boldsymbol{\psi}_1 = (\lambda_1, c_1, k_1, h_1, \beta_1, \xi_1, \lambda_2, c_2, k_2, h_2, \beta_2, \xi_2, \delta)$$

for the (Burr/GPD)^2-Clayton model

$$\boldsymbol{\psi}_2 = (\lambda_1, a_1, b_1, h_1, \beta_1, \xi_1, \lambda_2, a_2, b_2, h_2, \beta_2, \xi_2, \delta)$$

for the (log-Gamma/GPD)^2-Clayton model and

$$\boldsymbol{\psi}_3 = (\lambda_1, c_1, k_1, \lambda_2, c_2, k_2, \delta)$$

for the (Burr)^2-Clayton model. As explained in Chapter 2 of Volume I, the Bayes factors

$$B_{ij}(z) = \frac{\int_{\Psi_i} f_i(z \mid \boldsymbol{\psi}_i) \pi_i(\boldsymbol{\psi}_i) \, d\boldsymbol{\psi}_i}{\int_{\Psi_j} f_j(z \mid \boldsymbol{\psi}_j) \pi_j(\boldsymbol{\psi}_j) \, d\boldsymbol{\psi}_j}, \quad i, j \in \{1, 2, 3\}, \ i \neq j$$

can be approximated by the strongly consistent estimates

$$\tilde{B}_{ij}(z) = \frac{n_i^{-1} \sum_{k=1}^{n_i} f_i(z \mid \boldsymbol{\psi}_{i,k})}{n_j^{-1} \sum_{k=1}^{n_j} f_j(z \mid \boldsymbol{\psi}_{j,k})}, \quad i, j \in \{1, 2, 3\}, \ i \neq j$$

Table 14.5 Approximated Bayes factors for the (Burr/GPD)^2-Clayton model

(Burr/GPD)^2 vs (log-Gamma/GPD)^2	2.1×10^3
(Burr/GPD)^2 vs (Burr)^2	1.4×10^8

Results are given for Γ_1 priors. 10,000 simulations are used for calculation.

Here $\psi_{i,k}$, $k = 1, \ldots, n_i$, and $\psi_{j,k}$, $k = 1, \ldots, n_j$, are two independent samples generated from the prior distributions π_i and π_j, respectively, and z represents the fire insurance data for the period January–December 2002.

The strength of evidence in favour of the (Burr/GPD)^2-Clayton model versus the (log-Gamma/GPD)^2-Clayton or the (Burr)^2-Clayton model, respectively, can be evaluated according to Jeffreys's Bayes factor scale (see, for example, Gelman *et al* 1995). According to this scale, Bayes factors B_{ij} greater than 100 are considered as decisive evidence for model i against model j.) Following the results in Table 14.5, our (Burr/GPD)^2-Clayton model is clearly the best among the three competing models.

FINAL REMARKS

In the simulation study we have seen that the choice of the prior distributions plays an important role. We must be aware that decisions based on the posterior mean estimates and the posterior distributions are also affected by the priors. Therefore, the choice of a certain informative prior must be well founded, particularly when the data sets used for the analysis are small. Here the impact of the prior is usually higher than for large data sets.

In practice, it might also be useful to transform the data before starting the analysis, eg, by taking logarithms. Such transformations may change the dependence structure, and outliers may get closer to the rest of the data (or even further away). Note that Esmaeili and Klüppelberg (2010) have analysed the log-transformed fire insurance data set using maximum likelihood estimation. This is, of course, also a very reasonable approach, which leads to similar informative findings. Moreover, when we fitted several models to the fire insurance data and selected the best among these models using Bayes factors, this was intended to illustrate the procedure of model fitting and model selection. Of course, there may be other models which also describe the data very well.

The views expressed in this chapter are the sole responsibility of the authors and do not necessarily reflect those of UniCredit Group or any of its affiliates.

1 It should be made clear that we do not claim that the model in Equation 14.1 is the only possible structural model for operational risk or that its usage is particularly supported by empirical data. We only observe that these kinds of model are very popular and have a long history in the finance industry. As a matter of fact, it is worth mentioning that Equation 14.1 has been invented neither by the Basel committee nor the banking industry; instead it goes back to Filip Lundberg in 1903 in the context of insurance risk theory.
2 See Böcker and Klüppelberg (2008) and references therein.
3 See, for example, Cont and Tankov (2004) and references therein.
4 See also Böcker and Klüppelberg (2008) for a more detailed description of this approach.
5 See Böcker and Klüppelberg (2008) and Esmaeili and Klüppelberg (2010) for details about the subsequent results.
6 Again, see Esmaeili and Klüppelberg (2010).
7 Let us stress that this explicit choice is for demonstration. Any appropriate distribution can be used as prior instead.

REFERENCES

Basel Committee on Banking Supervision, 2004, *International Convergence of Capital Measurement and Capital Standards: A Revised Framework* (Basel: Bank for International Settlements).

Böcker, K., and C. Klüppelberg, 2005, "Operational VaR: A Closed-Form Solution", *Risk Magazine,* December, pp. 90–3.

Böcker, K., and C. Klüppelberg, 2008, "Modelling and Measuring Multivariate Operational Risk with Lévy Copulas", *Journal of Operational Risk* 3(2), pp. 3–27.

Cont, R., and P. Tankov, 2004, *Financial Modelling with Jump Processes* (Boca Raton, FL: Chapman & Hall/CRC).

Embrechts, P., C. Klüppelberg and T. Mikosch, 1997, *Modelling Extremal Events for Insurance and Finance* (Springer).

Esmaeili, H., and C. Klüppelberg, 2010, "Parameter Estimation of a Bivariate Compound Poisson Process", *Insurance: Mathematics and Economics,* doi:10.1016/j.insmatheco.2010.04.005.

Gelman, A., J. B. Carlin, H. S. Stern and D. B. Rubin, 1995, *Bayesian Data Analysis* (London: Chapman & Hall).

Index

(page numbers in italic type relate to tables or figures)

A

adaptive mixture of Student-*t* distributions (AdMit) procedure, 10–16
AdMitIS procedure, 9–10
  empirical illustration of, 16–24
advanced measurement approaches (AMAs), 371, 401
Alternative Investment Solutions (AIS), 98–9
Arch model, 3
ASRF, uncertainty of risk figures under, 219–25
asset-backed securities (ABSs), 243–6, 250, 273

B

Bayesian credit portfolio approach to predictions based on certain uncertainties, *see* certain uncertainties
Bayesian estimation, xx, 93
  of Arma–Garch processes with stable disturbances, 102–5
  credit risk parameters and, uncertainty in, 217–19
  Garch-type models and, 6–25
  of Lévy copulas for multivariate operational risks, 439–63
  of parameters of alpha-stable distribution in the unconditional setting, 101–2
Bayesian framework for operational risk (OR), 371–497, *376*, *383*, *384*, *385*, *386*, *387*, *388*, *390*, *391*, *392*, *393*, *395*, *396*
  application, 382–4
    data, 382
    normal-copula risk-measure results, 389–92
    perfect-dependence risk-measure results, 382–9
    Student-*t* copula risk-measure results, 392–4
  model, 372–82
    copula functions, 396–82
    marginal parameter estimates, 373–5
    normal copula, 378–82
    risk measures, 375–6
    Student-*t* copula, 380–2
  see also operational risk (OR)
Bayesian model averaging (BMA), 15–16, 22, *22*, *23*, *24*
Bayesian prediction of portfolio VaR and ES, 86–9, *88*
Bayesian procedure for portfolio allocation, 89–93
bivariate Clayton model, 443–4
Black–Scholes, xx, 142, 143, 144–5, 152–3, 161, 172
  delta edge, 157
bounded total-variance assumptions, 148–9
bounded volatility assumptions, 144–6
(Burr/GDP)^2 model, 446–8, 456–61

C

certain uncertainties, predictions based on, Bayesian credit portfolio approach to, 179–197

analysis of historic data, 186–90, *187, 188, 189, 190*
explained, 181–3
Markov chain Monte Carlo (MCMC) methods of estimation, 183–4
predictions, 190–5, *191, 192, 193, 194*
simple model, 184–6
collateralised debt obligations (CDOs), 241, 243–6, *244*, 248, 250, *252*, 269, 273, 275–6, *279*, 282, 302, 309
Comprehensive R Archive Network (CRAN), 10
copulas, Bayesian prediction of risk measurements using, 69–94
see also risk measurements using copulas
credit risk modelling 274, 277, *279, 283, 301, 305, 306, 308, 311*
financial crisis, model crisis and, 270–2
formula, implementation of, 290–1
Step 1, 291–3
Step 2, 297
Step 3, 397–302
Step 4, 302–8
formula, very general, 282–4, *283*
general mixture-model framework, 284–90
levels of valuation and, 272–82
rethinking, 269–316
simplifications (Level 2), 308–13
correlation structure and non-linear dependencies, 310–11
stochastic limit theorems, 309–10
simplifications (other areas), 312–13
suggested further reading concerning, 314–15

credit risk parameters, uncertainty in, 199–39
ASRF, uncertainty of risk figures under, 219–25
considered risk figures, 220–1
MCMC and, Bayesian approach with, 225
moment of maximum likelihood, estimation of, 221–5
Bayesian estimation and, 217–19
asymptotic single risk factor, 217–8
Gibbs sampler, 219
mixed binomial model, 217
empirical study concerning, 225–37, *227, 228, 229, 230, 231, 232, 233, 234, 235, 236, 237*
discussion of results, 226–7
S&P default, 226
simulation, 226
models, estimators, asymptotic normality and, 202–8
asymptotic single-risk-factor model, 205–7
estimation errors, 207–8
mixed binomial, 202–5
point estimators and, uncertainty of, 208–17
ASRF model, maximum likelihood estimate in, 213–16
ASRF model, moment estimator in, 208–13
asymptotic confidence intervals and, 216–17

D

DAX Index, 70, 72, 72, *81, 82, 82*–3, *83*, 84–6, *85, 86*, 91, *92*, 93

default risk *332, 333, 337, 338, 339, 340, 365*
  Bayesian approach to, 319–41
  excitation, 330–4
  expert information and, elicitation of, 321–7
  inference, 334–41
    by SMEs; 345–67 *see also main entry:* small and medium-sized companies
  statistical models for, 327–30
Default Risk Service, 336
derivative pricing:
  calibration and parameter uncertainty and, 151–60
    Bayesian approaches and, advantages and disadvantages of, 158–60
    Bayesian framework and, 155–7
    Bayesian pricing and hedging and, 157–8
    inverse problem and, 151–2
    regularisation and, 153–5
    well-posedness and, 152–3
  decision rules and, 169
  model uncertainty, calibration to reduce, 149–51
  model uncertainty's impact on, 137–72, *138, 139, 140, 167, 168*
  model uncertainty measures and, 160–8
    coherent, 165–6
    convex, 166
    risk-averaging, 162
    risk-differencing, 163
    worked example, 166–8
    worst-case, 163–5
  model uncertainty, sources and types of, 140–1
    incorrect calibration, 141
    incorrect model, 140–1
    incorrect solution, 141

  model-free, 143–51
    bounded total-variance assumptions, 148–9
    bounded volatility assumptions, 144–6
    super-replication, 146–7
  motivating examples, 137
    parameter uncertainty, 138–9
    specification uncertainty, 138
  recommended further reading concerning, 170–2
  risk and Knightian uncertainty concerning, 139–40
Dow Jones Industrial Average Index, 49, 70, 72, 72, *81, 82, 83,* 84, *85, 86, 88,* 91, *92,* 93
Dupire's Formula, 153

E

EGarch model, 17, *18, 19, 20, 21, 22, 23, 24*

G

Garch-type models, Bayesian estimation and combination of, 3–25
  AdMit procedure, 10–16
    algorithm *18*
  Bayesian estimation of, 4–10
    AdMitIS procedure, 9–10, 16–24, *19*
    Griddy–Gibbs sampler, 6–7, 9
    importance sampling (IS), 7
    Metropolis–Hastings (MH) algorithm, 8–9
GJR model, 3, *20,* 22, *23,* 24
Griddy–Gibbs sampler, 6–7, 9, 101

H

Hadamard's criteria, 152, 156
Hedge Fund Research Inc. 95, 98, 113

hedge funds:
  Bayesian inference for,
    95–134, *105*
    estimation of Arma–Garch
      processes with stable
      disturbances, 102–5
    estimation of parameters
      of alpha-stable
      distribution in
      unconditional setting,
      101–2
    literature review
      concerning, 97–8
    methodology concerning,
      100–11
    simulated data illustrates,
      105–7, *106*, *107*
    VaR and CVaR backtesting
      and, 110–11
    VaR and CVaR prediction
      concerning, 107–10
  data description for, 98–100
  empirical analysis
    concerning, 111–27, *112*,
    114, *115–16*, *118–19*, *120–1*,
    122–3, *124–5*, *126–7*, *128–9*,
    130–1, *132–3*
    risk forecasts on fund
      index data, comparisons
      of, 113–16
    risk forecasts on
      individual fund,
      comparison of, 116–18
    risk forecasts on many
      funds across different
      strategies, comparison of,
      118–27
  Kupiec and Christoffersen
    tests and, performance
    according to, 118–19
  loss function metric and,
    CVaR performance
    according to, 120–3
  risk performances for
    Sep.–Oct. 2008 concerning,
    123–7
  stable returns distribution of,
    95–136

methodology concerning,
  100–11

I

importance sampling (IS), 7
importance sampling (IS) with
  adaptive mixture of
  Student-*t* distributions, *see*
  AdMitIS methodology
integrated nested Laplace
  approximation (INLA),
  346–8, 350, 351, 354–6, *358*,
  359, *360*, *362*, 362–7 *passim*,
  363, *364*
  approximation error, 355–6
  software, 357
interpreted languages, 8

K

Kupiec and Christoffersen tests,
  110, *114–16*, 117
  performance according to,
    118–20

L

Lehman Brothers, 96, 113, 269,
  280
Lehmann–Scheffe Theorem,
  262–4
Lhoste, Ernest, 374
loss distribution approach
  (LDA), 371–2, 401
loss function metric, CVaR
  performance according to,
  120–3

M

Markov chain Monte Carlo
  (MCMC) procedures, 5, 7,
  31, 33–6, 37, 42, 50, 51–2,
  70, 80–1, 82, 83, 93, 97, 101,
  106, 166, 181, 183–4 201,
  207, 216, 218, 319, 321, 346,
  356, *358*, *360*, *361*, *364*, 372,
  418, 448
  alternative, 25
  Bayesian approach with, 315,
    234, 238

INLA as alternative to, 346
simulated SV data for 53
tailored, 60
MATHEMATICA, 8
MATLAB, 8, 141
Metropolis–Hastings (MH)
    algorithm, 8–9, 183
minimum-variance unbiased
    estimators (MVUEs),
    255–6, 257, 262–5
model uncertainty:
    calibration to reduce, 149–51
    decision rules and, 169
    impact of, on derivative
        pricing, 137–72, *138, 139,
        140, 167, 168*
    measures, 160–8
        coherent, 165–6
        convex, 166
        risk-averaging, 162
        risk-differencing, 163
        worked example, 166–8
        worst-case, 163–5
    recommended further
        reading concerning, 172–6
    sources and types of, 140–1
        incorrect calibration, 141
        incorrect model, 140–1
        incorrect solution, 141
    see also derivative pricing
mortgaged-backed structured
    securities *243, 244, 245,
    246, 251, 252, 254, 255, 256,
    257, 258, 259*
    crisis in, 241–66
    measurement uncertainty
        and, 255–9
    securitisation and, crisis in,
        242–7
    systematic risk and, exposure
        to, 247–55
        pooling assets does not
            mitigate, 250–1
        simple normal copula
            model, 257–9
        tranching liabilities
            leverages exposure to,
            251–2

multivariate stochastic volatility
    models, 46–51
    additional, 51
    Cholesky, 48–9
    factor, 49–50
    Wishart random processes,
        47–8

O

operational risk (OR), Basel
    Committee definition of,
    371
operational risk (OR), Bayesian
    framework for, 371–97,
    *376, 383, 384, 385, 386, 387,
    388, 390, 391, 392, 393, 395,
    396*
    application, 382–94
    data, 382
    normal-copula
        risk-measure results,
        389–2
    perfect-dependence
        risk-measure results,
        382–9
    Student-*t* copula
        risk-measure results,
        392–4
    model, 372–82
        copula functions, 376–82
        marginal parameter
            estimates, 373–5
        normal copula, 378–80
        risk measures, 375–6
        Student-*t* copula, 380–2
operational risk (OR), combining
    internal and external data
    and expert opinions for,
    401–35, *412, 413, 425, 430*
    Bayesian approach to, 404–7;
        see also operational risk
        (OR), Bayesian framework
        for
    conjugate prior
        distributions, 407
    iterative update procedure
        for priors, 406

posterior distribution, 405–6
predictive distribution, 405
conjugate prior extension, 418
general remarks, 433–5
heuristic approaches to, 403–4
loss frequency: Poisson model, 419–26
loss severities: Pareto model, 426–9
parameter uncertainty and, capital charge accounting for, 429–33
Poisson–Gamma example, 408–15
  empirical Bayesian, 414–15
  model, 409–11
  pure Bayesian, 411–13
prior parameters and, estimation of, 407–8
  pure Bayesian, 407–8
  empirical Bayesian, 408
operational risk (OR), multivariate, Lévy copulas for:
Bayesian estimation of, 439–63
bivariate Clayton model, 443–4
(Burr/GDP)^2 model, 446–8
general model, 443–8
fire-insurance data, analysis of, 454–62, *455*, *456*, *457*, *458*, *459*, *461*
Bayes factors, 461–2
(Burr/GDP)^2-Clayton model and, 456–61
MCMC algorithm, 448–50
  Gibbs sampling, 448–9
  initial values, burn-in, number of iterations, subsampling, 450
  proposal densities, choice of, 449–50
simulation study, 450–54, *451*, *452*
  illustrative example, 451–3

posterior mean estimates, quality of, 453–4, *454*

P

portfolio allocation, Bayesian procedure for, 89–93

Q

quantile, 70, 84, 86–8, 90, 109, 110, 180, *187*, 188, *189*, 191–5, *193*, *194*, 216, 220, 225, 304, 323, 325, 331, 332, 341, *358*, *360*, *365*, 366, 375, 385, 408, 429–33, 347, *458*

R

R, 8
relative numerical efficiency (RNE), 19, 21
risk measurements using copulas:
  basic concepts, 74–6
  Bayesian prediction of, 89–94
  copula–Garch models, 76–9
  introduced, 70
  model parameters, Bayesian inference for, 79–83
  portfolio allocation, Bayesian procedure for, 89–93
  portfolio VaR and ES, Bayesian prediction of, 86–9
  volatilities and dependence measures, prediction of, 83–6

S

sequential Monte Carlo (SMC), 31, 32, 45, 60
  posterior inference via, 36–42
small and medium-sized companies:
  data, 348–9
  defaults in, Bayesian modelling of, 345–67, *348*, *349*, *353*, *358*, *360*, *361*, *362*, *363*, *364*, *365*
  methods, 354–6

INLA, 354–6; *see also main entry:* integrated nested Laplace approximations (INLA)
  MCMC, 356
  model, 349–54
    Bayesian formulation, 350
    latent Gaussian, 354
    logistic regression, 349–50
  results, 357–66
    customer example, 365–6
    with informative prior, 359–65
    with vague prior, 357–9
stochastic volatility modelling:
  applications, 51–9
    example: with fat-tailed errors, 53–4
    example: with jumps, 56–8, *59*
    example: simple, 51–3
    example: with smooth transition, 53
    example: with time-varying loadings, 58–9, *60*
  Bayesian inference for, 31–62
  multivariate stochastic volatility models, 46–51
    additional, 69
    Cholesky, 48–9
    factor, 49–50
    simulated data *52*, *53*
    Wishart random processes, 47–8
  univariate, 31–46
    posterior inference via Markov chain Monte Carlo, 33–6
    Posterior inference via sequential Monte Carlo, 36–42
    SV model, 32–3, *56*, *57*, *58*
structured finance collateralised debt obligations (SFCDOs), 273
Student-*t* method, adaptive mixture of, *see* AdMit

procedure; *see also* AdMitIS methodology
subprime, 243, *244*, 245, *246*, 247, *265*,
  crisis, xxi, 113, 269, 273, 307
super-replication, 146–7

T

TGarch model, 3

U

univariate stochastic volatility models, 31–46
  posterior inference via Markov chain Monte Carlo, 33–6
    sampling parameters, 33–6
    sampling states jointly, 35–6
    sampling states one at a time, 34–5
  posterior inference via sequential Monte Carlo, 36–42
    Liu–West filter, 39–40, 52, 56
    particle learning, xv, 38, 40–2
  SV model, 31, 32–3
    correlated errors, 42
    Dirichlet process mixture (DPM), 43
    fat-tailed, skewed and scale mixture of normals, 42–3
    with jumps, 44
    long-memory, 43–4
    Markov-switching stochastic volatility, 45
    smooth-transition, 45–6
    volatility-volume, 46

V

volatility forecasting, 3, 171

Z

zero loss rates, 228, 230, 232, 237, 238